CRITICAL COMPA

RUSSIAN REVOLUTION
1914–1921

CRITICAL COMPANION TO THE RUSSIAN REVOLUTION 1914–1921

Edited by

Edward Acton

Professor of Modern European History
University of East Anglia, Norwich

Vladimir Iu. Cherniaev

Senior Research Scholar
Institute of Russian History, RAN, St Petersburg

William G. Rosenberg

Professor of Modern Russian and Soviet History
University of Michigan

A member of the Hodder Headline Group
LONDON

First published in Great Britain in 1997)y
Arnold, a member of the Hodder Headline Group,
338 Euston Road, London NW1 3BH

http://www.arnoldpublishers.com

Co-published in the United States of America by
Oxford University Press Inc.,
198 Madison Avenue, New York, NY10016

British Library Cataloguing in Publication Data
A catalogue record for this book is available from the British Library

Library of Congress Cataloging-in-Publication Data

.A catalog record for this book is available from the Library of Congress

ISBN 0 340 76365 5

1 2 3 4 5 6 7 8 9 10

Typeset by Phoenix Photosetting, Chatham, Kent

What do you think about this book? Or any other Arnold title?
Please send your comments to feedback.arnold@hodder.co.uk

Contents

VII   ECONOMIC ISSUES AND PROBLEMS OF EVERYDAY LIFE

VIII   NATIONALITY AND REGIONAL QUESTIONS

Contributors

Edward Acton
University of East Anglia
Alexander Herzen and the Role of the Intellectual Revolutionary (1979);
Rethinking the Russian Revolution (1990); *Russia: The Tsarist and Soviet
Legacy* (1995).

Olavi Arens
Armstrong State College
'The Estonian Maapäev during 1917', in V. Stanley Vardys and Romuald J.
Misiunas, eds., *The Baltic States in Peace and War, 1917–1945* (1978); 'The
Estonian Question at Brest-Litovsk', *Journal of Baltic Studies* 25 (1994).

Francesco Benvenuti
University of Bologna
The Bolsheviks and the Red Army, 1918–1922 (1988); 'Reforming the
Party: Organization and Structure, 1917–1990', in Catherine Merridale and
Christopher Ward, eds., *Perestroika: The Historical Perspective* (1991);
'Industry and Purge in the Donbass', *Europe-Asia Studies* 45 (1993).

Jane Burbank
University of Michigan
Intelligentsia and Revolution: Russian Views of Bolshevism, 1917–1921
(1986); 'Lenin and the Law in Revolutionary Russia', *Slavic Review* 54
(1995); 'Discipline and Punish in the Moscow Bar Association', *Russian
Review* 54 (1995); 'Were the Russian *Intelligenty* Organic Intellectuals?', in
Leon Fink, Stephen T. Leonard and Donald M. Reid, eds., *Intellectuals and
Public Life* (1996).

Vladimir Iur'evich Cherniaev
Institute of Russian History, RAN, St Petersburg
Editor and contributor, 'Rossiiskoe dvoevlastie i protsess samoopredeleniia
Finliandii', in *Anatomiia revoliutsii. 1917 god v Rossii: massy, partii, vlast'*

(1994); 'Eticheskii kommunizm epokhi grazhdanskoi voiny', in S. I. Polotov, ed., *Rabochie i rossiiskoe obshchestvo. Vtoraia polovina XIX–nachalo XX veka. Sbornik statei i materialov posviashchennyi pamiati O. N. Znamenskogo* (1994); 'Gibel' dumskoi monarkhii. Vremennoe pravitel'stvo i ego reformy', in B.V. Anan'ich, ed., *Vlast' i reformy. Ot samoderzhavnoi k sovetskoi Rossii* (1996); 'Uchenyi vlast' i revoliutsiia: parabola sud'by N.S. Tagantseva', in T.M. Kitanina, ed., *Intelligentsiia i rossiiskoe obshchestvo v nachale XX veka* (1996).

Barbara Evans Clements
University of Akron
Bolshevik Feminist: The Life of Aleksandra Kollontai (1979); with Barbara Alpern Engel and Christine D. Worobec, eds., *Russia's Women: Accommodation, Resistance, Transformation* (1991); *Daughters of Revolution: A History of Women in the USSR* (1994); *Bolshevik Women* (1997).

Robert Daniels
University of Vermont
The Conscience of the Revolution: Communist Opposition in Soviet Russia (1960); *Red October: The Bolshevik Revolution of 1917* (1968); *Trotsky, Stalin and Socialism* (1991); *The End of the Communist Revolution* (1993).

Andrew Ezergailis
Ithaca College
The 1917 Revolution in Latvia (1973); *The Latvian Impact on the Bolshevik Revolution* (1983); *The Holocaust in Latvia* (1996).

Orlando Figes
Trinity College, Cambridge
Peasant Russia, Civil War: The Volga Countryside in Revolution (1917–1921) (1989); *A People's Tragedy: The Russian Revolution, 1891–1924* (1996); 'The Russian Revolution of 1917 and its Language in the Village', *Russian Review* 56 (1997).

David S. Foglesong
Rutgers University
'Xenophon Kalamatiano: An American Spy in Revolutionary Russia?', *Intelligence and National Security* 6 (1991); 'A Missouri Democrat in Revolutionary Russia: Ambassador David R. Francis and the American Confrontation with Russian Radicalism in 1917', *Gateway Heritage* 12 (1992); 'The United States, Self-Determination, and the Struggle Against Bolshevism in the Eastern Baltic Region, 1918–1920', *Journal of Baltic Studies* 26 (1995); *America's Secret War Against Bolshevism: US Intervention in the Russian Civil War, 1917–1920* (1995).

Ziva Galili
Rutgers University
With Leopold Haimson and Richard Wortman, eds., *The Making of Three Russian Revolutionaries: Voices from the Menshevik Past* (1987); *The Menshevik Leaders in the Russian Revolution: Social Realities and Political Strategies* (1989); with Leopold Haimson and Albert P. Nenarokov, eds., *Men'sheviki v 1917 godu*, 4 vols. (1994–7).

Peter Gatrell
University of Manchester
The Tsarist Economy 1850–1917 (1986); 'The First World War and War Communism, 1914–1920', in Robert W. Davies, Mark Harrison and Steven G. Wheatcroft, eds., *The Soviet Economic Transformation, 1913–1945* (1993); *Government, Industry and Rearmament in Russia, 1900–1914: The Last Argument of Tsarism* (1994).

Israel Getzler
Hebrew University of Jerusalem
Martov: A Political Biography of a Russian Social Democrat (1967); intro. to Iu. O. Martov, *Zapiski sotsial-demokrata* (1975); *Kronstadt, 1917–1921: The Fate of a Soviet Democracy* (1983).

Mark von Hagen
Columbia University
Soldiers in the Proletarian Dictatorship: The Red Army and the Soviet Socialist State, 1917–1930 (1990); 'Does Ukraine Have a History?', *Slavic Review* 54 (1995); 'The Great War and the Mobilization of Ethnicity in the Russian Empire', in Barnett Rubin, ed., *Empire, Nations, Regions: Political Change and Order in the Former Soviet Space* (1996); with Karen Barkey, eds., *After Empire: Multiethnic Societies and Nation-Building. The Soviet Union and the Russian, Habsburg, and Ottoman Empires* (1997).

Tsuyoshi Hasegawa
University of California, Santa Barbara
The February Revolution: Petrograd, 1917 (1981); 'Crime, Police, and Mob Justice in Petrograd during the Russian Revolution of 1917', in Charles E. Timberlake, ed., *Religious and Secular Forces in Late Tsarist Russia* (1992); 'Crime and Police in Revolutionary Petrograd, March 1917–March 1918: Social History of the Russian Revolution Revisited', *Acta Slavica Iaponica* (1995).

Sergei Viktorovich Iarov
Institute of Russian History, RAN, St Petersburg
'Kronshtadtskii miatezh v vospriiatii petrogradskikh rabochikh (po neopublikovannym dokumentam)', *Zven'ia. Istoricheskii al'manakh* 2 (1992); 'Uchreditel'noe sobranie v politicheskikh diskussiiakh 1918 g.', in P.A.

Shishkin, ed., *Vspomogatel'nye istoricheskie distsipliny* (1994); 'Politi-cheskaia psikhologiia krest'ian pri perekhode k voennomu kommunizmu', *Reche. Al'manakh russkoi filosofii i kultury* 2 (1995); 'Krest'ianskie vol-neniia na severno-zapade Sovetskoi Rossii v 1918–1919 g.', in P. V. Danilov and T. Shanin, eds., *Krest'ianovedenie. Teoriia. Istoriia. Sovremennost'. Ezhegodnik* (1996).

Peter Kenez
University of California, Santa Cruz
Civil War in South Russia, 1918: The First Year of the Volunteer Army (1971); *Civil War in South Russia, 1919–1920: The Defeat of the Whites* (1977); *The Birth of the Propaganda State: Soviet Methods of Mass Mobilization, 1917–1929* (1985); *Cinema and Soviet Society, 1917–1953* (1992).

John D. Klier
University College, London
Russia Gathers Her Jews: The Origins of the 'Jewish Question' in Russia, 1772–1825 (1986); with S. Lambroza, eds., *Pogroms: Anti-Jewish Violence in Modern Russian History* (1992); *Imperial Russia's Jewish Question, 1855–1881* (1995).

Diane P. Koenker
University of Illinois
Moscow Workers and the 1917 Revolution (1981); ed., *Tret'ia vseross-iiskaia konferentsiia professional'nykh soiuzov, 1917: stenograficheskii otchet* (1982); with William G. Rosenberg, *Strikes and Revolution in Russia, 1917* (1989); with William G. Rosenberg and R. G. Suny, eds., *Party, State, and Society in the Russian Civil War* (1989).

Boris Ivanovich Kolonitskii
Institute of Russian History, RAN, St Petersburg
'Pravoekstremistskie sily v marte–oktiabre 1917 goda', in R. Sh. Ganelin, ed., *Natsional'naia pravaia prezhde i teper': Istoriko-sotsiologich. ocherki* (1992); 'Revolutionary Names: Russian Personal Names and Political Consciousness in the 1920s and 1930s', *Revolutionary Russia* 6 (1993); 'Antibourgeois Propaganda and Anti- "Burzhui" Consciousness in 1917', *Russian Review* 53 (1994); 'Sovety i kontrol' nad pechat'iu (mart–oktiabr' 1917 goda)', in S. E. Polotov, ed., *Rabochie i rossiiskoe obshchestvo. Vtoraia polovina XIX–nachalo XX veka. Sbornik statei i materialov, posvi-ashchennykh pamiati O. N. Znamenskogo* (1994); '"Rabochaia intelli-gentsiia" v trudakh L. M. Kleinborta', in N. N. Smirnov, ed., *Intelligentsiia i rossiiskoe obshchestvo v nachale XX veka* (1996).

Dominic Lieven
London School of Economics
Russia and the Origins of the First World War (1983); *Russia's Rulers Under the Old Regime* (1989); *The Aristocracy in Europe, 1815–1914* (1992); *Nicholas II, Emperor of All the Russias* (1993).

Lars T. Lih
Montreal, Quebec
Bread and Authority in Russia, 1914–1921 (1990); *The Bolshevik Sowing Committees of 1920: Apotheosis of War Communism?* (1990.); ed., *Stalin's Letters to Molotov, 1925–1936* (1995).

Alter L'vovich Litvin
Kazan University
Bez prava na mysl'. Istoriki v epokhy Bol'shogo Terrora (1994); *Krasnyi i belyi terror v Rossii. 1918–1922* (1995); ed., *Fanni Kaplan. Ili kto strelial v Lenina? Sbornik dokumentov* (1995); ed., *Levye esery i VChK. Sbornik dokumentov* (1996).

Silvana Malle
Organization for Economic Cooperation and Development, Paris
The Economic Organization of War Communism, 1918–1921 (1985); *Employment Planning in the Soviet Union: Continuity and Change* (1990).

Aleksei Rostislavovich Markov
St Petersburg
'Ot vrazhdebnosti k obshchemu iazyku: vokrug konfliktov po prizyvu studentov v armiiu v gody grazhdanskoi voiny', in B. A. Starkov; ed., *Sotsial'nye konflikty v sovetskoi istorii* (1995); 'Byl li seks pri sovetskoi vlasti?', *Rodina* 9 (1995).

Evan Mawdsley
University of Glasgow
The Russian Revolution and the Baltic Fleet (1978); *The Russian Civil War* (1987); 'Soldiers and Sailors', in R. Service, ed., *Society and Politics in the Russian Revolution* (1992).

Michael Melancon
Auburn University
'Stormy Petrels: The Socialist Revolutionaries in Russia's Labor Organizations, 1905–1914', *Carl Beck Papers* (1988); *The Socialist Revolutionaries and the Russian Anti-War Movement, 1914–1917* (1990); 'The Left Socialist Revolutionaries and the Bolshevik Uprising', in V. Brovkin, ed., *A Prelude to Catastrophe: Revolution, Civil Wars, and the New Order in the Russian Empire, 1917–1922* (1996).

Albert Pavlovich Nenarokov
Russian Independent Institute for Social and National Problems, Moscow
Vostochnyi front. 1918 (1969); *1917. Kratkaia istoriia, fotografii i doku-menty* (1976, 1977, 1979, 1987); *Vernost' dolgu. Marshal Sovetskogo Soiuza A. I. Egorov* (1973, 1978, 1983); *K edinstvu ravnykh. Kul'turnye faktory ob'edinitel'nogo dvizheniia sovetskikh narodov v 1917–1924* (1991); with Ziva Galili and Leopold Haimson, eds., *Men'sheviki v 1917 godu*, 4 vols. (1994–7).

Martha Brill Olcott
Colgate University and Carnegie Endowment for International Peace
The Soviet Multinational State: Readings and Documents (1990); *The Kazakhs* (2nd edn, 1995); *Central Asia's New States: Independence, Foreign Policy and Regional Security* (1996).

Daniel Orlovsky
Southern Methodist University, Dallas
The Limits of Reform: The Ministry of Internal Affairs in Imperial Russia, 1802–1881 (1981); 'Reform during Revolution: Governing the Provinces in 1917', in R. O. Crummey, ed., *Reform in Russia and the USSR: Past and Prospects* (1989); 'The Lower Middle Strata in Revolutionary Russia', in E. Clowes, S. Kassow and J. West, eds., *Civil Society in Late Imperial Russia* (1991); 'The Hidden Class: White-Collar Workers in the Soviet 1920s', in Lewis Siegelbaum and Ronald G. Suny, eds., *Making Workers Soviet: Power, Class and Identities* (1994).

Shane O'Rourke
University of York
'Warriors and Peasants: The Contradictions of Cossack Culture 1861–1914', Oxford D.Phil. (1994); 'Women in a Warrior Society: Don Cossack Women 1861–1914', in R. Marsh, ed., *Women in Russia and Ukraine* (1996).

Raymond Pearson
University of Ulster
The Russian Moderates and the Crisis of Tsarism, 1914–1917 (1977); *National Minorities in Eastern Europe, 1848–1945* (1983); *The Longman Companion to European Nationalism, 1789–1920* (1994).

Alexander Rabinowitch
Indiana University
Prelude to Revolution: The Petrograd Bolsheviks and the July 1917 Uprising (1968); *The Bolsheviks Come to Power: The Revolution of 1917 in Petrograd* (1976); with Sheila Fitzpatrick and Richard Stites, eds., *Russia in the Era of NEP: Explorations in Soviet Society and Culture* (1991).

Christopher Read
University of Warwick
Religion, Revolution and the Russian Intelligentsia: The 'Vekhi' Debate and its Intellectual Background, 1900–1912 (1979); *Culture and Power in Revolutionary Russia: The Intelligentsia and the Transition from Tsarism to Communism* (1990); *From Tsar to Soviets: The Russian People and their Revolution, 1917–1921* (1996).

William G. Rosenberg
University of Michigan
Liberals in the Russian Revolution: The Constitutional Democratic Party, 1917–1921 (1974); ed., *Bolshevik Visions: First Phase of the Cultural Revolution in Russia* (1984); with Diane P. Koenker, *Strikes and Revolution in Russia, 1917* (1989).

Robert Service
School of Slavonic and East European Studies, University of London
The Bolshevik Party in Revolution: A Study in Organizational Change 1917–1923 (1979); *The Russian Revolution, 1900–1927* (1986); *Lenin: A Political Life*, 3 vols. (1985, 1991, 1995); *A History of Twentieth-Century Russia* (1997).

Mikhail Vital'evich Shkarovskii
Central State Archive, St Petersburg
Peterburgskaia eparkhiia v gody gonenii i utrat 1917–1945 (1995); *Russkaia pravoslavnaia tserkov' i sovetskoe gosudarstvo v 1943–1964 gg. Ot peremiriia k novoi voine* (1995); 'The Russian Orthodox Church versus the State: The Josephite Movement, 1927–1940', *Slavic Review* 54 (1995); with N. Iu. Cherepnina, *Spravochnik po istorii pravoslavnykh monastyrei i soborov g. Sankt Peterburga 1917–1945 (po dokumentam TsGA SPb)* (1996).

Nikolai Nikolaevich Smirnov
Institute of Russian History, RAN, St Petersburg
'Petrogradskie rabochie i obrazovanie vremennógo koalitsionnogo pravitel'stva', in G. L. Sobolev, ed., *Piterskie rabochie v bor'be s kontrrevoliutsiei v 1917–1918 gg.* (1986); *Tretii Vserossiiskii s"ezd sovetov: istoriia sozyva, sostav, rabota* (1988); *Na perelome: Rossiiskoe uchitel'stvo nakanune i v dni revoliutsii 1917 goda* (1994); 'Rossiiskoe uchitel'stvo nakanune novoi revoliutsii', in V. Iu. Cherniaev, ed., *Anatomiia revoliutsii. 1917 god v Rossii: massy, partii, vlast'* (1994); 'Rossiiskaia intelligentsiia v gody pervoi mirovoi voiny i revoliutsii 1917 g. (Nekotorye voprosy istoriografii problemy)', in T. M. Kitanina, ed., *Intelligentsiia i rossiiskoe obshchestvo v nachale XX veka* (1996).

Steve Smith
University of Essex
Red Petrograd: Revolution in the Factories 1917–1918 (1983); trans. and ed., with Diane P. Koenker, *Notes of a Red Guard: The Autobiography of Eduard Dune* (1993); 'Workers against Foremen in Late-Imperial Russia', in Lewis Siegelbaum and Ronald G. Suny, eds., *Making Workers Soviet: Power, Class and Identities* (1994).

Richard Stites
Georgetown University
The Women's Liberation Movement in Russia: Feminism, Nihilism and Bolshevism, 1860–1930, 2nd edn. (1991); *Revolutionary Dreams: Utopian Vision and Experimental Life in the Russian Revolution* (1989); *Russian Popular Culture: Entertainment and Society since 1900* (1992).

Ronald G. Suny
University of Michigan
The Baku Commune, 1917–1918: Class and Nationality in the Russian Revolution (1972); *The Revenge of the Past: Nationalism, Revolution, and the Collapse of the Soviet Union* (1993); *Looking Toward Ararat: Armenia in Modern History* (1993); *The Making of the Georgian Nation* (1995).

Elizabeth Waters
London
Female Icons and Anti-Heroines: A Social History of the Soviet Union (1994).

Howard White
University of Bath
'Civil Rights and the Provisional Government', in Olga Crisp and Linda Edmondson, eds., *Civil Rights in Imperial Russia* (1989); 'The Urban Middle Classes', in Robert Service, ed., *Society and Politics in the Russian Revolution* (1992); '1917 in the Rear Garrisons', in Linda Edmondson and Peter Waldron, eds., *Economy and Society in Russia and the Soviet Union, 1860–1930* (1992).

Allan Wildman (deceased)
Ohio State University
The Making of a Workers' Revolution: Russian Social Democracy, 1891–1903 (1967); *The End of the Russian Imperial Army: The Old Army and the Soldiers' Revolt (March–April 1917)* (1980); *Vol. 2, The End of the Russian Imperial Army: The Road to Soviet Power and Peace* (1987).

Robert C. Williams
Davidson College
Culture in Exile. Russian Emigrés in Germany, 1881–1941 (1972); *Artists in Revolution: Portraits of the Russian Avant-Garde, 1905–1925* (1977); *The Other Bolsheviks: Lenin and His Critics* (1986).

Alan Wood
Lancaster University
With John Massey Stewart, *Siberia: Two Historical Perspectives* (1984); ed., *Siberia: Problems and Prospects for Regional Development* (1987); with Richard A. French, eds., *The Development of Siberia: People and Resources* (1989); ed., *The History of Siberia: From Russian Conquest to Revolution* (1991).

List of maps

Acknowledgements and note on transliteration and dates

In the course of preparing this volume we have between us accumulated too many debts to list. Some, however, must be singled out. Francis King acted as research assistant on the project. He brought to it a level of care and precision, technical skill and linguistic proficiency that are quite out of the ordinary, and he combined these with a truly formidable knowledge of the revolution. He translated all the Russian contributions into English, checked points and clarified issues in every single article, and solved a thousand and one editorial problems. At the British end, Steve Smith's wisdom and encouragement were crucial both at the outset and at the conclusion, and we received valuable advice from Colin Davis, Roy Davison, Simon Dixon and Peter Gatrell. Christopher Wheeler at Arnold not only conceived the idea for the volume but proved a model of patience and good counsel from first to last.

We are grateful to the British Academy for providing a substantial research grant to support the project, and to the Universities of East Anglia and Michigan for the grants and facilities which they provided.

Edward Acton
Vladimir Iu. Cherniaev
William G. Rosenberg

Note on transliteration and dates

Russian words have been transliterated according to a simplified version of the Library of Congress system. Exceptions have been made for certain names already familiar to the English and American reader, and for some names and words which have been transliterated directly from languages other than Russian.

Dates before 1 February 1918 are given according to the Julian Calendar (Old Style). This ran thirteen days behind the West's Gregorian Calendar which Russia adopted after the revolution, declaring the day following 31 January 1918 to be 14 February (New Style).

PART

I

INTRODUCTION

The Revolution and its Historians

The Critical Companion in Context

EDWARD ACTON

The model for this volume is the *Critical Dictionary of the French Revolution* published by François Furet and Mona Ozouf to mark the second centenary of 1789. The debt is an appropriate one. Just as the French revolution conditioned the long nineteenth century in Europe, so the repercussions of the Russian revolution have reverberated across the globe in the twentieth century. Like its French forerunner, the Russian upheaval challenged the prevailing socio-political order, recast international relations, and stamped its impress on the human imagination. And it, too, has generated a vast literature, both polemical and scholarly. The purpose here is to present in the most accessible and digestible form the finest fruits of contemporary research into the subject.

Content, scope, contributors

The volume consists of free-standing essays organized into seven sections: The Revolution as Event; Actors and the Question of Agency; Parties, Movements, Ideologies; Institutions and Institutional Cultures; Social Groups, Identities, Cultures and the Question of Consciousness; Economic Issues and Problems of Everyday Life; and Nationality and Regional Questions – together with an Index which includes supplementary material on some 500 participants touched upon *en passant*. These headings by no means exhaust the sub-categories into which recent and current work might be arranged. Nor is the list of essays in each section comprehensive. So vast was the scope of the revolution that no pretence at total coverage can be made. However, the formal table of contents only hints at the wealth of material which our contributors have woven into their analyses. Moreover, we have sought to identify a range of topics and themes – from those debated for decades to those only now being opened up, from workers to refugees, from events in Petrograd to those in Tashkent, from the geopolitical setting to the role of ritual, from issues of food supply to questions of identity – the illumination of which will cast light, if sometimes from an unexpected angle, across the sprawling canvas of the revolution.

So far as the number of essays commissioned is concerned, we have been constrained by our wish to provide space both for a succinct account of and for critical reflection upon the current state of learning. While the volume is designed to be accessible to readers with minimal prior knowledge, it seeks at the same time, unlike a general synthesis, a conventional reference book, or a 'definitive' dictionary, to press the limits of current knowledge, the questions that remain unanswered, the agenda for future research. Each entry, while taking core data as its point of departure, offers an interpretative and thematic treatment. We have encouraged the same critical and analytical approach to the problem of periodization. The central focus of the volume is upon the years of international war, revolution and civil war, 1914–1921, but some essays deliberately dwell upon what seems the most significant phase within that period, while others treat pre-revolutionary roots and precedents or anticipate developments in the 1920s and afterwards.

The collective profile of the contributors bears witness to the universal significance of the revolution. In contrast to the French prototype, where not surprisingly all but six of 24 contributors were from France, our quest for state-of-the-art resumés and reflection has led us across the globe. The 46 contributors come from the United States and Britain, from Australia and Japan, from Israel and Western Europe, and from Russia and the former Soviet Union. The roll-call is a distinguished one and includes many of the scholars who have made most impact upon the study of the revolution. The number of monographs and edited books for which they have been responsible runs into the hundreds, the number of articles is many times greater. Behind virtually every line in the book lies painstaking historical research and careful sifting of available sources – archival and published, public and private, official and illegal, literary and visual, military and civilian, political and social, economic and cultural, from the capital and from the provinces, Russian and non-Russian, retained within the fallen empire and scattered with the emigration.

A key consideration in deciding to launch the project was the opportunity to bring together Western and Russian work. Thanks to the energy and inspiration of our associate editor in St Petersburg, Vladimir Cherniaev, fifteen of the essays, as well as the Index of names, have been written in Russia – and a Russian edition is in preparation. The volume will thus serve as a bridge between work in Russia and in the West and, we hope, stimulate fresh lines of thought in both. For Russian scholars and students it will serve as a guide and entrée to recent and current work abroad. Outside Russia, it will draw attention to the generation of Russian scholars grappling with the revolution amidst the sound and fury of Russia's post-Soviet redefinition. Given the pivotal role the revolution has played in modern Russian history, their intellectual odyssey itself represents an important element in that re-definition. Moreover, they include in their number historians of the highest quality and, provided that the catastrophic decline in resources currently afflicting Russian academic life is reversed, their contributions are no doubt a harbinger of things to come. Should there be an international project conceived on similar lines to this volume two decades hence, the balance between Russian and non-Russian contributors is likely to have swung heavily towards the former.

Published to coincide with the eightieth anniversary of the October revolution, the volume presents the distilled essence of work which over the past quarter-century has transformed the way in which specialists view the revolution. At the same time, it points forward to the new issues and questions to which research and analysis are now turning. The need for a statement of this kind arises from two disparate phenomena which in the 1990s have converged to reshape profoundly the legacy that the twentieth century is destined to bequeath to the new millennium: the collapse of communism at a time of right-wing ideological ascendancy in the West, and the cultural upheaval often associated with the ever more capacious label 'post-modernism'. The impact which these developments are having upon the study of the Russian revolution reflects the manner in which controversy surrounding it has developed since 1917.

Controversy over the revolution

No other subject of historical research and debate has been more directly conditioned by conscious political manipulation. For seven decades a rigid and tendentious reading of the revolution confined the work of Soviet historians within narrow guidelines. It was propagated at school and university, in textbooks and films, in the street names, the monuments, the ritual and rhetoric of public life and became embedded in popular Soviet consciousness. In the West, meanwhile, historians were provoked by the claims of this reading to concentrate upon the same issues it raised – while contradicting every Soviet proposition and developing a virtual mirror-image interpretation of the revolution. And outside the communist world it was this avowedly partisan liberal Western version which moulded the popular image of the Bolshevik '*coup d'état*'. The passing of the Cold War and of the bi-polar world has brought the prolonged dialogue of the deaf to an abrupt halt and thereby opened the way for an agenda which is no longer framed by the impassioned partisanship born in 1917. The *Critical Companion* has been written to help bring this new agenda into focus, to publicize it, and to stimulate work upon it. At the same time, however, the political and intellectual context in which the denouement of the Cold War controversy has taken place by no means guarantees that *both* partisan versions will gently fade into oblivion. For whereas Soviet orthodoxy has been reduced to silence, the credibility and popular currency of its Western liberal counterpart have actually been enhanced by the total collapse of its old rival. The *Critical Companion* has been written, too, to bring home to the widest possible audience the glaring inadequacies which recent research has exposed in the traditional Western account as well as in Soviet orthodoxy. The key issues at stake may be depicted with greatest clarity by tracing the main contours of the historiographical debate.

The orthodox Soviet account, as it eventually crystallized, was designed to establish the legitimacy of the Bolshevik regime which emerged from the revolution. It portrayed the 'Great October Socialist Revolution' as the supreme event in world history, inaugurating the era of freedom in the saga of mankind, and blazing the trail for which all humanity was destined. It was based on the concoction of selections from the ideas of Marx and Lenin which came to be known as 'Marxism-Leninism'. It saw the revolution as a process governed by historical laws, the supreme vindication of the materialist analysis of history as the story of the progress of mankind and of its productive power. It described the revolution as the product of the ultimate class struggle, spawned by advanced capitalism, which pitted the bourgeois controllers of the means of production against the proletariat, the class destined to bring about socialism. And it placed at the very centre of the drama Lenin's 'party of a new type', the Bolshevik Party imbued with the scientific theory of revolutionary Marxism. It was the party which led each of the three revolutions – the 'dress rehearsal' of 1905–6, the overthrow of the tsar in February 1917, and the culminating triumph of October; it was the party which exposed the falsehoods both of the ruling class and of the bogus 'socialist' Mensheviks and Socialist Revolutionaries (SRs); it was the party which instilled into the vanguard of the proletariat class-consciousness and a real understanding of the nature of capitalist relations and the revolutionary process; and it was the party which organized and drew in its wake the less advanced but nevertheless democratic and oppressed strata of an unevenly developed society, enabling it to sweep the Provisional Government from power. The way was thereby opened for the establishment of Soviet democracy and the placing of state power in the hands of the working masses, led by the Bolshevik (in 1918 renamed Communist) Party. The war was brought to an end, private landownership abolished, industry nationalized, the right of self-determination of the national minorities recognized, and the groundwork laid for socialism. Massive obstacles were placed in the way of the new order. On top of the destruction caused by World War I were imposed the ravages of a civil war brought on by the support which foreign capitalists and their governments lent the savage counter-revolutionary efforts of Russia's defeated classes. Yet the party rallied the working masses to defend the revolution, mobilized the proletariat and peasantry in the Red Army, equipped and supplied the army despite the economic chaos, and drove the White Armies from Russia. Thus, guided by Lenin's inspired leadership, itself based on his total grasp of scientific Marxist theory, Soviet power was consolidated and the foundations established for the construction of the first socialist society.

The orthodox Soviet view developed and changed over time. It was at its most rigid and reached the heights of absurdity under Stalin. Following his death, daring spirits, including E. N. Burdzhalov and P. V. Volobuev, departed significantly from the party line. The late Soviet period saw numerous specialist studies based on a gradual expansion in the archival base made available. Some Soviet historians managed to publish innovative work, such as that of V. I. Startsev on high politics, which broke away from the tramlines of Marxism-Leninism. And with each new authoritative synthesis, the orthodox account became more detailed, more finely nuanced and more subtle. But, to the end, its key features remained in place.

The Marxist-Leninist version not only directly shaped Soviet historiography but also conditioned the debate abroad. This was not because it was accepted outside the USSR. Far from it. But historians committed to it were responsible for the selection of most of the archival material made available, they published the great bulk of relevant studies, and on the basis of this Marxist-Leninist interpretation of the revolution, they propounded a view of *world* history which challenged prevailing Western assumptions. In the West, historians devoted their energy to responding to Soviet assertions, exposing flaws in the Soviet view, and presenting an account which was diametrically at odds with it. Far from being law-governed, they argued, the revolution was the result of a chain of ghastly accidents. The tsar might have been a wise and able statesman, instead of the inadequate, hen-pecked political simpleton he was. The First World War might not have broken out at such a delicate moment in Russia's process of modernization and thus might have taken quite a different course and never involved the country in such terrible social and economic dislocation. The Provisional Government which came to power in February might not have been led by such incompetent, idealistic, naïve liberal politicians. It might have steered Russia along a democratic path had it been genuinely supported instead of fatally undermined by the dogmatic Menshevik and SR leaders. These narrow-minded ideologues agreed to form a coalition with the liberals and yet continued to denounce the war, attack the principle of private property, and undermine the authority of officers, managers and government officials alike. And the whole story might have turned out entirely differently had it not been for the ruthless power-hunger of the most extreme revolutionary intelligentsia: had the Bolsheviks not manipulated and brainwashed the simple Russian people, preaching their fantasies about class war, soviet power and socialism, and had they not decided to overthrow the legitimate government by conspiracy and force.

By the same token, according to this account, it was only the ruthlessness and superior organization of the Bolshevik regime which enabled it to survive after October. It faced massive popular opposition, immediately demonstrated by the Bolsheviks' stunning defeat in the Constituent Assembly elections of November–December 1917; the scale and breadth of the civil war demonstrated how shallow were its popular roots – foreign intervention played a decidedly peripheral role; it had the divisions and logistical handicaps suffered by the Whites to thank for its bloody victory in the civil war. The authoritarian nature of Bolshevism shone through every feature of the new order – the suppression of free speech; the forcible crushing of all opposition; the imposition of a one-party system; the fanatical, ideologically driven determination to replace the market and private enterprise with centralized control and planning of the entire economy. It was this vision which inspired 'war communism' and when in 1921 the Bolsheviks were forced to yield to popular pressure and adopt the New Economic Policy (NEP), they saw it as no more than a temporary pause before their mission could be resumed. The policies, the terror, and the bloodshed that accompanied Stalin's Five-Year Plans, collectivization and forced industrialization represented a direct product and fulfilment of the crime of October.

From the 1960s and early 1970s, however, the dissent of a few prominent pioneers from this mainline Western interpretation gave way to a substantial new historiographical wave. These younger historians, though sometimes collectively characterized in reductionist fashion as 'revisionists', were not in fact bound by a common philosophy of history, nor did they agree upon every aspect of their dissent. What distinguished them, rather, was their willingness to probe, criticize and where necessary repudiate the traditional view; their recognition of the extent to which it was inspired by Cold War hatred of all things 'left' – and especially the Soviet system – rather than by historical analysis; and their determination to subject received wisdom about the revolution to searching scrutiny, their commitment to social perspectives and quantitative methods already being widely applied in less sensitive fields, and their use of sources hitherto barely tapped. They undertook detailed re-examination of traditional assumptions about the imperial Russian economy. They delved more deeply into the structure and decision-making process – in foreign as well as domestic affairs – of the tsarist state and the Provisional Government, into the changing social composition, the internal debates and divisions, the organizational strengths and weaknesses, as well as the process of policy-formation, of the major political parties – Octobrist, Kadet, moderate socialist and Bolshevik. And, reflecting the growing influence of social history in the West, typified by the work of E. P. Thompson and the *Annales* school in France, they began to view the revolution 'from below', to shift the spotlight away from Nicholas II, Kerensky and Lenin, and to look instead at the experience and aspirations of workers, soldiers and peasants. In doing so, they challenged Soviet and traditional Western accounts alike.

The effect was to foreground the social polarization of tsarist Russia and underline the part played by objective processes in radicalizing the masses

and destroying in turn tsarism, Russian liberalism and the moderate socialist parties. A flow of fresh research highlighted the way in which the experience of the lower classes – the *proizvol* and land hunger from which
peasants suffered, the contemptuous treatment by officers and grim conditions which soldiers suffered, and the crude, authoritarian factory order
which workers suffered – led them to become increasingly radical and critical of the status quo. It emphasized the gradual spread of literacy, the
widening horizons, the growing sense of dignity among the lower orders,
and the way in which this encouraged them to revolt against the oppression,
the insecurity and the humiliation meted out to them by privileged society.
Greatest attention was devoted to workers, a series of studies showing how
the absence of civil and trade-union rights led workers to clash repeatedly
with the state and how the realization spread that it was only by political
change that they could substantially improve their own lives. The effect of
the work of this new generation, therefore, was to expose the inadequacy of
traditional Western emphasis on chance, on the poor leadership of tsar, liberals and moderate socialists, and to render implausible the treatment of
politics in a revolutionary situation as autonomous. For the same reasons,
the effect was to demythologize and play down the importance of the
revolutionary intelligentsia – and in doing so to cut down to size the role
attributed to the Bolshevik Party in Soviet hagiography. Comparative work
drew attention to the fact that in the West, too, there were extremist intellectuals who preached class war, revolution and socialism in the period, but
that in the West these ideas did not win much popular support. That they
did in Russia was not because of the brilliance or will-power or ruthlessness
or deception of the intelligentsia. It was because they expressed the very
aspirations towards which workers and peasants were led by their own
experience.

The implication of this work was that it was that support, rather than
superior organization or tactical genius, which enabled Lenin and his colleagues to come to power. Moreover, the success of Bolshevism during 1917
reflected not the party's centralization, unity and discipline but rather its
relatively open, flexible and democratic structure. Nor does the traditional
Western notion that the party was predominantly made up of radical intellectuals withstand close scrutiny: in 1917 the great majority of members
were urban workers and rank-and-file soldiers. And their migration towards
the Bolsheviks was not the product of brain-washing and infection by spell-
binding Bolshevik propaganda but part of a massive leftward shift clearly
registered even among those who continued to support the Mensheviks and
Socialist Revolutionaries. Nor was the October seizure of power an isolated
coup against the grain of developments across the country. The transfer of
power from the established local government bodies favoured by the
Provisional Government into the hands of workers', peasants' and soldiers'
soviets and committees was in many areas far advanced long before the
uprising in Petrograd. And the Constituent Assembly elections can only be

read as a conclusive popular repudiation of October if the Left SRs continue to be treated, as they have for so long, as a minor detail: had the electoral process permitted peasants to differentiate between SRs and the emergent Left SR party, it seems likely that the latter, in alliance with the Bolsheviks, would have secured a majority of deputies prepared to endorse October. Moreover, closer study of the Bolsheviks brought to light the competing currents and variety of agendas within 'Bolshevism' and the manner in which the economic and military nightmare of the post-October period privileged those currents pointing towards the policies of 'war communism'. In contrast to the picture presented in Soviet and traditional Western accounts, now thrown into sharp relief were the major elements of discontinuity between October and the regime that emerged from the civil war, and the drastic impact which that cataclysm had upon the party, its membership and its ethos. Equally revealing was the light thrown on the process by which the lower classes – whose power in 1917 had seemed irresistible as they swept away traditional authority, hierarchy and property relations, overthrew the ancient monarchy, and cut the ground from beneath the Provisional Government – were enfeebled during the civil war. After 1917, because they were divided, atomized and economically devastated, because they were alarmed at the threat that the Whites might reverse the social upheaval of 1917, because they were deprived of literate, ambitious, assertive strata recruited to serve the new state, and because, as a recent discussion in *Slavic Review* has suggested, of the disintegration of collective identities, workers and peasants proved unable to prevent the emergence of a highly centralized, bureaucratized and authoritarian regime.

By the late 1980s, the work of these historians who had exposed the flaws in Soviet and traditional Western interpretations alike was endorsed bymost Western specialists and was attracting increasingly sympathetic, albeit qualified, reviews from more outspoken Soviet historians. Although they constituted no single school of thought and although there were numerous differences of emphasis among them, they had laid the groundwork for major new syntheses, ranging from Tim McDaniel's reconceptualization of the contradiction between capitalism and autocracy (1988) to Orlando Figes's panoramic and richly coloured new narrative (1996). By no means all issues had been resolved: a recurrent criticism, voiced by leading figures who had themselves contributed to the flow of innovative work in the 1970s and 1980s, held that for all the new light that the view 'from below' had cast on the revolution, the interplay between organized political activity and mass social experience remained inadequately understood. Nevertheless, advocates of the traditional Western view were thrown onto the defensive, reduced to an ageing minority, and seemed in danger of losing the argument altogether. Alongside the numerous analyses based on Petrograd, there were appearing studies of the revolution as it unfolded in Moscow and Saratov, in Baku and Latvia. And broadly speaking, the conclusions in each place bore out the case against the traditional Western interpretation: to understand the

October revolution it is essential to grasp that political, social and economic conditions in the Russian empire had generated mass discontent and aspirations which the tsarist regime was finding it ever harder to contain; that the First World War and the period of the Provisional Government led workers, peasants and soldiers towards a deeper and deeper repudiation of the old order; that it was because Bolshevism articulated mass aspirations so well that the party attracted the support it did and seized power with such ease in October; that Bolshevism embraced a variety of competing ideological currents but that in responding to economic disaster and civil war, the new regime rapidly shed its democratic features and popular base and became ever more militarized and brutalized.

The collapse of Marxism-Leninism and the resurgence of the right

Since the 1980s, however, there has been a dramatic reversal of fortunes in the historiographical struggle over the revolution. The whole framework within which controversy had taken shape has been recast, on the one hand, making possible an extraordinary resurgence of the traditional Western view, while on the other breaking down the constraints born of Cold War polemic and opening up the field for fresh approaches.

In the first place, the collapse of the Communist Party of the Soviet Union (CPSU) and the USSR destroyed the orthodox Soviet account of the revolution. The Communist Party had been its driving force; its intellectual coherence depended on the notion that the party had led the Soviet people on a path irreversibly bound towards socialism and the ultimate utopia of communism. When the party went into terminal disarray, its leadership disbanded by Gorbachev and the whole organization banned by Yeltsin, it suddenly ceased to be possible to view the Bolshevik victory as the inauguration of a new, socialist stage in world history. The effect in terms of historiography was enormously liberating. The mould cast 80 years ago, the time-honoured Soviet/anti-Soviet paradigm, was finally broken. A whole new generation of Russian historians was set free. And the doors to the archives were at last unlocked. The result has been to allow facets of the revolution long ignored altogether, treated in almost formulaic terms, or at best pushed to the periphery to move towards centre stage. In the short term, however, scarcely less striking was the fillip given to adherents of the traditional Western view. Overnight, they saw their old enemy reduced to ashes and Soviet orthodoxy repudiated in its homeland. Inevitably, this seemed to vindicate those who had been most militant and categoric in their denunciation of each and every proposition endorsed by Marxism-Leninism. In the case of historians of the revolution, this meant adherents of the traditional Western view rather than those who had found fault with that view.

The Soviet collapse affected the whole world, but its primary impact, of course, has been in the former Soviet Union and Russia itself. Here it led to the furious repudiation of all things Soviet – the symbols, the monuments, the nomenclature, the novels, the films, the textbooks, the very language of the Soviet era were rejected and disdained. The removal of the incubus of Marxism-Leninism opened the way, in the medium term, to cultural renaissance and ideological pluralism. But the vigour of the initial rejection brought with it, during the Gaidar years at least, a violent ideological swing to the right, leap-frogging over social-democratic values to those of unvarnished capitalism. Thus where historiography was concerned, the warmest welcome in those years was not for revisionist ideas but for full-blooded traditional Western interpretations, for translations of liberal and right-wing memoirs. The greatest regret was not for communist critics of Stalin, such as N. I. Bukharin; not for the moderate socialist leaders of 1917, I. G. Tsereteli and V. M. Chernov; not even for Kerensky; but rather for the path of the right-wing liberal leader P. N. Miliukov, for tsarism's last dynamic minister, P. A. Stolypin, and even for Nicholas II himself, who was soon on the way to being considered for canonization by the Church. At the extreme there was a return to bizarre conspiracy theories to explain October, including brazen attempts to rehabilitate the long-discredited anti-semitic forgery, 'The Protocols of the Elders of Zion'.

Meanwhile, in the West the collapse of the USSR coincided with and sharply accentuated a period of right-wing political and intellectual ascendancy which had been epitomized by the governments of Ronald Reagan and Margaret Thatcher. Notions of collective action, collective control, collective ownership and state intervention were in full-scale retreat before the triumphant march of those preaching the free market and possessive individualism. And it seemed there could be no more powerful demonstration of the supposed superiority of the market over planning and of individualism over collectivism than for the entire Soviet enterprise to implode precisely at this moment. The effect, in terms of historical controversy, was to accentuate the swing to the right and to restore the confidence and credibility of traditional Western approaches.

The mood was captured to perfection when, with flawless timing, the long-time American doyen of Russian history viewed from the right, Richard Pipes, Professor of History at Harvard, published in 1990 a new thousand-page study of the revolution. In effect Pipes ignored the work of the whole generation engaged in social history and boldly reasserted the interpretation which their work had rendered implausible. And while reviews in specialist journals tore the book to shreds, in the quality press it was enthusiastically received and widely acclaimed as a definitive masterpiece. It was symptomatic of the intellectual climate that in 1993 the Norwegian Nobel Institute chose Pipes to deliver a prestigious new annual lecture series designed to address topics relevant to the Institute's work as secretariat to the awarders of the Nobel Peace Prize – and that the world's best-known university press subsequently published his ruminations. Pipes used his version of the revolution to proclaim the conclusive failure of the entire Enlightenment project. Exuding conservative triumphalism, he opened his lectures with Machiavelli's charming observation that 'He who abandons what is done for what ought to be done, will rather learn to bring about his own ruin'. The peasantry, he declared, 'held "freedom" of no account'; workers he portrayed as a wild mob creating 'that peculiar Russian air of generalized, unfocused violence – the urge to beat and destroy' and manipulated 'like a school of fish' by socialist leaders; most members of the Bolshevik Party in 1917–18 were lifelong professional revolutionaries; Lenin's authority was so great that his followers 'never undertook any action which he did not personally approve'. The revolution, he proclaimed, 'was the result not of insufferable conditions but of irreconcilable attitudes . . . attitudes rather than institutions or "objective" economic and social realities determine the course of politics'.

Each proposition flies in the face of the most detailed and meticulous specialist research; the overall picture painted is a mere caricature of the momentous social drama which that research is gradually recovering. It is as if, because the collapse of the USSR took place when the right was riding high in the West, a veil was about to be drawn over the implications of the best work of recent decades in an attempt to ensure that popular understanding of the revolution, in the East and West alike, would be based on old myths resuscitated.

The impact of post-modernism

Like the collapse of the USSR, the multi-faceted late-twentieth-century intellectual shift identified with the term 'post-modernist' has had an ambivalent impact on the study of the revolution. On the one hand, some of the repercussions of this shift have played a major role in shaping a new agenda for research. Contemporary emphasis on issues of culture and discourse, in particular, have sensitized historians to questions for too long treated as unproblematic. It has encouraged them to reappraise their own conceptual apparatus, to recognize and bring to light the presuppositions and implicit assumptions – be they about values, processes or relations, about progress, modernization or gender – embedded in the analytical language they themselves employ. No less important, it has encouraged them to approach with greater care the complex ways in which the various discourses of the historical subjects they study affected how those subjects understood and reacted to the world around them. Moreover, it has been the most intellectually adventurous historians who have proved most willing to grapple with the problems which the cultural perspective raises. It is they who, building on the innovative work of the 1970s and 1980s, are now giving deeper consideration to the relationship between being and consciousness, to the extent to which cultural formation, ideology, identity and discourse affect the way in which individuals and social groups interpret and respond to objective conditions, processes and experience. It is in these terms that they are refining the insights arising from earlier work, seeking to take further our understanding of the relationship between the social revolution and its political outcome – be it by unpacking the sense in which during 1917 the complex amalgam that was Bolshevism came to 'articulate' working-class aspirations; by tracing the way in which, after October, the discourse of class categories ceased to bind together and empower the lower orders and became instead a highly effective instrument of division, demonization and legitimation in the hands of the new regime; or by uncovering the profound impact which the revolution had on relations of power beyond those embodied in the formal institutions of state and property. Thus in a sense this 'new cultural history' constitutes an extension of the 'new social history' of the post-1960s' period and it is reflected in each of the sections which follow, both in essays dealing with familiar actors, parties, institutions, social groups, economic, regional and minority national problems, and in those exploring their under-studied counterparts, be it the Russian Orthodox Church, the press or the gender question. Throughout, there is a heightened concern to explore how hard reality, the flesh-and-blood experience of men and women, interacted with, was at once coloured by and itself informed, the specific conceptual tools and rival discourses available to them in the territories of the fallen tsar.

At the same time, however, other features of the same intellectual shift have contributed towards an intellectual climate which in many ways is more conducive to acceptance of the traditional Western approach than of the insights of its critics. For new awareness of the assumptions hidden in the language of supposedly value-free social analysis has all too easily been taken as grounds for repudiating the findings of social analysis altogether. Paradoxical as it may seem, it is historians whose methodology is rooted in the period preceding the explosion of social history in the 1960s and 1970s who stand to benefit from the extreme scepticism and crude relativism which these currents of thought have bred. The paradox is to be explained, at one level, by the fact that this scepticism, like the Pipesian approach to the past though from an entirely different direction, represents an attack upon the whole tradition of historical research which flows from the Enlightenment. It rejects faith in science, in reason, in deduction and induction; it tends to treat everything, every artefact, every event, every statement as a text which can be read a thousand different ways; it doubts our ability to know anything; it has no use for origins, causality or synthesis, and refuses to accept that one explanation is superior to another. At its most strident, it repudiates the rules of evidence and the distinction between objective and subjective, denies our ability to study and understand the past, and is ultimately incompatible with the writing of history. Yet its impact on the cultural and intellectual climate of the late twentieth century is undeniable. And, at least where the controversy over the Russian revolution is concerned, its impact has been to lend further comfort to champions of the traditional Western interpretation.

In the first place, this scepticism has thrown into question the notion of any 'grand narrative' in history. It has rejected the idea that there is a story to be told of progress, whether in terms of ideas or institutions, of human dignity or social mores, which we can recover and authenticate. It casts doubt not only on faith in reason in general but specifically on the notion of history as a rational tale of human striving. Clearly this not only clashes directly with any kind of Hegelian or Marxist or Christian approach to the past, but it also tends to undermine even the more modest assumptions which underlie recent work on the development of mass aspirations in late imperial Russia. Moreover, the general effect of this shapeless, agnostic attitude to the past is to predispose students reared under its influence towards the kind of approach that treats the Russian revolution, like every historical phenomenon, as dependent on chance and political misjudgement, and amounting to little more than a fluke.

Second, this current of scepticism, feeding as it does on the willingness of critical social analysis to reappraise its own concepts, casts particular doubt on historical approaches which lay emphasis on objective socio-economic conditions. It rejects any attempt to focus on social groups and strata defined in terms of their social role and common economic interests. It has no use for notions of class. Here, too, though it may have very little to say about what *can* be known and analysed, its negative message, its eagerness not only to deconstruct but to reject wholesale the terms and concepts on which social analysis depends, is much more damaging to the critical work of the post-1960s' generation than to the traditional Western view which has long relegated social categories and economic issues to the periphery.

Third, and a direct corollary of this, is the way in which the same scepticism, rooted in the notion that we are all prisoners of one discourse or another, tends not only to privilege the subjective but to treat it as autonomous. This implies that in so far as the study of the past makes any sense at all, human action and social change are to be explained in terms of the ideas, the values and mental images that people happen to have. It is this notion which has the gravest implications for a critical and reflective approach to the study of the past and which appears to lend most support to the traditional Western interpretation of the revolution. For if the autonomy and causal primacy of ideas are accepted, it follows that to understand the political outcome of the revolution there is no need to study the social dimension, to complement study of the mental world of men and women with analysis of their material experience. Once that primacy is accepted, it is but a short step to endorsing central features of the Pipesian interpretation – and above all the claim that the fundamental cause of the Russian revolution is to be found not in the realm of political, social and economic realities nor in the clash of interests, fears and aspirations born of these but in the autonomous world of ideas and attitudes, and at root, according to Pipes, in the propaganda, the language, the discourse infiltrated by socialist intellectuals.

A landmark

Thus the momentous developments which have refreshed the agenda for future research on the revolution have also threatened to obscure the light which recent work has thrown upon it. The drama still unfolding in the former Soviet Union has burst asunder the old fetters on free historical research while the contemporary intellectual shift has inspired new sensitivity both to the problems and to the importance of discourse analysis. But the same combination has also lent new plausibility to a partisan approach whose inadequacies have been exposed by contemporary critical research. It is against this background that the *Critical Companion* has been conceived. It represents a self-conscious landmark, bringing together in a single encyclopaedic volume a display of that critical work in all its richness and variety, a display which is at once considered and accessible, authoritative and emphatic. But it is a landmark erected on an intellectual landscape whose once fixed points are moving and melting before our very eyes and constructed at a supremely fluid and exhilarating moment in the historiography of the revolution.

Further reading

Acton E., *Rethinking the Russian Revolution* (London, Edward Arnold, 1990).

Appleby J., Hunt L. and Jacob M., *Telling the Truth about History* (New York, Norton, 1994).

Burdzhalov E. N., *Russia's Second Revolution: The February 1917 Uprising in Petrograd*, trans. and ed. by Raleigh, D. J. (Bloomington, Indiana University Press, 1987).

Figes O., *A People's Tragedy: The Russian Revolution 1891–1924* (London, Jonathan Cape, 1996).

Furet F. and Ozouf M., *The Critical Dictionary of the French Revolution* (Cambridge, MA, Belknap Press of Harvard University Press, 1989).

Haimson L., Rosenberg W. G. and Rieber A., discussants, 'The Problem of Social Identities in Early Twentieth-Century Russia', *Slavic Review* 47 (1989), pp. 1–38.

McDaniel T., *Autocracy, Capitalism and Revolution in Russia* (Berkeley, CA, University of California Press, 1988).

Pipes R., *The Russian Revolution, 1899–1919* (London, Collins Harvill, 1990).

Pipes R., *Communism: The Vanished Spectre* (Oxford, Oxford University Press, 1994).

Smith S., 'Writing the History of the Russian Revolution after the Fall of Communism', *Europe-Asia Studies* 46 (1994), pp. 563–78.

Startsev V. I., *Krakh Kerenshchiny* (Leningrad, Nauka, 1982).

Suny R. G., 'Revision and Retreat in the Historiography of 1917: Social History and Its Critics', *Russian Review* 53 (1994), pp. 165–82.

Volobvev P. V., *Ekonomicheskaia politika Vremennogo Pravitel'stva* (Moscow, 1962).

Interpreting Revolutionary Russia

WILLIAM G. ROSENBERG

Imperial Russia and the revolutionary experience

The cataclysm that engulfed the peoples and territories of imperial Russia as war and revolution brought the new Soviet empire into being touched directly more than 140 million people. While the short-hand label 'Russian revolution' generally signifies the radical political transition from tsarist to communist rule in nine short months during 1917, its multiple dimensions were linked not so much by the sharp moves from February to October, but by profound and irrevocable changes in life experience and expectation throughout the much broader period of world war and civil conflagration between 1914 and 1921. At different times, and for different people, these changes were sometimes felt with a hope that leavened anxieties and deprivations. For many, however, whether liberals who hoped in 1914 that the World War might bring political liberalization, moderate socialists who heralded in February the start of political and social democracy, or various radical enthusiasts who may have envisioned in October the promise of peace, land, and a new world order, the anticipation of betterment was quickly engulfed by anguish. No sequence of events in human history had as yet affected so many individuals so profoundly. Beneath all its complexity and contradiction, the Russian revolution was at its core a vast social trauma.

Comprehending the Russian revolution thus requires a grasp of the major events, parties, institutions and actors whose description and analysis by leading authorities make up most of this volume, but it requires, too, an effort to uncover the meanings of hope and disappointment, of anguish and anger, that were the constant accompaniments to revolutionary change. These subjectivities not only linked psychological and physical brutalities to various social and political mobilizations and facilitated different forms of action; they also gave events and actions their particular (and often contradictory) meanings, which are often not immediately apparent or even readily evidenced in any systematic way. All too often, the traumas of violence and deprivation are subsumed in 'objective' narratives of political events and social action, since it is actors and actions that are most easily recorded.

In the process, important commonalities of the revolutionary experience are displaced. Personal trauma in the years between 1914 and 1921 crossed social categories, ages, occupations and genders. It was found in the trenches and among the flood of wartime refugees so ably discussed below by Dominic Lieven and Peter Gatrell; by industrialists, gentry landowners and Daniel Orlovsky's 'middle strata'; by the workers and peasants, officers and soldiers discussed by Sergei Iarov, Orlando Figes, Evan Mawdsley and Peter Kenez; and everywhere, certainly, by women, as Barbara Clements eloquently testifies. It affected victors and vanquished, triumphant radical enthusiasts as well as their defeated and brutally repressed 'bourgeois' antagonists. For many, deprivation and anguish also became progressively worse, amplified by the collapse of hopeful efforts on which such enormous energy had been expended. The poignant diary of a brilliant academician like Iurii Vladimirovich Got'e has more in common than he might have liked with the many plaintive and despairing letters that ordinary workers and peasants sent to Lenin and other Bolshevik leaders during the civil war and which were secreted for so long in Soviet archives.

The recent opening of these archives and the ability now of Russian and non-Russian scholars alike to grapple freely with important historical issues everywhere as equals make this a timely moment to expand and enrich our understanding of revolutionary Russia, and finally, perhaps, to put aside the reductionist tendencies toward demonization and triumphalism that have characterized all Soviet historiography of this period and a good deal of Western writing as well. From more open perspectives, students may now more easily understand the processes and experiences that contextualized the events and actions which constitute core narratives, and at least complement the common and understandable tendency to identify 'who was to blame' with a more judicious comprehension of 'what was responsible' for a trauma that was universally felt.

This is not in any way to diminish the roles of Lenin, Bolshevism, or other political actors and movements in shaping the flow of events: from the outbreak of war in 1914, through the abdication of the tsar in March, the April and July crises of 1917, the radicalization of the factory and agrarian movements, to the October seizure of power, and the various episodes that map the civil war which raged across the former tsarist empire. Obviously, human agency is *always* responsible at some level for the havoc people wreak on each other; and both explaining and understanding Russia's revolutionary experience clearly requires careful attention to individuals, social groups and their political organizations, as the largest number of the contributions to this volume amply testify. At the same time, however, as other contributions suggest, the fullest explanations also require careful attention to deeply embedded cultural processes, to economic patterns and structures, to the forms, nature and locations of power, and especially to the relationship between ideologized discourses of various sorts, personal experiences, and both the longer and shorter patterns of structural change in late imperial Russia. In examining the role of ideology, in particular, one can perhaps find the initial connections between human agency, experience and social processes or structures, since ideologies helped give meaning to shared experience and generally mapped the various collective efforts to give shape to the context of upheaval and dislocation in which they were lodged.

Ideology as explanation and the representation of social identity

Virtually without exception, the ideological perspectives which are described in this volume and which Russia's principal actors and movements brought to the revolutionary epoch were grounded in some way in wishes to relieve at least some aspects of social distress and individual deprivation. The familiar tropes with which both radical and moderate socialists linked impoverishment and exploitation to the baneful institutions of private property and capitalism (and from this imagined a range of more or less idealized communitarian solutions) were the complement in important ways to liberal and conservative arguments about the inadequacies of the imperial Russian state and the urgency of effective governance based on the rule of law. Each was part of a broad public discourse about ways and means to relieve the social tensions that had come to wrack tsarist Russia, improve material well-being, and assure a secure future.

Like the pervasive dislocation of the epoch itself, this ideological wish for betterment is essential to understanding the great passion that characterized virtually all political activism between 1914 and 1921, as state power moved formally from the old regime to the Provisional Government, and then became so violently contested with the creation of the Bolshevik regime. Whatever their provenance, activist politics only seemed to bring increasing and more awful deprivations, first to one social sector, then to another. As perspectives on the ways in which social distress could be mitigated, socialist, liberal, and even conservatives' ideologies differed fundamentally, of course; and within these broad camps, the 'left', 'centre' and 'right' also sorted themselves out in terms of how, at what pace, and which particular attributes of imperial Russia's 'backwardness' could be alleviated. In the process, however, perspectives formed from (ideological) visions of Russia's appropriate future increasingly gave way to contending explanations about what was wrong with the present. Ideologies led as always to ready simplifications; and as we know, simplification is the root of intolerance and the core of stern authority. Especially after February, as the essays below by Michael Melancon, Ziva Galili, Albert Nenarokov, Israel Getzler and others on the SRs, Mensheviks, Kadets and their leaders nicely show in parallel, it was precisely because of a growing, and soon, indeed, certain conviction that one's political rivals were aggravating rather than ameliorating social conflict and distress that the grounds for common effort collapsed. Russia's devastating civil war emerged from this failure as well as from Lenin and the Bolsheviks' familiar urge for power.

One's sense of urgency about how and where matters were becoming worse in this period did not depend at first on ideology as much as on social location and perspective, that is, on social identity. Claims to increasingly scarce resources and the means to their access were both still tightly circumscribed by the bounds of outmoded social and ethnic paradigms, reflected for example before 1917 in a severely restricted electoral franchise and after February in the continuing systems of civil law and cultural bias, especially in non-Russian parts of the empire. The press for (revolutionary) activism thus cut broadly across the political spectrum. However much liberal zemstvo figures close to the peasants' and gentry's predicaments after 1914 understood the longer-term structural origins of deprivation in the countryside, for example, they recognized that solutions could not be long deferred by the state without increasingly serious social conflict; and however much moderate and radical socialists disagreed on the appropriate stages and timing of socio-economic transformation in industrial production and the distribution of commodities after 1917, the deterioration of Russia's mixed market economy itself soon made the question of access to, and especially control over commodities, a matter of sheer survival for many close to the factories and the fields. Similar differences in perspective increasingly divided nationalities, as the contributions below by Mark von Hagen, Olavi Arens, Andrew Ezergailis, John Klier, Martha Olcott and Ron Suny variously indicate. The urgency of local control is always related in some measure to the range and intensity of deprivations imposed on communities from outside.

The way social and political identities were consequently consolidated in this period, from the socio-cultural debris of the old order, increasing economic insecurity, and one's social position in the new, both complemented the processes whereby ideologies were simplified and increased their appeal. As they increasingly became *explanations* of lived experience and the putative reasons for political actions and social behaviour, social identities themselves became linked ever more to political causes. Thus the commitment of liberals and others to military victory against the Germans, although formulated ideologically in part as essential for Russia's commercial vitality after the war and hence popular social welfare, after February increasingly became, in the eyes of the left, an explanation for why men and women were dying. As Allan Wildman, Ziva Galili, Albert Nenarokov, Raymond Pearson and Boris Kolonitskii all suggest in this volume in different ways, the war itself became the specific fault of those who were now representing a reductively defined social stratum. In a similar way, defence of law and social order, always intrinsically a defence of established privilege, became increasingly the reason why wages were inadequate, prices were high, and food and fuel in scarce supply. Indeed, as imperial Russia's state-capitalist structure did begin to crumble, at once cause and consequence of the deprivations of war and revolution, the analytic logic of class differences and conflict became the insidious, ideologized passions of class warfare.

In the process, representations of 'worker' and 'peasant', 'bourgeois' and 'the intelligentsia', 'Ukrainian' and 'Russian', even 'Red' and 'White', moved from ideologically and socially constructed identities to powerful and antagonistic states of mind. The Bolsheviks increasingly gained and held power through coercive force, of course, but they gained and held this coercive force itself not simply because they were the best organized of the parties, but because their ideology, so cleverly reformulated by Lenin and others after the Leader's return in April 1917, became in its simplicities increasingly convincing and persuasive as an explanation for immediate social distress. Meanwhile, on the other side of the growing social divide, where anxiety and deprivation soon became no less acute, Bolshevik evil itself became the universal 'answer'. Among their other accomplishments, Lenin and the Bolsheviks most successfully cultivated the identification, representation and demonization of 'enemies', a process which curved whatever may have been the potential of revolutionary betterment into the ultimate anguish of Soviet Russia's never-ending civil wars.

Locations of power and the question of the state

The forms of power lodged in the ideological manipulation of political and social discourse – of which Lenin was past master – should give pause to those who believe coercive force alone brought the Bolshevik state into being. While the overthrow of the tsar, so carefully analysed in this volume by Tsuyoshi Hasegawa, obviously signified the political collapse of autocratic Russia, what constituted the essence of autocracy was not simply, and perhaps after 1905 not even primarily, its formal political institutions. It was rather an array of self-replicating and culturally legitimated social and cultural relations, ones that embodied their own forms of power and control and situated them in clearly marked locations. The thick social networks of the village community discussed below by Orlando Figes, the peasantry's complex relations with state officials and their gentry allies, the very ways land was owned and possessed, the urban ghettos and their links to the social hierarchies of the industrial workplace, the church and religious life discussed by Mikhail Shkarovskii, even the hierarchical tensions of student life and the heavily gendered role patterns within families described in the essays of Aleksei Markov, Elizabeth Waters and Barbara Clements – all these were fields of imperial Russian social practice structured by cultural forms and concepts of authority and maintained by direct and implicit political rights and powers. Each involved well-defined patterns of domination and subordination. All were formally justified by shared concerns about social order. Each was strengthened by an array of formal institutions and institutionalized traditions. Even diction and the use of impersonal speech reflected the ways power was located under the autocracy both within Russia itself, and in the vast non-Russian areas of the empire. As the impressive array of essays here on nationalities and regions collectively emphasize, military garrisons in these latter regions may have maintained tsarist control, but the extension of Russian fields of social dominance and subordination was the core of imperial power.

While the state and its officials were obviously the most visible objects of political struggle before 1917, contestation over these socially embedded forms of autocratic power constituted the revolution's deeper political undercurrent. Indeed, as Hasegawa indicates, while Duma and military leaders moved forward in February, convinced that new leadership would strengthen, not weaken, state authority, men and women in the capital, mobilized by food shortages and other pressing everyday needs, clearly sought and effected changes in the places and ways power itself was to be held. As Steve Smith, Diane Koenker and Allan Wildman detail, it was the confrontation against social practices *within* Petrograd factories and the garrison, and soon within Russian industry, the military, and especially the countryside more broadly, that after February began to alter both the nature of authority and understanding of where and how it was to be exercised.

Thus the devolution of power was one of the central currents of change in revolutionary Russia, just as it was at the end of the Soviet epoch. The ways in which established social institutions and relations lost authority and traditional political meaning were consequently as much a part of revolutionary politics in 1917 as the struggles among the parties for control of the state. The significance of the factory committee movement, for example, was not ultimately in the reformulation of production and work processes, as initially intended, but in the radical destabilization of lines of authority within the factory, and the accompanying shift of understanding about where the power to decide these questions should be located, and by whom. In the countryside, the expropriation of gentry land and the reabsorption of Stolypin's 'separators' back into the commune were more than simply the forceful assertion of peasant use rights: they radically disempowered all institutionalized forms of gentry control and revolved totally the traditional patterns of dominance and subordination between land owners and land users.

As in other great revolutions, these transforming shifts of power and authority were necessarily chaotic. They often occurred quite informally, and were not readily associated with specific events. But they speak to the importance of a revolutionary narrative that encompasses power in its social and cultural structures as well as its more formal politics and political institutions. In many places, they preceded the networks of committees, associations, and soviets that gave them institutional legitimacy, even if,

once legitimized in this way, they spread more rapidly; and they were quite
far advanced even if not complete by the time the Bolsheviks seized what
was left of the state. At the same time, however, since cultural systems of
domination and subordination involve far deeper structures than those that
define their institutional forms, it was also the case that, somewhat paradoxically, these transforming shifts were sometimes, in important ways, far
from revolutionary. In rural Russia, for example, the traditional gendering
of power relations may well have been strengthened as male-dominated village assemblies expanded their authority; and with few exceptions, men in
factories under workers' control were at best only marginally more willing
to share their new power with women than they were under the old regime.

If social order is an effect of institutionalized power, moreover, social disorder in 1917 was a further effect of shifting locations of power, while resistance to these processes was the foundation of civil war. For Kerensky (as
well as for other prominent figures in the Provisional Government), preserving state authority was thus the defining task of governance in 1917,
while for Bolsheviks and their supporters, extending the locations of power
past their points of greatest resistance was the defining mark of revolutionary commitment, at least until they themselves had to govern.

It is here that one can begin to look more closely at one of the most com-
monly held arguments about the state itself in this period: that its weakness
lay primarily in the debilitating effects of 'dual power', and that divided
authority with the Soviet made it impossible to stem 'the forces of decay'. If
we understand 'authority' to mean legitimated power, however, rather than
simply the ability to coerce, and if we understand a principal task of democratic states to be the mediation of contending claims about local boundaries
of power and authority, especially those embedded in social relations and
cultures, it can be argued that the Russian state lost its capacity to govern in
1917 not because its authority was compromised by the soviets and even less
because Miliukov and others initially identified its interests with military victory and imperialism. Rather, the state began to 'wither' because it lacked,
and indeed never had, the institutional capacity to mediate contending claims
about how power should be exercised locally, and because it was unable to
satisfy conflicting claims on its economic, social and cultural resources.

Here the distinction between state (in Russian, *gosudarstvo*) and government (*pravitel'stvo*) is of some importance, the former representing certain
general interests and practices, the latter reflecting changing programmatic
ways of defining them and assuring their effective implementation. The
devolution of power in 1917 effectively meant that the act of governing, or
the making and implementing of policy, shifted its location as well. In the
process, Kerensky's 'national' coalition regimes found themselves increasingly unable to argue or demonstrate convincingly that there was any unifying set of interests and practices that could be broadly reflected in a
democratic Russian state. Lenin may well have prescribed in *State and
Revolution* the ways Bolsheviks should use state power to smash resistance

and 'complete' the revolution, but a more fundamental task after October, and one that faced all civil war contenders, was the very reconstruction of the state itself. The success of the Red Army in a context of Allied intervention described below by Evan Mawdsley, Francesco Benvenuti and David Foglesong, and the accompanying militarization of Bolshevism that Robert Daniels, Sergei Iarov and Vladimir Cherniaev variously discuss, ultimately meant that the forms and means of post-revolutionary state formation would themselves become the thicker roots of Stalinism.

The economy as 'instituted process'

Both contemporary and retrospective concern with the most visible aspects of the devolution of power in the revolutionary period, and especially with the political consequences of a weakening state, has tended to veil the implications of both these processes for revolutionary Russia's economy, and hence the material well-being of its citizens. As much of British and West European history suggests, in historical circumstances where localities have adequate resources and can function economically without great dependence on the state, the collapse especially of imperial orders does not necessarily portend economic disaster. A signal characteristic of imperial Russia, however, was the extent and form of state participation in what might best be described as its 'partly commercialized' economy, and the particular ways, consequently, in which economic processes imbricated political, social and cultural institutions. Because of the relative absence of domestic investment capital, the costs of resource extraction and capital goods production, the relative inelasticity of mass consumer demand, a somewhat underdeveloped banking system, and above all, in the view of some, the absence of adequate standards of commercial morality and behaviour, the state itself in imperial Russia had historically carried a heavy economic load. Its economic power and influence were also culturally respected even if frequently challenged. Commercial activism, speculation, even petty trading bore various pejorative connotations in some circles well before Bolsheviks and others infused the term '*burzhui*' (bourgeois) with contempt. It was the state's offices and institutions which were broadly expected to help finance economic development (especially in heavy industry), manage major extractive industries, assure the flow of capital resources, provide fiscal security, regulate the market, and help relieve distress.

If the state's inadequacies in this regard fuelled a range of dissidence well before 1914, the outbreak of war compounded developmental and managerial responsibilities while adding heavy new distributive burdens. As was the case with other warring powers, the tsarist regime moved quickly to concentrate industrial and defence production and extend administrative control over market exchange. As the state's demand for military goods increased, direct state ownership expanded. In 1915, the Special Council for Defence began to regulate all military production and to provide a range of direct and indirect subsidies to major producers, often without any careful estimates of actual costs. By the autumn of 1915, state regulatory commissions were supervising transport, fuel and food distribution, and military procurements; by 1916, the domestic market in metals, chemicals, coal and leather goods was almost entirely under state control. Meanwhile, as Lars Lih's work has shown, the state's sudden need for huge quantities of foodstuffs left routine processes of economic exchange in a shambles in much of the countryside. Local state and military representatives soon had the power to requisition goods and embargo trading in essential supplies. Compulsory procurements, supported by coercive sanctions, became common, a harbinger of the confiscations that wreaked havoc in the civil war. Conservative liberals like Petr Struve and Aleksandr Krivoshein pressed to resolve the growing food supply crisis by extending price regulation to *all* foodstuffs, whether designated for the army or not. A. I. Shingarev, soon to become a prominent figure in the Provisional Government, railed with many others against the corruption and growing speculation these practices engendered, and demanded that the Ministry of Finance itself take strong measures to repress it. Here, too, the shadow of the cursed 'bagmen' (*meshochniki*) of the civil-war period could be seen in faint outline even before the overthrow of the tsar.

With the February revolution, moreover, it was the hope and expectation on both sides of the dual-power divide not that the state would become less engaged in managing Russia's deteriorating economy but, on the contrary, that its role would expand and its institutional practices would become more rational and effective. New laws on grain and fuel monopolies, new efforts to regulate prices, and an attempt to put new life into the growing number of state regulatory committees preoccupied Soviet and government figures alike, especially after the formation of the first coalition in May. This, in turn, increased both practical dependence on the state and popular expectations concerning its ability to address critical issues of individual and social welfare at precisely the moment when real power was shifting away from the centre and the capacities of state officials and institutions were weakening. While the Ministry of Finance and other high state offices soon faced what Shingarev described as a 'hurricane' of new claims, workers, peasants and the burgeoning network of soviets pressed for an expanded system of price and distribution controls. One fundamental concern was to control the rising cost of living. Another, and increasingly prevalent one, was to curb speculative excesses and 'unfair' profits. Behind both, however, was an even more pressing issue for those concerned with Russia's democratic future: the likelihood that continued shortages of food and other essentials would further exacerbate Russia's social and political polarization, and make any semblance of democratic government impossible.

By late summer, as Nikolai Smirnov indicates in his original essay below, popular hope in the ability of a Constituent Assembly to carry revolutionary Russia through its crisis had already faded. The solution increasingly seemed to be that the state itself should assume an ever more directive economic role. While the Ministry of Labour became deeply involved in trying to settle scores of labour–management disputes, agreeing in some instances to increase state procurement prices to assure higher wages, in others to expand procurements themselves, a newly reorganized State Economic Council debated further measures to extend regulatory control. At the same time, reports from various state food procurement groups indicated that the chances of meeting urban needs in the forthcoming winter were slim. In the countryside, bagmen were already subverting regulated grain procurements in massive numbers, the 'bootleggers', as Lars Lih has called them, of the prohibited grain trade. At the offices of the Ministry of Finance, meanwhile, as the economic situation everywhere deteriorated, more than 8,000 government engraving plant workers turned out some 30 million new paper roubles a day, an amount which by October was insufficient to meet the state's immediate needs.

Since economic exchange relations in revolutionary Russia, as everywhere, reflected cultural as well as economic values, an important consequence of the state's attempt to assert closer control over the economy in 1917 was its increasing identification with excesses over which, in fact, it had less and less control. Equally portentous was the growing identification of market practices themselves, and especially the legal protection of private ownership rights, with 'injustice' and 'unfairness', since they reflected the equities of accumulation and opportunities for wealth, not those of distribution. In these social and cultural terms, as well as in terms of more formal economic institutions, the economy was an 'instituted process' to use Karl Polanyi's term. Its vitality was not simply a matter of material well-being, but of preserving the system of social values which it reflected.

Although the 'withering' of the state was broadly welcomed in revolutionary Russia in so far as it signalled the end of coercive political controls, the weakening of its economic capacities was almost everywhere a disaster. And as the established processes of market exchange themselves deteriorated in 1917, so did the customs, habits and values that were their necessary accompaniment. Thus, while the task of state reconstruction after October was regarded as a political imperative for both Bolsheviks and their civil-war antagonists, it also constituted in the view of many the only real possibility to stave off total economic collapse. Well before the measures of war communism outlined below by Silvana Malle, the ground was prepared for disastrous cultural–economic experiments.

The significations of October

What did October signify in the process of Russia's revolutionary transformation? The interesting questions here are not whether October represented in some important way the coming to power of an authentic workers' and peasants' regime, nor whether 'proletarian dictatorship' had any but symbolic meaning. As is by now well known even and perhaps especially by former Soviet readers, the party's primary political task after October, aside from self-preservation, was to gain control *over* the inclinations and authority of workers' and peasants' institutions themselves and to subordinate completely the soviet core of the Soviet state, not integrate them into structures that reflected popular desires or interests in any but prescriptive ways. Although the party itself was socially based on the industrial workforce, many of whose most competent members were soon Bolshevik bosses and administrators, 'proletarian dictatorship' very quickly became an uncompromising dictatorship *over*, not by, industrial and agrarian labour. These issues are essentially about how the Bolsheviks themselves represented their coming to power, attempted to legitimize their regime, and linked themselves propagandistically to broader local and non-Russian revolutionary currents. Indeed, the hollowness of Bolshevik sloganeering was evident almost at once. By the spring of 1918, both the opposition to Leninist rule among workers and peasants that would later explode around Tambov and Kronstadt, and the party's readiness to use the vicious 'extraordinary measures' described so well below by Alter Litvin, were readily apparent. Endless repetition may have created sacred Soviet historical traditions but these are interesting only in terms of the developmental role of truth-claims, not because they help us understand October.

There are similar weaknesses in the questions of whether (or how) Leninism and early Bolshevism produced Stalinism (or even fascism, as some historians now claim), matters which have gained much attention especially since the collapse of the Soviet Union. Here polemics work in a different direction: as attempts to discredit not only the obvious Stalinist and fascist components of Leninism and early Bolshevik rule, but also efforts to understand the complex historical conjuncture that produced them, as if analysis was exculpation. Who would disagree that tragedy engulfed Russia in various horrific ways from the summer of 1914 onward, or that October vastly extended the suffering of Russian and other peoples of the old empire? The lessons of history are not in human evil but in understanding what produced it.

At least three analytically important and principally interesting issues have concerned those seriously seeking to understand October as a turning point in Russia's extended revolutionary process. The first is whether the Bolshevik seizure of the state was a narrow, conspiratorial coup, or whether there was sufficient support for Lenin's party to warrant regarding October as a popular revolution in ways comparable to February. Somewhat related is the question of teleology: whether the Bolsheviks' coming to power flowed logically, if not ineluctably, from both the longer- and shorter-term historical currents in which it was embedded. Finally, there was (and is) the connected issue of alternatives, both democratic and authoritarian, of crucial importance to contemporary activists as well as to historians. At question here are such matters as the viability of a Constituent Assembly and a constitutional order, had Lenin allowed such possibilities, or the potential for civil-war leaders like Kolchak or Denikin to consolidate viable all-Russian anti-Bolshevik regimes. This issue of 'alternatives' is not at its core a counter-factual one. It relates as much as the other two to the problem of locations of power and their relation to naked force; to the issue of agency, and the degree to which human behaviour and revolutionary practice related to the structural elements of Russia's revolutionary conjuncture; and to essential questions of governance: what was required, in other words, of any governing order at the time to achieve a modicum of social peace, stability, and well-being.

If 'coup' is used conceptually to emphasize the sudden, swift and forceful manner in which Bolshevik leaders seized state institutions on 25 October, clearly October was a *coup d'état* whether or not it had popular support. But in so far as 'coup' connotes the 'usurpation' of power by a narrow band of dedicated revolutionaries socially rooted in the radical intelligentsia, who artificially cloaked their own political ambitions with a self-styled defence of popular interests, as the notion is now frequently deployed, the essential linkages between Russia's revolution and October are lost, along with its world historical meaning. About Bolshevik brutality and passion for power there cannot be (and never has been) much dispute. Some of this clearly stemmed from the party's radical attack on the disciplinary constraints associated with both tsarism and capitalism; some related to the anger and brutality linked to subordination and repression; and some surely emerged from psychological drives and hostile distortions in perception whose essence is largely beyond recapture. But as Alexander Rabinowitch, Robert Service and other careful historians have shown, Bolshevism was also a movement of substantial breadth and diversity during the revolutionary period, the single-mindedness of Lenin and his April Theses notwithstanding: the notion of the party as a disciplined conspiratorial block determined from the start to seize power is and has always been a distorting caricature.

What Bolshevism brought to Russia's revolutionary conjuncture was a capacity for organization, an ideological clarity, and a social positioning that facilitated affiliation with the radical relocation of power and authority in 1917. While Bolsheviks shared some of these attributes with other radical groups, and while party affiliation was little barrier to cooperation in many local soviets and committees, it was their certainty of vision and its explanatory force that gained them purchase. As extensive work in the social history of 1917 has now demonstrated, the increasing polarization of society within Russia as well as elsewhere in the empire was hardly Lenin's doing. At best one can say that Bolsheviks both at the centre and elsewhere used their exceptional capacities of communication to exacerbate tensions and accelerate the processes of social conflict well underway.

As propaganda instruments, newspapers like *Soldatskaia Pravda* ('Soldiers' Truth') reflected brilliantly the simplifications and hostilities of a tabloid mentality almost perfectly suited to the dispositions and anxieties of those eager for ready explanations and longing for relief. But Bolsheviks were hardly alone in identifying the relative material deprivations of workers and peasants within the exploitative structures of Russian private and state capitalism. What particularly distinguished Lenin's followers was the capacity to turn social antagonism into class warfare and their eagerness for conflict rather than social peace. Everywhere in 1917 responsible socialists contested the established social and cultural balances of power and in one or another form pushed their revolution. Few imagined this transformation without resistance, conflict and even some degree of repression if a stable socialist order was ever to be achieved. It was Bolshevism, however, that most eagerly pushed conflict into warfare, turned antagonists into enemies, and took greatest advantage of the devolution of power before October to build local support. Bolsheviks gained authority within and through the soviets and more broadly because the reasons they gave for how and why this relocated power should be forcefully used were convincing. At important moments, they gave coherence to the popular anger, energy and compulsions that the revolution had released.

Here, perhaps, one can identify the most important elements of Bolshevik agency in 1917. It is not, that is, whether human practice, rather than the locations, structures or nature of power itself, is the key to understanding October, but how they articulated with one another: how they fit, interacted and moved historically. Lenin was hardly alone in craving power in 1917 wherever it was located, and shared sometimes deluded notions of self-importance and 'saviourdom' with Kerensky and his antagonists on the right. October signified the triumph of Leninist will not because of its urgency, but because in contrast to other individuals and movements whose lust for control was equally pressing, Bolshevism penetrated revolutionary Russia's structural and political deformations. By October Lenin *could* act when he wanted to. Others could not, even when all of Russia could read in the newspapers what the Bolshevik *vozhd'* was about. Hence the silence of effective resistance, however deep its sentiment, and the exultant noise of Bolshevik triumph, however shallow its reflection of popular needs and interests.

To identify the logic behind Bolshevik success, however, hardly implies that specific outcomes were inevitable in 1917 – notwithstanding the familiar teleology of most common revolutionary narratives. The world historical significance of the Russian revolution was neither that ordinary workers and peasants could take power into their own hands if they were effectively led by a relatively well-organized revolutionary band, nor that a dedicated political conspiracy could readily subvert an established and legitimate democratic order if only it bent its will to the task. Rather, what the Bolsheviks' coming to power signified was the enormous difficulty of popular governance at a conjunctural moment of deep socio-cultural and economic dislocation, and the way in which pressures for the rapid satisfaction of popular needs and interests in a society with relatively weak civil, legal and democratic political traditions carried a powerful disposition toward authoritarianism in some form. That Lenin and other Bolsheviks exploited this disposition more effectively than others certainly testifies to their single-minded determination. But the disposition itself reflects the urgent need in such moments for democratically inclined regimes to show convincingly the relationship between their policies and future social welfare needs, and how difficult at such conjunctures are the necessary tasks of using inherited state power, in either its ordinary or superordinate forms, as an instrument for democratization.

Any alternatives to Bolshevism in 1917 had to confront these limitations directly. The efforts made after February to enlist broad sectors of the empire's population in democratically reformulating Russia's state interests and the means to achieve them stalled because the boundaries of central and local power could not be effectively negotiated or defended. Even the boundaries of democratic Russia itself, within and among the many nations of the empire as well as within a highly competitive international world system, could not be presumptively defined, as the Bolsheviks themselves were rudely to discover. And here, the views of Russian liberals differed from most Russian Marxists not on whether the state had to begin broadly to service its peoples' needs while also defending its institutions and prerogatives, but on its relationship to Russia's dominant, and in some sectors, hegemonic social groupings.

In 1917, this meant war – literally, in terms of maintaining Russia's vast army and somehow containing the Germans; figuratively, but with ample instances of direct confrontation, in terms of defending state institutions, resources, powers and interests from those created and defined through the shifting locations of power. These two struggles could only be pursued effectively if the army remained intact and loyal (but to what?), and preserved for the state the coercive force necessary to maintain order (but for whom?); or if the state's own institutions and interests themselves were radically redefined, and its powers linked in mutually reinforcing ways the new, non-state power structures emerging throughout revolutionary Russian society. In other words, given the unlikelihood that the Provisional Government could keep the army intact, even perhaps without the June offensive, the only possibility for retaining politically democratic governance in 1917 required the state to mediate rather than exacerbate social conflict and to accommodate rather than contend with popular needs and the radical social changes they engendered. In a phrase, the revolutionary state had both to represent itself, and be accepted, as popular, essential and worth defending. October reflected the failure of democratic Russia to manage this awesome task every bit as much as it signified Leninist political determination.

Civil wars and the tragedy of competitive impossibilities

It is in these terms as well, finally, that one can identify the most important linkages between the pre- and post-October phases of Russia's revolutionary transformation. Lenin and his party inherited precisely these tasks of governance when they declared themselves Russia's rulers, whatever their views on democratic politics. So did the leadership of the Constituent Assembly, both before and after Lenin drove it from Petrograd, as well as the anti-Bolshevik Workers' Assembly movement, Denikin and his generals in South Russia, the 'Supreme Ruler' Admiral Kolchak in Omsk, the huge peasant partisan movements under Makhno and Antonov, and each of the movements within the empire for national independence. In all of these cases the reconstruction of the state in some form remained essential to providing basic human needs and securities. In each of these cases, too, pretensions to power brought the need to reconnect state and local interests in some way, and to rearticulate state authority with diffused forms of power and sharply antagonistic interests. The failures of human agency can neither be exculpated nor loaded with a singular causal burden. Even a synod of saints would have found the stage set for tragedy, the competitive aspirations and needs of embittered, hopeful and increasingly desperate people impossible to reconcile without force.

Some of the most interesting contributions to this volume touch on this cardinal aspect of the revolution's civil-war phase. At the level of formal politics, Nikolai Smirnov's essay on the Constituent Assembly depicts a noble effort to reconstitute state authority on exclusively moral foundations without access to power itself in any substantial form. That the democratic ideals the Assembly represented soon became central to much of the discourse of anti-Bolshevik protest within Soviet Russia speaks eloquently to the politically and socially democratic spirit of the revolutionary period as a whole, but also, paradoxically, to the ways in which the moral authority of the democratic state proved inversely proportional to its functional power.

As Litvin, Service and Francesco Benvenuti demonstrate, moreover, the Bolsheviks themselves hardly escaped this dilemma. One of the most salient features of revolutionary Russia in the aftermath of October is that no significant improvements could be made in the well-being of ordinary workers and peasants, the capstone of the Bolsheviks' own claim to legitimacy. For a few brief weeks workers' control over production may have improved matters at the margins, but the processes of economic collapse were related structurally to the absence of production capital, a rampant inflation fuelled by the printing press, shortages in fuel and other resources, transport problems, and the inability of unregulated markets to manage the distribution of scarce commodities in ways perceived as equitable. In these circumstances, and facing the additional pressures created by the massive demobilization of the army and the spontaneous 'nationalization' of factories by factory committees in the expectation that this would bring them state support, it is hardly surprising that Lenin and his comrades initiated measures to assume direct control over the economy, or began to implement through the Cheka 'extraordinary' measures of control. Radical ideologies were readily tuned to critical circumstances, radical ideologues only too eager to press the crisis forward into lethal social combat.

Indeed, for Bolsheviks the tasks of revolutionary state-building, although difficult and problematic in the extreme, were significantly easier than those assumed by the White movements in South Russia and Siberia precisely because a radical explanatory ideology *sanctioned* brutal force and defined a clear (if unworkable) set of 'solutions'. Violence could thus be formally linked in the civil war to exactly the same broad set of hopes and expectations that mobilized workers, peasants and soldiers against the tsar, however much practice increasingly belied both the Bolsheviks' claim in this regard and the possibility that popular hopes could be realized. It is hardly surprising that strong anti-Bolshevik currents quickly developed in factories and industrial centres, as well as, more predictably, in the countryside, nor that much of this dissidence was articulated in the available and familiar discourse of civil liberty and political democracy. What all resistance to Bolsheviks failed to offer, however, beyond the mitigation of civil violence and repression so many desperately desired, was a set of social policies and political practices designed to end Russia's turmoil in the name of a better Russian and regional future sufficiently convincing to sustain a massive and coordinated anti-Bolshevik mobilization.

This, more than any failure of military coordination, was the fatal weakness of the Whites and the inherent limitation of the independent peasant armies. The repressive policies of these forces were often indistinguishable in their brutality from those of the Reds (especially against the Jews), yet neither was accompanied by an ideologically coherent set of policies or aspirations. Although Generals Alekseev and Denikin both professed liberal sentiments, and while Denikin, Kolchak and Wrangel all relied in some way on conservatively liberal as well as reactionary advisors and aides, none believed democratic mechanisms were politically viable any longer in Russia's circumstances, none could rationalize contending claims over resources (especially land), and each relied on hopes for the lost order of 'indivisible' Russia's past rather than on coherent arguments about how to resolve the question of empire in ways that met hitherto subordinate interests. The reconstruction of an imperial 'White' state whose authority was in some way ideologically or constitutionally legitimized and whose power could again articulate with other forms of authority in revolutionary Russia was as impossible to achieve without the brutal repression of internal civil resistance as the Bolshevik hopes of creating a democratic proletarian order. Wrenching social chaos, still more human suffering, and cruel authoritarianism in many forms were the understandable effects of Russia's revolutionary predicament every bit as much as the dreams for betterment that for a brief historical moment, at least, were almost everywhere the source of genuine and inspiring celebration.

THE REVOLUTION
AS EVENT

Russia, Europe and World War I

DOMINIC LIEVEN

In the early twentieth century the Russian empire was both less powerful and less secure relative to its major great-power rivals than had been the case a century before. The most basic reason for this was that the industrial revolution, originating in Western Europe, had then spread unevenly across the continent. Although in the last 50 years of Imperial Russia's existence economic development was rapid, per capita GNP in Russia lagged far behind German, British, French and even Austrian levels in 1914. One result of this was that the effort to sustain the armed forces and defence industries of a modern great power strained both the Russian economy and domestic political stability. In addition, relative backwardness called into question the empire's ability to survive in a war against other great powers.

Geopolitical changes also worsened Russia's international position in the half-century before 1914. For much of the eighteenth and nineteenth centuries, Russia, like Great Britain, had benefited from its position on Europe's geographical periphery. Territorial expansion in the heart of the European continent was difficult, tending to unite a coalition of hostile powers against any potential hegemon. Expansion outside Europe was much easier, and both Britain and Russia were best placed for such expansion, partly because their geographical position gave them a security against European rivals which France, Austria and Prussia did not possess.

Imperial Russia had benefited, too, from the decline of its traditional rivals in Eastern Europe (Sweden, Poland and the Ottoman empire) and of their French ally and patron. The rise of two Germanic great powers in Central Europe (Prussia and the Habsburg Monarchy) was also to Russia's advantage because these two states were bitter rivals and competed for Russian support. In these circumstances the Romanovs' empire was able to secure control over both the Baltic provinces and almost the whole of present-day Ukraine, the latter becoming by 1900 the centre both of the empire's agriculture and of its heavy industry. Russia's geopolitical triumphs and its territorial expansion consolidated the legitimacy of the

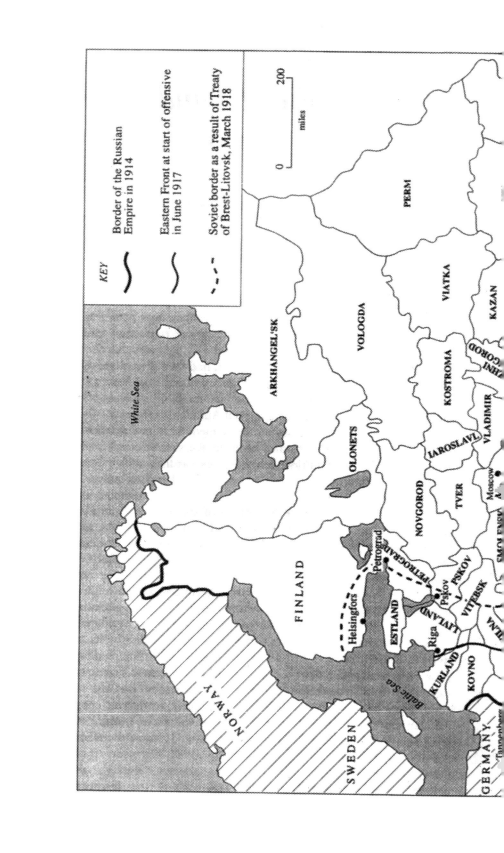

White Sea

ARKHANGEL'SK

VOLOGDA

OLONETS

PERM

VIATKA

KAZAN

KOSTROMA

IAROSLAVL

VLADIMIR

NIŽNII
GOROD

TVER

NOVGOROD

Moscow

SMOLENSK

FINLAND

Petrograd

PETROGRAD

PSKOV

Pskov

Helsingfors

VITEBSK

ESTLAND

LIVLAND

Riga

KURLAND

KOVNO

NORWAY

SWEDEN

Baltic Sea

GERMANY

Tannenberg

Map 1. The Eastern Front in World War I

autocratic regime and the alliance between crown and nobility, enabling the latter to acquire new estates in the fertile grainlands of the south. The eighteenth-century Russian aristocracy acknowledged their country's cultural inferiority to the West, as Ancient Romans had done with respect to Greece. Like the Romans, Russian elites could assuage their pride by reflecting on their empire's military and political triumphs.

In the last decades of Imperial Russia, however, matters became much more difficult. In the Crimean War (1854–56) Russia was defeated above all because a pre-industrial power could not hope to compete with more modern rivals. French and British troops travelled to the war by steamship and railway; British rifles outranged Russian artillery. The tsarist state lacked the resources to build a dense railway network or to equip its armed forces with the most modern military technology. Not only its armed forces and economy, but also its society and administrative system were revealed as backward. Defeat weakened the regime's legitimacy and the security of its western and Black Sea borders. The Polish rebellion of 1863 awakened fears that revolt among non-Russian peoples on the western borderlands would be backed by more powerful foreign states, thereby leading to the empire's disintegration. In 1863 these fears proved unfounded: British and French support for the Poles was purely verbal and neither country was in any case well placed geographically to intervene in Russia's western borderlands. With the unification of Germany in 1871, however, a new and potentially far more formidable threat emerged to Russia's control over her western frontier provinces, as well as, indeed, to her administrative and economic heartlands in European Russia and the Ukraine. The emergence of Japan as a major military and economic power by the early twentieth century was a further challenge to Russian security, particularly since Russian Asia was sparsely colonized, its communications with the empire's far-distant heartland were tenuous, and its southern borders were being turned into a power vacuum by the decline of the Ching empire.

Of the many possible threats to Russian security by 1900, however, the German one was the most dangerous, partly because of Germany's unique military and economic power, but also because the Hohenzollern empire was best placed to invade Russia's core territories. Military and economic power boosted Germany's arrogance and her ambitions. At the same time the strains of creating a new nation and of managing the political and psychological consequences of very rapid socio-economic modernization resulted in ever more resounding appeals to German nationalism as a means to unite society and sustain the legitimacy of its ruling elites. In addition, as the German economy boomed, Berlin inevitably acquired interests in regions traditionally seen as lying within the sphere of other powers. In the Russian case, this above all meant the Ottoman empire and Persia. The fact that the Hohenzollern Reich, though already Europe's most powerful state in 1900, contained less than half the world's Germans, was a further cause of concern to its neighbours. Pan-German propaganda fanned such fears, since it pointed to possibilities of almost unlimited German expansion, including into areas of the Russian empire inhabited by ethnic Germans.

Of the German communities living outside the Hohenzollerns' state, however, the largest and most important dwelt in the Habsburg Monarchy, whose dominant elites had traditionally more often than not been ethnic Germans. The 1879 German–Austrian alliance came to be rooted partly in common cultural sympathies, in a manner somewhat reminiscent of the later solidarity between Britain and the United States. With the rise of ethnic German nationalism and of conflict between Slavs and Germans within the Habsburg Monarchy it was a very moot point whether Vienna could for long have sustained a foreign policy not based on alliance with Berlin. This was doubly true because not only Austrian–German but also Hungarian elites saw their interests and sympathies as demanding close alignment with Germany. The latter was seen as sustaining not merely the Monarchy's external position against Russian competition in the Balkans but also the pre-eminence of the Germans and Hungarians within the Monarchy, as well as the latter's freedom from any conceivable German irredentist movement backed by Berlin. Although Bismarck attempted to balance between an absolute commitment to Austria–Hungary's survival and reassurance to Petersburg that Germany would never allow any challenge to essential Russian interests, his successors proved less skilful and less careful. Their abandonment in 1890 of the so-called Reinsurance Treaty with Russia led directly to the Franco-Russian alliance of 1894, which remained the central pillar of Russian foreign and military policy down to the Bolshevik seizure of power in 1917.

The logic underlying the Franco-Russian alliance was that Europe's two second-ranking powers were uniting to ensure that neither of their interests were trampled upon by the continent's potential hegemon, Germany. The alliance was designed to deter Germany from any such ambitions but also to defeat her in war should deterrence fail. The division of Europe into two military alliances made it almost certain that any conflict between great powers would engulf the entire continent. Nevertheless, in the first decade of Nicholas's reign Russia's relations with Berlin and Vienna were friendly. This was in part because much of Petersburg's attention was devoted to the Far East, which in turn made it easier to agree with Austria on a policy of supporting the status quo in the Balkans.

Russia's defeat by Japan in 1904–05 and the subsequent Russian revolution of 1905–06 changed matters very much for the worse. Awareness of Russian impotence encouraged first Germany and then Austria to defend their interests in the Moroccan Crisis of 1905–06 and in the 1908–09 Bosnian Crisis in a more aggressive manner than would otherwise have been the case. In Berlin's defence, however, it does need to be stressed that Germany did not seize the opportunity offered by Russia's weakness to impose its domination on Europe, as it could easily have done at any time between 1905 and 1909. The Russian government, acutely aware both of its international vulnerability and of its lack of prestige at home, became over-fearful of Austrian aggression in the Balkans after 1909, against which it helped to organize a league of Balkan states. The latter's existence in turn contributed to instability in the Balkan peninsula and to Russo-Austrian tensions. The tsarist regime's position was also challenged by the emergence of liberal–nationalist political parties in Russia which asserted their patriotic credentials by stressing Russia's mission in the Balkans and contrasting their own support for that mission with the government's caution and cowardice. Under all these pressures, a gap opened between Petersburg's strong rhetorical defence of its international interests and its actual willingness to stand up for these interests when challenged. Russia's rivals were thereby rather encouraged to discount Petersburg's pronouncements and to believe that pressure would bring rewards. This mattered in 1914.

In the period 1911–14 the Ottoman empire appeared to be on the verge of disintegration. Defeat by the Italians in 1911–12 and then by the Balkan League in 1912–13 was accompanied by political turmoil in Constantinople. The fate of the Ottoman lands and of the Balkans affected the interests of all the major European states and had major implications for the European balance of power. As regards the Balkans, the powers most involved were Austria and Russia. Both general staffs attached great importance to the support of the Balkan states' armies in the event of a European war. The likelier the latter became, the more this priority obsessed Petersburg and Vienna. For the Russians, Constantinople and the Straits possessed huge strategic and economic importance. In the event of a great power rival controlling the Straits, Russia's Black Sea trade and ports would be at the latter's mercy, as would the grain exports on which the empire's commerce and finances rested. Constantinople was also important to Austria, but still more so was the threat of Balkan nationalism to domestic stability within the multi-ethnic Habsburg empire. The Balkan wars of 1912–13 had greatly enlarged Serbian and Rumanian territory, together with the ambitions and self-confidence of Serbian and Rumanian nationalists. The Habsburg Monarchy contained large and discontented Serbian and Rumanian minorities. In 1914 Vienna feared that it would soon lose all its influence over the independent Balkan states, which in turn would contribute to its inability to control the Slav and Rumanian populations of the Monarchy. In more general terms, the rulers of the Habsburg state believed that a reassertion of the empire's power and vitality was essential in order to overawe its potential foreign and domestic enemies, and to contradict the widely prevalent assumption that the Monarchy was moribund and doomed to disappear in the era of nationalism and democracy. The Austrian ultimatum to Serbia of July 1914 was, of course, also designed to punish Belgrade for the assassination of the Archduke Franz Ferdinand: more basically, however, it aimed to turn Serbia into an Austrian protectorate and to reassert the Habsburg regime's power and prestige both in the Balkans and at home.

The Austrian ultimatum to Serbia faced the Russian government with a terrible dilemma. In 1914 Russia's rulers did not want war. Whatever hankering Nicholas II may ever have had for military glory had been wholly dissipated by the Japanese war. That conflict had taught the whole ruling elite that war and revolution were closely linked. Though war with Germany would be more popular than conflict with Japan had been, its burdens and dangers would also be infinitely greater. Russian generals usually had a deep respect for the German army, to which on the whole they felt their own army to be inferior. Above all, Russian leaders had every reason to feel that time was on their side. In strictly military terms, there was good reason to postpone conflict until the so-called 'Great Programme' of armaments was completed in 1917–18. In more general terms, Russia already controlled almost one-sixth of the world's land surface, whose hitherto largely untapped potential was now beginning to be developed at great speed. It was by no means only Petr Stolypin who believed that, given 20 years of peace, Russia would be transformed as regards its wealth, stability and power. Unfortunately for Russia, both the Germans and the Austrians were well aware of all the above facts. Both in Berlin and Vienna it was widely believed that fear of revolution would stop Russia from responding decisively to the Austro-German challenge: but it was also felt that war now was much preferable to a conflict a decade hence.

In fact, for the Russian government it was very difficult not to stand up to the Central Powers in July 1914. The regime's legitimacy was at stake, as were the patriotism, pride and self-esteem of the key decision-makers. Still more to the point was the conviction that weakness would fatally damage Russia's international position and her security. If Serbia became an Austrian protectorate, that would allow a very significant diversion of Habsburg troops from the southern to the Russian front in the event of a future war. If Russia tamely allowed its Serbian client to be gobbled by Austria, no other Balkan state would trust its protection against the Central Powers. All would move into the latter's camp, as probably would the Ottoman empire. Even France might have doubts about the usefulness of an ally so humiliatingly unable to stand up for its prestige and its vital interests. Above all, international relations in the pre-1914 era were seen to revolve around the willingness and ability of great powers to defend their interests. In the age of imperialism, empires that failed to do this were perceived as moribund and ripe for dismemberment. In the judgement of Russian statesmen, if the Central Powers got away with the abject humiliation of Russia in 1914 their appetites would be whetted rather than assuaged. At some point in the near future vital interests would be threatened for which Russia would have to fight, in which case it made sense to risk fighting now, in the hope that this would deter Berlin and Vienna, but in the certainty that if war ensued Serbia and France would fight beside Russia, and possibly Britain and certain other states as well.

The logic which took the tsarist regime to war in 1914 also made any subsequent separate peace with Germany impossible, even had Berlin been willing to buy Russia off with generous terms. Nicholas II believed that his personal honour was tied to the Franco-British alliance. He also knew that Russia's elites, including her generals, were wholly committed to victory and would never allow him to make peace with Germany on any other terms. Any attempt by him to negotiate with Berlin would have been political suicide. Above all, however, to make a separate peace with Germany would have meant allowing Berlin to switch all its troops to the western front, with the high risk before 1917 that this would have resulted in the defeat of France and German hegemony in Europe. An isolated Russia which had abandoned its allies would clearly have been in no position to contest this hegemony. If German domination of Europe had been unacceptable to Russia before 1914, it was likely to be even more so after a victory bought at the expense of great suffering had increased German appetites and stirred up German passions.

Nor was there any military reason for Russia to seek a separate peace between August 1914 and March 1917. Too much attention is usually paid to the defeats of Tannenburg in 1914 and Gorlice–Tarnow in 1915. Russia's military effort in the First World War amounted to much more than this. If on the whole the Russian army proved inferior to the German forces, that was usually true of the French and British as well. Moreover, during the Brusilov offensive in 1916 Russian forces had shown themselves quite capable of routing large German units. Russian armies usually showed themselves superior to Austrian forces of comparable size, and their performance against the Ottomans in 1914–16 was very much superior to that of British forces operating in Gallipoli, Egypt and Mesopotamia. The Russian defence industry performed miracles in 1916 and if there were legitimate doubts as to whether this level of production could be fully sustained in 1917, the same was true of the war economies of a number of other belligerents. It is true that Rumania's defeat necessitated a major redeployment of troops and supplies to the southern front in the weeks before the revolution and that this, together with a particularly severe winter, played havoc with railway movements on the home front. Nevertheless, in military terms there was absolutely no reason to believe that Russia had lost the war in February 1917.

Indeed, when one raised one's eyes from the eastern front and looked at the Allies' overall position, the probability of Russian victory was very great, so long as the home front could hold. Although the British empire was potentially the most powerful of the Allied states, in 1914–16 France and Russia had carried the overwhelming burden of the war on land. Not until July 1916 on the Somme were British forces committed *en masse* against the Germans, and even then the British armies, though courageous to a fault, lacked proper training and were commanded by amateur officers and generals who lacked any experience of controlling masses of men. Even so, in the summer of 1916 the combined impact of the Somme, Verdun and the

Brusilov offensive had brought the Central Powers within sight of collapse. A similar but better coordinated effort, with British power now peaking, held out excellent prospects for 1917. Still more to the point, by February 1917 the German campaign of unrestricted submarine warfare made American involvement in the war in the immediate future a near certainty: the Allied superiority in resources would thereby become overwhelming.

Once stalemate set in on the battlefield in 1914, the First World War became as much as anything a contest over which belligerent's home front would collapse first. This fate befell Russia in large part because even its upper and middle classes, let alone organized labour, were more hostile to the existing regime and less integrated into the legal political order than was the case even in Italy, let alone in France, Germany or Britain in 1914. In addition, opposition to the regime was less divided along ethnic lines than was the case in Austria–Hungary, and Russia was more geographically isolated from military and economic assistance from its allies than was the case with any of the other major belligerents. Nevertheless, unrest on the domestic front was by no means confined to Russia. The Italian home front seemed on the verge of collapse after the defeat of Caporetto in 1917 and the French army suffered major mutinies that year. In the United Kingdom the attempt to impose conscription in Ireland made that country ungovernable and led quickly to civil war. In both Germany and Austria revolution at home played a vital role in 1918, though in contrast to Russia it is true that revolution followed decisive military defeats and was set off in part by the correct sense that the war was unwinnable.

The winter of 1916–17 was decisive not just for the outcome of the First World War but also for the history of twentieth-century Europe. Events on the domestic and military fronts were closely connected. In the winter of 1915–16 in both Germany and Austria pressure on civilian food consumption had been very severe. The winter of 1916–17 proved worse. The conviction of the German military leadership that the Central Powers' home fronts could not sustain too much further pressure on this scale was an important factor in their decision to launch unrestricted submarine warfare in the winter of 1916–17, thereby (so they hoped) driving Britain out of the war and breaking the Allied blockade. By this supreme piece of miscalculation and folly the German leadership brought the United States into the war at almost precisely the moment when the overthrow of the imperial regime was preparing Russia to leave it. Even without American involvement it is unlikely, though not impossible, that the Germans, by 1917–18, could have secured outright military victory on the western front. It is even more improbable, however, that the British and French on their own could have defeated Germany or forced the abandonment of the Treaty of Brest-Litovsk, which established German hegemony throughout Central and Eastern Europe. With the Russian empire disintegrating and Russia itself in the throes of revolution and civil war, the Germans only needed a peace of exhaustion on the western front to give them an excellent chance of establishing their hegemony in most of Europe. Without American involvement such a peace would have been within their power by 1918–19.

The overthrow of the monarchy led very quickly to the disintegration of the Russian army as an effective fighting force. The Provisional Government contributed to this disintegration by its commitment to an offensive in the summer of 1917. The Bolsheviks made an even greater contribution by their pacifist propaganda. Much of this propaganda was thoroughly dishonest, since it pretended that a compromise peace was possible with Imperial Germany. Had the Bolsheviks ever admitted in 1917 their willingness to concede the terms finally agreed at Brest-Litovsk their popularity would have plummeted. At Brest-Litovsk Lenin took a calculated risk, believing that either a revolution in Germany or Allied victory would save him from most of the peace treaty's consequences.

In the short run Lenin was to be proved correct but in the longer term grave consequences were to flow from the collapse of Russia's war effort and the Bolsheviks' separate peace with Germany. At Versailles in 1919 the victorious Western powers created a European settlement at the expense of both Germany and Russia, both of which were viewed as defeated countries. Since Germany and Russia remained potentially the continent's most powerful states, this fact in itself more or less guaranteed that the peace settlement would be unstable. America's retreat into isolation and Britain's need to sustain a worldwide empire on the basis of shrinking relative resources made this even more likely. The French army on its own could not sustain a European settlement whose founding principles were the defeat and humiliation of Germany, the limited dismemberment of both the German and Russian empires, and the creation of a *cordon sanitaire* of weak states in Eastern Europe against the communist threat.

It is true that when a German danger re-emerged in the 1930s an effort was made to resurrect the old Franco-Russian–British alliance against it. The existence of a thoroughly anti-communist string of buffer states, however, made effective Soviet military intervention against Germany very difficult. In addition, Paris and, in particular, London loathed and deeply distrusted Stalin's regime, whose commitment to the European territorial and socio-political status quo they well knew to be purely temporary and tactical. On their side the Soviet leadership was not wrong to believe that many members of the British elite would have been only too happy to see Hitler and Stalin at each other's throats. Given Britain's lack of an army and France's determination to fight a defensive war behind the Maginot Line it was also realistic to expect that in any Allied war against Germany the Soviet army would be forced to do most of the fighting. In the late 1930s Stalin was faced with a dilemma familiar to tsarist statesmen in the early twentieth century. Either he could seek to deter and if necessary defeat German expansionism in alliance with Britain and France, or he could do a deal with Berlin, accepting or even encouraging the latter's conflict with

London and Paris for hegemony in Western Europe and on the seas. Although in 1939 Russia's leaders made the opposite choice to the one adopted in 1900–1914, in both cases the consequences for the Russian people were devastating. The fact that the decision and its appalling consequences had to be made twice within the space of a quarter-century owed much, however, to the events of 1917–18.

Further reading

Hasegawa T., *The February Revolution: Petrograd 1917* (Seattle and London, University of Washington Press, 1981).

Jones D. R., 'Imperial Russia's Forces at War', in A. R. Millett and W. Murray, eds., *Military Effectiveness,* vol. l: *The First World War* (Boston, Allen and Unwin, 1988).

Lieven D., *Russia and the Origins of the First World War* (London, Macmillan, 1983).

Ropponen R., *Die Kraft Russlands* (Helsinki, Historiallisia tutkimuksia No. 74, 1968).

Rostunov I. I., *Russkii front pervoi mirovoi voiny* (Moscow, Nauka, 1976).

Stone N., *The Eastern Front 1914–1918* (London, Hodder & Stoughton, 1975).

The February Revolution

TSUYOSHI HASEGAWA

Despite the recent debate on the nature of the October revolution, there is a general consensus on the basic nature of the February revolution. With the notable exception of George Katkov, who seeks the cause of the revolution in a conspiracy of Freemasons, liberals and German money, a majority of historians see it as a genuine revolution joined and supported by a broad spectrum of society, a revolution whose root cause can be traced to the inherent contradictions of the tsarist regime. This does not mean, however, that historians are unanimous on all aspects of the February revolution. Indeed, lively debates have emerged on certain aspects of the revolution.

The impact of World War I

For the past three decades historians have produced an impressive array of monographs, convincingly establishing that the tsarist regime was pregnant with irreconcilable internal contradictions that it had no capacity to resolve. One needs to stress, however, that the existence of such contradictions does not in itself make a revolution inevitable. While Leopold Haimson has argued that the war did not alter the fundamental nature of these contradictions, in my view World War I had the most direct and decisive impact, triggering the February revolution.

First, it was during the war that erosion of tsarist authority proceeded with catastrophic speed, gnawing at the frail foundations on which autocracy stood. The Rasputin affair (*Rasputinshchina*) dealt a deadly blow to tsarist authority, and caused the mass desertion of the tsar by supporters of the autocracy.

Second, the war made the break between the autocracy and the liberals irrevocable. Sensing the approaching storm from below, they formed a 'Progressive Bloc' in the Duma, and tried to convince the tsar to form a 'ministry of confidence' that would enjoy the trust of the country. However, when their olive branch was consistently met with intransigent rejection from the tsar, the radical wing of the liberals sought to utilize the revolutionary movement, while another group centred around A. I. Guchkov plotted a palace coup. But the majority of the liberals led by P. N. Miliukov refused to undertake either course for fear that such action might provoke a mass uprising from below which they believed would sweep away not only the state but also society. The formation of Masonic ties, emphasized by Katkov, can be interpreted as a desperate attempt by the radical intelligentsia, in opposition to the mainstream liberals, to create a forum for opposition that cut across party lines, for the avowed purpose of overthrowing the government, while seeking a vital link with the mass movement.

Third, wartime conditions were responsible for revitalizing the workers' strike movement, which, after the summer of 1915, grew in frequency as well as militancy. As Michael Melancon's recent work demonstrates, the radical revolutionary parties, which realigned themselves in common opposition to the war, increased their influence among the working class at the expense of the 'defencists' who supported the war and advocated collaboration with the bourgeoisie. The acute systemic crisis of tsarism also radicalized the defencists, who were as eager as the radical revolutionaries to overthrow the regime.

Fourth, World War I greatly altered the nature of the army. During the war, the officer corps was heavily recruited from the urban middle class, and opposition sentiments spread among the officers. The high command increasingly regarded the tsar as a political impediment to the successful prosecution of the war, and no longer felt that the fate of the nation was tied to his salvation. As for the peasant-soldiers, they went to war devoid of the sense of patriotism that was prevalent among the educated elite. In the third winter of the war, war-weariness and war fatigue clearly gnawed at the morale of the soldiers, who could no longer be insulated from political propaganda against Rasputin and the tsarina – the 'German woman'.

Finally, the war changed the nature of the national economy and society as a whole. Whereas in the political realm, the tsarist government plunged into a collision course with the liberals, on the economic and social level it was forced to mobilize social organizations for total war. Matsuzato Kimitaka argues that what should impress historians is not that the February revolution took place at all, but rather how quickly the tsarist regime succeeded in creating a system of wartime mobilization which was resilient enough to withstand three years of war. What was fatal, in his view, was not the tsarist government's inability to carry out national mobilization in total war, but rather its failure to coordinate competing interests with regard to food supply after the second half of 1916. When the government decided to introduce a ration system in Petrograd, demonstrations by women workers provided the spark that caused the conflagration.

KEY

State institutions
Major factories
Barracks
Major railway stations
Railway lines

Okhrana Headquarters (Khabalov's HQ in February)
Marinskii Palace (Pre-Parliament in October)
Smolny Institute (Congress of Soviets in October)
Tauride Palace (State Duma/Petrograd Soviet)

VYBORG
DISTRICT

SMOLNY
INSTITUTE

TAURIDE

FINLAND
STATION

PETER PAUL
AND FORTRESS

Neva

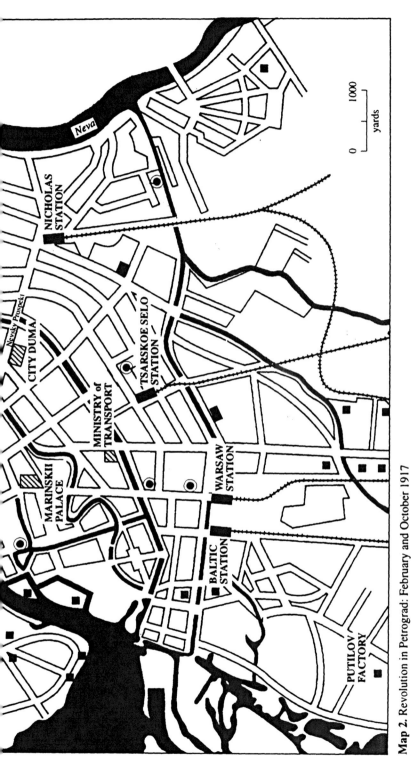

Map 2. Revolution in Petrograd: February and October 1917

Revolt

Process

The insurrection had two aspects: the workers' strikes and demonstrations and the soldiers' mutiny. The February revolution began on 23 February 1917 with the strike of women workers in the textile mills in the Vyborg District in Petrograd who went out on the streets with a single demand – 'Bread!' The strike immediately spread to the neighbouring metallurgical factories and its leadership was quickly taken over by more experienced activists. By 25 February, the workers' movement had developed into a general strike that paralysed the normal functioning of the capital. On 26 February government troops systematically fired upon the demonstrators for the first time. The government's determination led even the veteran leaders of the revolutionary parties to predict that the movement was coming to an end. But the order to fire pushed the soldiers to an inevitable choice between conscience and discipline.

The exact process of the soldiers' mutiny cannot be established precisely. Early on the morning of 27 February the soldiers of the Volynskii Regiment revolted. The mutiny quickly spread to the neighbouring military units, whose barracks were adjacent to those of the Volynskii Regiment. By noon, unruly masses of soldiers, joined by sympathetic crowds, put the north-eastern section of the central city beyond the control of the government. On the other side of the Neva in the working-class Vyborg District, a second armed revolt was taking place, this one led by determined worker activists. In early afternoon the two revolts were linked. After establishing the Tauride Palace as its centre, the insurrection spread to all parts of the city. By late night almost all the reserve battalions in the city had joined. The cabinet resigned and the ministers fled. The insurrection had triumphed in Petrograd.

Spontaneity and leadership in the workers' revolt

Traditional liberal historiography has viewed the February revolution as 'leaderless, spontaneous, and anonymous'. In contrast, official Soviet historiography long held the view that the workers' revolt was led by the Bolshevik Party. In 1956 the Soviet historian E. N. Burdzhalov challenged the official view, suggesting that in addition to the Bolsheviks, a number of socialist groups including the Left SRs, *Mezhraiontsy*, and the internationalist wing of the Mensheviks, also played a role in the strike movement. Burdzhalov also challenged the myth of monolithic Bolshevik leadership by pointing out the differences between the Russian Bureau led by A. G. Shliapnikov and the Bolshevik activists of the Vyborg District Committee.

Although the questions raised by Burdzhalov were not pursued by Soviet historians, who were subjected to the subsequent ideological retrenchment, they were taken up by Western historians. The present author developed the thesis that the workers' revolt was sustained by a group of committed revolutionary-worker activists. Burdzhalov's suggestion that groups other than the Bolsheviks actively worked behind the workers' movement was most forcefully argued by Melancon, who attributed the most important role in the February revolt to the Left SRs and *Mezhraiontsy*.

David Longley, however, has dismissed the whole debate over 'consciousness' and 'spontaneity' as specious. In his view, the issue was artificially concocted by Soviet memoirists in the context of the internal power struggle during the 1920s. He specifically questions the generally accepted interpretation that seeks to date the origin of the February revolution in the women's strike in the Vyborg District on 23 February, and criticizes the Vyborg-centred interpretation. Instead, he proposes that the Putilov strike on 22 February be seriously considered as the beginning of the revolution, and contends that the insurrection was led by non-party people, 'who simply rose to the occasion'.

Closer examination of the archival evidence reveals numerous references to 'hooligan activities' by demonstrators, mostly women and youths, who broke shop windows, looted goods and disrupted the functioning of trams. This gives credence to Joan Neuberger's pioneering work on hooliganism in the earlier period, and supports her insistence that hooligan crimes should be examined as a part of a revolutionary movement against the regime. The debate on spontaneity and leadership is far from settled. The challenging task for historians is to examine the workers' movement during the February days on its own terms, unfettered by the narrow framework established by Soviet historiography, while not dismissing it as a spontaneous, incomprehensible outburst.

The soldiers' revolt and the government's incompetence

What assured the victory of the insurrection was not the workers' movement but the soldiers' mutiny. Here it is more difficult to claim a direct link between the soldiers' actions and revolutionary propaganda. As Allan Wildman argues, the internal logic inherent in the Russian military during the war was more responsible for these actions. Nor was the soldiers' revolt so explosive as to engulf the entire Petrograd garrison instantaneously. Many soldiers defiantly resisted the appeal to join the revolt, while others remained neutral until the victory of the insurrection was assured late in the evening. The majority of soldiers reacted to the insurrection more ambiguously than has been believed.

Once the soldiers mutinied, they became a disorganized, anarchical, unruly mob, heeding no authority. They made no conscious and coordinated efforts to take over strategic positions, leaving the strongholds of the government forces and crucial communications centres untouched. A careful analysis of the loyal troops' reaction to the insurrection leads one to dismiss the view that the loyal forces 'melted away as soon as they came into contact with the revolutionary mobs'. The loyal troops who responded to Petrograd Military District Commander General S. S. Khabalov's summons did not disintegrate until the ineptitude of the commanding authority rendered their resistance meaningless. Some units actively resisted assaults by the insurgents. This situation has prompted Katkov to argue that the insurrection could have been crushed by a small detachment of troops led by determined and capable officers.

Indeed, as Katkov argues, the authorities displayed incredible ineptitude, lack of foresight, loss of nerve, bad judgement, and an absence of leadership, qualities that were more responsible for the disintegration of the loyal troops than the soldiers' eagerness to join the mutiny. This incompetence was by no means an accident, however, but was rooted in the structural weakness of the regime itself. The fact that the grave responsibility for the security in the capital was entrusted to such incompetent military and civilian leaders demonstrated the organic decay of the tsarist system. Moreover, this ineptitude underlines the pervasive psychological doubt about the use of force against the popular insurrection. The reaction of many commanding officers to the insurrection revealed their lack of commitment to the regime and their fear that an attempt at suppression would provoke bloody retaliation. As for the soldiers, there was little doubt that they found the task of internal repression to be repugnant. Nicholas's order to shoot pushed them into a corner where there remained no room for ambiguity between discipline and conscience.

By its very nature the soldiers' revolt imparted radicalism to the revolution. The line between defiance and discipline was a matter of life and death. Once the soldiers acted against discipline, there was no turning back, while the success of the mutiny depended on whether they could induce others to join in. The dynamics of the soldiers' mutiny also determined the actions of the rest of the soldiers. The mutiny completely obliterated the neutral ground: either soldiers should uphold discipline or they should join the insurrection. Once the soldiers crossed the line against discipline, their personal security could be guaranteed only by making sure that the old order would not be restored. This fear of reprisal further radicalized the revolution.

Formation of the Petrograd Soviet

While lawlessness and chaos began to reign in the streets on 27 February, two centres of power, the Petrograd Soviet of Workers' and Soldiers' Deputies and the Provisional Committee of the State Duma (Duma

Committee) were created in the Tauride Palace. The Petrograd Soviet was formed on the initiative of the leaders of the Workers' Group just freed from prison, who envisaged the Soviet as no more than a coordinating centre for the strike movement. The leadership of the Petrograd Soviet was immediately taken by a self-appointed Executive Committee, which was in turn dominated by three socialist intellectuals, N. N. Sukhanov, N. D. Sokolov and Iu. M. Steklov. During the crucial days between 27 February and 4 March, these three socialists defined the problem of power, and gave the Petrograd Soviet its initial direction.

On the question of power, they consistently maintained that a provisional government ought to be a bourgeois government. What determined this notion was not merely the dogmatic Marxist assumption that a bourgeois-democratic revolution should precede a proletarian-socialist revolution, but rather the pressing reality that revolutionary power emanating solely from the insurgent masses could not possibly have any chance of survival. They were painfully aware that the insurrection was turning into chaos and anarchy, and that a punitive detachment sent from the front was approaching the capital. The only way to prevent a civil war and to save the insurrection appeared to rest in expanding the revolution to involve the Duma liberals who had stood ambiguously on the sidelines.

The challenge to this notion came from the insurgent masses themselves. The overwhelming support that the Petrograd Soviet received from the insurgent masses began to transform it into something more than its initial organizers had envisaged. Contrary to the general assumption that from its inception the Petrograd Soviet firmly established itself as a revolutionary power and that it 'transferred' the power it had held to the bourgeoisie, the Petrograd Soviet's control over the insurgents was fragile at best during these first three days.

Petrograd workers quickly responded to the call of the Executive Committee to send their delegates. Although a complete list of the factories and organizations that conducted elections does not exist, it seems clear that the sudden inclusion of the workers and shop and office clerks who had stood outside the strike movement during the war contributed to the increase in influence of the moderate socialists at the expense of the radical socialists. These delegates had divergent political opinions, but despite this divergence, their allegiance clearly belonged to the Petrograd Soviet rather than to the Duma Committee. To cope with the breakdown of order and to consolidate the gains of the revolution, the factory workers quickly created workers' militia in their factories and living quarters. They jealously guarded the independence of these forces, and resisted attempts to integrate them into a unified city militia.

But the most decisive factor that determined the character of the Petrograd Soviet was the 'soldiers' question'. On 28 February the Military Commission of the Duma Committee issued 'Rodzianko's order' which instructed soldiers and officers to return to their barracks and submit to new military discipline. Viewing this as an attempt to restore the old order, the soldiers' delegates stormed into the plenary Soviet session on 1 March, and dictated their demands to the reluctant leaders of the Executive Committee, which had no choice but to issue Order Number One in the name of the Petrograd Soviet. The soldiers' actions catapulted the Petrograd Soviet into the centre of power, to which insurgent soldiers chose to pledge allegiance.

Thus the decisive and unbridgeable gulf that separated the lower strata of society from the 'privileged' strata became apparent. Alarmed by the possibility that the insurgents might push the Petrograd Soviet to assume governmental power, the Soviet Executive Committee decided to hasten the formation of a bourgeois provisional government by negotiating directly with the Duma Committee.

Formation of the Duma Committee

On the evening of 27 February, three basic facts confronted the Duma liberals: first, the triumphant insurrection had created its centre in the Petrograd Soviet; second, the intransigent tsar, backed by the high command, was determined to crush the insurrection; and finally, they themselves, centred in the Duma, served as the sole authority in the capital after the collapse of the tsarist cabinet. The insurrection provided the general background to the February revolution, but the actions of the liberals, who actively sought to resolve the first two irreconcilable facts by capitalizing on the third, determined the specific course of the revolution.

The most difficult question that the liberals faced during the February revolution was the legitimacy of the government that they intended to create. On the one hand, they sought continuity with the old regime by trying to obtain the tsar's sanction to form a government. Yet the insurgents constantly pushed the liberals in a radical direction, and forced them to accept the revolution itself as the source of legitimacy. There was an inherent contradiction between these two sources of legitimacy and, in the end, the Provisional Government, by seeking both, was left with none.

Initially, the Duma's reaction to the insurrection was slow and hesitant. When the capital was taken over by the insurgents, the Duma deputies held only a 'private meeting'. They rejected proposals for creating a military dictatorship and for declaring the Duma to be the constituent assembly. Miliukov's non-committal proposal to 'wait and see' prevailed.

It was the insurgent soldiers who pushed the wavering Duma deputies in a radical direction. Having defied military discipline and their sacred oath to the tsar, they sought an authority that would anoint their action with legitimacy, and poured into the Tauride Palace to obtain that sanction from the Duma. The Duma reacted to this, with reluctance, by forming the Duma Committee, whose stated objective was to restore order in the capital as the sole legitimate authority in the absence of any government.

The Duma Committee's actions were clearly revolutionary, although they were intended to restrain the further intensification of the revolution rather than to promote it. The Duma Committee sanctioned the arrests of the former tsarist ministers, officials and the police, took over the government apparatus by appointing its own commissars, approved the creation of the city militia to replace the old police and took over the Military Commission created by the Petrograd Soviet. But because its ultimate goals – the restoration of order and the prevention of further revolutionary development – were basically at variance with the aspirations of the insurgents, it failed to gain their acceptance. The only way to regain legitimacy in the eyes of the insurgents was to secure the acceptance of the Petrograd Soviet. When the Soviet Executive Committee proposed to negotiate on the terms for the 'transfer of power' to the Provisional Government, the liberals leapt at the opportunity.

This policy failed. The insurgents enforced their will without much consideration of their leaders' intentions. The manner in which the soldiers issued Order Number One, the refusal of the insurgents to surrender their weapons, and the rejection by workers of the merger of their own militia with the city militia, all indicated the failure of the Provisional Government's attempt to gain the insurgents' support. When Miliukov announced the formation of the Provisional Government on 2 March, the masses reacted with hostility, asking Miliukov: 'Who elected you?' Miliukov improvised an answer: 'The revolution has elected us.' He knew and they knew that this answer was not exactly truthful. For their part, the Soviet leaders, despite their intention to help the bourgeoisie form the Provisional Government, could not give it unconditional support, lest they themselves lose their own credibility among the insurgents. Their qualified support made the existence of the Provisional Government precarious: it existed only on the sufferance of the Petrograd Soviet.

The abdication of Nicholas II and end of the counterrevolution

Nicholas II reacted to the news of the insurrection in Petrograd in two ways: politically and personally. Politically, his decision was simple and categorical. Rejecting all forms of compromise, he decided to send a punitive detachment commanded by General N. I. Ivanov to quell the revolution. General M. V. Alekseev, the chief of staff, made arrangements to send a sizeable force to assist Ivanov. Leaving the military operation solely in the hands of Alekseev and Ivanov, Nicholas focused his entire attention on joining his family in Tsarskoe Selo. The tsar left Mogilev on 28 February, physically removing himself from the centre of decision-making.

There is no question about the decisive role played by the Duma

Committee in halting the counterrevolutionary forces and in forcing
Nicholas to abdicate. The Duma Committee's commissar to the Ministry of
Transport, A. A. Bublikov, succeeded in placing the entire railway network
through which the counterrevolutionary troops and Nicholas travelled
under the control of the Duma Committee. Through careful manipulation
of information, the Duma Committee delayed the movement of Ivanov's
punitive detachment and the reinforcements, and prevented Nicholas's train
from reaching Tsarskoe Selo.

Military leaders, too, played an important role in halting the counterrevolutionary expedition and in forcing Nicholas's abdication. Initially, the
high command supported Nicholas's resolve to crush the revolution by
force. As soon as it learned that power had been transferred to the Duma
liberals, however, it fully cooperated with the Duma Committee, and
decided to halt the punitive detachment without the approval of the tsar.
Furthermore, gullibly trusting the veracity of the Duma Committee's manipulated information, the military leaders collectively exerted pressure on
Nicholas to abdicate. Isolated from his family and deserted by all of his
trusted military leaders, Nicholas acquiesced.

What ultimately determined the actions of the military leaders was their
desire to preserve the fighting capacity of the armed forces. There was no
doubt that the officers and the soldiers would be reluctant to fulfil the
assignment of crushing the revolution. If the order to suppress the revolution had been implemented, there might have been an open rebellion within
the expeditionary forces themselves. Military suppression of the revolution,
even if successful, would have irreparably tarnished Russia's image in the
eyes of its democratic allies, while the subsequent political uncertainty
might have paralysed Russia's ability to continue the war. In this sense, the
military leaders and the Duma liberals shared an interest in avoiding bloodshed. This lack of will on the part of the military leaders, which was nurtured by their psychology and political orientation, was also an expression
of the profound malaise of the dying regime.

The abdication of Grand Duke Mikhail and the formation of the Provisional Government

The Duma Committee decided to take power on the evening of 27 February,
but it did not immediately proclaim itself to be a provisional government. In
fact, the first list of members of the Provisional Government, which was significantly different from the composition of the Duma Committee, was not
compiled until 1 March, and its formation was not announced until 3
March. The delay in the formation of the Provisional Government and the
difference in composition between it and the Duma Committee resulted
from an intense power struggle among the liberal leaders, which was

integrally connected with the question of the legitimacy of the Provisional Government.

On 1 March, under pressure from various liberal quarters, Miliukov compiled the list of the Provisional Government. M. V. Rodzianko, who had clearly become unacceptable to the insurgents, was removed from the list, and Prince G. E. L'vov was recommended for the posts of premier and Minister of Internal Affairs. Simultaneously, the Provisional Government consciously severed its institutional ties with the Duma and the Duma Committee, seeking to persuade the insurgent masses that its legitimacy stemmed from the revolution itself. Miliukov, the architect of the Provisional Government, appointed himself Foreign Minister, while Guchkov was selected as War and Navy Minister. The inclusion of Kerensky as Minister of Justice assured the vital link with the Petrograd Soviet.

An important but unresolved historiographical question is how influential the Masonic organization was in determining the composition of the Provisional Government. Although Katkov made this question a central part of his interpretation of the February revolution, most historians have avoided the issue. In my view, Masonic ties played a crucial role during the February revolution on two important occasions: the selection of Provisional Government ministers and the abdication of Grand Duke Mikhail. Five members, Kerensky, N. V. Nekrasov, A. I. Konovalov, M. I. Tereshchenko and I. N. Efremov are known to have belonged to the secret political Masonic organization. Yet it is difficult to prove on the existing evidence any 'conspiracy' by the Freemasons. Additional evidence, especially the use of the hitherto closed Kuskova archives, and further examination of the role of Konovalov, whose activities during the revolution remain mysteriously obscure, will be required to reach a definitive conclusion on this question.

The final act of the February revolution was the abdication of the Grand Duke Mikhail, which drove the last nail into the coffin of the monarchical system in Russia. The Duma liberals at first sought Nicholas's abdication in favour of his son, Aleksei, under Mikhail's regency. In other words, initially the liberals did not intend to destroy the monarchy. Two significant events took place to change their view. The first was the angry reaction of the masses to the preservation of the monarchy. The second was the unexpected decision by Nicholas to abdicate, not only on his own behalf but also on behalf of his son, in favour of Mikhail.

These new developments again caused a dynamic shift of political power among the Duma liberals. Miliukov considered it crucial to obtain legitimacy for the Provisional Government from the old regime and to secure legal and institutional continuity between them. Kerensky, Konovalov and Nekrasov – and here one might be able to talk about the second crucial influence of the Masonic ties – sought to destroy the monarchical system and found the Provisional Government on a republican basis.

The role played by Rodzianko was decisive in Mikhail's abdication.

Rodzianko may have been truly frightened by the spectre of the further popular unrest which the preservation of the monarchy might have unleashed. Yet his personal ambition also played a part. Hoping to recover his prestige, seriously damaged by 'Rodzianko's order', Rodzianko attempted to bolster the image of the Duma and himself by joining the radical wing of the liberals.

On 3 March, the members of the Duma Committee and the Provisional Government met with Grand Duke Mikhail. Kerensky, supported by Nekrasov, Konovalov and Tereshchenko, presented the case for his abdication, while Miliukov singlehandedly made a case for the preservation of the monarchy. Having consulted in private with Rodzianko and Prince G. E. L'vov, Mikhail decided not to accept the throne. The monarchical system thus ended unceremoniously. During the night of 3 March, two manifestos, one announcing Nicholas's abdication and another announcing Mikhail's refusal to take the throne, were printed side by side in various newspapers. The February revolution was now complete.

Conclusion

The most important result of the February revolution was the collapse of the tsarist state. The only authority that had held the institutions, bureaucracy, society and peoples of the empire together was suddenly, completely and unequivocally struck down. The Provisional Government had neither the authority nor an ideology powerful and coherent enough to integrate what was left from the tsarist state and what emerged from the insurrection into a single state. Nor could the Petrograd Soviet, whose leaders were most eager to avoid the mantle of state power, have filled the vacuum created by the collapse of the old regime. This situation is best characterized as 'disintegration of state power' rather than the traditional concept of 'dual power', since real power did not rest in either body. Real power instead filtered down to the multifarious lower organs, which jealously guarded it. This condition was reinforced by the profound revolution in the consciousness of the masses, who were suddenly awakened with confidence in their ability to decide their own fate, but who at the same time were possessed by the constant fear that this fragile power might be taken back at any moment by their real and imaginary class enemies. The February revolution thus marked both the end of the old regime and the beginning of a new revolutionary process.

Further reading

Burdzhalov E. N., *Vtoraia russkaia revoliutsiia: Moskva, front, periferiia* (Moscow, Nauka, 1971).

Burdzhalov E. N., *Russia's Second Revolution: The February 1917 Uprising in Petrograd*, tr. and ed. Donald J. Raleigh (Bloomington, Indiana University Press, 1987).

Cherniaev V. I., ed., *Anatomiia revoliutsii. 1917 god v Rossii: massy, partii, vlast'* (St Petersburg, Glagol, 1994).

Ferro M., *The Russian Revolution of February 1917* (London, Routledge and Kegan Paul, 1972).

Haimson L., 'The Problem of Social Stability in Urban Russia 1905–1917', *Slavic Review* 23, 4 (1964) pp. 619–42, and 24, 1 (1965) pp. 1–22.

Hasegawa T., *The February Revolution: Petrograd, 1917* (Seattle and London, University of Washington Press, 1981).

Katkov G., *Russia 1917: The February Revolution* (London, Collins, 1969).

Leiberov I. P., *Na shturm samoderzhaviia: Petrogradskii proletariat v gody pervoi mirovoi voiny i fevral'skoi revoliutsii* (Moscow, Mysl', 1979).

Longley D., 'Iakovlev's Question, or the Historiography of the Problem of Spontaneity and Leadership in the Russian Revolution of February 1917', in E. R. Frankel, J. Frankel and B. Knei-Paz, eds., *Revolution in Russia: Reassessments of 1917* (Cambridge, Cambridge University Press, 1992), pp. 365–87.

Matsuzato Kimitaka, 'Sôryokusensô to chihôtôchi: daiichiji sekaitaisenki roshia no shokuryôjigyô to nôjishidô' [Total War and Local Rule: Food Supply and Agrarian Leadership] (Ph.D. dissertation, Tokyo University, 1995).

Melancon M., *The Socialist Revolutionaries and the Russian Anti-War Movement, 1914–1917* (Columbus, Ohio State University Press, 1990).

Mel'gunov S. P., *Martovskie dni 1917 goda* (Paris, Editeurs Réunis, 1961).

Neuberger J., *Hooliganism: Crime, Culture and Power in St Petersburg 1900–1914* (Berkeley, University of California Press, 1993).

Wildman A., *The End of the Russian Imperial Army*, vol 1: *The Old Army and the Soldiers' Revolt (March–April 1917)* (Princeton, Princeton University Press, 1980).

The April Crisis

ZIVA GALILI

In most histories of 1917, the 'April Crisis' figures as the first in a series of major political crises marking the path from the February revolution to the October seizure of power and as a harbinger of the polarized and radicalized landscape of later months. For two days on 20 and 21 April social mistrust and hostility were abundantly evident on the streets of Petrograd – in the direct clashes between the supporters of the Soviet and the middle-class counter-demonstrators who rallied to the cause of the Provisional Government, as well as the widely differing expectations that motivated them. The unfolding of the crisis exposed a powerful undercurrent of social conflict, compounded by the critical weakness of the government's political authority. Yet, chronologically, the crisis was located at a time marked by relative fluidity, when the unfolding of the revolution did not appear predetermined and the principal political actors believed that new political alternatives could be shaped to contain societal conflicts and bolster political authority. As a result, this mildest of revolutionary crises, notable for its theatricality more than the brute force displayed, produced the swiftest and most dramatic political consequences.

Miliukov's diplomatic note

The immediate and most easily reducible cause of the April Crisis was a conflict over the definition of Russia's foreign policy goals that pitted the Petrograd Soviet against the Provisional Government, especially its Foreign Minister P. N. Miliukov. Initially, foreign policy issues had not been included in the 'dual power' agreement which made the Petrograd Soviet's support for the Provisional Government conditional on the fulfilment of certain demands. But in mid-March, with the revolution secure and the Soviet's authority among its followers increasing, the internationalist framers of 'dual power' began to claim a national and international role for the

Petrograd Soviet in ending the war. 'An Appeal to All the Peoples of the World', authored by N. N. Sukhanov and approved by the Executive Committee (11 March) and the full Soviet (14 March), repudiated the war in general and the belligerents' 'acquisitionist ambitions' in particular. A week later, the Executive Committee turned its attention to the practical means of making this sentiment the cornerstone of Russia's foreign policy. By then, the Menshevik leader I. G. Tsereteli and his group of 'Siberian Zimmerwaldists' had returned from exile to take the lead in shaping the Soviet's policy *vis-à-vis* the war and the Provisional Government. Their 're-volutionary defencist' policy consisted of a bipartite insistence on peace 'without annexations and indemnities' and support for maintaining the army's defensive capabilities, as well as a preference for relying on quiet negotiations to ensure the government's compliance.

Tsereteli's modulated policy appeared to have achieved a victory of sorts on 27 March, when three days of tense negotiations led to the issuance of the Provisional Government's 'Declaration on War Aims', renouncing 'domination over other nations' and 'seizure of their national possessions'. However, in addressing the Russian people rather than the Allies, the proclamation of 27 March pointed to significant differences between the Soviet and the Foreign Minister over Russia's war aims and the Soviet's role in defining them. In interviews and statements preceding the government's declaration, Miliukov had insisted on Russia's right to Constantinople and the Dardanelles and had labelled 'Peace without Annexations' a German formulation. After 27 March, he showed little inclination to accommodate the Soviet's demand that the declaration be reissued as a formal diplomatic note to Russia's allies. When forced to issue such a note by pressure from the Soviet, fellow Kadets, and a visiting delegation of Allied socialists, he was determined to use the occasion to restate Russia's intention to pursue the war and reap the promised rewards of victory.

The Petrograd Soviet, meanwhile, had publicly made its support of the government's Freedom Loan conditional on the issuing of Miliukov's promised note. Its leaders had misled themselves and their followers into expecting Miliukov to include their revolutionary goal of 'democratic peace' in Russia's agenda for international diplomacy. The stage was thus set for the disappointment and sense of betrayal with which leaders and followers alike received Miliukov's diplomatic note, issued on 18 April and made public in the morning newspapers on 20 April. The note had the effect of negating rather than affirming the policy implications of the 27 March de-claration, for attached to the text of the declaration was a letter in which the Foreign Minister promised that Russia would continue the war to a 'decisive victory', 'fully observe' her treaty obligations, and eventually participate in the establishment of 'guarantees and sanctions' – terms suspiciously remin-iscent of the objectionable annexations and indemnities.

Yet, of all the issues raised by the April Crisis, the conflict over foreign policy was the easiest to settle. During the night of 20 April negotiators for

the Executive Committee and the Provisional Government, led respectively
by Tsereteli and the left Kadet N. V. Nekrasov, agreed on a compromise text
for a supplementary note in which annexations were again repudiated and
the offending terms 'guarantees' and 'sanctions' explained as references to
international tribunals, limitations on armaments, etc. Though the Executive
Committee was not greatly impressed by this compromise (it voted on 21
April by 34 to 19 in favour of accepting it, but called for increased control
by the Soviet over the government's foreign policy), the full Petrograd Soviet
voted later that day by 2,000 to 13 for a resolution that described the compromise as 'a great achievement for democracy'. The cabinet and the
Provisional Committee of the State Duma also gave their approval to the
new text. The ostensible reason for the crisis was thus removed.

Social confrontation

While the conflict over war and foreign policy would remain a persistent issue
with grave implications, two other factors present in the April Crisis – social
conflict and the shakiness of political authority – were to become, if anything, more crucial to the fate of the revolution. The first of these has long
since dominated the narrative of 1917. Social historians of the revolution
broadly agree that throughout 1917 social tensions became increasingly
focused on the central divide between the 'haves' and 'have nots', even as
other social fault-lines formed and changed in ever more complicated patterns. Moreover, they agree that at several crucial junctures this central divide
easily overshadowed the complexity and ambiguity of social relations. The
conflict concerning Miliukov's note was clearly such a juncture. It united disparate groups around a sense of mistrust and betrayal and presented the
advocates of non-conciliation with ready audiences among the disillusioned
and disoriented. The Bolsheviks as well as the Kadets seized the opportunity.

   Alexander Rabinowitch's study of the Bolshevik Party provides a careful
yet emphatic assessment of Bolshevik influence in the early stages of the crisis: 'Rank-and-file party members from garrison regiments and factories
undoubtedly helped to provoke the street demonstrations in the first place.'
Later, a leaflet distributed by radical dissidents from the Bolshevik Petersburg
Committee was 'primarily responsible for the sudden appearance among
demonstrators of "Down with the Provisional Government" banners' on 21
April. Even so, during the first day of the demonstrations, the majority of
workers and soldiers in the streets of Petrograd protested not against the government as such but against its refusal to follow the Soviet's lead in revising
Russia's foreign policy. Their banners were either those left over from May
Day (18 April in the Russian calendar), which called for peace and brotherhood, or new, hastily prepared ones with the slogan 'Down with Miliukov
and Guchkov!' Only a small number of them, the more radical Vyborg District
workers, advocated the resignation of the entire cabinet.

But if the mood of the demonstrators on 20 April appears mild from the perspective of events to come, this was not how it registered with the Kadet Central Committee. Responding to attacks on the Kadet ministers and more broadly to the Soviet's presumption in questioning the authority of the government, the committee ended a long meeting on the night of 20 April with a militant declaration calling upon loyal citizens of Russia to demonstrate against 'anarchy' and for the authority of the Provisional Government. The next day, thousands of Kadet supporters, reinforced by well-to-do citizens, *intelligenty* and shopkeepers, reclaimed the capital's central avenues and converged on the Mariinskii Palace, where Miliukov and Minister of War A. I. Guchkov appeared before them as representatives of the government. The sight of the 'bourgeois' demonstrators with banners declaring 'Down with Anarchy!' and 'Long Live Miliukov!' was probably crucial in determining the mood of the worker and soldier demonstrators on this second day of the crisis. A sense of betrayed trust and a renewed belligerency was apparent. Many demonstrators were now armed and violent clashes broke out between the opposing groups.

These patterns of a crystallizing social conflict, feeding on long-standing mistrust and perceptions of betrayal and fanned by the opponents of social conciliation, would emerge again and with much greater clarity and force during the July Days. And yet, the April Crisis was not merely the first in an escalating series of social confrontations, for it was located within a unique phase in the unfolding of social relations – near the conclusion of a seven-week period of unprecedented concessions to workers' various demands, of remarkable order and self-discipline in the factories and on the front, a time when conciliation and compromise could still be presented as the engine of change. The next two months would see an erosion in the efficacy of conciliation. In the factories, a second wave of workers' demands would yield significant new concessions, but these would be obtained more often than not through strike action. On the front, the shift would be swifter as demoralization and disintegration would rapidly set in. But on 20 and 21 April the optimism born of the February victory had not yet been frustrated by a recalcitrant government, increasingly entrenched employers, persistently demanding workers, and demoralized soldiers. The meagre victory over Miliukov's note could be embraced as real and concordant with the Soviet's perceived power, while the successful efforts of the Soviet's leaders at containing the crisis were taken as proof of their responsibility and influence with their followers.

The political crisis

Ultimately, it was in the political sphere that the April Crisis most dramatically exposed as well as fed the contradictions inherent in the political arrangements born of the February revolution. The crisis developed well within the framework of 'dual power', both as crafted by the Executive Committee of the Petrograd Soviet in its early days, and as re-interpreted by the Soviet's new 'revolutionary defencist' leadership. And yet, this demonstration of the efficacy of 'dual power' in forestalling anarchy and yielding a political compromise only helped to precipitate a major realignment of political forces and a most significant move from a policy of 'dual power' to one of coalition.

From the outset, the leadership of the Petrograd Soviet demonstrated a sense of its own strength and responsibility. Declaring Miliukov's note to have 'destroyed the compromise that had made cooperation with the government possible', the Executive Committee committed itself to seeing the note immediately revised, though initially it was divided between those who would have the cabinet pressured through demonstrations and those who recommended quiet negotiations with the ministers. The arrival of the first groups of demonstrators in front of the Tauride Palace early on 20 April resolved the argument in favour of negotiations; an appeal was promptly issued to the masses of the city to avoid any demonstration not authorized by the Soviet. The leaders did not disagree with the political goal of the demonstrators, but they were determined to avoid an unorganized display of force that could undermine the government's shaky authority or provoke violent clashes in the streets. For this reason, when news arrived on 21 April of just such clashes, the full Soviet moved to ban all demonstrations in Petrograd for two days. Yet concern for the government's authority did not deter the Executive Committee from issuing a proclamation forbidding the troops from following any and all orders not sanctioned by the Soviet. Backed by the soldiers, the Soviet thus easily neutralized an earlier order from the military commander of Petrograd (General L. G. Kornilov) for the troops to come to the defence of the government.

The April Crisis demonstrated just how weak the Provisional Government had become, deprived of the single most important means of exercising its authority. Coupled with the spectre of social conflict, the weakness of central authority aroused a widespread desire for a formal expression of unity, especially among those intermediary social and political groups that had hoped to prevent polarization. Intelligentsia organizations, elected local authorities, soldiers' and officers' organizations, and peasant soviets all appealed to the Petrograd Soviet and the Provisional Government to form a coalition. Within days, the same demand was voiced by those closest to the two centres of political authority: on the Provisional Government's side, the Moscow Committee of Public Organizations, the Moscow Kadets, ministers Kerensky and Nekrasov, and eventually Prime Minister G. E. L'vov; on the Soviet's side, the Party of Socialist Revolutionaries and the Menshevik faction of the Petrograd Soviet, who now joined the Trudoviks and the group of right-wing Social Democrats around the newspaper *Den'* ('The Day') in advocating coalition.

Within the cabinet, the crisis accelerated a rift that had been in the making since mid-March. Miliukov and Guchkov, supported by A. I. Shingarev, F. I. Rodichev and leading Kadets outside the cabinet, advocated uncircumscribed authority for the government, which alone could speak for Russia's national interests, and rejected special influence over state policy for the Soviet – a merely 'partisan' institution. Confronting them with a renewed sense of urgency, seeking to strengthen the government's political authority by coopting the moderate leaders of the Soviet, were four fellow cabinet ministers: Nekrasov, undaunted by the defeat of his left Kadet line at the party's congress in late March; Kerensky, the popular Trudovik; A. I. Konovalov, the Moscow entrepreneur active in the Party of Progressists and the wartime public organizations; and M. I. Tereshchenko, a non-party 'repentant capitalist'.

The intensified search for stronger political authority and the contest over the best means toward this goal precipitated the announcement on 29 April of Guchkov's resignation from the post of Minister of War. At the most transparent level, Guchkov's resignation underscored the threat of anarchy, especially in the army, and was followed by a flood of appeals to the Soviet from soldiers' committees and officers sympathetic to democracy that it join the government to prevent further disintegration of the army. Guchkov's underlying motives in resigning were stated in his address to a commemorative meeting of the members of all four State Dumas on 27 April, when he attacked the Soviet's sponsorship of dual power and 'multi power', which had resulted in 'no power' and threatened the country with civil war. But if Guchkov's resignation marked the crystallization of the anti-democratic forces, it also signalled their departure from the Provisional Government, for on 2 May, Miliukov too would resign in protest over the invitation issued by Prime Minister L'vov to the Petrograd Soviet to join in a coalition government.

The political aftermath of the April Crisis, especially Guchkov's resignation, underscored the dangers inherent in the weakness of the government's political authority and the potential threat of anti-democratic mobilization, while also promising the consolidation of a liberal political bloc eager to cooperate with the moderate leadership of the Soviet and willing to accept its most urgent demands. These dangers and promises played a crucial role in dramatically changing the position of the Petrograd Mensheviks on the question of socialist participation in government. From the early days of the revolution, the Mensheviks had led the Petrograd Soviet in rejecting such participation in favour of 'dual power'. Even after Tsereteli had emerged in late March as the principal articulator of Menshevik policy, interpreting 'dual power' not so much as a framework for pressure on the government as for cooperation with all the 'vital' (i.e. progressive) forces of the nation, Mensheviks, including the 'revolutionary defencist' centrist faction, held firmly to their rejection of coalition. As late as 25 April, the party's leadership adopted a resolution (drafted by Tsereteli's closest ally, F. I. Dan) which stated more fully than ever before the ideological and political arguments the Mensheviks had mustered over the years to resist coalition government. On 28 April, the Mensheviks led the Executive Committee in rejecting Prince L'vov's first invitation to join the government. Thus, it was the reversal of their position on the evening of 1 May that allowed a majority in favour of coalition to coalesce at a meeting of the Executive Committee later that night and opened the way to negotiations over the shape and programme of the new coalition cabinet, which began on 2 May.

With the establishment of coalition government the April Crisis and its political aftermath came to an ending of sorts. Coalition was the crisis's principal legacy, one that persisted for the rest of the year, just like the social conflict and shaky political authority it was designed to remedy. Perhaps more than any other crisis in 1917, the April Crisis tempts the historian to disentangle 'objective' events and realities from their apprehension and translation into policy through human agency. In the case of the Menshevik leaders of the Petrograd Soviet, agency clearly involved the refraction of the revolution's changing realities through a combination of ideology, past experience and expectations specific to Menshevism; but just as clearly, the events of late April first reinforced, then overshadowed ideological convictions. More broadly, the significant impact of the April Crisis on a range of political leaders and policy decisions was most likely due not merely to the exigencies it represented, but also to the perception that political alternatives were still possible, a perception that was already tempered in late April but not yet overshadowed by an increasingly acute sense of how quickly these possibilities might vanish. This perceived fluidity in turn was rooted in the prevailing tenor of social relations, but rooted as well in the power of chronology and the simple fact that alternatives remained operative for as long as they had not been tried and discarded.

Further reading

Galili Z., *The Menshevik Leaders in the Russian Revolution: Social Realities and Political Strategies* (Princeton, Princeton University Press, 1989).

Rabinowitch A., *Prelude to Revolution* (Bloomington, Indiana University Press, 1968).

Rosenberg W. G., *Liberals in the Russian Revolution, 1917–1921* (Princeton, Princeton University Press, 1974).

Tsereteli I. G., *Vospominaniia o fevral'skoi revoliutsii*, 2 vols. (Paris and The Hague, Mouton, 1968).

Voitinskii V. S., *God pobed i porazhenii*, ed. Iu. Fel'shtinskii (New York, Chalidze Publications, 1990).

The Breakdown of the Imperial Army in 1917

ALLAN WILDMAN

Modern mass conscripted armies are mirrors of nations, particularly in wartime. Correspondingly, in 1917 the Russian army was a major arena of the revolutionary process and an important component in the complexion of power, replicating the inversion of authority and fragmentation along class lines, as well as the bifurcation into formal and representative modes of power. Moreover, the great mobilizing issue for both the masses and the political elites was the continuation of the war at the front. The Bolsheviks prevailed because they gave voice to the front soldiers' urgent desire for peace, whereas other parties failed to do so. Three times in 1917, in March, August and October, the front army was summoned to reverse revolutionary developments in the rear, and floundered on the soldiers' unwillingness to obey their officers. The upheaval in the front army proved to be decisive for the outcome of the 1917 revolution.

The army in the February revolution

At the time of the February revolution the Russian Imperial Army numbered around nine million men and had endured two and a half years of unrelenting trench warfare, suffering five and a half million casualties, nearly two million of them fatalities. Though themselves beset by great trials, the front soldiers also heard of strikes, riots and starvation by letters from home, and by word of mouth from those returning after leave and from replacement companies. In the autumn of 1916 mutinies by whole regiments and divisions were triggered by orders to move up to the front.

The official announcement of the tsar's abdication on 3 March was interpreted by front soldiers as confirmation of their expectations of peace. Soldiers deeply distrusted the versions they were given by their officers, convinced the latter were deliberately withholding pronouncements of the new government on peace. The result was a rash of incidents and arrests of

senior officers, followed by nominations of new officers of their own choice
and organized efforts to send deputations to the rear.

Soon normal discipline and military order broke down entirely, fed by
ever fresh political news – of the formation of the Provisional Government
and the Soviet, of the massive revolt of the Petrograd garrison, of other barracks revolts and local revolutions in the immediate rear, of new laws and
decrees on peace and changes in military rules. The text of Order Number
One of the Petrograd Soviet reached the front via radio, telegraph and the
published version in the first issue of the *Izvestiia* ('News') of the Petrograd
Soviet, and was taken by soldiers and officers alike to be an order of the new
government. The abolition of the death penalty and the vesting of disciplinary authority in elected soldier–officer courts deprived the command of its
awesome punitive powers. Attempts by officers to delay the announcement
of these rights in the hope of having them reversed or modified only exacerbated tensions and fuelled the determination of soldiers to get authentic
information directly from Petrograd and the Soviet, which was now becoming the new symbol of authority.

Conflicts over these issues led to the first spontaneously formed soldiers'
committees, which officers themselves soon came to regard as necessary to
restore calm. The result in a matter of two or three weeks was an inversion
of military order at the front which replicated the system of 'dual power' in
the rear. In the last two weeks of March a system of soldier-officer committees from the company up to the army and front level was put in place, confirmed by orders of higher commanders and Supreme Headquarters itself.
Initiators and organizers were often wartime officers, educated non-coms
(veterinarians, doctors) and literate workers who had past associations
with politics or the revolutionary movement. Nearly all identified themselves as 'socialists'. They were responding in this to the universal sentiment of the soldiers, who were predominantly peasant in background and
wished nothing so much as to have their interests represented in the new
order.

General M. V. Alekseev, who assumed command of the army after
Nicholas's removal, reluctantly conceded such arrangements in a general
order of 30 March. However, two armies on the northern front, the Fifth
and Twelfth, had already called army congresses of elected deputies which
ratified a system of committees by 15 March; and on the western front, a
general order approved already existing committees on 17 March, as did the
Special Army on the south-western front and the Sixth Army on the
Rumanian front. Others followed somewhat later. The process culminated
in a massive Congress of the Western Front on 7–17 April in Minsk that featured patriotic, pro-war speeches by generals and major political figures.
But soviet-oriented elements held sway, and the resolutions passed reflected
the Petrograd Soviet position on war and peace, 'control' over the
Provisional Government and other issues. The formula of representation
was four soldiers and one officer from every division. Almost universally the

soldiers' committees at the front were joint soldier-officer committees, and lower officers of socialist persuasion predominated in the leadership.

The first soldier–officer deputations to Petrograd were alarmed over rumours that war production was lagging and that the Soviet was hampering the work of the Provisional Government. The non-socialist press played up these notes of conflict to put pressure on the Soviet and the factory workers. The result was a rash of sharp encounters between soldiers and workers on factory premises and in public meetings. But the danger of rift soon dissipated as workers assured soldiers of their desire to support their brothers at the front, blaming fuel shortages, obstruction by managers, and the 'bourgeois press' for intentionally trying to drive a wedge between them in order to reverse the gains of the revolution.

Front representatives became directly involved in soviet politics by attending the All-Russian Conference of Soviets at the end of March where they learned of the distinction between the Soviet's peace policy of a democratic peace based on 'no annexations and indemnities' (and until then a war of defence), and that of the 'bourgeois' groups who favoured 'war to complete victory'. The soldier deputations and many of the officers returned to their units fully identifying themselves with the Soviet's position. When conveyed to the trench soldiers, this information confirmed the latter's conviction that the revolution meant a speedy peace and that the *burzhui* (bourgeois) elements in the government required close watching. A crisis in power had passed, but the allegiance of the front committees was now firmly welded to the authority of the Petrograd Soviet.

Fuller information on the politics of the rear did not, however, bring a return to military discipline or soldier-officer harmony. Incidents leading to the arrest and removal of senior officers continued on an alarming scale, routine military duties were neglected, and fraternization with the enemy became endemic, the latter encouraged by German intelligence officers claiming to be socialists. Soldiers' committees (and their officer component) were now frequently caught in the middle, on the one hand, fully endorsing the Soviet peace formula in its most 'revolutionary defencist' variant and therefore anxious to maintain military discipline and submission to officer authority, and on the other speaking for the soldier constituency and revolutionary goals. Often they sought to mediate soldier-officer conflicts with the approval of the higher command, more and more falling into the role of 'enforcers' of discipline (higher committees often more strictly than lower). On other occasions, however, 'to restore calm' committees recommended removing officers or yielding to the demands of angry soldiers. To avoid conflict with their constituents, committee men seldom opposed fraternization openly.

Bolsheviks along with socialists of all persuasions had played a significant role in committee activity in March and April, their behaviour scarcely distinguishable from the others. Some were even 'defencist'. Until the end of April few front Bolsheviks were in touch with the party leadership and Lenin was still engaged in a battle within his own party over his 'April Theses'. One finds very little anti-war agitation conducted by Bolsheviks in these weeks. Menshevik and Socialist Revolutionary committee men frequently worked in harmony with Bolsheviks for the common goals of the revolution.

The April Crisis and its aftermath at the front

The political crisis in the capital over Foreign Minister P. N. Miliukov's 'Note' to the Allies of 18 April that led to the formation of the coalition government and Kerensky's assumption of the portfolio of the Ministry of Defence had the paradoxical effect of committing the socialists in the cabinet to a defensive war until Germany responded to peace overtures. Kerensky immediately made it clear that he felt that Germany would not make peace, nor would the Allies take the Russian peace policy seriously, until the 'revolutionary army' inflicted a major defeat on the enemy. With great zeal he made an extensive tour of the front, speaking before army and front 'congresses' and large throngs of soldiers in an effort to fire up enthusiasm for a new offensive. He found an especially receptive audience among soldier-officer committee men frustrated over their declining influence with their constituency, and looking on Kerensky as the embodiment of their vision of the revolution.

They proved totally unable, however, to convey their enthusiasm to rank-and-file troops, who persisted in disruptive behaviour and were increasingly disillusioned with the socialist leaders in Petrograd. In fact many units, to the despair of committee orators, passed resolutions condemning the idea of an offensive and calling on the Soviet to countermand it. Soldiers were all the more disenchanted when prominent Soviet leaders like M. I. Skobelev, V. B. Stankevich and the 'author' of Order Number One, N. D. Sokolov, descended on the front to tell them they must prepare for the offensive and obey orders without question. In June Sokolov was beaten and nearly lynched.

The front committee leaders now found themselves representing the Soviet leadership and the government to the front rather than the reverse, and correspondingly they suffered a diminution in authority. It was within this widening gulf with the mass of peasant and lower-class soldiers over the question of an offensive that the Bolsheviks found their opportunity. Nearly every front, army and corps committee was now headed at the front by a coalition of Menshevik and Socialist Revolutionary committee men and up to the eve of the October revolution they loyally supported the policies of the Soviet Executive Committee and the coalition government, Kerensky remaining the symbolic figure. This was a profound reversal of power relationships, for which there was a high price to pay in October and November.

Meanwhile, soldiers in the capital, anxious not to be sent to the front, rapidly slipped out of the control of the Soviet-oriented committees and welcomed Bolshevik agitators into their barracks. A special Military Organization of the Bolshevik-Party-trained agitators disrupted meetings called by the pro-Soviet elements, and introduced anti-war resolutions or radical amendments to the resolutions of the regular committees, which ever more frequently were approved. The decision of the Soviet Executive Committee to support sending replacements to the front was easily exploited by the Bolsheviks to convince the soldier masses that they had been betrayed by the socialist leadership which now supported the 'capitalist' Provisional Government and pursued 'imperialist war aims' in league with the 'bourgeois' Allies. When replacements did embark for the front they carried the virus of these attitudes with them, along with large packets of *Pravda* ('The Truth') and the new Bolshevik organ *Soldatskaia Pravda* ('Soldiers' Truth'). Also a fair number of front Bolsheviks had by then visited Petrograd, acquainted themselves with the new orientation of the party and adopted it as corresponding to the shaping mood of the trench soldiers.

Many front Bolsheviks thus became conduits of vigorous agitation against the scheduled offensive. They were frequently expelled from the regular committees or remained a vexing element within them: the comradely solidarity of the early months was gone. Bolshevik agitation against the war at the front, which was a trickle in early May, became a flood by early June. Whole regiments mutinied, disobeyed orders on troop movements, committed violence against their officers and pro-war agitators, and some formed independent 'republics' behind the lines. Often agitators having no party association picked up Bolshevik slogans and arguments from the press or tours to the rear, as did German agents who spread them through fraternization.

The virus of 'Bolshevism' spread rapidly because the anti-offensive slogans reinforced the peace longings of the soldiers. It provided the language and the crude arguments they needed in confrontations with official 'persuaders'. 'Bolshevik republics' sprang up on the northern front in the two Latvian brigades and the 436th Novladozhskii Regiment (which put out the highly effective newspaper *Okopnaia Pravda* ('Trench Truth')), the 20th Grenadier Regiment on the western front, and two Finnish rifle regiments and the Guards Grenadier Regiment on the south-western front, but other 'republics' also appeared with no known Bolshevik connections (Second Grenadier Division, western front, several Siberian regiments on the south-western front, the 163rd Infantry Regiment on the Rumanian front). The Grenadier and Guards regiments were in constant turmoil.

The June offensive

As the date for the offensive drew near and elaborate preparations were set in motion, including massive concentrations of heavy artillery, special government 'commissars' (almost all of them Soviet-oriented defencists) collaborated closely with committees to bring shaken units back under control and convince them that revolutionary duty required them to obey orders. Kerensky himself again toured the front, mustering all the eloquence at his command in addressing huge assemblies of the soldiers designated for attack. In the guards units he faced down the troublesome Grenadiers and won over most of the remainder who now swore to obey orders and moved into position for the attack.

On 16 June a massive artillery bombardment began along a 50-mile stretch on the sector on the south-western front designated for the initial thrust. Two days later Russian soldiers poured out of the trenches led by committee persuaders bearing huge red banners. Initial successes by the Eleventh Army soon stalled as units taking heavy casualties demanded to be withdrawn and replacement units refused to move up. By 20 June further action had to be cancelled to deal with a new rash of mutinies in the rear. The Seventh Army to the south had even less success after taking 15,000 casualties (the German and Austro-Hungarian losses were even higher). On the Rumanian front General Kornilov's Eighth Army accomplished the only significant success, passing two spurs of the Carpathians and taking the Galician town of Kalush, but other attacks on the northern and western fronts triggered immediate and massive revolts. Whole units fled to the rear, fanning out over the countryside. Huge round-up actions were necessary, which led to mass arrests and the dismantling of large formations. All further operations on these fronts were cancelled.

The news of the defeat rocked the capital on the eve of the July Days and fed into a mood of mass hysteria by both pro-government and soviet elements. Shortly thereafter the Germans launched a major counter-offensive opposite the Galician city of Tarnopol, propelling the Eleventh, Seventh and Eighth armies into a disorganized retreat. According to an official communiqué, cowardly soldiers of the 607th Regiment 'opened up the front to the enemy' without a fight, allowing the German hordes to pour through until all the ground gained in the Brusilov offensive of the year before was yielded back to the enemy. (This version was later proven false by an official investigation.) 'Bolshevism' in collusion with the German general staff was blamed for the morass both at the front and in the rear. Kerensky and other Soviet figures lent their authority to these versions, and all parties called for 'strong state [or revolutionary] authority', including restoration of the death penalty at the front. On 12 July, backed by the socialist ministers, a decree on the death penalty for desertion, flight and disobedience to orders during battle, to be enforced by new field 'revolutionary courts', was transmitted by wire to the front. Other decrees initiated by Kerensky proscribed 'meetings' and discussions of orders at the front and the circulation of Bolshevik newspapers, specifically *Pravda, Soldatskaia Pravda*, and *Okopnaia Pravda*. Bolshevik and other agitators were arrested on a large scale. Others disappeared underground. Punitive operations under the supervision of commissars and committees were mounted against the most incorrigible units and several of the most famous were disbanded, although some of these efforts failed, and resulted in a rash of lynchings, including that of Commissar Linde and General Girshfeld who tried to disband the Third Infantry Division, and of Colonel Bykov, commander of the First Guards Rifle Regiment.

Polarization and radicalization: the Kornilov fiasco

In the course of these developments many generals and lower officers became aggressively reassertive, blaming the failure of the offensive not just on the Bolsheviks, but on committees, the soviets and the entire revolutionary settlement. They welcomed and eagerly sought to make use of the new repressive measures. General Lavr Kornilov first attracted the attention of the public and the generalship by ordering the shooting of deserters on the south-western front on 8 July and threatening to resign his command if the government did not approve the restoration of the death penalty. Impressed that Kornilov alone of the front commanders did not call for the abolition of front committees, Kerensky appointed him as commander in chief to replace General Brusilov.

Kornilov was instantaneously transformed into a figure representing the hopes of a resurgent right, overshadowing the Provisional Government, now perceived to be weak and vacillating. Kerensky by this risky step was deprived of enhanced prestige when he became Minister President of a new coalition government on 23 July. Kornilov vigorously pressed Kerensky to restore the disciplinary powers of officers, curb committees, army congresses and other meetings, and extend the death penalty to the rear, news of which circulated in the press. However, Kerensky deftly avoided committing himself, fearing alienating the pro-Soviet elements.

The rivalry between Kornilov and Kerensky came to a climax at the Moscow State Conference in mid-August where a series of military and civilian figures denounced the entire system of soviets and committees and called for a strong, unitary, authoritarian government. Nearly all groups of the centre and right, including most Kadets, now looked to Kornilov to rescue the country from the clutches of the left with little discrimination between Bolsheviks and other socialists, or between the Kerensky cabinet and the Soviet.

At the front the higher level committees, which had thus far favoured draconian punitive measures, now mobilized for a defence of revolutionary institutions. In August soldiers, committees and officers nevertheless observed an uneasy truce, taking advantage of a lull in military action. Ordinary soldiers, extremely resentful at having been blamed by the press and the command for the collapse of the front, now averred that the officers had strangely absented themselves (an officer who lit a cigarette at night was 'signalling the enemy'). They viewed the fall of Riga on 21 August as a deliberate effort by the command to discredit the revolution, inverting the mythology of the higher officers and the civilian right. Kornilov was already a symbol to them of counterrevolution because he favoured the death penalty and attacked the Soviet. Psychologically soldiers were prepared to take on Kornilov well before their committees were.

Kornilov's efforts to occupy the capital with the Third Cavalry Corps under General Krymov had little chance of success once Kerensky was alerted to his intentions through V. N. L'vov's clumsy attempt to act as an intermediary. Krymov's main force was intercepted by the local soviet at Luga some 80 miles from the capital when it was alerted by Kerensky's circular telegram removing Kornilov as a traitor. Railroad workers disabled trains, the local garrison of Cossacks agitated fellow Cossacks in Krymov's force, other agitators mobilized by the Soviet arrived shortly thereafter and needed only to explain the 'counterrevolutionary' designs of Kornilov to neutralize the expedition.

Many civilian politicians and generals tried to persuade Kerensky to reinstate Kornilov for the salvation of the country, but when Kornilov released a proclamation denouncing the Provisional Government for being in the clutches of Germans and Bolsheviks, most of them withdrew their support, including key commanders on the northern and western fronts. Only General Denikin and several of his army commanders on the south-western front sought to continue the campaign, openly declaring their support for Kornilov. Their attempts to close down wire and radio communications at staff headquarters only encouraged staff units, committees, commissars and enlisted men to take over various headquarters and 'control' communications. In a matter of hours virtually all headquarters that could have been centres of Kornilov's support were in the hands of revolutionary forces. The reaction of the committees and soldiers went far beyond any real threat posed by Kornilov. Even on the northern and western fronts where most generals were loyal to the Provisional Government, committees supported by soldiers established elaborate controls over communications and even operative orders. For the first time since the early days of the revolution common soldiers and their committees acted in close concert to 'save the revolution'.

Kerensky's personal reputation was permanently impaired when he gave credence to rumours that he had encouraged Kornilov but then lost his nerve, by issuing stern orders to dismantle all the special measures of control over the command. Most committees obeyed with reluctance, but the soldiers were now looking for a radical alternative to Kerensky and the very idea of a coalition government with the 'bourgeoisie'. They found it difficult to believe that the Soviet leadership still supported a government that would not simply declare an end to the war.

Rejuvenated Bolsheviks gained considerable credibility at the front because they alone called for an immediate end to the war and the radical resolution of what was uppermost on most soldier-peasants' minds, the land question; likewise, they alone called for a new government based on the soviets which conformed to the soldiers' mythic conception of their own power. Organized Bolshevik forces at the front, especially on the south-western and Rumanian fronts, were by no means in a position to capitalize on this mood in the month of September. But the soldiers announced their determination to end the war by refusing to build winter bunkers, by hounding their officers as 'Kornilovites', by calling meetings without the consent of their committees to pass resolutions against the war, and by sending deputations to the Soviet to demand it take over the government. Many resolutions with a touch of folk irony called for the death penalty for all Kornilovites. From late September through October whole regiments and divisions initiated 'peace actions' with the enemy. Most were defused by promises to terminate work on entrenchments and by authorizing 'meetings' and deputations to the rear, but harried commanders were now at the mercy of their men.

Higher soldier-officer committees were very slow to face up to the magnitude of this groundswell of soldier resistance, remaining loyal to the Soviet leadership and the Provisional Government, while preparing for elections to the Constituent Assembly. Many still blamed the mood on a handful of Bolshevik and German agents. When the Soviet Executive Committee, yielding to mass pressure, authorized the convocation of a Second Congress of Soviets, most army committees refused to send delegations, well aware that to do so would force by-elections that could only bring in a new levy of Bolshevik representatives. When the Soviet leadership insisted that they send authorized deputations to prevent an easy Bolshevik takeover, they fell between two stools – half sent deputations and half did not, just enough to give the congress legitimacy, but not enough to prevent a pro-Bolshevik majority. Their resistance gave the Bolsheviks their much needed argument to authorize new elections to committees and army-wide congresses.

The army in October

By the time of the October coup in Petrograd this process was only beginning, but the effect was to neutralize the front committees as a source of support for the coalition government and Kerensky. Kerensky, forced to flee the capital to Pskov, the northern front headquarters, sought to raise an expeditionary force counting on the loyal support of army commissars and committees. Initially a number of committees passed resolutions of support, but faced by the soldiers' own determination not to be drawn into a civil war, declined to raise military units. Only a small force of 1,200 Cossacks responded, and they were soon confronted by a hastily assembled force of Red Guards and Baltic sailors at Pulkovo Heights outside Petrograd on 28 October. After a brief skirmish the Cossacks agreed to surrender Kerensky if they were given orders to return to their Don homeland. Kerensky fled in disguise.

The Supreme Command under General Dukhonin, chief commissar Stankevich and the Headquarters' representatives of the army committees engaged in frenetic efforts to mobilize the loyal elements in the army committees, but the effort floundered due to a massive turnover in the committees themselves as a direct response to the news of the October coup. Pro-Bolshevik elements and other leftists equally committed to ending the war and transferring land to the peasants were able to force by-elections to lower committees and the immediate convocation of army-level congresses to elect a new leadership. Within a week on the northern and western fronts this resulted in the replacement of the old defencist leadership by leftist coalitions with the Bolsheviks usually commanding a plurality, if not an absolute majority. Many of the resolutions passed by the congresses reflected compromises with other leftist factions; hence, they seldom endorsed Lenin's formula of an all-Bolshevik government and took an ambivalent stance towards the resolutions of the Second Congress of Soviets, including the recognition of the Council of People's Commissars (*Sovnarkom*). They were more inclined to support the Railroad Union (*Vikzhel*') formula of an 'all-socialist government from the Popular Socialists to the Bolsheviks' until the meeting of the Constituent Assembly and a policy of 'no civil war', but *Vikzhel*''s sponsorship of negotiations collapsed on 2 November. In fact, many front Bolsheviks were 'conciliationists' and sought resolution of the question of power through votes in the democratic bodies and elections to the Constituent Assembly rather than by force of arms. Due to weaker forces and poor communications, the process took much longer on the south-western and Rumanian fronts, but even there by 1 December the old leadership was ousted at army and front congresses, though there was a much smaller Bolshevik presence in the new leftist coalitions.

The results of elections to the Constituent Assembly, which took place flawlessly at the front due to the careful preparations of the old committees, reflected the same pattern: on the northern and western fronts the Bolsheviks obtained 48 per cent and 66 per cent of the vote respectively whereas on the south-western and Rumanian fronts they received around 24 per cent (in the Ninth Army only 11 per cent). However, a new surge in favour of the Bolsheviks occurred as a result of *Sovnarkom*'s appeal to the front on 8 November, signed by Lenin, Stalin (as Commissar of Nationalities) and the newly appointed 'commander in chief' N. V. Krylenko, for every regiment to undertake its own armistice negotiations with the enemy. In response many units at the front eagerly took up 'negotiations' across the wire, overshadowing the general armistice negotiations at Brest-Litovsk.

With the armistice process well under way, Krylenko and a small force of Baltic sailors made their way to Supreme Headquarters and occupied it on 20 November. In spite of Dukhonin's efforts to surrender peacefully and Krylenko's efforts to defend him, Dukhonin was brutally murdered. New congresses on the south-western and Rumanian fronts ratified the shift towards recognition of Soviet power and Bolshevik positions on the war, the agrarian settlement, and other issues. Bolshevik-dominated Military Revolutionary Committees assumed authority over a rapidly dwindling front army, as regional contests in the Ukraine, the Don Republic and the Caucasus signified the total collapse of the old empire and the Imperial Army. The peasant-soldiers demobilized themselves, anxious to return to their homesteads to participate in the massive redistribution of the land.

The committee revolution at the front paralleled the Bolshevik assumption of power in the capital and ensured that the Provisional Government could never return. It was not an unequivocal endorsement of Bolshevik ascendancy, but of the idea of Soviet power and peace, which had assumed mythic proportions. Most soldiers at the front and even many front Bolsheviks expected the Bolsheviks to share power with other socialist parties and opposed the resolution of matters by force of arms. They heartily endorsed Constituent Assembly elections because they were persuaded the assembly would ratify Soviet power and peace. Lenin's personal reputation, despite his intransigence over an all-Bolshevik government, soared at the front because he had successfully forced the issue of the armistice, but many soldiers were not actually sure whether he was a Bolshevik or an SR. It was the consistent promise of immediate peace, and conversely the belated and ambivalent positions of the other socialist parties, that solidified Bolshevik support at the front. In the peasant-soldiers' view, what had taken place was a 'Soviet revolution' which had brought about peace and finally confirmed their entitlement to the land. Though this was but a moment in the long drama of 1917 and was soon overtaken by new developments in 1918, it was, perhaps ironically, the most potent factor of all in facilitating the transfer of power from a discredited Provisional Government headed by Kerensky to a Bolshevik dictatorship.

Further reading

Gen. Denikin A. I., *Ocherki russkoi smuty*, 5 vols. (Paris, J. Polovozky et Cie, 1921–6).

Frenkin M. S., *Russkaia armiia i revoliutsiia 1917–1918* (Munich, Logos, 1978).

Gaponenko L. S., ed., *Revoliutsionnnoe dvizhenie v russkoi armii 27 fevralia–24 oktiabria 1917 goda. Sbornik dokumentov* (Moscow, Nauka 1968).

Gen. Golovin N. N., *The Russian Army in the World War* (Yale, Yale University Press, 1931).

Katkov G., *The Kornilov Affair: Kerensky and the Breakup of the Russian Army* (London and New York, Longman, 1980).

Gen. Knox A., *With the Russian Army, 1914–1917*, 2 vols. (New York, Arno Press, 1971).

Miller V. I., *Soldatskie komitety russkoi armii v 1917 godu* (Moscow, Nauka, 1974).

Wettig G., 'Die Rolle der russischen Armee im revolutionären Machtkampf 1917', *Forschungen zur Osteuropäischen Geschichte*, 12 (1967).

Wildman A. K., *The End of the Russian Imperial Army*, 2 vols. (Princeton, Princeton University Press, 1980, 1987).

The October Revolution

ALEXANDER RABINOWITCH

During the October 1917 revolution, the Provisional Government headed by Aleksandr Kerensky was overthrown, the Bolsheviks came to power, and the Soviet regime that would rule Russia for more than 70 years came into being. To understand the dynamics of the October revolution, it is essential to take account of the results of the February revolution.

Especially significant was the emergence of two potential national governments out of the rubble of the old regime. One was the officially recognized Provisional Government, initially dominated by prominent liberals and, after April, by an uneasy coalition of liberals and moderate socialists. The other was the Soviet (first the Petrograd Soviet and, after July, All-Russian Soviet Executive Committees), controlled by moderate socialists until the autumn of 1917 and in principle representative of a nationwide network of workers', peasants' and soldiers' soviets. Under the moderate socialists, the Petrograd Soviet recognized the legitimacy of the Provisional Government and, with qualifications, supported its policies of delaying fundamental political, economic and social reform (including convocation of a Constituent Assembly), in the interests of national defence.

As economic conditions worsened and as carnage at the front continued, popular pressure grew on the moderate socialists to take power into their own hands. With some exceptions, the unfolding of this process was most advanced in Petrograd, then the Russian capital. Events there inevitably shaped developments elsewhere. However, of equal importance in influencing developments nationally, disaffection with government policies and attraction to immediate radical change were growing throughout Russia. Meanwhile, revolutionary workers, peasants, and soldiers were increasingly taking matters into their own hands.

Lenin and the Bolshevik Party, April–July

The elemental forces unleashed by the February revolution could not be stopped in midstream. Virtually alone among Russia's political leaders, Lenin understood that. Returning to Russia from emigration in April 1917, Lenin quickly torpedoed the movement towards the unification of Bolsheviks and Mensheviks then underway, and positioned the Bolshevik Party on the extreme left of the Russian political spectrum with the battle cry, 'All Power to the Soviets!' Yet it is extremely important to note that in 1917, the slogan 'All Power to the Soviets' stood not for a Bolshevik dictatorship, but for an end to coalition with the bourgeoisie and for 'people's power' exercised through representative, multi-party soviets. The Bolsheviks also stood for immediate peace, fundamental land reform and 'workers' control' in the factories. Amid burgeoning disenchantment with the results of the February revolution, this programme was attractive to workers, peasants and soldiers throughout Russia. In Petrograd, its popular magnetism was vividly reflected on 18 June, when the Bolsheviks successfully transformed a mass demonstration planned as a show of strength by the moderate socialist Soviet leadership into a powerful expression of grass roots support for the Bolshevik platform.

Tailoring the Bolshevik programme so that it would reflect popular aspirations was one of Lenin's most important contributions to the development of the revolution. However, contrary to traditional interpretations, in 1917 Lenin was not the all-powerful leader of a monolithic party. Bolshevik leaders fell into three distinct groups: Lenin and also Trotsky, among others, who viewed the establishment of revolutionary soviet power in Russia less as an end in itself than as a stepping stone to an immediate international socialist revolution; an influential group of significantly more moderate national party leaders led by Lev Kamenev for whom transfer of power to the soviets was primarily a vehicle for building a strong alliance of likeminded groups who would form a caretaker all-socialist coalition government pending convocation of the Constituent Assembly; and a middle group of often quite independent-minded leaders, whose views on the development of the revolution tended to fluctuate in response to their perceptions of the prevailing situation. Recognition of these divisions at all levels of the party is essential for an understanding of many otherwise puzzling moments in the development of the October revolution.

Likewise, in 1917, Lenin's pre-revolutionary conception of the small, united, centralized party was discarded. Decision-making became more democratic and decentralized, the relatively free exchange of ideas was tolerated, if not encouraged, and tens of thousands of new members, whose aspirations helped shape policy, were welcomed into the party. The risks of this loose party structure and fluid, dynamic relationship between the party and its constituency were revealed in mid-summer. Thus on 1 July, the

Bolshevik Central Committee began preparing for a left-socialist congress aimed at unifying all internationalist elements of the 'Social Democracy' (including the Menshevik-Internationalists and the left wing of the SR party, the Left SRs) in support of common goals. Yet only two days later, radical elements of the Bolshevik Petersburg Committee and the party's Military Organization, responsive to their militant constituencies, encouraged the abortive July uprising in Petrograd against the wishes of Lenin and the Central Committee. (The latter considered such action premature because it would be opposed by peasants in the countryside and soldiers at the front.) This unauthorized action prompted the arrest of leading Bolsheviks, forced Lenin to go into hiding, and brought preparations for a left-socialist congress to a quick halt. In the long run, however, the Bolsheviks' organizational flexibility (not only in Petrograd but in Moscow and in other major cities), as well as their relative openness and responsiveness, and their extensive, carefully cultivated connections in factories, local workers' organizations, and military garrisons, were to be important sources of the party's strength.

The aftermath of the July Days

Organizational damage to the party after the July Days was much less severe than might have been expected. Meanwhile, economic conditions continued to deteriorate, the initially promising June offensive was transformed into yet another military débâcle, and the danger of counterrevolution appeared to be increasing. As a result, support for the Bolshevik programme once again began rising even before General Lavr Kornilov's unsuccessful military *putsch* at the end of August caused it to skyrocket.

The march on Petrograd of General Kornilov's forces was halted by the action of all socialist groups working together under the aegis of the soviets. However, the role of the Bolsheviks was critical because of their close organizational links to the revolutionary masses and their ability quickly to mobilize factory workers, garrison soldiers and Baltic fleet sailors. Thus, the rapid defeat of Kornilov had the dual effect of further enhancing the stature of the Bolsheviks at a popular level and providing a powerful stimulus to the idea of all socialist groups banding together for the success of the revolution.

On 1 September, the Petrograd Soviet adopted a resolution proposed by Kamenev calling for exclusion of the bourgeoisie from power and the creation of a new, exclusively socialist national government composed of representatives of the revolutionary proletariat and peasantry. Among the tasks of this new government would be proclamation of a democratic republic, promulgation of a land reform programme, institution of workers' control in factories, nationalization of key branches of industry, the arrangement of a universal democratic peace, and immediate convocation of a Constituent Assembly. Passage of this resolution enabled the Bolsheviks to gain effective control of the Petrograd Soviet, a development that would greatly facilitate their assumption of power in October. Of more immediate consequence, however, the All-Russian Soviet Executive Committees rejected the idea of replacing the Provisional Government with an exclusively socialist, soviet government. So too did the so-called Democratic State Conference, which met in Petrograd from 14 to 22 September. Still, the Democratic State Conference reflected the striking growth within the moderate socialist camps of left Menshevik and Left SR groups, which supported much of the Bolshevik platform as passed by the Petrograd Soviet on 1 September. Moreover, the failure of the Democratic State Conference to respond to popular aspirations for an immediate change in the government refocused attention on the soviets as the arbiter of national politics.

Preparations for October

On 21 September, the Bolsheviks and Left SRs joined forces in calling for the early convocation of a second All-Russian Congress of Soviets. This basic orientation towards the creation of a homogeneous socialist government by the Second Congress of Soviets was to define the political activity of the Bolsheviks, as well as the Left SRs and Menshevik-Internationalists, throughout the latter part of September and the first ten days of October.

During August and September, Lenin had tried his best to influence Bolshevik policy from his hiding-place in Finland. After the July Days, he had campaigned with only very mixed success to persuade his colleagues to abandon the goal of transferring power to the soviets and to prepare for an armed uprising. Subsequently, even he was so impressed by the ease with which the Bolsheviks, Mensheviks and SRs working together had defeated Kornilov that in his essay 'On Compromises', in early September, he allowed for the possibility that the revolution might yet develop peacefully if the national Soviet leadership took power into its own hands without further delay.

Lenin's mood of moderation was short-lived. In mid-September he renewed his emphasis on revolutionary violence. Such factors as the strong position of the extreme left in Finland, the winning of majority support in the Petrograd and Moscow soviets, the massive social upheaval among land-hungry peasants in the countryside, the continuing disintegration of the army at the front and the soldiers' increasingly insistent demands for immediate peace, and signs of revolutionary unrest in the German fleet encouraged Lenin to hope that seizure of power by the Bolsheviks would have strong support in the cities and would no longer be solidly opposed by the provinces and the front, and that creation of a genuinely revolutionary government in Russia would serve as a catalyst for mass rebellions in other European countries. Moreover, as soon as Lenin sensed the possibility of creating an extreme left government through a quick one-stage revolution, his interest in 'compromise' with the moderate socialist parties cooled.

Somewhat contradictorily, Lenin also seems to have become genuinely alarmed that the government might somehow still manage to deflate the revolution by negotiating a separate peace, surrendering Petrograd to the Germans, manipulating elections to the Constituent Assembly, or provoking a disorganized insurrection. He also seems to have worried that if the party delayed too long, it would lose influence among the masses and become powerless to halt Russia's slide into complete anarchy. For all these reasons, on 12 and 14 September (just as the Democratic State Conference was getting underway), Lenin wrote two blistering letters to the Central Committee demanding that the party walk out of the Democratic State Conference and organize an immediate armed uprising 'without losing an instant'.

To Bolshevik leaders in Petrograd, these letters came as a bolt from the blue. Guided in part by Lenin's earlier moderation, they were working closely with the Menshevik-Internationalists and the Left SRs to try to persuade a majority of the Democratic State Conference to take upon itself the task of forming a homogeneous socialist government. 'We all gasped', N. I. Bukharin was later to recall. The Central Committee met in emergency session on the evening of 15 September, within hours of Lenin's mid-September letters being received in Petrograd. Participants at this meeting included not only members of the party's top leadership normally in Petrograd but also several Central Committee members temporarily in the capital for the Democratic State Conference. All were cool to Lenin's entreaties; indeed, what appears to have concerned the committee most of all was to ensure that the substance of Lenin's messages be kept secret. Moreover, during the rest of September militant essays from Lenin intended for the Bolshevik press were systematically suppressed in favour of his more moderate writings, thereby creating the illusion that he was still thinking along those lines.

Lenin reacted with fury. The Bolshevik leadership in Petrograd, in concert with other left groups, was pursuing a steady course aimed at the creation of a homogeneous socialist government at a nationwide Congress of Soviets, which at the insistence of leftist delegates to the Democratic State Conference was scheduled for 20 October. Roughly simultaneously, the Bolshevik Central Committee, with the approval of Bolshevik delegates to the Democratic State Conference, decided to convene an emergency party congress on 17 October, just prior to the start of the Soviet Congress. To Lenin, these decisions indicated that the party was letting the last golden moments when power could be seized slip away. First from Finland, and then, by the end of September, from a hideout on the northern outskirts of Petrograd, he delivered a series of stinging rebukes to his party colleagues, accompanied by ever more insistent demands that the Provisional Government be overthrown at once.

Lenin argued his case in person at a historic meeting of the Bolshevik Central Committee on 10 October. At issue was the reversal of the strategy aimed at peaceful transfer of power to multi-party soviets that had been the key to the party's extraordinary rise in influence and authority among the revolutionary masses since April. Beyond this, he also had somehow to persuade his party colleagues that the existing situation was so critical that a decision on this question could not be delayed until the emergency party congress which, judging by the thrust of related intra-party discussions during the Democratic State Conference, would have strongly resisted the seizure of power before the imminent Second All-Russian Congress of Soviets. Attending this meeting were 12 of the committee's 21 members. Proponents and opponents of immediate armed action against the Provisional Government argued their cases passionately and at length. Ultimately, 10 of the 12 Central Committee members at the meeting yielded to Lenin and agreed to make immediate preparations for the seizure of power 'the order of the day', thus pre-empting the scheduled party congress – which was never held.

Divisions within the leadership

Despite this green light for the organization of an armed uprising, little was done to accomplish the goal for roughly two weeks. For one thing, right Bolsheviks such as Kamenev and Grigorii Zinoviev (who were present at the 10 October meeting), along with the prominent Moscow Bolsheviks Aleksei Rykov and Viktor Nogin (who were not), vigorously opposed Lenin's course. In the summer of 1917, they had rejected Lenin's idea that conditions were rapidly ripening for an early socialist revolution. Rather, they became steadfast advocates of the formation by the Soviet leadership of a homogeneous, democratic, multi-party socialist government that would hold power until the convocation of the Constituent Assembly. Barring precipitous action by the Bolsheviks, they were convinced that the Constituent Assembly would be strongly influenced by revolutionary socialist groups and would construct a democratic soviet-based political system. In part because of the correspondence between their views and the views of other left-socialist groups, right Bolsheviks such as Kamenev, Zinoviev, Rykov, Nogin, and also the trade-union leader David Riazanov, were among the party's most authoritative leaders in 1917. Both Soviet and Western historians have traditionally interpreted their arguments against organization of an armed uprising in late September and October 1917 as a sign of lack of courage. Yet in the light of subsequent events, their warnings about the long-term dangers of an exclusively Bolshevik assumption of power in backward Russia and of reliance on early decisive socialist revolutions abroad appear remarkably prophetic.

Another, more significant factor that worked against the organization of an immediate armed uprising was the opposition of Central Committee members such as Trotsky and radically inclined local Petrograd party leaders who were attracted to the idea of an early socialist revolution in Russia but were sceptical about whether workers and soldiers could be mobilized behind the kind of 'immediate bayonet charge' demanded by Lenin. In part because of their continuing interaction with workers and soldiers, these leaders on the spot possessed a more realistic appreciation than Lenin of the party's influence and authority among the masses, and of popular attachment to the soviets as legitimate democratic institutions in which all genuinely revolutionary groups would work together in support of common goals. Then too, many of these leaders (albeit not Trotsky), as well as their counterparts around the country, were themselves genuinely sympathetic to an all-socialist collaboration and did not want to damage prospects for its realization. Also, as a result of the first-hand impact of the Kornilov experience, they were much less concerned than Lenin about the Provisional Government's capacity to damage the left.

Despite these concerns, in response to the Central Committee's decision of 10 October, local-level Bolshevik leaders in Petrograd explored possibilities for starting a popular uprising. After several days, however, many were forced to conclude that for the moment the party was technically unprepared to initiate an immediate mass uprising and that, in any case, most workers and soldiers would probably not be responsive if the party called for a rising before the Congress of Soviets (which by now had been rescheduled from 20 to 25 October). Moreover, they recognized that by usurping the prerogatives of the national Congress of Soviets, they would jeopardize possibilities for collaboration with such potentially important allies as the Left SRs and Menshevik-Internationalists. Further, they risked loss of support in such mass organizations as trade unions, factory committees and the Petrograd Soviet; and, most ominous of all, they would increase the danger of opposition by troops on the nearby northern front.

In the face of these obstacles to organization of an immediate armed uprising, the following approach gradually suggested itself: (1) that the soviets (because of their stature in the eyes of workers and soldiers), and not party groups, should be employed for the overthrow of the Provisional Government; (2) that for the broadest support, any attack on the government should be masked as a defensive operation on behalf of the Soviet; (3) thus that action should be delayed until a suitable excuse for giving battle presented itself; (4) that to undercut potential resistance and to maximize the possibility of success, every opportunity should be utilized to subvert the authority of the Provisional Government peacefully; and (5) that the formal overthrow of the existing government should be linked with and legitimized by the decisions of the Second Congress of Soviets. To be sure, this more subtle approach carried the risk that the Provisional Government might not be overthrown prior to the Congress of Soviets. Among top party leaders in Petrograd, however, only Lenin seems to have been at all concerned about that possibility.

The Bolsheviks come to power and the Second Congress of Soviets

Against this background, the Provisional Government's announcement in the second week of October of plans to move the bulk of the Petrograd garrison to the front was a windfall for the Bolsheviks. It provided an effective immediate 'cause' around which a decisive struggle against the Provisional Government could be waged. With the party's encouragement, garrison soldiers quickly concluded that history was repeating itself – that as in the Kornilov affair, the government, in league with the military high command, was once again bent on stifling the revolution. Actually, so great was popular mistrust of the Provisional Government's intentions at this time that even moderate socialist leaders recognized that garrison troops would not respond to orders not in some way controlled by the Petrograd Soviet. Hence it was a Menshevik who initially proposed that a special committee be established by the Soviet to clarify the problem of Petrograd's security and to draw up a plan for the defence of the city which could be popularly supported. Between 20 and 24 October, this ostensibly non-party committee, the Military-Revolutionary Committee of the Petrograd Soviet, successfully substituted its own representatives for government commissars in major garrison units, arms depots and other key military points. At the same time, the Military-Revolutionary Committee secured agreement from virtually the whole garrison that troop orders not countersigned by the Military-Revolutionary Committee would be considered invalid. In effect, the Provisional Government was disarmed without a shot being fired.

In response to the Military Revolutionary Committee's actions, Kerensky initiated steps early on the morning of 24 October to suppress the left. This act made the armed uprising that Lenin had been demanding for weeks feasible. Yet even after this, a majority of the Bolshevik Central Committee opposed any attempt to overthrow the Provisional Government before the opening of the Congress of Soviets, now less than 24 hours away. It required Lenin's personal intervention before dawn on 25 October, under circumstances that are still obscure, to launch offensive operations against the Provisional Government. During the rest of the day, all pretence that the Military-Revolutionary Committee was simply defending the revolution and attempting to maintain the status quo pending the expression of the congress's will was dropped. Instead an all-out effort was made to confront congress delegates with the overthrow of the Provisional Government before the start of their deliberations; this effort culminated late that night with the occupation of the Winter Palace (seat of the Provisional Government). Hours earlier, a proclamation drafted by Lenin announcing the Provisional Government's overthrow had been telegraphed around the country.

In retrospect, it appears that Lenin's basic purpose in insisting on the overthrow of the Provisional Government before the opening of the Congress of Soviets was to eliminate any possibility that the congress would form a socialist coalition in which the moderate socialists might have had a significant voice. If this was the case, Lenin's strategy succeeded brilliantly. On the eve of the opening of the congress, before the initiation of the military operations that culminated in the seizure of the Winter Palace, it appeared all but certain that efforts to establish a multi-party democratic socialist government pledged to a programme of peace and fundamental reform would at last bear fruit. The isolation of the Provisional Government in the prevailing circumstances was clearly reflected in an event that took place on the evening of 24 October at the 'Preparliament', a pseudo-parliament created by the Democratic State Conference. After a passionate, at times almost hysterical appeal by Kerensky for an endorsement of his crackdown on the Bolsheviks, a majority of delegates supported a resolution demanding, among other things, that the Provisional Government either commit itself to the immediate enunciation of a radical land reform and peace programme or step down. Joining the Left SRs and Menshevik-Internationalists in support of this resolution, in effect a vote of no confidence in Kerensky, were several prominent moderate socialists who had previously been among the Provisional Government's staunch supporters.

Early indications of the composition of the congress seemed similarly promising, as were the arriving congress delegates' official positions on the government question. According to a preliminary report by the Credentials Committee, 300 of the 670 delegates to the congress were Bolsheviks, 193 were SRs (of whom more than half were Left SRs), 68 were Mensheviks, 14 were Menshevik-Internationalists, and the remainder were either affiliated with one of a number of smaller political groups or did not belong to any formal organization. An overwhelming number of delegates, some 505 of them, were firmly committed to transfer of 'All Power to the Soviets', that is, to the creation of a Soviet government that reflected the party composition of the congress. The vastly strengthened position of left factions within the Menshevik and SR camps was apparent at delegate caucuses before the start of the congress itself. Thus at a meeting of the Menshevik faction on the morning of 25 October, a majority of delegates agreed to call for the complete reconstruction of the cabinet and specifically stipulated that the new government be 'homogeneous' and 'democratic'. At an initial SR caucus at about the same time, it turned out that the Left SRs had a sizeable majority. A resolution proposed there by the SR Central Committee was defeated by a vote of 92 to 60, after which the majority agreed to contact the Menshevik-Internationalists, evidently to coordinate efforts to form a multi-party democratic socialist government at the congress. Equally significant, following this victory some Left SR leaders retained hope that the entire SR faction might stick together behind the programme of the left.

It is important to keep in mind this spirit of reconciliation in order to grasp the full import of the Bolsheviks' belated attack on the Provisional Government. The beginning of the congress's deliberations on the evening of 25 October was punctuated by the boom of cannon firing on the Winter Palace. The effect was a good deal more damaging to the prospects for forming a broadly based coalition government than it was to the Winter Palace. In response to the independent Bolshevik uprising, the Mensheviks and SRs moved rightward, withdrew from the congress, and joined the ranks of those opposing Soviet power. A short while later, Iulii Martov, on behalf of the Menshevik-Internationalists, attempted to persuade the congress to declare a recess while a delegation was sent to sound out all socialist organizations about the creation of a broadly representative socialist government. His proposal was rejected, after which the Menshevik-Internationalists also withdrew from the congress. Now, apart from the Bolsheviks, only the Left SRs remained.

From then on, the Second All-Russian Congress of Soviets degenerated into a boisterous celebration of revolution during which Lenin and Trotsky superintended rapid-fire passage of bombastic, primarily propagandistic decrees on the proclamation of Soviet power everywhere in Russia, immediate peace, and land reform. In the ensuing din, as these decrees were hurriedly telegraphed around the country, intermittent efforts by the Left SRs (supported by moderate Bolsheviks) to awaken a semblance of caution among the delegates, and, in this connection, to refocus their attention on the critical importance of re-establishing common ground with the moderate socialists, were barely heard and got nowhere. Still, as the congress drew to a close shortly before dawn on 27 October, the Left SRs remained hopeful of serving as intermediaries in somehow bringing all socialist groups together in a new government. They refused the Bolsheviks' invitation to accept posts in the new Soviet government. Consequently, the first Council of People's Commissars, headed by Lenin, was made up exclusively of Bolsheviks. According to the decree sanctioning the formation of this government, it was to be responsible to a new Executive Committee formed by the congress, and to serve only until the convocation of the Constituent Assembly.

The consolidation of one-party rule

While efforts to establish a multi-party Soviet government suffered a severe setback at the Second All-Russian Congress of Soviets, they did not stop there. Initial opposition to the one-party government which had been created there coalesced around an organization called the All-Russian Committee for the Salvation of the Motherland and the Revolution, formed by the Petrograd City Duma on 26 October. Included in the leadership of the committee were representatives of the city duma, the former Soviet Executive Committees, and the moderate socialists who had walked out of the Soviet Congress. Among other things, the Committee for the Salvation of the Motherland and the Revolution encouraged 'sit-down' strikes of civil servants and set about organizing a military insurrection in Petrograd, timed to coincide with an attack from outside the city by a Cossack force supporting Kerensky and led by General P. N. Krasnov.

Meanwhile, cooler heads were attempting to serve as intermediaries between the two sides. Prominent among these mediators were the Menshevik-Internationalists and the Left SRs, the latter being of special importance to the Bolsheviks because of their strength among peasants in the countryside. Among a myriad of labour organizations seeking to play a similar role was the All-Russian Executive Committee of the Union of Railwaymen (*Vikzhel'*). *Vikzhel'* threatened a nationwide rail stoppage at midnight on 29 October if the Bolsheviks refused to participate in negotiations aimed at the creation of a homogeneous socialist government responsible to the soviets and including representatives of all socialist groups.

Intense discussions under *Vikzhel'*'s auspices about the make-up and structure of a new government were held in Petrograd from 29 October to 5 November. With Kamenev in charge of negotiations for the Bolsheviks, they started well. Indeed, on 2 November even the Bolshevik press reported that they were nearing a successful conclusion. However, the negotiations ultimately foundered, primarily because of impossibly high demands made by the moderate socialists (essentially requiring repudiation of Soviet power and most of what had been accomplished by the Second All-Russian Congress of Soviets), the Bolsheviks' defeat of the military insurrection organized by the Committee for Salvation of the Motherland and the Revolution and of the loyalist Cossack force led by General Krasnov, and the consolidation of soviet power in Moscow. These developments immeasurably strengthened support for the hardline policies of Lenin and Trotsky, enabling them successfully to torpedo the negotiations.

To be sure, during the run-up to the Constituent Assembly in December, Bolshevik moderates were to make a valiant bid to mobilize the party's delegation in support of the Constituent Assembly's right to define Russia's future political system. However, by then they had been squeezed out of the party leadership and this effort also failed. In retrospect, the results of the Second All-Russian Congress of Soviets and the failure of the *Vikzhel'* negotiations proved to be decisive, not only in ending possibilities for the creation of a homogeneous socialist coalition government, but also in making a long and bloody civil war inevitable. The Bolsheviks had come to power, and the Soviet era in Russia's history had begun.

Further reading

Akademiia nauk SSSR, Institut istorii, Leningradskoe otdelenie, *Oktiabr'skoe vooruzhennoe vosstanie: Semnadtsatyi god v Petrograde*, 2 vols. (Leningrad, Nauka, 1967).

Institut marksizma-leninizma pri TsK KPSS, *Protokoly Tsentral'nogo komiteta RSDRP(b): Avgust 1917–fevral' 1918* (Moscow, Gosizdat, 1958).

Kudelli P. F., ed., *Pervyi legal'nyi Peterburgskii komitet Bol'shevikov v 1917g: Sbornik materialov i protokolov zasedanii Peterburgskogo komiteta RSDRP(b) i ego Ispolnitel'noi komissii za 1917 g*. (Moscow-Leningrad, Gosizdat, 1927).

Mel'gunov S. P., *Kak bol'sheviki zakhvatili vlast'* (Paris, Editions la Renaissance, 1953).

Rabinowitch A., *The Bolsheviks Come to Power: The Revolution of 1917 in Petrograd* (New York, W. W. Norton, 1976).

Wildman A. K., *The End of the Russian Imperial Army*, vol. 2: *The Road to Soviet Power and Peace* (Princeton, Princeton University Press, 1987).

The Civil War
The Military Campaigns

EVAN MAWDSLEY

Introduction

'Civil war' takes different forms. This chapter will outline and evaluate events on the formal military 'fronts' rather than unorganized conflict between the population and government forces. Although there have been interesting recent debates among Russian historians about chronology and causation, this article will follow the accepted notion that civil war followed, rather than preceded, the October revolution and the overthrow of Kerensky's Provisional Government. The post-communist view of E. G. Gimpel'son is compelling: 'Our civil war was unavoidable because the Bolshevik Party decided to establish the dictatorship of the proletariat and by doing this to lead the country on the socialist path'.

The civil war and the democratic anti-Bolsheviks, October 1917 to November 1918

The 'triumphal march of Soviet power'

The first 'campaign' in the winter of 1917–18 went very well for the Bolsheviks. After the neutralization of a few anti-Bolshevik military detachments in Petrograd and Moscow the civil war took the form of a projection of Bolshevik power across the land mass of the former Russian empire. Historians in Russia will probably not again use Lenin's phrase, the 'triumphal march of Soviet power', but it is not an unreasonable description of what occurred.

The early centres of resistance were not Kerensky strongholds, but places with a particular national or territorial identity or with conservative characteristics where the internal 'seizure of Soviet power' did not apply. The

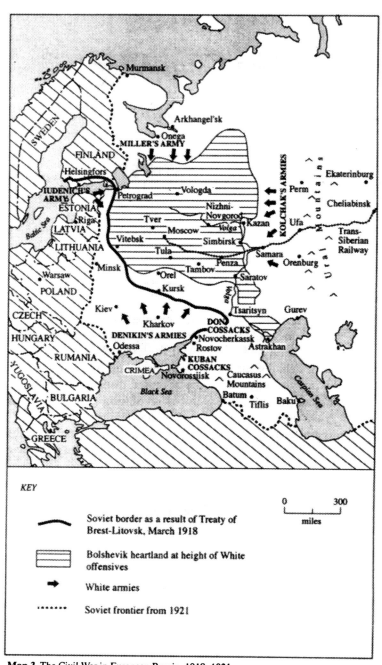

KEY

Soviet border as a result of Treaty of Brest-Litovsk, March 1918	
Bolshevik heartland at height of White offensives	
White armies	
Soviet frontier from 1921	

Map 3. The Civil War in European Russia, 1918–1921

Cossack lands of the northern Caucasus and the southern Urals were especially important. Kiev, the prospective capital of an inchoate Ukrainian entity, was another centre. Detachments of Red Guards – armed workers, soldiers and sailors – spread out to break this resistance. They came from Petrograd and Moscow and from regional pro-Soviet centres; the term 'railway *(eshelonnaia)* war' is not inappropriate here. One of the 'campaigns' was against the Orenburg Cossacks in the southern Urals, under Ataman A. I. Dutov. More extensive was that led by V. A. Antonov-Ovseenko against the Don Cossacks of Ataman Kaledin at Novocherkassk. The war with Kaledin provided an excuse for an attack on the Ukrainian government, the Rada. At the end of January 1918 its forces were driven from Kiev and a month later the Don Cossacks and Russian nationalists and conservatives who had rallied to 'the Don' were driven from Rostov. Lenin could declare the civil war won.

Whether the Bolsheviks could have kept control of all they had won during the railway war is an academic question. In reality the external situation reopened the internal conflict. Between February 1918 and the middle of the summer German, Austrian and Turkish armies occupied Estonia, Latvia, Belorussia, the Ukraine and parts of the Transcaucasus. They spared central Russia but in the territories they occupied Soviet power was overthrown, left-wing groups were driven underground, and conservative nationalists encouraged. The Central Powers' advance also provoked in May 1918 a 'mutiny' by the pro-Allied Czechoslovak Legion, 40,000 men, strung along the railway from the Volga to Vladivostok. Moscow lost control over the central Volga region, the Urals and Siberia, and it was cut off from Central Asia. This extraordinary development was symptomatic of how weak the Bolshevik hold had been on the periphery in the first place.

Komuch *and the Cossacks*

In the summer of 1918 the situation was set for a new and bloodier round of fighting. Many historians date the beginning of the civil war from this time, thereby putting the onus on 'external' action in the form of the Czechoslovak uprising. Whatever the case, the situation appeared very threatening. The Communist zone was ringed by enemies. A Socialist-Revolutionary-led counter-government appeared at Samara (later Kuibyshev), the 'Committee of Members of the Constituent Assembly', or *Komuch*. Fortunately for the Communists, the 'eastern' front was the only active one and the anti-Communist forces numbered only a few thousand Czechoslovaks aided by detachments of a small *Komuch* 'People's Army'. But it erupted when the resources of the infant Red Army were concentrated in the western 'screens' facing the Central Powers. A hastily formed Eastern Army Group *(Front)* broke apart in July and August, partly due to the rebellion of its Left SR commander. (To avoid confusion, the Russian word *front*, used in both World Wars as well as in the civil war, will be translated here as 'army group', i.e. a formation of up to five 'armies' controlled from one headquarters; a 'front' in the English sense – the eastern front, the southern front – sometimes involved several army groups.)

The Communists lost the strategic Volga towns of Simbirsk and Kazan as the enemy seemingly raced down the river towards Moscow. The Reds held out partly because they were able to shift detachments from the west and partly because they had their own 'special' troops in the form of the Latvian riflemen, commanded by a Latvian colonel named I. I. Vācietis. It was important, too, that once the Left SR uprising was put down there was no effective political challenge to the Communists in Moscow or elsewhere in the Communist zone. Kazan was re-taken in September, with the direct participation of the People's Commissar for War, Trotsky. Simbirsk and Samara were soon recaptured, and by November 1918 the reconstructed Eastern Army Group had pushed the anti-Bolshevik forces back from the Volga to the Urals.

The late summer and early autumn was a political and military test for the 'democratic counterrevolution', and one that it failed. The political short-comings of *Komuch* and its eastern rival, the Provisional Siberian Government, do not concern us directly here. Neither do the faults of their common successor, the Provisional All-Russian Government. What matters is that none of these governments were able either to create effective mobile military forces or to foment serious unrest in the Soviet zone; they were not even able to hold the formidable obstacle of the River Volga.

The Volga front seemed the most important because of its relative proximity to Moscow. In retrospect the successes much further south had greater consequences for 1919. The Don Cossacks cleared their 'host' region and the Volunteer Army took control of the Kuban, the region further south. This might not have happened had Austro-German troops not covered the western flank of the Don or had Red troops not been concentrated on the middle Volga front. But the main anti-Bolshevik 'base area' was established without any Allied involvement.

Things were different in North Russia. There the Allies did directly intervene, but in tiny numbers and in a sparsely inhabited region whose only value was as a base for further Allied involvement. There was no direct danger to the Soviet government because the forces involved were small, because they were far from Moscow and Petrograd, and because they were there more to prevent German activity than to mount an offensive. The position on the Pacific coast was generally similar. The Japanese sent a larger numbers of troops, but they in no way threatened Soviet power in Europe. Unlike the northern intervention, Vladivostok opened a railway route to an anti-Bolshevik centre in the hinterland, but it was an extremely long one.

The first year of the civil war was not directly a White versus Red struggle. The Central Powers had a strong influence on the periphery, Allied leverage was extremely limited, and – above all – 'White' participation was limited. The 'democratic counterrevolution', however, proved unable to mount an effective military or political challenge to Soviet rule. The most important consequence of this was that the Communists had twelve months to consolidate their hold over central Russia, the zone from which they would fight the next two years of the civil war. Even after the amputation of Siberia, Central Asia, the Transcaucasus, the Ukraine, Belorussia, Poland and the Baltic provinces that base territory had an area of a million square miles, a population of 60 million, and – above all – most of the resources of the wartime Imperial Russian Army. Already by the end of 1918 there were 500,000 *krasnoarmeitsy* (Red Army personnel), a force that dwarfed all the Bolsheviks' internal opponents. The Volga campaign had served as a kind of dress rehearsal for 1919 during which, due especially to Trotsky's influence, a 'regular' form of Red Army had been created, commanded by trained ex-imperial officers and manned by peasant conscripts.

The civil war and the Whites, November 1918 to November 1920

The western offensive

Stalinist historiography traditionally periodized the civil war as the First, Second, and Third 'Campaigns of the Entente'. In fact, the civil war could be seen as the mirror image of that – as a series of attacks into the periphery of the former Russian empire from the Communist core. The first of these had been the 'railway war'. A year later the end of the First World War meant not a concentric onslaught against Bolshevism but a Bolshevik offensive to the west, vast in geographical scope and involving a substantial proportion of available Red forces. This was directed partly into what in the 1990s came to be called the 'near abroad', the peripheral territories traditionally held by the Russian state but now out of Moscow's control. Red forces advanced into the Baltic states, Belorussia, and the Ukraine on the heels of the departing German and Austro-Hungarian armies. To be fair, it was also conceived as an attempt to take control of the periphery before the expected arrival of large numbers of Allied troops (a threat which never emerged), and it had the support of underground Communists. It was also, however, partly conceived as a step in the campaign to spread communism to the West and to support the revolution in Central Europe.

The Red western campaign was not as successful as Moscow had hoped, but it took a lot of ground. The border nationalists no longer had Germany and Austria to protect them, and the Allies were not prepared or able to provide an alternative. The French presence in Odessa from December 1918 to April 1919 was a complete failure, although a unique combination of the

Royal Navy and remnants of the German Army helped turn back the Red advance on Estonia and Latvia.

Siberia and the Urals, 1919–1920

The defeat of Germany and her allies was only the first of two key developments in the late autumn of 1918. The other was the domination of the anti-Bolshevik movement gained by the Whites. The centre-left radicals, Czechs, and Cossack atamans were replaced by conservative and 'all-Russia-minded' military officers. The key event was Admiral Kolchak's coup in Omsk, the Siberian capital of the SR-dominated Provisional All-Russian Government, on 18 November. There was, however, a parallel if more gradual development in the south, with a shift in the balance between General Denikin's Volunteer Army and its embattled comrades in arms, the Don Cossacks. The creation on 8 January 1919 of a unified command, the Armed Forces of South Russia (AFSR), marked the subordination of the Cossacks to White leadership.

The overture to the climactic year 1919 was a local Soviet defeat, the 'Perm catastrophe' of December 1918. Kolchak's right-flank army advanced rapidly across the Urals to retake the city of Perm. It was not until March 1919, however, that Kolchak was able to mount a general offensive. The Siberians could no longer rely on the backbone of the Czechoslovak Legion, but the Siberian forces had been built up to an extent, and Moscow was preoccupied with the campaigns in the southern and western borderlands. Kolchak's Western Army under General M. V. Khanzhin quickly re-took much of what had been lost in the previous autumn and threatened to reach the Volga crossings. It was, however, a short-lived success. White forces were inadequate, and Kolchak had probably attacked as much for political objectives – Allied recognition and aid – as military ones. His new divisions were far from ready. The Reds were able to reinforce the Eastern Army Group, putting in place larger and more effective forces. Peasant dissatisfaction with the Kolchak regime was not obviously a factor. The Reds held on to the eastern side of the Volga, and in May 1919 they took the offensive themselves. This would turn out to be a non-stop advance deep into Siberia – partly over the objections of Vācietis, now the overall Red Army commander, who had wanted to stop at the Urals in order to transfer troops back to more threatened sectors of the ring of fronts.

Kolchak attempted to regain the initiative at the Ural passes in July 1919 but was undone by the loss of Cheliabinsk. Out in the Siberian steppe the Whites tried another counterattack in September but failed. The Reds for their part were able to bypass the collapsing Kolchak armies and take Omsk, almost by a *coup de main*, on 14 November 1919. The year-old government of 'Supreme Ruler' Kolchak had been a military failure. He had failed to create effective field forces. This was partly because the Siberian peasants were reluctant to serve. Active peasant partisan resistance to Kolchak, threatening his lines of communications, was probably less of a factor, at least until the position was hopeless. A most important element was demographic. Kolchak in Siberia could not hope to compete with the resources of Russia proper. Whether the Siberians were enthusiastic or not they numbered at most eight million, compared to the 60 million in the Communist hinterland.

South Russia, 1919–1920

The southern front was the most dramatic of the civil war, and probably also the most important. The AFSR was better led and equipped than anything in Siberia, and it benefited especially from large numbers of Don and Kuban Cossacks. Not only was it initially created without any help from the Allies, but its early successes into the early summer of 1919 were achieved before the arrival of significant amounts of Allied military *matériel*. (No Allied infantry served with Denikin, although a handful of British pilots and tank crews took part.) The Red Army command also regarded the southeast as the key front and devoted major resources to trying, without success, to finish off the Don Cossacks before Allied aid could arrive. In the meantime, the Volunteer Army were able in the winter of 1918–19 to consolidate their rear by clearing the Red 'Caspian-Caucasus Army Group' out of the North Caucasus. Denikin was then able to transfer mobile troops to the Don front and to repel a ring of Red attacks; General Mai-Maevskii carried out here one of the most brilliant operations of the war.

In May 1919, just as Kolchak's reverses began, the AFSR burst out of the Don–Donbas region. The Red armies were overextended and their reserves had now been sent to stop Kolchak. Allied support had some impact, though so far more on White morale than White *matériel*. Extreme Red 'de-cossackization' policies had driven the mass of the Cossacks into the anti-Bolshevik camp. Above all the Whites had more effective troops, with perhaps 45–50,000 AFSR frontline soldiers driving back Red forces nearly twice their strength. By the end of June all components of the AFSR had made dramatic progress into Soviet territory. The Volunteer Army had taken Kharkov, one of the great industrial cities of the Russian empire, and broken across the Dnepr into the right-bank Ukraine. The Don Army had regained control of the expanse of the Don Cossack region. General Wrangel's Caucasus Army had finally taken Tsaritsyn (later Stalingrad, and then Volgograd), the 'Red Verdun', breaking Red communications with the Caucasus. The result was great alarm in Moscow and a radical shake-up of the Red Army command.

The Whites had to pause to rebuild their units and consolidate (militarily) the expanse of territory they had taken. They were being vigorously counterattacked by the Reds under their new commander S. S. Kamenev, who in

August 1919 began an attack from the eastern end of the southern front into the Don territory, designed to drive down the right bank of the Volga deep into the AFSR rear. This was the occasion for another of the major strategic controversies from the civil war. The plan involved an indirect rather than a direct defence of Moscow. In 'grand-strategic terms' it also blocked any link between Denikin and Kolchak and allowed troops to be shifted from the Kolchak front if necessary on interior lines. In the event it failed to make much progress, and the AFSR was able to renew its attack further west. Kursk and Orel fell in short order and at the end of November 1919 Moscow was under threat – although the Whites were still 250 miles from the Red capital. In the end, however, the AFSR was stopped. It was overstretched and outnumbered (100,000 men versus 150,000 Reds in October 1919). Orlando Figes has suggested that a key feature in the autumn of 1919 was a return of peasant deserters, partly from fear of Denikin and partly for seasonal reasons. In any event, this was a Red victory inflicted by weight of numbers rather than by cunning strategy.

The AFSR was soon in headlong retreat back to the Don. The Reds had meanwhile created a remarkable mobile force in the form of S. M. Budennyi's Cavalry Army (*Konarmiia*). *Konarmiia* not only neutralized the early AFSR superiority in (Cossack) cavalry, but also provided a war-winning force. Denikin was not even able to hold out on the River Don at the start of the New Year. At the end of March 1920 he was forced to evacuate Novorossiisk and move by sea to the Crimea. With the North Caucasus the Whites lost their greatest advantage, the Don and Kuban Cossacks. It is worth remembering, however, that even before the fiasco of the winter of 1919–20 this base area only contained perhaps ten million people, a fraction of Moscow's resources. Denikin was never able to raise more than 100,000 effectives (in October 1919), and like Kolchak he had been taking on numerically stronger Red forces, in this case 50 per cent greater in strength.

The Kolchak and Denikin campaigns of 1919 were the most substantial threats to Soviet power. They were coupled with a much smaller advance by a 'North-western Army' operating from Estonia against Petrograd in May and again in November 1919, and also with pressure from small White and Allied detachments based on the northern ports of Murmansk and Arkhangel'sk (Archangel). General Iudenich's army was interned in Estonia in November 1919, and although the northern Whites held on over the winter, after the departure of the Allied detachments they were crushed by Red forces moving up the railways. Arkhangel'sk fell in February 1920 and Murmansk in March.

The destruction of the Whites, 1920

The military campaigns from the spring to the autumn of 1920 were – overall – actually more intense than those of 1919, but in one sense they were less important. The campaigns in 1918 and 1919 were for the survival of the Soviet government. By the spring of 1920 the Moscow government was under no direct military threat. Where the Red Army was fighting the Russian Whites in 1920 it was fighting remnants, small in number, and remote from the vital centres of urban Russia. The remnants of the Siberian White armies simply fled east along the Trans-Siberian Railway. Kolchak himself was captured and executed at Irkutsk in February 1920. The Siberian Whites, now dominated by the notorious Ataman Semenov, were briefly able to hold up a further advance beyond Chita (east of Lake Baikal), but in the autumn they pulled back to the Pacific coast. There they held out until the withdrawal of their Japanese protectors in October 1922, an event which marked the end of the civil war.

The army of General Wrangel in the Crimea was more worthy of the Red Army's attention, although this survival of Denikin's army in the Crimea was an oversight. In June 1920 Wrangel's 'Russian Army' broke north out of the Crimea proper into the grain areas of the North Tauride – in what was called the 'Third Entente Campaign'. Wrangel lacked sufficient strength to make any further advance in the face of an enlarged Red Army, and in November 1920 a counter-offensive under M. V. Frunze pushed him back, stormed the Perekop Isthmus into the Crimea, and drove the last of the European White Armies and several hundred thousand refugees into exile.

The campaign in Poland

The most serious military operations of 1920 were between Red and Polish forces. The 'Soviet-Polish War' is often not seen as part of the Russian civil war, but that seems an arbitrary judgement based on hindsight. Most of Poland was in the Russian empire up to 1914, and the campaign against the so-called 'White Poles' (belopoliaki) was part of general Red strategy. There had been low-level fighting and substantial movement of the fronts throughout 1919. In addition, the Polish campaign was part of a larger expansionist mission, aimed at spreading communism to Germany across Poland.

The immediate cause of full-scale war was a Polish invasion of the Ukraine in late April 1920. The short-term aim of this Polish advance was to pre-empt a Soviet move into the western borderlands (re-taking, in turn, territory occupied by the Poles in 1919). The longer-term one was to incorporate those borderlands in an Eastern European federation centred on Warsaw. In the event, the Poles held Kiev for little more than a month before being driven out and nearly encircled by A. I. Egorov's South-western Army Group, spearheaded by Budennyi's Cavalry Army, now re-deployed from the Don. The main activity, however, was north of the Pripet marshes where M. N. Tukhachevskii's Western Army Group pushed the Poles back 400 miles to the Vistula. This involved a series of offensives launched in May and July and supported by Red cavalry. In August 1920 a confused battle was fought east of Warsaw where the overextended Western Army Group had its left flank turned by the Poles and had to make a hasty retreat out of the trap. One cause of the defeat was the South-western Army Group's failure to move in support, a blunder later blamed on Egorov's commissar, Stalin. More important was the strength, both qualitative and quantitative, of the Polish Army and the fact that it and the stability of the Polish government had been underestimated. The Polish Army numbered 740,000 in August 1920, compared to 100,000 in the AFSR ten months before. The Red Army was still not able to conduct long-distance operations on a front where it could not 'live off' the enemy for replacement manpower and supplies; Tukhachevskii had only 40,000 men when he reached the Vistula. In any event a Soviet-Polish armistice was achieved in October 1920, allowing Wrangel to be finished off in the following month, and bringing to an end the major campaigns of the civil war.

The character of the civil war

There has been a renewal of interest in the civil war in post-communist Russia. Even in the Gorbachev period more objective works appeared and there was a flood of reprints of White memoirs and inter-war monographs, most notably N. E. Kakurin's classic account. Since 1991 much of the re-thinking has been done together with Western specialists. In 1993 it was reported that the Institute of Russian History of the Russian Academy of Sciences was working on a six-volume history of the civil war. It is hard to know whether the new Russian work will change our understanding of events, or simply introduce a more rounded approach that has been common in the West for the last thirty years, i.e. breaking away from one-sided sympathy for the Reds and giving a balanced view of Trotsky and other figures.

In any event, important new information has become available. One of the most remarkable sources is a 1993 volume of statistical data on Red Army losses, edited by G. F. Krivosheev. There are many reasons to doubt the precision of the figures, but they do give new insights into the scale and concentration of the civil war fighting. The overall figures for 1918–20 give 250,000 Red Army soldiers who were killed or who died in frontline dressing stations out of a total of 700,000 in the 'died and missing' (*bezvozvrat-nye poteri*) category. In this category 410,000 were listed as having died of wounds or sickness; the majority were in fact probably sick, based on the other category of loss, 'wounded and sick' (*sanitarnye poteri*), which comprised 540,000 wounded and no fewer than 3,790,000 sick. According to other figures Red Army losses were much higher in 1920 than in 1919. The 1919 figure may have been somewhat understated due to the incomplete record-keeping in that chaotic period. The greater strength of the Red Army in 1920 (a paper strength of 4,420,000 in July 1920 compared to 2,320,000 in July 1919) was undoubtedly also a factor; disease was the major cause of losses, and the higher the number of soldiers the higher the losses. The relative weight of the Polish campaign, however, is remarkable: this intense fighting accounted for about two-thirds of known *frontline* losses in 1920.

In contrast, in 1921 and 1922 only 10,000 soldiers were killed or died in frontline dressing stations (i.e. compared to 250,000 in 1918–20). In this period 'sick and wounded' comprised 2,460,000 sick and only 10,000 wounded (i.e. compared to 540,000 wounded in 1918–20). This suggests that of the 210,000 *deaths* from 'wounds and sickness' the latter was once again the largest cause. These statistics do not support the argument made by Vladimir Brovkin, Richard Pipes and others that there was a very high level of internal fighting in the post-1920 period. The losses for 1921–22 were not insignificant, and they do not take account of losses of Cheka and other non-army units. Nevertheless, if the figures are reasonably accurate, they indicate that the burden on the Red Army was greatly reduced after the liquidation of the formal fronts against the Whites in late 1920.

Pipes's new books on the revolution and its consequences have excited much controversy, but it is hard to disagree with his conclusion that 'the victory of the Red Army was a foregone conclusion'. A basic cause of the Red military victory was a *degree* of control – throughout the period 1917–20 – over the Great-Russian heartland. We now know more about the significant levels of anti-Communist unrest within this heartland, but it is going too far to argue, as Vladimir Brovkin does, that 'the magnitude of the Bolshevik war against peasants on the internal front eclipsed by far the frontline civil war against the Whites'. The heartland contained a mass of population and a physical expanse that the counterrevolutionaries could not overcome. This core also contained most of the surviving human and equipment resources of the Imperial Russian Army, and the Soviet side had a year's head-start over their opponents in the race to prepare for civil war. Fighting on interior lines they were able to deal with their ring of enemies one at a time.

The anti-Bolsheviks, for their part, were mostly perched on the periphery. The realities of geography meant that they could not give mutual support – indeed could hardly communicate with one another. For the 'White' (i.e. conservative military) element of the anti-Bolshevik movement there were political paradoxes. Great-Russian nationalists and advocates of a restored and unified Great-Russian state, they were based in regions dominated by non-Russians and autonomy-minded Cossacks. Their peripheral bases did, especially after November 1918, give the Whites access to the world oceans and Allied support. 'Intervention' was, however, on a tiny scale in European Russia, if this is measured by involvement of troops in fighting. Allied intervention was important for anti-Communist morale, at least in early 1919. British provision of *matériel* – especially to Denikin and Kolchak – was very substantial. But even the guns and greatcoats provided were only a fraction of what the Reds inherited from tsarist stocks.

Other political factors are harder to weigh up. The organized anti-Bolshevik forces changed over time, and until the end of 1918 were based partly on a continuation of the 1917 revolution and partly on popular regionalism (of the Cossack or Siberian variety). These forces could not sustain political stability; they also could not develop effective or even politically reliable armies. The Whites, dominant after November 1918, possessed military talent in abundance but very limited capacity for state-building or for the rallying of popular support.

Richard Pipes makes the interesting suggestion that the White defeat was partly due to a lack of popular patriotism, i.e. the Russian population's inability to put their material interests before true *national* interests. Pipes's perspective here is Great Russian, and another aspect that might have been developed – in the light of the events of 1991 – is the weakness of 'local' patriotism, the weakness of national identity among some of the larger ethnic minorities. Pipes's more general point may well have been true for the critical year 1919. By the end of that year, however, the Moscow government had become the only alternative for national rebirth; Russian patriotism was now one of Lenin's sources of strength.

Further reading

Azovtsev N. N., *et al.*, eds., *Grazhdanskaia voina v SSSR*, 2 vols. (Moscow, Voenizdat, 1980, 1986).

Brovkin V. N., *Behind the Front Lines of the Civil War: Political Parties and Social Movement in Russia, 1918–1922* (Princeton, Princeton University Press, 1994).

'The Civil War in Russia: A Roundtable Discussion', *Russian Studies in History* 32, 4 (Spring 1994).

Fiddick T. C., *Russia's Retreat from Poland, 1920: From Permanent Revolution to Peaceful Coexistence* (New York, St Martin's Press, 1990).

Figes O., 'The Red Army and Mass Mobilization during the Russian Civil War, 1918–1920', *Past and Present* 129 (1990).

Genis V. L., 'Raskazachivanie v Sovetskoi Rossii', *Voprosy istorii* 1 (1994).

Kakurin N. E., *Kak srazhalas' revoliutsiia*, 2nd edn (Moscow, Politizdat, 1990).

Kavtaradze A. G., *Voennye spetsialisty na sluzhbe Respubliki Sovetov 1917–1920 gg.* (Moscow, Nauka, 1988).

Khromov S. S., *et al.*, eds., *Grazhdanskaia voina i voennaia interventsiia v SSSR: Entsiklopediia*, 2nd edn (Moscow, Sovetskaia Entsiklopediia, 1987).

Krivosheev G. F., *et al.*, eds., *Grif sekretnosti sniat: Poteri vooruzhennykh sil SSSR v voinakh, boevykh deistviiakh i voennykh konfliktov: Statisticheskoe issledovanie* (Moscow, Voennoe izdatel'stvo, 1993).

Lincoln W. B., *Red Victory: A History of the Russian Civil War* (New York, Simon and Schuster, 1989).

Litvin A. L., Polikarpov V. D. and Spirin L. M., 'Grazhdanskaia voina. Lomka starykh dogm i stereotipov', in V. S. Lel'chuk, ed., *Istoriki sporiat. 13 besed* (Moscow, Politizdat, 1988), pp. 46–83.

Mawdsley E., *The Russian Civil War* (Boston, Allen and Unwin, 1987).

Nenarokov A. P., *et al.*, *Revvoensovet Respubliki (6 sent. 1918–28 avg. 1923 g.)* (Moscow, Politizdat, 1991).

Pipes R., *Russia under the Bolshevik Regime, 1919–1924* (New York, Knopf, 1994).

Poliakov I. A. 'Grazhdanskaia voina v Rossii (poiska novogo videniia)', *Istoriia SSSR* 2 (1990).

Poliakov I. A. and Igritskii, I. I., eds., *Grazhdanskaia voina v Rossii: Perekrestok mnenii* (Moscow, Nauka, 1994).

Swain G., *The Origins of the Russian Civil War* (London, Longman, 1995).

Ushakov A. I., *Istoriia grazhdanskoi voiny v literature russkogo zarubezh'ia* (Moscow, ITsRM, 1993).

Foreign Intervention

DAVID S. FOGLESONG

Western and Soviet historiography

No aspect of the history of revolutionary Russia has been the ground for more entrenched polemical warfare than foreign intervention in the civil war. During the long decades of antagonism between Soviet Russia and the West, historians of the interventions divided into two major camps. Most Western scholars viewed 'intervention' as consisting almost exclusively of the military expeditions that the Allied and Associated powers sent to northern Russia and Siberia in the summer of 1918, at the height of Germany's last offensive in France. From that relatively narrow vantage point, 'orthodox' or 'traditional' historians concluded that intervention was motivated primarily by the strategic concerns and coalition politics of the war against Germany. They frequently denied that ideological hostility to Bolshevism was a significant factor – at least until the Armistice of 11 November 1918. In the opposing camp, Soviet writers (joined in some respects by 'revisionist' or 'New Left' historians in the West) tended to view 'intervention' more broadly as a variety of efforts by the Western powers, ranging from clandestine plots to military campaigns, designed to overthrow the Bolshevik government. While Soviet authors' identification of the main organizer of intervention varied over time, they repeatedly charged that Allied imperialists had instigated the conspiracies and launched the invasions in order to smother the fires of socialist revolution.

In the post-Cold War era, historians in Russia and the West who seek to break out of the old interpretive trenches may find a sensible starting point in the recognition that foreign intervention involved much more than the expeditions to Arkhangel'sk and Vladivostok – even more multifarious activity than Bolshevik leaders suspected – but that the foreign actions were more hesitant and disjointed than the single-minded crusade depicted by many Soviet writers. While bridging the division over definitions of 'intervention', it is also possible to overcome the false dichotomy between strategic and ideological motives. British and French policy-makers' desperate effort to revive resistance to Germany on the eastern front in 1918 did not blind them to the rising danger of Bolshevik contagion, and waging the World War did not keep the Allies from pursuing long-term political and economic goals in Eurasia. Foreign intervention in Russia *was* in many respects an outgrowth of the Allies' war against the Central Powers, but in affirming that fact one must not forget how World War I originated in the global rivalry of European powers for territory, markets, natural resources and political dominance.

While works on the civil war have often separated military and diplomatic from social and political history, thereby largely divorcing developments inside Russia from the world outside, it is essential to recall that the civil war was an international struggle: a war in which not only Russians and Ukrainians but also Latvians, Estonians, Czechs, Germans, Americans and many other nationalities fought and died; a war waged not only behind the lines in Russia but also in the parliaments and streets of foreign countries; a struggle between Reds and Whites not only to mobilize the bodies and sympathies of Russian peasants but also to win the hearts and open the purses of foreign sympathizers. Approaching the civil war as a major event in international history is essential to understand the peculiar, unconventional nature of foreign intervention: widespread and diverse, since the vulnerabilities and disruptions of Russia were too tempting and too ominous to be ignored; yet hesitant and furtive, since foreign powers' interests diverged and their actions were constrained by popular sentiments in the era of the 'new diplomacy'.

Espionage, propaganda, financial aid, counter-propaganda and covert action, February 1917–July 1918

When the tsarist autocracy collapsed and the Russian empire began to disintegrate in 1917, competition intensified between foreign states vying for political influence, popular allegiance, strategic resources and future export markets from the Baltic to the Pacific and from the Arctic Circle to the Black Sea. With the World War entering its climactic stage, this escalating competition triggered the first phase of foreign intervention, which centred on espionage, propaganda and the encouragement of revolts or coups. As Russians gradually withdrew from World War I, Germany sought to accelerate and the Allies sought to halt or reverse that process, chiefly through propaganda campaigns and financial subsidies to Russian political groups. While the exact amounts and specific channels for much of the German aid to the Bolsheviks remain uncertain, George Katkov, Fritz Fischer, Winfried Baumgart, Z. A. B. Zeman, and other historians have established that by the end of 1917 Germany had spent roughly 30 million marks for propaganda in Russia, and German funds seem to have contributed to the expanding circulation of Bolshevik newspapers in 1917. To counteract 'German intrigue' and peace propaganda, the French, British and American governments dispatched several special missions charged with keeping Russia in the war and preventing anti-war socialists from taking power. While French representatives made pro-war speeches and alerted the Provisional Government to alleged German–Bolshevik connections, Allied officers encouraged General L. G. Kornilov to suppress 'disorder', Anglo-American agent Somerset Maugham subsidized pro-Ally propaganda, and American financier William Boyce Thompson contributed a million dollars to the moderate socialist Committee on Civic Education in Free Russia. Although Bolsheviks, their moderate socialist opponents and many historians portrayed such American, Allied and German actions as uniquely sinister cases of foreign meddling in Russian politics, they should instead be seen as part of the burgeoning multi-lateral competition in intelligence, counter-intelligence, and propaganda in revolutionary Russia.

From the Bolshevik seizure of power through the spring of 1918, foreign efforts to influence developments in Russia continued to rely heavily on propaganda and secret financial support for Russian groups. While Germany expended about three million marks per month for Russian propaganda in the first half of 1918, the American Committee on Public Information (CPI) blanketed Russian cities with hundreds of thousands of posters and pamphlets stressing Wilsonian idealism, and at the same time CPI representatives stealthily purchased supposed evidence that the Bolsheviks were German agents. As Germany continued for a time to give money to the Bolshevik Party, British, French and American representatives tried to deliver funds to anti-Bolshevik forces in southern Russia which they hoped would be able to block German access to Russian resources and form a 'nucleus' for the regeneration of a pro-Ally Russia. Pursuant to a December 1917 spheres-of-influence agreement, French attempts to support such anti-Bolshevik groups focused especially on the Ukraine, where French citizens had invested heavily in the chemical and metallurgical industries, while British efforts focused on the oil-rich Transcaucasian region. Although Allied and American representatives were able to transmit only a fraction of the hundreds of millions of roubles promised in the winter of 1917–18, anti-Bolshevik officers continued to regard foreign financial assistance as crucial to their success, and the arrival of larger sums in the spring and summer of 1918 contributed to the resurgence of the Volunteer Army.

After Red units drove the Volunteers into the Kuban in February 1918, American officials sought to encourage and support other forces who might oppose Bolshevik and German domination of Russia, including a Cossack band under G. M. Semenov in eastern Siberia and clandestine organizations in northern and central European Russia. The most important of the underground formations was Boris Savinkov's Union for Defence of Motherland

and Liberty, which launched a revolt at Iaroslavl and Rybinsk in early July, when it mistakenly expected imminent Entente reinforcement from the north. Anticipating clashes between Allied and Red forces, in July and August British, French and American diplomats, officers and intelligence agents participated in several other covert moves against the Soviet regime (which they regarded as a *de facto* ally of Germany), including a British attempt to suborn the Bolsheviks' Latvian guards and French and American military attachés' supervision of the sabotage of railroads, bridges and warehouses that the Red Army needed to use. (Although the broad outlines of these covert actions are well known, a full account of the struggle between the Cheka and foreign intelligence agencies will require new access to classified and restricted files in Russian and Western archives.)

Military intervention in North Russia, Siberia and South Russia, 1918–1919

Overlapping with the intensification of the 'secret war' was a third phase of relatively open military intervention that unfolded after the Soviet government signed and ratified the Treaty of Brest-Litovsk in March 1918. While the company of Royal Marines that went ashore at Murmansk in early March was welcomed by the local Soviet and condoned by Trotsky, the central Soviet government protested vigorously against the British and Japanese landing of small detachments at Vladivostok in April, and by May most Allied leaders had abandoned hopes for a Bolshevik invitation to intervene. Since the hard-pressed Allies did not have able-bodied troops to spare for campaigns in Russia, they lobbied relentlessly for American and Japanese expeditions. Rightly suspecting that Japanese military leaders had no intention of driving across Siberia to engage German armies but were determined to establish a sphere of influence in the Amur basin that would conflict with America's Open Door policy, President Woodrow Wilson and his advisors repeatedly resisted proposals for Japanese intervention. However, by late May, amid a flurry of allegations that the Bolsheviks were German agents, reports that the Soviet government was about to fall, and urgent appeals for action from anti-Bolshevik Russians, Wilson agreed to contribute American soldiers to an Allied expedition that would safeguard military stockpiles in northern Russia and secure a base area where patriotic Russians could outfit an army and organize a government.

After fighting erupted between Red forces and pro-Ally Czechoslovakian legionnaires along the Trans-Siberian Railway at the end of May 1918, Wilson and his advisors became more amenable to intervention in Siberia, since they believed that the Czech soldiers would not provoke a 'yellow peril' reaction among their Slavic brethren, while the alleged threats to the Czech Legion from Austro-Hungarian and German prisoners of war would help to justify military intervention to the American people. Although Wilson privately recognized that his course amounted to an undeclared war against Soviet Russia, neither he nor the Allied governments dared to make a candid public acknowledgement of the implicit anti-Bolshevik thrust of their policies, in part because they feared that would alienate liberals and socialists whose support they needed in the war against Germany. Thus, while the British, French and American people were denied full information, public opinion still acted as a negative check on the scale and development of intervention in the widening civil war.

On 17 July Wilson's final formal approval of military expeditions to Siberia and north Russia was conveyed to Allied and Japanese leaders, who quickly began trying to evade Wilson's stipulations that the expeditions should be small forces which would be limited to indirect roles in support of Czech and Russian armies. The commander of the 9,000-man American Expeditionary Force in Siberia, General William S. Graves, persistently tried to follow Wilson's guidelines by restricting American troops to guarding Vladivostok and patrolling the eastern end of the Trans-Siberian Railway – even in the face of later State Department pressure for more active coopera-tion with anti-Bolshevik forces. However, the scope of foreign action still greatly exceeded Wilson's injunctions. Although Washington tried to limit Japan to fewer than 12,000 men, by November 1918 Tokyo had dispatched more than 70,000 troops to eastern Siberia, where they remained until 1922. In northern Russia, US Ambassador David Francis authorized the British command to use the 4,500 American soldiers on the front lines against the Red Army, up to 200 miles inside Russia. Although Wilson tried to rein in the deployment of the US forces in the autumn of 1918, they suf-fered more than 500 total casualties before being finally withdrawn in June 1919. The British and French battalions in north Russia also had more men killed and wounded than the brigades sent to Siberia and southern Russia. With Russian war-weariness, apathy and social polarization aggravated by monarchist officers' plotting against socialist ministers and by the high-handedness of Allied commanders at Arkhangel'sk, the head of the 'Provisional Government of the Northern Region', N. V. Chaikovskii and his associates were unable to raise significant Russian forces. The Allied units consequently played more direct and central roles in the fighting in the north than on other fronts. (The effect of foreign intervention on the ability of anti-Bolsheviks, especially moderate socialists, to mobilize armies in the different regions is a subject that warrants further research.)

Although victory in the war against Germany was assured by October 1918, in that month French Premier Georges Clemenceau ordered military intervention in southern Russia to ensure the elimination of German hege-mony, the destruction of Bolshevism, and the protection of French eco-nomic interests. However, the French and Greek forces that reached Odessa in December showed even less enthusiasm for fighting than the Allied sol-diers in northern Russia and Siberia, who were uncertain of the purposes of the expeditions after the Armistice. Already at the end of 1918, facing sharp criticism from the left, Clemenceau and Foreign Minister Stéphane Pichon announced that French units would only form a defensive front and that active operations against the Bolsheviks would have to be conducted by Russian armies. In April 1919, following a Red Army offensive and a mutiny of the French Black Sea fleet, Allied forces were hastily evacuated from Odessa.

In late 1918 and early 1919 Britain and the United States also began moving towards withdrawal of their military forces from Russia. Although the British War Office dispatched two divisions to Transcaucasia in November 1918, at almost the same time the war cabinet decided against expanding military intervention elsewhere in Russia. In February 1919, after months of mounting criticism of intervention by soldiers' relatives, newspaper editors and members of Congress, President Wilson ordered the return of the north Russian expedition as soon as possible. Early in March the British cabinet followed suit, deciding to withdraw forces from north Russia and the Transcaucasus later that year.

Financial and military aid to anti-Bolshevik forces, 1919–1920: Russian propaganda and Western opinion

While retreating from direct military intervention in 1919, the Allies and the United States escalated their indirect intervention in the civil war by increasing shipments of supplies to White armies and to anti-Bolshevik nationalist forces in the borderlands of the former Russian empire. The British shipped massive amounts of war *matériel* (worth more than 100 million pounds) to the Whites, especially to the armies under General A. I. Denikin in the south and Admiral A. V. Kolchak in Siberia. With the approval of the US Treasury and State Department, the Russian embassy in Washington, headed by B. A. Bakhmeteff, utilized credits extended to the former Provisional Government to send more than $50 million worth of supplies to Siberia and south Russia. The United States also supported anti-Bolshevik campaigns with more than $5 million worth of 'humanitarian' aid that the American Relief Administration and American Red Cross distributed, particularly to the Russian North-western Army in the Baltic region, commanded by General N. N. Iudenich. Amid rising doubts about the capacity of White forces to resurrect a great Russian counterweight to Germany, in 1920 the French suspended aid to Denikin and expanded military assistance to Polish forces, who used the *matériel* to launch a war against Soviet Russia in April. After the Red Army counterattack imperiled Warsaw in the summer, France resumed aid to the Volunteer Army and granted *de facto* recognition to the government of Baron P. N. Wrangel, though the extension of credits to

Wrangel was inhibited by French leaders' anticipation of parliamentary opposition and public demonstrations.

Recognizing the important bearing of foreign support on the outcome of the civil war, different Russian political groups sought to increase, redirect or terminate such assistance. Liberal representatives of the former Provisional Government in France, Britain and the United States organized propaganda campaigns in which they argued that to repay Russians for their enormous sacrifices from 1914 to 1917 and to fulfil the objectives of the war against Germany the Western countries should help patriotic Russians defeat the Bolshevik menace, liberate Russia from German domination, and establish a strong Russian democracy. Such publicity was offset, however, by reports about monarchist coups, terror and pogroms in White territories that stoked Western peoples' fears of contributing to a restoration of tsarist oppression. The liberal anti-Bolshevik propaganda was also undercut by *émigré* leaders of the Socialist Revolutionary Party who, embittered by the lack of Allied support for moderate socialists in Siberia in 1918 and angered by the Kadet–Cossack coup at Omsk in November 1918, urged the Allies not to send aid to the reactionary dictatorships of Kolchak and Denikin. Finally, Bolshevik representatives who believed the fate of Soviet Russia hinged on breaking through the Allied economic blockade and cutting off aid to the Whites strained to mobilize Western working-class protests against intervention and to induce Western capitalists to pressure their governments for normalized economic and diplomatic relations with Soviet Russia. The struggle between conservative, liberal, moderate socialist and communist Russians to influence public opinion and government policy in the West is one dimension of the international history of the civil war that awaits further research. Analysis of *émigré* publications and the archival records of Russian embassies, military missions and information bureaux should clarify how Russians portrayed the struggle over the future of their country and how they understood the problems of rallying foreign support for Bolshevik and anti-Bolshevik movements.

Impact and legacy of intervention

The overall effect of foreign intervention in Russia remains uncertain. Although Entente and American money and *matériel* were clearly vital in supporting and equipping anti-Bolshevik forces, it is more difficult to gauge how much dependence on foreign aid sapped the morale of White officers, how important hopes for Allied recognition and supplies were in prompting premature military offensives and lack of interest in building local popular support, and how far foreign representatives' arrogance and disdain for White leaders undermined the Whites' popular prestige. It has often been suggested that foreign intervention assisted the Red victory by helping Bolsheviks to portray their opponents as tools of rapacious imperialists and

to blame economic problems in Soviet Russia on hostile capitalist encircle-
ment, yet there has been little systematic research on such Bolshevik propaganda or on the attitudes of Russian soldiers, workers and peasants towards
such issues.

During the Cold War, Western scholars often downplayed the impact of
Allied intervention on Soviet world views, arguing that it only confirmed
Bolshevik leaders' ideological expectations of capitalist hostility and claiming that later Soviet charges about widespread Western subversion were
merely propaganda. In this as in other areas, new scholarship may move
beyond false dichotomies and polarized positions towards more sophisticated and nuanced interpretations. It was one thing to *expect* imperialist
intervention on theoretical grounds; it was quite another thing to *experience*
Western antipathy towards Bolshevism during the protracted civil war – to
feel the anti-Soviet thrust of intervention on one's own skin, as Mikhail
Levidov put it in an early Soviet study. As scholars analyse the way 'intervention' figured in the war scare of 1927, the anti-American propaganda
campaign of 1948–53, and the Khrushchev-line historiography of 1958–63,
they may uncover a complicated interplay between the authentic memories
of people who lived through the years of intervention, on the one hand, and
cynical manipulation by Communist leaders and ideologists, on the other.
Similarly, as historians examine newly opened records concerning Soviet
foreign relations after the civil war, they may find a complex interaction
between fear of a new intervention, perception of cracks in Western opposition, and the drive to exploit divisions between the capitalist powers which
was also a long-term legacy of the 1917–21 period.

Further reading

Baumgart W., *Deutsche Ostpolitik 1918: Von Brest-Litowsk bis zum Ende
des ersten Weltkrieges* (Vienna, Oldenbourg, 1966).
Brinkley G. A., *The Volunteer Army and Allied Intervention in South
Russia. 1917-1921* (Notre Dame, IN, University of Notre Dame Press,
1966).
Carley M. J., *Revolution and Intervention: The French Government and the
Russian Civil War, 1917–1919* (Montreal, McGill-Queens University
Press, 1983).
Debo R. K., *Revolution and Survival: The Foreign Policy of Soviet Russia,
1917–1918* (Toronto, Toronto University Press, 1979).
Debo R. K., *Survival and Consolidation: The Foreign Policy of Soviet
Russia. 1918–1921* (Montreal, McGill-Queens University Press, 1992).
Foglesong D. S., *America's Secret War Against Bolshevism: US Intervention
in the Russian Civil War, 1917–1920* (Chapel Hill, University of North
Carolina Press, 1995).

Ganelin R. S., *Sovetsko-amerikanskie otnosheniia v kontse 1917–nachale 1918 g.* (Leningrad, Nauka, 1975).

Goldin V. I., *Interventsiia i antibol'shevistskoe dvizhenie na Russkom Severe. 1918–1920* (Moscow, Izdatel'stvo MGU, 1993).

Katkov G., *Russia 1917: The February Revolution* (London, Collins, 1969).

Kennan G. F., *Soviet-American Relations, 1917–1920*, 2 vols. (Princeton, Princeton University Press, 1956 and 1958).

Levidov M., *K istorii soiuznoi interventsii v Rossii* (Leningrad, Priboi, 1925).

Morley J. W., *The Japanese Thrust into Siberia, 1918* (New York, Columbia University Press, 1957).

Petracchi G., 'Ideology and Realpolitik: Italo-Soviet Relations, 1917–1933', *Journal of Italian History* 2, 3 (Winter 1979), pp. 473–519.

Thompson J. M., *Russia, Bolshevism, and the Versailles Peace* (Princeton, Princeton University Press, 1967).

Ullman R. H., *Anglo-Soviet Relations, 1917–1921*, 3 vols. (Princeton, Princeton University Press, 1961, 1968, 1972).

Unterberger B. M., *The United States, Revolutionary Russia, and the Rise of Czechoslovakia* (Chapel Hill, University of North Carolina Press, 1989).

Zeman Z. A. B., ed., *Germany and Revolution in Russia. 1915–1918* (Oxford, Oxford University Press, 1958).

The Tenth Congress of the Communist Party and the Transition to NEP

SERGEI V. IAROV

Although the Tenth Congress of the Russian Communist Party (RKP(b)) is widely regarded as one of the most important events in Soviet history, disagreements remain about its real significance. In part, this stems from the political ambiguity of its decisions. The congress is usually associated with Russia's transition to the New Economic Policy (NEP). However, it was not until some time later that the necessity of a complete break with the war-communist system was appreciated, and the term 'NEP' was invented. The congress resolution 'On Party Unity' led to divisions within the party, as it was primarily an instrument of repression which set firm limits on political compromises inside the party. The decisions on the trade unions, which were debated hotly and at great length, proved to be of little real value. The change in economic policy made it necessary to make substantial corrections to them. The particular significance of the congress lay elsewhere – it posed and tried to solve an unprecedentedly wide range of the most urgent social and political problems, which continued to concern Russian society for decades thereafter.

The basic historical source for studying the Tenth Congress is the stenographic report, which was first published in 1921 and republished in 1933 and 1963 with ever increasing numbers of appendices and footnotes. All these editions lack accounts of the eighth, ninth and tenth sessions of the congress which took place on 12 and 13 March 1921. These were closed sessions and, the published versions claimed, 'minutes were not taken'.

The party discussion on the trade unions around the end of 1920 and the beginning of 1921 is widely perceived as the background to the Tenth Congress. There are good reasons for this: the sharp polemics around the trade-union question continued at the congress. The January 1921 plenum of the RKP(b) Central Committee (CC) permitted delegates to be elected on the basis of 'platforms', that is, according to their attitude to one or another trade-union programme. The importance of this has sometimes been overstated, particularly if one compares it to the situation at the Eighth Congress of the RKP(b) in 1919, at which the 'Left Communists' held factional sessions in spite of an official prohibition.

The Tenth Congress was originally scheduled to begin on 6 February 1921, but was postponed for one month without explanation, finally opening in Moscow on 8 March. It had a wide-ranging agenda, including reports on the political and organizational work of the CC, the Control Commission, the RKP(b) delegation to the Communist International (Comintern), the Main Political Education Committee (*Glavpolitprosvet*) and the Party History Commission (*Istpart*). Among the other major questions considered by the 990 delegates were the party's national and trade-union policies, party unity and party construction, the USSR's foreign policy, replacement of food requisitioning with a tax in kind, and the fuel crisis.

The congress discussions opened after three reports which took up the whole of the second session: the CC's political report introduced by Lenin, its organizational report given by N. N. Krestinskii, and A. A. Sol'ts's Control Commission report. Arguments centred around the pre-congress polemics and particularly the party crisis. Neither Lenin's supporters nor their opponents disputed the existence of this crisis; the basic disagreements concerned its analysis and how to end it.

The party crisis: bureaucratization and disunity

In the motion proposed by the 'Workers' Opposition' on the CC political report, it was claimed that 'in the most important areas and on the most important questions of Communist construction there have been a series of deviations showing a lack of trust in the creative powers of the working class and concessions to the petty bourgeoisie and the bourgeois-*chinovnik* castes'. This accusation was developed in the speech of Aleksandra Kollontai, one of the leaders of the Workers' Opposition. Having stressed that there were many alien elements in the party, she concluded that 'the Central Committee has had to adapt to them, to manoeuvre instead of following its line clearly and distinctly. We can see how this deviation and adaptation affects both the question of our relations with the trade unions and the international question.' It is not difficult to decipher Kollontai's remarks. She noted, first, the RKP(b)'s moderation in its criticism of the bureaucratic trade-union apparatus and its refusal to reorganize it completely. Second, she clearly had in mind the call for different political systems to coexist – which was shortly thereafter advanced, albeit with many qualifications, in the report of L. B. Kamenev.

One cannot agree with Lenin's dismissal of these criticisms as mere demagogy, since they were not unfounded. However, many of the opposition's assessments of the general situation within the party were certainly scholastic. It is clear that they had been formulated with the aid of standard ideological clichés, and they made debatable claims concerning the supposed causes of real phenomena. The idea that there is a direct connection between the social origins of the people making up a state institution and the policies of that institution was commonplace for orthodox Communist propagandists, and is, indeed, not unique to them. However, in this case it did not take account of the specific political structures of Soviet Russia, their hierarchical nature and the quasi-collective method of decision-taking.

The features of the crisis itself were presented in far more concrete terms by representatives of various party blocs. The most important of these features were that the party was becoming 'clogged' with people of non-proletarian origin while workers were leaving it, that there was a gulf between the party leadership and the ordinary membership and an unwillingness to recruit rank-and-file Communists to responsible positions. There was a struggle against dissent in Bolshevik ranks, a lack of democracy, the formation of special castes of 'leaders' and a caste mentality. Nobody actually denied that these were real tendencies, although the opposition presented them apocalyptically while the RKP(b) CC majority saw them merely as natural problems of party growth. In all the speeches by opposition representatives one can clearly see their concern to lay the main emphasis on the subjective rather than the objective causes of the crisis. They regarded it as being the fault of individuals and groups, rather than a result of social changes in Russia. Their accusations were both an instrument of political struggle and an attempt at a political analysis which suggested a cure. However, it is obvious that this sort of diagnosis cannot be accurate or unbiased. The resolution moved by Lenin's supporters and passed by the congress, 'On Questions of Party Construction', gave the appearance of a deeper understanding of the reasons for the party crisis, although its assessments were evidently an exercise in apologetics. The resolution explained inequalities among Communists in terms of economic priorities in wartime – in order to obtain particularly essential items, it was necessary to pay more for them. The war was also used to justify the militarization and centralization of party organizations. The words 'necessity' and 'inevitability' occurred frequently, and were the universal riposte to Lenin's opponents. 'Inevitable' causes give rise to 'inevitable' consequences: 'centralization has developed a tendency to turn into bureaucratization and alienation from the masses, battle-orders often became distorted into unnecessary coercion, essential privileges became the basis for all kinds of abuses, the necessary curtailment of party organs weakened the spirit of party life'. These conclusions did not, however, shed any light on how these 'excesses' came about, why measures which were in theory benign, in practice took on 'distorted forms' and, finally, whether the military factor alone could account for these striking changes.

The subsequent development of Soviet society showed clearly that the bureaucratization of all its administrative organs, in particular the most basic one, the Communist Party, was pre-programmed, inherent in the logic of their development. The war was able to intensify and even caricature this process, but it was not the sole cause. The multiplication and reproduction of bureaucratic structures were inevitable both because of their internal laws of development and because the new political order created a most favourable environment for them. However, nobody criticized that political order at the congress, and it would seem that nobody realized its intimate connection with the widening gulf between top and bottom.

The opposition proposed a range of measures to overcome the party crisis, and to restore its democratic appearance and its lost 'revolutionariness'. These were a 'purge' and the establishment of strict conditions for admission to the RKP(b); its democratization; and the 'normalization' of the leadership. A purge was made necessary by what the opposition saw as a process of - 'erosion' of the party by people from non-proletarian backgrounds. The alternative report on party construction presented to the congress by S. P. Medvedev for the Workers' Opposition openly proposed that 'only those elements who are fully committed to the standpoint of the working class and the Communist revolution should remain in the party', a criterion that was hazy, ill-defined and arbitrarily formulated. This sort of rhetoric was characteristic of other reports, speeches, contributions and proposed theoretical platforms at the congress, which shows the ideological dominance of a type of discourse in which practical considerations were certainly not at the forefront.

Moreover, Medvedev showed himself to be meticulous in his proposals for ensuring that 'the non-working class elements who join the ranks of the party understand workers' psychology': 'anybody who joins our party from outside the working class or peasantry should be required to work for a given period ... in a factory and to learn the basic processes of physical labour'. He was inclined not to limit this measure to 'dubious' party members alone: 'it is necessary that all party members serve a certain time in the factories'. When one reads these words it is difficult to get away from the idea that Medvedev wanted to solve a political problem by – literally – 'physical' means, compelling RKP(b) members to work shoulder to shoulder in the hope that this production 'friction' would kindle the flame of party comradeship.

A layer of utopianism, albeit less obvious, was also to be found in other prescriptions for curing the party's ailments, especially measures considered for 'normalizing' the upper ranks of the party. In particular it was said that the majority in the leading organs of the party should consist of workers who remained at the bench, and that it was essential to free Communist functionaries from many of their additional responsibilities, which would permit them to live in the midst of the masses instead of squandering their time on trivial matters.

The views of Lenin and his supporters, expressed in the congress resolution 'On Questions of Party Construction', were more moderate, although there was essentially nothing new in their list of anti-bureaucratic measures. It also proposed purging the party of non-Communist elements, only not on the basis of their social origin, but 'by an accurate assessment of the work of all individual RKP(b) members, both in their employment and as party members'. It recommended that the names of all new recruits to the party be publicized, that the preparatory 'candidate' stage of membership for people not of working-class or peasant origin be lengthened, and that Communists be brought into 'responsible work'. These were clearly palliative measures, as, in effect, was the entire resolution. Overall, it was more pragmatic than the opposition documents. However, some of the 'general measures to normalize the party' which it proposed were extremely abstract and intentionally indistinct. For example, the opposition's categorical demand that Communists be required to work at the bench was reflected here as follows: 'it is essential that all party members in responsible positions are periodically released from these positions so that at all times a section of even the busiest party workers is working in the thick of proletarian life in agitational and propaganda work'.

It is important to note that almost everybody at this congress habitually confused the concepts 'party' and 'society', and in their remarks it is difficult to distinguish between specifically party as opposed to state or 'Soviet' bureaucratism. This was not accidental. As V. N. Maksimovskii, a representative of the 'Group of Democratic Centralists' correctly observed: 'a whole range of failings in our party apparatus stem from the fact that our party is the ruling party, that it is linked to state power, and that we cannot separate the crisis of the party centre from the crisis of the Soviet centres'. The delegates realized that party and social maladies were interdependent, but they proposed a variety of different cures. This was shown particularly clearly in the discussion about permissible and impermissible forms of democracy, which was recognized, not only by the opposition, to be one of the main ways to cure the Soviet regime. In the report on party construction N. I. Bukharin openly declared that since the RKP(b) is the organization of the most advanced workers, the greatest degree of democratism is possible only within its ranks. Outside the party, as he put it, 'there is a descending curve of democratism'.

Not even his opponents challenged him on this. Although one of them did favour the application of a number of norms of party democracy in state administration, he found it necessary to stress that this was permissible only 'within the bounds of the general class relationship'. This hazy formulation reaffirmed the principle of political inequality between different social groups, which was fixed in the Soviet constitution and itself set limits on the application of democracy. In effect, representatives of the most diverse platforms were in agreement with Bukharin. For example, N. Osinskii (V. V. Obolenskii) admitted that one could not advance the slogan of independent workers' action, in case it was used against the ruling party. Trotsky expressed similar ideas: 'Of course, workers' democracy is the only method by which the masses can be increasingly involved in political life ... But all this is on condition ... that this formal aspect is subject to the dictatorship of the party, which stands for the basic interests of the working class even during temporary fluctuations in the mood of the class itself.'

Thus recognition was given to an extremely complex and indirect mechanism for applying the democratic 'cudgel' against bureaucrats. First of all democracy should be established within the party and then partially applied, in measured doses, in other spheres. The limits within which it was to be applied were to be set not 'from below' but 'from above', that is, by the very structures which were the main objects of anti-bureaucratic criticism. It is not difficult to appreciate that the democracy these measures bestowed was negligible, and that this approach to combating bureaucracy was utopian.

Of course, it was not this alone which gave the green light to bureaucratism. One thing, however, is beyond doubt: if it was possible to decide which classes could enjoy the benefits of democracy and to what extent, it was not too difficult to consider another problem – how much democracy should be distributed among the Communists themselves.

The discussion on party unity, which concluded with the adoption of an eponymous resolution, was not on the congress's original agenda. It evidently arose as a reaction to the trade-union discussion. However, as Leonard Schapiro, Robert Daniels and Adam Ulam have shown, that is not the full story. It was based on an exaggerated view of the scale of the split in the party and of the dangers of different platforms. All the documents and accounts that have been preserved show that Lenin was undoubtedly the key figure in the argument about party unity which erupted at the congress. He did not take part in the discussions about Communist agitation or about the national question, and ignored a whole range of other important questions the delegates discussed. But there was one question on which he touched time and again, even when it was not related to the subject on which he was speaking – the struggle against deviations. On this matter his speech was remarkably emotional, categorical and scathing, and contrasted even with the interventions of other speakers who were not always restrained in their choice of words. Lenin's philippics against the opposition are an eloquent testimony not only to his political temperament, but also to the frame of mind in which he composed the resolution 'On Party Unity'. One of the major features of his political thinking was an aversion to any kind of dissenting ideas which went beyond the boundaries of orthodoxy, and to factionalism which destroyed the monolithic nature of the party. This feeling derived from the experience of his struggle for dominance within the party, which had been accompanied by internal Bolshevik squabbles and other unpleasantnesses, in which it was difficult to distinguish personal from political factors. It is important to bear this in mind when considering the ferocity of Lenin's reaction to the emergence of opposition platforms, which, after all, could only muster a few dozen votes from the hundreds of delegates present.

Two factors convinced Lenin of the correctness of his fundamentalist views. First, there was the political disorder within Russia – to Lenin, the roar of the Kronstadt cannons was an unanswerable argument against turning the party into a debating society. Second, there was the sheer number of different platforms – an unprecedented phenomenon within the Communist Party. During the civil war, apart from the Left Communists and the 'Military Opposition', there had not been any influential opposition currents.

Lenin did not propose to dispense with all the established party rituals and, in general, recognized the possibility of sharp arguments within the RKP(b). But he insisted on a sharp delineation between discussion as such and the formation of separate factions, in dispute with one another and capable of splitting the party. For all its apparent logic, this presentation of the problem was profoundly contradictory. Freedom of discussion must inevitably reveal differences of opinion and thereby distinguish groups supporting one or another point of view. They might not necessarily form into factions, but it would not be possible to prevent the establishment of links, even only unofficial ones, between people with similar views. For this reason party polemics would hardly have remained confined to special publications and journals as Lenin suggested, but would inevitably have spread to the lower party organizations. In arguing the need to adopt this resolution, Lenin frequently referred to the dangerous political situation in the country, which required total and unconditional party unity. Nonetheless, his speeches, and the congress documents which reflected them, did not give any clear indication of the political circumstances in which the resolution would retain its relevance. This allowed its arbitrary criteria to become established and thereby conferred permanent status on an extraordinary, temporary act.

A key point in the discussion on party unity was the debate on point four of the motion which stated, in particular, that 'anybody expressing criticisms should take into account the position of the party among the enemies which surround it'. A. Z. Kamenskii, a representative of the Democratic Centralists, pointed to the contradictory character of that position: 'Where, we may ask, are these criticisms being expressed? ... In front of party members? Then it is ridiculous to make such a suggestion! ... What criteria could anyone use to decide what is and is not dangerous? Would comrades be punished for not knowing that something or other is dangerous to the party? ... All this raises an endless number of questions. And how could we have discussions like this if we cannot tell which ideas will be deemed to be absolutely dangerous for the party's internal cohesion and which ones will be approved?' This was said in the discussion of the draft motion, but, despite the convincing arguments against it, the point was retained in the version which was passed. The resolution itself could have been regarded as nothing more than a rhetorical declaration, had it not been for point seven, which detailed the procedure for exclusion from the party and from its leading organs. The congress decided against publishing the resolution, and it became widely known only three years later.

The political significance of the resolution 'On Party Unity' only became apparent later, in the course of the power struggle which erupted among

Lenin's heirs after his death. In essence, there had always been methods for purging the leadership of the party, and there was hardly any need for a special law to lay down procedures. While Lenin remained alive, it had been more of a preventative measure. Oppositionists were removed from the Central Committee by manoeuvring behind the scenes in the election of CC members at congresses. This had been done successfully at the Tenth Congress. The overwhelming majority of the delegates, who supported Lenin, had decided in advance in the closed session which oppositionists would be elected onto the CC and which would not. There was no reason why these methods could not have been used at other party congresses in the course of the debates between 1923 and 1929.

The resolution 'On Party Unity' had an ideological, rather than a practical significance. Its value was determined by two circumstances which were not without importance for party ethics. First, it made it possible to show that somebody had been removed from the upper echelons of the party for factional activities, rather than for any other reason. This made it far more difficult for the excluded party leaders to regain their former political influence than would have been the case if their fall had been a result of secret intrigues, little understood by the party rank-and-file. Second, the resolution itself was made public in the name of Lenin, and its use clearly demonstrated that it was an anti-Leninist deviation which was being denounced. In circumstances in which Lenin's authority was virtually sacred, reference to this resolution as the reason for party ostracism without fail heralded a downturn in one's political career.

Western historians have drawn attention to the contradiction between the congress resolutions 'On the Question of Party Construction' and 'On the Role and Tasks of the Trade Unions', on the one hand, and 'On Party Unity' and 'On the Syndicalist and Anarchist Deviation in Our Party', on the other. However, these documents have far more in common than is often considered to be the case. The first two documents permitted moderate criticism of the party and trade-union leaderships and a similarly limited democratization of the RKP(b) and the All-Russian Central Council of Trade Unions (VTsSPS), while the second two supplemented the code of party and trade-union democratic norms with an article setting out the punishments to be applied to those who went beyond the bounds of moderation. The difference between the two sets of documents was that the first of them was extremely vague about the penalties for disobedience, while the second set spelled them out in excessive detail, even citing the particular example of the Workers' Opposition.

NEP

Turning now to NEP, the role played by the congress in its origins was more modest than that traditionally ascribed to it. The question of who was the originator of NEP is a complex one. As the dust settled after the arguments of the Tenth Congress, Trotsky was the first to declare publicly that he had proposed it before anyone else, referring to his note 'Basic Questions of our Food and Agrarian Policy', presented to the CC on 20 March 1920. Sharp objections to this claim became commonplace in Soviet historiography, and a simple list of the works which disputed Trotsky's claim would take up several pages. However, the criticism of his theses has usually been based on a one-sided interpretation of point three, which proposed 'supplementing compulsory requisitioning with compulsory tilling and cultivation'. It is not difficult to show that this proposal is in keeping with the politics of war communism. However, Trotsky's critics generally ignore the first point in his project, which was that it was possible to replace 'confiscation of surpluses with a certain percentage deduction (a kind of progressive income tax), calculated so that it would still be advantageous to increase cultivation'. This was precisely the measure from which NEP subsequently developed. It is remarkable that the second point in Trotsky's project almost exactly anticipated the vacillations of NEP in its initial stages. The semi-illicit word 'trade' was replaced by the indistinct formula 'distribution to the peasants of industrial products'.

Trotsky's project was cautious, and it is possible that this was one of the reasons it was so indistinct. The reference to compulsory cultivation was not accidental – it was a safety precaution in case this economic innovation were to misfire. In any case, Trotsky's theses were far from original. The measures he proposed were obvious to many economists at the time. They could see no other way of overcoming Russia's economic collapse. Trotsky's service was in defining the circle beyond which the Bolsheviks would not risk stepping in the first stages of the NEP experiment. He formulated its first step, and, like those who followed him in 1921, he did not imagine that it would be necessary to take a second and a third step before the economic structure would acquire the necessary stability. If we want to find a system of measures which anticipated NEP, we should not look to Trotsky, but to the Menshevik programme *What Is To Be Done?* published in 1919. Schapiro has noted the almost complete correlation between the Menshevik document and NEP, although the question of 'who was first' means little here. This closeness was not so much the result of ideological interplay as of an appreciation of obvious economic facts, the only difference being that it took some people longer to appreciate them than others.

The CC rejected Trotsky's draft at the end of March 1920 by eleven votes to four. The minutes of this meeting are not extant, but, judging from Trotsky's subsequent memoirs, it was the spectre of free trade which caused the greatest alarm in the party's inner sanctum. The author of the project was 'accused of being a free-trader'. It is characteristic that Lenin was named as one of the sharpest critics of Trotsky's theses.

However, within a few months Lenin was one of those who, cautiously at first, then more insistently, began to look for a way out of the economic crisis in methods quite alien to those of war communism. The immediate impetus for Lenin's reassessment of his views was provided by the discussion on the peasant question at the Eighth Congress of Soviets in December 1920. In the course of this discussion Lenin made a number of noteworthy practical suggestions, showing a readiness to take a realistic approach to the needs of the countryside. He was lukewarm in his assessment of the future of collective farming and frequently referred to the desirability of 'relying on the hard-working farmer' and of rewarding them – individually, not collectively. It is true that the congress decision 'On Measures to Strengthen and Develop Peasant Agriculture' rested overall on the principles of war communism, and even extended them. It was proposed, for example, to combat reductions in sowing and inadequate seed supply by forming special sowing commissions. Moreover, they clearly took no account of the peasants' lack of interest in expanding the area under cultivation. The question of whether the decisions of the congress should be considered to be forerunners of NEP or whether they should be regarded as war-communist measures was long debated by Soviet historians from the mid-1960s. The most categorical proponents of the two viewpoints were E. B. Genkina and Iu. A. Poliakov.

The documents of the Eighth Congress of Soviets are certainly not imbued with the spirit of NEP. However, the discussion of the peasant question at the congress clearly showed the same pragmatic mood which was to become decisive in the formation of NEP. Following these congress debates, a commission was established to consider and, as far as possible, alleviate the position of the countryside. Its proposals, which were submitted to the CC at the beginning of 1921, did not envisage radical changes in the policy towards the peasantry. On 4 February 1921 Lenin spoke at the Moscow Metalworkers' Conference – a conference which openly demanded the abolition of requisitioning and its replacement by a tax in kind. In his speech Lenin refrained from mentioning the tax and merely made a casual reference to a possible re-examination of 'the relationship between workers and peasants'. Nonetheless, he soon ceased vacillating. On 8 February 1921 the Politburo appointed a commission to devise a solution to the peasant question, and Lenin gave it his 'Preparatory Rough Draft of Theses on the Peasants'. Its first point was 'to grant the wish of the non-party peasants for the replacement of requisitioning [the confiscation of surpluses] by a grain tax'. Its second point proposed a reduction in the volume of this new tax compared to the previous requisitions. This second measure may not have been directly connected to a radical change in agrarian policy. It was rather a reformulation of previously proposed palliative measures to alleviate the situation of the peasantry. At any rate there were no suggestions at that stage that a large number of people should be taken off state rations, which some historians have claimed would explain the reduction in the overall volume of food deliveries envisaged by the tax. Both of Lenin's points are entirely in accord with the metalworkers' resolution mentioned above. In the same 'rough draft' he proposed reducing the percentage of tax deductions in accordance with the 'diligence of the cultivator', and, finally, 'extending the freedom for the cultivator to use his surplus after tax in local economic circulation on condition that the tax is paid quickly and in full'. This last point is particularly important. It represents the quintessence of Lenin's ideas on trade as they stood in February 1921. The taboo on the word 'trade' itself remained, replaced instead by the indistinct formulation 'freedom to use surpluses', and this 'freedom' was to be confined to the local level and subject to various other conditions to limit the extent of these concessions.

Lenin's 'rough draft' became the basis for the broader and more concrete motion 'On the Replacement of Requisitioning by a Tax in Kind', prepared for the Tenth Congress. Two new commissions set up in February 1921 by the CC refined and polished it in turn. The members of these commissions were L. B. Kamenev, Osinskii, N. I. Muralov, P. Popov and A. D. Tsiurupa. Essentially, the motion was prepared in private and was not the subject of any kind of broad preparatory discussion. At the end of February *Pravda* carried a few articles on the question, but, as Lenin later remarked, 'nobody responded to them'. Clearly even the proponents of requisitioning realized the necessity and inevitability of its abolition. This atmosphere of apathy extended to the auditorium at the Tenth Congress. Lenin presented the main report on the replacement of requisitioning by a tax in kind. The most interesting feature of his speech is that it provided the first theoretical foundation for this economic revolution in terms of Bolshevik ideological canons. It was here, in a concentrated form, that Lenin presented the ideas which were later to become a pivot of the official ideological structure. He attempted to show the compatibility of this economic innovation with traditional conceptions of socialism. He did not deny the possibility of 'capitalist restoration', but his assessments were, overall, as optimistic as they were pragmatic: 'Is it possible to a certain extent to restore freedom of trade, freedom of capitalism for small farmers, without thereby destroying the roots of the political power of the proletariat? It is possible, because it is a question of the extent. If we were able to acquire even a small quantity of goods and retain them in the hands of the state ... and were able to put these goods into circulation, we would be able, as a state, to add economic power to our political power.'

There is no agreement among historians about what were the main factors which facilitated the transition to NEP. In Soviet literature the majority opinion is that the introduction of NEP was predetermined above all by the need to rethink the relationship between the authorities and the peasantry after the end of the civil war. This process was presented as inevitable, and the economic and political crisis of 1921 was just an event which accelerated it. On the other hand, many Western authors regard the crisis of 1921 as the basic reason for the renunciation of war communism. Some have even linked it to the Kronstadt uprising, although it merely provided additional arguments in favour of a decision which had in principle been taken several weeks earlier.

There was not much response among the congress delegates to the question of replacing requisitioning by taxation. Tsiurupa and E. A. Preobrazhenskii, who spoke after Lenin, had virtually no quarrel with Lenin's proposal and only dealt with particular aspects of it. Even M. I. Frumkin, who worked in the food apparatus and who proposed an alternative motion on the abolition of requisitioning, did not dispute the necessity of introducing the tax, and requested only that it be postponed. The stenographic report of the congress omits detailed data about voting on congress resolutions. However, the latest evidence suggests the vote was almost unanimous. The document itself consisted of nine points, which enumerated in detail the general principles for assessing and collecting the tax, and particularly stressed its progressive character. The farmers were to receive details of the size of the tax before work began on the spring sowing. It is noteworthy that all members of the village communities, regardless of their property status, were to be involved in setting the individual apportionment of this tax. Attempts to grant this right to the rural poor alone were quashed by Lenin himself in the final editing of the resolution in March 1921. However, the authorities' sympathies with the rural poor did manifest themselves, for example, in point four of the resolution, which stated that 'the poorest peasant households may be exempted from some, and in exceptional cases, from all forms of the tax in kind'. In addition, tax reductions were proposed for 'diligent peasant farmers' who increased their sown areas.

The most difficult task was to define the limits and forms in which the peasants could sell their surpluses after tax. This exchange, which was partially to replace the principle of total state distribution, was intended to be organized in the following way – farmers were to be allowed to exchange their products for any others, but only within the confines of 'local economic circulation'. Those who voluntarily sold their produce to the state over and above the tax level, were allowed to take advantage of the state 'fund of agricultural equipment and consumer goods'. It was this part of the document which remained most abstract and indistinct. It did not provide answers to the most basic questions: what is understood by exchange, does it mean sale or something else, and what forms should it take? It did not take account of the fact that an inadequately formulated law is most likely to be broken. To a certain extent these inadequacies were rectified at the March 1921 session of the Soviet Central Executive Committee (VTsIK), which decreed that exchange was to take place through cooperatives, bazaars and markets. Here too, the word 'trade' was not used.

The Tenth Congress was undoubtedly of crucial importance in the stabilization of the Soviet political regime at the start of the 1920s. It did not propose a fully functional model of the relationship between rulers and ruled, but it was able to soften the sharp contradictions between them by codifying ethical norms. The extent to which it moved towards NEP was very modest, but it opened the way to radical economic innovation. The congress brought together the ingredients for the subsequent ideological unification of the country. There were objective reasons for the mixed nature of the congress's political outcome. It was the embodiment of a 'transitional' state order, which did away with the remnants of post-revolutionary anarchy, but was still a long way from being a classical authoritarian dictatorship.

Further reading

Daniels R. V., *The Conscience of the Revolution: Communist Opposition in Soviet Russia* (Oxford, Oxford University Press, 1960).

Desiatyi s"ezd RKP(b), stenograficheskii otchet (Moscow, Politizdat, 1963).

Fitzpatrick S., Rabinowitch A. and Stites R., eds., *Russia in the Era of NEP: Explorations in Soviet Society and Culture* (Bloomington, Indiana University Press, 1991).

Genkina E. B., *Gosudarstvennaia deiatel'nost' V. I. Lenina 1921–1923 gg.* (Moscow, Nauka, 1964).

Kim M. I., ed., *Novaia ekonomicheskaia politika. Voprosy teorii i istorii, sbornik statei* (Moscow, Nauka, 1974).

Poliakov Iu. A., *Perekhod k NEPu i sovetskoe krest'ianstvo* (Moscow, AN SSSR, 1967).

Schapiro L., *The Origin of the Communist Autocracy* (London, Macmillan, 1977).

Ulam A. B., *Lenin and the Bolsheviks: The Intellectual and Political History of the Triumph of Communism in Russia* (London, Secker and Warburg, 1966).

ACTORS AND THE
QUESTION OF AGENCY

Chernov

MICHAEL MELANCON

Born the son of a local treasury official of peasant origin, Viktor Mikhailovich Chernov (1873–1952) grew up in Saratov province in comfortable circumstances. During 1892 he entered the Moscow University law school, where he quickly joined student revolutionary circles. After his 1894 arrest, he spent the years 1895–99 in exile in Tambov province, where his successful organizing activities among the peasantry marked an important stage in his life and that of Russia. Upon his return from exile, he emigrated to Western Europe, where he began the task of converting reluctant proto-Socialist-Revolutionary groups to the peasant cause. The 1902 peasant uprisings across the south of Russia justified Chernov's urgings and gave rise to the Socialist-Revolutionary Party (PSR) in its historically familiar form.

Chernov quickly established his reputation as the chief theorist and formulator of programmes for the new party. His neo-populist theory described a triad of revolutionary classes as the basis for Russia's impending revolution: the radicalized intelligentsia, the proletariat and the peasantry as the main army (whose participation he described as the *sine qua non* of a Russian revolution). Russia's weak, unassertive bourgeoisie, Chernov maintained, would be unable to overthrow the autocracy, the task falling instead to the intelligentsia–workers–peasantry, who would provide the impetus toward socialism. Chernov's writings thus contained proletarian- and peasant-oriented programmes: for workers, an eight-hour day, minimum wage, unionization and workers' control; and for peasants, land socialization that entailed the transfer of all land to the peasantry and its cultivation according to communal and peasant labour norms until the (voluntary) introduction of advanced agricultural usages. Although influenced by Marxist writings, Chernov followed N. K. Mikhailovskii in introducing subjective, individualist and ethical elements into his theories, demarcating them from orthodox Marxism's objective historical laws. His lifelong interest in ethical problems notwithstanding, Chernov continued the tradition of the

Narodnaia Volia in espousing terrorism against the autocracy (an example of his thinking about subjective factors).

At the end of the 1905–07 revolution, which he witnessed at first hand upon his return to St Petersburg, Chernov offered a critique of his party and of the entire socialist movement in failing to overthrow tsarism: because of their enforced underground existence, the parties had not mastered the techniques of coordinating society's multifarious revolutionary impulses. Chernov then firmly guided the PSR onto a continued radical path that rejected both the reformism of the Popular Socialists, who split off from the right wing, and the extremism of the Maximalists (adherents of factory and peasant terrorism) on the left. The PSR devoted itself to mass propaganda and organizing in pursuit of the elusive socialist revolution.

With the 1908 revelation of E. F. Azef as a police spy, massive debates broke out within the party about the appropriateness of continued terrorism. Because of ethical misgivings and the enormous costs to the party, Chernov allied with M. A. Natanson and N. I. Rakitnikov to argue successfully for an end to SR terrorism. During 1910, Chernov opposed a new reformist heresy within the party, this time led by the estimable A. R. Gots, N. D. Avksentiev, M. V. Vishniak and E. K. Breshko-Breshkovskaia; once again, his staunchness won the day, as the party firmly rejected the idea of abandoning the revolutionary path.

Immediately after the outbreak of the war, Chernov participated in a conference in Switzerland of SR *émigré* leaders to determine the party's wartime policies. Pre-war attitudes towards the necessity for or lack of continued revolutionary activities against tsarism largely determined approaches to the war issue; thus Avksentiev led a group who wished to postpone socialist goals for the war's duration, whereas Chernov and Natanson argued strongly in favour of utilizing the war to further the revolutionary cause. No agreement being feasible between two such divergent views, the internationalist and defencist SRs, both in the migration (as it was called) and inside Russia, soon went separate ways until the February revolution.

With the aid of Natanson and B. D. Kamkov, Chernov published the anti-war newspapers *Mysl'* ('Thought') and *Zhizn'* ('Life') and helped create the ultimately predominant internationalist movement within the PSR. Albeit in softer tones than Natanson, during 1914 and 1915 Chernov espoused a position that advocated the Russian government's defeat as a precursor of socialist revolution. His writings were so influential and he wielded such personal authority that tsarist agents reporting on the alliance of *émigré* anti-war socialists (SRs, Bolsheviks and Mensheviks) described Chernov as its predominant leader. Although he attended the 1915 Zimmerwald Conference, he failed to sign its famous anti-war manifesto and did not participate in the 1916 Kienthal Conference, whereas Natanson enthusiastically participated in both; during 1916 and early 1917, Chernov played a markedly lesser role in SR *émigré* affairs than earlier, perhaps signifying a dampening of his anti-war fervour (his memoirs never touched on this sensitive issue).

Upon the Russian revolution's outbreak, Chernov, like other internationalists, at first found his return home blocked by Allied governments reluctant to unleash *émigré* anti-war socialists on Russia's fragile new polity. Even so, he rejected travel through Germany (the path ultimately taken by Lenin and numerous other Bolsheviks, Mensheviks, SRs and anarchists), preferring the hazardous submarine-infested North Sea passage.

Chernov's arrival on 8 April marked a signal moment in SR history and of the Russian revolution, just as Lenin's return five days earlier did (with vastly different nuance) for his party and the revolution. Whereas Lenin badgered the Bolsheviks back from their conciliationist stances toward radical ones, Chernov allied himself for several fateful months with his former opponents, SR defencists such as Avksentiev and Gots, thus, in effect, strengthening the party's post-February reformist tilt. In both the Petrograd Soviet Executive Committee and, a few weeks later, the Provisional Government, Chernov at once played a role commensurate with his high standing as a socialist leader. Sergei Sossinskii, the author of a new dissertation about Chernov, notes that it was he who first suggested that the Petrograd Soviet's declaration on peace be transmitted by the Provisional Government to the Allies; Foreign Minister P. N. Miliukov's attempt to subvert the peace-oriented message by appending a secret note launched the April Crisis that brought down the first government.

Similarly, Chernov was at the centre of the SR (and eventually Menshevik) group that espoused a socialist–liberal coalition in the new government, which he entered as Minister of Agriculture. Chernov's positions during the spring and summer of 1917 the government and the war certainly warrant the assertion that he had softened his lifelong radicalism, an evaluation his own memoirs confirmed without explanation. Chernov's voluminous contemporary writings at least outline rationales for his positions and activities. He felt that the relative disorganization of the socialist movement necessitated initial support for the liberal Provisional Government since propertied (*tsenzovye*) elements were temporarily in a better position to govern.

Socialist entry into the Provisional Government in alliance with liberals, an idea socialists had traditionally anathematized, provided a thornier problem. Chernov made his entry conditional upon socialist control of the labour, agriculture and food-supply ministries, which, he argued, provided the basis for reconstructing the country on socialist initiative, a formulation not at odds with his thinking about a rapid development toward socialism and quite different from right-wing SR and Menshevik motivations. As regards the war, despite his continued sincere insistence that Russia renounce Allied war aims and work toward peace on the basis of a renewed Socialist International, Chernov became an unalloyed revolutionary defencist, who even supported the June offensive because 'without an offence, there is no defence'. His supporting argument that Russia's new government had renounced war aims seems thin in light of the rather obvious liberal-moderate socialist dedication to the war (Chernov himself had contributed greatly to the political demise of 'Miliukov-Dardanelskii', as he had called the then Foreign Minister).

Meanwhile, within the party Chernov's role was equally great, although during this period in an indirect way. In aligning himself with moderates and thus leaving the Central Committee and the party under their control, Chernov ensured that legions of his supporters among SR activists would follow him (albeit temporarily and uneasily) in his revolutionary defencism and support for the Provisional Government, whereas most had a clear preference for rapid action on land reform, an end to the war and the creation of an all-socialist government. It was precisely this circumstance that fuelled the rapidly growing leftist SR movement, led and peopled by Chernov's pre-February party allies. At the party's May congress, Chernov attempted to negotiate a middle path between left and right. His rightward tilt on the important issues of war and government offered especially little succour to the left, as symbolized by the congress's election of a single leftist, Natanson, to the new Central Committee (leftists had roughly 20 per cent of the delegates and won up to 40 per cent of the votes). This set the stage for increasingly intractable intra-party conflict and the SRs' final split.

Within the government, Chernov's sanguine hopes about reconstructing the country through socialist control of key ministries also proved barren. True, under his guidance, the Ministry of Agriculture organized central and local land committees aimed at land redistribution; even so, the protracted organizational task as yet offered little to impatient peasants. Leaving the country's vast social problems unaddressed, the government delayed Constituent Assembly elections and during June launched the ruinously unsuccessful military offensive. This was the context of the July disorders that brought down the coalition government (Chernov himself was almost lynched outside the Soviet Executive Committee premises).

Chernov's precise role in the reconstruction of the Provisional Government with a socialist majority and headed by Kerensky is unclear, as is his attitude toward the new government's attempted repression of radicals (Bolsheviks, Left SRs and left Mensheviks). A reasonable surmise is that the new government's authoritarian proclivities were foreign to Chernov, as suggested by his near-resignation later in July (supposedly in response to the liberal press's accusations about his alleged German ties) and his actual resignation on 26 August, just as the Kornilov episode began. From this time forward, Chernov launched a barrage of criticism against the Provisional Government on the land question and the war and dedicated himself to dragging the party away from its rightist positions toward the left-centre, doubtlessly his preferred placement on a political spectrum, whence he could attack both right and left within the party and in the realm of public discourse.

The Bolshevik seizure of power galvanized Chernov into unwonted action as he travelled to army headquarters at Mogilev, where he joined Kerensky in attempting to organize armed resistance to the Bolsheviks and to establish a non-Bolshevik alternative government. With the failure of this endeavour, he remained away from Petrograd (perhaps expecting arrest at the hands of the new government) until his late-November return for the Fourth SR Congress. Chernov and his left-centrist positions (meaningful negotiations for peace, transfer of land to the land committees and a socialist government) completely dominated the SR Congress, as the rightist leaders lost all influence in the eyes of most delegates. Unfortunately, the broader unity within the mass of party cadres and supporters that the new positions might have created earlier in the year was now irrevocably lost. Expelled by the Central Committee for breaking party discipline, the Left SRs held a separate congress that founded a new party which quickly encroached upon the SRs' peasant, worker and soldier following.

Since Chernov and the SRs adamantly rejected the new Soviet government, which the Left SRs entered in December, they based all their plans upon the upcoming Constituent Assembly. The elections had provided the SRs with a resounding victory, especially among the peasantry. Because of perceived threats to the Constituent Assembly from the Bolsheviks (henceforth Communists) and the Left SRs, Chernov associated himself with the Committee for the Defence of the Constituent Assembly. Consisting of moderate and centrist SRs and Mensheviks, this committee undertook to mobilize political and, if necessary, military support for the assembly (the archival records of the committee suggest, however, a certain torpor on the part of society). Seemingly without hindrance, the Constituent Assembly opened on 5 January with a comfortable moderate socialist majority. The Bolsheviks and Left SRs put forward M. A. Spiridonova as chair, but Chernov, the moderate nominee, handily won the election.

During the famous one-day existence of the Constituent Assembly, Chernov displayed exemplary courage and statesmanship under the most trying, indeed dangerous, circumstances. Ignoring the Communist–Left SR walkout, not to mention the bullying of half-drunk hostile armed guards (thugs is the better term), Chernov calmly led the assembled delegates through the futile passage of new laws on the land and the pronouncement of the country as a democratic federated republic. Finally, under direct physical duress, Chernov agreed to the early morning closing of the first and last session. With the subsequent locking of the assembly hall and shooting of pro-Constituent Assembly worker demonstrators, Russia's gathering of democratically elected legislators and the SRs' hopes of dominating the nation's affairs came to a permanent halt.

Although the PSR continued to function openly, Chernov again went underground, as he had for so much of his life. From Moscow he witnessed helplessly the growing chasm between the Communists and all other socialists, the repression of the workers' movement when it turned its support back toward the Menshevik–SR alliance, and the crushing of democratically elected soviets, culminating in the forcible expulsion of SRs and Mensheviks from the soviets during June.

In the light of the Red Terror, Chernov and many other SRs headed south-east. Chernov left Moscow during May, arriving after a hazardous journey in Samara on 19 September. There he joined the balance of the SR Central Committee which dominated Samara's brief-lived *Komuch* government (Committee of the Constituent Assembly). Chernov immediately reasserted his authority by persuading the PSR to withdraw support from the Directory, an anti-Bolshevik government that had arisen in Ufa. Chernov's criticism of the Directory focused on its conservative orientation, despite the fact that two out of its five members were SRs, albeit rightist ones (Avksentiev and V. M. Zenzinov).

This introduced Chernov's last notable contribution to revolutionary discourse, the so-called 'third force' between the extremes of right and left (Whites and Reds), entailing a faith in democracy and in the people, symbolized by his term *narodovlastie*. Regardless, the third force (centrist SRs and Mensheviks) found themselves crushed between the anvil and hammer of the White and Red armies, after which Chernov and the SRs, hunted by both sides, again entered underground life.

By late 1918 Chernov espoused arming SRs for the people's democratic cause but, out of fear of a White victory, abstained from the Left SR policy of sponsoring anti-Bolshevik peasant uprisings. He also steadfastly rejected the early 1919 anti-White accommodation with the Communists reached by V. K. Volskii, N. V. Sviatitskii and K. S. Burevoi. Legalized briefly during March 1919, the PSR under Chernov's leadership continued its criticism of Communist policies until a new round of arrests drove him and others to escape abroad in early 1920. Despite dogged pursual, his third path had found no firm ground in the cataclysmic civil war. Until his death in 1952, Chernov lived in Western Europe and America.

The failure of Chernov's cause – that is, of the populist narrative he formulated for early twentieth-century Russia – constituted a tragedy of the first order. His neo-populist analysis of Russia's social structure was closer to the mark than anything Marxist theory offered; for example, his theory of Russia's revolutionary classes foreshadowed even the USSR's latter-day definition of its social basis (intelligentsia, proletariat and peasantry). With its huge peasantry, Russia required leaders knowledgeable about and sympathetic toward peasant aspirations; within or at the head of a government, Chernov could have fulfilled this role. Similarly, his democratic fervour contrasts well with Leninist indifference toward democratic processes.

Chernov's political failure, however, issued primarily from his own inadequacies. Unfortunately, the softness of will he emphasized in his self-critical memoirs (as regards his 1917 failure to oppose the right SRs) was not the real problem since often in his life he stood adamantly against formidable opponents. Rather, Chernov utterly lacked a sense of political timing. Having vacillated when firmness would have counted after February 1917, he acted only when Bolshevik encroachments and the split in the PSR were far advanced. Similarly, just after 25 October he engaged in quixotic attempts to form a non-Bolshevik government in Mogilev, thus missing the joint socialist negotiations in the capital. His dignified performance at the Constituent Assembly also poses a question about why he did not throw his considerable stature behind its earlier election. Possessing in full measure invaluable traits of character and profound insight, he did not know when and where to take appropriate action, a lack which, combined with his personal self-abnegation, fatally damaged him as a political leader in revolutionary Russia.

Until quite recently, historical writing about Chernov consisted of one dissertation about his theories, supplemented by comments in various histories of the PSR. Sossinskii's new dissertation advances our knowledge about Chernov's activities during 1917–20; his proposed full-length biography of Chernov based upon archives will certainly aid us in evaluating the career of this key figure in early twentieth-century Russian history.

Further reading

Chernov V. M., *Zapiski sotsialista-revoliutsionera* (Berlin, Izdatel'stvo Z. I. Grzhebina, 1922).

Chernov V. M., *Rozhdenie revoliutsionnoi Rossii (Fevral'skaia revoliutsiia)* (Paris, Iubileinyi komitet po izdaniiu trudov V. M. Chernova, 1934).

Chernov V. M., *The Great Russian Revolution* (New Haven, Yale University Press, 1936).

Chernov V. M., *Pered burei*, 2nd edn (Moscow, Mezhdunarodnye otnosheniia, 1993).

Cross T. B., 'Victor Chernov: Reason and Will in a Morality for Revolution' (Ph.D. dissertation, Indiana University, 1968).

Mikhailovich 'Chernov, Viktor', in P. V. Volobuev *et al.*, eds., *Politicheskie deiateli Rossii. 1917. Biograficheskii slovar'* (Moscow, Nauchnoe izdatel'stvo Bol'shaia rossiiskaia entsiklopediia, 1993), pp. 347–51.

Sossinskii S. B., 'Pages from the Life of Victor Chernov' (Ph.D. dissertation, Boston University, 1995).

Kerensky

BORIS I. KOLONITSKII

It is impossible to imagine the February revolution without Aleksandr Fedorovich Kerensky (1884–1970), 'the central and most popular figure of the revolution', as N. N. Sukhanov put it. Kerensky personified the revolution. He held some of the most important posts in the Provisional Governments of 1917. In March and April he was Minister of Justice, and from May to August he was War and Naval Minister. From 8 July he was head of the Provisional Government, and from 30 August he was commander in chief. However, a list of these posts alone cannot convey either Kerensky's real authority, or the power he enjoyed from the outset in the first revolutionary cabinet.

Lenin wrote of the first Provisional Government that 'the democrat Kerensky was invited into the new government in order to create the impression of popular representation, in order to have a democratic windbag who would make impressive but meaningless proclamations to the people, while the Guchkovs and the L'vovs continued with their anti-popular activities'. Lenin's assessment was quite incorrect. In fact, the 35-year-old Minister of Justice had considerable influence, and it was frequently his position which determined the cabinet's decisions. Even at that time he was being referred to as the 'only ... man in the Cabinet who had any power' (R. H. Bruce Lockhart), 'the most influential member of the government and a strong man' (Sir George Buchanan), 'the real Prime Minister' (V. M. Zenzinov), 'the most influential minister' (Z. N. Gippius) and 'the strongest man in the Council of Ministers' (Arthur Ransome). P. N. Miliukov stated that 'although he had not yet become a "powerful force" within the state, Kerensky had certainly already attained such a status within the government'. In a conversation with the French socialist Albert Thomas, Kerensky claimed that his position within the cabinet was 'special', and that without him everything would 'collapse'. This notion of the Minister of Justice's particular influence was widely shared – innumerable petitions and resolutions containing demands quite unrelated to his official competence were addressed to him personally.

Some of his contemporaries ascribed Kerensky's influence, and even his entry into the Provisional Government, to the Masonic solidarity of certain members of the cabinet. The influence of the 'Supreme Council of the Peoples of Russia' has received a great deal of attention from certain historians, notably George Katkov. However, the reason for Kerensky's authority had already been discerned in 1917. He was 'the right person in the right place'. This expression was used, quite independently, by people of such diverse political persuasions as Nicholas II, Gippius and V. V. Shul'gin. Kerensky was very well placed – in conditions of dual power he was both a member of the government and a deputy chairman of the Executive Committee of the Petrograd Soviet. According to I. V. Gessen, the decision to bring Kerensky into the government was influenced by the fact that he already had a prominent role in the Soviet. G. L. Sobolev has suggested that the organizers of the Petrograd Soviet put Kerensky forward for a government post in the hope of using his authority to strengthen their own position. Kerensky's influence was also taken into account in forming the Provisional Duma Committee – his name was placed second in the official list of members of the committee, after that of M. V. Rodzianko, the chairman.

At the time when the power structures of revolutionary Russia were being created, Kerensky already enjoyed considerable authority. He was known as a defence lawyer at political trials, as a member of the commission which investigated the Lena events of 1912, and as one of the most outspoken members of the Duma. He was known in all manner of legal, semi-legal and illegal circles among the radical intelligentsia. However, his influence was above all a consequence of his actions between 23 and 27 February 1917, which were both decisive and effective: his call to disobey the tsar's decree on the dissolution of the Duma, his bold speeches to soldiers in revolt, the arrest of the tsarist ministers, and his personal contact with the centres of the movement. Among the more prominent political figures, only Kerensky acted so quickly, boldly and brilliantly. As V. B. Stankevich put it: 'He was the only person who gave himself completely to the spontaneous mass movement with enthusiasm and complete trust. Only he could honestly and truthfully talk with soldiers as "we".' Sukhanov also wrote about Kerensky's unique role: 'the indispensable Kerensky of the last days of tsarism, the ubiquitous Kerensky of the February–March days'. In such circumstances certain conservative deputies such as Shul'gin even regarded him as a revolutionary 'dictator'.

However, Kerensky's influence was not only a result of his presence in the institutions of power. The political life of the country between February and October 1917 was shaped by an understanding between the so-called 'living forces in the country' – the soviets and committees led by moderate socialists, and the liberals. Although he was formally connected with the Socialist Revolutionaries, Kerensky was not partisan, and his political position was exactly in between the two camps, at the fulcrum of Russian political life.

He personified this agreement, he symbolized 'the coalition of all the living forces in the country', as M. I. Skobelev put it. To I. G. Tsereteli, Kerensky represented the 'democratic intelligentsia', on the edge of 'soviet', 'socialist' and 'purely bourgeois' democracy. He noted that Kerensky tried to play the role of a 'national' figure, and that his ideal was 'non-party and supra-party power'. His opponents dubbed him 'the mathematical centre of Russian Bonapartism'. In Sukhanov's words: 'He was destined to become the mathematical point at which the harsh and, to him, incomprehensible forces of the revolution crossed.' Both left- and right-wing critics, such as P. E. Dybenko and Iu. V. Got'e, reproached him for 'sitting on two stools'. He considered himself to be the expression of the 'all-national character of the revolution', and was, in the words of N. A. Rozhkov, 'an intransigent defender of coalition', a politician of compromise. His political fate, his very existence as a politician, depended on the preservation of that agreement.

Although right-wingers such as V. M. Purishkevich called Kerensky 'the minister for civil war' in the summer of 1917, this assertion was unfounded. As Lenin put it, Kerensky's government 'wanted to harmonize the interests of landowners and peasants, workers and bosses, labour and capital'. He attempted to revive the coalition when there was already no basis for it, he preached compromise to those who rejected it, he tried to prevent civil war when it had already become practically inevitable. This does not, of course, absolve him or other leading politicians of responsibility for the fact that while he was in power the country slid slowly but surely towards civil war.

However, his political position does not in itself explain the Kerensky phenomenon. His influence in the power structures was primarily the result of his enormous popularity within the country. To cite Buchanan: 'From the very beginning Kerensky was the central figure in the revolutionary drama, and alone among his colleagues enjoyed evident support on the part of the masses.' Not one of the revolutionaries of 1917 enjoyed that sort of honour. Kerensky was the charismatic leader of revolutionary Russia – to challenge the 'people's tribune' was, in the early days, simply dangerous.

How can Kerensky's 'dizzying' influence be explained? Many years later he wrote about February: 'That was the historical moment which gave birth to "my Russia", an ideal Russia which took the place of that Russia which had been defiled and polluted by Rasputin and the universally hated monarchy.' There were few revolutionaries who could have said that. F. A. Stepun, a supporter and colleague of Kerensky, called him 'the only . . . true-born son of the revolution' among the members of the government. This not entirely dispassionate characterization can be extended: outside the ranks of the cabinet there were very few leading political figures who would have identified themselves so fully with the revolution. For liberals it was excessively radical, cutting across their ideals and developing in a direction which was 'to the left of common sense'. The socialists considered it to be a 'bourgeois' revolution and looked for a way out of the crisis and its problems by 'deepening' the revolution. Kerensky identified with February completely, and his position fitted well the euphoric, excited, carnival mood of the 'masses' in the initial phase of the revolution. Both the character and the political position of the 'Minister of People's Justice' were close to their political culture.

Kerensky was not closely involved with party politics. Sukhanov had grounds for calling him an 'undemocratic democrat'. Kerensky's own particular political convictions were underpinned neither by participation in mass democratic organizations, nor by a knowledge of Western democratic models. (He scornfully admitted the latter himself in various speeches of 1917.) In 'his own' party, the Socialist Revolutionaries, Kerensky was seen either as a novice or as an outsider – at the party congress he did not gain enough votes to be elected onto the Central Committee. As Tsereteli put it, Kerensky did not have fixed views on social or agrarian questions, nor on industrial regulation, issues which acquired immense importance as the revolution developed. At a later stage his lack of strong connections with political parties and of tried and tested political colleagues would have serious consequences for Kerensky. However, in the initial phase of the revolution, not to be strongly identified with any party was a kind of political trump-card. 'Strength lies in unity' was one of the most popular slogans. To be 'partisan' was seen as a threat to that unity. The politicized masses were irritated by inter-party arguments and polemics.

Kerensky's political style also corresponded to the initial, carnival period of the revolution. As Dietrich Geyer has observed, at a time when history had become theatre, the pathos of accomplished agitators was a factor of state importance, and Kerensky was an invaluable figure both for the Soviet and for the government. He was a remarkable speaker and improvisator, a fine actor, an 'impressionist-politician' as Sukhanov and V. M. Chernov put it, who could catch instinctively the mood of an audience, reflect it subtly and brilliantly and thereby significantly amplify that mood. Kerensky was the outstanding 'star' at post-revolutionary 'concert-meetings' at which speeches by ministers would be interspersed with performances by actors. People went 'to see Kerensky', and the label of 'popular minister' was not accidental. Describing the 'Kerensky phenomenon', contemporaries used such phrases as a 'frenzy of enthusiasm' (Lockhart), and 'the psychosis of the crowd' (V. D. Nabokov). These often negative assessments in fact confirm the remarkable success of his performances.

The revolution had an immediate effect on Kerensky's external appearance. According to Miliukov he declared that the masses were not able to recognize power 'in a coat'. In just a few post-revolutionary photographs Kerensky appeared 'in a coat', but he soon 'democratized' his appearance and dressed himself in a black jacket, which to Lockhart resembled 'ski-ing kit over a black Russian workman's blouse'. Even at this early stage there was a noticeable 'militarization' of Kerensky's appearance, which Stepun regarded as a 'tribute to the revolutionary epoch and his role within it'. After he had been made War and Navy Minister, he wore a semi-military costume, and at the front he appeared in a field shirt and puttees, but for everyday wear he chose an elegant field jacket. Kerensky could be considered to have started the fashion adopted by the first generations of the Soviet *nomenklatura* – in the 1920s such jackets became known as *vozhdevki* (a leader's jacket), and later as *Stalinki* (a Stalin jacket).

It was no accident that Kerensky, with his intuition and talent for acting, adopted the 'Napoleonic pose' in which he was frequently photographed and caricatured. That image initially impressed his enthusiastic audiences.

It has been observed many times that one cannot fully grasp the effect of Kerensky's speeches on the basis of their textual content alone. However, they do give an impression of Kerensky's style as a politician. Both his famous speech at the conference of delegates from the front in which he denounced 'rebellious slaves', and his strange speech at the closure of the Moscow State Conference were a kind of public confession, which his detractors described as 'hysterical ravings'. According to S. P. Mel'gunov, many at the latter conference thought Kerensky had lost his mind, and A. I. Shingarev commented that 'Kerensky was either playing Hamlet, or he had lapsed into the psychopathic hysteria of Fedor Ivanovich' (Tsar Fedor I). Kerensky saw himself as a 'moral politician', for whom not only pragmatic success, but also sincerity and fidelity to a certain ethical position were important. This could be seen particularly clearly in his attitude to the death penalty and to the use of force in politics. He knew that many of his political friends and supporters would judge and assess him as a 'moral politician', a person with 'clean hands'. This is not surprising; the Petersburg Religious-Philosophical Society, whose meetings Kerensky had occasionally attended, had sometimes considered political problems through a religious–ethical prism. Like many other intellectuals, Kerensky had a syncretic (moral–religious–political) consciousness. It was from this point of view that the people from that circle initially assessed him. According to N. Berdiaev, when A. Belyi saw Kerensky the politician in the spring, Belyi used the expression 'the birth of the new man' – a phrase used by many representatives of the Russian 'silver age'.

That does not mean that in his speeches and his actions Kerensky was always sincere and above politicking. As early as March and April 1917, he gave diametrically opposed accounts of the Soviet to different audiences. He was a master of political intrigue. However, the image, appearance and reputation of a 'moral' politician were very important to Kerensky. In this sort of political culture his 'confessional speeches' were absolutely natural. The 'passionate sincerity' of Kerensky's speeches corresponded to the mood of the moment. The mass political consciousness of the first months of the revolution was also a syncretic moral–religious–political consciousness.

The other image upon which Kerensky modelled himself was that of 'master of men's minds', a creative and artistic politician. He had even been called 'the poet of the revolution'. Such acts as throwing flowers (a gesture copied from the theatre), his unexpected conducting of the Volynskii regimental orchestra, the bows and the kisses were all quite in keeping with this cultural orientation. Apart from the generally theatrical style of political life at that time, this sort of behaviour can be explained in terms of national traditions. For several generations of the Russian intelligentsia art, and particularly literature, were surrogates for politics and ideology – the aestheticization of politics was a consequence of the politicization of aesthetics. It is not surprising that some of Kerensky's supporters referred to themselves as his 'admirers' and 'worshippers'.

A striking feature of Kerensky's speeches was his notion that he had been 'chosen'. Tsereteli noted his conviction 'that he was a providential figure, destined to save Russia'. Miliukov wrote that Kerensky 'identified the revolution with his own person'. This malicious assessment nonetheless contains an element of truth – Kerensky did regard himself as a unique and irreplaceable political leader, as the personification of 'Russian democracy'. He frequently claimed that the only alternative to him was anarchy, chaos and dictatorship, and demanded not only trust, but faith. In his speeches there were invariably just two subjects of the political process – Kerensky himself, the revolutionary leader, and the revolutionary people. Those closest to him regarded him in the same way, 'all Russia immediately recognized its leader in him . . . They knew, loved and believed in him' recalled his wife, O. L. Kerenskaia.

Many 'realistic' politicians also recognized his unique role. Gessen wrote that 'the revolution revolved around Kerensky', and also called him the 'axle of the revolution'. A. I. Putilov declared in 1917 that Kerensky was 'the only strong personality the revolution has produced'.

The propaganda campaign around the 'people's minister' would appear to have reinforced his sense of destiny. The press called him 'the knight of the revolution', 'the lion heart', 'the first love of the revolution', 'the people's tribune', 'the genius of Russian freedom', 'the sun of Russia's freedom', 'the people's leader', 'the leader of freedom', 'the saviour of the fatherland', 'the hero-minister', 'the prophet and hero of the revolution', 'the Prometheus of the Russian revolution', 'the good genius of free Russia', 'the leader of the Russian revolution', and 'the pride and joy of the revolution'. (This last phrase was later used by Trotsky to describe the Kronstadt sailors.) By June 1917 'Long live the people's leader Kerensky!' had become almost an official greeting. It was used by Kerensky's future opponent L. G. Kornilov to greet him on a visit to the front. Special badges and medals dedicated to Kerensky were produced. One of them was particularly telling – on the top side 'a depiction of A. F. Kerensky bedecked with flowers, looking to the right', and on the other side the slogan 'the glorious, wise, true and beloved leader of the people – 1917'.

It should be borne in mind that many of the most prominent representatives of the intelligentsia took part in this glorification. Kerensky had connections in many of the clans of the radical intelligentsia through friendship as well as personal and professional relationships. Consequently he was 'their' man in the world of politics. Kerensky had the authority of the intelligentsia on his side, and his cult was a manifestation of the intelligentsia's caste solidarity. It was no accident that in 1917 he was elected to such organizations of the intelligentsia as the Free Economic Society and the Teachers' Union. He frequently regarded himself as an 'intellectual-politician', as Dybenko and M. M. Zoshchenko noted. Subsequently caricatures of Kerensky played a certain role in inflaming anti-intellectual attitudes in Soviet Russia.

In 1917, M. I. Tsvetaeva, P. A. Olenin-Volgar' and A. S. Roslavlev wrote poems devoted to Kerensky. I. E. Repin painted his portrait. Vladimir I. Nemirovich-Danchenko, K. S. Stanislavskii and the collective of the Moscow Arts Theatre addressed Kerensky thus: 'you personify the ideal of the free citizen, which the human soul has cherished throughout the ages, and which the poets and the artists of the world have passed on from generation to generation'. Vasilii I. Nemirovich-Danchenko described the impression made upon him by a speech by Kerensky thus: 'When you listen to him, you feel as if all your nerves are stretching out towards him and joining with his in one knot.' The academician S. A. Vengerov wrote: 'I am always irritated when they call Kerensky the Russian Danton. He is Kerensky, and that is enough to make him immortal.' A. I. Kuprin called Kerensky 'the people's heart': 'In every age and among all nations in severely testing times, there has been an inscrutable and direct spiritual receiver, a divine resonator, a mysterious mouthpiece for the people's will, which I call the living, beating heart of the people.' One cannot help noticing that these are not purely political assessments of Kerensky – they are combined with ethical and aesthetic judgements. Some of these judgements reflect an assessment of the immediate political situation, but many of the writers were being perfectly sincere. According to Gippius, even in the autumn of 1917 certain members of the Petrograd intelligentsia regarded Kerensky as 'sacred' and would not tolerate any criticism of him. Of course, many intellectuals had other views, but Kerensky was still very popular in that milieu.

The Kerensky cult became the most important factor in Russian political life. According to Lockhart 'for four months [he] was worshipped as a god'. Once he had become War Minister, despite his completely non-military past, he enjoyed enormous influence in the army. The resolutions of military committees referred to him as 'the people's minister', 'the irreplaceable leader of the revolutionary forces', 'a tireless fighter for an idea', 'beloved leader', 'the true leader of Russian democracy', 'the symbol of democracy' and 'our supreme leader'. Of course, the positions of army organizations did not always coincide with the attitudes of the rank-and-file soldiers. However, we can find similar assessments in letters from ordinary soldiers: 'I live in the trenches, but I forget all my troubles and am happy that at the head of our people's revolutionary army there is such a glorious and beloved leader Minister Kerensky.' His speeches were regarded as 'the most sincere, coming from the soul of the most sincere person'.

So, very shortly after the most radical anti-monarchist revolution, in a political atmosphere dominated by democratic ideology there emerged, without any external compulsion, a cult of a single leader and saviour. This gave Nabokov grounds for speaking of the 'idolization' of Kerensky. An example of this can be found in the poem by L. Kannegiser (who subsequently assassinated M. S. Uritskii), whose lyrical hero is prepared to die for his motherland, inspired by a vision of Russia's leader and saviour: 'Russia, freedom, Kerensky on a white horse'.

'The Kerensky phenomenon' was caused by three factors: the 'people's minister' himself, the propagandists of his cult and his audience. The creators of the cult adopted a variety of models. The image of Kerensky as leader was influenced by the tradition of the leader of the liberation movement, the image of the artist as master of men's minds, the militarist tradition of the World War military leader, and the age-old tradition of deification of the sovereign, the head of state. According to contemporary accounts many peasants believed Kerensky to be the 'new tsar'. The rupture in the institutions of power in the course of the February revolution led to a situation in which the law ceased to be the source and instrument of power, the state lost its monopoly on the legitimate use of force, and a break with the former political tradition was declared. In such circumstances the personal authority of a politician, his image in the mass consciousness, acquired importance in the exercise of power. The revolutionary mass looked for, chose and elevated its charismatic leader.

However, the cult of the leader of the revolution was soon put to the test. The political criticisms of his opponents on both the left and the right were increasingly directed against Kerensky himself, once he had become War Minister.

The authority of the 'people's minister' was undermined by the failure of the 'Kerensky–Brusilov' June offensive. Many people at the time regarded the idea of an offensive as adventurist. It was said that the offensive was undertaken under pressure from the Allies. Kerensky himself refuted this, showing that the decision was taken above all because of the internal situation.

After the July crisis Kerensky, as head of the government, reached the summit of power. He personally picked the 'government of salvation of the revolution', and the power of the head of government was significantly increased. However, it was at precisely this point that his popularity began to melt rapidly away. This fall in his authority led to increasing criticism of his positions, and to a broadening of the front of his opponents. As enthusiasm for the idea of coalition waned, there was a corresponding increase in attacks on Kerensky from both left and right. The most striking manifestation of Kerensky's tarnished image was the circulation of all sorts of rumours.

In right-wing circles Kerensky's supposedly Jewish origins were discussed. Rumours of his moral 'dissolution' were more widespread. The transfer of the seat of government to the Winter Palace, Kerensky's use of the tsar's personal apartments and the imperial train, his 'Bonapartist style', and, not least, his break-up with his wife provided fertile soil for this sort of gossip. It was even said that one of the tsar's daughters had become his lover. Kerensky was accused of having resurrected a 'court atmosphere', of drug abuse, of embezzlement of state property and of using the personal effects of the tsar's family. It was claimed that he used the tsarina's bed-linen. This last rumour was supposed to show the effeminate nature of the leader, which was also true of the sobriquet 'the new Alexandra Fedorovna', supposedly coined by V. Khlebnikov. Right-wingers even suggested that Kerensky was the puppet of German agents and that he was secretly preparing a deal with the enemy. Gossip about Kerensky was spread in salons, on the street and in the classroom. It even found its way into the newspapers and into diplomatic reports.

Kerensky's manners and external appearance, which had earlier been seen as an example of his democratic nature and military courage, became an object of ridicule. To his former political friends, like D. V. Filosofov, he resembled 'a chauffeur in a wealthy household'.

The Kornilov affair dealt a fatal blow to the Kerensky cult. He found himself in a situation in which both left and right considered him to be a traitor. The events have always been a matter for controversy. Stepun described the conflict as 'the final act of a tragic misunderstanding'. Kerensky himself justified his actions during those days by claiming that there was a 'counter-revolutionary movement' in the *Stavka*. His testimony should be treated with great caution. He did not mention his own intrigues against Kornilov, which were recounted by V. V. Vyrubov. On the other hand, Kornilov accused Kerensky of 'great provocation', and this charge was repeated by many former Kornilovites in the emigration. Katkov reached similar conclusions, and claimed that Kornilov did not intend any kind of conspiracy against the government. However, those who argue this line fail to mention the actions and plans of V. S. Zavoiko and his associates, and their influence within the *Stavka*. It is easy to see that the advocates of this view are actually in agreement with Lenin (and therefore with many authors of the Soviet period), who called Kerensky a Kornilovite 'who fell out with Kornilov by chance'.

Kerensky's victory over Kornilov was his own political defeat, in that his political base, the coalition of 'living forces', was undermined, and his personal authority plummeted. As Bessie Beatty put it: 'Kerensky, trying like the true democrat he was to please everyone, succeeded in pleasing no one. Attacked from above and below, from within and without, there seemed little hope for him.' His room for political manoeuvre was very limited. Even before Kornilov's move, he observed with reason: 'If I move to the left, I have an army without a general staff, and if I move to the right, I have a general staff without an army.' Kerensky's isolation was further reinforced as his relations with several of the Allied missions soured. It was not just the balance of political forces which had changed, the political climate had changed as well. The enthusiasm and the fashion for politics which characterized

March 1917, which had fitted so well with Kerensky's own mood and political style, gave way to disillusionment, depression and disenchantment with politics. Just as the euphoric atmosphere of March created the magnetic attraction of the 'impressionist-politician', so the subsequent depression could not help but undermine it. Although resolutions expressing firm support still came in from village communities and from military committees, his charisma was fading relentlessly.

It was particularly painful for Kerensky to be rejected by people of his own circle and caste, members of the radical intelligentsia. Many of them began to reproach him for the very actions and gestures for which they had previously lauded him. They never considered their own responsibility for the Kerensky cult. The 'diary' of Gippius, who knew Kerensky well, is particularly telling in this respect. In the spring she 'believed' in him as the 'only' politician who could 'deal' with the situation, whereas from August onwards she denounced him in sharp and unreasonable terms. The style of her condemnation is significant. The early version of the 'diary' contained accusations of 'dissolution' and of drug abuse. She judged him in aesthetic terms: 'without the slightest beauty'. Kerensky's femininity was stressed: 'he gives way to everyone almost like a woman'; 'a revolutionary old woman'. She continued this theme in a poem of 1918 which described the former leader as 'capricious like a woman'. He was still regarded as a unique politician, but in negative terms: 'slave of the Bolsheviks', 'Russia is sinking in a bloody ditch, and he is to blame'.

In their judgement of Kerensky, many refined intellectuals followed the same path as the millions of semi-literate soldiers in the trenches. If at first he, and only he, was seen as a single and all-powerful leader, the saviour of the country, now the former idol was regarded as a miserable windbag, an old woman, and the main, if not the only, source of all Russia's woes. Kerensky came to personify the crisis: the perjorative term *Kerenshchina* was coined and was used avidly by people in the most diverse political camps. Describing the mass political consciousness of the 'young democracy', Chernov noted a strong tendency to 'personalize' ideas, a 'fetishism of personalities'. With Kerensky evidently in mind, Chernov warned that 'a crowd of fetishists will react just as savages do when their fetishes fail to deliver: they will tear them down, beat them and trample them into the dirt'. Previously this mass political consciousness sought a way out of the crisis by giving more power to Kerensky; now it expected miracles from his removal. In the autumn of 1917 the Bolsheviks and their allies were able to play on this sort of mass attitude, waging a propaganda campaign against 'the traitor Kerensky'.

'A weak politician', 'spineless', 'hysterical', 'an actor' and 'a windbag' – Russian memoirists and historians of both left and right concurred in their contemptuous assessments of Kerensky, which reflected the attitudes of 1917. They contain a considerable amount of truth. Nonetheless, they tell us more about their authors than about Kerensky. Both the Kerensky cult of 1917 and subsequent writings about him, including the apologetic literature, are monuments to the specific political culture of the revolutionary period.

The overthrow of the monarchy and the spread of anti-monarchist attitudes did not overcome Russia's authoritarian and patriarchal political culture – it only led to its mutation. At the centre of the revolutionary political culture there remained the image of the 'strong politician', a single and all-powerful leader and saviour, endowed with the highest moral qualities and almost divine powers. An unconditional and unreserved 'faith' in the 'true' leader was considered to be a public duty. All problems could be solved by giving him more power. As William Rosenberg has observed, the potential of state power as a mechanism for solving the most diverse problems was exaggerated fantastically, and 'government' and 'power' were considered synonymous. There was a crucial contradiction between this sort of political culture and the democratic ideology of the initial stages of the revolution. There was also a contradiction between the peculiar democratic ideology and the 'leaderist' political culture of Kerensky himself, his colleagues and supporters.

However, the deepening crisis led to the desecration of the leader's image. His amorality was stressed, his behaviour was judged aesthetically as 'ugly', and he lost his masculinity in the public perception. The authoritarian and patriarchal political culture placed the blame for the situation on the leader alone, and examined neither its own responsibility for the emergence of the leader cult, nor its own mistakes and illusions.

The propagandist phrase 'first love of the revolution' sums up the Kerensky phenomenon extremely well. (This is appropriately used in the title of Richard Abraham's book – the only scholarly biography of Kerensky.) The attitude of the Russian revolution to its chosen leaders bore the stamp of that first romantic love. The Kerensky cult influenced the other sub-cultures of the revolution and counterrevolution, such as the cult of Lenin and the other Bolshevik leaders, and the cult of Kornilov and the other 'White' leaders. Caricatures of Kerensky played a certain role in the creation of these new cults – the feminine image of the 'weak' and 'sickly' failed politician was contrasted to the healthy masculinity of the 'real', 'powerful' leaders. The legend according to which Kerensky dressed in women's clothes in order to escape from Gatchina, also played a part in this.

Shortly after his political downfall, when still living in hiding, Kerensky emerged as a chronicler of the revolution. His first book, devoted to the Kornilov affair, appeared as early as 1918. In this, and in other works by Kerensky, there is a strong undertone of self-justification. Although they are irreplaceable historical sources, these grand self-portraits should be approached warily, and need to be scrutinized closely against other sources. This is particularly true of his final memoirs. Kerensky as a memoirist and as a historian not only passes over important facts in silence, he also rationalizes, modernizes and Westernizes the ideals and motives, the words and deeds of Kerensky the politician of 1917, distorting the picture of the 'true and beloved leader' of the February revolution.

Further reading

Works by A. F. Kerensky

Delo Kornilova (Moscow, Zadruga, 1918).

Izdaleka: Sbornik statei 1920–1921 (Paris, Russkoe izdatel'stvo Ia. Polovotskogo i ko., 1922).

'Gatchina', Sovremennye zapiski (Paris, 1922), pp. 147–80.

Catastrophe: Kerensky's Own Story of the Russian Revolution (New York, D. Appleton, 1927).

'Soyuzniki i Vremennoe Pravitel'stvo', Sovremennye zapiski 55 (Paris, 1934).

The Crucifixion of Liberty (New York, John Day, 1934).

Browder R. P. and Kerensky A. F., eds., The Russian Provisional Government, 1917: Documents, 3 vols. (Stanford, Stanford University Press, 1961–2).

Russia and History's Turning Point (London, Cassell, 1966).

Other works

Aleksandr Fedorovich Kerenskii (Po materialam Departamenta politsii) (Petrograd, tip. Akts. o-va 'Narod i Trud', 1917).

Abraham R., Kerensky: The First Love of the Revolution (London, Sidgwick and Jackson, 1987).

Fontenot M., 'Symbolism in Persuasion: The Influence of the Merezhkovskii Circle on the Rhetoric of Aleksandr Fedorovich Kerenskii', Canadian-American Slavic Studies 26, 1–3 (1992), pp. 241–65.

Golikov A. G., 'Fenomen Kerenskogo', Otechestvennaia istoriia 5 (1992), pp. 60–73.

Gorinov M. M., 'Kerenskii', in P. V. Volobuev et al., eds., Politicheskie deiateli Rossii, 1917. Biograficheskii slovar' (Moscow, Nauchnoe izdatel'stvo Bol'shaia rossiiskaia entsiklopediia, 1993), pp. 143–9.

Kolonitskii B. I., A. F. Kerenskii i krug Merezhkovskikh. 1917 god, in Petrogradskaia intelligentsiia v 1917 godu, otv. red. O. N. Znamenskii (Moscow-Leningrad, Izdanie Instituta istorii SSSR AN SSSR, 1990).

Sobolev G. L., compiler and author of introductory article, Aleksandr Kerenskii. Liubov' i nenavist' revoliutsii: Dnevniki, stat'i, ocherki i vospominaniia sovremennikov (Cheboksary, Izdatel'stvo Chuvashkogo universiteta, 1993).

Startsev V. I., 'Begstvo Kerenskogo', Voprosy istorii 11 (1966), pp. 204–6.

Startsev V. I., Krakh kerenshchiny (Leningrad, Izdatel'stvo 'Nauka', Leningradskoe otdelenie, 1982).

Sverchkov D. F., Kerenskii (Leningrad, Priboi, 1927).

Zoshchenko M., 'Besslavnyi konets', Literaturnyi sovremennik 1 (1938), pp. 223–63.

Lenin

ROBERT SERVICE

Lenin was born in 1870 in Simbirsk, the son of a province-level schools inspector; and in the October revolution, after a lifetime spent in revolutionary activity mainly abroad, he became the leader of the world's first socialist state. His real name was Vladimir Il'ich Ul'ianov; Lenin was the pseudonym he used only after the turn of the century. Within the ethnic compound of his ancestry were Kalmyk, Jewish and Swedish elements; but he was brought up as a Russian. He was an outstanding pupil at school (where his headmaster was the father of the future Minister-President of the Provisional Government, Aleksandr Kerensky), but his older brother, Aleksandr, was hanged for involvement with a populist-terrorist group in 1887. Quickly, young Vladimir too became engaged in revolutionary politics. Expelled for this activity from Kazan University, he took an external degree in law at St Petersburg University but continued to participate in revolutionary populist circles. He worked briefly as a lawyer before joining clandestine Marxist circles. He was arrested in 1895 and sent into Siberian exile. Upon release, he emigrated in 1900 and associated himself with Georgii Plekhanov – who was the founding figure in Russian Marxism – and co-edited the revolutionary journal *Iskra* ('The Spark'). At the Second Congress of the Russian Social-Democratic Labour Party (1903) there was a split, largely caused by the objections taken to Lenin's organizational manipulativeness. Lenin's group were the self-styled Majoritarians (*Bol'sheviki*); his opponents, who were led by his ex-colleagues on the *Iskra* board, called themselves the Minoritarians (*Men'sheviki*).

The split did not then become permanent, even though Lenin's factional polemics became notorious. In January 1905 both the Bolsheviks and the Mensheviks were caught unawares by the sudden revolutionary crisis in Russia. Lenin returned to St Petersburg from Switzerland only in November, and found it useful to sanction re-unification with the Mensheviks since he needed to restrain his own faction's radicals. The tsarist repression, however, was severe and effective. Lenin re-emigrated in

1907 and spent the next decade moving between Switzerland, Italy, France and Austrian Poland while attempting to maintain the *émigré* bodies of the Bolsheviks in good fettle. In 1912 he managed to hold a Bolshevik Party conference in Prague, a conference for which he claimed the right to act in the name of the entire Russian Social-Democratic Labour Party.

As a result of the February revolution he was able at last to return to Russia. By agreement with the German government he travelled by sealed train from Switzerland, where he had had to spend most of the First World War, across central Europe. Arriving in Petrograd on 3 April 1917, he revealed his 'April Theses', which called upon socialists to take power in Russia. In October his Bolshevik Party overthrew the Provisional Government through the agency of the Military-Revolutionary Committee of the Petrograd Soviet. This action was sanctioned by the Second Congress of Soviets, then in session in the capital. Lenin became Chairman of the Council of People's Commissars (*Sovnarkom*). From then until his death in January 1924 he was the most influential leader in the Soviet government and the Bolshevik Party.

His rise to prominence among Russian Marxists had its origins in some extraordinary ideas. He had always had a preoccupation with doctrinal matters. Like his mentor Plekhanov and his idols Marx and Engels, Lenin contended that no revolutionary movement was worth joining unless the scientific validity of its diagnosis of current politics and economics was demonstrable. He rejected the Russian populist notions about the virtues of the peasants, their land commune and their egalitarian traditions, as romantic sentimentality. In his earliest writings, especially his book *The Development of Capitalism in Russia* (1899), he sought to prove that capitalist techniques of production, finance and trade already dominated in the Russian empire. Such techniques, he asserted, prevailed not only in the urban but also in the rural sector. But at the same time he believed that capitalism would not fully flourish until such time as the tsarist regime had been eliminated. From this he concluded that the post-Romanov stage in Russia's development would be constituted by capitalist consolidation. Thereafter a further revolution – namely a socialist one – would be attempted.

Even more controversial was Lenin's booklet *What Is To Be Done?*. Published in Munich in 1902, it urged that the Russian Social-Democratic Labour Party's organization should be highly centralized and disciplined and that its members should agree to work actively on the party's behalf in the difficult conditions of tsarism. This was interpreted by his Marxist critics as a disguised reversion to those methods employed by Russian populist terrorists which were conventionally disowned by most Marxists. The Mensheviks were especially firm in their hostility to Lenin after the Second Party Congress in 1903.

This organizational dispute acquired a strategical dimension in 1905: Lenin urged that the workers should seek out the peasantry as their main revolutionary ally, whereas the Mensheviks proposed a coalition between the working class and the bourgeoisie. Furthermore, Lenin dropped any commitment to installing parliamentary democracy after tsarism's overthrow. Instead he called for 'a provisional revolutionary democratic dictatorship of the proletariat and the peasantry' – and he made no secret that such a dictatorship should, if necessary, undertake a mass terror in order to prevent counterrevolution. Even the peasants would not be free from firm state regulation. The land would be nationalized and peasant households were to be prevented from following any customary practices inimical to the expansion of a capitalist economy. Lenin claimed that he was simply applying Marxist principles to the developing circumstances of Russia; but his critics repeated that his proclivity for dictatorship and terror bore the imprint of Russian agrarian terrorism.

There was truth in the assertions of both sides. In some ways Lenin was a continuer of Marxist ideas, and undoubtedly he was an assiduous student of Marx, Engels and Plekhanov. In other ways, perhaps unconsciously, he resuscitated the arch-authoritarian legacy of the most violent thinkers in the Russian populist tradition.

What is clear is that Leninist thinking elicited a positive response among many Russian Social Democrats. No-one turned more young people to Bolshevism than he. Even after the introduction of a State Duma in 1906 there was harassment of the political parties, and this environment in Russia stimulated rebels to go to extremes in their ideas. Without this environment, Lenin would have remained an obscure scribbler studying arcane aspects of Marxist thought in Swiss libraries. It also helped his cause that he wrote in pungent prose. To be sure, his literary prowess should not be overstated; for he wrote the twentieth century's most thuddingly dull booklet on epistemology, *Materialism and Empiriocriticism* (1909), which touched the depths of inelegance. But what was wanted by Bolsheviks was not stylistic panache but a muscular assertiveness that would see off the intellectual attacks on Bolshevism. Lenin's style therefore was positively attractive to them.

Beyond question, Lenin was assertive. He had boundless confidence in his own abilities and in every situation he appeared to assume that only he had the correct policy and could supply the correct leadership. The notion of 'orthodoxy' was essential to his emergent image. He was a born leader. At no time did he ever give the glimmer of a sign that he doubted that he could guide the party to eventual victory.

There was an unpleasantly bossy side to his personality. Fellow Bolshevik leaders of intellectual distinction sooner or later fell out with him. The prime example was Aleksandr Bogdanov, who broke with Lenin in 1908. He expected his close associates to be bright and industrious but to constitute no challenge to him as Bolshevik leader. He was extremely combative whenever any of them crossed him – indeed, he was combative in virtually all situations. Bolsheviks before 1917, it should be mentioned, thought he overdid this. His propensity to discern items of grand principle in apparently innocuous details of philosophy or rural social organization mystified his otherwise adoring Russian followers. Many of them put it down to his having stayed too long in 'the Alpine air', which was a reference to the amount of time he spent far from his native land.

But this was not the only side to him. Lenin, unlike several of his rivals, had no airs and graces. Certainly he gave the impression that the revolution in Russia would go to the dogs if he did not somehow remain at the helm of his party: he sensed that he was a man of destiny. Yet he behaved modestly. He was an approachable, hard-working party boss, willing to lend a hand when one of his comrades got into a scrape. He met the trains of revolutionaries arriving in Switzerland, and even helped one of them with his part-time carting job.

Once in power, this side to his personality endured. He proved adept at keeping the juddering jealousies of Trotsky, Stalin and G. E. Zinoviev within acceptable limits. He was a punctilious chairman of *Sovnarkom* and the Party Central Committee and insisted that Bolsheviks should attend conscientiously to the practical tasks of government. Despite an initial diffidence about mass oratory as well as a rather schoolmasterly style of verbal delivery, Lenin came to be able to rouse crowds as efficiently as the party's firebrand speakers. He managed to communicate at several levels simultaneously. In every speech there was something not only for the sophisticated Marxist but also for the rank-and-file party member (who typically had not read Marx or Engels). These multi-faceted accomplishments of writer, theorist, organizer and speaker were crucial ingredients in his ability to lead a party.

For this to be appreciated it has to be understood how weak his position had been even within his own faction of the Russian Social-Democratic Labour Party immediately before the fall of the tsarist regime in February 1917. The Great War virtually cut him off from his usual Russian intermediaries – and he was fortunate that he was released from custody in the opening days of hostilities by the Habsburg police in August 1914. Returning to Switzerland, he was rarely able to give effective direction to his organizations in Russia.

Even if contact had been easier, however, it is doubtful that he would have dominated the Bolsheviks at that time. Among his problems were the eccentric policies he adopted. There were many Russian revolutionaries, including Mensheviks and Socialist Revolutionaries (SRs), who agreed with him in condemning those socialists across Europe who supported the war efforts of their respective governments. Such revolutionaries met in two conferences at Zimmerwald and Kienthal in Switzerland in 1915–16. But Lenin could not get on with them. He wanted no talk of an end to the war as the main aim. Instead he proposed the objective of turning the European 'imperialist war' between the two great military coalitions into a continental class war. His slogan was 'European civil war'. Equally unattractive to most of his fellow Bolsheviks was his call for them to espouse the defeat of Russia in the war. They thought it illogical to castigate all sides in the fighting as nefarious imperialists and then to argue that it would be better for German rather than Russian imperialism to triumph.

Yet the breakdown of the Romanov monarchy gave him an opportunity to re-impose himself. The German government had every reason to facilitate his return home and to subsidize his subsequent activities. Whatever else he stood for, he would predictably do damage to the Russian war effort.

And he came back to a Russia which offered a scenario of revolution different from what anyone, including himself, had anticipated. The anti-tsarist revolution had occurred in the course of the most intensely contested war in recorded history. The war was not going well for Russia on the eastern front. Economic disequilibrium was already beginning to have an effect. The administration inherited from the old regime was disintegrating and social dislocation was accelerating. Such a situation placed a premium on rapid political reactivity. Few parties came close to having the necessary flexibility. The Mensheviks and SRs were doctrinally inhibited from taking power even though they could easily have obtained it without much bloodshed. Even many Bolshevik leaders felt that they could not support an insurrectionary strategy despite the fact that traditional Bolshevism had expected tsarism to be supplanted by a temporary socialist dictatorship. Such a dictatorship had been projected to promulgate civic freedoms and to consolidate capitalism; but the liberal-led Provisional Government was already discharging this task. The need for insurrection seemed to have disappeared.

But into this environment of growing chaos leapt Lenin. Barely had he arrived at the Finland Station in Petrograd than he announced his 'April Theses', which demanded that power should be transferred as soon as possible to a socialist government.

He gave few arguments as to why traditional Bolshevism should be abandoned; he simply affirmed that the bourgeois stage of the revolution was already completed – an odd remark inasmuch as he had previously maintained that capitalism in Russia had to be thoroughly modernized before 'the socialist transition' should be attempted. And yet throughout the war he had also declared that Europe, including Russia, stood on the brink of a new era in the history of humanity: socialist revolution. He had added that advanced forms of capitalism were predominant in the financial and industrial sectors of the Russian imperial economy. In any case, traditional Bolshevism had always called for a provisional socialist dictatorship to be installed as soon as tsarism had been overthrown. The Bolshevik conception of a bourgeois-democratic revolution had always been a peculiar one.

Lenin spent most of his polemical energy on practical points. Above all, he declared that any failure by the country's socialists to seize power would result in Russia being handed over to counterrevolutionary forces. The war would be fought to the bitter end. Workers would lose their newly-won rights to form parties and trade unions without governmental interference.

Peasants would never get the land. The non-Russian nations and ethnic groups would suffer from official oppression.

Consequently he urged socialists to take power, and asserted that this could be done through the agency of the various mass organizations. Initially he trusted that it could be effected through the soviets; but when it became apparent that the Mensheviks and SRs might hold onto majorities inside them, he was determined to turn to other mass organizations. The main consideration for him was not procedural nicety but action. Popular support could be increased by slogans such as peace, bread, land and freedom. Specific policies could be developed to win over particular groups. To the industrial labour-force Lenin offered 'workers' control'. To the peasantry he offered 'land socialization'. To the non-Russians he offered 'national self-determination'. To everyone he offered a 'peace without annexations or indemnities'. Revolution in Russia, he affirmed, would be the first fire in a conflagration which would soon affect all Europe and North America.

These policies were acceptable to radical socialists, especially Bolsheviks, who were uneasy about the liberal-led Provisional Government after the February revolution. At the Seventh Conference of the Bolsheviks in late April he got his way. There were, of course, problems. The July Days led to a warrant being put out for his arrest and he fled to Finland. Returning on 10 October, however, he persuaded the Bolshevik Central Committee that the time had arrived for the seizure of power. After a little argument and only a little more organization, this plan was implemented to coincide with the opening session of the Second Congress of Soviets of Workers' and Soldiers' Deputies on 25 October 1917.

And so Lenin came to power as the result of an extraordinary general situation in the Russian empire. It is inconceivable that a *Sovnarkom* would have been created in times of peace or economic well-being. But he knew very well how to exploit this situation. His ideas were already radical and ruthless; they were also kept deliberately flexible. Bolsheviks – or at least most of them – would have responded enthusiastically to anyone who had proposed a clear-cut revolutionary strategy to get rid of the Provisional Government. But whether they would so readily have followed others exactly at the moment and in the way ordained by Lenin is much less certain. His personal insistence was of cardinal importance, then, in making the October revolution happen in October.

And his influence over events continued to be decisive. Several of these events were vital to the establishment of the kind of regime that the USSR became. In the first weeks after the October revolution, he steeled the Central Committee against compromise with the Mensheviks and the Socialist Revolutionaries. He also was the moving spirit behind the formation of the Cheka (Extraordinary Commission) in December 1917, and his was the wilfulness that left the Bolshevik Central Committee in no doubt that it was desirable to close down the Constituent Assembly. Without

Lenin, furthermore, it is by no means clear that the Bolsheviks would have signed the Treaty of Brest-Litovsk and avoided an invasion by the Central Powers in March 1918. Time after time he exerted a moulding impact upon his party's deliberations in the early months of 'Soviet power'.

In the civil war this impact was undiminished. He insisted that his party should take seriously the 'national question' and should build a federal structure for the socialist state. He also initiated various discussions on international socialist strategy in 1918–20.

It is hard to believe, too, that anyone but he could have convinced the Bolshevik Party about the urgent need to introduce the New Economic Policy in 1921. The hostility to a reversion to capitalistic tendencies in the economy was wide and deep among Bolsheviks. Lenin had to use all his forensic talent at the Tenth Party Congress in March 1921 to confirm the permission for the private grain trade to be resumed. This victory, however, was only provisional. Two months later at the Tenth Party Conference there were more severe questions for him; but again, albeit after a bruising debate, he protected the New Economic Policy. By then he had a reputation as a revolutionary who could react dynamically in dangerous situations. There had been doubters about his merits at every conjuncture. The October revolution and the Treaty of Brest-Litovsk had nearly lost him the position of leader of his party. But he had eventually triumphed; and had he been unable to introduce the New Economic Policy, the Soviet regime would almost certainly have fallen to popular revolts.

If Lenin had a major influence on policy, he also exercised formative authority over institutions. Together with Trotsky, he ensured that the *Sovnarkom* should exclude all but the Left SRs (and in summer 1918 he ruthlessly excluded them too). Having set up the Cheka, he ensured that its leader Feliks Dzerzhinskii was unencumbered by restraints in acting against counterrevolutionaries. Together with Stalin, moreover, he established the People's Commissariat for Nationality Affairs. And it was Lenin – more than anyone else – who made the arrangements for the founding congress of the Third (Communist) International (Comintern) in Petrograd in March 1919.

His greatest institutional innovation, however, was the inception of the one-party state. In fact he had no blueprint for this. The emergence of the party as the supreme agency of the Soviet state in 1918–19 happened more under the direct influence of Central Committee Secretary Iakov Sverdlov than of Lenin. But the ideological, political and organizational groundwork had been laid by Lenin. He it was who had written about leadership and dictatorship in 1902–05. He had ensured, too, that his party had come to share power with no other party within months of the October revolution. He had repeatedly had recourse to the Party Central Committee rather than *Sovnarkom* when he encountered resistance to his proposals. The creation of a one-party state stemmed from these earlier phenomena. Once created, moreover, the one-party state was held rigidly in place by Lenin; and he would allow not the slightest derogation from its precepts. At the end of the civil war, when he no longer needed Mensheviks and SRs to fight in the Red Army, he drove their organizations out of existence.

Lenin also had an influence at a still deeper level – at the level of attitudes. Several characteristically Bolshevik attitudes were affected by him. Throughout his career he stressed and re-stressed the need for leadership. He also urged that politics could not be a matter of sentimentality: Bolshevism, he emphasized, was 'scientific'. By this he meant that it was true and unchallengeable. He denied that any other political tendency had a claim to similar status. His thought incarnated intolerance. He advocated dictatorship and terror.

In *The State and Revolution* (written in 1917), furthermore, he went out of his way to disown any absolute commitment to either 'democracy' or 'freedom'. 'Democracy', according to Lenin, was simply a transitional form of state organization. The ultimate objective of Marxism was a society in which the state had 'withered away'. In such a society the principle would be enshrined: from each according to his talents, to each according to his needs. This would involve a total absence of exploitation or oppression. The very need for any state, even a democratic one, would have disappeared. Similarly he was unladen by a commitment to freedom. The point was to move Russia and Europe from capitalism through the dictatorship of the proletariat to communism. The means whereby this could be achieved did not necessarily have to involve freedom. Civic rights grounded in constitution, law and customary tolerance were a matter of indifference to Lenin. This ideological heritage left a deep imprint upon Bolshevik consciousness.

And yet the influence should not be exaggerated. Lenin did not invent most of these attitudes for Russian revolutionaries. They pre-dated him. The populist terrorists in the 1860s–1880s had developed many of them; and they were not entirely absent from certain trends in European nineteenth-century socialism and anarchism. Furthermore, several of the Russian Marxists did not need Lenin to resuscitate this tradition for them. It had not been Lenin but Plekhanov who had first pleaded the case for scientific, anti-sentimental and dictatorial policies. And several of Lenin's contemporaries – Trotsky comes immediately to mind – were developing the tradition at the same time as him. Lenin had the greatest but not the sole influence.

Nor should we overstate the scope of Lenin's influence in other ways. It must always be taken into account that Lenin had little regular direct contact with Russia before April 1917. He emigrated in 1900 and spent less than two further years – 1905 to 1907 – in Russia. His influence, therefore, was confined to what he could achieve by his journalism, his correspondence, his face-to-face meetings with visitors from Russia and his speeches at occasional congresses. Even in 1917 his contact with Bolsheviks and the rest of society was not uninterrupted. Arriving in Petrograd in early April, he fled again in early July and returned to a fitful, clandestine presence in the capital only in mid-October. Admittedly he wrote regularly for *Pravda* ('The Truth'), but the circulation of this central party newspaper was seldom more than 90,000 copies. No photographs of him were published, no film appeared. His appearances at mass meetings were rare.

Admittedly, his fame rose steeply after the October revolution. Nevertheless, knowledge about him was not universal. Held up by a gang of robbers in a Moscow street in 1919, he was unrecognized even though he gave them his name – and the local district soviet bureaucrats did not believe that he was who he said he was either. It was only during the period of the New Economic Policy that his plans and activities became known truly widely.

Nor must it be forgotten that even those people – mainly Bolshevik leaders and activists – who were acquainted with Lenin and Leninism did not always accept his demands. Recurrently in 1917 he met opposition to his policies, and this continued after the October revolution. On most questions of importance to him he got his way. But he paid the price of allowing others to have their head on other questions. He had to handle the Bolshevik Party carefully if he was to maintain his leadership and hold his party to policies that would keep them in power. Furthermore, much of what was done by the Bolsheviks resulted from their collective will more than from the specific intervention of Lenin. The administrative machinery of government and party during the civil war was ramshackle. Communications were maintained only faultily, and a huge responsibility was laid upon local political bodies to show initiative. It is very far from having been the case that Lenin simply had to express an opinion for it to be implemented automatically.

Thus he had to deal with the Politburo, the Central Committee and the successive party congresses and conferences with finesse; and he had to see off overt opposition in the form of the Left Communists, the Military Opposition, the Democratic Centralists, the Workers' Opposition and the various factions hostile to him in the trade-union controversy. He also had to tread warily in respect of the opinions of Bolsheviks who were generally in agreement with him.

He was aware that his grip on the leadership had to be constantly reinforced. Having always been prone to headaches and insomnia, he suffered a series of minor strokes in adulthood. By the winter of 1921–2 he was having to take time off political work and in May 1922 he had a major stroke. At first he relied upon Stalin, the Central Committee General Secretary, to act as a conduit to the central party leadership. But quickly the two men fell out. Stalin wished to engorge the other Soviet republics established in 1919–21 into the existing Russian Soviet Federated Socialist Republic (RSFSR), whereas Lenin suggested the formation of a federal Union of Soviet Socialist Republics (USSR). To Lenin's horror, Stalin was also willing to countenance a partial relaxation of the state foreign-trade monopoly; and Stalin annoyed him, too, by failing to act against the bureaucratic tendencies both in the Party Central Committee Secretariat and in the Workers' and Peasants' Inspectorate.

Becoming fit enough to resume a modicum of public activity, Lenin compelled Stalin to drop the plan to enlarge the RSFSR at the expense of the other Soviet republics. He also allied himself with Trotsky on the question of the state foreign-trade monopoly, and they beat Stalin in December 'without having to fire a single shot'. Lenin wrote what became known as his political testament in the winter of 1922–3 and called for the removal of Stalin from the General Secretaryship: 'He is too crude.'

The dispute between Lenin and Stalin has been romanticized into a clash between two fundamentally different attitudes to revolution. But Lenin did not want to dismantle the one-party, one-ideology state. He did not wish to democratize the internal life of the party. He did not countenance strict adherence to constitutional and legal propriety. He did not intend to offer the freedom of national self-determination. Even in calling for Stalin's removal from the General Secretaryship, he was not campaigning for Stalin's elimination from Soviet public life. Differences certainly existed between Lenin and Stalin, and undoubtedly the subsequent history of the USSR would have been different if Lenin had not died when he did. It is hard to imagine him clambering up to quite the scale of violence applied by Stalin to the peasantry in the years of mass collectivization. It is virtually inconceivable that Lenin would have wiped out the cadres from party, government, army, economy and intelligentsia as Stalin did in 1937–8. Nevertheless, Lenin's USSR would have been no haven for a democratic, humanitarian socialism.

Of equal importance is the fact that the precedents and instrumentalities of later horrors were placed at Stalin's disposal by the period of Lenin's rule. Lenin had laid the foundations of dictatorship and lawlessness. Lenin had consolidated the principle of state penetration of the whole society, its economy and its culture. Lenin had practised terror and advocated revolutionary amoralism. His widow, N. K. Krupskaia, opined that had he survived his fatal heart attack in January 1924, Lenin would have ended his days in one of Stalin's jails. If so, he could hardly have held himself free from blame for such a misfortune: he himself was the creator of the regime that resorted to Stalinist barbarism.

This, however, does not exhaust the record of Lenin's impact. Leninism, after all, was applied not only in Russia but – at its farthest extent by the mid-1980s – across an area that amounted to well over a third of the entire globe. In some countries it succeeded by dint of local revolutionary movements. In others it was imported by foreign armies. But in most countries it found political, economic and cultural material to work with. Invented in Russia, Leninism provided broadly deployable methods and doctrine of revolution. It offered, or at least appeared to offer, a realistic alternative to a capitalist world order that had no fundamental answer to many questions of economic exploitation, political oppression and national discrimination.

Such questions still require to be answered six years after the dismantling of the USSR, the CPSU and Soviet Marxism-Leninism. Not for nothing have the remains of Lenin's corpse been allowed to rest in the marble mausoleum outside the Kremlin wall on Red Square.

Further reading

Daniels R. V., *The Conscience of the Revolution: Communist Opposition in Soviet Russia* (Cambridge MA, Harvard University Press, 1960).

Harding N., *Lenin's Political Thought,* 2 vols. (London, Macmillan, 1977, 1981).

Lewin M., *Lenin's Last Struggle* (London, Faber, 1969).

Polan A., *Lenin and the End of Politics* (London, 1984).

Rigby T. H., *Lenin's Government: Sovnarkom 1917–1922* (Cambridge, Cambridge University Press, 1979).

Schapiro L., *The Communist Party of the Soviet Union* (London, Methuen, 1970).

Service R., *Lenin: A Political Life,* 3 vols. (London, Macmillan, 1985–95).

Martov

ISRAEL GETZLER

Iulii Osipovich Martov (1873–1923) returned to Russia from Switzerland on 9 May 1917, virtually the last socialist leader to do so, by means of the same controversial 'sealed train' procedure used by Lenin at the end of March. Indeed, the idea for the arrangement whereby Russian revolutionaries would be exchanged for interned German civilians had been Martov's, not Lenin's; yet while Lenin had eagerly taken advantage of the German offer, Martov wasted six precious weeks attempting to persuade his party comrades, the leaders of the Petrograd Soviet, to secure the Provisional Government's sanction. The Petrograd Menshevik leaders' less than lukewarm response to his urgent cables and letters and their eventual vetoing of the deal boded ill for Martov's future leadership.

That leadership had rested on his role as founder and principal ideologist of the Menshevik Party, on his intellectual brilliance and moral stature, and on the trust, bordering on love, which he inspired – but certainly not on his organizational talents and political skills. For those, he relied on Fedor Dan, his brother-in-law and the Menshevik Party's 'chief of staff'.

Martov's leadership of the fractious and pluralist Menshevik Party had already been eroded during the war when the party split into 'internationalists' and a variety of 'defencists'. Martov, a founder and pillar of the Zimmerwald peace movement, now stood out as a passionate spokesman of internationalism and as an acerbic critic of the G. V. Plekhanov and A. N. Potresov varieties of defencism. His conciliatory efforts to keep the party together, notably his adamant refusal to disown his defencist comrades, proved of no avail. In the aftermath of the February revolution, it fell to the charismatic and less internationalist I. G. Tsereteli to unite the large majority of Mensheviks on a compromise platform of 'revolutionary defencism'. Worse still, Tsereteli and his associates Dan, M. I. Skobelev and N. S. Chkheidze cavalierly ignored Martov's urgent cable from Copenhagen on 1 May – 'any participation in a coalition government is impermissible' – and confronted him with a *fait accompli*, by joining the Provisional Government just days before his return.

'Something irreparable has happened', he reported to his close friend Nadezhda Kristi on 22 May:

> Our comrades who, since the beginning of the revolution, have drifted from the Zimmerwald line into a very questionable mishmash of internationalism and the duty to 'defend the revolution' on the one hand, and, on the other, 'loyalty to the Allies', have committed the ultimate stupidity: they have joined the government on the basis of a simple promise that the question of a revision of the war's aims will be raised with the Allies, whereas what they should have insisted on was that the government raise the question of immediate peace.

Worse still, when he lashed out at Tsereteli and the Menshevik leadership at the All-Russian Menshevik Conference in May for joining the government, pandemonium broke loose and he was brutally shouted down.

Had Martov, like Lenin, arrived back early in April, he would have had at least a fighting chance of challenging Tsereteli's 'political line' and of preventing his comrades from joining the government: both the Petrograd and Moscow Menshevik party organizations were dead set against coalition, as were the Georgian Mensheviks led by Noe Zhordania. Tsereteli and Dan, who in the end tilted the balance in favour of coalition, were themselves in doubt. Moreover, entry into coalition was against long-accepted Menshevik doctrine and the self-denying ordinance which prescribed social-democratic abstention from power in Russia's bourgeois revolution, a position Martov was fully convinced had been 'brilliantly confirmed' by the February revolution in contrast to the flawed ideas of Lenin and Trotsky.

Martov's dilemma now was whether to split the party, as his Petrograd supporters led by Iurii Larin urged, or to remain within it as the provincial delegates demanded. He decided on something in between: to form an opposition faction of Menshevik-Internationalists within the party in the hope that it could reconvert the revolutionary-defencist majority in time for the Menshevik congress planned for late July, when Tsereteli had pledged that 'all questions will be under review again'.

A harsher reception and a final break with Tsereteli awaited Martov at the First Congress of Soviets in June, where his faction of Menshevik-Internationalists numbered only 35 out of the total 1,090 delegates. At the very outset, Martov launched his protest against the deportation of Robert Grimm (the Zimmerwald secretary) for being implicated in German peace offers. Seething with anger, he charged Tsereteli with supporting Grimm's deportation and having high-handedly gone behind the back of the Executive Committee of the Petrograd Soviet to whom he was responsible. This attack, as Martov soon found out, was widely seen as little less than *lèse-majesté* and produced an immediate uproar in which he was angrily shouted down. As he wrote to Kristi, he now realized that 'for the majority of the assembly names such as Aksel'rod and Martov have no meaning', while 'our internationalist position is to them that very same Bolshevism which they understand as "separate peace" and "civil war"'.

From then on, Martov became a persistent critic of Tsereteli's policies, especially on coalitionism and on peace and war. As the government prepared for the June offensive, Martov's alternative was an ultimatum to the Allies to start peace negotiations. He fiercely denounced the offensive which to him meant that Russia, effectively out of the hostilities since March, would now voluntarily go back into a war that was bound to end 'in Sedan'.

It took Martov a long time to abandon his taboo on power. In response to a letter from Kristi in April 1917, in which she raised the question of a socialist 'seizure of power', he explained that even in Russia's present revolutionary situation, where a proletarian assumption of power was feasible because it would be supported by the peasantry and by the peasant soldiers, it was still undesirable.

> The peasants may give their support to the seizure of power by socialists, but they will expect from them such things as an end to their poverty together with the preservation of their smallholdings , and a 'war to the finish', etc, etc. Thus such an adventure would either end in a tragic *Krach* when they wake up to it that they have made a mistake, or, more likely, in our doing what Engels termed 'the work of another class'.

The role of the socialists had to remain one of implacably critical opposition. As late as June, Martov was still demanding the recall of the socialist ministers from the coalition government. Then came the government crisis caused by the walkout of the Kadet ministers on 2 July. This, Martov concluded, meant that 'the entire organized bourgeoisie had walked out on state power':

> History demands that we take power into our own hands and I believe that the entire revolutionary democracy of Russia will support us. That government of the democracy will take Russia to the Constituent Assembly, but, above all, it will take Russia out of the war which is strangling the revolution and its achievements.

But the July Days drowned out Martov's call for a democratic, popular-front type of government with the Bolshevik war-cry 'All Power to the Soviets!' Those demonstrations, in turn, gave Tsereteli the opportunity to dismiss Martov's proposal on the grounds that it represented a major change in policy over which the provincial soviets must be consulted. Meanwhile, Kerensky was able to form a second coalition government, and, in Martov's view, on worse terms than the first: its socialist ministers were no longer to be responsible to the soviets.

By mid-August, Martov realized that he had failed to convert the Menshevik majority. At the so-called (August) Unification Congress one-third of the delegates supported him, but two-thirds had moved to the right, towards class collaboration or, in Tsereteli's favourite expression, 'cooperation with the living forces of the country'. This was highlighted at the State Conference on 15 August when, in response to the widely applauded conciliatory speech of Aleksandr Bublikov, leader of the industrialists, Tsereteli and Bublikov 'shook hands amidst a resounding ovation'.

Martov's remaining in the Menshevik Party while fiercely criticizing its leadership and exposing its policies both played into the hands of the Bolsheviks and boomeranged on his own Menshevik-Internationalist faction. Many of the faction's Petrograd members went with Larin when he joined the Bolsheviks in late August – he claimed to have taken 1,000 workers with him – in protest, as Martov later put it, 'against our coexistence with the defencists'.

If Martov's conception of a 'government of the democracy' ever had any chance of being accepted it was in mid-September in the wider forum of the Democratic Conference, whose predominant mood was very much against coalition with the Kadets. Martov, the sharpest critic of coalitionism, was elected as spokesman of the majority both of the Menshevik faction (Tsereteli was elected spokesman of the minority) and of the Soviet *curia* (Dan was spokesman of the minority). Leading Bolshevik spokesmen, such as L. B. Kamenev, were pledged not to overthrow a 'homogeneous democratic ministry', should one emerge, even after Lenin, from his hiding place in Finland, sent two letters to prod the party into readying itself for the seizure of power.

That anti-coalition mood was initially translated into narrow majorities voting against coalition with the Kadets, and somewhat more comfortable majorities voting for the principle of coalition in the abstract. Martov implored delegates to vote for coalition, but without the Kadets, if only to serve as a directive for the formation of a new government. But the final resolution in that spirit was roundly defeated (813 to 183 with 80 abstentions) by the combined vote of the Bolsheviks and the entire centre and right wing. In effect, Tsereteli had again thwarted Martov, this time by his control of the Central Executive Committee of Soviets which had given the cooperatives and the municipalities – known to favour coalition with the Kadets – more than their fair share of representation.

When the Second All-Russian Congress of Soviets opened on 25 October, Martov – on behalf of the Menshevik-Internationalists and the Jewish Workers' Party, Poalei Tsion – proposed that the first item on the agenda be 'the question of the peaceful resolution of the crisis' created by the Bolshevik insurrection. The proposal was greeted with stormy applause by the entire congress, a majority of whose delegates understood 'All Power to the Soviets!' to mean a broadly based government of the soviet parties and not a narrow Bolshevik government. A. V. Lunacharsky, on behalf of the Bolshevik faction, declared that the Bolsheviks had no objections. Martov's proposal was passed unanimously. At that crucial moment, Lev Khinchuk, on behalf of the Mensheviks, read out a declaration roundly denouncing the 'Bolshevik military conspiracy', echoed by Mikhail Gendelman, on behalf of the SRs, and Genrikh Erlikh, on behalf of the Bundists. Then, to the catcalls of the Bolsheviks, they all stalked out of the hall, as much in fury, as Martov later remarked, as out of conviction that 'victorious Lenin could not last more than three days, not even in Petrograd'. This was a blow to Martov who had entreated them 'not to walk out of the congress' but to stand their ground and 'give Lenin a run for his money'. When he then urged the formation of an all-socialist commission to negotiate the establishment of a 'government of the democracy', Trotsky pounced on the walk-out to neutralize the embarrassing proposal:

Now, when our insurrection is victorious, you tell us: renounce your victory, make concessions, compromise; with whom, I ask, with whom ought we to compromise? With those wretched groups who have walked out or who are making this proposal? ... No! No compromise is possible here! To those who have walked out, and to those who make such proposals, we must say: you are pitiful isolated individuals; you are bankrupts; your role is played out; go where you belong from now on – into the dustbin of history!

'Then we shall leave!' Martov shouted amidst the applause which greeted Trotsky's speech, and so saying, he too walked out accompanied by his supporters.

At the end of October, Martov, together with Rafail Abramovich, made further attempts to negotiate a broadly based socialist government. But on 2 November Lenin cracked the whip: there would be no more negotiations, which had only been tolerated as 'a diplomatic cover for military action'. To make things worse for Martov, the Left SRs, who had so far held out against Lenin's invitation to join the Council of People's Commissars (*Sovnarkom*) unless it co-opted representatives of all soviet parties, joined it in December as junior partners and basically on Bolshevik terms. This put an end to Martov's hopes that, with the help of the moderate Bolsheviks and the Left SRs, it would still be possible to prevent the consolidation of a Bolshevik minority dictatorship. He now became the leader of the Mensheviks in opposition to the Bolshevik regime.

Having lost both his party and his closest ally, Dan, to Tsereteli, Martov was no match for the major political leaders of 1917, P. N. Miliukov, Kerensky, Tsereteli and, in the end, Trotsky and Lenin. These were charismatic figures, great orators and consummate politicians, hell-bent on winning power and devoid of any doubt as to the wisdom of their policies, *and* they had political parties to back them up. Martov, on the other hand, was indifferent to personal power, instead believing in and practising collective leadership; he was too honest, decent and impulsive to dissimulate. He could be brilliant and fascinating as a speaker in smaller assemblies, but not in the mass meetings of 1905 and 1917. His superb intelligence and his great talent as a writer were not of great use to him in 1917 when he had no newspaper under his control and, until late in September, had to rely on the hospitality of *Novaia zhizn'* ('New Life') run by Maksim Gorky and N. N. Sukhanov. His loyalty to his friends, his reliance on and trust in political colleagues, and his fairness even to political enemies such as the Bolsheviks under persecution in the post-July Days period, which totally ignored all political expediency, were no more political assets than was his great belief in the power of argument and persuasion. While all his virtues make him one of the most attractive and loved figures of the Russian revolutionary movement and of European socialism, they did not equip him for political leadership in 1917.

Still, it can be argued that Martov's broadly based 'government of the democracy' – some sort of popular-front government to which he only came round as late as the July Days – made far better sense than Tsereteli's single-minded and inflexible pursuit of cooperation with the so-called 'living forces of the country' which produced one coalition government after another marked by 'organized, collective inactivity'. It can also be argued that Martov's demand for an active peace policy including an ultimatum to the Allies would at least have prevented the disastrous Kerensky offensive of June/July 1917, even if it could not have taken Russia out of the war – for no-one, not even Lenin, would have dared to advocate a separate peace.

Martov's failure to lead his party or even influence its policies in 1917 contrasts sharply with his firm leadership of the Mensheviks in opposition (until the end of 1920) and in exile (until his death on 4 April 1923), and the general acceptance by his party of his complex but consistent two-pronged (*dvuedinaia*) semi-loyal, semi-implacable policy *vis-à-vis* the Bolshevik dictatorship. One major reason for Martov's subsequent ascendancy was the stark fact that it was a solidly beaten party and a much chastened revolutionary-defencist majority led by Dan that rallied to him at the Extraordinary Congress of the Menshevik Party early in December 1917. Moreover, his opposition to and fierce critique of the Bolsheviks' headlong plunge into socialism was fully in tune with the Mensheviks' understanding of the 'bourgeois' limitations of the Russian revolution and their abhorrence of minority dictatorship and the terror. His dual policy of supporting the Bolsheviks in the struggle against White restoration and foreign intervention while indicting and exposing the terrorist dictatorship, made good sense to those who could neither bring themselves to join the Whites nor throw in their lot with the Bolsheviks. Led by Martov they sought desperately to find a place for themselves as an opposition within the Soviet system which, willy-nilly, they accepted 'as a fact of life though not in principle'.

When a small right wing, including Aleksandr Potresov and Vladimir Levitskii (Martov's youngest brother), joined the anti-Bolshevik Union for the Regeneration of Russia, the Committee of Members of the Constituent Assembly (*Komuch*) and other anti-Bolshevik coalitions, they were given short shrift by Martov and expelled from the party. Along with Dan,

Abramovich, and the majority of Mensheviks, Martov remained convinced that a violent overthrow of the Bolshevik regime would not be followed by the victory of liberal-bourgeois or social democracy but by counterrevolution. That outcome he feared even more than he detested Bolshevism, which he and other Mensheviks regarded as not yet beyond redemption.

Even after 1920, when Martov had become the leader of a party that was to all intents and purposes in exile, the Mensheviks continued to accept his revised dual policy, now far more implacable and far less loyal. His last major article, 'Our Platform', enjoined his party not only to keep clear of all anti-Bolshevik coalitions but also to shun the Bolshevik regime – which was in danger of degenerating even further into a Caesarist–Bonapartist dictatorship – while doing its best to prevent the Comintern from taking over the socialist parties of the West. Martov's 'line of social democracy' became, after his death, the guideline not only of the Mensheviks but also of the Labour and Socialist International which, at its foundation congress in May 1923, adopted a two-pronged Menshevik resolution which determined its attitude to the Soviet Union until the Nazi–Soviet pact of August 1939.

Martov's success as leader of his party in opposition and in exile, and his lasting influence on the Mensheviks and on the Labour and Socialist International, owed much to his personifying and expressing more than any other socialist leader that mixture of realism, despair and moral-humanitarian commitment with which Menshevism and European social democracy confronted the Bolshevik perversion of the Russian revolution. Small wonder that so many recognized in Martov the true conscience of the Russian revolution.

Further reading

'Iz lichnoi perepiski Iu. O. Martova s N. S. Kristi', in Z. Galili and A. P. Nenarokov, eds., *Men'sheviki v 1917 godu*, vol. 1 (Moscow, 1994), pp. 242–50, 456–9, 588–91.

Aronson G., et al., eds., *Martov i ego blizkie* (New York, 1959).

Getzler I., *Martov: A Political Biography of a Russian Social Democrat* (Cambridge and Melbourne, Cambridge University Press, 1967).

Martov I. O., *Zapiski Sotsial-demokrata* (Cambridge MA, Oriental Research Partners, 1978).

[This article is based on research that was first published in *The Slavonic and East European Review* 72, 3 (July 1994). Copyright 1994, University of London. All rights reserved.]

Miliukov

RAYMOND PEARSON

Entering 1917 as the most influential opposition politician in the tsarist empire, Pavel Miliukov (1859–1943) became the greatest political casualty of the Russian revolutionary era of 1917–21. In the West, Miliukov's reputation as the 'spokesman for imperial Russia's nascent liberal movement' earned a contemporary and retrospective esteem which has only comparatively recently come under critical scrutiny. Within Russia and later among the Russian *émigré* diaspora, Miliukov's obsessive and insatiable appetite for politics attracted jealous criticism from party colleagues as well as vituperative attack from political rivals to the left and right, earning him only grudging respect as an indefatigable fighter-in-defeat. Once dismissed as the 'chief ideologist of the Russian imperialist bourgeoisie' by Soviet historiography, Miliukov has enjoyed an unexpected rehabilitation under glasnost: historically embodying an alternative to both tsarism and Bolshevism in the crucial years 1917–21, he has been represented as the tragically vanquished champion of a constitutional 'middle road' whose European orientation and liberal principles have become more relevant than ever before in the post-Soviet Russia of the 1990s.

Born on 15 January 1859, the son of a Moscow municipal architect, Pavel Nikolaevich Miliukov became an archetypal member of the Russian intelligentsia, studying at Moscow University from 1877 to 1882. Spending his formative years weathering the shift in political climate from the reforming era of Alexander II to the reactionary era of Alexander III, Miliukov became assistant professor in history at Moscow University through the dispiriting years from 1886 to 1894. Surviving the unpredictable patronage of Vasilii Kliuchevskii, the doyen of Russian historians, he successfully defended his master's dissertation in 1892 and produced a series of valuable historical studies in the later 1890s. Increasingly drawn to oppositional politics, however, Miliukov was deprived of his university post and sentenced to internal exile in Riazan for sympathy with student demonstrations in 1895–7. Barred from domestic teaching, he took up positions abroad, notably at the University of Sofia in Bulgaria, where he developed his interest in Russia's relations with the smaller Slav states of the Balkans. On the eve of the new century, the thwarted 40-year-old Miliukov was experiencing a career blockage which only reinforced the commitment to oppositional politics which had earlier blighted his otherwise promising academic prospects.

Over the first five years of the twentieth century, Miliukov completed his conversion from professional academic to oppositional politician through the classic nexus of 'creed' (ideological conviction), 'need' (tsarist harassment) and 'greed' (career frustration). Having already served his apprenticeship in the craft of political journalism, in 1902 he co-founded and contributed regularly to *Osvobozhdenie* ('Liberation'), the Stuttgart-published journal which promoted the establishment of the Union of Liberation in 1903–04, trying in particular to attract cautious and moderate zemstvo opinion to the radical banner. Always an admirer of the liberal West and still without regular gainful employment, Miliukov spent much of the 1903–04 period abroad, especially enjoying lecture tours in the USA to publicize the emerging Russian liberal cause.

In the spring of the turning-point year of 1905, he returned from America to join the campaign against a tsarist establishment reeling from defeat in the Russo-Japanese War and erupting social discontent, and became chairman of the newly established Union of Unions, a militant coalition of professional associations. By October 1905, he was the prime mover in the foundation of the Constitutional-Democratic (or Kadet) Party, formed by an expedient alliance of zemstvo gentry and urban professionals. Elected onto the central committee of the Kadet Party at its Foundation Congress, Miliukov was soon appointed joint editor of the new Kadet daily newspaper *Rech'* ('Speech').

Although 1906 was a year of first triumph and then disaster for the Kadet Party, Miliukov's career featured a degree of good fortune lacking in the past. He took overall responsibility for the party's electoral campaign for the First Duma, elected in April 1906, and deserved much of the credit for a Kadet triumph at the polls which made the party by far the largest 'faction' within the Duma. Although excluded from standing as a candidate on a residence technicality, Miliukov contrived both to 'rule the Duma from the buffet-room' and to represent the Duma in clandestine negotiations with the tsarist government for a 'Duma Ministry'.

When an impasse in relations between the radical Duma and resurgent tsarist regime resulted in the dissolution of the First Duma in July 1906, Miliukov was a leading advocate of the deputies decamping to Vyborg in Finland to issue a parliamentary challenge to the government. Although drafting the 'Vyborg Appeal' threatening 'not a kopek to the treasury, not a soldier to the army', Miliukov could not legally join Kadet deputies in signing the act of defiance. As a consequence, when the government prosecuted the Vyborg signatories for sedition, securing a three-month prison sentence and a lifetime suspension of political rights for the accused, Miliukov escaped punishment. While nearly the entire first generation of Kadet leaders was now barred from standing for future Dumas, Miliukov almost alone among his colleagues not only survived but could capitalize on the Kadet disaster of summer 1906: the fortuitous and sole 'beneficiary of Vyborg' among all the 'victims of Vyborg', Miliukov was set to dominate the Kadet faction in all subsequent Dumas through until 1917 itself.

Although again debarred from standing for the brief Second Duma in 1907, Miliukov was elected to lead the numerically reduced Kadet faction in the Third Duma (1907–12) and Fourth Duma (1912–17). Throughout this decade, Miliukov's principal tasks were to attempt to reconcile the warring left and right wings of the Kadet Party, and to maintain Kadet morale in an era of tsarist revanche. Right-wingers in the party blamed Miliukov for making the Vyborg Appeal too radical, especially as its author had escaped unscathed after leading his comrades into political oblivion. Left-wingers accused Miliukov of too readily settling for what amounted to collaboration with the tsarist administration headed by Petr Stolypin and his electorally fixed Third and Fourth Dumas. Though under constant sniping from both Kadet wings, the 'great conciliator' steered a middle course of measured compromise between the liberal ideals of 1905 and the harsh realities of tsarist recovery, steadily building up his authority, even indispensability within the party.

The accusation of accommodationism or collaborationism levelled against Miliukov, especially after his speech in London in 1909 identifying himself as belonging 'to His Majesty's Opposition, not to the opposition to His Majesty', became even more marked with Russia's entry into the First World War. From the instant the war was announced, Miliukov demanded a suspension of politics and unconditional *union sacrée* of government and society behind the Russian war effort. Even when military disaster rocked Russian society in mid-1915, the sole political recourse countenanced by Miliukov was the creation of a Progressive Bloc composed of the moderate factions of the Fourth Duma, which made only modest requests of tsarist government, principally 'a ministry enjoying the confidence of the public', in return for confirmation of full backing.

By 1916, Miliukov's 'patriotic defencism' was laying him open to attack as the conscious or unwitting stooge of a tsarist regime whose unpopularity was approaching crisis point. Aware of the collapse in his political credibility outside and inside the Kadet Party, Miliukov chose to assert his independence by a speech in the Duma on 1 November 1916 in which a succession of criticisms of the tsarist government were each followed by the rhetorical question 'Is this stupidity or treason?' Miliukov was (much later) to claim that his unstated answer was actually 'stupidity' but the almost hysterical public reaction was to presume guilt to a charge of 'treason'. Although alarmed by the swell of populist applause, Miliukov was content to bask in his new-found reputation (and later in 1917 to accept credit for launching what was retrospectively claimed by the Kadets as the 'storm-signal of the Russian revolution').

In February 1917 'the central figure of bourgeois Russia' proved the most reluctant of revolutionaries. Under mounting pressure from the re-established Petrograd Soviet but in mortal dread of tsarist repression, Miliukov organized from members of the Duma a Provisional Committee 'to restore order', a body cautiously designated so as to offer tsarism no pretext for inflicting another 'Vyborg' on the liberal cause. Miliukov then accepted the necessity of a Provisional Government to act as a caretaker administration until the convening of a democratic Constituent Assembly. As undisputed 'king-maker' of a Provisional Government whose cabinet was recruited from the Progressive Bloc, Miliukov included Aleksandr Kerensky out of political tokenism, excluded his long-time rival, the Duma President Mikhail Rodzianko, and reserved for himself the prestigious post of Foreign Minister.

When Tsar Nicholas II abdicated in favour of his younger brother, Miliukov attempted to persuade Grand Duke Mikhail to accept the crown as a constitutional monarch until the Constituent Assembly made a definitive decision about the constitution of Russia. Mikhail, however, preferred the advice of Rodzianko and Kerensky, declining the crown until and unless offered by the Constituent Assembly. Although no monarchist by conviction, Miliukov was so dismayed by what he regarded as this cowardly and crass tactical blunder that he had to be dissuaded from resigning from the Provisional Government by a Kadet Party delegation.

The *éminence grise* of the Provisional Government was all too soon in difficulties. His lengthy Duma experience had been training for parliamentary opposition, not for the rough-and-tumble of executive politics in revolutionary 1917. On 18 April, Miliukov dispatched a formal diplomatic 'note' to Russia's allies reaffirming Russia's commitment to 'war until final victory', the price of which was the annexation of Ottoman territories already agreed in secret treaties contracted by the tsarist government, which would effectively convert the Black Sea into a Russian lake. A Soviet-orchestrated public outcry at the 'tsarist imperialism' of 'Miliukov-Dardanel'skii' created an 'April Crisis' which could only be resolved by the forced resignation of Miliukov on 2 May and a reconstitution of the Provisional Government involving the shedding of the right-wing members of its cabinet in favour of the political left.

Back in opposition after only two months in ministerial office, a humiliated Miliukov attempted to counter the leftward drift of the coalition Provisional Government. The triumphalist unity with which the Kadets greeted the February revolution came under intolerable strain: the right-wingers within the party gained the ascendancy and Miliukov put up no resistance to the rightward surge of Kadet politics, withdrawing all remaining Kadets from the Provisional Government in July. His privilege-and-property prevarication over such burning contemporary issues as autonomy for the non-Russians, redistribution of the land to the peasantry and the elections to the Constituent Assembly provoked widespread disillusionment. When the Kornilov Affair rocked the Provisional Government in August–September 1917, Miliukov and the Kadets were universally believed to back, and even to have instigated, the army high command's commitment to political counterrevolution.

Whatever the precise degree of Kadet complicity in the failed Kornilov coup, Miliukov was now tarred with a reactionary brush and, after the Petrograd coup of October 1917, was targeted as an enemy of the new Bolshevik regime. In fear of reprisals which indeed claimed the lives of other Kadet leaders in 1917 and early 1918, Miliukov quit Petrograd for the south of Russia to head the Political Council attached to the White Volunteer Army commanded by General Alekseev, lobbying tirelessly for greater Allied intervention to oust the Bolshevik regime. In early summer 1918, in a policy turnabout whose naked desperation was matched only by its consummately bad timing, Miliukov publicly converted to a so-called 'German orientation': given the unwillingness or incapacity of the French, British and American Allies to dislodge Bolshevism, the greater military force of Germany must be harnessed to the anti-Bolshevik crusade. No sooner had the 'German orientation' been announced, creating consternation among all left Kadets and then schism in the party, than the Allied defeat of the German spring offensive on the western front confirmed that Germany was about to lose the First World War.

Having switched from Russian super-patriot to German collaborator in the space of a single year, a discredited Miliukov emigrated via Kiev and Jassy to Paris to organize international and Russian *émigré* support for the White movement. With his recent unconsummated affair with Germany alienating all Allied governments, he was in reality an embarrassment to the Whites, which did not prevent or inhibit him from unconditionally endorsing from 1918 to 1920 what critics dubbed the White 'Regressive Bloc', notwithstanding its authoritarian character and programme. With the final defeat and expulsion from Russian soil of the last White army of General Wrangel in November 1920, Miliukov's redoubtable political energies became confined to the faction-riven Russian *émigré* arena. Shamelessly jettisoning his recent right Kadet affiliation, he launched a 'new tactic' of alliance between the left Kadets and Socialist Revolutionaries to form a left-of-centre bloc against Bolshevism from 1921. Having antagonized almost everyone by his series of political *volte-faces*, Miliukov was by now deeply distrusted and unpopular (and was lucky to survive a monarchist assassination attempt in Berlin in 1922 which claimed the life of his host Vladimir Nabokov).

As chief editor of the largest Russian *émigré* newspaper *Poslednie Novosti* ('The Latest News') from 1921 to June 1940, Miliukov dedicated himself to preserving 'Russia abroad' as 'Bolshevik barbarism' transformed the new Soviet Union into a cultural wasteland. He retained into old age his characteristic capacity to surprise: on the death of his formidable wife Anna Sergeevna (whom he had married in 1887), the talented amateur violinist scandalized *émigré* society by promptly marrying a concert pianist of less than half his age. An intriguing postscript to Miliukov's political career came with the fall of France in 1940, when he was approached by Nazi Germany to serve as a collaborator in a future 'Vichy Russia'. Spurning this offer of a revival of his 'German orientation', Miliukov lived long enough both to denounce the German invasion of Russia and, virtually on his deathbed, to rejoice at the news of the Russian victory at Stalingrad. An *émigré* from his homeland for the last 20 years of his life, outliving almost all his political generation to become (in his own phrase) 'the last of the Mohicans' of Russian liberalism, Miliukov died at the age of 84 at Aix-les-Bains in Savoy on 3 March 1943.

In retrospect, Miliukov was spectacularly unsuccessful as a politician and statesman, spending the overwhelming majority of his long political career – all but two months in early 1917 – in opposition, successively condemning tsarist reaction in the Duma, denouncing Bolshevism within Russia and castigating the Soviet Union from Western Europe, all with near-negligible historical effect.

Although there is conspicuously no historiographical consensus about Miliukov, his personal career failure has always been closely identified with the broader fate of liberalism in Russia. At one extreme, the charitable view traditional to Western historiography is that Miliukov was a hapless prisoner of circumstance. Liberalism was chronologically premature and therefore anachronistic in late tsarist Russia, where societal modernization had still to produce a substantial supportive middle class. European liberalism was also geographically inappropriate and therefore misplaced in revolutionary Russia, where educational levels fell woefully short of Western norms. By this deterministic interpretation, Miliukov can personally bear no responsibility for the train of events which saw Russian liberals reduced to a threatened and then extinct political species over the period 1917–21. On the contrary, he deserves sympathy as a doomed martyr to the irreconcilable incompatibility between European liberalism and early twentieth-century Russia.

At the other extreme, bitter condemnation of Miliukov's political conduct suffuses *émigré* memoirs. According to this indictment, liberalism's admittedly daunting task was rendered insuperable by Miliukov's at best tactless, increasingly quixotic leadership. He was never as 'European' or 'liberal' as his credulous clique of admirers suggested: while consistently striking an anti-authoritarian pose, his own authoritarianism within the Kadet Party was legendary. Luckier than he deserved in his pre-1917 career, Miliukov disgraced himself and the cause of liberalism by a string of crass political misjudgements over the period 1917–21, a record of 'stupidity or treason' for which he was punished by over 20 years of richly deserved exile from Russia. What he termed political realism was too often either craven collaborationism or naked opportunism. The result was a career remarkable for its sequence of disconcerting tactical switches: from militant radical to constitutional accommodationist in 1905–06; from tsarist collaborator to patriotic critic in 1915–16; from pro-Allied loyalist to pro-German opportunist in 1917–18; and from pro-right to pro-left opponent of Bolshevism in 1920–1. Notwithstanding the long political odds against the successful implementation of liberalism in Russia, Miliukov had the egregious distinction of rendering liberalism's likely failure absolutely certain.

The conventional Soviet line and the modern Western view occupy median positions between the poles, acknowledging the overarching suprahuman forces which consigned Russian liberalism to the 'dustbin of history' but reserving a degree of responsibility and even blame for Miliukov personally. A politician only effective in the insulated constitutional environment of the Duma, he was painfully at a loss in the hurly-burly of revolutionary, mass politics. Emerging as the supreme 'politician among academics' within the closed world of the Kadet Party and Progressive Bloc, he proved only 'an academic among politicians' in revolutionary 1917, easily outclassed and outplayed by Lenin, Trotsky and even Kerensky. At the same time, like any politician, Miliukov was constrained by the principle *je suis leur chef, donc je les suis* and could not have maintained his virtually unchallenged leadership of the Kadet Party throughout its 15-year existence without substantial, if not majority support for his line of strategy. By this argument, the blame for Kadet failure should not be laid exclusively at the door of Miliukov, who has been unjustly (even guiltily) made the supreme scapegoat for liberal disaster.

In the last (or rather latest) analysis, Miliukov's politics seem incorrigibly inconsistent, his performance unpardonably contradictory and his legacy irretrievably flawed. Over his long political career from the 1890s to the 1940s, Miliukov shifted spasmodically from the radical left through the centre to the far (but not furthest) right, and then convulsively back again to the moderate left. The short-term result of his bizarre performance over the critical revolutionary era was increasing isolation and consequent political impotence, precipitated by his alienation of virtually the entire spectrum of Russian contemporary opinion. The long-term result has been a simmering controversy among participants, spectators and then historians about Miliukov's personal motives, political judgement and historical role which has actually grown over the years and, particularly for the crucial but still under-researched period 1917–21, remains far from final resolution.

Further reading

Dumova N. G., *Liberal v Rossii: tragediia nesovmestimosti. Istoricheskii portret P. N. Miliukova*, vol. 1 (Moscow, Institut Rossiiskoi Istorii RAN, 1993), volumes 2 and 3 forthcoming.

Evreinov B. A., ed., *Sbornik statei, posviashchennykh Pavlu Nikolaevichu Miliukovu, 1859–1929* (Prague, red. kom., 1929).

Miliukov P. N., *Istoria vtoroi russkoi revoliutsii*, 3 vols. (Sofia, Rossiisko-bolgarskoe knigoizdatel'stvo, 1921–4).

Miliukov P. N., *Political Memoirs, 1905–1917* (Ann Arbor, University of Michigan Press, 1967).

Miliukov P. N., *The Russian Revolution*, vol. 1: *The Revolution Divided: Spring 1917*; vol. 2: *Kornilov or Lenin? Summer 1917*; vol. 3: *The Agony of the Provisional Government* (Gulf Breeze, FL, Academic International Press, 1978, 1984 and 1987).

Riha T., *A Russian European: Paul Miliukov in Russian Politics* (South Bend, IN, Notre Dame University Press, 1969).

Stockdale M. K., *Pavel Miliukov and the Quest for a Liberal Russia, 1880–1918* (Ithaca, NY, Cornell University Press, 1996).

Nicholas II

DOMINIC LIEVEN

Nicholas II was born on 18 May 1868. He was the oldest child of the Tsarevich Alexander, heir to the Russian throne, and Marie Fedorovna, born Princess Dagmar of Denmark. When Nicholas's grandfather was assassinated in 1881 his father succeeded to the throne as Alexander III, reigning until his sudden death in 1894, aged only 49.

Alexander and Marie were devoted to each other and their five children. The imperial couple had limited intellectual or aesthetic interests, Alexander III being a straightforward, conscientious but not very intelligent man, who loved the outdoors and maintained strict standards in his personal life. Less well educated and cosmopolitan than his father, Alexander III saw himself as embodying Russian traditions, values and interests. The family circle in which Nicholas grew up was untroubled, intimate and unsophisticated. Its influence was strengthened by the fact that the young prince was educated entirely at home, without the company of other boys save for his brother George. The Empress Marie, like the other Danish princesses of her generation, was a devoted and possessive mother whose children matured late. Though taught by some of the best professors in the empire and showing many signs of intelligence, Nicholas's formal education was completed before he reached the age of 20. There followed a carefree period as a junior officer in the Guards and a grand tour around the world in 1890–91, after which began Nicholas's rather gentle introduction into the business of government, whose high point was his chairmanship of the Siberian Railway Committee from 1893.

The completely unexpected death of his father forced Nicholas to take on immense responsibilities that he was as yet neither professionally nor emotionally ready to bear. Unlike, for instance, his German cousin, Wilhelm II, Nicholas came to the throne with no independent political standpoint of his own, no 'crown prince's party' and a deep respect for the political legacy of a strong-willed and rather overpowering father whom he loved. Nicholas's first notable public statement was a reaffirmation of that commitment to autocracy on which his father's rule had been based.

The determination to preserve autocracy is indeed the strongest single thread that runs through Nicholas II's political thinking. The emperor believed that responsibility for Russia's fate had been laid on his shoulders by God and history. He therefore had no right to evade that responsibility. Where matters crucial to Russia's future were at stake, he must retain the final word.

In addition, ruling Russia was not only a personal but also a family responsibility, of which he was the trustee rather than the outright possessor. In his own way Nicholas was a great populist. He believed fervently in the basic decency, courage, patriotism and religious faith of the ordinary Russian, which for the emperor meant above all the peasant and soldier. He saw himself as the guardian and protector of a people as yet too uneducated and unsophisticated for any form of democracy, and easily exploited and led astray by members of the educated classes. The warm and affectionate relationships that reigned between the Romanov children and the servants and soldiers who worked in their palaces added emotional strength to this populism, which drew intellectual inspiration from a tradition of conservative and Orthodox moral and political thought whose most famous spokesman was Fedor Dostoevsky.

An innocent childhood and an education devoted to inculcating purity of heart and selfless patriotism were a poor preparation for a working life at the heart of Russian politics. Nicholas's values were also far removed from those of the modern capitalist society that his own government's policies were helping to create in Russia. Among educated Russians he found officers, priests and landowners most congenial. A basically gentle, sensitive and well-meaning man, Nicholas could never have sustained his belief in his role as tsar had he not been convinced of the Russian people's fundamental support for the monarchy. The warm reception he always drew from the people, especially in the countryside and in the armed forces, confirmed this naïve faith. So too did his wife, the Empress Alexandra, whose fears for her family's safety, highly strung and religious personality, and deep alienation from Petersburg society all contributed to her passionate need to believe in the union of tsar and people.

It would, however, be wrong to explain Nicholas's commitment to autocracy in these terms alone. His political views also had a very strong rational core. The emperor believed that only an authoritarian regime sheltering behind the monarchy's legitimacy could hold together a vast and multi-ethnic empire, develop its human and natural resources, defend it against outside enemies and maintain a peaceful balance between sharply conflicting classes and nationalities. Nicholas inherited this conviction from his father and ancestors, but it was confirmed by the increasingly virulent social and ethnic conflicts that occurred in his reign. Great multi-ethnic empires created by conquest are not easily preserved by democratic means in an increasingly nationalist age. Russia's rulers looked at rampant ethnic disputes in the neighbouring Habsburg empire and the way in which they threatened that empire's existence and weakened its military and geopolitical effectiveness. This strengthened their determination to use authoritarian means to preserve and consolidate their empire's Russian identity. More important, like other educated Russians, Nicholas II was a member of the European society of his day and shared its elites' conviction that private property, education and high European culture were the foundations of civilization and progress, and therefore also of a country's power. Nicholas did not believe these values would survive in contemporary Russia unless protected by an authoritarian regime. The near social revolution of 1905–06, the first two Dumas' commitment to the expropriation of private land, and the growth of extreme socialist parties ready to exploit civil rights in the cause of the complete destruction of the existing polity and society strengthened this view, whose roots lay in an awareness of the cultural gulf that separated the world of Russia's European elites from that of the masses. Throughout the reigns of the last three Romanov monarchs, tough-minded authoritarian senior officials were on hand to remind wavering emperors of these fears.

Though committed to the principle of autocracy, Nicholas found it very difficult effectively to fulfil the role of autocrat. This was partly because of his personality. His sensitivity, impressionability and aversion to arguments and to abrasive personalities all counted against him, as did his basic distaste for and distrust of politics and politicians, and his fear of being controlled or manipulated by them. The emperor never had political friends or intimates on whose loyalty or counsel he could rely. His job as autocrat was, however, an impossible one. To be head of state and head of government for virtually the whole of one's adult life is more than the human frame is designed for. Even tough professional Western politicians seldom survive in the top office above a decade, nor do the countries they govern face crises on the scale of those undermining Nicholas's Russia. By 1915–17 the emperor was showing signs of physical and mental collapse. He survived the stresses of his office by cultivating an artificial restraint, optimism and detachment which his critics saw as indifference. Had Nicholas found a Richelieu or a Bismarck to run his government his problems would have lessened. But the Russian monarchical tradition expected the tsar to rule, not to hide behind a prime minister or the universally distrusted bureaucracy, especially in periods of crisis and danger. In any case Russia's domestic problems were more intractable than the Prussian constitutional crisis of 1862–6 and a Bismarckian-style solution to internal dangers through some crushing military victory was beyond Russia's power.

Nicholas was served by some very able ministers, of whom Sergei Witte and Petr Stolypin are the best known. He allowed Witte to dominate much of governmental policy in the 1890s, and Stolypin in the years 1906 to 1911. Both men's policies aroused enormous opposition among the key elites, however, and entailed serious dangers. The Western Zemstvo Crisis of 1911, when Stolypin clashed head-on with conservatives in the State Council and cajoled Nicholas into supporting him, finally wrecked the emperor's trust in his minister but Nicholas also had deeper rooted doubts as to whether political stability in Russia was best served by gearing policies to the wishes of the Duma majority or by accepting the limits imposed on government authority by semi-constitutional and semi-parliamentary politics.

Like all Russian monarchs since Nicholas I (1825–55), Nicholas II distrusted the bureaucracy and found it increasingly hard to control. The job became more difficult as the administration grew in size and complexity. Between 1880 and 1914 the number of civil servants in Petersburg alone grew from 23,000 to 52,000. The Russian government was involved in industrialization and the transformation of peasant agriculture. It was also waging a secret war against a well-developed revolutionary movement. In general by contemporary European standards the scale of governmental activity in Russia was very great, while the extent to which it was controlled by law, public opinion or parliamentary scrutiny was very limited. This helps to explain many of the bureaucracy's inefficiencies and its unpopularity. But from the rulers' perspective, the legal and parliamentary controls needed to improve bureaucratic effectiveness and popularity would undermine the police state on whose existence the tsarist social order, political stability and the multi-national empire depended.

In other great bureaucratic empires rulers used special groups (e.g. eunuchs, imperial slaves or foreigners) as private imperial watchdogs over the administration. In many cases terror was employed systematically as a means of control. None of these options was open to a Russian monarch in Victorian and Edwardian Europe. Presiding over the transition from an aristocratic and patrimonial polity to a bureaucratic state, Nicholas I had concentrated power in his Personal Chancellery and used the gendarmerie subordinated to this Chancellery's Third Section as an elite body designed to supervise the rest of the administration on the ruler's behalf. The gendarmerie never fulfilled this role efficiently, however, and after 1855 the emperor's Personal Chancellery lost its power to the ministries. An attempt by Alexander III to restore part of the Chancellery's power in 1894 foundered against bureaucratic opposition, while Nicholas II's only attempt to work through a species of personal secretariat headed by Dmitri Trepov in 1905–06 was furiously opposed by the Prime Minister, Sergei Witte.

Nicholas II could stop any prime minister from effectively controlling and coordinating governmental policy but he could not do the job himself. Senior officialdom, and indeed broader socio-economic elites, were unwilling to accept the principle of popular sovereignty and were probably correct to believe that their power and property would not survive its coming. They therefore had little choice but to accept the only alternative principle of legitimacy, namely the sovereignty of the monarch. Russia's ruling elites, however, found it a frustrating and impossible task to control the embodiment of that sovereignty, Nicholas II.

The emperor began to make a real personal impact on politics around the turn of the century, impelled both by his own growing experience in government and by clear signs of domestic political crisis, which was accompanied by universal denunciations of bureaucratic rule. The emperor's attempt to reassert personal control merely worsened matters, however, and the Far Eastern policy with which he was most associated led to the disastrous war with Japan. In the wake of that war and the 1905 revolution a Council of Ministers, a parliament and a prime minister were created, with the intention of putting constraints on the monarch. Even in more modern Imperial Germany, however, parliament, chancellor and ministers never succeeded in fully controlling Wilhelm II in peacetime, though efforts to publicize sexual and other scandals in the Kaiser's private entourage (the Eulenberg affair) had their parallels in A. I. Guchkov's efforts to use the Rasputin affair to push the Romanovs out of active politics. During World War I the German military and conservative elites did succeed in capturing Wilhelm II and took the Hohenzollern monarchy down with them when defeated in 1918. Nicholas, by contrast, manoeuvred successfully to retain his independence but at the price of isolating the monarchy from most Russian political, social and military elites, who refused to back him in the face of mass revolt in Petrograd in 1917. Nicholas himself was a patriot, devoted to his army and to Russia's honour and security. When his generals told him that his abdication was necessary for the war's successful prosecution he gave way with little struggle.

The immediate prelude to revolution was the crisis of summer 1915. In June 1915 Nicholas dismissed those ministers least acceptable to the Duma in an attempt to sustain a united war effort. Over the summer, however, further pressure built up and in September the Progressive Bloc was formed within the legislature, calling for the creation of a government based on the support of the Duma's majority. Despite pressure from most of his ministers, Nicholas refused the Bloc's demands. He saw them as a major step towards parliamentary government. He also believed that the ministry created to satisfy the Bloc's demand would prove unable to master the wartime crisis, which would inevitably lead to calls for further changes and involve the disintegration of governmental authority.

Refusal of the Duma's demands isolated Nicholas, however, and lost him the support of many of the bureaucracy's most efficient and respected senior cadres. Since the emperor needed at least the tacit cooperation of public elements (such as the zemstvos and War Industry Committees) in the war effort, he could not re-appoint Nikolai Maklakov or any other member of the small band of authoritarian bureaucrats in the Ministry of Internal Affairs. At a time of growing domestic economic and political crisis, the pool of available candidates for key ministerial posts and the calibre of appointments shrank, with obvious effects on the regime's legitimacy and effectiveness.

The last tsarist Minister of Internal Affairs, Aleksandr Protopopov, though supported by the Empress Alexandra, was a senior Duma politician from the Octobrist Party with excellent connections in industrial circles. Not merely, however, did hopes that his appointment would smooth relations with the Duma prove futile, Protopopov also showed himself a hopelessly ineffective head of the vital ministry for combating revolution at a time of supreme political crisis. Had Nicholas and the Progressive Bloc come to an agreement in 1915, it is possible that the key ministries could have been run by experienced bureaucrats for whose activities the legislature would have shared some responsibility. Instead the crown was lumbered with sole responsibility for the inefficiency of a parliamentarian promoted beyond his competence and subjected to the hysterical abuse of his former colleagues.

After the revolution Nicholas was arrested and held in increasingly strict confinement first in Tsarskoe Selo, then in Tobolsk and finally in Ekaterinburg. In July 1918 he, his wife and children, and the family's servants were killed. The evidence strongly suggests that orders for their death came personally from Lenin.

Further reading

Bokhanov A. N., *Sumerki Monarkhii* (Moscow, Nauka, 1993).

Lieven D., *Nicholas II: Emperor of all the Russias* (London, John Murray, 1993).

Nicholas II, *The Letters of the Tsar to the Tsaritsa, 1914–1917,* trans. A. L. Hynes, ed. C. E. Vulliamy (Hattiesburg, MS, Academic International Press, 1970).

Verner A., *The Crisis of Russian Autocracy: Nicholas II and the 1905 Revolution* (Princeton, Princeton University Press, 1990).

Spiridonova

ALEXANDER RABINOWITCH

Maria Aleksandrovna Spiridonova (1884–1941) is one of the Russian revolution's most interesting and important, yet tragic and little-known
figures. A prototype revolutionary terrorist in late tsarist times, she became
a leader of the radical agrarian socialist Left SR party after the October 1917
revolution and was the joint Bolshevik–Left SR nominee for the presidency
of the Constituent Assembly. However, after she masterminded the assassination of Count Wilhelm Mirbach, the German ambassador to Soviet
Russia, in July 1918, the Bolsheviks forced her into oblivion. Spiridonova
spent most of the remaining 23 years of her life in exile or in Soviet prisons
and labour camps.

Born into the family of a minor, non-hereditary Tambov noble in 1884,
Spiridonova first gained national attention at the age of 20 when she assassinated G. N. Luzhnovskii, a district Okhrana official in Tambov province.
The Tambov SR Committee had marked Luzhnovskii for execution because
of his brutal suppression of rebellious peasants. Impelled by an enduring
idealism, the youthful Spiridonova, already a member of an SR terrorist
squad, volunteered for the task. Following her arrest for the crime, lurid,
sensationalized press reports that she had been tortured and abused sexually
by the police and prison personnel provoked a storm of sympathy. She was
initially sentenced to death by hanging, but domestic and international pressure forced tsarist officials to reduce her punishment to life imprisonment.
Probably due in no small part to the efforts of her SR comrades,
Spiridonova was mythologized from this time on as a 'martyr-heroine' who
had willingly sacrificed herself to help suffering peasants.

By February 1917, when she was liberated from a women's prison in
Nerchinsk after the overthrow of Nicholas II, Russian peasants regarded her
as a kind of saint. Spiridonova travelled from Siberia to Moscow as a delegate to the Third SR National Congress at the end of May 1917 but failed
to win a place on the SR Central Committee elected by the congress. None
the less, she remained at the centre of events, becoming deeply involved

in the leadership of the Petrograd SR organization, then already dominated by Left SRs, and also in work with peasant soviets.

After the October revolution, which Spiridonova hailed, she was among prominent Left SRs who sought the creation of a Soviet government that was representative of all socialist parties. However, in mid-November 1917, after efforts to construct a broadly based socialist coalition failed, she strongly supported the short-lived Bolshevik–Left SR government. During the struggle over the signing and ratification of the Treaty of Brest-Litovsk, Spiridonova, then a member of the Left SR Central Committee, was one of only a very few prominent members of that relatively new party to support Lenin's policy of immediate peace.

Throughout these first months after October, Spiridonova and Lenin had a personally respectful, if not always constructive, working relationship. However, by the late spring of 1918 their association had soured (as had the Bolshevik–Left SR relationship generally). The primary cause for this breakdown, at least for Spiridonova, was the brutal Bolshevik grain procurement policy and the devastating impact on the peasantry of the government's vast territorial and increasingly onerous economic concessions to Imperial Germany. As head of the Peasant Section of the Central Executive Committee of the All-Russian Soviet of Workers', Peasants' and Soldiers' Deputies, then a highly visible and influential political position, Spiridonova was well attuned to the deepening misery of peasants throughout the country.

By this time popular disenchantment with Bolshevik rule was well advanced, not only in rural but also in urban Russia. The primary beneficiaries of this nationwide grass-roots shift of public opinion were the Left SRs. During the second half of June 1918, it was an open question which of the two parties would have a majority at the Fifth All-Russian Congress of Soviets, scheduled to convene in Moscow on 4 July.

In this uncertain and fluid situation the Left SR Central Committee, at a meeting on 24 June, resolved to employ terrorism against high German officials, if necessary, to provoke immediate termination of the Brest-Litovsk treaty. When the Fifth Congress of Soviets opened in Moscow's Bolshoi Theatre on the evening of 4 July, it became clear to the Left SRs that the Bolsheviks had effectively fabricated a sizeable majority and, consequently, that there was no prospect of using the congress to force a fundamental change in the government's pro-German, anti-peasant policies. Spiridonova and her colleagues concluded that resolute action outside the congress along the lines sanctioned by the Left SR Central Committee on 24 June was unavoidable.

On the afternoon of 6 July, during a recess in the Congress of Soviets, Left SRs Iakov Bliumkin and Nikolai Andreev gained entry into the German embassy, where they assassinated Count Wilhelm Mirbach, the ambassador. From that point on, however, all Left SR plans and expectations went awry. The Left SR leadership had expected that the killing of Mirbach would provoke an immediate German military attack; in the event, Lenin's government successfully mollified the Germans. The Left SRs were also confident that radical Bolsheviks, the 'Left Communists', were sympathetic to their concerns and would ultimately support their action. However, with the survival of Bolshevik power seemingly hanging by a thread, even the most extreme Left Communists maintained party discipline. Finally, the Left SRs were confident that Mirbach's assassination would spark decisive socialist revolutions abroad; however, nothing of the kind occurred.

Instead, Lenin, for one, appears to have decided that the killing of Mirbach provided a fortuitous opportunity to put an end to the growing Left SR threat. Thus, Bolshevik authorities immediately portrayed Mirbach's assassination as an uprising against Soviet power. With this justification, they mobilized sufficient troops to isolate and defeat Left SR military forces, although not without considerable anxiety about the development of the operation and its eventual outcome.

On the afternoon of 6 July, soon after the assassination, Spiridonova rushed to the Bolshoi Theatre to deliver an open letter to the Bolshevik Central Committee and to speak at a scheduled evening session of the Fifth Congress. The letter has never been published, and the evening session did not take place. However, later statements by Spiridonova make clear that her purpose in going to the Bolshoi was to take exclusive responsibility for Mirbach's killing. She also expected to be given a chance to explain and justify Left SR aims and to plead for support of them. When Spiridonova arrived at the Bolshoi, the more than 400 Left SR congress delegates were milling around in confusion. Prohibited from leaving the theatre, the delegates were held there under difficult conditions for more than two days, after which 'the main culprits' were sent to dungeons in the Kremlin. Moreover, the Peasant Section, the centre of Spiridonova's activity, was officially dissolved.

Bliumkin and Andreev evaded capture, as did 11 of 14 other Left SR leaders indicted in connection with Mirbach's assassination (perhaps because of sympathy for them within the Cheka). However, an undisclosed number of other Left SRs were summarily shot. Spiridonova herself was held in a Kremlin cell where, as in 1906, she claimed to have awaited death joyfully, as the ultimate sacrifice for the revolutionary cause. She also anticipated a public trial, during which she would be able to articulate the revolutionary message she had tried to voice on 6 July. However, neither hope was realized. To avoid sympathetic crowds, her trial, originally announced for 1 December, was moved up to 27 November. On that day she was tried in secrecy and sentenced to a year in prison. (The following day, she was amnestied at the direction of the Presidium of the Central Executive Committee.)

Spiridonova briefly resumed political activity, marginally rejuvenating the Left SR Party and maintaining an exhausting schedule of speeches to worker and peasant groups. Her stature as 'the soul' of the Left SR party remained unchallenged despite the fact that she was among a minority of Left SRs who staunchly opposed attempts at reconciliation with the Bolsheviks. One of the Cheka agents assigned to her noted in a report at this time: 'within the Left SR party something akin to a fetish has come to surround Spiridonova's name: Maria Aleksandrovna is literally worshipped. Her life of suffering is being used as a general symbol for the suffering and oppression of the entire working class.'

In her speeches of this period, Spiridonova denounced the Soviet government's domestic and foreign policies as a betrayal of the revolution and predicted the Bolsheviks' early downfall. However, she distanced herself from the Left SRs' ultra-left terrorist wing. Moreover, she steadfastly continued to support the ideal of 'toiling people's' power exercised through democratic soviets.

None the less, at the height of the civil war all political attacks on the Bolsheviks were considered a crime against the Soviet state. In January 1919, after Spiridonova delivered a particularly derisive speech, the Moscow Cheka rearrested her. On 24 February 1919 she was tried before the Moscow Revolutionary Tribunal. Nikolai Bukharin, the only witness for the prosecution, charged that Spiridonova was mentally ill and 'a menace in the prevailing environment'. The tribunal judged Spiridonova guilty of slandering Soviet power and individual Soviet leaders, thereby aiding the counterrevolution, and sentenced her to 'isolation from political and social activity by means of incarceration in a sanitorium for a year'.

From the time of her first beatings and confinement in 1906, Spiridonova's physical and mental condition had been fragile. Among other things, she suffered hearing loss and periodic bouts of tuberculosis, typhus, shingles, dysentery, hysteria and depression. After her arrest and sentencing in February 1919, her health quickly deteriorated. Instead of being sent to a sanitorium she was incarcerated in a 'narrow hole' of a cell carved out of a crowded, noisy Kremlin guards barracks. Concerned about her worsening condition and aided by a sympathetic guard, the Left SRs successfully arranged her escape on 2 April 1919. (During her many years of confinement, Spiridonova demonstrated an uncanny ability to win the sympathy of her guards, a trait that became part of the Spiridonova 'myth'.)

From the spring of 1919 until she was rearrested on 26 October 1920 (her last months of relative freedom), Spiridonova hid in Moscow under the name Onufrieva. Despite her worsening health, she participated in party meetings and wrote extensively. At the time of her recapture, she was bedridden with typhus and a nervous disorder. Held under house-arrest for a month, she was subsequently transferred to a Cheka infirmary and, still later, to a psychiatric prison. In July 1921, appeals to allow Spiridonova to leave Russia by participants in an international women's congress meeting in Moscow were rejected because, as Trotsky is said to have put it, she 'was still too dangerous to be at liberty or be permitted abroad'. It seems likely that such thinking was influenced by the abortive Kronstadt uprising against Bolshevik rule in February 1921, as well as by an ominous wave of peasant rebellions that swept rural Russia in the early 1920s. Finally, on 18 November 1921 Spiridonova was released into the custody of two Left SRs on condition that henceforth she refrain from all political activity. There is no evidence that she ever violated this condition.

With one of her closest comrades, Aleksandra Izmailovich, to care for her, and under around-the-clock police surveillance, Spiridonova was moved to a dacha near Moscow. Probably because of their perceptions of the threat posed by Spiridonova's name amid continually expanding turbulence among peasants in the countryside, the Soviet authorities still considered her and other leading Left SRs security risks. On 16 May 1923, by which time large numbers of former moderate socialist and liberal party leaders had been either forced or permitted to emigrate, Spiridonova was suddenly rearrested and sentenced to three years of administrative exile for the unsubstantiated crime of having made preparations to flee abroad.

Spiridonova's administrative exile lasted not three but fourteen years. For the remainder of the 1920s she resided in Kaluga (1923–5), Samarkand (1925–8), and Tashkent (1928–30). In 1930, following Stalin's consolidation of power, Spiridonova was again arrested. Charged with maintaining contacts abroad, she was sentenced to three more years of administrative exile (the term was extended twice), this time in Ufa, capital of the Bashkir Republic. Long cut off from any kind of political activity, she worked as a senior economic planner in an agricultural bank.

In exile her once voluminous correspondence dwindled to a trickle and her personal contacts were limited almost exclusively to a relatively small group of former Left SR exiles in Ufa. None the less, on 8 February 1937 she was rearrested; this time, she was charged with attempting to help unite all former opposition parties and groups into a counterrevolutionary centre, and with carrying out terrorist acts against the leadership of the Bashkir Republic. Refusing to yield to torture, she staunchly rebutted the charges against her, both orally and in writing. She was tried on 7 January 1938, found guilty, and sentenced to 25 years imprisonment.

Spiridonova's end came on 11 September 1941, as the invading Germans approached the prison in Orel where she was incarcerated. She and 156 other political prisoners were sentenced to be shot for 'conducting defeatist propaganda among prisoners and plotting to flee the prison in order to renew subversive activities [against Soviet power]'. Immediately led out of the prison, she, along with the other condemned prisoners, were transported to the nearby Medvedev Woods. Earlier, trees in a secluded section of the woods had been uprooted and burial trenches prepared. After all the prisoners had been shot by a special NKVD operations group brought in from Moscow, the trenches were covered with dirt and the trees replanted.

Seventeen years later, in November 1958, Irina Kakhovskaia, Spiridonova's close friend and party comrade who had been amnestied following Stalin's death, petitioned the Main Prosecutor of the USSR for Spiridonova's posthumous rehabilitation. The petition was denied. Not until 1990 were the 1941 charges against Spiridonova rescinded. Finally, in 1992, Spiridonova was exonerated of the charges for which she had been imprisoned and exiled beginning in 1918, and was fully rehabilitated.

Further reading

Bezberezh'ev S. V., 'Maria Aleksandrova Spiridonova', in *Rossiia na rubezhe vekov: Istoricheskie portrety* (Moscow, Politizdat, 1991).

Boniece S., 'Maria Spiridonova, 1884–1918: Feminine Martyrdom and Revolutionary Mythmaking' (Ph.D. dissertation, Indiana University, 1995).

Gusev K. V., *Eserovskaia bogoroditsa* (Moscow, Luch, 1992).

Kakhovskaia I. K., 'V TsK KPSS', in Roy Medvedev, ed., *1964–1970: Politicheskii dnevnik* (Amsterdam, Herzen Foundation, 1972).

Leont'ev I. V., 'Spiridonova, M. A.', in P. V. Volobuev *et al.,* eds., *Politicheskie deiateli Rossii: 1917 Biograficheskii slovar'* (Moscow, Nauchnoe izdatel'stvo Bol'shaia rossiiskaia entsiklopediia, 1993).

Rabinowitch A., 'Maria Spiridonova's Last Testament', *The Russian Review* 54 (1995).

Steinberg I., *Spiridonova, Revolutionary Terrorist* (London, Methuen, 1935).

'Tragediia v Medvedevskom lesu: O rasstrele politzakliuchennykh Orlovskoi tiur'my', *Izvestiia TsK KPSS* 11 (1990).

Trotsky

VLADIMIR IU. CHERNIAEV

On 26 October 1879, at Ianovka farmstead in Elizavetgrad uezd, Kherson gubernia in southern Ukraine, a son, Leiba, was born to Anna and David Bronstein, a secularized Jewish couple. He was to go down in history under the name of Lev (Leon) Trotsky. The family was interested only in making a living. As it became richer, it acquired land, and erected a windmill and a brick house. Lev went to school in Odessa, at St Paul's *Realschule,* and completed his secondary education at Nikolaev. He was an able pupil, ambitious, quarrelsome and hot-tempered, with a strong sense of fairness. His father wanted him to work in his mill, but Lev had been seized by a bookish attraction to revolution. He criticized Populism (*narodnichestvo*) for its mustiness and Marxism for its narrowness, although at the time his conceptions of both were hazy.

Under the name 'L'vov', he headed the 'South-Russian Workers' Union', and, as he later recognized,

> If it had been possible for anyone to look at all this with a 'sober' eye, at this group of young people, scurrying about in the half-darkness around a miserable hectograph, what a sorry, fantastic thing it would have seemed to imagine that they could, in this way, overthrow a mighty state that was centuries old! And yet this sorry fantasy became a reality within a single generation; and only eight years separated those nights from 1905, and not quite twenty from 1917.

On 20 January 1898 he was arrested for the first time, and, after serving two years in prison in Odessa, he was exiled to Ust'-Kut, Eastern Siberia, for four years. Before he left for Siberia, he married Aleksandra Sokolovskaia, a fellow member of the South-Russian Workers' Union, who was to be the mother of his two daughters. He found work as a bookkeeper with a millionaire merchant, published articles in the liberal newspaper *Vostochnoe obozrenie* ('Eastern Review'), and composed leaflets. At that time Social Democrats were obsessed with the idea of creating a centralized party. In

August 1902 he escaped from exile. He filled out a blank internal passport, mischievously adopting the surname of the chief warder of the Odessa prison: Trotsky. In Samara Lev Trotsky became a writer on the illegal social-democratic paper *Iskra* ('The Spark'). He later left Russia, crossing the border into Austria with a group of smugglers. In Paris he met Natal'ia Sedova, who later became a close friend, his second wife, and the mother of his two sons. He was taken round London by the editor of *Iskra*, Vladimir Il'ich Lenin. This was their first period of collaboration.

At the Second Congress of the Russian Social-Democratic Labour Party (RSDRP) (1903), Trotsky rejected Lenin's principle of subordinating the individual to the party, preferring a free union of like-minded people. He set out his views in the pamphlet *Our Political Tasks*, first published in Geneva in 1904, which he dedicated to his mentor, the Menshevik P. B. Aksel'rod. Lenin described it as 'the most brazen lies'. In response, Trotsky called Lenin a dictator and a usurper, and accused him of Jacobinism. Trotsky also broke with the Mensheviks, rejecting the idea of seeking agreements with the liberal parties, and became a non-factional Social Democrat.

Trotsky was in his element during the revolution of 1905. He came to St Petersburg illegally and produced the *Russkaia gazeta* ('Russian Gazette') with his friend A. L. Parvus. Using the name 'Ianovskii', he was the ideological leader of the Petersburg Soviet of Workers' Deputies in his capacity as the editor of its *Izvestiia* ('News'), its deputy chairman and, from 27 November 1905 until his arrest on 3 December, its chairman. He agitated among the workers for the idea of an armed uprising. In his book *Results and Prospects*, which he wrote in Kresty prison in 1906, he advanced what came to be known as the theory of 'permanent revolution'. Russia's combination of modernity and backwardness created the conditions for an uninterrupted revolution which would go beyond bourgeois-democratic change to socialism. He argued that a workers-led government, initially supported by the peasants and then sustained by revolutionary socialist governments in the West, could use the dictatorship of the proletariat to cross the gulf between the RSDRP minimum and maximum programmes. His pamphlet, *Our Tactics in the Struggle for the Constituent Assembly*, was published in 1906 in Moscow by the Bolsheviks, because their positions corresponded. Trotsky's behaviour when his case came to court was brave and dignified. He was sentenced to 25 years' exile (until 1931) north of the Arctic circle, from whence it was impossible to escape. Therefore he escaped *en route* to his place of exile, on reindeer, disguising himself as an engineer on Baron Toll's polar expedition. Having reached Finland, Trotsky wrote a short book, *There and Back Again*, describing his adventures. It was published in 1907 in St Petersburg, and Trotsky was able to use the royalties from it to go abroad.

At the Fifth RSDRP Congress (1907), Lenin favoured a *rapprochement* with Trotsky, but Trotsky soon became enamoured of the idea of party unity, proposed merging the Bolshevik and Menshevik factions and jettisoning the irreconcilables on both sides, and condemned the Bolshevik 'expropriations' (bank robberies), one of the organizers of which was I. V. Stalin. From 1908 to 1912 in Vienna Trotsky published a paper aimed at workers called *Pravda* ('The Truth'). His brother-in-law, L. B. Kamenev, was unable to recruit him to the Bolsheviks, and was recalled from *Pravda*'s editorial board by Lenin.

Lenin denounced Trotsky as 'the vilest careerist', a 'rogue' and so on. Trotsky protested against the Bolsheviks' appropriation of the title of his newspaper *Pravda*. The Bolsheviks boycotted the August 1912 conference of the RSDRP convened by Trotsky in Vienna, and the bloc of tendencies and groups which resulted from the conference soon broke up. In 1913 the *Okhranka* intercepted a letter from Trotsky to the Menshevik N. S. Chkheidze, in which he said: 'The entire edifice of Leninism at present is built on lies and falsification, and bears the poisonous seeds of its own disintegration. There seems to be some kind of pointless purpose in the way that all this is blown up into a wretched squabble by the master Lenin, that professional exploiter of all that is backward in the Russian labour movement.' Stalin was later to make clever use of that letter in his struggle with Trotsky.

Trotsky regarded World War I as the revolt of capitalism's productive forces on a global scale against private property and state borders. Against Lenin's revolutionary defeatism and call to turn the imperialist war into a civil war, he advanced the slogan 'Peace without victors or vanquished!' In September 1916, the newspaper *Nashe slovo* ('Our Word'), on which he worked with the Menshevik leader Iu. O. Martov, was closed down by the French authorities. Trotsky was expelled from Paris to Spain, where he was arrested. He spent New Year's Day, 1917, on a steamer bound for New York. He described his experiences in a book, *It Happened in Spain*. In New York he worked closely with N. I. Bukharin.

Once he had heard about the February revolution, Trotsky hurried to return to Russia. The British authorities arrested him *en route* and interned him in a prisoner-of-war camp in Amherst, Canada. It was the new Russian Minster of Foreign Affairs, P. N. Miliukov, who obtained his release. On the morning of 4 May he met with a triumphant reception in Petrograd. He was coopted onto the Executive Committee of the Petrograd Soviet, and became the leader of the Interdistrict Organization of the RSDRP (the *Mezhraionka*). This was a smallish group of centrist internationalists. As yet it is unclear what induced Lenin immediately to propose a merger with the Bolsheviks and to offer Trotsky a place on the Bolshevik Central Committee. It is possible that Trotsky had a good source of finance. He refused the offer at first, although he stood for the removal of the liberal-reformist Provisional Government which included Mensheviks and Socialist Revolutionaries, and for the establishment of the dictatorship of the proletariat. During the July Days he rescued the Minister of Agriculture V. M. Chernov, who had been seized by a group of anarchists while trying to pacify the angry crowds. However, following the suppression of the July Days demonstrations and the measures taken against Bolsheviks and anarchist communists, Trotsky again found himself in the Kresty prison. The *Mezhraionka* merged with the Bolsheviks at the latter's Sixth Congress in July–August 1917, and Trotsky was elected to the Bolshevik Central Committee while he was still in prison. On 2 September he was among those released on bail in the aftermath of the Kornilov affair, and on 25 September he became the head of the Bolshevized Petrograd Soviet, fashioning its Military-Revolutionary Committee into an organ of insurrection. The insurrection began, as Lenin had demanded, before the Second Congress of Soviets opened, but depended for success, as Trotsky had calculated, on identification with the soviets rather than the party alone, and on the support of the congress. The day of victory was Trotsky's thirty-eighth birthday. He was at the height of his glory, and was unmoved by A. M. Gorky's angry words about 'Mr. Trotsky's frenzied dance on the ruins of Russia'.

October 1917, with its fury and inspiration, welded the two leaders together. Lenin proposed that Trotsky head the Council of People's Commissars (*Sovnarkom*). Trotsky refused the honour, so Lenin became its Chairman, while Trotsky became People's Commissar of Foreign Affairs. They both opposed the pressure, spearheaded by the executive of the railway union (*Vikzhel'*), for an all-socialist coalition and the entry of the SRs and Mensheviks into the *Sovnarkom*. Their tactical disagreements over the Brest-Litovsk peace negotiations – during which Trotsky advocated a policy of 'neither war nor peace', while Lenin insisted that they must settle with the Germans at all costs – merely reflected different assessments of the imminence of the world revolution.

In April 1918, Trotsky became the Commissar for War and the Navy, and from 2 September he was also the Chairman of the Revolutionary Military Council of the Republic (*Revvoensovet*). In 1920 he also took on the post of People's Commissar of Transport. Trotsky bears a great deal of responsibility both for the victory of the Red Army in the civil war, and for the establishment of a one-party authoritarian state with its apparatus for ruthlessly suppressing dissent. As a Jacobin in spirit, he was not frightened by the smell of freshly spilled blood. He was an ideologist and practician of the Red Terror. He despised 'bourgeois democracy'; he believed that spinelessness and soft-heartedness would destroy the revolution, and that the suppression of the propertied classes and political opponents would clear the historical arena for socialism. He was the initiator of concentration camps, compulsory 'labour armies' and the militarization of labour, and the state takeover of trade unions. Trotsky was implicated in many practices which were to become standard in the Stalin era, including summary executions. Between 1922 and 1929 the towns of Gatchina and Iuzovka were named 'Trotsk' in his honour. The arrogant tone of his articles on *Literature and Revolution*, published in Moscow in 1923, was later to be further developed by Stalin's *protégé* and militant champion of cultural conformism, A. A. Zhdanov. Trotsky considered the intelligentsia to be thoroughly bourgeois, and he was one of those who approved the expulsion in

1922 of several prominent liberal academics, philosophers, writers and public figures.

In his last political testament, the *Letter to the Congress* (winter 1922–3), Lenin considered his possible successsors, recognized that Trotsky was the most able member of the Central Committee, and requested that Stalin be removed from the position of party General Secretary. It remains a mystery why Trotsky did not offer fuller support to Lenin in his fight against Stalin in 1922–3. Trotsky was later to suggest that Stalin might have poisoned Lenin. He regarded Lenin's mausoleum with its mummified body as an insult to revolutionary consciousness, and wrote: 'His ideas have been chopped up into quotations for false prophets. With their preserved corpse they have fought against the living Lenin and against Trotsky. The masses have been deafened, confused and terrorized ... The dictatorship of the apparatus over the party has been established.'

The power struggle took the form of a discussion about who were the real 'Leninists', in the course of which the notion of a 'Trotskyist deviation' was thought up. Although he remained true to the idea of an iron proletarian dictatorship through the party, Trotsky published a pamphlet, *The New Course* (1923), in which he launched a campaign for democracy within the party. He advocated the election of all party officials, the right of criticism, and measures to attract industrial workers and youth, amongst whom he had many supporters. Another aspect of the argument was whether it was possible to construct socialism in a single country. In view of the cultural and technological backwardness of the USSR, Trotsky did not think it would be feasible without the spread of revolution to the West and the East, along with the most rapid possible industrialization and collectivization. However, the idea of world revolution held little attraction for the Soviet population, which had suffered so much from wars and experiments in 'barrack-room communism', and in 1923–4 the leading position was taken by a triumvirate of Stalin, Kamenev and G. E. Zinoviev. 'The leaden rump of the revolution outweighed the head of the party,' complained Trotsky. His political power began to decline precipitately: on 26 January 1925 he was removed from his posts as Commissar for War and Chairman of the *Revvoensovet*; on 23 October 1926 from the Politburo; on 27 September 1927 from the Communist International (Comintern) which he had helped found; in October from the Central Committee; and on 14 November 1927 from the party itself.

On 7 November 1927, at a demonstration to mark the tenth anniversary of the October revolution, Stalin organized a display of 'popular anger', and stones were thrown at Trotsky. On 16 January 1928 he was exiled to Alma-Ata. He regarded his defeat as a kind of Thermidor, threatening the gains of the revolution. Later, in his book on Stalin, he pointed to the reasons for this Thermidor: the consequences of NEP, the restoration of free trade, the rejection of egalitarianism, the growth of the bourgeoisie and a bureaucratic degeneration of the party. He wrote: 'Within the party there have formed special shock brigades of careerists, embezzlers, debauched children of the bureaucracy, shameless and cynical elements, those who seek personal revenge . . . those who have got rich quick, and those who have abandoned their ideals.' In 1927 the GPU, the successor to the Cheka, had become 'an instrument of the bureaucracy against the people and against the party'. However, Trotsky himself had played no small part in the creation of the totalitarian regime which had gained mastery over the entire resources of the country, while the process of bourgeois degeneration took longer than he anticipated. It lasted for another half-century and was completed by 'perestroika', the collapse of the CPSU, and criminal privatization, in which the former party *nomenklatura* began to acquire former state and public property for itself.

When the question of expelling Trotsky from the USSR was discussed in the Politburo, only Bukharin, A. I. Rykov, M. P. Tomskii and V. V. Kuibyshev spoke against. On 12 February 1929, Trotsky was forcibly put onto a steamer, ironically called *Il'ich*, and sent to Istanbul. In 1932 he was stripped of his Soviet citizenship. His exile began on the island of Prinkipo in the Sea of Marmora. From 24 July 1933 he lived in the south of France; from 18 July 1935 in Norway; and from 9 January 1937 in Mexico. Only the Mexican government did not regard him as *persona non grata*. The other governments tried to get rid of him as soon as possible, in order to avoid arguments with Stalin, against whom Trotsky waged a furious ideological battle in his journal, *Bulletin of the Opposition (Bolshevik-Leninists)*, and in such books as *My Life* (1929), and *The Stalin School of Falsification* (1932). Trotsky watched with bitterness as the revolution, in the shape of Stalin, devoured its children, and the Soviet regime took on features very akin to fascism. His colleagues of October 1917 perished; his brother, his sister, his son Sergei, and his nephews, all of whom were unconnected with politics, were shot. N. K. Krupskaia, N. I. Podvoiskii and others rewrote their memoirs, amending their assessments of Trotsky's character and activities, distorting or keeping silent about his role in the revolution. At the beginning of 1935, after the murder of S. M. Kirov, Trotsky's books were removed from Soviet libraries, and almost all were destroyed. Only a few copies were retained in closed sections of certain libraries.

At the Moscow trial of the fictitious 'Trotskyite-Zinovievite Terrorist Centre' (of Kamenev, Zinoviev and others) in August 1936, Trotsky was charged with White-Guard and fascist terror against the leaders of the party and government, and was to be arrested and tried if found on Soviet territory. In reality it was Trotsky who was hiding from Stalin's terrorists, and was demanding an international investigation into Soviet trials. In his book *The Revolution Betrayed* (1936) Trotsky wrote that Stalinism was not a type of Bolshevism, and argued the need for a new revolution in the USSR and the creation of a new, revolutionary International. All those who sympathized with him outside the USSR had been expelled from the Comintern, such as Alfred Rosmer and Boris Souvarine in France, and the Maslow-Fischer group in Germany. The Fourth International was founded in Alfred

Rosmer's apartment on the outskirts of Paris in 1938. The basis of its ideology was Trotsky's theory of permanent revolution.

Trotsky predicted that World War II would develop after the fashion of
World War I and would bring about working-class struggles in the different
countries, uprisings and new revolutions. Otherwise socialism would be
defeated forever. The borders of the USSR, which he continued to consider
as a kind of workers' state, were just temporary trenches in the class struggle.
The future lay with a Socialist United States of Europe and of the whole world.
On 25 April 1940, in an open letter to the Soviet workers, 'You are Being
Deceived!', Trotsky explained that the CPSU and the Comintern were completely rotten, and that the aim of the Fourth International was to cleanse the
USSR of its parasitic bureaucracy and to spread the October revolution over
the whole world. He proclaimed: 'Down with Cain-Stalin and his camarilla!
Long live the USSR, the bastion of the workers! Long live the world socialist
revolution!' However, Trotsky's words did not reach their addressees. As a
politician he was bankrupt. Stalin, with his bandit conception of Marxism,
remained on top in the USSR, and he was already gunning for Trotsky.

In 1938 Lev Sedov, Trotsky's eldest son and closest collaborator, the
editor and publisher of the *Bulletin of the Opposition*, was poisoned in
Paris. In 1940, Trotsky's villa in Coyoacan was attacked by an armed band
led by the Mexican communist painter David Alfaro Siquieros, who apparently intended to kill him. Ramon Mercader, a lieutenant and commissar of
the Spanish republican army, communist and NKVD agent, was more successful. He gained entry to Trotsky's inner circle in the guise of a Belgian
journalist. On 20 August 1940 he drove an icepick into Trotsky's skull. The
blood soaked the manuscript of Trotsky's final book, *Stalin*.

The leader of the October revolution was buried with full ceremony in the
garden of his villa in Coyoacan, which was turned into a museum. A red flag
was raised over his grave, and the headstone was engraved with a hammer
and sickle. His wife, N. I. Sedova, was buried alongside him in 1962.

Trotsky's assassin was released from jail in 1960. He felt no remorse,
worked for a period in the Institute of General History in Moscow, and then
lived in Cuba where he died in 1978. He was buried in Moscow, and his
gravestone in the Kuntsevskoe cemetery bears the legend: 'Hero of the
Soviet Union Lopez Ramon Ivanovich'.

For almost half a century the name of Trotsky, shrouded in Stalinist lies,
was a term of political abuse in the USSR. The most detailed scholarly biography of Trotsky was written by the former Polish communist and
Trotskyist Isaac Deutscher, and was published in three volumes in London
between 1954 and 1963. Although Deutscher was sympathetic to Trotsky,
he took a fairly critical view of his activities. There are valuable insights and
observations in other Western studies, notably that of Pierre Broué.
Collections of Trotsky's papers in foreign archives have also been published.
In the USSR they were available to very few people, and Trotsky's name was
expunged from the official history of the revolution. For a time the Soviet

censors prohibited all mention of Trotsky, even in a negative context, and his surname was generally omitted when historical documents from the revolution of 1917 were published in the USSR.

This ban on the use of Trotsky's name was lifted by the Soviet authorities only in 1988. His books were released from the closed sections of libraries and began to be republished. In 1991 a Russian translation of the third volume of Deutscher's trilogy, *The Prophet Outcast*, was published in the USSR. The full trilogy has still not been translated. Soviet biographical publications dealing with Trotsky started by patching up the disintegrating Stalinist schemas: there was a partial recognition of Trotsky's revolutionary and military services, a depiction of Trotskyism as an opponent of Leninism before 1917, and as a deviation from the general line of the party after Lenin's death. They aroused interest by containing facts, which had often been lifted from the works of Western historians, rather than by the depth of their analyses. Afterwards, historians began to divide into two camps: those who idealized Trotsky's activity and even credited him with devising the New Economic Policy; and those who had a sharply negative attitude towards him, such as the military historians published in *Voenno-istorich-eskii zhurnal* ('Military-Historical Journal'). As Russian archives have become more accessible, publications have begun to contain materials which are new to Western historians. For example, the Moscow historian N. A. Vasetskii's book on Trotsky cites for the first time documents from the Russian Department of Police in 1916, alleging Trotsky's collaboration with the Austro-Hungarian secret services.

The greatest interest among Russian readers has been aroused by the trilogy on Lenin, Stalin and Trotsky by the military historian D. A. Volkogonov, who has enjoyed sole access to secret party archives. The evolution of the views of this historian is also interesting. In *Triumph and Tragedy*, his book on Stalin, the first fragment of which was published in *Pravda* on 9 September 1988, he counterposed the 'demon of the revolution' Trotsky to its supposed 'angel' Lenin. By the time he published his books on Trotsky (1992) and Lenin (1994), he presented Trotsky as very close to Lenin, and the views of both of them as very like those of Stalin. Even after his death, Volkogonov has been subject to a great deal of criticism for this evolution from various authors, who have masked their biases in favour of one or other of the three leaders with justified criticisms of Volkogonov's careless use of historical sources and his inaccurate rendering of the names of certain figures.

Trotsky's archive has been dispersed around the world. He took two wagon-loads of documents with him into emigration. Those he sold in 1937 are kept in the archive of the Second International at the International Institute of Social History in Amsterdam. Materials relating to the 1920s, before his expulsion from the USSR, were given to the Houghton Library of Harvard University in Cambridge, Massachusetts, and documents from 1929 and afterwards, along with the manuscripts of his books, are in the Hoover Institution on War, Revolution and Peace in Stanford, California. In Moscow, the Russian Centre for the Preservation and Study of Documents of Recent History (RTsKhIDNI, formerly the Central Party Archive of the Institute of Marxism-Leninism) holds the minutes of Politburo meetings and other documents on Trotsky's activities and Stalin's struggle against him. There are also documents concerning Trotsky in the Archive of the President of the Russian Federation (formerly the Sixth Sector of the General Department of the CPSU CC), the Archive of the Federal Security Service and the Archive of the Russian Overseas Intelligence Service. However, these last three archives are not open to researchers. In order to gain a more profound understanding of the personality and activities of Trotsky, a key figure in the Russian revolution and the Soviet state, it will be necessary to locate and critically assess these documents scattered around the globe.

Further reading

Broué P., *Trotsky* (Paris, Fayard, 1988).

Deutscher I., *The Prophet Armed: Trotsky 1879–1921,* second edn (Oxford, Oxford University Press, 1970).

Deutscher I., *The Prophet Unarmed: Trotsky 1921–1929,* second edn (Oxford, Oxford University Press, 1970).

Deutscher I., *The Prophet Outcast: Trotsky 1929–1940,* second edn (Oxford, Oxford University Press, 1970).

Fel'shtinskii I., ed., *Arkhiv Trotskogo. Kommunisticheskaia oppozitsiia v SSSR. 1923–1927,* 4 vols. (Moscow, Terra, 1990).

Knei-Paz B., *The Social and Political Thought of Leon Trotsky* (Oxford, Clarendon, 1978).

Meijer J. M., ed., *The Trotsky Papers,* 2 vols. (Paris and The Hague, Mouton, 1964, 1971).

Paramonova N. B., Finogenova S. P. and Cherniaev V. Iu., *Raboty L. D. Trotskogo v fondakh Biblioteki Akademii nauk SSSR* (St Petersburg, Biblioteka RAN, 1991).

Rogovin V. Z., *Byla li al'ternativa? 'Trotskizm': vzgliad cherez gody* (Moscow, Terra, 1992).

Rogovin V. Z., *Vlast' i oppozitsii* (Moscow, T-vo zhurnal 'Teatr', 1993).

Trotsky L. D., *The History of the Russian Revolution* (London, Gollancz, 1965).

Trotsky L. D., *The Revolution Betrayed* (New York, Merit, 1965).

Trotsky L. D., *Stalin* (London, Panther, 1969).

Trotsky L. D., *My Life* (New York, Pathfinder, 1970).

Trotsky L. D., *The Stalin School of Falsification* (New York, Pathfinder, 1972).

Vasetskii N. A., *Trotskii. Opyt politicheskoi biografii* (Moscow, Respublika, 1992).

Volkogonov D. A., *Trotsky: Eternal Revolutionary,* trans. and ed. Harold Shukman (London, HarperCollins, 1996).

Tsereteli

ZIVA GALILI AND ALBERT P. NENAROKOV

History has not been kind to Iraklii Georgievich Tsereteli (1881–1960), the Georgian-born Menshevik leader of the Petrograd Soviet and the All-Russian Executive Committee of Soviets (VTsIK). Not only is his name often missing from the histories of the revolution but, when mentioned, he is presented as the executor – not the strategist or tactician – of political accommodation between the Soviet and the Provisional Government. His one biography (*A Democrat in the Russian Revolution* by W. H. Roobol) is not widely known. The layman vaguely identifies him as a second-tier Kerensky. But a more proper comparison would be with Lenin. No less than his Bolshevik nemesis, Tsereteli was known for an unshakeable conviction in his own political conception and strategy, for his ability to hold sway over doubting collaborators and, not least, for his crucial impact on the period that bears his mark. At every significant turn, from the second half of March to October 1917, it was Tsereteli who articulated the political strategy that was followed by mainstream Mensheviks and Socialist Revolutionaries and determined the political course of the soviets and the so-called 'democratic camp'. This singular role is all the more striking because Tsereteli's conception of the revolution did not sit comfortably with any one of the established wings of the Menshevik Party on the eve of 1917, be it internationalism or defencism. Indeed, Tsereteli (again, like Lenin) embodied the role an individual could play in a historical event so patently moved and shaped by crowds, popular organizations and parties.

Like Kerensky, Tsereteli embodied the early victories and the eventual defeat of a democratic conception of the Russian revolution. But his strength was not as a popular tribune. Tsereteli was a politicians' politician. His naturally aristocratic bearing, the ascetic halo of a man who had spent many years in prison, and the confidence of one who had always been a leader joined in a commanding personality which, together with the power of argumentation, made him highly persuasive with fellow socialists and progressive-minded ministers. He appeared brave, honest, even moralistic, but also realistic. This was the case particularly in the first half of 1917, when his conception captured the mood of broad segments of Russian society and the strategies he fashioned appeared workable. But his influence continued long after the optimism of the early period waned, when his idealized broad national unity, embodied and anchored in a coalition government, had become unworkable.

To understand Tsereteli's political conceptions, it is necessary to sort out the layers of influence left by a peculiar revolutionary career in which short periods of intensive political activity and prominence were interspersed by long years of distant isolation. The earliest and deepest layer was left by Tsereteli's childhood environment in Georgia (where he was born in 1881), by his family of Russified and Westernized Georgian intelligentsia of aristocratic origins, and by the early history of Georgian social democracy. From his influential, Westernized father and uncle, Tsereteli inherited a fundamental, even deterministic faith in progress which underlay his Marxism. His social-democratic convictions were distinguished by their optimism about Russian society. In the political hegemony enjoyed by the Georgian social democrats he saw confirmation of his father's argument that the intelligentsia was destined to lead the nation in the difficult transition from autocracy to democracy.

Tsereteli's formative experience with Russian public life began during the protests of 1901 and 1902, when he became a leader of the 'political' wing of the student movement in Moscow. Arrest and illness kept him away from politics during 1905 and 1906, but he made a triumphant return in 1907 at the head of the Georgian, and later the all-Russian, social-democratic faction in the Second State Duma. At the Second Duma, he was able to test a strategy of cooperation between Social Democrats and other oppositional forces, and do so with the blessing of the Central Committee of the RSDRP, where the Mensheviks held a majority in 1907. Based on this experience, he developed two principal arguments: first, that Russian social democracy could successfully organize the peasantry and receive its full support in the struggle against autocracy; and second, that the policy of limited cooperation with the Kadets placed the Social Democrats in a good position to convince the bourgeoisie to join in concerted opposition to the tsarist government. During years of imprisonment from 1907 to 1913 he held fast to his conclusion that a good portion of Russia's educated society could be counted among the progressive forces.

A third and crucial stage in the development of Tsereteli's ideas took place during the First World War, when he lived as an exile in the village of Usol'e, outside Irkutsk in eastern Siberia. Tsereteli proclaimed himself an internationalist, but his insistence on socialist 'absolute neutrality' did not stem from the common internationalist interpretation of the war as 'imperialist'. Instead, Tsereteli based his denunciation on autocracy's role in the conduct of the war. More broadly, he saw war as posing an obstacle to progress and threatening the solidarity of the social-democratic movements of Europe, thus depriving the weaker Russian movement of its natural sources of support. A corollary of these ideas was the belief that a democracy might be justified in taking up arms to defend its national territory and that Russian democracy, in particular, could not be made to pay the price of a separate peace. This last point was also rooted in Tsereteli's respect (unusual among Russian Social Democrats) for the importance of stable political structures, particularly during a time of unsettling social and political change.

Together, these ideas undergirded the strategy of 'revolutionary defencism' which Tsereteli would enunciate in 1917. At the same time he was also drawing on his old optimism about Russia's political development and on his reading of the wartime experience to develop an integrated conception of a revolution led by social democracy but resting on the united 'vital forces of the nation'. He believed that the wartime 'public organizations', especially the Union of Cities and the War Industry Committees, contained the bourgeoisie's 'healthy, progressive' elements and that these had formed the kind of cooperation with the working class essential for Russia's safe transition to democracy. On a more personal level, Tsereteli argued that the unity of opinion between himself, his closest colleagues among Irkutsk's Social Democrats, and those Socialist-Revolutionary exiles who thought of themselves as 'neutral internationalists' exemplified the war's impact on the Russian revolutionary movement at large. He thus positioned himself and the tight group of his supporters to serve as the linchpin of a concerted effort to link a broad spectrum of Russia's competing political leaderships around the task of democratizing the country.

The February revolution was seen by Tsereteli as the realization of his ideas. The revolution, he observed, was a democratic, national revolution carried out by the 'vital forces of the country', among whom he counted not only the soviets' socialist leaders, the workers and the soldiers but also the peasantry and the progressive bourgeoisie. Although he believed that Russia's revolution was an 'all-national' one and its immediate goal democracy, not socialism, he felt that the country's backwardness made the leadership role of the socialist intelligentsia crucial – in promoting the alliance of the 'vital forces', on the one hand, and safeguarding freedom and the revolutionary spirit, on the other. In this scheme, moreover, the soviets were also assigned the all-important task of ensuring the stability of the Russian polity. Military defence of the revolution was one aspect of this task, as well as a guarantee that Russia would continue to play the crucial role Tsereteli had seen for it in the promotion of peace.

Neglected by historians, Tsereteli's first ten days in Petrograd marked a dramatic change in the strategies pursued by the Petrograd Soviet. The Soviet's stance of internationalism and conditional tolerance of the Provisional Government was replaced by two basic strategies, formulated in direct response to the political realities which Tsereteli found in Petrograd upon his return on 20 March: first, the strategy of 'revolutionary defencism' which combined socialist support for military defence with direct negotiations with the Provisional Government to advance the cause of comprehensive peace; and second, a general strategy of direct contact and cooperation between the leaders of the soviets and the Provisional Government with the aim of realizing the democratic goals of the revolution to their fullest without threatening the 'unity of the vital forces'.

Several factors made this dramatic change possible. First, there was the Executive Committee of the Petrograd Soviet, until now dominated by the Menshevik and Independent Social Democrats who had initiated and supported the policy of 'dual power' and *kontrol'*, but falling increasingly into disarray caused as much by internal inconsistencies as by the incalcitrance of the Provisional Government. Then there was the atmosphere around these two political centres – already tense, but not yet hardened by the experience of repeated confrontations, and still open to new possibilities. Finally, there was Tsereteli – the 'prince' of Georgian social democracy and the legendary orator of the suppressed Second Duma, now returning from long years of solitary imprisonment and exile. His slogans and strategies were perfectly suited to reconcile the socialists' internal inconsistencies; his ability to speak to the ministers of the Provisional Government with natural ease provided a welcome and still credible alternative to the stalemate between the Soviet and the Provisional Government. Not least, his deftness at constructing a grand narrative of an all-national revolution (not surprisingly, one that recast his own, long-evolving conception), found resonance among the Soviet's socialist leaders as well as its mass following.

The early victories in the Executive Committee and with the Provisional Government, coming on the eve of the All-Russian Conference of Soviets (29 March–3 April), launched Tsereteli into the position of prominence he would hold in the all-Russian organs of the soviets until October. His formula of revolutionary defence became the rallying point for centrists in the Menshevik and Socialist Revolutionary factions, who now joined in one Revolutionary Defencist bloc that enlisted the support of most delegates from the army and the provinces. To this sympathetic gathering Tsereteli argued that the just-completed negotiations over foreign policy showed the 'responsible' representatives of the bourgeoisie in the cabinet to have renounced the 'narrow class policy' on war which had characterized their class in the past. He used this example to urge a policy of cooperation with the responsible elements of the propertied and educated classes, which understood the national tasks of the day. But while implying that *kontrol'* by the Soviet over the Provisional Government was not as necessary as the architects of dual power had believed, he stopped short of recommending the strategy that appeared to follow from his conception – i.e., the establishment of a coalition government – for it violated the axiomatic Menshevik doctrine against socialist participation in a bourgeois government. Within a month, however, Menshevik enthusiasm for Tsereteli's vision of the soviets as the guarantors of Russia's safe transition to democracy linked with shifting political realities to force a rethinking of the party's stand on coalition.

The April Crisis and its aftermath exposed the weakness of the Provisional Government, its disunity, and the need for the Soviet to shoulder a greater share of national responsibility. Tsereteli was already the first among equals in the Soviet's 'Star Chamber', the handful of Menshevik and Socialist-Revolutionary centrist leaders who led the Petrograd Soviet in public and determined its policies behind closed doors. Now, he became the architect of the first coalition government in Russia. Presenting the coalition as the embodiment both of national unity and of the strength and responsibility of the soviets (here, again, he was the author of a winning narrative), he nevertheless insisted that socialist participation be minimal, relying on cooperation with the 'bourgeois' ministers rather than a socialist majority in the cabinet to bring about the reforms that were the socialists' main justification for participation in government.

The two months from the establishment of the first coalition to the crisis of early July marked the zenith of Tsereteli's influence. Designated the Minister of Post and Telegraph, in fact he personified the coalition – first among the leaders of the soviets and the socialist leader most trusted by the 'progressive' ministers. Yet, his political construct and the political arrangement that it made possible – the 'unity of the vital forces' and the coalition government – were already under attack. His fellow Mensheviks' sweeping support of coalition at their May Conference gave way to doubts. Expressed behind the closed doors of the party's Organizational Committee (protocols of which have recently come to light), Menshevik disenchantment peaked on 14 June with a serious reconsideration of socialist withdrawal from coalition.

Tsereteli's response to the disappointments of coalition was telling: he explored every possibility for redefining the contours of coalition, but never wavered in advocating the basic strategy. In June he continued to hail the unity of the vital forces, blaming the Bolsheviks alone for the rise of radical displays in Petrograd, and seeking to redefine 'democracy' by excluding the Bolsheviks from it. The events of early July forced him to face the failure of the coalition he had authored two months earlier. He made himself the putative architect of a new form of coalition – not with the vital forces at large, but with the more progressive, democratic forces which the new Radical Democratic Party now hoped to gather around itself. While implicitly narrowing further the definition of the 'vital forces', this constellation underscored the unity of purpose between Tsereteli and the Progressists and Left Kadets who joined in the new party, especially N. V. Nekrasov and I. N. Efremov. All the greater, then, was the disappointment, when it became apparent that, in the conditions that had developed by the summer of 1917, the new party and those close to it in the cabinet (especially M. I. Tereshchenko and Kerensky) could not stand their ground against pressure

from the Kadets and the organized entrepreneurs. Tsereteli declined to join
the second coalition which came into office on 23 July without a programmatic statement.

Years later, when he sat down to write his memoirs of 1917, Tsereteli saw
this moment as the end of his fruitful work on behalf of his conception of
the revolution. The memoirs – a two-volume account, detailed and sober,
though naturally self-acquitting – do not cover the last three months of the
revolution, thus adding to the perception that the polarization of society
during these months had emptied political initiatives and solutions of their
significance and had paralysed the Mensheviks. The recently published
documentary history of the Menshevik Party shows that this was not so. It
thus behoves the historian to take a fresh look at Tsereteli's words and
actions in the post-July period.

A close reading of Tsereteli's public addresses in July and August reveals
a gradual rhetorical substitution of 'state interest' for the increasingly hol-
low slogan of the 'united vital forces'. Not that he wavered in his advocacy
of unity and coalition, but his assessment of the Russian revolution (if not
his ideal conception of it) underwent a profound adjustment: no longer a
national revolution, carried by broadly based forces, united by the democratic intelligentsia into a putative 'nation', but a revolution threatened by
widening social and political chasms and dependent on the will and courage
of the moderate political leaders, themselves increasingly isolated. In the
aftermath of the crisis of early July their most pressing task was to take
every necessary measure to ensure the stability and survival of the revolutionary regime.

The language of his arguments was still revolutionary. Speaking to an
emergency plenary of VTsIK on 17 July, Tsereteli addressed the need to
strengthen 'revolutionary order'. He agreed with the many critics of the
Provisional Government from among the provincial and army delegates and
the warnings of his closest colleague F. I. Dan that it was necessary to find a
way to 'strike at anarchy without striking at the revolution itself'. And when
he stated that the Provisional Government had to be given 'unlimited
powers' to fight anarchy 'in all of its manifestations', it was with the
argument that anarchy and counterrevolution fed on each other. But
already on 24 July, in urging VTsIK to accept and support the cabinet just
established, Tsereteli spoke openly of an important change occurring in the
'relations of the democratic organizations to power': whereas previously the
Soviet exercised *kontrol'*, extended help, and participated in the exercise of
power, 'now, full power must be handed over to the Provisional Government' and the Soviet must not interfere in its work.

As a rallying slogan, 'the interest of state' did not have quite the appeal,
the sweeping optimism that had made Tsereteli's rhetoric of unity so successful in the soviets. Indeed, it competed with and contradicted the narrative of a united revolution. Nor did it have historical resonance among
Mensheviks. But this was rhetoric for a revolution and a party in crisis. It

helped Tsereteli unite around himself not an enthusiastic majority, but a disillusioned yet determined core, most of whose members were embroiled in the work of the soviets and the government and bore the attending burden of responsibility. These men had seen their most fearful expectations about coalition realized, had wavered between fear of Bolshevik-inspired extremism and the danger of counterrevolution, and they welcomed Tsereteli's formulations which justified the measures they generally agreed were necessary.

Another political construct of the time – the 'democratic programme' – also served as common ground for Tsereteli and the core of Menshevik veteran centrists . In the aftermath of the second coalition's refusal to be bound by any programmatic statement, least of all the so-called July 8 programme of relatively radical reforms, the 'democratic programme' became not only a necessary part of any campaign against anarchy and extremism, but also the focus of new Menshevik initiatives to define and mobilize those forces that could still be counted on the side of the revolution. Their most prominent success came at the Moscow State Conference (12–15 August), when all the 'democratic' groups, socialist and non-socialist, endorsed the 'August 14 programme'. By giving the 'democratic programme' equal place with 'state interest', Tsereteli strengthened his claim to the support of its strongest advocates – B. O. Bogdanov, N. S. Chkheidze and, most importantly, Dan. Indeed, new documentation reveals Dan's public pronouncements in July to have been much closer to Tsereteli's than had been previously assumed. The two men appear to have worked in full unison through all the tribulations and concessions preceding the formation of the second coalition. Thus, as late as the Unification Congress of the Menshevik Party in the second half of August, and in spite of the prolonged crisis of coalition, Tsereteli commanded a sufficiently strong base of support in the party to ensure its unity and the primacy of his strategies.

General Kornilov's attempted coup in late August emboldened the Mensheviks to launch anew the search for a political alternative to coalition government. Significantly, the initiative was now seized by Dan and Bogdanov, who advocated an all-democratic government charged with implementing the democratic programme of 14 August and accountable to a new public democratic body. Tsereteli, in contrast, declared the coup and its failure to have exonerated the strategy of coalition. He argued that the Kadets' reported involvement with Kornilov did not exclude the party as such from potential participation in government, and demanded that Kerensky be given a free hand in shaping a new, plenipotentiary cabinet. The soviets, he stressed, must not block the new chance to unify the 'truly vital forces'.

This was Tsereteli's last-ditch defence of coalition and he pursued it with tenacity, singlemindedness and opportunism reminiscent above all of Lenin. Of his old supporters, M. I. Skobelev, K. A. Gvozdev and Chkheidze were closest to his current thinking. Others had to be won over repeatedly, most

notably Dan and Bogdanov (the latter confessed to the Democratic Conference that after six months as a coalition supporter he had become an
advocate of a government accountable to democracy alone). In the weeks
leading to the convocation of the Democratic Conference, Tsereteli pressed
his case with arguments that addressed the immediate political concerns of
Mensheviks of Dan's and Bogdanov's stripe, calling for a new government
that would be willing to implement the democratic programme and accept
public accountability. With warnings against workers' extremism ('The
conscious elements must struggle against this *stikhiia* . . .') and a corresponding stress on the need for a strong government enjoying broad support
from society, he also tapped into old and new fears. Thus, when the
Democratic Conference opened, Dan was again the tireless, impeccable supporter of Tsereteli and his coalition strategy, allowing only for a slightly
greater emphasis on the 'programme'.

The Democratic Conference (14–22 September) was at once Tsereteli's
grandest, most natural arena and the scene of his greatest disappointment.
The delegates (about 1,500 of them) came from soviets, the army, labour
organizations, co-operatives, zemstvos and municipalities, national organizations and parties – the whole, diverse 'democracy'. But democracy (like
the Menshevik Party itself) was hopelessly divided, voting now for coalition,
now against it, always by the slightest of margins. Tsereteli argued, cajoled
and even cheated the revolutionary parliament of Russia into following the
political path he considered least harmful. He relied on Dan to ram through
the Menshevik Central Committee a resolution calling on the Democratic
Conference to create a representative standing body (the Preparliament) and
authorize it 'to support the organization of power' by Kerensky. He then
presented this resolution to the deadlocked Democratic Conference as a
document he himself had drafted for the conference's Presidium. He also
made one critical addition to the original Central Committee resolution: a
provision allowing the new government to supplement the democratic
Preparliament with representatives of the propertied groups, should the latter join the cabinet. The body that resulted from this resolution lacked any
binding power, nor was there any incentive for its opposing wings to work
out their differences. Dan, Bogdanov and others fought on to push through
this Preparliament the most crucial elements of the democratic programme.
Tsereteli himself left Petrograd on 5 October, travelling to Georgia to be
reunited with his family. He would be back only after the Bolshevik seizure
of power.

At the Democratic Conference, the magic orator of March and April, the
Georgian prince, the valiant 'knight of coalition' (in A. N. Potresov's words)
was reincarnated as a tough, determined politician. The conception animat-
ing him was largely unchanged, but the revolutionary circumstances could
not have been more different. Tsereteli's optimism finally cracked. V. D.
Nabokov reported him betraying signs of panic for the first time. And
Tsereteli himself summed up his deepest disappointment in a speech to an

audience of Georgian Social Democrats in Tiflis. He complained that the Russian democratic intelligentsia, 'unlike that of Georgia', had proven incapable of fulfilling its role in the revolution and had left the leaders of revolutionary democracy with the dismal choice between coalition and a government of the soviets. Facing this choice even Iu. O. Martov, leader of the Menshevik Internationalists, declared at one point during the Democratic Conference his preference for coalition without the Kadets over the alternative. But as Dan was to discover during the final days of the Provisional Government, coalition remained a barrier to the very reforms that could have helped it avoid a Bolshevik takeover. All of Tsereteli's logic and realism, his convictions and persuasiveness, his personal magic and oratorical powers could not make the coalition government a workable political solution.

Still, Tsereteli's role in Russia's revolution was not yet exhausted. After his return to Petrograd on 7 November, no longer standing at his party's head, he threw himself into the task of shaping new strategies intended to hold back a civil war and towards this purpose even supported Martov, his political opponent for many months and the leader of a new Menshevik majority. Tsereteli's continued significance to any effort at bringing together Russia's democratic forces was recognized in the decision of the new Menshevik leadership to entrust him as the party's chief spokesman at the opening of the Constituent Assembly. His significance to the efforts at democratic consolidation throughout 1917 must become once again (as it was for many contemporaries) part of our understanding of the optimistic hopes and tragic disillusions of that year, and the main lens through which to approach the life and work of this enigmatic man.

Further reading

Galili Z., *The Menshevik Leaders in the Russian Revolution: Social Realities and Political Strategies* (Princeton, Princeton University Press, 1989).

Galili Z. and Nenarokov A. P., 'Krizis koalitsionnoi politiki i usilenie tsentrobezhnykh tendentsii men'shevistskoi partii', in *Men'sheviki v 1917 godu*, vol. 2 (Moscow, Progress-Akademiia and Rospen, 1995).

Nenarokov A. P., 'Upushchennaia vozmozhnost' edineniia demokraticheskikh sil pri reshenii voprosa o vlasti', in *Men'sheviki v 1917 godu*, vol. 3, part I (Moscow, Rospen, 1996).

Nikolaevskii B. I., 'I.G. Tsereteli: Stranitsy biografi', *Sotsialisticheskii vestnik* (1959), no. 6: 119–22; no. 7: 141–3; no. 8/9: 159-64; no. 10: 196–200; no. 11: 219–23; no. 12: 243–5.

Roobol W. H., *Tsereteli: A Democrat in the Russian Revolution* (The Hague, Martinus Nijhoff, 1976)

Tsereteli I. G., *Vospominanicia o Fevral'skoi revoliutsii*, 2 vols. (Paris and the Hague, Mouton, 1968).

The White Generals

VLADIMIR IU. CHERNIAEV

The term 'White generals' denotes the military leaders of the White movement in Russia and thereafter in the emigration, who sought to overthrow
Bolshevik power and recreate a unitary state – 'Great Russia, one and indivisible'. It is a common mistake to extend the term 'White generals' to those
Cossack atamans and generals who, although they fought on the White side,
were fighting for the independence of the Cossack regions. These Cossack
leaders did not recognize the authority of the leaders of the White movement, and they retained their separate identity in the emigration.

The White generals won their positions as a result of their talents and
courage on the battlefield. Their social origins were not of great importance.
The leading White generals M. V. Alekseev, L. G. Kornilov and A. I.
Denikin were born into poorer and more proletarian families than, say,
Lenin or Trotsky. Alekseev's and Denikin's ancestors had been serfs. Baron
P. N. Wrangel came from the old aristocracy, A. V. Kolchak, N. N. Iudenich
and E. K. Miller were descended from the nobility. Their views had been
formed not so much by their social origins as by their membership of the
officer caste, which was closed and conservative, with its own traditions and
codes of honour. The officers were bound by oath to serve the throne, and
the tsarist authorities took pains to keep them away from liberal or socialist
influences. However, contact with the intelligentsia infected the officers with
liberalism, and military failures in World War I gave rise to doubts about
the ability of Nicholas II, as commander in chief, to lead Russia to victory.

The key figure among them in February 1917 was Nicholas II's chief of
staff, General-Adjutant M. V. Alekseev. He had previously taught future
generals at the General Staff's Nikolaevskaia Academy, and in the war
against Japan he had been Quartermaster-General of the Third Army.
During World War I he had commanded the north-western and western
fronts, and on 18 August 1915 he took charge of the *Stavka* headquarters,
and became commander of the entire Russian army with the Tsar as nominal commander in chief. Having quietly joined the liberal opposition,

Alekseev proposed strengthening Russia's power and ability to wage war by creating a government of national confidence with liberal participation, but subordinate to the dictatorship of the head of the *Stavka* (i.e., to himself), preserving the juridical status of the tsar. In June 1916 Nicholas rejected this scheme, and this determined Alekseev's role in his subsequent abdication. It was on his initiative that, at the decisive moment in the February revolution, the commanders of the front armies and the naval fleets, including Grand Duke Nikolai Nikolaevich and Admiral Kolchak, called on the tsar to abdicate in favour of his son. It seemed to them that the revolution was directed against Nicholas, and would be completed by his abdication. It was Alekseev who told the ex-tsar he was under arrest, and he subsequently took the position of commander in chief.

To the generals, winning the war was more important than conserving the monarchical form of government. In their eyes, it was not the Provisional Government's republican type of administration which prevented this. It was rather the government's inability to prevent the collapse of the army and the country itself, the interference of soviets and elected soldiers' organizations in military matters, and the Bolsheviks' calls for fraternization with the enemy and the replacement of the army by the general arming of the people. Alekseev and Denikin, the head of his general staff, demanded firm measures by the government to strengthen the army. This led to their dismissal from their posts at the end of May 1917, and they joined the secret movement of army commanders for a military dictatorship. They were not aiming at the restoration of the monarchy. Instead, they favoured first Admiral Kolchak, and later General Kornilov as dictator.

The 37-year-old Kolchak was a noted polar explorer, a learned hydrographer, oceanologist and glaciologist, who had been awarded the golden sabre for his courage in the defence of Port Arthur during the war with Japan. He was the State Duma's naval expert, had assisted in the creation of the naval general staff, and had been in charge of working out its programme of naval ship-building. During World War I he had laid a shield of mines to protect Petrograd against naval attack, and had taken part in assaults on German shipping convoys. In June 1916 he headed the Black Sea Fleet, created a flotilla on the Danube, and was preparing to storm the Bosporus, but these plans were upset by the revolution. On 6 June 1917 the Sevastopol Soviet removed him for resisting their intervention in the fleet's affairs, and the Provisional Government, preferring to be rid of Kolchak, sent him to the USA in early August at the head of a naval mission.

The 47-year-old Kornilov was no less remarkable a person. He was a fearless military intelligence officer who had secretly penetrated regions of Asia inaccessible to Europeans owing to his knowledge of local languages and his Asiatic appearance. He had written geographical studies and was a talented military commander. In the war against Japan he had commanded a brigade, and in World War I he commanded a division, which had become known as the 'steel division' for its tenacity. In July 1916 he was the first general to escape after being taken prisoner. He was put in charge of a corps and, in March 1917, of the Petrograd Military Region. It was Kornilov who arrested the tsar's family. During the April Crisis he had wanted to use cannon fire in the manner of Napoleon Bonaparte to disperse demonstrators demanding the resignation of the government, but the artillerymen refused to obey him. In the June Offensive it was his Eighth Army that had the greatest successes at the front. On 7 July he was put in charge of the southwestern front. He got the Provisional Government to reintroduce the death penalty at the front for military offences, and he banned Bolshevik agitators and papers. On 19 July he handed this front over to Denikin and became commander in chief.

At the end of August, Kornilov was at the head of an attempted military-republican coup which aimed to disperse the soviets, destroy the Bolsheviks, and establish under his leadership a powerful Council of National Defence, in which he expected Alekseev and Kolchak to take part. This unsuccessful attempted coup represented the starting point of the White movement. It fell to Alekseev to arrest the Kornilovites. In an album produced by the arrestees, Kornilov penned the slogan: 'The more difficult the situation, the more boldly we must press forward'. Alongside him in prison were his colleagues and fellow generals: his chief of staff A. S. Lukomskii, the Quartermaster-General of the *Stavka* I. P. Romanovskii, Denikin and his chief of staff S. L. Markov, and the commander of the Eleventh Special Army, I. G. Erdeli. Their discussions in prison gave rise to the programme of the White movement.

After the Bolshevik revolution, Alekseev's secret officers' organization moved from Petrograd and Moscow to the Don, and became the nucleus of the Volunteer Army, joined by the Kornilovites who had fled to the south. Rivalry arose between Alekseev and Kornilov. Denikin helped overcome this by means of a compromise: Kornilov became commander in chief, while Alekseev became supreme leader, with responsibility for civil administration, finances and foreign relations. In Soviet historiography, all the White generals were depicted as fervent monarchists. However, Kornilov, Denikin and some others did not want to see the restoration of the Romanov dynasty, and adopted the idea of not prejudging the question. This idea had emerged in the February revolution as a compromise between the liberals and socialists, and had been rejected from the outset by the Bolsheviks. In its political declaration the Volunteer Army promised to create a provisional strong supreme authority, to restore civil rights, freedom of speech and of the press, to denationalize industry and convoke a Constituent Assembly, in order freely to determine the will of the people on the desired form of government and solution of the land question. The Volunteer Army chief of staff, Lukomskii, attempted to convince Kornilov of the necessity for a period of dictatorship followed by the election of a new Constituent Assembly by propertied elements, but Kornilov argued that events themselves would show what approach to take.

On 13 April 1918, during the First Kuban Campaign (the 'Ice March'), Kornilov was killed in the storming of Ekaterinodar. He was succeeded by his assistant, the 45-year-old Denikin. Denikin's first military experience had been in the war with Japan, in which he had repulsed attacks with bayonets and carried out cavalry raids into the enemy's rear. He was a talented writer, and had published war stories and satirical articles about military life. During World War I his division of riflemen became known as the 'Iron Division', and was expanded into a brigade. He avoided sacrificing his men needlessly. For his personal courage he had been awarded a diamond-encrusted weapon of St George.

Denikin was an officer of liberal-republican views. He took Kadets such as Countess S. V. Panina and N. I. Astrov as advisers, although he was concerned not to alienate those further to the right. He ordered that the murder of the tsar's family be marked by a requiem in the army, but rejected Alekseev's suggestion that the army adopt the monarchist standard. Neither the inhabitants of the Don, the Kuban, and Stavropol', where the Volunteer Army was based, nor the governments of the Entente states, on whose assistance the army was counting, wished for the restoration of tsarism. Additionally, it could have led to dissension within the army. As Denikin wrote in one of his letters: 'If I raise the republican flag, I lose half my volunteers, and if I raise the monarchist flag, I lose the other half. But we have to save Russia.' For this reason the army's slogan was not any specific form of government, but 'Great Russia, one and indivisible'.

Soviet and Western historians often interpret this slogan as a manifestation of Russian nationalism. However, it clearly expressed a patriotic urge to recreate the power, prosperity and unity of the motherland, which had been broken up and destroyed by the revolution and the humiliating (particularly for the military) terms of the Brest-Litovsk peace. There was indeed widespread nationalism in the Volunteer Army, but it was alien to Denikin, the son of a Russian father and a Polish Catholic mother. Denikin shared the views of the liberal historian V. O. Kliuchevskii on the national, religious and cultural unity of the three branches of the Russian people: the Great Russians, Little Russians (Ukrainians) and Belorussians. Denikin believed that the Ukrainian question had been inspired by Germany and Austria-Hungary, which intended to use chauvinists to weaken Russia and make the conquered Slavic peoples the manure ('*Düngervölker*') in which German culture could flourish. He considered the Ukrainian leader S. V. Petliura a traitor and a rogue, and rejected the idea of allying with him against the Bolsheviks.

From October 1918, following the death of Alekseev, both military and civil power were held by Denikin. Generals A. M. Dragomirov and Lukomskii became his deputies. Both favoured the restoration of the house of Romanov and, despite Denikin's opposition, monarchist propaganda developed among the troops. In the spring of 1919 Denikin asked his Special Council, the highest organ of civil administration, to draw up some regulations for the parts of South Russia occupied by his forces. They were intended to facilitate the transfer of land to peasants with little land, either by voluntary agreement or by compulsory sale, and to devise labour laws envisaging an eight-hour day, health protection, the development of insurance, trade unions and so on, in conjunction with employers and workers. However, the return to the landowners of livestock and equipment seized by peasants was accompanied by acts of gross violence, while the factory owners dismissed all the awkward workers once they got their enterprises back. This led to worker and peasant hostility to the White movement.

Denikin did not recognize the authority of the SR-Kadet Ufa Directory which was formed on 23 September 1918 in the sole and short-lived attempt to create a civilian anti-Bolshevik government claiming to rule over the whole of Russia. On 18 November it was overthrown and in its place Kolchak declared himself Supreme Ruler of the Russian State as well as commander in chief and established his dictatorship in Siberia, the Urals and the Far East. His declared aims were to create an army capable of fighting, to rout Bolshevism, and to establish the rule of law 'so that the people can choose the form of government it wants without hindrance, and realize the great ideas of freedom'. It was, however, the harshest of the White regimes. It shot peasants, workers and soldiers for insubordination, closed down inconvenient newspapers and broke up trade unions. Even the opponents of the Bolsheviks regarded it as the darkest reaction, as 'Bolshevism in reverse'. Kolchak recognized all the treaties and obligations of the tsarist government, restored pre-revolutionary taxes and duties as well as introducing new ones, gave large subsidies to industrialists, merchants and bankers, and paid handsomely for military supplies from Britain, France and Japan. Those peasants who had received land from the Bolsheviks ceased to own it and became leaseholders, whilst prosperous farms were encouraged. The Kadet Professor N. V. Ustrialov, a close associate of Kolchak, remarked that 'as a dictator Kolchak was completely created by circumstances which demanded dictatorship'. By mobilizing the male population between 18 and 43 with at least four years' education, Kolchak created an army of 400,000 men.

In early January 1919 Denikin informed Kolchak of his total and unbreakable allegiance, but did not recognize his supremacy until 12 June. This hesitation was the result of personal rivalry. Denikin's entourage wanted him to have the supreme role. Kolchak rewarded this eventual recognition by making Denikin deputy commander in chief.

General Iudenich had recognized Kolchak's authority in January 1919. In 1915 and 1916 he had distinguished himself by taking Erzerum and Trapezund, thus thwarting Turkey's planned seizure of the Suez Canal. In 1919 he was in Finland, preparing a march on Petrograd. On 10 June Kolchak named him commander in chief of the troops in the north-west of Russia, but refused to recognize the independence of Finland, Estonia, Latvia and Lithuania. As a result of this, Finland and Estonia became unwilling to take part militarily in the assault on Petrograd. Without the support from Finland and Estonia on which he had been counting, Iudenich was routed on reaching the outskirts of Petrograd. The remnants of his army in Estonia were disarmed and demobilized, and Iudenich himself went to Britain and ceased to be involved in the White movement.

On 30 April the supremacy of Kolchak was recognized by the Provisional Government of the Northern Region in Arkhangel'sk. The leading role in this government was played by General E. K. Miller, who had shown himself to be a good strategist in World War I. He had been wounded in a soldiers' riot in April 1917 and had subsequently been dispatched to Italy as a *Stavka* representative. By February 1920 he had been defeated, and Miller and his general staff escaped into exile on icebreakers, under fire from workers and sailors who had risen against them. He was later reproached by many for having left the remnants of his army at the mercy of the victors, having believed British promises to evacuate them.

The offensive which Kolchak launched in March 1919 with the aim of linking up with Denikin's forces ended in a Red Army counteroffensive. On 5 January 1920 Kolchak relinquished the title of Supreme Ruler in favour of Denikin, who had been regarded as his deputy. He was subsequently arrested by the Czech Legion, handed over to the SR and Menshevik-dominated Political Centre in Irkutsk, tried by the local Military-Revolutionary Committee and, on 7 February 1920, shot.

Denikin's troops' assault on Moscow in the summer of 1919, which coincided with Iudenich's forces' march on Petrograd and the retreat of Kolchak's army, was the most dangerous moment for Lenin's government. Denikin demanded that his army guarantee the inviolability of the persons and property of civilians regardless of their status, nationality or religion, but was none the less unable to prevent looting and pogroms. His subordinate General V. Z. Mai-Maevskii, commander of the Volunteer Army, believed looting to be the motor of military success, and permitted his soldiers to sack Khar'kov for three days. General A. G. Shkuro, commander of the Kuban Army, extorted levies from urban Jews. Some generals were particularly noted for their pillaging. Other generals, such as Baron Wrangel, A. P. Kutepov and Ia. A. Slashchov, attempted to combat looting by publicly hanging thieves from posts to deter others, but this did little to change the overall picture. Wrangel later recalled: 'One of the major reasons for the collapse of General Denikin's army was its lack of any firm notion of right or sense of legality. The troops were debauched, and the military courts under the chief military and naval procurator were powerless.' The population, particularly that part of it which had not had any experience of the looting and pogroms perpetrated on the Bolshevik side, began to detest the White Army, which facilitated its defeat. When Denikin's forces were routed, it was Slashchov who saved the Crimea, preventing a Red Army force ten times larger from crossing the Crimean Isthmus. This allowed the front to be reformed after the catastrophe at Novorossiisk and the White troops' capitulation at Sochi, and postponed the collapse of the White Army for another year.

On 22 March 1920 Denikin surrendered his post to his main opponent in the White movement, Baron Wrangel. During World War I, Wrangel had been the first to be awarded the Order of St George for taking two German field guns in a cavalry attack, and in 1919 he commanded the Caucasian and later the Volunteer Army. Comparing Wrangel with Denikin, a participant in and historian of the White movement D. Lehovich wrote:

> Wrangel had an attractive appearance and the bearing of an officer of one of the best cavalry regiments of the old Imperial Guard. He was impetuous, nervous, impatient, powerful and sharp, but at the same time he was a practical realist and was extremely flexible in political matters. Denikin was an inflexible person who had never sought political power. At that time he was disenchanted with his colleagues, restrained and laconic, and retained within himself, for all the twists and turns of fate, certain romantic and idealistic characteristics. He concentrated these in the inner world of his principles and his view of life which, alas, diverged sharply from reality. Wrangel was naturally a born leader and dictator, whereas Denikin regarded dictatorship as just a passing phase, inevitable in conditions of civil chaos.

Wrangel removed the Kadets from power, and even regarded the Octobrists with suspicion. He remained a convinced monarchist. Pressure from the Entente countries compelled his government to carry out 'left-wing policies with right-wing hands'. However, these right-wing hands did not share the 'left-wing prejudices of parliamentarism and democracy', and under more favourable circumstances could soon have returned to 'the right cause'. Wrangel was prepared to form any alliances necessary in his attempt to establish a second, independent White Russia within Tauride gubernia, and hoped to incorporate the Don region and the North Caucasus. Unlike Denikin, he was intolerant of internal opposition. He militarized and bureaucratized the civil authorities, and renamed his forces the 'Russian Army', stressing that they were fighting for the whole of Russia.

Denikin thought it improper to give military awards in a civil war between Russians, and soldiers who distinguished themselves were rewarded with promotion alone. Kolchak, Iudenich and the Don atamans bestowed the traditional awards for military services. Wrangel, unlike Denikin, not only awarded the George Cross, but also created the Order of St Nicholas the Miracle-Worker, with a ribbon of the national tricolour bearing the legend 'Faith will save Russia'.

On 25 May 1920 Wrangel published a land decree in the hope of winning peasant sympathy. It distributed land to the peasants, for which they would have to pay the state in cash or grain over 25 years. However, this measure was too late to win the peasants to his side. Wrangel introduced volost zem-stvos, established order in the rear, strengthened his army and launched an offensive, declaring that the Russian people should have the chance to choose its rulers itself. During the war between Soviet Russia and Poland, Wrangel refused to establish a joint command with the Polish leader Józef Piłsudski for political reasons. Once this war had ended, the Red Army could devote all its forces to Wrangel, and on 17 November 1920 the remnants of his army left the Crimea for Constantinople.

Abroad, the White generals were no longer seen as useful by their former military allies. Denikin lived in Britain, Belgium and Hungary, and in 1925 he settled in France. In Britain he had rejected P. N. Miliukov's suggestion that he assume titular supreme power, calling instead for support for Wrangel. He started writing his multi-volume work *The Russian Turmoil*, in which he described the 1917 revolution and civil war as both a historian and a memoirist, and frankly admitted his own mistakes. Many former generals and officers found employment as workers and drivers in Paris, Sofia and other cities. General N. F. Ern worked as a farm labourer in Paraguay before being invited to become a professor at the Military Academy. He distinguished himself in the war with Bolivia and became a Paraguayan lieutenant-general. The former commander of the troops of the Odessa region and governor-general of Odessa, A. V. Shvarts, later worked for many years as a professor in the Academy of the Argentinian General Staff.

After the Soviet Central Executive Committee had decreed an amnesty, Slashchov returned to Moscow in November 1921. He had been demoted to the ranks by a court of honour for quarreling with Wrangel. From 1922 he lectured on tactics at the 'Vystrel' school for top officers, published articles against Wrangel, and called on officers to return home. He was shot on 11 January 1929. The official version of this story was that his murderer killed him in revenge for the execution of one of his relatives.

In the hope of preserving his army from disintegration, in 1924 Baron Wrangel founded and headed the Russian All-Military Union (ROVS). Its members were obliged to remain battle-ready and to refrain from participating in political organizations. Wrangel believed that it was necessary to keep monarchists and republicans together in order to maintain the unity of the army and continue the White struggle. He kept to the centrist position of not pre-judging the issue, although Lukomskii and others were demanding that the ROVS advance the slogan of monarchism.

The claim of Grand Duke Kirill Vladimirovich to the Russian throne caused a split among the monarchists into 'legitimists' (Kirill's supporters), and the supporters of the Grand Duke Nikolai Nikolaevich, who could not forgive Kirill for betraying the tsar in the February revolution, nor for his subsequent calls to unite tsarist and Soviet power. Relations between the White generals and Grand Duke Nikolai were also difficult. Alekseev had convinced him not to take part in the fratricidal civil war. Kolchak had been put forward as a counterweight to the idea of calling on the grand duke to be leader. In the period of the White Army's collapse, Wrangel did not consider it possible to proclaim Nikolai as leader, but on 16 November 1924 he announced his recognition of Nikolai, handed the leadership of the army and military organizations over to him, and seconded Kutepov to him to lead secret operations within the USSR. However, in spite of Wrangel's warnings, Kutepov and the grand duke became involved in the so-called 'Trust' operation, which had been skilfully prepared by the OGPU, and which did grave damage to the White cause.

Wrangel's closest colleagues were the generals P. N. Shatilov and A. A. von Lampe, who published the journal *Beloe delo* ('The White Cause'), along with A. I. Guchkov and the philosopher I. A. Il'in. Wrangel was preparing to create a secret organization to carry out work within the USSR, but he died on 25 April 1928. His children believed he had been poisoned by an OGPU agent.

Wrangel's successor as head of the ROVS, Kutepov, sent terrorists into the USSR through Finland, but they were quickly eliminated. This was because Kutepov's circle included such Soviet agents as the White general N. V. Skoblin, his wife the singer N. V. Plevitskaia, and the former Moscow industrialist and member of the Provisional Government S. N. Tret'iakov. On 26 January 1930, Kutepov was kidnapped by OGPU agents on the streets of Paris. He died in a prison cell in Moscow as a result of frequent injections, without having said a word to his interrogators. The next head of the ROVS, General Miller, was also seized on the streets of Paris on 22 September 1937. In Moscow he was kept in prison under the name of Ivanov and, after lengthy interrogation, was shot on 11 May 1939. Skoblin, who had been involved in the kidnap of Miller, fled back to the USSR from France. It later became known that he was also connected with the fascist Abwehr, and had helped it get materials into the USSR, including that which was used in the trial of M. I. Tukhachevskii and other marshals. Plevitskaia died in prison in France.

Subsequent heads of the ROVS were the former commander of Wrangel's Don Corps F. F. Abramov and, from 1938 to 1957, Wrangel's former chief of staff General A. P. Arkhangel'skii, who laid the basis for ROVS's cooperation with the new generation of *émigrés* in the National Labour Union (NTS).

Denikin kept aloof from political groups, ROVS and the Grand Duke Nikolai Nikolaevich, whom he did not believe capable of playing a serious role. Denikin warned the *émigrés* against Nazism, and considered that a war launched by Germany would lead not to the liberation, but to the enslavement of the Russian people. The day Germany invaded the USSR, the White General P. S. Makhrov, a member of the 'Union of Defencists' which favoured aiding the USSR in the event of military invasion, posted a request to the Soviet ambassador in Paris asking to be admitted into the Soviet army. As a result he found himself in a Nazi concentration camp. The former Quartermaster-General of the Volunteer Army and head of the ROVS office, General P. A. Kusonskii, was also arrested and beaten to death in a concentration camp by the Nazis.

However, most of the White generals decided to make use of Germany in their struggle for a White Russia. An ROVS department head, von Lampe, offered volunteers to the Wehrmacht for the war against the USSR. General N. N. Golovin, who had set up advanced military courses in the emigration along the lines of the general staff's Nikolaevskaia Academy, trained Russian officers for the Wehrmacht. In 1941 General B. A. Shteifon created and headed a Russian Corps which was integrated into the Wehrmacht and fought against the Yugoslav partisans. Generals Arkhangel'skii, Abramov, Dragomirov, von Lampe, Shkuro and others took part in A. A. Vlasov's 'Russian Liberation Army'. The assets of Wrangel's army were given to the 'Committee for the Liberation of the Peoples of Russia', set up by Vlasov in November 1944 in Prague as a pro-German Russian government.

The White collaborators with the Nazis accused Denikin of defecting to the camp of the 'Jew-Masons'. He was held under house arrest and his premises were searched. He secretly put General P. K. Pisarev, who had commanded a corps in Wrangel's army, in charge of the Union of Defencists. In an address marking the 27th anniversary of the Volunteer Army on 15 November 1944, Denikin called Nazi collaborators 'scum', declared that 'the fate of Russia is more important than the fate of the emigration', and wished the Soviet army victory. However, his hopes that the national enthusiasm in the USSR which the war had produced would lead to the ousting of the Stalin regime as well as the Nazis, were unfounded. Depressed by the fact that part of the emigration had come under the influence of Stalin, in December 1945 Denikin moved to the USA. He was writing a book, *The Second World War, Russia and Abroad*, and some memoirs, *The Path of a Russian Officer*, but this work was interrupted by his death.

By the 1980s the remaining participants in the White cause with the rank of general had died. The White movement failed in Russia not only because of its leaders' inadequate military skills and insufficient assistance from its allies, but also because of the generals' personal ambitions and rivalries and their inability to advance a rallying call and programme to attract the majority of Russia's population. By abolishing the Soviet decrees they reinstated the democratic laws of the Provisional Government, but were unable to guarantee observance of these laws. Their arbitrariness, along with the White terror, turned the population against them. In the emigration they held fast to the idea of not pre-judging Russia's governmental system, but, for all the vitality of the idea, it failed to bring results.

In Soviet historiography the White generals were uniformly depicted as counterrevolutionary monarchists. It retrospectively belittled or ignored their roles in the Russo-Japanese war and World War I, and did not mention their scientific achievements. It was not until the 1990s that scholarly biographical essays and books on the White generals began to appear. These included K. A. Bogdanov's *Admiral Kolchak*, which was based on archival sources and appeared in 1993, and the collection of essays by military historians

World War I in the Memoirs of Russian Military Leaders, published in Moscow in 1994. The literature published outside Russia is much fuller, including D. Lehovich's well-documented *White Against Red: The Life of General Anton Denikin*, S. P. Mel'gunov's *Tragedy of Admiral Kolchak*, Peter Kenez's two-volume *Civil War in South Russia*, and R. Luckett's *The White Generals: An Account of the White Movement in the Russian Civil War*. However, as yet there are no good scholarly biographies of such leading military figures as Alekseev, Kornilov, Wrangel, Iudenich or Miller, who became the leaders of the White Army.

Most of the documents on the White generals are located outside Russia, particularly in the USA and France. In the Bakhmetiev Archive, in the Department of Rare Manuscripts of the Library of Columbia University in New York, there are the personal deposits of Denikin, Iudenich, Kutepov, Shatilov, Makhrov, von Lampe and others. In the Hoover Institute in Stanford the collections of Baron Wrangel and his mother, and of Generals Miller, Lukomskii, von Lampe and others, as well as the deposit on Iudenich's North-Western Army, are accessible to researchers. There are further documents relating to Wrangel in the private collection of his son P. P. Wrangel (Southampton, New York State), and in the Mark Bristol collection at the US Library of Congress. A collection of top secret ROVS materials is held at the Holy Trinity Monastery of the Russian Orthodox Church Abroad in Jordanville, New York State. In Western Europe the most valuable materials are held in the Archive of the Society of Adherents of Russian History in Paris and in the private collection of Lavr Chapron du Larre (the grandson of General Kornilov) in Brussels.

In Russia, materials on the pre-revolutionary lives and works of the White generals are held in the Russian State Military-Historical Archive in Moscow, and materials on Admiral Kolchak are in the Russian State Naval Archive in St Petersburg. The basic materials about their activities in the civil war and the emigration are kept in the State Archive of the Russian Federation (with deposits on Alekseev, Denikin, Kolchak and others), and in the Centre for the Preservation of Historical Documentary Collections (formerly the secret Central State Special Archive).

Further reading

Bogdanov K. A., *Admiral Kolchak* (St Petersburg, Sudostroenie, 1993).
Bortnevskii V., *Beloe delo. Liudi i sobytiia* (St Petersburg, Geia, 1993).
Denikin A. I., *The Russian Turmoil: Memoirs Military, Social and Political* (London, Hutchinson, n.d.).
Denisov S. V., compiler, *Belaia Rossiia. Al'bom No. 1* (New York, Glavnoe pravlenie Zarubezhnogo soiuza russkikh voennykh invalidov, 1937).
Figes O., *A People's Tragedy: The Russian Revolution 1891–1924* (London, Jonathan Cape, 1996).

Goldin V. I., compiler, *Belyi Sever. 1918–1920. Memuary i dokumenty*, 2 vols. (Arkhangel'sk, Informatsionnoe Agentstvo 'Argus', 1993).

Kenez P., *Civil War in South Russia, 1918: The First Year of the Volunteer Army* (Berkeley, University of California Press, 1971).

Kenez P., *Civil War in South Russia, 1919–1920: The Defeat of the Whites* (Berkeley, University of California Press, 1977).

Lehovich D. V., *White Against Red: The Life of General Anton Denikin* (New York, Norton, 1974).

Lockett R., *The White Generals: An Account of the White Movement in the Russian Civil War* (New York, Viking, 1971).

Makhrov P. S., *V Beloi armii generala Denikina. Zapiski nachal'nika shtaba Glavnokomanduiushchego Vooruzhennymi Silami Iuga Rossii* (St Petersburg, Logos, 1994).

Mawdsley E., *The Russian Civil War* (Boston, Unwin Hyman, 1987).

Mel'gunov S. P., *Tragediia Admirala Kolchak* (Belgrade, 1930).

Mlechin L., *Set' Moskva-OGPU-Parizh* (supplement to journal *Konets veka*, 1991).

Poliakov I. A. and Igritskii I. I., eds., *Grazhdanskaia voina v Rossii: perekrestok mnenii* (Moscow, Nauka, 1994).

Portugalskii R. M. *et al.*, eds., *Pervaia mirovaia v zhizneopisaniiakh russkikh voenachal'nikov* (Moscow, Elakos, 1994).

Prianishnikov B., *Nezrimaia pautina. VChK-GPU-NKVD protiv Beloi emigratsii* (St Petersburg, Chas pik, 1993).

Shchegolev P. E., ed., *Iudenich pod Petrogradom. Iz belykh memuarov* (Leningrad, Sovetskii pisatel', 1991).

Slashchov-Krymskii I. A., *Belyi Krym. 1920 g. Memuary i dokumenty* (Moscow, Nauka, 1990).

Wrangel P. N., *Always with Honor* (New York, Robert Spellar, 1957).

PARTIES, MOVEMENTS, IDEOLOGIES

Anarchists

VLADIMIR IU. CHERNIAEV

The anarchist ideal of having no government, and the communistic aspirations which go with it, are always present in one form or another in society. They flare up at times when a society is becoming less prosperous, and die down when the society is flourishing. Hopes of realizing anarchist ideas arose in the nineteenth century, when the French economist and sociologist Pierre-Joseph Proudhon proposed that an anarchist republic, in which freedom 'was the mother, not the daughter, of order', could be established through peaceful reforms. Later, Russian revolutionary *émigrés*, the noblemen M. A. Bakunin and Prince P. A. Kropotkin, made anarchism into a revolutionary ideological system.

The Bakuninist conception of a 'worldwide revolution' involved the destruction of the state as having exhausted its historical role. It envisaged the forcible reconstruction of society on the bases of collectivism, self-government and socialism (i.e. equality and the abolition of exploitation), turning it into a fraternal union of free, autonomous, productive associations, which would voluntarily come together in a united Europe and a world federation. Bakunin followed the principle that 'freedom without socialism is injustice, while socialism without freedom is slavery', and warned that Karl Marx's ideas on the dictatorship of the proletariat could only be realized in the form of an authoritarian state communism, in which state property would become the property of state officials.

The apostle of anarchist communism, Kropotkin, considered that the reconstruction of society would be a lengthy process. Evolution would prepare for the revolution, and the latter would give direction to further evolution. Reaction could slow down evolution for a time, but society would inevitably pass through socialism to anarchist communism. State authority was hostile to the natural right of individual freedom, and would fall along with capitalism, to be replaced by people's rule (*narodopravstvo*). Unlike the 'overbearing communism' of Marx, 'free communism', a synthesis of economic and political liberty, would be able to guarantee the freedom of the individual in the communes in which everybody would work, collectively, without payment. Kropotkin considered the most powerful force in the struggle for economic freedom to be the cooperative movement, and the universal means to attain general freedom – an anarchist federation without laws, courts, prisons (i.e. schools of crime), coercion or executions.

Two early organizations of Russian anarchists were founded in Geneva by G. I. and L. Gogeliia – in 1900, the 'Group of Russian Anarchists Abroad', and in 1903, 'Bread and Freedom', which was supported by Kropotkin. Other groups later arose in the US, Germany, France and Bulgaria. The main centres of anarchism in the Russian empire were Bialystok, where the first group was founded in 1903, Odessa and Ekaterinoslav. The First and Second Congresses of Bread and Freedom, held in London in 1904 and 1906 with Kropotkin present, adopted policies of destroying capitalism and the state by means of a general strike, decentralizing industry, and uniting physical and mental labour. They rejected participation in the newly established State Duma, and though condemning terror, recognized the right to employ it in self-defence.

The extremist wing of anarchist communism was represented by the 'Black Flag Group' of I. S. Grossman-Roshchin and others, who advocated indiscriminate terror; and a group known as the *beznachal'tsy*, who rejected any moral scruples in the struggle against the autocracy and who favoured 'direct action' such as killing and robbery. Along with the Socialist Revolutionaries, the anarchist communists carried out 'expropriations' to get funds. In December 1905, their bands fought alongside SRs, Bolsheviks and Mensheviks on the barricades in Moscow.

Subsequent tendencies within anarchism developed their own tactics. The syndicalists, such as G. B. Sandomirskii and Ia. Novomirskii (D. I. Kirillovskii), agitated for the transfer of enterprises to the trade unions as the highest form of workers' organization, and for struggle against the state through strikes, sabotage and expropriations. The individualists, such as Professor A. A. Borovoi, saw their goal as freedom for individuality, and private property as its guarantor. Associational anarchism, represented by Lev Chernyi (P. D. Turchaninov), proposed uniting individualism and collectivism by creating producers' associations, but it was also in favour of terror against the autocracy.

By 1907, there were more than 5,000 anarchists organized in 255 groups in 180 towns and villages in the Russian empire. They included craftsmen, peasants, small traders, intellectuals and workers. They were drawn from various nationalities, including Russians and Ukrainians, and about one half of them were Jews from the Pale of Settlement, the territory to which Jews were restricted, consisting of the Polish provinces and those of the west and south-west.

Others who tended towards anarchism without becoming involved in the movement were the followers of L. N. Tolstoy (essentially a Christian sect), Jan Wacław Machajski, who represented a tendency in Marxism hostile to the intelligentsia, V. A. Posse and the communist-cooperators, and, after 1917, the ethical communists.

Following the defeat of the 1905 revolution the anarchist movement disintegrated, and by 1914 there were only seven groups left. The anarchists were split over World War I. Some, such as Kropotkin, and the prisoners in Schlüsselburg fortress P. F. Vinogradov and I. P. Zhuk, favoured Russia's military victory. Others, such as Grossman-Roshchin and A. Iu. Ge, were internationalists and defeatists. At the start of 1917 there were a few hundred anarchists at liberty, and those who were in prison were released after the February revolution. Anarchists took part in the uprising in Petrograd, and gained influence among soldiers and sailors, particularly on the naval base of Kronstadt. Among the anarchists who returned from emigration were Kropotkin, V. M. Volin (Eikhenbaum), V. S. Shatov and E. Z. Iarchuk. An attempt to unite the anarchists at a conference held in Khar'kov on 18–22 July 1917 was not successful.

'The Anarcho-Syndicalist Propaganda Union' of Volin, G. P. Maksimov (Grigorii Lapot'), Iarchuk and others gained control of a number of trade unions, demanded the replacement of the state with a federation of syndicates, collaborated with the Bolsheviks in the Central Council of Factory Committees and encouraged workers to take over the factories. In practice, these takeovers followed the same pattern: seizure – sell-off of raw materials and property – collapse of production.

The anarchist communists remained the strongest and most militant current. Their Petrograd federation, led by I. S. Bleikhman (N. Solntsev), called for a social revolution: the overthrow of the Provisional Government, the transfer of enterprises, land and foodstuffs to the workers for common use, the replacement of trade by natural exchange between communes, and the establishment of a union between these communes. They placed economic equality above political equality, considering that even an angel, given power, would grow horns and a tail.

The veteran anarcho-syndicalist Sandomirskii pointed with horror at the personal enrichment of those anarchist communists who had seized the well-appointed private residences of aristocrats and merchants. Kropotkin paid a visit to their headquarters at the former dacha of General P. P. Durnovo, a member of the defunct State Council, and was appalled at the convergence between anarchist communists and common criminals. Although he rejected Kerensky's invitation to join the government, Kropotkin was sympathetic to him and to Prince G. E. L'vov, the Provisional Government's first prime minister, and considered that the activities of the anarchists and Bolsheviks would help the Germans win the war. He saw the soviets as instruments for building the new order, but, unlike such figures as Bleikhman and Iarchuk, was not invited to join them. These other anarchists considered that, as an anarchist, Kropotkin was finished.

A destructive role in the construction of a democratic order was played by the informal alliance between the anarchists and the Bolsheviks, who were pragmatically extending their social support on the basis of the most impatiently revolutionary sections of society. The Bolsheviks manipulated the anarchists skilfully, while distancing themselves from anarchism verbally in order to deflect criticism from the right. Lenin recalled in 1921: 'I have met and talked with few anarchists in my life, but all the same I have seen enough of them. I sometimes succeeded in reaching agreement with them about aims, but never as regards principles.' The leaflets and papers issued by the anarchists in 1917 show convincingly the similarity of their approach with that of the Bolsheviks. They denounced the war and presented a simplistic view of the ease with which Russia could get out of it. They displayed the inertia of revolutionary underground thinking: they advocated solving problems by force and the right of expropriation; they called for the arming of the whole population; they rejected the spiritual values of the past, particularly religion; they replaced morality with revolutionary expediency and law with force; they hated a society which was incompatible with all this and strove to tear it down in order to create a new, classless society on their own model. The anarchist road seemed shorter than the Bolshevik one, but both shared the conviction that it was a crime to hold back the revolution, and that the one in Russia would be completed by the world revolution and the total annihilation of capitalism.

In the course of the political crises of 1917 the anarchist communists came close to the left Bolsheviks in their desire to overthrow the Provisional Government. The First All-Russian Congress of Soviets in early June condemned the anarchist communists' seizure of the printworks of the newspaper *Russkaia volia* ('Russian Freedom'), and the government demanded that they vacate the Durnovo dacha. Bolsheviks took part in the campaign to get resolutions passed by workers and soldiers in defence of the anarchists and, during the June crisis, they participated in the Durnovo dacha's Military-Revolutionary Committee. Following the demonstrations on 18 June the anarchist communists liberated some of their sympathizers, as well as some people accused of spying, from Kresty prison. In response, the government arranged that the Durnovo dacha be stormed, in the course of which the anarchist and criminal Sh. A. Asnin was killed. On 3 July anarchist communists together with left Bolsheviks brought soldiers out on a demonstration, seized the Peter and Paul Fortress, surrounded the Tauride Palace in which the Soviet leadership was based, and demanded that it take state power. When the government suppressed the demonstrations, Bleikhman was hidden by the Bolshevik S. S. Zorin (Gomberg).

Anarchist communists and syndicalists helped the Bolsheviks overthrow the Provisional Government. Bleikhman, Iarchuk, V. S. Shatov and others joined the Petrograd Military-Revolutionary Committee. K. V. Akashev brought artillery out of the Winter Palace, and Zhuk, A. G. Zhelezniakov, A. V. Mokrousov and other anarchists took part in storming it. Anarchists helped the Bolsheviks seize power in Moscow and in the provinces.

Zhelezniakov, as chief of the guard at the Tauride Palace, carried out the Bolsheviks' order to disperse the All-Russian Constituent Assembly on 6 January 1918.

By 1918, there were anarchist organizations in 130 towns, and around 40 anarchist newspapers and journals were being published. As they consolidated their power, the Bolsheviks began to bring the anarchists to heel, disarming their 'black guards': in Ekaterinburg in November 1917, in Khar'kov in December, in Samara and Kamenskoe in January–February 1918, in Moscow on 11–12 April, and in Petrograd on 22–23 April. However, at a meeting of the Petrograd Soviet, M. S. Uritskii, the head of the Petrograd Cheka, assured the anarchists that there was not and would not be any ideological struggle against anarchism. The arrested anarchists were released.

Zhelezniakov, Zhuk, Vinogradov, N. A. Kalandarishvili and other anarchists fought and died on the Bolshevik side in the civil war. One of the 26 Baku commissars who were shot in 1918 was the anarchist E. A. Berg; Denikin's counter-intelligence agency killed Ge; Shatov took part in the defence of Petrograd in 1919; and the Crimean insurrectionary army in 1920 was commanded by Mokrousov. Such anarchists considered themselves to be part and parcel of Soviet power, and were known as 'soviet anarchists'.

The anarchist communist Nestor I. Makhno, who had been a prisoner of the tsarist authorities, formed a revolutionary insurrectionary army in the Ukraine in 1918. At one stage it numbered 80,000. With its cavalry and machine-gun carts it fought against the Austrians and Germans, then against S. Petliura's and Denikin's forces, causing chaos behind their front lines. Its ideological leadership in 1919 and 1920 was provided by the secretariat of the *Nabat* ('Tocsin') anarchist federation, led by Volin, P. A. Arshinov and others, who joined its Military-Revolutionary Committee and called for a 'third revolution'. Its attempt to create an anarchist republic centred around Guliai-Pole led to the disintegration of the economy and of social life, and ended in a break with *Nabat*, which was liquidated by the Ukrainian Cheka in November 1920. The Makhnovites were noted for their cruelty, drunkenness and debauchery, dubbed 'the dictatorship of syphilis'. Their alliance with the Red Army was sporadic, and was punctuated by breaks and mutual settling of scores. In 1921 Makhno fled to Romania, with a Red Army division in pursuit. After three years in prison he settled in Paris and wrote his memoirs. In accordance with his final wishes, the urn containing his ashes was buried in Père Lachaise cemetery, along the wall where the Paris Communards lie.

In the spring of 1919 a movement of 'underground anarchists' arose, based in Moscow with affiliated bodies in Samara and Khar'kov. They considered the 'soviet anarchists' to be complicit in repression, and Bolshevik power to be a new form of autocracy, against which they declared war with dynamite. On 25 September 1919 they threw a bomb into a room during a session of the Moscow Committee of the Communist Party (RKP(b)), at which Lenin was expected to be present. Twelve people were killed, including V. M. Zagorskii, the secretary of the Moscow Committee, and 55 were injured, including N. I. Bukharin, A. F. Miasnikov, M. S. Ol'minskii, G. I. Safarov, Iu. M. Steklov and E. M. Iaroslavskii. Following this action, the underground anarchists published a declaration which accused the Bolsheviks of suppressing freedom, turning the soviets and the trade-union leaderships into lackeys, and enslaving and silencing the workers. It called for the overthrow of both Red and White statists by partisan bands, and for the creation of a confederation on the basis of voluntary agreements and free initiatives. The Cheka liquidated this movement. Although the legal anarchists condemned the terrorists, they were also subject to mass arrests. The Cheka closed their clubs and confiscated anarchist literature.

The anarcho-syndicalists considered that the RKP(b) policy of nationalization and centralization of the economy was leading to state capitalism, the worst form of exploitation of the workers. Workers' unions should be the basis of a socialist society, not to gain privileges for selected members of the RKP(b), but to ensure equal rights for everybody. In some respects these views coincided with those expressed by the 'Workers' Opposition' within the RKP(b) (A. G. Shliapnikov, S. P. Medvedev, A. M. Kollontai and others), which was condemned at the Tenth and Eleventh RKP(b) Congresses and then broke up.

From January 1918 Kropotkin led the Moscow League of Federalists, which considered the return to state centralism to be harmful. The League saw Russia's future as a federative democratic republic, a voluntary union of free regions and nationalities with a high degree of local autonomy. Kropotkin enjoyed mutually respectful relations with Lenin, and wrote several approving comments in his copy of Lenin's *State and Revolution*, although Kropotkin saw the question more in terms of 'state *or* revolution'. Lenin talked with him in the Kremlin, had almost all his books in his library, proposed publishing a complete collection of Kropotkin's works, and thought especially highly of his *Fields, Factories and Workshops*. In particular, the book's proposal to create schools which gave training in production skills was implemented under the supervision of N. K. Krupskaia.

It pained Kropotkin to watch the Bolsheviks demonstrate how *not* to make a revolution. The construction of state communism by means of dictatorship was turning the soviets, the trade unions and the cooperatives into bureaucratic appendages of the RKP(b), untrammelled power was leading to atrocities, the revolution was being condemned to bankruptcy, and the word 'socialism' was becoming a term of abuse. Under Kropotkin's influence, in November 1918 Lenin revoked the right of local Cheka organs to execute people without trials or investigations. In April 1919 Kropotkin admitted that for the ordinary people, the word 'soviet' had become 'synonymous with hunger, summary executions, all kinds of violence and secret killings'. His hopes that, through their mistakes, the Bolsheviks would arrive at the ideal of individual freedom, had been destroyed.

Anarchists were released from Moscow's jails on their word of honour for one day to take part in Kropotkin's funeral, which took place on 13 February 1921. Anarchists bearing black flags and Bolsheviks bearing red ones followed Kropotkin's bier from the House of Unions to the Novodevichii cemetery. This was their last joint demonstration. In 1923, the All-Russian Committee to Immortalize the Memory of Kropotkin, the secretary of which was the anarchist-federalist N. K. Lebedev, Kroptokin's executor, opened a Kropotkin museum and archive in the house where he had been born, and formed the 'Black Cross' to aid needy and imprisoned anarchists. Kropotkin committees and groups were formed in Petrograd, Khar'kov and Rostov-on-Don, as well as in Britain, France and Germany.

Anarchist sailors took an active part in the spontaneous uprising on Kronstadt in March 1921, demanding genuinely free elections to the soviets. Once this uprising had been harshly suppressed, the RKP(b) began to rid itself of its former allies. The former secretary of the Moscow Federation of Anarchist Groups, Lev Chernyi, was shot on a criminal charge. On 5 January 1922 ten anarchists were expelled from the country, including Volin, Maksimov and Iarchuk. Only Iarchuk returned, with Bukharin's help, in 1925. He joined the RKP(b), but was repressed in 1930. In 1924 A. L. Gordin emigrated to the USA, and his group of anarchist universalists fell apart. Grossman-Roshchin's attempts to reconcile anarchism with Leninism ended with his declaration in the mid-1920s that he had become a Marxist.

In the 1920s, the anarchist mystics A. A. Karelin, A. A. Solonovich and N. I. Proferansov formed a network of secret orders in Moscow, Leningrad, Nizhnii Novgorod and Khar'kov. In Moscow, the 'Order of the Spirit' established a 'Brotherhood of Charity' for acts of anonymous philanthropy. A 'Temple of Arts' led by Iu. A. Zavadskii brought actors together. These circles discussed philosophy, art and history. Borovoi spoke out as an opponent of mysticism.

In order to combat anarchism Stalin created a 'Department for Counteragitation and Disorganization' within the OGPU, headed by M. A. Trilisser. Trilisser was also head of the Foreign Department of the OGPU and, under the name Moskvin, secretary of the Executive Committee of the Communist International. He was himself executed in 1938. Trilisser's department stirred up arguments among the anarchists and between them and the Kropotkin committee, and fabricated anarchist documents. Arshinov, who was living in Paris and edited the anarchist journal *Delo truda* ('The Cause of Labour'), collaborated with the OGPU until he was unmasked in 1930 and expelled from France. In 1932 he returned to the USSR from the US, and was shot in 1937.

In 1929 and 1930, the remnants of the anarchist movement from the revolutionary period were destroyed. The authorities closed the anarcho-syndicalist *Golos truda* ('Voice of Labour') publishing house, sent Borovoi into exile, and arrested the participants in the anarchist orders. Akashev, Novomirskii, Sandomirskii, Solonovich and others were executed or died in

GULAG camps, which were headed by the former anarchist L. I. Kogan. The former head of Makhno's counter-intelligence, L. N. Zin'kovskii (Leva Zadov) was also working for the NKVD. The Kropotkin museums were closed in 1938 and 1939, and the censorship permitted his name to be mentioned only in connection with his seven works on geography and geology. The publication of the collected works of Bakunin was halted after the fourth volume, in 1935. The authorities banned publications on anarchism in order to obliterate it from society's memory. They succeeded in this – although towns, villages and streets retained the names of Bakunin, Kropotkin or Zhelezniakov, citizens no longer associated these names with anarchists, who were now seen as bandits and enemies of socialism.

The anarchist movement was reborn in the USSR during the 'perestroika' period, in conditions of social liberalization and of the deformed, 'flea-market' economy which resulted from the resistance of part of the party-state *nomenklatura* to the transition to a free market. In 1988 some students of history at the Herzen Pedagogical Institute in Leningrad founded an 'Anarcho-Syndicalist Free Association' with the slogan 'To a free federation without coercion or power!', and in 1990 they formed an 'Association of Anarchist Movements'. The 'Confederation of Anarcho-Syndicalists', which emerged in 1989 and has groups in ten cities, follows the ideas of Bakunin. The syndicalists demand the transfer of state enterprises and property to their own work collectives. In 1989 there were lectures commemorating the 175th anniversary of Bakunin's birth, in which philosophers and historians argued that it was necessary to draw practical lessons from his attempt to work out the principles of a self-developing socio-economic system. In the same year the 'Confederation of Anarchists of the Ukraine' was formed in Khar'kov.

A new impetus to the development of anarchism has been provided by the collapse of the USSR. The First Congress of Anarchists of Eastern Europe took place in August 1992 near Kaliningrad, and included anarchists and punks from Russia, Tatarstan, Ukraine, Belorussia and Lithuania. The former *nomenklatura*'s retention of power and its appropriation of state and public property in the course of criminal privatization, the unprecedented growth of corruption, crime and unemployment, and the state's practice of delaying the payment of wages are all tending to foster anarchist communist sentiments in that part of the population which is getting poorer. Present-day anarchism is still weak, divided and peaceable (only the Petersburg 'Anarcho-Communist Revolutionary Union' has declared itself opposed to non-violence) and is not able to play the role it played in the three Russian revolutions.

Soviet historiography on the anarchists' part in the revolution was ideologically directed towards glorification of the victory of the ruling party and justification of its repression of the anarchists. In the 1920s and 1930s, the works of historians such as B. I. Gorev, V. N. Zalezhskii and M. Ravich-Cherkasskii, and of Bolshevik publicists such as K. B. Radek,

E. A. Preobrazhenskii and Ia. A. Iakovlev, were dominated by political accusations. The apogee of falsification was E. M. Iaroslavskii's *History of Anarchism in Russia*, published in Moscow in 1939. Thereafter, nothing was published on anarchism until the mid-1960s. The exception was Stalin's article of 1906–7 'Anarchism or Socialism?', which appeared in the first volume of his *Works*, published in 1946, and which served to reinforce the view of anarchists as the most malicious enemies of socialism and communism.

The subsequent generation of Soviet historians, such as S. N. Kanev, V. V. Komin and E. M. Kornoukhov, produced new facts from state and party archives, within the limits imposed by the censorship. However, it was only after the fall of the CPSU and the removal of censorship that a scientific study of anarchism became possible. The latest generation of historians, including V. V. Kriven'kii, V. D. Ermakov, O. A. Ignat'eva and A. L. Nikitin in Russia, and V. F. Verstiuk and V. A. Savchenko in the Ukraine, have taken the first steps in that direction. However, in certain historical works there has been a tendency to romanticize and make heroes of the anarchists, particularly Makhno.

Works on Russian anarchism published abroad had little impact on Soviet historiography owing to the ideological resistance of Soviet historians and the fact that the works of Western historians and anarchist *émigrés* were virtually inaccessible in the USSR – they were either not in the libraries at all, or were held in closed sections. The greatest contribution to the study of Russian anarchism has been that of Paul Avrich, whose monograph and collection of documents are as yet unrivalled both in Russia and in the West. There is valuable information on anarchist activities to be found also in Alexander Rabinowitch's *Prelude to Revolution*, S. A. Smith's *Red Petrograd*, Diane Koenker's *Moscow Workers and the 1917 Revolution*, and D. J. Raleigh's *Revolution on the Volga*.

It remains for historians to determine more carefully the views and positions of the different anarchist currents and groupings, to investigate the activities and fate of individual anarchists, but, above all, to seek out and publish documents by anarchist individuals and organizations, scattered around archives in Russia, Ukraine, the Caucasus and abroad.

Further reading

Avrich P., *The Russian Anarchists* (Princeton, Princeton University Press, 1967).

Avrich P. ed., *The Anarchists in the Russian Revolution* (London, Thames and Hudson, 1973).

Ermakov V. D., *Rossiiskii anarkhizm i anarkhisty (vtoraia polovina XIX – konets XX vekov)* (St Petersburg, Nestor, 1996).

Gorelik G. *et al.*, *Goneniia na anarkhizm v Sovetskoi Rossii* (Berlin, Gruppa russkikh anarkhistov v Germanii, 1922).

Iarchuk E., *Kronshtadt v russkoi revoliutsii* (New York, izdanie Ispol'nitel'nogo komiteta professional'nykh soiuzov g. N'iu Iork, 1923).

Koenker D., *Moscow Workers and the 1917 Revolution* (Princeton, Princeton University Press, 1981).

Kropotkin P. A., *The Conquest of Bread and Other Writings*, ed. M. Shatz (Cambridge, Cambridge University Press, 1995).

Makhno N. I., *Russkaia revoliutsiia na Ukraine*, 3 vols. (Paris, Biblioteka Makhnovtsev, 1929; Komitet N. Makhno, 1936, 1937).

Nikitin A. L., 'Zakliuchitel'nyi etap razvitiia anarkhistskoi mysli v Rossii', *Voprosy filosofii* 8 (1991), pp. 89–101.

Rabinowitch A., *Prelude to Revolution* (Bloomington, Indiana University Press, 1968).

Raleigh D. J., *Revolution on the Volga: 1917 in Saratov* (Ithaca, Cornell University Press, 1986).

Smith S. A., *Red Petrograd: Revolution in the Factories 1917–1918* (Cambridge, Cambridge University Press, 1983).

Verstiuk V. F., compiler, *Nestor Ivanovich Makhno: Vospominaniia, materialy i dokumenty* (Kiev, Dzvin, 1991).

Zevelev A. I., ed., *Istoriia politicheskikh partii Rossii* (Moscow, Vysshaia shkola, 1994).

The Bolshevik Party

ROBERT SERVICE

The Bolsheviks were the political party that triumphed in the October revolution of 1917. They founded a Soviet state and announced that the era of European socialist revolution had arrived. Their survival and self-consolidation in power had a decisive impact on the history of their country, their continent and the rest of the world, an impact that has not disappeared along with the disintegration of the USSR.

The origins of Bolshevism were pretty inauspicious. At the Second Congress of the Russian Social-Democratic Labour Party (RSDRP) in 1903, held in Brussels and London, the group of delegates associated with the *émigré* journal *Iskra* ('The Spark') was victorious. Its version of Marxism, in terms of doctrine and policy, carried the day and the group dominated all the discussions. But at the moment of their triumph, the Iskraites fell into disagreement among themselves about the new party rules; for until then the party had existed only as a name. Lenin wanted a formulation of rules that implied stricter conditions for admittance to membership than his opponents wanted. He was defeated on this, but by careful lobbying managed to secure a majority for his supporters on the new central party bodies. He proceeded to call his sub-group within the party the Majoritarians (*Bol'sheviki* or Bolsheviks) while the opposing sub-group permitted themselves to be called the Minoritarians (*Men'sheviki* or Mensheviks).

In the emigration these factions struggled bitterly. The Bolsheviks themselves split into contending sub-factions – and the doctrinal father of Russian Marxism, Georgii Plekhanov, left them altogether and allied himself with the Mensheviks. In particular, Lenin's schismatic manoeuvres and polemical style came in for criticism. Meanwhile the party organizations in the Russian empire were distinctly reluctant to concede that differences among their distant leaders about questions of party organization were so important as to merit the risk of tearing the RSDRP apart on a permanent basis. At the most there were only 12,000 party members by late 1904, and they were hard-pressed to keep pace with the increasing agitation in the labour movement across the empire. Only a handful of self-styled Bolsheviks were keen to maintain organizations entirely separate from those of the Mensheviks.

The Bolshevik attitude to the working class also impeded the faction in its political activity. Lenin's *What Is To Be Done?* (1902) had claimed that the workers, if left to themselves, were capable of rising only to the level of 'trade-union consciousness'. Accordingly, he argued, it would require leadership by intellectuals to elevate the working class to a consciousness that was truly socialist. And this attitude was shared by most Bolsheviks as they tried to elaborate their policies in respect of the revolutionary crisis that gripped Russia in 1905. Workers in many cities formed strike committees which became virtual organs of local self-government and which were called 'soviets' (in English, councils). But the Bolshevik distrust of the potential of autonomous working-class politics meant that the faction was slow to participate in the soviets. As revolutionaries, the Bolsheviks were too doctrinaire for their own practical good.

For Lenin, this was a sign of intolerable self-indulgence and on his return to St Petersburg in November 1905 he insisted that Bolsheviks should participate in the soviets. For tactical reasons, he also sought to recombine the Bolsheviks and Mensheviks in the RSDRP: he needed the Mensheviks to restrain the over-zealous commitment of most of his Bolsheviks to armed insurrection. A Fourth Party Congress was held in April 1906 where reunification took place and a joint Central Committee was formed. By the end of the year the RSDRP had about 150,000 members. It was the major political force in the labour movement – and the Bolsheviks were a strong component in the party's leadership.

Yet the seeds of factional conflict had not been crushed. The experience of 1905–06 induced Bolsheviks to work out a general revolutionary strategy. Their objective, as they had decided at their separate 'Third Party Congress' in April 1905, was to overthrow the tsarist regime and institute a 'provisional revolutionary democratic dictatorship of the proletariat and the peasantry'. This would be a dictatorship by socialist parties; it would exclude the 'bourgeois parties': indeed, its aim would be to prevent a counter-revolutionary compromise between the overthrown emperor and the middle classes. According to Lenin, a class alliance between workers and peasants was the sole guarantee that Russia could break with her 'feudal', autocratic past and institute both a democratic state order and a flourishing capitalist economy. To this end he recommended that the dictatorship should abolish private landownership and should transfer the agricultural land at a peppercorn rent to those peasants who actively worked it. The dictatorship would be ruthless and, as the congress agreed, should not flinch from the application of mass terror.

Mensheviks objected that this strategy, despite Lenin's protestations about holding to a two-stage Marxian schema, was essentially a proposal for a one-stage socialist dictatorship. They argued that such a dictatorship would never introduce democracy or facilitate the development of capitalism. For them, the crucial strategic objective should be to cement a class alliance not with peasants (whom they thought of as being ignorant and unreliable) but with the industrial and professional sections of the urban middle classes (whom they regarded as the most progressive sections of the Russian propertied elite).

Thus the RSDRP remained strategically divided even after its organizational re-unification. The two main factions cooperated in the soviets, in the trade unions and in public propaganda. But the tsarist regime reasserted its strength in 1906, and used both the stick and the carrot. First, a rising of Moscow workers in December 1905 was crushed; and then elections were held to a State Duma in 1906 in order to win over middle-class opinion. The regime's harassment of the socialist parties was relentless. In 1907, difficulties became so great that practically all the Marxist leaders recognized that the counterrevolution was irresistible, and they again went into the emigration. This exodus involved Lenin and the Bolshevik leadership. Defeat for the revolution pushed the RSDRP back into internal disputes. Lenin immediately set about forming his own separate Bolshevik organization. He had trouble from Aleksandr Bogdanov, who regarded his attitude to the working class as altogether too authoritarian. In 1908 there was a conclusive split between Lenin and Bogdanov; each of them went on to claim he alone represented the authentic spirit of Bolshevism. And so Bolshevik activity abroad again became a saga of bickering in Swiss coffee houses and library foyers.

In the Russian empire, however, the RSDRP began to recover its confidence. After much vacillation, it decided to participate in the elections to the Second and subsequent State Dumas. Social-democratic deputies entered the Duma on the party's ticket. The faction also succeeded in publishing a legal party newspaper, *Pravda* ('The Truth'), in St Petersburg from 1912 and printed books and pamphlets in Russia. It supplied activists to penetrate the legal trade unions and these activists were at the forefront of the strike movement which accompanied the industrial upturn of the years immediately before the First World War. Building on these successes, Lenin was striving almost openly to form his own separate party of Bolsheviks. A self-proclaimed Party Conference was held in Prague in January 1912 which was an overwhelmingly Bolshevik gathering; the other factions of the RSDRP were issued invitations either not at all or too late for them to be able to attend.

But there were underlying problems that Lenin failed to solve. One was that not everyone in his faction accepted the desirability of a separate Bolshevik Party masquerading as the legitimate, exclusive expression of the RSDRP; a second was that the Bolshevik faction remained small and poorly coordinated. The outbreak of the Great War brusquely accentuated these problems. Not all Bolsheviks were willing to oppose the national war effort – some even volunteered to fight in the forces against the Central Powers. Above all, few condoned Lenin's idea that they should campaign for

Russia's defeat and for the engagement in a 'European civil war'. Links between Switzerland (where Lenin spent much of the war period) and Russia were sundered most of the time. Links between the various Bolshevik organizations in Russia were frail and intermittent. Bolshevik Duma deputies were arrested and sent into administrative exile in Siberia, and most local organizations fell into inactivity. A Russian Bureau of the Bolshevik Central Committee operated under the leadership of Aleksandr Shliapnikov, but its impact on the strike movement in Russia was minimal.

None the less the street demonstrations in Petrograd – as St Petersburg had been re-named – in the last days of February 1917 gave the local activists a chance to assert themselves. They participated in the formation of the Petrograd Soviet (although the Mensheviks and Socialist Revolutionaries, it must be added, took the leading posts). As the Provisional Government came into existence and as prominent Bolsheviks such as Lev Kamenev and Iosif Stalin returned from internal exile in Siberia, the Russian Bureau of the Central Committee found ways to cooperate with the Mensheviks and to offer combined pressure on the Provisional Government. Re-unification of the two factions was widely expected.

But this was by no means a foregone conclusion. Shliapnikov and others felt that Kamenev and Stalin were altogether too pro-Menshevik. Furthermore, many Bolsheviks elsewhere were aghast at a policy of 'conditional support' for the Provisional Government – and Bolsheviks of such a type were bound to increase in number as the general ineffectualness of the Provisional Government in tackling problems became known in the country. Into this fluid situation Lenin interposed himself upon his return from Switzerland in April. He called for socialists to assume power and for a package of basic social and economic reforms to be implemented; he demanded universal peace in Europe. Immediately a controversy broke out, and those Bolsheviks who supported Kamenev's policy left the faction or, like Kamenev himself, coped with the new radicalism by attempting to moderate it. Meanwhile, some Mensheviks decided that, after all, such radicalism appealed to them. And tens of thousands of radically inclined workers were quickly recruited into the ranks of Bolshevism. All these factors enabled Lenin to make a decisive break with the Mensheviks and – admittedly over the ensuing months – to constitute a separate party at last: the RSDRP (Bolsheviks).

In fact, Lenin's long years in exile had left him insensitive to certain currents in contemporary Russian society. He had to attune himself fast and, if the party was to gain in popularity, to drop several of his favourite slogans. He ceased talking openly about 'European civil war'. He swapped 'land nationalization' as an objective for what the peasants asked for: 'land socialization'. For most of the year he stopped calling for a socialist 'dictatorship'; and he picked up the slogan of 'workers' control' from the practice of Petrograd labour forces. The Bolshevik central party leaders prodded him in this direction; it was not a one-man Central Committee. And Kamenev in particular felt that the mollifying of Lenin's language foretold a transition towards policies that would allow an accommodation between Bolshevism and the rest of Russian socialism.

The organization of the party was not so very unlike that of the other parties. The Bolshevik party was a mass party. Its ordinary party members elected their local committees; local party conferences sent delegates to assemblies in Petrograd where policies were debated and central party bodies were elected. These central party bodies supplied a central newspaper, a set of current directives and such personnel as they could spare. The Bolsheviks called this 'democratic centralism'. But how democratic was it and how centralist in reality? In the main, there was ample room for discussion at the local level. And without the support of local delegates to the Seventh Party Conference – support that was freely given – Lenin's radicalism would perhaps not have won the day. There was also a formulation of policies on major current issues at the Sixth Party Congress in August. On the other hand, certain strategic decisions were taken without reference to local party members. The most striking instance was the Central Committee decision on 10 October 1917 to set about organizing a seizure of state power. Only a few major Bolsheviks from 'the localities' were initiated into the plot.

Of course, there has also to be recognition that any broader discussion would have endangered the success of the revolutionary exercise. As it was, Kamenev and G. E. Zinoviev leaked the 10 October Central Committee decision to the socialist press. The general strategy of a socialist seizure of power, moreover, had not been adopted in secret by the Bolsheviks. Every newspaper reader in the country had known since April that the Bolshevik Party aimed to overthrow the Provisional Government.

Outside these critical moments, in any case, there were several obstacles to centralist dominion. Communications across the country were patchy and *Pravda* was widely distributed only in Petrograd. At each level of the official organizational hierarchy there were committees kicking against the traces of hierarchical instructions. Local Bolshevik committees, while upholding ideas of centralism in theory, acted in practice as independent agencies of socialist revolution. They set their own policies, both domestic and international. Thus their behaviour introduced an anarchic jaggedness to the neat pattern of democratic centralism. The nub of the matter is that the Bolshevik leaders and activists were not democrats by principled choice. They were masters of factional manipulation. They had a theory of revolution based on leadership and command; they had an instinctive distrust of the working class's capacity to make its own revolution. They wanted results and were willing to ditch any procedure in the service of that cause.

Furthermore, it is altogether inaccurate to describe the Bolsheviks as a highly coordinated party in 1917. Recruitment was massive: by the end of the year there were about 300,000 members. But the recruits knew next to nothing of Marx and Engels and had not read much of Lenin. Even their attendance at party meetings was irregular. Nevertheless, they had their indispensable uses. For instance, they provided the personnel to staff the factory-workshop committees and the soldiers' committees. They were also very effective, down-to-earth communicators of the party's diagnosis of the baleful effects of the Provisional Government's policies.

But a clash in objectives between most party rank-and-filers and their leaders was already in the making. For the established leadership at central and local levels had had to simplify the contents of Bolshevism in order to weld the party together. This meant that few rank-and-file members knew that the Central Committee intended to wage a 'revolutionary war' if a European socialist revolution did not occur when the Bolsheviks seized power in Russia. Similarly, peasants did not know that state-run collective farms were an ultimate party objective and workers were given no notion of the tight labour discipline expected in the longer term. The assumption of most leaders was that these aspects of Bolshevism would be accepted by the rest of the party and by the whole of the working class once the revolution had been made and the workers had – with the assistance of the party's propagandists – come to understand their basic interests. Nevertheless, Bolshevik leaders were not entirely frank about their long-term objectives.

Nor, however, were they simply deceivers. For they had convinced themselves that the revolution would be easier than it turned out to be. If they deceived others, it was partly because they had already deceived themselves. Even Lenin, as hard-boiled a pragmatist as the Bolsheviks possessed, was sure that things would turn out all right upon the assumption of power under Bolshevik guidance.

Among his reasons for growing optimism was the effectiveness of the Bolshevik mass party in penetrating the mass organizations that sprang up in the cities between February and October 1917. Their first successes came with the organizations nearest to the point of industrial activity: the factory-workshop committees. Bolsheviks held a majority in them in Petrograd in May 1917. Steadily they made gains also in the trade unions, and by summer they dominated certain local soviets. By early September they were winning votes in both the Petrograd and Moscow Soviets. The slogan of 'all power to the soviets' – which Lenin sought to drop after the July Days (when the Petrograd Soviet had permitted the Provisional Government to hunt down the Bolshevik leaders and to proscribe Lenin) – was resumed. Most Bolsheviks looked forward to the Provisional Government's overthrow and the installation of an all-socialist coalition government. Consequently it is inappropriate to suggest that the Bolsheviks had no toehold in the mass revolutionary movement of 1917: they could not have come to power without such a toe-hold.

The seizure of power allowed Lenin, together with his ally Trotsky, to give yet another decisive jerk on the steering-wheel of party policy. Against expectation, they refused to admit the Mensheviks and Socialist Revolutionaries into the new Soviet government. This was debated in the

Bolshevik Central Committee, and after a few weeks of uncertainty the will of Lenin and Trotsky prevailed. Whenever there was disagreement at the apex of the party in the ensuing years, furthermore, there was broad discussion inside central party bodies before policies were settled. The crucial instance is the dispute over the proposed separate peace with the Central Powers in early 1918. Until Lenin could persuade the Bolshevik Central Committee, there could be no ratification of the Treaty of Brest-Litovsk in March 1918.

In other ways there was rapid change in the party. The most obvious manifestation occurred with internal factional wrangling. By and large, the Bolsheviks were spared controversies before the October revolution because they agreed on two fundamental policies: first, the desirability and possibility of a socialist government in Russia; second, the imminence of European socialist revolution. Everything else was dwarfed by this consensus until the party held power. The need for precise policies in government instantly divided the party. In addition to the issue of separate peace, the following questions were extremely contentious: the scope of state intervention; the attitude to national self-determination; the use of 'bourgeois specialists'; and wage differentials. On these matters, Lenin urged prudent policies that would secure the party in power whereas others – and they may well have constituted a majority of central and local leaders in 1917–18 – felt that a betrayal of the party's pre-October commitments was taking place. At the height of the Brest-Litovsk dispute in January–March 1918, Lenin's critics became known as the Left Communists.

Lenin and Iakov Sverdlov, the Central Committee Secretary, exploited every opportunity to push their policies on the rest of the party. There is more than a hint that the Seventh Party Congress in March 1918, when the party's name was changed to the Russian Communist Party (Bolsheviks), was preceded by propaganda and organizational dispensations which deliberately favoured Lenin's declared supporters. But the victory was still impermanent. Left Communists refused to work in the Bolshevik Central Committee and *Sovnarkom* after being defeated at the Party Congress; and whereas their leader N. I. Bukharin was quickly reconciled to Lenin, the other Left Communists were extremely restive.

The stimulus to political consolidation came from unexpected quarters. In July 1918 the Left Socialist Revolutionaries, who had served as junior partners in *Sovnarkom* since December 1918, organized armed action against the Bolsheviks. This followed a series of disturbing developments on the Volga, especially the revolt of the Czechoslovak Legion and the same Legion's agreement to fight its way into central Russia on behalf of the *Komuch* government (which consisted of Socialist Revolutionaries elected as deputies to the Constituent Assembly). Thus the Bolsheviks faced a threat from within and outside the area under their rule. This was decisive in rallying Bolsheviks of all orientations to the Central Committee. Important, too, were the shifts in Lenin's economic policy. The food shortage in central and northern Russia, particularly after the loss of Ukraine through the Treaty of Brest-Litovsk, induced the Soviet authorities to declare a food dictatorship. Lenin thereby signalled that he was shelving his own more moderate initial measures on the agrarian question. He and his supporters in *Sovnarkom* also sanctioned a large-scale campaign of industrial nationalization. The Bolsheviks strode onwards towards a one-party dictatorship by a party that increasingly acquired the internal coordination it had never previously possessed.

The subsequent campaigns of the civil war reinforced the centralist imperatives. Such imperatives would anyway have had to be accepted by the party if the Bolsheviks were to maintain a monopoly of power. But the protracted military conflict between the Red and White Armies destroyed any lingering possibility that the loose organizational features of the Bolshevik Party would endure. Every policy was conditioned by the life-and-death struggle against Kolchak, Denikin and Iudenich. And the transition to authoritarian modes was accelerated by the party's long-standing paeans to the virtues of a centralized party. Bolsheviks at last began to practise what they had for a long time preached.

This combination of situation, accident and ideology also had an effect on the inter-institutional arrangements made within the Soviet state. Initially most Bolshevik central leaders had taken for granted that control over the state would be ensured by the setting of broad lines of policy in the party and by the appointment of the party's representatives into the main state institutions. The leadership had not bargained for the confusion that would exist among the institutions. In the second half of 1918 and the first quarter of 1919 it was decided that a supreme state agency had to be imposed, and the most reliable such agency from the Bolshevik viewpoint was the party itself. To all intents and purposes the party became the dominant wielder of comprehensive state authority. Its bodies at central and local levels became the highest executive organs. *Sovnarkom* and the other governmental agencies were made dependent on the regular instructions and sanctions provided by party committees.

This did not occur on the basis of a blueprint; on the contrary, neither Lenin's *State and Revolution* (1917–18) nor Bukharin's various programmatic writings had much mentioned the topic of relations between party and government. And so the specific form the Soviet party–state took was invented to the accompaniment of a great deal of improvisation. But the extempore actions were certainly undertaken, too, within a frame of the Bolshevik Party's general assumptions and inclinations. Ideology played its part. Indeed, many local Bolsheviks, while welcoming the internal party reorganization and the party's role as supreme state agency, felt that not enough attention was given either to the practical demands of governance or to organizational theory. Criticisms of this kind came from Nizhnii Novgorod party chief Lazar' Kaganovich, who did not care a fig for internal party democracy. They also came from Timofei Sapronov and others in the

Moscow City Party Organization who felt that a system of running the party that was both more efficient and more democratic ought to be introduced. Both Kaganovich and Sapronov, despite their disagreements, argued that the entire internal apparatus of the party needed to be overhauled.

Sverdlov had already taken account of the problem and from January 1919 he set about reorganizing the central party bodies. The Central Committee's work had been affected by the unavoidable need to send some of its members to other cities and to the various war fronts. In order to maintain continuity and consensus in decision-making it was resolved to set up two inner sub-committees, the Political Bureau (or Politburo) and the Organizational Bureau (or Orgburo), to handle affairs in the period between the rare Central Committee meetings. Sverdlov was also instructed to establish a set of departments in the Secretariat so that the much-enlarged functions of the party as supreme state agency could be properly discharged. He died in March 1919, but the reorganization was continued by his successor Elena Stasova (and indeed by her triple successors in 1920, N. N. Krestinskii, E. A. Preobrazhenskii and L. P. Serebriakov). Analogous reorganizations were put in hand lower down the party's structure. And as an ever smaller proportion of experienced party leaders could be spared for party work, a single official was designated to be responsible for each local committee. In 1917–19 the leading official was called the chairman; in 1920 the holder of this influential post was given the fresh title of committee secretary.

The emphasis on hierarchy and discipline was accompanied by an impatience with prolonged discussion. Open party meetings were infrequent and were described dismissively as *mitingovanie* (pointless meetings). Not everyone approved of the trend. Many of the ordinary rank-and-file members who had joined the party in 1917 were disappointed by the party's political and economic policies – and they left the party in disgust. Furthermore, malcontents were expelled after 1918 in the internal campaigns known as 'purges' (*chistki*).

Until the October revolution, the Bolshevik Party consisted mainly of working-class recruits; it is estimated that three-fifths of the rank-and-filers were drawn from the industrial labour-force. But this changed rapidly during the civil war. And by 1921, according to official records, only 44 per cent of party members were of working-class background – and indubitably even this proportion was greatly exaggerated. Their place was taken by persons who joined for a variety of reasons. Some saw the Bolsheviks as defenders of Russia against foreign aggression. Others saw them as the architects of a meritocratic society which would soon lose its specifically Bolshevik features. Others again were blatantly on the make and joined the Bolsheviks out of a desire to deploy power and have some of the small but attractive privileges associated with involvement with the party. The extent of these privileges was not offered unconditionally. In the civil war, Bolsheviks ruled while 'sitting on their suit-cases'. At any time the Whites might have defeated the Red Army and then any

Bolshevik taken prisoner could expect, at best, a quick death by firing-squad. Most officials also underwent a worsening of their health in these years. When all such caveats are made, however, it is undeniable that the party began to lose its connection with the working-class aspirations of 1917 and became a party of leaders which told the working class what to do.

Civilian party leaders occasionally referred to their party, without pejorative intent, as a militarized party. This was true in another sense. Most Bolsheviks in 1919–20 were located not in the cities but in the armed forces. The extrusion of democratic procedures was faster in the party in the Red Army than elsewhere. The elective hierarchy of party committees was abruptly abolished and replaced by political commissars. Indeed, the commissars were made subject to a non-party body, the Revolutionary–Military Council of the Republic headed by Trotsky. They were enjoined to spread the centrally produced propaganda to the troops and to control the officers in the Red Army. The task of Bolsheviks serving in the Red Army was not to question policies, but to obey. And this highly hierarchical and disciplinary approach put the steel into similar tendencies in the civilian party organizations.

Objection to such developments was taken by a series of internal party 'oppositions'. They had a hotchpotch of ideas. The first was the so-called Military Opposition. This was led behind the scenes by Stalin and was a loosely assembled group which criticized Trotsky's management of the Red Army. Some disliked the use of former Imperial officers; some wanted greater stress on purely party work in the armed forces; and a few called for more democratic modes of decision-making. The dispute was defused by modifications to policy made at the Eighth Party Congress in March 1919. Much more serious was the oppositionist group which gelled in 1919–20: the Democratic Centralists. These demanded in particular that centralism should be balanced by broad, collective discussions. Led by T. V. Sapronov and N. Osinskii, they were rejected by most party leaders even in the localities as offering a project inappropriate to the state's wartime needs. Still more irritating to the growing consensus of party officialdom was the Workers' Opposition which stood for a role to be given to workers and peasants in deliberations undertaken on their behalf. The Workers' Opposition demanded that the party should share power with the soviets and the trade unions; but its activities were to be denounced by Lenin at the Tenth Party Congress in March 1921.

And so none of these oppositions made much headway. Bolshevik Party officials could occasionally see the point of their criticisms; but they sensed that, despite mistakes and deficiencies, the central party bodies were dedicated, confident and at least as efficient as any conceivable alternative set of leaders. Moreover, the internal party regime was becoming more authoritarian – as the oppositionists insistently declared. This regime was turned upon its critics, who were sent to jobs outside the capital if their recalcitrance persisted. Ukraine was a dumping ground for Democratic Centralists.

Not that this was a party of automatons. Bolsheviks in civilian and military party organizations alike still believed that their struggle would lead ultimately to the transformation of societies around the globe. No longer would there be oppression or exploitation. The communist era was at hand. Buoyed up by their victories in the civil war, Bolshevik leaders assumed that the methods either introduced or strengthened during the years of the military conflict – methods of authoritarian organization in party, state and society – offered the most reliable means to realize the old Bolshevik objectives in peacetime. Whether by deliberate purpose or otherwise, the objectives themselves had undergone alterations. No longer was there much balance between the revolution from above and the revolution from below. Bolsheviks aimed at an imposed revolutionary settlement. The casualty of this kind of thinking was any serious commitment to autonomous popular self-administration which had appeared in Bolshevik pronouncements in 1917. Such utopianism had never been without strong elements of authoritarianism. But by the end of the civil war authoritarian assumptions were at the unchallengeable core of Bolshevism.

Utopianism itself did not disappear; essentially it, too, became authoritarian. By the close of the civil war it was so prevalent in the party that the wartime economic stringencies were assumed to provide the model for postwar reconstruction. When Trotsky suggested modifications to official agricultural policies in February 1920, he was howled down in the Politburo by Lenin; and Lenin got his come-uppance when he proposed material incentives for peasant agriculture at the Eighth Congress of Soviets in December 1920: the Congress basically rejected his desired reform. Only the emergency of peasant rebellions in a large number of Russian and Ukrainian provinces in the remaining months of the winter allowed Lenin to insist on a change of policy away from grain requisitioning towards a graduated tax in kind set at a lower level of state procurement of grain. First the Politburo in February 1921 and then the Tenth Party Congress in March sanctioned the turnabout.

By then it was abundantly evident that a new political and social order had been brought into being and that the party was its crucial component. Could things have been otherwise? The starting point for any sensible discussion must be that the party (or faction, as it was before 1917!) had always been dictatorial in its prescriptions for socialist revolution. It had always been vanguardist; it had never ceased to manifest impatience with the niceties of constitution, legality and custom. Its mass popularity and mass party recruitment in 1917 submerged but did not drown this tendency in Bolshevism. This tendency, furthermore, resurfaced ultra-vigorously after the October revolution. Perhaps dictatorialism might have been checked if the party had not been isolated in politics; but of course Lenin could not conceive of any other form of administration. And once the dictatorship had been established, it was bound to get nastier if it was to survive. In turn this meant that the party would have to become less and less democratic in its internal life. The ban on factional activity introduced by Lenin at the Tenth Party Congress in March 1921 was a logical completion of an organizational sequence in motion over several years.

Yet we must not exaggerate. The party at the end of the civil war was certainly centralist, disciplinary and hierarchical. But it should also be emphasized that this was in comparison with the party of the years of tsarism and revolution. Communications remained ramshackle even after the civil war. Disobedience, even if it was mainly of a passive kind, was pervasive; and once a central party leader decided to break ranks with the Politburo, as Trotsky did in 1923, factional activity was scarcely containable.

Factionalism was not the only problem for the leaders who sought to discipline the party. Its internal regime gave rise to mechanisms whereby party officials sought to defend themselves against unwanted pressure from above. Hence the cliental links that were constructed by leaders at all levels. Hence the 'family groups'. Hence the local 'nests' that were built by the party's representatives in all public institutions. And each time the central leadership faced such impediments to its control, it tried to reactivate the party by purges, by re-appointments and by one-issue campaigns. This served only to goad the local officials further into inventing ever more devious methods to close off their committees and organizations from central interference. Such interactions were already detectable during and immediately after the civil war. The party was vital for revolutionary change, but its internal organization and external political functions had an impact upon what kind of change was practicable and at what price. It was a blunt instrument that was bound to produce changes of a crude kind. A one-party state ruled in the name of an unchallengeable ideology is hardly likely to produce a society of voluntary cooperation. The likeliest result is the sullen society which was already typical of the USSR in the 1920s.

None the less, from the Second Congress of the Communist International in July–August 1920 this same party was proffered as the model for communist parties worldwide. The conditions for membership of the Communist International were based explicitly upon the Bolshevik Party's rules. By the 1980s such parties were in power across a territory covering a third of the earth's surface. From a little, squashed acorn in 1903 a set of gnarled, distended oaks had grown. Not all of them have yet been felled; and even where, as in Russia, this has been accomplished, the roots of the tree have a capacity for self-regeneration.

By comparison with its later features, of course, the Bolshevik Party of 1921 was far from being monolithic. It still laid a stress upon the need for practical results rather than procedures. It was still very far from valuing the quiet, dutiful carrying out of orders. The party was a bureaucratic organization, but it was a bureaucratic organization of stupendous dynamism. The party remained loyal to its leadership and, through its central and local apparatuses, ready to follow it in the interests of enhancing the prospects of revolution. Such a party could survive the death of Lenin in January 1924. Its was a pliant party only insofar as the basic precepts of Marxism-Leninism seemed to be protected. The New Economic Policy embodied a temporary economic retreat which was deeply unpopular with Bolshevik Party officials. The leader who identified himself with allegiance to Lenin and yet eventually displayed his impatience with these measures of compromise was Stalin. Not by accident did Stalin win the factional struggle that opened between him and Bukharin, the New Economic Policy's defender, in 1928–9.

And so Stalin won the struggle for the Lenin succession only partly because he was an effective administrator. Never was a man underestimated so devastatingly. N. N. Sukhanov called him a 'grey blur'. For Trotsky, the most arrogant and self-preening of Bolsheviks, he was a mindless bureaucrat. What Stalin's rivals failed to comprehend was that he understood his party better than anyone. He knew how to approach dismantling the New Economic Policy. Timing was important. Language, cunning and determination, too. For the Bolshevik Party had to be handled with care. It had not ceased to have explosive qualities for its putative leaders.

Why does this matter in more general terms? The answer is surely that only by studying the Bolshevik Party in the round may we hope to gauge the limits of flexibility within the political system of which the party was the core. There always were ideological and organizational constraints. This was understood by Lenin even though he hated the fact that occasionally he could not get his 'Leninist' party to do his bidding. This was one of the reasons why Stalin sought to exterminate the party's leading cadres in 1937–8; for the Bolshevik Party was not a mere engine at a leader's control even during the early 1930s. If we are to understand the history of the Russian revolution, we must engage in something wider than leaderology – to use Lenin's phrase. We must look at the ideology, organizational mechanisms, social composition and political role of the party as a whole. On this, at least, we may agree with the otherwise doleful outpourings, the mind-numbing asseverations of successive official Soviet history books. Indeed, the development of Bolshevism is a much more complex and intriguing topic than most of its historians, in either East or West, have yet recognized. Bolshevism as history lived, lives and will live!

Further reading

Benvenuti F., *The Bolsheviks and the Red Army, 1918–1922* (Cambridge, Cambridge University Press, 1988).

Elwood R. C., *Russian Social Democracy in the Underground: A Study of the RSDRP in the Ukraine, 1907–1914* (Assen, Van Goorcum, 1971).

Keep J. H. L., *The Rise of Social-Democracy in Russia* (Oxford, Clarendon Press, 1963).

McKean R., *St Petersburg between the Revolutions: Workers and Revolutionaries, June 1907–February 1917* (New Haven and London, Yale University Press, 1990).

Rabinowitch A., *The Bolsheviks Come to Power: The Revolution of 1917 in Petrograd* (New York, Norton, 1976).

Rigby T. H., *Communist Party Membership in the USSR, 1917–1967* (Princeton, NJ, Princeton University Press, 1968).

Sakwa R., *Soviet Communists in Power: A Study of Moscow during the Civil War 1918–1921* (London, Macmillan, 1988).

Schapiro L., *The Communist Party of the Soviet Union*, 2nd edn (London, Methuen, 1970).

Service R., *The Bolshevik Party in Revolution: A Study in Organizational Change 1917–1923* (London, Macmillan, 1979).

The Communist Opposition

From Brest-Litovsk to the Tenth Party Congress

ROBERT V. DANIELS

Introduction

A striking feature of the Russian revolution was the persistence of political pluralism within the victorious Communist Party throughout the most violent and uncertain period of revolutionary struggle, the era of war communism between 1918 and 1921. Though opposition outside the party was suppressed step by step between January and July 1918, internal communist opposition to Lenin's policies continued active and vocal until after the end of the civil war. This opposition served significantly to document the changing methods and direction of the nascent Soviet regime. The more famous struggle for the succession to Lenin in the 1920s was less free and less profound in the issues it raised than the controversies of the war communism era. Not until General Secretary Mikhail Gorbachev opened the way for political reform in the 1980s was a comparable debate possible over the fundamental principles of the Soviet system.

The issue of coalition, Brest-Litovsk and the Left Communists

Post-revolutionary opposition to the communist leadership can be divided into three phases, or four if the months immediately following the October revolution are included. In those early days opposition came from the right wing of the party, an echo of misgivings about the forcible one-party seizure of power in October 1917. Grigorii Zinoviev, Lev Kamenev, the future prime minister Aleksei Rykov, and others who had resisted the October action actually resigned their seats in the Bolshevik Central Committee and the new Council of People's Commissars (4 November 1917) as they vainly demanded the formation of a multi-party coalition government. The only result of this protest was the temporary inclusion of the Left Socialist-Revolutionary Party in the Council of People's Commissars.

In January 1918 political lines within the Bolshevik Party were completely recast when Lenin abruptly came out for acceptance of the demands made by Germany in the negotiations at Brest-Litovsk to end Russia's participation in World War I. In this shift he was now supported by the characteristically cautious right wing of the party – who remained his staunch allies until his death in 1924 – but was opposed on the left by Nikolai Bukharin and his followers who had been the most ardent supporters of the revolutionary takeover and the party dictatorship. This realignment set up the ongoing confrontation between Lenin and the left opposition that continued in one form or another until 1921 and had its echoes throughout the 1920s.

Bukharin and the opponents of peace in 1918 contended that the agreement with Germany would hamstring revolutionary Russia's mission to spread the socialist revolution internationally, and would thereby sacrifice the opportunity to win the foreign support that they deemed essential for the survival of the proletarian revolution in Russia itself. As Bukharin contended at the Seventh Party Congress (7 March 1918), 'The conditions of the peace . . . reduce to nothing the international significance of the Russian revolution . . . The way out . . . is revolutionary war against German imperialism.' He and his supporters were prepared to fall back to Siberia and wage guerrilla war against the enemy while appealing to the European workers to overthrow their respective governments and come to the aid of revolutionary Russia. If the Russian revolution were thrown back upon itself, they feared, it would be obliged to compromise with bourgeois elements and turn into a system of state capitalism. 'If the Russian revolution were overthrown by violence on the part of the bourgeois counterrevolution,' declared the internationalist Karl Radek, 'it would rise again like a phoenix; if, however, it lost its socialist character and by this disappointed the working masses, this blow would have ten times more terrible consequences for the future of the Russian and international revolutions.'

Denoting themselves the 'Left Communists', the Bukharin group mustered four votes against Lenin's five in the crucial decision by the Bolshevik Central Committee on 28 February 1918 to accept Germany's peace terms, while four other Central Committee members, following Leon Trotsky's formula of 'No war, no peace', abstained. Lenin's narrow victory, made possible by the split on the left, established the survival of the revolutionary Russian state as the first priority of Soviet foreign policy, and relegated international revolution to the secondary, instrumental role that it continued to play throughout the life of the Soviet regime.

In their outrage at the peace, the Left Communists held talks with the Left Socialist Revolutionaries, who were equally opposed to the treaty, with the object (legitimate in a democratic state) of removing Lenin as head of the government, forming a new ruling coalition, and resuming the war. Though the Left Communists quickly backed out of the scheme, it was recalled and used against Bukharin when he was sentenced to death in the Moscow trial of 1938, with the new allegation that the opposition had planned to kill Lenin.

Following endorsement of the Treaty of Brest-Litovsk by the Seventh Party Congress in March 1918, the Left Communists (now led by the economist Valerian Osinskii-Obolenskii) broadened their oppositional stance to issues of internal policy. In particular, they denounced Lenin's steps to create a new bureaucratic chain of command in government and industry at the expense of the revolutionary philosophy of the soviets and workers' control touted by Lenin himself in his 1917 tract, *State and Revolution*. In their short-lived journal, *Kommunist*, the Left Communists warned of 'the deviation of Soviet power and the majority of the party on the ruinous path of petty-bourgeois policies', and threatened that 'the left wing of the party will have to stand in the position of an effective and responsible proletarian opposition'.

The military opposition and the Democratic Centralists

Upon the outbreak of civil war in May 1918 the communist revolution took a sharp turn to the left, with increased repression against all remaining non-communist parties, sweeping nationalization of private enterprise, and forcible requisitioning of food from the peasantry. Viewing the civil war as a fight for the immediate implementation of the utopian communist goal, the Left Communists temporarily closed ranks with the party majority in a life-and-death struggle for survival. The programme adopted by the Communist Party at its Eighth Congress in March 1919 embodied the spirit of the left in affirming 'proletarian democracy', 'suppression of the resistance of the exploiters', and 'eventually the abolition of state authority'.

Nevertheless, after the collapse of Germany in November 1918 eased pressure on the Soviet regime, new disagreements broke out between the leadership of the party and its left-wing elements. At the core of these new controversies was the degree of centralized power and autocratic methods being exercised by Lenin's government. One focus of contention was the new Red Army as Trotsky had set it up, with conventional military command and discipline and the employment of former tsarist officers – the 'military specialists' or *spetsy*. This trend was resisted by communists still enamoured of the democratized army of 1917 and informal guerrilla tactics. Led by the Left Communist Vladimir Smirnov, and initially with Joseph Stalin's encouragement, this 'Military Opposition' challenged Lenin and Trotsky at the Eighth Party Congress, particularly over the abolition of elected party committees in the army. At a secret session of the congress they won over a third of the delegates for their alternative.

Soon afterwards, led by Smirnov, Osinskii and Timofei Sapronov, the leftists formed the 'Group of Democratic Centralists' (more accurately, democratic anti-centralists), to challenge the whole direction of the communist regime. They questioned Moscow's growing supremacy over the provinces, the primacy of executive organs over the soviets, and the dominance of party institutions over the government and other institutions at all levels. Defending the egalitarian ideal and the 'collegial principle' of administration by committees, the Democratic Centralists underscored the excesses of military methods occurring throughout the political and economic system and the trend to hierarchies of individual authority.

A particularly strong centre of decentralist sentiment, capitalizing on the issue of minority autonomy, was the Ukraine. The issue of the national minorities in the Russian empire had divided left and right Bolsheviks before the revolution, with the former (notably Iurii Piatakov) calling for 'proletarian internationalism' and the latter (including Lenin) endorsing national self-determination. In practice, when the leftists led by Piatakov and the Democratic Centralist Andrei Bubnov gained control of the Communist Party in the Ukraine during the civil war, the positions were reversed, the left advocating decentralization and the right insisting on centralism. In April 1920 Moscow ordered a thorough purge of the elected Ukrainian leadership, and put an end to this base of opposition.

The 'Workers' Opposition' and the trade-union controversy

By mid-1920, as a communist victory in the civil war appeared assured, the left opposition again became invigorated, both in the form of the Democratic Centralists and in a new group based on the trade unions that took the name 'Workers' Opposition'. Led by Aleksandr Shliapnikov (the first Bolshevik Commissar of Labour and one of the anti-dictatorship protesters of November 1917), Aleksandra Kollontai (the Bolshevik feminist, first Commissar of Social Welfare, and a Left Communist in 1918), and the metalworkers' leader S. P. Medvedev, the Workers' Opposition harked back to the workers' control movement of 1917 and called for the trade unions to run industry independently of the party: 'The organization of the administration of the economy [should] belong to the All-Russian Congress of Producers, united in trade production unions, who elect the central organs that administer the whole economy of the Republic.' Shliapnikov proposed a three-way 'separation of powers' between the party, the soviets and the trade unions, while Kollontai denounced both bourgeois experts and communist bureaucrats and protested, 'The working class, *as a class* . . .

becomes an ever less important factor in the affairs of the Soviet republic.' The Workers' Opposition wanted to expel all non-proletarians from the party and require officials to perform manual labour at least three months a year.

A high point of left opposition sentiment came at the Ninth Party Conference in September 1920, as support for both the Democratic Centralists and the Workers' Opposition peaked. Almost half the party members in Moscow supported one or the other or the parallel group led by E. N. Ignatov. The Ninth Conference adopted a remarkable resolution affirming the norms of democracy and free criticism within the party, and calling for steps to curb bureaucracy and eliminate economic inequality.

In the autumn and winter of 1920–21 the most divisive controversy yet in the history of the Soviet republic broke out over the future role of the trade unions in the communist system, and by implication over the prospects and methods for implementing the new society. On the left were the Workers' Opposition and the Democratic Centralists, upholding the economic primacy of the trade unions and looking to the rapid realization of the anti-state ideal of 1917. Unfortunately for the left, the old proletarian base of the party had largely dissolved during the civil war, as industry was idled, workers were drawn into the army and the bureaucracy if they did not simply quit the party and go back to their ancestral villages, and wartime casualties took their toll. Where workers remained politically active they often preferred the Mensheviks, especially in Petrograd.

Meanwhile, just as in the Brest-Litovsk controversy, a fissure opened up between the communist centre led by Trotsky and the right wing of the party who rallied around Lenin. The Trotskyists, joined now by Bukharin, believed in the need for maximum coercion in the spirit of war communism to institute the new society. They proceeded from two controversial initiatives of Trotsky's – labour armies, and *Tsektran*, the Central Committee for Transport, set up in August 1920 to merge the rail and water transport unions with the Commissariat of Communications under military-style party officers. On this model the centrists called for 'governmentalizing' and militarizing the trade unions in order to absorb them into the centralized structure of management and discipline. Lenin, however, was moving towards a more cautious and long-term conception of the transition to socialism. First through a so-called 'buffer' group led by Zinoviev, and then directly, he called for the trade unions to revert to their conventional role as defenders of the interests of the workers while management remained the prerogative of the system of 'state capitalism'. An acrimonious public debate, the broadest since the Brest-Litovsk controversy and unmatched again until the Gorbachev era, extended from the Eighth Congress of Soviets in December 1920 to the Tenth Party Congress in March 1921. However, relying for his base on the Petrograd party organization controlled by Zinoviev, Lenin was able as before to prevail in most party organizations when they chose their delegates to the congress. Still, he barely came out ahead in the Moscow organization against the combined forces of the left opposition and the Trotskyists.

The Tenth Party Congress and the suppression of the opposition

All of the issues raised by the left opposition – party democracy, decentralization of power, and the status of the workers and trade unions – were abruptly resolved at the Tenth Congress. The congress happened to coincide with the revolt against communist rule by troops and sailors at the Kronstadt naval base outside Petrograd, whose grievances echoed the complaints of the left opposition. Lenin seized the occasion of this threat as an excuse to suppress his opponents within the party and silence utopian hopes for an early transition to the communist ideal. To this end, he had the congress adopt two decisive resolutions. One, 'On the Syndicalist and Anarchist Deviation in Our Party', condemned the Workers' Opposition as a 'petty-bourgeois' heresy. Foolishly the Democratic Centralists broke ranks with the Workers' Opposition to endorse this excommunication. The second resolution, 'On Party Unity', banned further activity or formal platforms by any organized factions within the party. A secret clause authorized the Central Committee by a two-thirds vote to expel any of its own members deemed guilty of factionalism.

These moves effectively ended the free exchange of ideas within the party, at the same time that Lenin announced a retreat in the revolution by adopting the New Economic Policy, compromising with small-scale private enterprise and the peasantry, and relegating the trade unions to the limited role they had under capitalism. Simultaneously Lenin punished the Trotsky faction by removing them from their strategic positions in the party Secretariat and Central Committee, as he turned to Stalin to be the top organization man under the new rules of party discipline. Lenin and Trotsky remained at odds until the Soviet leader's last months of activity in 1922–3. The stage was now set for the vocal but ultimately futile effort by former oppositionists throughout the 1920s to deny to Stalin the political succession and the fate of the revolution.

Echoes of the opposition of the war communism era continued to be heard. In March 1922 the Workers' Opposition vainly appealed to the Communist International (Comintern) against the suppression of 'workers' democracy' in Russia. In 1923, one of their number, Gavriil Miasnikov, organized a new anti-bureaucratic movement, the 'Workers' Group', but it was quickly suppressed. The Democratic Centralists made common cause with the Trotskyists in the 'New Course' controversy over party democracy in December 1923–January 1924, the first in the series of fruitless efforts by the left opposition of the 1920s to reverse the trend towards totalitarianism.

They appeared again as a separate group in 1927 to plead for the restoration of democracy in the party, only to be expelled at the same time as the Trotskyists at the Fifteenth Party Congress in December of that year. With few exceptions the leaders of the 1918–21 oppositions were liquidated in the purges of 1936–38, without benefit of trial. An exception was Aleksandra Kollontai, who survived to serve as a Soviet diplomat until her death in 1952.

Background and philosophy of the opposition

The roots of the communist opposition of 1918–21 go well back into the pre-revolutionary history of the Bolshevik movement, especially in the emigration. From the revolution of 1905 onwards, the Bolshevik faction of the Russian Social-Democratic Workers' Party was divided over political tactics, as the revolutionary purists, led by Lenin's initial second in command, the philosopher–economist Aleksandr Bogdanov, disputed Lenin's decision to take part in the tsarist Duma. In 1917 Lenin veered to the left to call for a new revolution by the Bolsheviks, in which he was backed by left Bolsheviks such as Bukharin, together with the group of radical anti-war Social Democrats around Trotsky who rallied to support the Bolshevik leader. These elements then became the nucleus of the left opposition to Lenin as he determined to make peace with Germany and supplant the direct democracy of 1917 with new structures of hierarchical authority.

Bogdanov's influence continued to be felt in the movement to create a distinct proletarian culture. Based on the theory that all culture and values are class-bound, this effort was embodied between 1918 and 1921 in the Proletkul't organization that Bogdanov headed. Disbanded by the party, Proletkul't nevertheless had an echo in the anti-bureaucratic 'Workers' Truth' organization that surfaced in 1923 to call for a new 'Workers' Party'. Like Miasnikov's Workers' Group, the Workers' Truth was quickly broken up by the police. Nevertheless, Bogdanov's doctrines and some of his disciples, including the historian Mikhail Pokrovskii and the former Democratic Centralist Bubnov (as Commissar of Education), were briefly influential in what is often termed Stalin's 'cultural revolution' of 1928–32.

In terms of personal background, a disproportionate number of the left opposition leaders were connected with experience in the pre-revolutionary emigration. Lenin, an *émigré* himself, used these people in 1917 to press his own radical agenda, but subsequently he always managed to overcome them by appealing to members from the pre-revolutionary Russian underground, usually workers, who had risen to the lower and middle levels of the post-revolutionary party bureaucracy. Typically impatient with theoretical disputations and democratic challenges to their own status, these *apparatchiki* provided the authoritarian nucleus for Stalin's rise to dominance in the party and the destruction of all opposition groups.

A consistent set of ideas, grounded in the *émigré* experience, ran from one manifestation of the left opposition to the next. They were semi-anarchist utopians, with an unbounded faith in the workers. They were anti-intellectual intellectuals or semi-intellectuals, particularly when it came to the employment of the 'technical intelligentsia' in positions of authority over the workers. (This theme was temporarily revived by Stalin with his anti-expert show trials during the upheaval of 1928–32.) The oppositionists were internationalist and messianic about the impact of the Russian revolution on the rest of the world, an impulse that mobilized them behind Lenin's drive for power in 1917 and just as emphatically turned them against him in 1918.

The left opposition believed ardently in the processes of democracy and political pluralism, but only for the working class and (after November 1917) within the framework of the single 'proletarian' party, a fatal limitation as it turned out. They recognized from an early moment the drift of the new Soviet system away from the direct democracy and egalitarianism of 1917, and towards bureaucratic authoritarianism, in the dominance of the party over the state (i.e., the elected soviets), of the centre over local authority, and of individuals over the committees and other elected bodies that they were supposed to serve. They returned again and again to the principle of the direct participation of the masses in administering their own destiny, in government, in the military and in industrial relations. They disliked the money economy as a survival of capitalism, and looked forward to an egalitarian 'natural economy' under communism. On the other hand, they had little interest in the peasantry and made little of the potential issue of rural suffering. In failing, they nevertheless created a record of protest documenting the evolution of the system, at least politically and in the urban sector, away from the utopianism of 1917.

The failure of the opposition

Many factors contributed to the failure of the left opposition of 1918–21. The small Russian working class on which the opposition intended to rely was dissipated by the conditions of war communism. The opposition's anti-bureaucratic and anti-expert philosophy ran directly counter to the technology-based requirements of modern life, and moreover defied the centralist habits of the Russian political tradition. Outside of Moscow and a few provincial centres, the opposition had no significant social base. It was usually divided, as it was between the Trotsky and Bukharin factions in the Brest-Litovsk controversy, and between the Democratic Centralists, the Workers' Opposition and the Trotskyists in 1920–21. It lacked strong leaders able to stand up effectively to Lenin; Trotsky had the necessary charisma, but he was inclined to authoritarianism himself and vacillated at key moments. The oppositionists were personally honest and dedicated individuals who protested at Lenin's authoritarianism within the communist regime. Unfortunately, bewitched by the mythology of the dictatorship of the proletariat, they failed (with few exceptions) to challenge the communist monopoly of power or to question the terror tactics used against non-communists, until they fell victim themselves when the one-party system was constricted into a one-faction system and then into a one-man system.

What if the left opposition had in fact succeeded at some point in checking the rush of the communist regime towards ruthless authoritarianism? Would their idealism and naïvety have exposed them to the revenge of the counterrevolution? Or would their fervour have carried them into the same sort of centralist expedients that the communist leadership in fact accepted? In any case, success for the utopians would have been contrary to all historical precedent: the one-party dictatorship and the requirements of political survival in a society racked by revolution and civil war reduced the anarchistic aspirations of the left to a misty dream.

Previous and subsequent parallels

For the communist opposition of 1918–21 to be fully understood, it has to be placed in the context of other great revolutions of history and the characteristic unfolding of the revolutionary process. Revolutions typically move from a moderate, liberal phase (in Russia, the Provisional Government of 1917) to a radical, extremist phase (the Bolshevik dictatorship), before they retreat and evolve into totalitarian dictatorship (the New Economic Policy and then Stalinism). Within the extremist phase there is another characteristic development, the emergence of a utopian, ultra-radical tendency in opposition to the more pragmatic radicals in power. Such were the Levellers and the Fifth Monarchy Men in the English revolution of the seventeenth century (democratic visionaries and religious millenarians, respectively), and the French revolutionary factions known as the Enragés and the Hébertistes (advocates for the Parisian working class) along with the proto-communist Gracchus Babeuf and his 'conspiracy of the equals'. Similarly, the sequence of opposition efforts in Russia from the Left Communists to the Workers' Opposition represented the force of utopian purism ranged against the perceived abuses of power and sacrifices of principle by the revolutionary government.

In Russia as in the earlier instances the ultra-radicals inevitably failed, but their stance established a new benchmark for subsequent revolutionary experiments elsewhere. The anti-bureaucratic, anti-expert, and egalitarian sentiments of the Russian left opposition briefly stirred up a current of sympathy in the new communist parties in Europe, though it was denounced by Lenin as a 'childhood disease of left communism'. Yugoslav communism after 1948 revived the Russian anti-statist ideas of 1917, and Josip Broz

Tito's programme of 'workers' self-management' bore a strong theoretical resemblance to the programme of the Workers' Opposition. Similar notions, notably in the military organization and tactics exemplified by Che Guevara, coloured the early years of the communist revolution in Cuba. Most striking was the echo of the Russian opposition in the so-called 'cultural revolution' in Communist China in the 1960s, including the introduction of communes, the concepts of proletarian culture and participatory democracy, and radical egalitarianism. Violent anti-intellectual and anti-expert purges in China included the idea broached by the Workers' Opposition of subjecting officials and specialists to obligatory manual labour. Finally, a related spirit of anti-managerialism distinguished the wave of student protest movements in Europe and the Americas in 1968. In none of these instances, however, was the parallel with the Russian opposition acknowledged.

The history of the early left opposition still has relevance after the collapse of the Soviet regime, even though post-communist thinking in Russia ignores it almost completely. It puts the Russian revolution in a broader perspective, demonstrating that the communist movement was not initially monolithic, and that there were alternative hopes and intentions, however impractical. The same sense of an alternative, of a higher social ideal, if not precisely the utopianism of 1917–21, could potentially play an important role in the reinvigoration of public life in Russia and other former Soviet republics under post-communist conditions.

Further reading

Anweiler O., *The Soviets: The Russian Workers', Peasants' and Soldiers' Councils, 1905–1921* (New York, Pantheon Books, 1974).

Bettelheim C., *Class Struggles in the USSR: First Period, 1917–1923* (New York, Monthly Review Press, 1976).

Daniels R. V., *The Conscience of the Revolution: Communist Opposition in Soviet Russia* (Cambridge, MA, Harvard University Press, 1960).

Daniels R. V., 'The Left Communists', *Problems of Communism* XVI (November–December 1967).

Daniels R. V., 'Socialist Alternatives in the Trade Union Controversy', in Daniels, *Trotsky, Stalin, and Socialism* (Boulder, CO, Westview Press, 1991).

Eighth Congress of the RKP(b): Stenogram of the Sessions of the Military Section of the Congress, 20 and 21 March 1919, and of the Closed Session of the Congress, 21 March 1919, *Izvestiia TsK KPSS*, 9, 10, 11 (1989).

Farnsworth B., *Alexandra Kollontai: Socialism, Feminism and the Bolshevik Revolution* (Stanford, CA, Stanford University Press, 1980).

Hagen M. von, *Soldiers in the Proletarian Dictatorship: The Red Army and* the Soviet Socialist State, 1917–1930 (Ithaca, NY, Cornell University Press, 1990).

Holmes L. E., For the Revolution Redeemed: The Workers' Opposition in the Bolshevik Party, 1919–1921 (The Carl Beck Papers in Russian and East European Studies, no. 802, Pittsburgh, University of Pittsburgh Center for Russian and East European Studies, 1990).

Kollontai A., The Workers' Opposition (Chicago, Kerr, 1921).

Kowalski R. J., The Bolshevik Party in Conflict (Pittsburgh, University of Pittsburgh Press, 1991).

Sakwa R., Soviet Communists in Power: A Study of Moscow during the Civil War, 1918–1921 (London, Macmillan, 1988).

Schapiro L. B., The Origins of the Communist Autocracy: Political Opposition in the Soviet State, First Phase, 1917–1922 (London, Macmillan, 1977).

Service R., The Bolshevik Party in Revolution: A Study in Organizational Change, 1917–1923 (London, Macmillan, 1979).

The Constitutional
Democratic Party (Kadets)

WILLIAM G. ROSENBERG

Kadet attempts to lead Russia towards a constitutional democracy in 1917 represented the culmination of many years' effort to 'Westernize' Imperial Russia into a nation and empire governed and ruled by law. The intellectual origins of this difficult undertaking can be traced back to eighteenth-century Enlightenment thinkers like Montesquieu and Beccaria, especially as their views were refracted through the humanism of Alexander Herzen and the jurisprudence of Boris Chicherin. Its political roots lay in nineteenth-century processes of professionalization engendered by the Great Reforms of the 1860s, especially in law, and in the autocracy's resistance to the premises of civic freedom that professional life required. Russian liberalism coalesced in the 1890s around Russia's major universities and urban professional centres, but also in the countryside around the zemstvos, where young doctors, teachers and attorneys confronted superstition and arbitrariness (*proizvol*) in their every effort to improve popular welfare. When the Kadet Party was formed in 1905, and officially registered as the Party of People's Freedom – *Partiia narodnoi svobody* – it presented itself as seeking a 'rule-of-law state' in the interests of all classes, nationalities and peoples, in contrast to the social partisanship of parties on the left. Whether this transformation might better come to Russia by evolutionary or radical means remained a point of contention throughout the party's history. Kadets seldom disagreed about programme, but seldom agreed about tactics.

Before 1917, this contention stemmed from the political implications of Kadet commitments to transcending narrow social partisanship (*nadpartiinost'*) and struggling 'not only for workers and peasants, but for the welfare and prosperity of all classes, of the entire Russian state', as a popular party pamphlet described it. This broad nationalism rather than any conscious partisanship was the core of a common Kadet outlook which transcended tactical differences and which shaped the party's programme. Kadets believed land should be transferred to Russia's peasantry, but that landlords had to be compensated for their loss; that national and ethnic groups should enjoy full civil freedoms, but that citizenship presupposed loyalty to the empire; that workers had the right to an eight-hour workday and other gains, but that these must not unduly disrupt production or threaten a firm's viability; that Russia had to become a constitutional and parliamentary monarchy, whose representatives were elected on the basis of universal, equal, direct and secret elections without regard to religion, nationality or gender, but that federalism could not work in Russia because nationalities were not numerically or culturally equal, and equal rights for women would have to wait until the country was 'ready'.

While distancing themselves in this way from particular social interests in order to advance what they regarded as the interests of state and society as a whole, Kadets thus promoted Russia's political liberalization in ways that held established social boundaries in some check. Although hardly defenders of the existing order, they were consequently attacked as a 'bourgeois' party by their antagonists on the left. Indeed, their very reluctance to defend particular social interests left the party without a strong social base. Kadets reflected the interests of Russia's commercial and propertied classes only in their promotion of civil liberties, their insistence that social conflict be mediated in ways that respected the interests of contending groups, their defence of property rights and relations, and their promotion of legal processes and the rule of law. Of the 26 members elected to the party's Central Committee at its Foundation Congress in 1905, nine were attorneys and nine were professors (including three professors of law). Not a single member was properly a representative of Russia's trading or commercial circles.

Between 1905 and 1917, 'left' Kadets like M. L. Mandel'shtam, N. V. Nekrasov and N. I. Astrov were particularly concerned that the party strengthen its ties with 'living social forces' among the proletariat and the peasantry in order to gain broader political support. This 'conciliationist' tendency found particular resonance among Kadet groups in Moscow and provincial cities, especially those close to the zemstvos. But V. A. Maklakov and other 'right' Kadets close to the centres of imperial power in St Petersburg worried more about the dangers of radicalism than party weakness, and insisted that the best course was Russia's liberalization 'from above'. Between these divisive tendencies, P. N. Miliukov, A. I. Shingarev, V. D. Nabokov, M. M. Vinaver, F. F. Kokoshkin and other activists struggled to hold their party in balance. With Bolsheviks and other radical Social Democrats boycotting the elections, Kadets won strong majorities in almost all urban areas of European Russia during the first Duma elections, particularly in Moscow and St Petersburg. Understandably, party leaders fully expected that in one way or another the evolving stresses of Russia's archaic autocracy would eventually bring them to power.

When Kadets finally realized these ambitions during the February revolution, however, circumstances were extremely inauspicious for liberal rule. As Miliukov and his colleagues took leading positions in the first Provisional Government, strong pressures to satisfy the immediate needs of

Russia's workers, peasants and soldiers, on the one hand, and to resolve the impending crisis in production and goods distribution, on the other, limited the possibilities for mediating conflict with reforms that protected contending social interests. Most difficult of all was the cultivation of respect for the rule of law and the creation of adequate means to defend it. This required broad acceptance of the authority and legitimacy of the new regime, conditions which Kadet figures like Miliukov and Nabokov insisted had to transcend the narrower (and more partisan) question of how well it functioned in response to social needs and demands. As political legitimacy became increasingly tied to functionality in 1917, however, workers and peasants both in Russia proper and in the empire's many ethnic enclaves and territories looked increasingly to their own popularly elected local councils (soviets) as Russia's appropriate authorities, while in the eyes of commercial and industrial interests the regime's legitimacy depended upon its ability to impose a 'lawful' social order. In the worsening economic and social circumstances created most immediately by Russia's engagement in the war, the liberals' insistence on 'legality' and 'statesmanship' (*gosudarstvennost'*) was inherently vulnerable to a wide array of contradictory challenges.

While Kadets dominated the government between March and May 1917, they took the lead in establishing full civil liberties, rationalizing industrial production and the prosecution of the war, and laying the groundwork for constitutional reform. This for both right and left Kadets was the very essence of the revolution, its historical justification. Municipal elections were set up for the empire's cities and towns; new legislation created elected district local government bodies in the countryside through the zemstvos; factory committees were formally authorized for all industrial enterprises; and representative land committees were established in rural areas to work through problems of food production and distribution, including those related to the actual possession and use of land. On 24 and 25 March, more than 300 delegates to the Seventh Kadet Party Congress strongly supported these efforts. The congress also urged unanimously that a Constituent Assembly be convened in the shortest possible time compatible with assuring a fair and proper election, so that major questions like land reform could be resolved by a duly constituted representative government. Kadets in the meantime would refine their own programme on this and other questions, build their party organization, and work everywhere to maintain the law and order essential to liberal democracy. Six weeks later at the Eighth Party Congress, the party reaffirmed its resistance to 'deepening' the revolution with premature reforms and to the dangers of 'Balkanization' implicit in nationality aspirations and federalism. A majority of 77 to 33 also affirmed the party's commitment to compensating landowners whose property was taken, rather than allowing the free redistribution of land.

The two strongest points of disagreement at the Seventh and Eighth Congresses concerned the closely related issues of war and empire, questions that also touched more fundamental conceptions of democratic forms and hence the liberal position towards the revolution. As articulated by Miliukov, Kokoshkin, A. A. Kornilov and F. I. Rodichev, the majority position favoured a 'Great and Indivisible Russia' and 'war to complete victory', which included Russia gaining control over the Dardanelles and the annexation in some form of Constantinople. Kadets denied these were the 'strivings of imperialism', as Rodichev put it, but simply a means of guaranteeing the freedom, independence and economic vitality of a post-war democratic Russia. A minority of Kadets denounced these views as chauvinistic and without practical meaning, and pressed the party to support Russia's reconstitution as a voluntary federation, a democratic *federated* republic that would provide constituent entities with substantial if not full autonomy. Kadets, after all, supported independence for Finland and Poland. But the majority remained strongly against supporting equivalent opportunities for other constituent regions of the Russian empire, even though some recognized this to be an issue on which Russia's military success, and indeed its very future, might depend.

The implications and consequences of Kadet views on these issues were soon apparent. 'War to complete victory' and 'Great and Indivisible Russia' not only positioned the party in direct opposition to soviet insistence on 'Peace without Annexations and Indemnities'; it encouraged the disaffection of Ukrainians, Turks and others from the Provisional Government's cause and strengthened local movements for independence. The manner in which liberal discourse represented both the Russian state and revolutionary society also allowed clearer boundaries to be drawn between Kadet and soviet conceptions of participatory democracy. Kadets championed civil liberties, supported the role factory and land committees gave to workers and peasants in the resolution of disputes, and welcomed the creation of an open civil sphere in which unions, nationality groups, and all sorts of other political formations could press their positions, including the soviets. But Kadets strongly denied the prerogatives of these participatory forms and forums to resolve constitutive issues of state policy. These could only be done 'lawfully', that is, according to existing (largely tsarist) law and within an overarching commitment to the rule of law.

The first two political crises of the provisional regime turned on these issues. After the publication of Miliukov's note to the Allies reaffirming Russia's pre-revolutionary war aims and the subsequent street protests, the Kadets' most prominent figure resigned his position as Foreign Minister and took the other Kadets with him from the government. Liberals returned to the cabinet without Miliukov only after leading members of the Petrograd Soviet agreed to take positions as well, creating a coalition Kadets hoped would temper participatory democracy in favour of its restraining legal analogue, and only after it became clear that the reconstituted cabinet would press a military offensive. Two months later, as the offensive stalled, Kadets again quit the government in protest at an agreement signed in Kiev promising the Ukraine and its governing Rada substantial autonomy. Kadets regarded this as a dangerous and unacceptable usurpation of the prerogatives of the Constituent Assembly, and hence certain to accelerate the rapidly growing tendencies towards social and political disintegration.

Kadet leaders did not know it, but their withdrawal from the government came just as dissident soldiers and Petrograd workers were about to begin the massive July Days demonstrations. The confluence of events had the effect not of bringing the Kadet Party back in defence of the embattled regime, but of further dividing its leadership and raising again the issue of *gosudarstvennost'*. Left and moderate party figures like Nekrasov, Astrov and N. M. Kishkin recognized in the July Days the fact of deepening social polarization. No less concerned about legality than Miliukov and those on the party's right, they again argued in favour of greater accommodation with Russia's 'living social forces' as a way of preserving liberal influence over the political course of events. Miliukov, Nabokov, P. D. Dolgorukov and others welcomed Kerensky's suppression of the July demonstrations and the arrest of its Bolshevik leaders, but saw a strengthening of state authority rather than further acquiescence to popular pressures as the only way ultimately to preserve democratic institutions, social order and the rule of law. While the left Kadets rejoined a government now essentially pledged to implement the Soviet's '8 July Declaration', one that, among other things, promised radical land reform with no guarantees of compensation to landowners, Miliukov, Rodichev, Maklakov and others began to contemplate the likelihood of more extensive civil conflict and the consequent need for a more authoritarian regime. Just as the June offensive marked the effective collapse of the Russian army, the three-week July crisis effectively marked an end to democratic state power itself in 1917, but most Kadets could not come to terms with the shift of authority to increasingly radical soviets any more than they could accept the end of a 'Great Russian State'.

In the process, the Kadets' *relative* political support in the empire's cities and towns held more or less steady, reflecting the deepening processes of social polarization that the revolution itself now encompassed. In some places, Kadet support actually increased, at least in so far as this can be measured by urban voting. In Moscow, the party gained only 17 per cent of the vote for the city duma on 25 June, but 27 per cent in the district dumas in September (and 35 per cent in the Constituent Assembly balloting in November). In Petrograd, the percentages went from 22 per cent in May to 21 per cent in August (and to 26 per cent in November). Elsewhere, increases over the summer were comparable for municipal elections, although the party remained virtually without support in the countryside, and ultimately returned only around 5 per cent of the total vote to the Constituent Assembly. Since the numbers of voters themselves declined steeply over time, however, these figures revealed not an increase in any *actual* support for the party that could be used to political advantage but the degree to which the Kadets as a whole were increasingly the symbolic political leaders of anti-soviet Russia. The 'bourgeois' representation Lenin and the Bolsheviks so vigorously pressed on the party was becoming a comprehensible and plausible description of political location, however spurious it remained in terms of the party's programmatic orientation.

Hence the party was readily identified as the instigator of General Kornilov's coup attempt in August even though its role was a passive one and the ties even of prominent party figures with the army command were tenuous at best. At the Ninth Party Congress that convened on 23 July, Miliukov and other prominent Kadets abandoned any effort at conciliation and aligned themselves squarely with the right. The country was in chaos: 'chaos in the army, chaos in foreign policy, chaos in industry, and chaos in nationality questions'. Kadets resolved to struggle against the sectarian left, 'a most critical danger', and to 'dedicate all forces to saving the Motherland!' At the Moscow Conference just before the coup attempt, Maklakov, Rodichev and Miliukov continued to speak with unrestrained hostility against the soviets and the left, refusing to pledge their support to Kerensky even though their Central Committee colleagues held prominent posts in his cabinet. Rodichev even exhorted Kornilov to 'Save Russia, and a grateful people will revere you', an encouragement that reflected broad Kadet sentiment if not the party's involvement in the conspiracy. The 'deep dark masses' also entered prominently into Kadet discourse in August, symbolizing even further disassociation from conceptions of democracy as participatory politics not carefully institutionalized and governed by law, or as unrestrained (illegal) social levelling. The party came to represent, in effect, the forces of Russia's polarized social and political right, without becoming its creation or active agent. The Kadets endured this posture through the last weeks of the provisional regime and took it with them into the throes of civil war.

The last (Tenth) Kadet Congress in free Russia took place in early October. Party leaders remained divided between those like Kishkin and A. I. Konovalov, who accepted posts in Kerensky's last cabinet in the hope that they could help it survive long enough for the Constituent Assembly to convene, and those like Miliukov, who thought Kerensky needed a psychiatrist (and that Kishkin himself should volunteer for the job if he was so determined to be of assistance), but who offered no practical alternatives. The party's primary focus was on the Constituent Assembly elections. In the provinces, conciliatory Kadets returned from the congress seeking electoral alliances with moderate socialists; in urban areas, most local groups sought support from the right. Both tendencies represented themselves as defending liberty, social justice, Russian national unity and the rule of law. Each was extremely pessimistic about the future. Neither was successful.

Thus, the Bolsheviks coming to power was hardly a surprise for Kadets. Indeed, on 19 October, the official party newspaper *Svobodnyi narod* ('Free People') began a daily column entitled 'Bolshevik Preparations', and Miliukov's apartment was put under armed guard. When Kerensky fled on 26 October, he appointed Konovalov as democratic Russia's last acting prime minister, and granted Kishkin 'extraordinary powers' to restore order. While the Central Committee urged Russians not to recognize the Bolsheviks, the Provisional Government collapsed as it had begun: nominally under Kadet Party control.

The task of open resistance was, of course, hopeless, and not simply because Kadets lacked the power to fight. Party leaders clung to the notion that resistance could only be through and by 'legitimate' bodies and 'legal' means. When a group of right SRs, Popular Socialists and moderate Social Democrats organized the Committee to Save the Fatherland on 26 October, A. I. Shingarev, Vinaver, Miliukov and others considered it just another effort to 'usurp' power. Kadets also opposed efforts by Tsereteli and others to form an anti-Bolshevik 'democratic centre' on the grounds that it would displace the prerogatives of the Constituent Assembly. Even after the arrest of Shingarev, Kokoshkin and other leading Kadets who were elected to the Constituent Assembly in November, Kadet–socialist cooperation became as much a victim of the Bolshevik coup as the coalition government it had constructed. Thus, once the Constituent Assembly itself was dispersed (followed shortly by the brutal murders of Kokoshkin and Shingarev), and all pretence of 'legal' resistance disappeared, most Kadets found themselves with little alternative to supporting the anti-Bolshevik armies beginning to form in South Russia and Siberia.

At a secret Kadet conference in Moscow on 14–17 May 1918, the continued hopes of Astrov and others that the Kadets might attempt to broaden their social base by drafting new proposals for reform were cast aside in favour of defending the 'national purpose'. Kadets would support all 'general-national' (*obshchenatsional'nye*) efforts to reconstruct a free Russian state whether they came from the right or left, providing they were dedicated to national unification, regional autonomy (rather than independence), the civil equality of nationalities, religious freedom and 'basic political reform'. They would not 'under any circumstances' solicit assistance against Lenin from the Germans, as Miliukov and others now in Rostov and Kiev were proposing; and they would organize in Moscow a 'National Centre' to help form a broadly based anti-German and anti-Bolshevik alliance in support of the military forces of Generals Alekseev and Denikin organizing in South Russia. The centre would also try to organize an anti-Bolshevik uprising in the capitals, hopefully timed to coincide with an attack by other anti-Bolshevik forces.

The May 1918 meeting set broad party strategy for the whole civil war period, but the party's Central Committee was able to meet for only a few additional weeks in Moscow before a concerted effort by the Cheka forced its members to flee. *Nash vek* ('Our Age'), the party paper published throughout the spring, was closed on 11 May. Vinaver and Astrov were among those who left to join Alekseev and Denikin, while others headed for Ufa and Omsk to link up with anti-Bolshevik efforts there. In the ensuing months, Kadets committed themselves in different ways and degrees to providing political leadership to Russia's various anti-Bolshevik forces in the interests of restoring an indivisible Russian state.

The task necessitated a range of compromises to liberal programmes and beliefs, reflecting further the priority now for Kadets of state over social and even civic interests. As in February 1917, the integrity of Russia's legitimate state order was the necessary foundation for any effort at social or political reform, rather than, as most socialists argued, reform constituting the basis of state legitimacy. Precisely because Kadets understood that legitimacy was a contested concept, they re-emphasized the importance of law and tradition, despite their tsarist foundations. Authority, in turn, depended on law, not on social purpose; and law required an appropriate coercive apparatus to assure its effectiveness. Here was the party's quintessential statism, not simply reaffirmed but substantially strengthened by the experience of 1917. What October represented was not simply the Bolsheviks' illegal usurpation of power, but a move towards social and political radicalism corrosive not only to liberal values and Russian social order, but to the whole Western European system of progressive national development. As Miliukov himself expressed it in May 1918, 'the law of national self-preservation' stood higher than any 'moral commitments'. The difficulty for most Kadets in the course of the civil war was that the White armies were far from noble defenders of these principles of *gosudarstvennost'*. As Kadets took positions of responsibility in successive White regimes, their moral commitments were repeatedly compromised along with their statist objectives by the indiscriminate brutalities perpetrated by the Whites, in some places fully commensurate with those of the Bolsheviks.

Thus in Kiev, I. A. Kistiakovskii, N. P. Vasilenko and several other prominent Kadets disregarded the directives of the party's Central Committee and acquiesced to German rule, working closely with the puppet Hetman Skoropadskii. Along with Miliukov, who himself briefly became an advocate of this 'German orientation', they hoped both to subvert the Ukrainian independence movement and to rupture the Brest-Litovsk peace by enlisting Germany further to the anti-Bolshevik cause. In South Russia, two conservative Central Committee members, V. A. Stepanov and K. N. Sokolov, took responsibility for organizing the civil administration of territories occupied by Denikin's Volunteer Army, insisting that regional political and social interests be subordinated absolutely to the army's needs. In the Ukraine, Kadets were consequently identified with the increasing harshness and brutality of German rule, especially as that army began in the late summer its disorderly retreat; and in the Kuban and South Russia, the White army's dictatorial authority increasingly compromised Kadet legalist pretensions, tainting the party with the inevitable excesses of military reaction.

While the exigencies of Russia's horrific civil conflict may have left Russia's liberals with no practical alternatives if they wanted to support the White cause, there were three grave weaknesses in their position, as several leading Kadets themselves recognized. First, it was very unlikely, as events were to demonstrate, that the anti-Bolshevik armies could succeed without a reasonably broad base of social support. Second, a broad political coalition was necessary to rally other parties and political movements, and take greatest possible advantage of the organizations and dissidents still functioning inside and outside of Bolshevik-controlled regions. And third, as Miliukov himself argued at a party conference in Ekaterinodar, subordination to the military was likely to minimize if not eclipse the party's role in post-war politics if the Whites were to win. The party's proper course was therefore to address itself seriously to local and regional interests, attempt to reformulate a popular social programme, reach out towards a broader political coalition, and demand the generals' adherence as a condition for joining ranks.

At virtually all Kadet party gatherings in South Russia and Siberia during the civil war, however, this latter position was held only by a small minority of party figures. As General Denikin formed the Armed Forces of South Russia in late 1918, Stepanov, Sokolov and others became uncompromising adherents of strict military dictatorship. Nikolai Astrov, who also worked closely with Denikin, attempted to play a moderating role, and struggled to prevent the escalating pattern of abuses by military field commanders, but his voice and his efforts were literally drowned by other party colleagues who turned the South Russian propaganda effort in a crudely nationalist, anti-populist, and at times anti-semitic direction. A similar pattern developed in Siberia under Admiral Kolchak after an armed coup against a moderate anti-Bolshevik Directorate brought him to power as 'Supreme Ruler' in November 1918. Here a self-styled 'Eastern Section' of the Kadet Central Committee became a forceful advocate of dictatorship, soon evoking the enmity even of the transplanted liberal newspaper *Russkie (Otechestvennye) vedomosti* ('Russian (Fatherland) News').

The only place where Kadets self-consciously adhered to the party's traditional programme and principles during the civil war was in the Crimea, where party luminaries like Vinaver, I. I. Petrunkevich, and Nabokov helped create a popular autonomous Kadet regime. Working closely with local zemstvo and Tatar leaders, including many prominent local socialists, the Kadets succeeded in organizing what they regarded as a model liberal administration, responsible to a regional parliament. Nabokov soon headed a special commission to re-establish effective judicial institutions; Vinaver led efforts to accommodate Tatar interests and assure broad-based civil liberties; and Solomon Krym, acting as 'Head of Government', implemented a broad local government reform and a limited but economically effective 'provisional' land reform, both of which were to be in effect until the convocation of an all-Russian Constituent Assembly. The popularity of these efforts was apparent in local elections. In Simferopol, for example, voters for a new city duma in late January 1919 returned 18 Kadets, 17 Tatars, 13 Social Democrats, 11 SRs, three Zionists, three Industrialists and two non-party delegates.

Events, of course, quickly overtook these conciliationist efforts, while in South Russia and Siberia the White movement's failure to secure popular support and to coordinate their armies led to its rapid dissolution once the Bolsheviks were able to sustain an assault. In both regions resistance behind the White lines was as serious as Bolshevik opposition at the front; and much of this was directed at the White regimes as well as their military administrations. In the last months of the civil war in South Russia, 'right' Kadet leaders gathered in Kharkov to demand unconditional support for military dictatorship, 'the basic guarantee that *gosudarstvennye* principles will triumph over anarchistic, mutinous, and separatist ones'. Their more moderate and conciliationist colleagues already recognized, however, that a radically 'new course' was necessary if any anti-Bolshevik efforts were to be salvaged.

It was not until the party leadership gathered in emigration, however, that these long-term divisions within Kadet ranks led to a formal rupture. Most Kadets left South Russia and Siberia in the spring and summer of 1920. In Paris, many established contacts with other *émigrés* grouped around the conservative Russian National Committee; in London and Berlin, they linked with various organizations to provide *émigré* relief; and in Constantinople and Sofia, they worked closely with General Wrangel and the remnants of the White armies. The newspapers *Poslednie novosti* ('The Latest News'), edited in Paris by Miliukov, and *Rul'* ('The Rudder'), which Nabokov and B. E. Nol'de edited in Berlin, became the dominant liberal voices of the *émigré* community.

In this setting of defeat and discouragement, the last chapter of Kadet history focused on analysing Russia's revolutionary experience and reconsidering the party's tactics, a matter for some of great importance. Miliukov, in particular, still imagined the Kadets had a role to play in Russia's future, partly because the massive social and economic dislocation the country had experienced made it seem unlikely that the Bolsheviks could survive, partly because he simply had difficulty contemplating permanent exile. In late 1920, consequently, he developed the outlines of what he called 'the New Tactic'. Oriented towards the satisfaction of 'popular aspirations', Miliukov's strategy was to 'turn the party to the left' in the hope that a massive insurrection inside Russia would call on *émigré* leaders to head a politically democratic state. Together with Vinaver and other party leaders in Paris, Miliukov hoped, finally, to form a firm tactical alliance with moderate socialists. His goal was to organize an 'all-Russian political coalition' committed to a federal democratic parliamentary republic, full autonomous rights for national minorities, and full recognition of the peasantry's claim to land.

The Kronstadt rebellion in March 1921 gave Miliukov and his supporters brief hope, but neither the Kadet leadership as a whole nor the *émigré* socialist parties gave the 'New Tactic' any chance of success. For the socialists, Kadets remained unacceptable representatives of the Russian right, as undoubtedly they were popularly perceived in Russia as well; and most within the party's thinning leadership ranks agreed with the Prague SR paper *Volia Rossii* ('Russia's Freedom') that the new tactic was 'cruelly mistaken'. The reason for this was not to be found simply in the Kadets' rightist representations, however, as the SRs averred, but in the ways the radical relocation of power in revolutionary Russia had destroyed the very possibility of liberal statism, a process begun almost the moment the party's leaders joined the Provisional Government in February 1917. Tactical political alliances in support of a 'Great and Indivisible' democratic Russian state had little if any relevance to the actual alignments and commitments of Russia's remaining 'living social forces', however much they reflected a new and admirable effort to take these forces finally into careful account. In June, this last effort at 'conciliation', one that conceivably could have strengthened the Provisional Government in the spring of 1917 had Miliukov and others then pressed their energies in that direction, again divided members of the party's Central Committee who gathered in Paris to discuss it. One month later, the party effectively broke apart.

Further reading

Dumova N. G., *Kadetskaia kontrrevoliutsiia i ee razgrom, Oktiabr' 1917–1920 gg.* (Moscow, Nauka, 1982).

Dumova N. G., *Kadetskaia partiia v period pervoi mirovoi voiny i Fevral'skoi revoliutsii* (Moscow, Nauka, 1988).

Medlin V. D. and Parsons, S. L., eds., *V. D. Nabokov and the Russian Provisional Government, 1917* (New Haven and London, Yale University Press, 1976).

Miliukov P. N., *Istoriia vtoroi russkoi revoliutsii*, 3 vols. (Sofia, Rossiisko-bolgarskoe knigoizdatel'stvo, 1921–4).

Rosenberg W. G., *Liberals in the Russian Revolution: The Constitutional Democratic Party, 1917–1921* (Princeton, Princeton University Press, 1974).

The Mensheviks in 1917

From Democrats to Statists

ZIVA GALILI AND ALBERT P. NENAROKOV

The history of the Menshevik Party in 1917, cast into the 'dustbin of history' by Lev Trotsky on the day the Bolsheviks seized power, has gradually been restored: first in a unique project that sought to record the retrospective views of *émigré* party veterans as they neared the end of their lives in the late 1950s and early 1960s; then, as the subject of a monographic study; and recently in a documentary publication, which demonstrates beyond doubt the Mensheviks' decisive role in shaping and implementing the political strategies of the soviets in 1917, from February to October. Bolshevik victory was very much the Mensheviks' defeat. But it is worth remembering that even in 1917, each of the two parties was still eager to appropriate the appellation RSDRP (Russian Social-Democratic Labour Party), each still used the other to define its unique position and cement its ranks, and each, in turn, still showed susceptibility to the appeal of social-democratic unity. The process of mutual demarcation and self-definition, which had begun at the Second Congress of the RSDRP in 1903, had not been fully completed even if more than a decade of factional struggle had solidified the elements of world view, political culture and practice that tended to mark a Menshevik from a Bolshevik.

Before the revolution

As Marxists, the Mensheviks tended to value not only the analytical framework and predictive powers of that doctrine, but its cosmopolitan point of view and the promise of a universalistic society. This can partly be explained by the preponderance among Mensheviks of ethnic minorities (Georgians and Jews) and the party's decidedly urban character. As Social Democrats, they subscribed to the scheme worked out by G. V. Plekhanov in the 1880s, according to which a bourgeois revolution would precede a capitalist, and later a socialist, transformation of Russia. Although they assigned a hegemonic position to the working class and its social-democratic party in this 'bourgeois' phase, the Mensheviks never tired of quoting Marx in arguing that political formations rested on socio-economic processes, that certain developments had to wait their turn, and that human will could not change the laws of history. The revolutionary initiation of 1905 invested this caution with the emotional power of fervent expectations and brutal repression. As refracted through the prism of their ideology, the unfolding of the first revolution gave credence to the central elements of Menshevik doctrine established at the First Conference of Menshevik Activists in May 1905, and were held as axiomatic well into 1917: that a transfer of power could come about only through a process of social change; that social democracy could organize and prepare the workers for such a transfer but could not decide the moment at which it would occur; and finally, since whatever provisional regime replaced tsarist rule would be bound to concern itself with the building of a bourgeois order, Social Democrats could not give it unconditional support, much less join it, lest they curtail their independence as a proletarian party and be driven into opposing their own worker following. Beyond this point of consensus, the experience of 1905 had the effect of uncovering not only the lines demarcating Mensheviks from Bolsheviks, but also those dividing Mensheviks themselves.

Already by 1906, A. N. Potresov proposed a programme of what Lenin would call 'liquidationism': eliminate the party underground and abandon the notion of the revolutionary party as the activator of social forces. Liquidationism thus involved the transformation of social democracy from a party of the revolutionary intelligentsia into a party of the masses, capable of competing for influence in the newly open national and local political arenas. In particular, trade unions, workers' cooperatives, workers' clubs and similar local proletarian organizations were now re-conceived by Mensheviks as schools for workers' self-activity (*samodeiatel'nost'*) and democratic political action. As such, Potresov's programme rankled with *emigré* Mensheviks, who remained emotionally, if not always practically, committed to the party's role in uniting and directing a fragmented labour movement. These tactical disagreements were at least partially solved when S. O. Ezhov, P. A. Garvi, and many other *praktiki*, that is, Mensheviks who had made themselves into bookkeepers, secretaries and organizers in the worker-run organizations, began in 1911 joining the so-called Initiative Groups which combined this legal work with involvement in a revived Menshevik underground. More persistent were the disagreements between the liquidationist publicists (*literatory* in Menshevik parlance) and their *émigré* critics. Men like Potresov, F. A. Cherevanin, E. Maevskii, V. O. Levitskii and B. I. Gorev saw in the growth of the urban sector in Russian society and the emergence of a new socio-political group – variously labelled the 'democratic intelligentsia', 'urban democracy', or simply 'the intermediary strata of the city' – the promise of an urban coalition between this new democracy and the progressive bourgeoisie, one that would hasten Russia's democratic transformation and secure it from social polarization and anarchy. In contrast, Iu. O. Martov, A. S. Martynov, S. Iu. Semkovskii and, for a while, F. I. Dan doubted that the young urban democracy could gain hegemony, prevent its bourgeois ally from excluding the lower strata from political life, or act with sufficient independence from the bourgeoisie and its parties.

The First World War deepened some of these disagreements while partially blurring others. The *émigrés* around Martov held to an internationalist doctrine. They saw the war as imperialist and looked to the Socialist International to impose a universal, just peace on the warring governments. In contrast, Potresov and the Liquidationists insisted that the tasks of self-defence demanded the participation of all the 'vital forces' of Russia, the socialist intelligentsia included, and argued further that an anti-tsarist alliance (which had failed to materialize in the proto-revolutionary wave of 1913–14) might still be forged around these tasks. Other Mensheviks who spent the war years in Russia, including some who called themselves Internationalists (most notably I. G. Tsereteli) but especially those who entered the work of the wartime public organizations, became more optimistic about an alliance of all the 'vital forces of the country' – the slogan that would guide Tsereteli in the construction and re-construction of coalition in the Provisional Government in 1917.

Thus, the internally divided Mensheviks did not come to 1917 with a well-articulated tactical solution to the question of power. Aside from a political culture which involved work in legal labour and public organizations and fostered an activism that was often belied by the party's self-ascribed position as the moderate faction of Russian social democracy, the more concrete elements of a general 'Menshevik' approach included the twin injunctions against socialist participation in a bourgeois government and a premature move towards socialism; a conviction that, for the revolution to traverse safely the distance from autocracy to social and political democracy, the working class and its party would need the cooperation of larger, stronger, better-educated groups in Russian society; and corresponding strategies intended to secure political arrangements that would allow the soviets to cooperate with the Provisional Government while also guiding its policies, and to contain the social processes unleashed by the revolution.

Rethinking the narrative of 1917

These goals – shared by most Mensheviks in 1917, open to many interpretations, and implemented within this range by the centrist Menshevik faction, the Revolutionary Defencists – have been poorly understood in both Western and Soviet historiography. Constructed with the Bolsheviks' victory as its overwhelming referential point, the narrative of 1917 is presented as a linear plot, gathering force from one crisis to another. Historians no less than memoirists have allowed what Potresov called 'class instinct' (as distinct from 'class consciousness') to influence their stories, with the result that the central goals and projects of the revolution – a democratic transformation of the polity, a democratic integration of society – have been blurred by emphasis on the struggle for power as such or, alternatively, on a crescendo of anarchy and social conflict that dwarfed all political action. In assessing the specifically Menshevik strategies that were directed towards preventing social polarization, the tendency has been to view them as lacking political realism from the start, being hide-bound by the doctrine of 'bourgeois revolution', and lacking as well in political resolve. Some elements of this historiographic consensus were addressed in Ziva Galili's 1989 study of *The Menshevik Leaders in the Russian Revolution*, but even this work left standing the notion that the polarization of social relations in the post-July period had finally paralysed the Mensheviks and, moreover, emptied all political initiatives and solutions of historical significance.

All of this needs rethinking in the light of the new four-part documentary history, *The Mensheviks in 1917*, published in Moscow between 1994 and 1997. As a scholarly enterprise, this work is indebted to the new access to a cross-section of archival materials in Russia and abroad and the new opportunities for collaboration between Russian and Western historians. As a documentary publication, it establishes the Menshevik leaders of the Petrograd Soviet and the all-Russian network of soviets not only in the context of the factional struggle within their own party (that is, between their own Revolutionary Defencist faction and their Defencist and Internationalist critics; between Mensheviks in the capital, the provinces and the army; and between labour activists and cabinet ministers), but also in the context of the organs of the soviets themselves, where these leaders, and the Socialist Revolutionaries who dutifully followed them, struggled to establish a succession of political strategies against pressures and criticism from the other socialist parties and groups. Additionally, it situates the Menshevik leadership solidly within the context of the three national convocations that dominated formal political life in the second half of 1917: the Moscow State Conference, the Democratic Conference, and the so-called Preparliament. Here intra-Menshevik divisions refracted and augmented the great political rifts of Russian society and polity that so facilitated the Bolsheviks coming to power.

Of the many issues that these new documents force to the fore, the most encompassing is that of the periodization of the revolutionary narrative. In pointing to the central concern of all Mensheviks with their self-assumed, yet necessary role of uniting disparate social forces around the historical task of Russia's democratic reconstruction (a concern that was at the heart of Menshevik factional struggles), the new documentation redirects our reading of the Russian revolution. The political crises and slogans (such as the April Theses, the April and July crises, and the *Kornilovshchina*) which have been cast as propelling the class confrontation and the struggle for power, may alternatively be read as symptoms of a prevailing political culture, and as constituent parts of three principal stages in the unfolding of the revolution. The first of these, which saw both the victory of coalition policies over the initial duality of authority and the crisis of these policies, lasted from February to the end of August; the second, the stage of missed opportunities to unify Russia's democratic forces and thereby resolve the question of power, lasted from the beginning of September to the October coup; finally, in the third stage, the ultimate collapse of efforts aimed at integrating society, and the parallel establishment of soviet power as an instrument of a one-party policy, underlay the period from the October coup until the dispersal of the Constituent Assembly in early January 1918.

In dedicating a volume to each of the last two stages, the new documentary history of Menshevism in 1917 redresses a long-standing imbalance. Despite the voluminous body of literature devoted to them, the second and third periods have not been subjected to thorough scholarly scrutiny, nor sufficiently commented upon by the participants. (The only significant exception is the 'notebook' of N. N. Sukhanov, the Internationalist Social Democrat whose personal recollections have shaped much of our understanding of the choices and decisions facing socialist leaders in 1917.) The new documentary history finally allows detailed examination of the debates surrounding the largely unknown attempts to create a homogeneous democratic government after Kornilov, and opens up a whole vista of activities immediately preceding and following October: the efforts at ensuring open public discussion of the most urgent problems of domestic and foreign politics; the contest over the structure and the actual exercise of political authority; the strategy on the part of some Mensheviks of actively resisting the regime that emerged from the October seizure of power by the Bolsheviks; and the struggle by others for a homogeneous socialist government, that is, a government embracing all the socialist parties represented in the soviets – Bolsheviks, Mensheviks, SRs and Popular Socialists (NS).

The Mensheviks and the role of the state

This new periodization is dictated by the logic inherent in the evolution of political processes as documented in the participants' understanding of those events, but the recovered documents significantly modify our perceptions of what occurred in Russia in 1917 in other ways as well. First and foremost is the question which we have chosen for special consideration here, namely, the prevailing conceptions and representations of the state as power (in the Russian sense of *vlast'*). It is now clear that the Mensheviks, having ascended to the Olympian heights of politics through the actual power of the soviets, found themselves in a situation in which greater political influence went along with immeasurably greater responsibility and an unavoidable need to make difficult decisions, a situation made all the more tortuous by inner strife within the party and a constant worry about party unity. In 1917, it was the Mensheviks who played *the* key role in the essential and complex processes related to the formation of democratic structures of authority and who relied on them to impart greater integration to Russia's fractious society. Time and again, Mensheviks of various tendencies had to balance ideology against the social and political realities of the moment. In its effort to provide conditional support for the Provisional Government by the soviets, the party attempted, concurrently, to retain its authority with the masses supporting the soviets and to exert pressure on the government to resolve problems of critical importance to *all* groups in Russian society, thereby helping the new government's political consolidation. This explains the acute clash of attitudes over the exercise of dual power and, above all, over the interpretation of what in fact the soviets were – one of the sources for the formation of a new democratic authority, or organs of self-government generated by the revolution itself.

The primary critique of this perspective came, of course, from Lenin, who viewed the soviets as a form of organizing political authority and whose call, in his April Theses, for casting this view into political formulas, enshrined the existing split between the political forces in Russia. Among other consequences, Lenin's pronouncement warped the processes of comprehension and generalization because it distracted and disfigured a real understanding of the soviets' role and place in the social life of the country. Yet criticism also came from among the Mensheviks themselves. With their initial almost limitless influence within the soviets, there was among them from the outset considerable ambivalence and inconsistency in relation to dual power.

The Mensheviks whose views were fully expressed by Dan (Tsereteli's most trusted and influential ally in the Menshevik leadership) considered pressure and *kontrol'* by the new democratic structures of power to be of key importance in their conditional collaboration with the census (propertied) Provisional Government. Dan's followers believed that only the soviets could secure the influence of 'revolutionary democracy' upon the character of political and economic reforms as well as upon the government's conduct of foreign policy. More conciliatory from the outset was the strategy of Tsereteli and the Defencist leader Potresov, who sought to avoid the necessity of exerting pressure on the Provisional Government by the soviets. This strategy, however, was called into question after P. N. Miliukov sent his famous diplomatic note to the Allies on 18 April, confirming Russia's intention to continue the war to a 'decisive victory'.

Moreover, from the beginning of the revolution there also existed a third point of view, that of the Menshevik *praktiki*. Through their work in the Labour Section of the Petrograd Soviet, men like B. O. Bogdanov and K. A. Gvozdev were the first to begin cooperating of their own accord with the Provisional Government, viewing themselves as a crucial link in the management of the economy and the salvation of the country and the state. In their own direct experience as mediators between workers and management they saw proof that some Russian entrepreneurs, typified by A. I. Konovalov (the Progressist entrepreneur who became Minister of Trade and Industry in the Provisional Government), were willing to provide the conditions for an open, self-regulating workers' movement, whose creation had consumed much of the Mensheviks' efforts since 1907. Yet already in late April, the same experience showed that some of the so-called propertied circles would have to be coerced into cooperation because of their inertia and even open opposition.

Similar conclusions were reached by the Mensheviks who were in charge of the Economic Section of the Petrograd Soviet, namely V. G. Groman and Cherevanin. Both men were economists and statisticians and veteran Liquidationists, whose work in the wartime public organizations had, to a large extent, determined their optimism regarding cooperation between socialists and public groups, including the commercial–industrial elements. Groman and Cherevanin were also keenly aware, even more so than their fellow *praktiki*, that only pressure by themselves and their allies among the technical intelligentsia could force the government and the entrepreneurial class at large to accept the economic measures they considered critical for Russia's survival.

The April Crisis strengthened these Mensheviks' belief that only socialist participation in the exercise of power could ensure an authoritative government as well as make it possible to implement the socially integrative policy the party considered necessary. What was not entirely expected was the dramatic transformation in the Mensheviks who joined the coalition government. This change, which can best be summarized as the transformation of democrats into statists *(gosudarstvenniki)*, involved a re-definition of the functions of the state as well as a shift in the Mensheviks' own self-perception.

Prior to the formation of coalition, as William Rosenberg has properly observed, 'the Soviet and the Provisional Government had rejected a potential role for the state as an instrument of social or class interests; it was constructed as a supra-party space for struggle, not an instrument of class privileges or social domination'. Indeed, the very appearance of the soviets and their coalescence into a vertically organized network so soon after the February revolution, gave largely spontaneous expression to a broadly based desire to replace the dominant conception of the state as an instrument of power with the emerging understanding of the state as an agent for social integration. However, Menshevik participation in government entailed an expansion in the state's functional significance in various spheres of social and economic life, and this (again, in Rosenberg's words) gave renewed strength to the state's traditional 'tendency to interfere, at the expense of its tendency to defend civil order. In the process, the boundary between state and society did not become clearer, as the consolidation of a new democratic order in Russia required, but instead became weaker.' At the same time, the Mensheviks directly involved in governmental work were driven by the burden of responsibility and more subtle changes in self-perception to see themselves as custodians of the Russian state, and to recognize the Provisional Government of which they were now members as the only appropriate locus of political authority.

From democrats to statists

This process, however, was neither straightforward nor simple. Thus, in the immediate wake of the dual July crises, the predominant Menshevik perception of the soviets appeared only marginally changed. To be sure, this moment was detrimental to Menshevik strategy in two ways: while the Kadets' withdrawal from the government cast doubt on the coalition's premise of collaboration between the representatives of the soviets and the non-socialist ministers, the mass anti-government demonstrations in Petrograd divided leaders from those led in the soviets. Still, the Mensheviks did not give up their reliance on the soviets as full participants in the formation of a new coalition, though the differences in the attitudes of various factions became more and more distinct.

A majority among the centrist Revolutionary Defencists favoured a new cabinet established along the former coalition principles, at first demanding that it commit itself to the programme of radical change accepted by the First Congress of Soviets (3 to 24 June), but retreating from this when it proved unacceptable to the soviets' coalitionary partners. Another group of centrists was prepared to accept a broad coalition, in which the existing government would be joined by all the constituent elements of 'revolutionary democracy' (i.e. the soviets, the socialist parties represented in them, and the plethora of labour and army organizations), as well as by elements of the so-called 'non-socialist democracy' (zemstvos, various branches of local self-government, cooperatives, professional unions of teachers, engineers, doctors and other employees). The Menshevik Internationalists, as is well known, rejected from the start the notion of socialist participation in coalition, and in July began calling (especially through the Petrograd Organization of the party, where they held a majority) for a transfer of power to the soviets, with the proviso that this be achieved not through coercion but through the soviets' organizational channels and political influence.

Reflected in the first of these positions was the new and emerging attitude of the *gosudarstvenniki*. This was evident in a hitherto unpublished speech of the Menshevik Minister of Labour M. I. Skobelev to the joint plenum (16–24 July) of the All-Russian Central Executive Committee of Soviets (VTsIK): 'No one in the government doubts the role and importance of local democratic organs in the struggle against economic destruction, but only the government can establish such organs.' Skobelev's perspective makes understandable Tsereteli's juxtaposition during those days of a strong executive power and a soviet 'incapable of realizing anything'. Tsereteli viewed the soviets as purely representative organizations, and called on them not 'to interfere with the power of the whole people', namely, the coalition government. One should note that these words were uttered long before the 'bolshevization' of soviets. Moreover, this position fully coincided with the view articulated by representatives of the propertied groups, as expressed by N. V. Nekrasov – the most radical of the Russian liberals – who on 21 July challenged the Menshevik-SR leaders by saying: 'Take this power into your hands and bear the responsibility for the fate of Russia. But if you lack the resolve to do so, relinquish power to the coalition government and then do not interfere in its work.' Even more surprising was the reflection of these new realities in the dynamic evolution of the Internationalist position, as expressed by the Committee of the Petrograd Organization. In a short period of time, the Committee significantly broadened its understanding of the essence of the 'soviet ministry' it had called for, and allowed for 'those bourgeois ministers who had not yet resigned' to continue their participation in the government while also demanding that it be strictly accountable to the soviets.

The August Congress of the RSDRP(o) failed to find a way out of the crisis of coalition politics. And in spite of its claim to represent the united (*ob'edinennaia*) wing of Russian social democracy, neither did it move a single step closer to the establishment of a truly unified workers' party, one possessing a sober, carefully balanced, specific and effective plan of action for the construction of a democratic state. On the other hand, new documentation offers abundant evidence that during the two months from the August Congress to the Second Congress of Soviets Menshevik policy was dynamic and creative, if ultimately unsuccessful.

First, there are the newly discovered protocols of the Central Committee elected at the August Congress, which together with the deciphered drafts of more detailed unofficial protocol notes make for something of a historical sensation. These documents convey the personal stand taken by each speaker, a rich spectrum of assessments and judgements at times entirely unexpected and often at odds with the notions entertained by several generations of students of Menshevism. They illuminate the logic that governed the changing attitude on the part of various Menshevik groups towards the idea of coalition, and document the search for organizational principles that would allow an accountable government to interact with the new democratic Preparliament, eventually convened early in October.

During this time, all the parties leading the soviets, in the centre as well as the provinces, saw a further decline in their prestige and authority, and none more so than the Mensheviks. Those Mensheviks who were 'more sensitive to the situation', as Ezhov put it, began revising their tactics. From their six-month experience with revolution they concluded that it was not worthwhile 'to buy a coalition with the propertied classes at the expense of democratic policy', for it only increased the workers' distrust, and cast them into the 'opposition camp'. Ezhov, like other party leaders who represented competing trends within Menshevism, insisted that in weighing their policy decisions the socialists should take into consideration the sentiments prevailing among a majority of the workers without, however, 'turning into Bolsheviks'.

Since the struggle for the masses went on mostly within the soviets themselves, there is a special value in a second new source for this period: the records of sessions (*ad hoc* and united, open and closed) of the VTsIK and the Petrograd Soviet, now carefully reconstructed from archival and press materials. In one instance after another, the new documentation shows the Mensheviks actively, though unsuccessfully, seeking to seize the initiative in the ongoing definition of the Russian revolution and its prospects. In the process, internal divisions deepened and undermined the goal of uniting all the democratic forces. Calls for a nationally responsible approach, and even the successful effort at the Moscow State Conference (12–15 August) to convince representatives of the so-called 'non-soviet democracy' (cooperatives, zemstvos and municipal self-government, etc.) to form a united 'democratic front' behind the August 14 Programme of democratic reforms, could not thwart the combative statements of the rightist forces or their repeated success in realizing their goal of complete governmental independence from the soviets.

The Kornilov coup in late August opened before the Menshevik leadership a comparatively easy and quick way out of the crisis of the policy of coalition and the attending crisis in the party's own ranks. For a moment, it appeared as if both the general's coup and Kerensky's initially uncertain response to it confirmed the correctness of the Mensheviks' overall approach to power as registered in the decisions of the August 'Unification' Congress. Thus, both the critics of the coalition policy and the supporters of the unity of the nation's 'vital forces' agreed that first and most urgently it was necessary to unite the broadest possible segments of society and, above all, revolutionary democracy itself under the banner of the defence of the government. At the same time, even Menshevik centrists could not fail to recognize the growing power of Bolshevik slogans among the soviets' following. Any delay in realizing the programmatic measures they had themselves endorsed on 6 May, 8 July and 14 August threatened to deprive the party and its leadership in the soviets of political initiative. Hence, in September the Mensheviks set out to achieve this goal with renewed dynamism and purposefulness, exploiting to the maximum the advantages of their centrist position, which had not yet been wholly discredited.

But their hopes were buried once and for all at the Democratic Conference (14–22 September). The behaviour of the political parties, social groups and organizations represented at the Conference was reminiscent of the behaviour of so many characters in Krylov's famous fables. The

Menshevik centrists, headed by Tsereteli, called for the formation of a government that would unite 'the vital forces of the nation' without regard to class, party or national interests and aspirations. The Menshevik Internationalists, as well as the left-wing SRs and the Bolsheviks, all demanded (although in different forms) that social control over the provisional regime be strengthened and that the forms of government accountability be more strictly defined. This could be done by linking the regime either to the soviets, to whom the Bolsheviks and like-minded people from other parties were now inclined to transfer authority, or, until the convocation of the Constituent Assembly, to a new organ (the Preparliament) that would include representatives not only from the soviets but also from other public organizations and groups and would exclude only those directly involved in the Kornilov affair. This, it seemed, was exactly what Russian society craved for, and what could still save it from extremism.

Class instinct (again, in Potresov's reading of the term) continued, however, to divide the delegates at the Democratic Conference both on the question of immediate goals and on their possible allies and partners. They seem to have become accustomed *ad absurdum* not to listen or trust one another. None of those participating in the debates noticed that in their general approach they were little different from the much castigated propertied supporters of General Kornilov. Just like Kornilov's supporters, everyone agreed that the main task of any government was to strengthen its governing functions. Some demanded a strengthening of the government to prevent industrial collapse and military defeat, others added that it would also be in the interests of the nation's 'vital forces', while a third group argued for it in terms of a dictatorship of the proletariat and peasantry. Thus, all the delegates contributed in one way or another to the fateful decision to invest state power with a special 'omnipotent role, interfering in everything'.

Exactly two months later, in an article published in the first issue of the newspaper *Klich* ('The Call'), Dan admitted that at the Democratic Conference the Mensheviks could have delivered the votes to ensure a stable majority against coalition, although, in his opinion, even this could not have ensured a realistic chance for an 'all-democratic power' because 'democracy' itself (meaning cooperators, representatives of zemstvos, municipalities and peasants' soviets) expressed no desire to participate without representatives of the propertied groups. Years later, this thought was repeated almost verbatim by V. S. Voitinskii (also a close Tsereteli ally), but he frankly added that neither did the Bolsheviks express 'even the smallest desire to join a government with the other socialist parties on a compromise platform acceptable to broad segments of democracy'. This could only be written at the end of the 1920s – not only long after October and the civil war, but also after the first years of NEP, when it had become only too clear that the Bolsheviks were there, indeed, 'in earnest and for a long time to come'. In November 1917 Dan could not write like this. He was well aware that L. B. Kamenev and some other Bolsheviks held a special position,

agreeing to support a socialist government and its compromise platform
before the Congress of Soviets. This 'moderate Bolshevik' stance was apparent not only in the statements by Kamenev and others at the Democratic
Conference but also in the negotiations held after October under the patronage of *Vikzhel'*, the central organ of the union of railroad workers and
employees.

Drawing on this knowledge in an article on the last days of the
Provisional Government published in 1923, Dan attributed the failure of the
Democratic Conference above all to the intolerance displayed by the official
representatives of VTsIK, and in this he was more accurate than Voitinskii,
other memoirists, and later scholars of 1917. The very reason and logic for
convening the Democratic Conference – that is, the realization that it was
essential to establish a homogeneous democratic government – were dealt a
blow by the refusal from the outset of Tsereteli and other official representatives of VTsIK to break with the propertied elements or to accept the
necessity of the 'formation of a purely democratic power'. (Dan himself
reluctantly supported this position.) In Dan's retrospective words, this
turned the Conference into 'an arena of totally unnecessary and even harm-
fully intensified altercations with the Bolsheviks'. For in fact, as Dan correctly asserted, at the Democratic Conference there was only one realistic
possibility – to form a 'soviet government' and not an 'all-democratic' one.

Later on, Dan also admitted that 'the constitution of the Preparliament
was seriously vitiated compared to the initial drafts because of the resistance
of the government'. The Provisional Council of the Russian Republic, as the
Preparliament was formally called, was relegated to a merely consultative
role. Nevertheless, the Menshevik leaders of VTsIK still hoped for success in
replacing the coalition with a purely democratic government, capable of
realizing quickly and resolutely the main points of the August 14 programme. Mensheviks had always valued the power of practice to change
institutions *de facto* and now they looked to joint work in the
Preparliament, which opened on 7 October, hoping that in the course of this
the non-soviet democracy might be emboldened 'to break ties with its
social-political conservatism' and accept a 'parliamentary' way of reforming
the government. The Menshevik leaders, then, hoped that the Menshevik
faction in the Preparliament would succeed in forging 'a left majority' with
the aim of forming, later on, a purely democratic 'left' government.
However, as Dan admitted in his 1923 article, there was little chance of
accomplishing this since so much time had been lost and events were developing with 'dizzying speed'.

Indeed, the Mensheviks' programme of withdrawing from the war
(founded on the slogans 'Peace without Annexations and Indemnities! The
Realization of the Right of Nations to Sovereignty!') was rejected outright
by the propertied circles, as were their other suggestions – especially the
regulation of agrarian relations and industrial production, combating the
pogrom movement and other violations of order, and the organization of

provisioning for the population and the army. Having given in to the propertied elements in questions regarding the character and formation of the government, having surrendered under pressure from these circles the idea of a cabinet accountable to the Preparliament created by the Democratic Conference, the Mensheviks found themselves unable to combat either rightist or leftist extremism. This was the result, to a large extent, of the speed with which they had been transformed from democrats into *gosudarstvenniki*, a transformation so rapid that it prevented them from noticing when and where the central power of the state once again lost touch with society. At the end of September, Tsereteli himself stated that 'in the country of revolutionary democracy, authority has been organized without any democratic support'. Now, when all failed, he redirected his attention to the 'enormous role of the soviets', which 'aggregate the opinions of the masses', and consequently are 'the active wing of democracy'. In truth, it was not only the state that lost touch with democracy, but so too did the democrats-turned-statists. Later the same road would be traversed by the Bolsheviks, who would use the soviets for the dictatorship of the proletariat and poor peasantry, making them into the instrument of a one-party political system.

Menshevik defeat in 1917 spelled the end both for the party's new-born statism and for its long-standing ideals and practices for the construction of social and political democracy in Russia. This defeat has obscured for many decades the Mensheviks' political activism and leadership in the revolution. But the brevity of what should be recognized as the 'Menshevik phase' of the revolution can also be a source for new insights, especially now that we can take full measure of Menshevik activities in 1917, of the complex patterns of their internal divisions, and the many permutations of their respective positions, most importantly that of the party's Revolutionary Defencist leaders. We know that as the moderate wing of Russian social democracy, the Mensheviks were tragically torn in 1917 between an abiding commitment to the advancement of the workers' immediate economic goals and long-term political and social ideals, and an equally steadfast conviction that these goals required a prolonged period of cooperation with other social forces. We have also learned that as architects and leaders of the soviets (the 'active wing of democracy') they saw their own commitment to the democratization of institutions and practices gradually give way: first to a sense of responsibility for the revolutionary project, which led them into the coalition government; and then, in the face of war, revolution and an incipient civil war, to a concern with safeguarding the very structures of state they had set out to transform. Menshevik statism cannot be blamed on personal hunger for power nor on the experience of exercising power. May it be attributed, then, to the interaction between their own social and democratic project and the realities of a fully enacted revolution, attended by deep, sweeping social and political processes? Was Russia's democratic revolution preordained to come full circle, to return to the reimposition of an all-encompassing state, having given society only a fleeting chance to generate the intermediary structures and frameworks that could have limited the scope of the state? The history of Menshevism in 1917 poses these questions afresh for historians to ponder.

Further reading

Basil J. D., *The Mensheviks in the Revolution of 1917* (Columbus, OH, Slavica Publishers, 1984).

Galili Z., *The Menshevik Leaders in the Russian Revolution: Social Realities and Political Strategies* (Princeton, Princeton University Press, 1989; Russian edition, 1993).

Galili Z., Haimson L. and Nenarokov A. P., eds., *Men'sheviki v 1917 godu*, 3 vols. in 4 parts (Moscow, 1994–7).

Volume I, *Ot ianvaria do iiul'skikh sobytii* (Moscow, Progress-Akademiia, 1994).

Volume II, *Ot iiul'skikh sobytii do kornilovskogo miatezha* (Moscow, Progress-Akademiia and Rospen, 1995).

Volume III, Part One, *Ot Kornilovskogo miatezha do Vremennogo Demokraticheskogo Soveta Rossiiskoi Respubliki (avgust-pervaia dekada oktiabria)* (Moscow, Rospen, 1996).

Volume III, Part Two, *Ot Vremennogo Demokraticheskogo Soveta Rossiiskoi Respubliki do kontsa goda* (Moscow, Rospen, 1997).

Haimson L., ed., *The Mensheviks: From the Revolution of 1917 to the Second World War* (Chicago, University of Chicago Press, 1963).

Haimson L., Galili Z. and Wortman R., eds., *The Making of Three Russian Revolutionaries: Voice from the Menshevik Past* (Cambridge, Cambridge University Press, 1987).

Ruban N. V., *Oktiabr'skaia revoliutsiia i krakh men'shevizma (mart 1917–1918 god)* (Moscow, 1968).

Sukhanov N. N., *Zapiski o revoliutsii*, 7 books in 3 vols. (Moscow, Izdatel'stvo politicheskoi literatury & 'Respublika', 1991–2).

Tsereteli I. G., *Vospominaniia o fevral'skoi revoliutsii*. 2 vols. (Paris and The Hague, Mouton, 1968).

The Socialist-Revolutionary Party (SRs), 1917–1920

MICHAEL MELANCON

As World War I approached its third year and the tsarist regime its demise, the Party of Socialist Revolutionaries (PSR) faced enormous challenges. Like other oppositionist movements, it had suffered heavily at the outbreak of war from sharp police repression. Disputes about the war had riven the party, with many hallowed leaders – A. A. Argunov, N. D. Avksent'ev and E. K. Breshko-Breshkovskaia – supporting Russia's war effort and others – V. M. Chernov, M. A. Natanson, and N. I. Rakitnikov – opposing it. Most top party leaders languished in West European or Siberian exile. Even so, the February revolution would soon catapult the PSR, for a time, into a pre-eminent position as Russia's largest party.

The SRs' remarkable, albeit ephemeral, post-February success reflects party history prior to the event. The Azef scandal led the SRs to abandon the practice of terrorism (while dangling its threat as a kind of Damocletian sword over the regime). In response to the 1908 police destruction of their committees, they introduced a successful campaign to win a firmer footing in Russia's proletarian organizations (labour unions, cooperatives, cultural associations and insurance funds). Meanwhile, P. A. Stolypin's repression of the peasant movement forced the PSR back to its pre-1902 status as a primarily urban-oriented organization; it intended to renew mass peasant-oriented work when possible and for that reason devoted some attention and publishing to peasant matters, but expended most efforts elsewhere.

Like the Social Democrats (SDs), the post-1905 PSR experienced lively debates, first about the efficacy and ethics of terrorism and then, beginning in 1910, about the necessity for continuing underground organizational work as opposed to legal endeavours in public organizations. The onset of the war wrought new divergences that largely paralleled earlier ones: the intelligentsia minority who had already renounced revolutionary activities supported the war effort, whereas most activists, following Chernov's lead, retained their radical outlook by coming out against the war. The leftist Natanson–B. D. Kamkov alignment (with Chernov's cautious support) even espoused the defeat of the tsarist government as a precursor to its over-throw. The anti-war sentiment of most SR cadres induced the pro-war leaders in the emigration and inside Russia to withdraw from party work for the war's duration.

By mid-1915, SR agitational and organizational work (as well as that of other revolutionaries) progressed more smoothly than earlier in the war. SR influence increased in wartime Petrograd's huge industries and those of other urban centres, as party organizations issued anti-war and anti-tsarist leaflets, participated in strikes, and recruited workers to the revolutionary cause. In these endeavours, PSR members allied themselves closely with internationalist Social Democrats (anti-war Mensheviks and Bolsheviks), whose efforts paralleled but did not surpass their own. In their propaganda at the fronts and in rear garrisons, the SRs successfully relied on their long-term attention to the armed forces, their staunch anti-war positions, and their land programme, whereas Social-Democratic efforts in this milieu were less methodical. With efforts in the village restricted to occasional peasant-directed leaflets, the PSR remained a largely urban-based organ-ization that devoted most of its energy to workers and soldiers. SR activities against the war, tsarism and capitalism, along with those of the Social Democrats, contributed to the revolutionary overthrow of the tsarist regime, a circumstance that calls into question prevailing theories about the February revolution's spontaneity. Certainly, traditional descriptions of the SRs as peasant-oriented intellectuals, reliant on terrorism and bereft of organizational ties with mass social elements are quite wide of the mark.

With the old regime's collapse of late February 1917, the PSR embarked on its new entirely legal life. Nationwide, the SRs joined other socialists in setting up and manning the network of soviets, public committees, factory, soldier and peasant committees and militias that replaced the administrative and police organs of the old regime. Unchallenged in organizing peasant and soldier-oriented institutions, the SRs rivalled, but did not equal, the Social Democrats (especially the Mensheviks) within the worker milieu. They took a special interest in factory committees, which SR cadres entered in large numbers; additionally, many factories throughout the country elected SR deputies to workers' soviets, a matter obscured by the social-democratic focus of most studies.

Nevertheless, SR leaders clearly yielded to their Menshevik SD allies in terms of numbers and activism in many urban soviet executive committees. Indeed, the SRs spread their forces quite thinly: as opposed to the Social Democrats' proletarian orientation, the PSR's broad programmatic injunc-tion required it to launch efforts among workers, peasants and soldiers, not to mention intelligentsia. In addition, many SR leaders entered the numer-ous 'public committees' which attempted to wield local power. Somewhat later in the year, SRs won elections as mayors of most cities and dominated urban dumas across the nation. The limited (although still substantial) SR role in urban soviet executive committees has produced a misleading perception that the SDs took the initiatives in revolutionary organizing, whereas an objective analysis might note the breadth of SR efforts among workers, soldiers and peasants and in public institutions.

Meanwhile, the SR organization underwent rapid, indeed phenomenal, growth. More than any other political organization, the SRs were the chief initial beneficiaries of the February revolution. Renewed party organizations held conferences, elected committees and launched newspapers. They founded clubs and libraries, issued masses of propagandistic literature, instituted agitational schools and sent speakers to factories, garrison units and to the fronts. From the intelligentsia, workers, soldiers and peasants, recruits flooded in (soon drawing the snide epithet 'March SRs'). The Petrograd organization alone came to count over 40,000 members, whereas nationally the party could boast many hundreds of thousands. By April, Chernov and other *émigré* leaders were returning to Russia to join those who had been living legally in the empire's cities or who had recently arrived from Siberian exile or hard labour. The euphoria of the victory over tsarism induced party members of hostile tendencies to submerge their differences in a common effort to reforge a single SR party, which even proffered a welcoming hand to the quite moderate fellow-populist Trudoviks and Popular Socialists. Ostensibly, a formidable organization had arisen that promised to exercise a decisive role in revolutionary Russia's future.

Heady achievements and bright prospects aside, the PSR faced serious problems. Enlistees flooded in while party structures were still rudimentary, rendering control difficult, a problem exacerbated by the SRs' post-February broad-spectrum (big tent) approach. Smaller enrolments or later ones (as with the Mensheviks and Bolsheviks respectively) might have ensured a salutary modicum of ideological conformity. As matters stood, the SR left and right soon accused one another of inheriting the 'March SRs', a significant proportion of whose support (whatever side it was on) ultimately proved flaccid and undependable.

The growing split in the party constituted a second major problem. The post-February melding of profoundly differing tendencies was not blessed with success. The very conferences that launched the rapidly waxing organizations witnessed the first clashes about the war, the nature of the revolution, and the new government. In most places, moderates initially won out. (An analogous process occurred among the Mensheviks and in the soviets.) By definition, most SR leaders living legally inside Russia prior to the February revolution were moderates, whereas the vast majority of leftist leaders were in one exile or another. Thus moderates such as Kerensky and V. M. Zenzinov in Petrograd and V. V. Rudnev, D. S. Firsov (Rozenblium) and M. Ia. Gendel'man in Moscow established their sway over local organizations and, ultimately, the new SR Central Committee.

Several factors boosted this process. The defencist intelligentsia, who for years had refrained from illegal party work, now streamed back into the party, where they comprised an articulate pool of support for the right. The argument used to establish the party's new moderation espoused caution in the face of possible reaction against the revolution and ringingly proclaimed the need for 'consolidating revolutionary gains' in preparation for future accomplishments, a programme that, as regards the war, came to be called 'revolutionary defencism'. Within the PSR, as well as within the soviets, the mass recruits generally heeded the ubiquitous moderate voices, although rank-and-file workers and soldiers maintained an edge of suspicion. The outnumbered and outshone leftists were obliged to await the arrival of new forces, which eventually appeared in the persons of B. D. Kamkov, Natanson and M. A. Spiridonova. However, upon his return Chernov unexpectedly tacked to the right, allying himself with the staunchly moderate A. R. Gots, Avksent'ev and Zenzinov and, such was his prestige, drawing with him radical activists across the country. Consequently, the Left SR leaders found themselves excluded from shaping party policy. The die was cast: the PSR's leadership established its definitive pre-October orientation that included revolutionary defencism on the war, steady support for the Provisional Government, and a willingness to delay action on reforms for workers and peasants and as regards Constituent Assembly elections.

Although all socialist organizations initially rejected entry into the Provisional Government (of his own volition Kerensky independently became Minister of Justice), almost at once moderate SRs began to urge an official socialist presence in the Provisional Government, a movement that accelerated with the April Crisis over Miliukov's note. During April, with Chernov's approval and eventual involvement, the PSR, over strong leftist objections, reoriented itself towards entry into the government, an idea that the Menshevik SDs also eventually sanctioned. In the SR view, only a socialist presence could invest the government with sufficient authority to carry out its mandate of introducing democratic reforms and holding Constituent Assembly elections. (By contrast, many rank-and-file SRs viewed entry as a desirable first step towards a socialist government.) Thus, in early May, prominent SRs and Mensheviks joined liberals in the government; Chernov became Minister of Agriculture, while Kerensky moved from Justice to the more important Ministry of War. Conditional support for the Provisional Government (on the basis of the famous 'in so far as' formula) now transmogrified into identification with it.

As of May and June 1917, the PSR's position still seemed unassailable. Party rolls were growing at a breakneck pace; SR factions in soviets likewise expanded and solidified. Front committees as well as soldiers' soviets and garrison committees were SR bastions. SRs everywhere presided over district and provincial peasant conferences; the late May Congress of Peasant Soviets elected an All-Russian Executive Committee that replicated the PSR's own leadership. During May, June and July, sweeping SR victories in city duma elections (often absolute majorities) added to the party's sense of well-being.

Nevertheless, the PSR's travails had already begun. At the First All-

Russian Conference of Soviets during late March and again at the First Congress of Soviets during June, the enormous SR delegations had some leftists who broke discipline in allying with other radicals (Bolsheviks and left Mensheviks) to speak openly against the Provisional Government and the war, thus implicitly criticizing the Central Committee's policies. The Kronstadt, Kazan and Kharkov organizations were outright leftist, while the huge Petrograd organization veered ever closer to radical positions; furthermore, many nominally moderate organizations passed resolutions on the war or the land that smacked of leftism. Although most peasant soviets and the peasant All-Russian Executive Committee still remained safely under moderate control, the Kazan, Mogilev, Penza and Kharkov peasant soviets were under Left SR sway and began passing land to the peasantry. Events at the SR congress during May revealed the true state of affairs: up to 40 per cent of the delegates voted for left-inspired resolutions. In general, the right wing of Avksent'ev, Breshko-Breshkovskaia, Argunov and M. V. Vishniak had little support, whereas the numerically predominant centre found itself trapped in the crossfire of the left–right war that commenced at the congress.

The PSR's special plight reflected its tortured position. By dint of theory, programme, cadres and history, the party was radical, that is, aimed at the rapid development of socialism. Even during 1917, much SR activity had a profoundly revolutionary cast. For example, the Petrograd SRs first suggested the idea of national congresses of worker, soldier and peasant soviets; in one stroke, Order Number One, formulated by soldier-SRs in the Petrograd Soviet, revolutionized Russia's vast military. SRs (along with Mensheviks) took the lead in organizing factory committees and militias (later known as Red Guards), both of which epitomized worker militancy and reflected the concept of workers' control. Likewise, SR-organized peasant soviets often pushed for transfer of private land to the peasants. Furthermore, numerous SR-dominated soviets (Kronstadt, Kazan, Penza, Samara and Turkestan) acted in virtual independence of the centre (as befitted SR theory about local autonomy), in effect achieving local soviet power. All such activities reflected deep-seated SR (populist) outlooks on the nature of Russian society and her appropriate path of development.

Thus, on the one hand, most SRs took their traditions seriously, whereas, on the other, the Central Committee and a significant number of local leaders tried to brake further deepening of the revolution; additionally, by entering the liberal-oriented Provisional Government, the top leaders effectively negated hallowed SR theory about the quick transition to socialism. A core of party intellectuals had, in effect, taken upon themselves the task of guiding the party and the nation along an evolutionary path. The resulting discordant notes within the party grew shriller with each passing month, achieving full cacophony after the Provisional Government's June offensive. With their quite literal understanding of 'revolutionary defencism' and 'support for the Provisional Government to the extent that . . .', most SR cadres viewed the military offensive as a betrayal of elementary revolutionary commitments, signalling an end to support for the government.

The massive July Days demonstrations in Petrograd and other centres represented disappointed SR worker and soldier expectations as much as Bolshevik manoeuvrings. The radical SR Northern Regional Committee came out for the demonstrations; marchers bore a veritable sea of banners with the SR slogan 'Land and Freedom', as well as with calls for Soviet power and an end to the Provisional Government. Nevertheless, the SRs (and Mensheviks) in the All-Russian Central Executive Committee of Worker and Soldier Soviets (VTsIK) decided to reconstitute the Provisional Government with a socialist majority and with Kerensky, the person most directly linked to the failed offensive, as head of government. In order to restore order, Kerensky then reinstituted the death penalty at the front and ordered the arrest of Lenin and other leading Bolsheviks, as well as numerous leftist SRs and Mensheviks.

As SR leaders in essence took over the Provisional Government, the deepening crisis within the PSR now shadowed the crisis in the country. The party was at the pinnacle of power, the very exercise of which proved a millstone: every crisis, every perception of failed revolutionary promise, was now blamed on the SRs (and their Menshevik allies). Furthermore, the Provisional Government's waning mass support deprived it of the wherewithal to wage an effective struggle against the Bolsheviks and other leftists, nor could it prevent further disorders and economic collapse. Thus, the Bolsheviks soon re-emerged as revolutionary martyrs, whose cause now progressed in lock step with waning SR-Menshevik worker and soldier support.

Both within the party and on the public scene, the Left SR movement advanced. During August and September, many SR organizations came under leftist control or split; likewise, peasant executive committees moved into opposition to the Provisional Government. To worsen matters for the moderate leadership, upon resigning his post as Minister of Agriculture in late August, Chernov laid down a barrage of criticism of the government (and the Central Committee) about the land and the war. Still, the Central Committee remained adamant in its unquestioning support for the government and Kerensky. The late-August Kornilov affair transformed the waning of SR worker–soldier support into a stampede, only partially stemmed by Left SR initiatives.

During the last two months of the Provisional Government, the SR Central Committee carried out a desperate kind of holding action, punctuated by occasional petulant outbursts, as when it 'expelled' the Voronezh, Tashkent and Petrograd organizations for leftism. It resisted pressures for a new party congress and an all-Russian congress of soviets. The Central Committee placed on its agenda, postponed, and never returned to the distressing question of the party's burgeoning left flank. It banked on success in the Constituent Assembly elections, which, after numerous delays, were scheduled for November. In putting together party electoral lists, the Central Committee weighted the balance heavily in favour of moderate SRs. The impeccable calculation, had fate not intervened in the guise of the new Soviet government, was that the peasantry would vote for SR slates, thus propelling the same moderate group that dominated the party, the Provisional Government, the peasant soviets, and (along with the Mensheviks) the VTsIK, into control of the Constituent Assembly as well.

Thus, the SR leadership did not welcome the Second Congress of Soviets, which the VTsIK (still under SR-Menshevik domination) reluctantly summoned for 25 October. At first, the SRs discouraged moderate socialists from attending, only to abandon this policy out of fear that a boycott would leave the field to radicals (predictably, a significant majority of the delegates at the congress were leftists). In the event, the congress found itself confronted with the Bolsheviks' long-heralded overthrow of the Provisional Government.

The Bolshevik *démarche* reunited Chernov and the rest of the Central Committee while at the same time immeasurably widening the gap between them and the left. The so-called right SRs (joined by the right Mensheviks) left the Congress of Soviets in protest at the use of force against the government, thus creating a Bolshevik majority that proceeded to recognize the overthrow and sanction a new Bolshevik-led Soviet government. The Left SRs, stepchildren in their own party, now pressured the Bolsheviks to negotiate the establishment of an all-socialist government, including the SRs and Mensheviks. Finding themselves threatened with a strike by railway workers (whose national union operated under Left SR influence), the Bolsheviks agreed to the negotiations, which lasted well into November; at one point, feeling isolated and under military pressure, the Bolsheviks tentatively agreed to broaden the government and, *mirabile dictu*, the SRs agreed to enter a government with them, while the Mensheviks agreed at least to support such a government. Unfortunately, the SR-Menshevik formula for the proposed government excluded Lenin and Trotsky, a condition the Bolsheviks, emerging from the perceived military threat, were happy to reject. The breakdown of the negotiations led to the final split within the SR party, after which the two sides held separate congresses; during December, the Left SRs joined the Bolsheviks as junior partners in the Soviet government.

In the Constituent Assembly elections later in November, peasants rewarded long-term SR attention with a massive vote that gave them, along with allied groups such as the Ukrainian SRs and the Armenian Dashniaks, roughly 60 per cent of the delegates overall, partially compensating for massive worker–soldier defections. Already concerned about potential moves against the Constituent Assembly (veiled warnings emanated from the Left SRs and the Bolsheviks), the SRs and Mensheviks formed a Committee for the Constituent Assembly's Defence, the records of which indicate society's ambivalence.

Meanwhile, late in the month the SRs held their party congress without the bothersome leftists. Now firmly under Chernov's wing, the delegates staunchly rejected the rightist policies that had led to such malign results and adopted a series of resolutions worked out personally by Chernov on war, land and the issue of socialist power. The new orientation placed the party firmly at the left-centre, close to earlier Left SR positions (the Mensheviks underwent a similarly belated leftward evolution). A savage irony lies in the virtual certainty that had the SRs adopted such stances earlier, the party would have retained much of its mass support, thus creating a bulwark against Bolshevik ascendancy; at this late stage, the SRs could not convincingly recast themselves in roles appropriate for the fervent populist narrative, the chief exponent of which became the Left SRs, who proceeded to encroach heavily on the party's remaining considerable mass following.

With the forcible dismissal of the Constituent Assembly in early January, the SRs – who boycotted the new Bolshevik–Left SR-dominated VTsIK – now, perforce, abandoned the centre stage they had occupied since the February revolution. Their last measurable contact with a portion of their original social base occurred during the upswing of worker support for Mensheviks and SRs in many cities during the spring of 1918; the Bolsheviks responded by arresting the newly elected Menshevik–SR executive committees and, during June 1918, by outlawing the SRs and Mensheviks from the soviets. Likewise, the factory assembly movement, which in Petrograd, Nizhnii Novgorod and other places developed under SR influence, ultimately failed to survive Bolshevik oppression. Tragically, by mid-1918 the SRs (and their Menshevik allies) had resumed the illegal status they had occupied under tsarism.

By summer, many SRs had fled to the south and to the east where they instituted a series of governments, ostensibly based upon the Constituent Assembly, in Samara, Ufa and Siberia aimed at recreating moderate socialist or socialist-liberal alternatives to the Bolsheviks. The failure of these governments to garner firm support from local workers and peasants – repeat Provisional Government performances proved unpopular – contributed to their military weakness and their demise at the hands of burgeoning fully armed White movements that viewed them as little different from the Bolsheviks.

By the autumn of 1918, the SRs, who still maintained a Central Committee and other institutions on Russian soil, were trapped between the two sides of the gruesome Russian civil war. The main group under Chernov's leadership manoeuvred between the Red–White Scylla and Charybdis, trying to prevent a counterrevolutionary White victory without openly supporting the Communist dictatorship, although a smaller group under the leadership of V. K. Vol'skii and N. V. Sviatitskii reached an anti-White accommodation with the Bolsheviks during mid-1919. For the balance of the civil war, the SRs maintained a surprising degree of activism, holding conferences, printing literature and addressing meetings. As the civil war wound down during 1920 in favour of the Soviet government, the Cheka closed in, decimating the central organs of the party inside Russia, after which Chernov made a daring escape abroad. Piecemeal activities continued for a year or two; heavy arrests and the famous 1922 trial put the quietus to the PSR inside Russia.

The PSR's gravest failure during 1917 was its lack of a clear political physiognomy. Many commentators have failed to realize the extent to which the rightist group, with Chernov's temporary passive connivance, distorted the party's theory and programme by supporting the liberal-oriented Provisional Government; likewise, the right's ardent support for the war repulsed many SR cadres and worker–soldier–peasant adherents. The consequence was a stream of defections towards the left, so that from spring 1917 onwards SRs and SR organizations lay arrayed on a political spectrum all the way from extreme left to near liberal. This opened the possibility of large early enrolments but precluded development of a clear programme for a society undergoing revolution.

Right SR rationales concerned support for the war and for Russia's continued membership in the Western alliance against Germany. The right SR intellectuals, who had rejected revolutionism even before the war, were committed to evolution towards socialism within a capitalist state, an essentially Menshevik position having nothing in common with SR theory or practice. In effect, they had abandoned the traditional populist-SR discourse about Russia's unique development and replaced it with a new one that reflected contemporary moderate European socialism. The right SRs had thus come to view themselves as guardians of the Russian state, veritable *gosudarstvenniki* (having much in common with the Constitutional Democrats), which explains their ardent defencism, their interest in the Provisional Government and local all-class public committees, and their nugatory attempts at state-building on the Volga and in Siberia during 1918. Perhaps defensible in and of themselves, these positions signified that those holding them were no longer SRs, especially since the enormous majority of SR activists and, more importantly, worker–peasant–soldier cadres continued to view Russian realities through the lens of radical discourse. The right SR bureaucratic seizure of control over the party and its official positions led directly to the party's loss of support, to the party split and, in a sense, to the Bolshevik seizure of power.

Existing studies of the PSR from 1914 through 1917 by K. V. Gusev and Oliver Radkey, as well as my own work, offer a framework but leave many questions unanswered; for example, Radkey's thorough examination of the central party leadership during 1917 provides limited information about local organizations. Similarly, topics such as SR activism within the peasant, soldier and worker milieu and among various nationalities remain blank pages. However, central and local archives have wide holdings about all aspects of SR history. The State Archive of the Russian Federation (now GARF, formerly TsGAOR) in Moscow has holdings on local SR party

organizations which it began to declassify in 1993; its holdings from the
police archives (pre-1917) and from various institutions during 1917 and
later have a wealth of data about the SRs. The Russian Centre for the
Preservation and Study of Documents of Recent History (RTsKhIDNI,
formerly TsPA IML) in Moscow has two major collections of interest: fond
274 and fond 564 with documents of the SR and Left SR parties.

Further reading

Gusev K. V., *Partiia eserov ot melko-burzhuaznogo revoliutsionizma k
kontrrevoliutsii* (Moscow, Mysl', 1975).

Hildermeier M., *Die sozialrevolutionäre Partei Russlands: Agrarsozialismus
und Modernisierung im Zarenreich (1900–1914)* (Cologne and Vienna,
Böhlau, 1978).

Melancon M., *The Socialist Revolutionaries and the Russian Anti-War
Movement, 1914–1917* (Columbus, Ohio State University Press, 1990).

Perrie M., *The Agrarian Policies of the Russian Socialist-Revolutionary
Party from its Origins through the Revolution of 1905–1907*
(Cambridge, Cambridge University Press, 1976).

Radkey O., *The Agrarian Foes of Bolshevism: Promise and Default of the
Russian Socialist Revolutionaries, February–October 1917* (New York,
Columbia University Press, 1958).

Radkey O., *The Sickle Under the Hammer: The Russian Socialist
Revolutionaries in the Early Months of Soviet Rule* (New York,
Columbia University Press, 1963).

Rice C., *Russian Workers and the Socialist-Revolutionary Party through the
Revolution of 1905–1907* (Basingstoke, Macmillan, 1988).

The Left Socialist Revolutionaries, 1917–1918

MICHAEL MELANCON

The Left Socialist-Revolutionary Party, which officially formed during November 1917, had its origins in wartime SR internationalism and, more directly, in the leftist movement within the party after the February revolution. The war's outbreak in 1914 marked an immediate, ultimately irremediable divide between those favouring continuation of the war in alliance with the Western democracies (defencism) and those who adhered to socialist anti-war internationalism. Under the leadership of V. M. Chernov, N. I. Rakitnikov and M. A. Natanson, the SR party (PSR) as a whole, including activist cadres and the party's worker, soldier, peasant and student following, took the internationalist stance; an arch-leftist group under Natanson and B. D. Kamkov even espoused the Russian government's defeat as a first step towards socialist revolution. Most organizations conducted the vigorous propaganda against war, tsar and capital appropriate to populism's traditional hostility towards both autocracy and capitalism.

Although N. D. Avksent'ev, E. K. Breshko-Breshkovskaia, A. A. Argunov and other figures supported the war, defencism found wide adherence only within the SR intelligentsia. Virtually identical in personnel, following and outlook with an earlier faction that had renounced revolutionary activities in favour of legal operations in existing social institutions, the smaller pro-war group 'sat out' the war in isolation from SR organizations. In principle, while they opposed the tsarist regime (but eschewed illegal means of struggle, especially during the war) they also demurred from sponsoring rapid socialist development. Their sharp divagation from traditional SR theory notwithstanding, they did not sever party ties but rather set about transforming the PSR according to their own lights.

The February revolution unexpectedly changed the balance of power within the party in favour of the defencists. Numerous activists and leaders hearkened to 'revolutionary defencism' which held the new revolutionary Russia worth defending. Even Chernov adopted this stance and in other ways inclined to the right, just as previously he had leaned to the left (albeit not so far as the Natanson–Kamkov wing). The rightward reorientation received a big boost from the inrush of defencist leaders and intelligentsia who for years had remained aloof from the illegal organizations. The defencist intelligentsia plus the revolutionary defencists (with Chernov at their fore) vanquished the leftists. Only those who had espoused the defeat of the tsarist regime as a precursor of a socialist revolution still adhered to anti-war positions and now also rejected the liberal-oriented Provisional Government in favour of a proposed Soviet-based socialist one. Even upon their return from European or Siberian exile, leftist leaders found themselves helpless to stem the tide. The formerly radical PSR now displayed a reformist and gradualist face, as the Central Committee, tightly under right SR control, firmly supported the war and the Provisional Government.

The post-February PSR attempted to bind together persons of two conflicting discursive worlds. The articulate rightist intellectuals, who established control of party organizations by persuading workers, soldiers and peasants of the need for caution, still often employed the rhetoric of revolution when making public speeches, whereas their actions and writings disclosed a reformism that mandated the task of consolidating the Russian state under the control of the educated bourgeoisie (*zhivye sily* – 'living forces' was the catchphrase employed). On the contrary, the leftist activists undertook to preserve unsullied the original SR (populist) mindset about Russia's uniqueness: the tsarist regime's demise at the hands of the workers and soldiers (peasants in uniform) set the stage for socialism rather than capitalism. Bereft of Chernov and his legions of followers, the leftists yielded control of the party but remained convinced that most activists shared their outlook.

The leftists had the task of propagating their views in order to regain the allegiance of mass party elements. They rejected a party split since, on the one hand, they overestimated the prospects of taking control from within and, on the other, they could hardly contemplate a party without Chernov and Rakitnikov. None the less, they openly staked out radical positions. At the late-March Soviet Conference and at other national, regional and local gatherings of the spring and summer, they opposed the war and the Provisional Government, advocated a socialist government, and urged reforms for workers, soldiers and peasants. They blocked with like-minded Bolsheviks and left Mensheviks to offer joint resolutions that were, until later in the year, regularly defeated by moderate SR-Menshevik majorities.

The Left SR failure to control the party organization did not signify lack of resources or popular support. Centres of Left SR strength formed quickly, to be joined regularly by new ones. With its huge sailor and soldier contingents, the Kronstadt SR organization at once became a leftist bastion that contributed heavily to the Kronstadt Soviet's famous radicalism. The similar Helsinki and Revel organizations also developed along leftist lines, as did the soldier-oriented Pskov SRs. Meanwhile, the enormous Petrograd organization, with its worker, soldier and intelligentsia components, started from a left-centrist position, and moved steadily leftward throughout the year. Thus, the SR Northern Regional Committee (including Kamkov and A. N. Ustinov) became a left-wing fortress that published its own newspaper, *Zemlia i volia* ('Land and Freedom'). At the fronts, Left SRs blocked with leftist Social Democrats to propagandize soldiers. The Ufa, Tomsk and Kazan SR organizations soon occupied leftist positions and the Kharkov organization coined for itself the future party's title 'Left SR-Internationalist'. These centres served as dissemination points for Left SR ideas throughout the Urals, the Volga region, Siberia, the Ukraine and beyond.

Existing research allows for the construction of only the roughest model for the early development of leftism within given SR organizations. The sailor-oriented Kronstadt, Revel and Helsinki organizations moved quickly to the left, whereas Black Sea fleet organizations remained moderate much longer; the party organization in Kharkov consisted of workers and intelligentsia, in Tomsk, soldiers and intellectuals, in Kazan, workers, soldiers, students and peasants, and so forth. Local organizations' alignments had less to do with their class make-up than with their leadership groups. Where strong leftist groups gathered, the organization leaned to the left; where moderate intellectuals predominated (as, prototypically, in Saratov, Moscow and Samara), organizations with identical mass bases as leftist ones tacked rightward. Within moderate organizations, leftism eventually arose directly from worker, soldier or peasant associated cadres, buttressing the Left SR argument that mass-level cadres shared their aspirations. Although the SR intelligentsia milieu never fell under leftist sway to the extent of other party elements, the Left SR leadership consisted largely of intellectuals. The typical Left SR national or local leader was an intellectual who had entered the realm of party activism during the period 1905–07, suffered arrest and exile, believed in the need for illegal revolutionary work, and opposed the war to the point of defeatism. The party intelligentsia's defencist proclivities ensured that during 1917 few new intellectual cadres rallied to the Left SR cause, so that the middle-level leadership of the Left SR movement and, later, party issued directly from soldier, worker and peasant elements.

By late spring, the leftist movement within the PSR was gathering strength, coterminously with Bolshevik accretions of support in soviets and other mass organizations. The Left SR contingent at the May party congress counted about 20 per cent of the delegates but on some important questions won 40 per cent of the votes. In order to coordinate their affairs nationally, the leftists created an organizational bureau, drawing threats from the Central Committee, which the moderate majority re-elected denuded of leftists except for Natanson, thus blithely ignoring actual alignments of strength. Left-oriented SR newspapers and orators warned of Bolshevik successes in excoriating moderate SR-Menshevik policies. They accused the

Central Committee of abandoning hallowed SR doctrine and, thereby, the party's traditional mass base in favour of appealing to middle social strata, the inevitable result of which, they admonished, would be further alienation of support.

After the July disorders, the rise of the SR Kerensky to head the Provisional Government enchained the Central Committee to its ruinous course. The Kerensky government further roiled the waters of party life by carrying out widespread arrests of Left SRs, along with Bolsheviks and left Mensheviks, and by its involvement in the Kornilov affair. Late summer developments justified the Left SRs' dire forecasts: worker–soldier support fell away from the SRs (and Mensheviks). Simultaneously, the Left SRs took control of party organizations from Petrograd to Tashkent, as worker–soldier–peasant cadres revolted against the intellectuals. Other organizations simply split, largely along intelligentsia (SR) and mass cadre (Left SR) lines.

Left SRs Kamkov, M. A. Spiridonova and I. Z. Shteinberg called for party and soviet congresses, which they expected would yield radical results. They felt that only an all-socialist government based upon the soviets would have the authority to carry out revolutionary reforms on the war, the land and the economy, ending the drift towards social and economic chaos; the leitmotif of their analysis was the avoidance of civil war by means of a unified democracy (the mass elements that supported socialism). In pursuit of these goals, the Left SRs continued to act jointly with the Bolsheviks and left Mensheviks. By late summer, Left SR factions in various soviets and at regional and national conferences either predominated (as at the Black Sea fleet and national railway workers' congresses) or, more commonly, combined with somewhat larger Bolshevik ones to outvote still sizeable SR–Menshevik contingents. During the weeks prior to the opening of the Second Congress of Soviets (25 October), the Left SRs, now in essence acting as a separate party, forged their own path quite distinct from the SR–Menshevik alliance and from the Bolsheviks. Expecting the upcoming soviet congress's dismissal of the Provisional Government, they tried to shortcircuit unilateral Bolshevik steps. They decried splits among revolutionary elements (foreboding civil war), an outlook many Bolsheviks and left Mensheviks shared.

At the Congress of Soviets, the Left SRs undertook to re-unite the Bolsheviks with the moderate SRs and Mensheviks, who abandoned the gathering in protest at the Bolsheviks' use of force. As earlier and for the same reasons, they strove to create an inclusive all-socialist government. Using their influence in *Vikzhel'* (the national railway workers' executive committee), the Left SRs enforced the famous negotiations between the Bolsheviks, who felt themselves under military pressure, and the SRs and Mensheviks. Agreement about an all-socialist government seemed imminent, but the SR-Menshevik exclusion of Lenin and Trotsky from the proposed government and the fading of anti-Bolshevik military pressure sabotaged the negotiations.

The Left SRs continued to pressure Bolsheviks towards the desired concessions, with perhaps greater prospects for success than is realized: the concept of an all-socialist government garnered enormous support (whereas one-party rule had none); numerous Bolsheviks from the Central Committee downward shared the Left SR position; and the Left SRs had waxing support in important institutions such as the peasant soviets. Thus, while refusing Bolshevik offers to enter the new Soviet government, the Left SRs attempted to create the conditions for a broader government. When this proved futile, the Left SRs entered the Soviet government in mid-December. Fear of a one-party dictatorship and hopes of moderating Bolshevik actions, against which they protested vigorously, motivated the Left SRs. Since complete Bolshevik isolation, they argued, would threaten soviet power itself, which they ardently supported, the only recourse was to ally with the Bolsheviks and fight for a better day. Thus they helped unify the All-Russian Executive Committee of Worker and Soldier Soviets (VTsIK) and the Peasant Soviet Executive Committee, which they dominated. The Left SRs thereby achieved a majority in the VTsIK (the new government's legislature), which partially ameliorated their junior status in the Soviet of Peoples' Commissars (*Sovnarkom*), where they held, among others, the commissariats of agriculture, justice and communications.

From their first entrance into the *Sovnarkom*, they fought Bolshevik violations of civil rights as symbolized by the Cheka's unlimited power. *Sovnarkom*'s tendency to govern without the VTsIK's sanction, a fateful step for the new government, was also a bone of contention between Left SRs and Bolsheviks. Nevertheless, the Left SRs still shared common ground with the Bolsheviks on significant questions such as the need to end the war, establish soviet power, transfer all land to the peasants, and institute workers' control (later events revealed conflicting assumptions about these concepts). The Left SRs and Bolsheviks (now Communists) cooperated in dismissing the Constituent Assembly, elections for which, both felt, the SR Central Committee had distorted by loading the party's tickets with moderates.

By late November 1917, the Left SRs had held their founding congress, which instituted the Central Committee and local party organizations. Even as they dealt with weighty governmental matters, the Left SRs confronted the task of launching a new party organization. The divorce from the rest of the party was painful and destructive; the SRs held on to much of the party's intellectual resources and, for the most part, its headquarter premises, newspapers and presses. Even so, the Left SRs experienced rapid organizational advances, symbolic of which was the enormous success of their central newspaper *Znamia truda* ('Banner of Labour'). Its masthead read like a checklist of much of Russia's high cultural intelligentsia (A. A. Blok, Andrei Belyi and R. V. Ivanov-Razumnik), who despite the SR intelligentsia's moderate tendency, flocked to the Left SR cause. The Left SR Party's social bedrock was its worker, soldier, sailor and, above all, peasant following, which, despite SR and Communist competition, seemed to grow by the hour.

At the January 1918 Third Congress of Soviets, summoned as a stand-in for the Constituent Assembly, the Left SRs eschewed the majority in the new VTsIK and, more significantly, *Sovnarkom* that their (small) preponderance over the Communists offered. Their as yet inchoate organizational status dissuaded them from assuming a leading role in the government (a quite rational decision also suggestive of an absence of the will to power). In any case, as quid pro quo for allowing the Communists a continued hold on the government, the Left SRs formulated the land socialization.law, which fulfilled the promises of Lenin's post-October land decree (itself simply a gloss of SR programmes). In this one stroke, the Left SRs believed they had laid the groundwork for socialism and for their own future (Russia as a 'vast commune from sea to sea' was a typical Left SR conceit).

Throughout January and February 1918, Communist–Left SR relations worsened. After rancorous debate, the Left SRs won admission to the Cheka (V. A. Aleksandrovich became F. E. Dzerzhinskii's assistant) as a remedy for the Communists' alleged misuse of the state police apparatus. The Brest-Litovsk treaty delivered the *coup de grâce*. Socialist internationalism had always insisted on a revolutionary peace 'without annexations or reparations', whereas Lenin's treaty awarded Germany vast territories and other benefits. Thus no inconsistency can be laid to the Left SRs or to the Communist majority that opposed the peace terms. Rather than a conventional military response, the Left SRs (and their Left Communist allies) envisioned opposing the meagre available German forces with a people's uprising organized through the soviets, which also overwhelmingly opposed the treaty.

Against the advice of some leaders (Spiridonova, Natanson and A. L. Kolegaev), the Left SRs resigned from the government in March 1918, thus creating the one-party government they had so feared. Still, aided by their disassociation from the government and the Communists, whose standing among all mass elements sunk vertiginously, their cause within the soviets prospered; the release of personnel from government responsibilities also proved a boon to party-building.

With the Left SR withdrawal from *Sovnarkom* and the Commissariat of Justice, which Shteinberg had used to moderate Communist actions, Lenin's government now launched the full-scale Red Terror. Additionally, the government responded to food shortages, exacerbated by the Brest-Litovsk terms, by organizing armed detachments to seize grain from the peasants, a policy the Left SRs abhorred. At the head of the VTsIK's peasant section, Spiridonova and the Left SRs attempted to maintain the peasants' revolutionary spirit and protect them from Communist blows. During a period when the SRs and Mensheviks made a distinct comeback among workers in large cities (drawing repressive measures from the Communists and the June exclusion of those two parties from the soviets), the Left SRs garnered more and more support in rural, town and provincial soviets, thus setting the stage for a final clash.

As the Fifth Congress of Soviets gathered, the Left SRs, who felt (accurately) that they should have a majority, prepared to form a government. When flagrant Communist manipulation of mandates dashed these expectations, the Central Committee decided upon the assassination of Count Mirbach, the German representative to Soviet Russia. The desperate intention was to break the peace and, ultimately, loosen the Communist hold on power. Left SR miscalculations included their belief that the act would attract massive popular support. Instead, Lenin quickly reassured already weakened Germany and, inside Soviet Russia, portrayed the murder as an attempt to seize power. Subsequent Left SR exclusion from the soviets created the one-party state, while the Cheka turned its malign force upon the party.

Despite losses from executions and arrests, the Left SRs survived and by the autumn of 1918 noted a new growth in party organizations in connection with heightened support from workers, peasants and even Red Army soldiers. The post-July splinter parties (Revolutionary Communists and Peoples' Communists) not only failed to collect mass support, but many of their members drifted back to the Left SRs. During the autumn of 1918, the Left SRs resolved, finally, to overthrow the Communist regime, which they now conceived as destructive of the Russian revolution (a year earlier they had feared a Bolshevik collapse as harmful to the revolution). They led massive peasant uprisings in protest against the Poor Peasant Committees (kombedy); they also helped spark and lead workers' strikes and demonstrations that continued well into 1919 and beyond. During 1919 the Cheka linked the Left SRs directly to massive strikes and uprisings among workers, soldiers and peasants so threatening that Sovnarkom granted Dzerzhinskii extraordinary powers against them. None the less, even two years later, the Kronstadt uprising and other anti-Communist disorders occurred at Left SR instigation. Thus the history of the Left SR party and activism, although never blessed with success, continued long beyond the usually ascribed mid-1918 termination point. The party's actual demise, like that of the SRs and Mensheviks, pertains to the period after the civil war.

The gravamen of the Left SR case against the Communists concerned allegations about indiscriminate terrorism, policies inimical to peasant–worker interests, and, above all, the supplanting of soviet power with an overcentralized one-party dictatorship. The Left SRs insisted that only they remained true to the original idea of 'soviet power' (societal support for which clearly remained strong throughout the civil war period and which underlay the Kronstadt uprising).

Despite several fateful errors in their brief history, Left SR analysis merited contemporaneous consideration and even today offers food for thought. Their basic outlook about a rapid transformation towards socialism involved a not unrealistic estimate of Russia's socio-economic realities.

During 1917, they accurately diagnosed the lack of firm support for moderate SR policies, which, among other problems, ignored the party's official programme and opened it to attack from the left. In a country with Russia's social structure, appealing to middle elements of society, as the Central Committee did, was suicidal; had the party instead come out against the war and for a socialist government, history would have moved differently. The Left SRs later regretted not splitting earlier from the PSR, doubtless their first grave misstep.

When the Bolsheviks threatened unilateral action against the Provisional Government, the Left SRs warned that such initiatives heightened civil tension. Only the democratic social elements acting in unison, they argued, could prevent or quell civil conflict, a consideration that underlay their vehement support for an inclusive all-socialist government before and after the October events. Formidable obstacles notwithstanding, such a government would have commanded enthusiastic support from an overwhelming majority of the population, across all socialist party lines. This approach (one might call it jump-starting democracy) deserves greater examination than it has received.

Entry into the government and participation in the Cheka, along with complicity in the closing of the Constituent Assembly, strike many observers as a betrayal of principles or spineless toadying to the Communists, whereas they were attempts to maintain soviet power – a genuine Left SR goal – and hinder Communist abuses of power. Leaving the government in March 1918 struck some Left SR leaders as petulant, depriving them of the possibility of influencing events; but it also enabled the party to shore up its organization to the point where it could challenge the Communists. Their on-the-spot critique of one-party power and 'blind centralization' cut directly to the heart of the most harmful tendencies of Communist rule.

The assassination of Mirbach was the Left SRs' most striking, almost inexplicable error. They overestimated popular response to the act (the Brest-Litovsk treaty itself was abysmally unpopular) and underestimated the ability of the Leninist leadership to utilize the act to damage their party, which then had broader support than any other in Russia. A simple overthrow of the Communists, well within the Left SRs' military capabilities, might have been better. Perhaps Left SR dedication to democratic power (wielded through the auspices of mass-based, elected organizations) was an Achilles' heel in Russia's catastrophic situation and against such opponents as the Communists. Occurring under the shadow of the civil war, subsequent Left SR activities remain outside the scope of existing research and analysis. Left SR idealism remained forever untested by the wielding of power; their forte was impassioned opposition.

My study and those of K. V. Gusev and Lutz Haefner (the last based upon Russian archives) closely scrutinize, respectively, the Left SR movement during the war and 1917–18. Studies in preparation (my manuscript about the Left SRs during 1917–19 and two biographies of Spiridonova) will also use archival sources. Still, the field remains wide open. Important figures (Natanson, Kamkov and Shteinberg) await biographers. The party's activities at the local and regional levels and among mass social elements, especially the peasants, require further study, as do the Ukrainian Left SR Party, the Left SR movement among Russia's literary intelligentsia, and the party's ethnic and gender components (besides Ukrainians, sizeable support came from Belorussian, Jewish, Tatar, Turkic and various eastern nationalities; no other major party had women leaders equal to Spiridonova, A. A. Bitsenko, Irina Kakhovskaia, Aleksandra Izmailovich and Ada Lebedeva). The archival sources mentioned on pp. 289–90 also pertain to the Left SRs. Of special interest in GARF are collections on *Vikzhel'*, *Sovnarkom*, the VTsIK and the NKVD; of interest in RTsKhIDNI are fond 564 about the PLSR and the collections of the Communist Central Committee (fond 17) and its Secretariat (op. 4). Additionally, the collection of the Peoples' Commissariat of Agriculture (fond 478) in the Russian State Archive of the Economy (RGAE) in Moscow has rich holdings on the Left SRs during 1918.

Further reading

Gusev K. V., *Krakh partii levykh eserov* (Moscow, Izdatel'stvo sotsial'no-ekonomicheskoi literatury, 1963).

Haefner L., *Die Partei der Linken Sozialrevolutionäre in der Russischen Revolution von 1917/1918* (Cologne, Böhlau, 1994).

Melancon M., *The Socialist Revolutionaries and the Russian Anti-War Movement, 1914–1917* (Columbus, Ohio State University Press, 1990).

INSTITUTIONS AND INSTITUTIONAL CULTURES

The Soviet State

ROBERT SERVICE

From its outset the Soviet state was an extraordinary political order, and it is only our retrospective knowledge that sometimes prevents us from acknowledging the fact. Its basic features were already in place within two years of the October revolution. Attempts to distinguish entirely separate periods of the history of the USSR are doomed to failure: the only sensible way to make sense of that history is to recognize that the regime which was established in 1917–19 was maintained intact through to the late 1980s.

In formal terms it was a state that underwent much change both territorially and constitutionally. The Russian Soviet Federative Socialist Republic (RSFSR) was proclaimed in January 1918 and acquired its constitution in June 1918. The area under its control waned and, eventually, waxed in the course of the civil war. Initially after the October revolution the republic held most of the towns in central and northern Russia, and Kiev was occupied some months later; but the Treaty of Brest-Litovsk hacked away all the non-Russian provinces from the control of *Sovnarkom* (the Council of People's Commissars), and the existence of *Komuch* (the 'Committee of Members of the Constituent Assembly' government in Samara) meant that there was also a military struggle in Russia. By late 1919, however, the Red Army had gained possession of nearly all Russia and moved into Ukraine and Belorussia. The question arose as to what relations should prevail between the RSFSR and the newly reconquered regions of the former Russian empire. At first the Bolshevik Party Politburo's policy was to get the RSFSR to sign bilateral treaties with the new Soviet republics. Although many leading Bolsheviks outside the Politburo considered this to be an unnecessary indulgence towards nationalist sentiment, the existence of several Soviet republics was undoubtedly useful in inducing non-Russians to believe that they would prosper more readily under the Reds than under the Whites. A permanent constitutional settlement was left until after the civil war; and as the civil war ended, so Stalin and others pressed for the other Soviet republics to be transferred to an expanded RSFSR.

This proposal was strenuously resisted by Lenin, who in mid-1922 convinced the central party leadership of the need to establish a union of Soviet Socialist Republics (USSR). The union would have a formal federal structure and the RSFSR would be simply the largest Soviet republic enjoying equality of power and status with all the rest within the union.

Nevertheless, the reality was that this structure was underpinned by infrangible centralist foundations. For the USSR was a one-party state. To most intents and purposes it had been such a state since the definitive rupture between the Bolsheviks and the Left Socialist Revolutionaries in July 1918. Other parties, notably the Mensheviks, were permitted a hobbled existence during the civil war. But Lenin and his closest associates were always intent on strengthening their party's control over the governmental apparatus and on excluding all other political tendencies from power. To be sure, an explicit promulgation of a one-party state was not made. But the arrest of leading members of parties judged hostile to socialism went on from the October revolution. Persecution of groups and organizations of Mensheviks, Socialist Revolutionaries (SRs) and Left Socialist Revolutionaries (Left SRs) proceeded throughout the civil war and a show trial was held of prominent SRs in 1922. By then all the other parties in the non-Russian regions in the territory under Soviet rule had also been subjected to comprehensive persecution. The USSR was directed by a single party, the Russian Communist Party (Bolsheviks), which tolerated no rival to its supremacy.

This party, furthermore, truly ruled over its one-party state. In the first months after the October revolution there had been uncertainty about how things would be arranged. The Bolshevik Central Committee acted on the implicit assumption that it could enhance the interests of revolutionary advance mainly by setting broad guidelines in policy and dispatching the party's best representatives to head the various state institutions. From November 1917 the situation became complicated when the Left SRs agreed to enter *Sovnarkom* as coalition members. Much bargaining had to take place between the two parties before any additional guidelines in policy could be agreed. Tensions were inevitable, but on most matters there was successful compromise between the Bolsheviks and the Left SRs – and the Basic Law introduced on the agrarian question in February 1918 was a sign of this.

Yet the Brest-Litovsk controversy thrust the Bolsheviks into internal dispute of the most intense kind. Before proceeding to discussions with the Left SRs, they persistently tried to formulate their own discrete policy on war and peace. Thus the party constituted the institution most readily able to offer clear leadership in an environment of chaos and conflict. Of course, the Bolsheviks had a long tradition before 1917 of organizing themselves in separation from other political groupings even within the Russian Social-Democratic Labour Party. What is more, their general doctrines inclined them to envisage the party – their separate party! – as a prime agency of victorious socialist revolution. And most of their prominent leaders had developed as politicians within a milieu of strong factional loyalty to Bolshevism. Already in spring 1918, therefore, there were murmurings that the party had to be conserved as an autonomous institution if the October revolution was to endure.

There was an organizational as well as a political aspect to such a development. *Sovnarkom* inherited a highly dislocated state order. The Bolsheviks themselves had done their utmost to disrupt the official administration before they took power. When power was seized in the October revolution, central ministries could seldom rely upon their instructions being obeyed 'in the localities' (*na mestakh*). A vertical line of command had virtually disappeared from practical affairs. Meanwhile there was also horizontal confusion. The various state bodies at each level of the territorially based hierarchy acted with little regard for each other's wishes. Uncooperativeness was more the norm than the exception.

Indeed, these difficulties were aggravated by the October revolution in various important ways. Most ministries were simply re-named as 'People's Commissariats' and were enjoined to continue uninterrupted with the business of government. But the Bolsheviks also established wholly new agencies for the discharge of public functions. Not only did they transform the soviets into governmental institutions, but they also encouraged the factory-workshop committees, the trade unions, the soldiers' committees and the village land communes to carry through an anti-capitalist revolution in whatever way they saw fit. The result was an extraordinary mish-mash of competing, clashing authorities. Furthermore, alongside the existing 'mass organizations' such as the soviets, the Bolsheviks invented several organizations of their own. Whenever they discerned a task which was not being adequately handled by a people's commissariat, their habit was to establish an additional body. Two of the most notable examples were the People's Commissariat for Nationality Affairs and the Extraordinary Commission (or Cheka). Both of them were set up as a means of prioritizing measures which might otherwise have lacked urgency of application; but both of them also had functions which overlapped with those of existing people's commissariats. No wonder there was administrative disarray not only in the capital but also in the provinces. This was not the end of the list of inherited and self-inflicted problems. For the Bolsheviks added further to the disarray by installing several *ad hoc*, temporary bodies to deal with specific emergencies. Thus in January 1918, *Sovnarkom* decided to appoint plenipotentiaries under Aleksandr Shliapnikov to impose dictatorial authority on the country's railway system.

This was the first of such plenipotentiary bodies, whose effect was to bring urgency to a particular topic of concern of official policy-makers at the expense of other concerns. Chaos mounted. The Soviet state was being governed by a mass of competing agencies whose officials often had little more to use to assert themselves than a hastily scribbled mandate given to them in Petrograd. All too often the mandate was insufficient in itself and a gun was carried by officials who anticipated problems. Indeed, guns were carried also for reasons of personal safety. Lenin himself went nowhere without his Browning pistol – not that this did him much good when he was held up by robbers in Moscow in 1919.

At the centre itself there was no less chaos than elsewhere. *Sovnarkom* was formally the government. But *Sovnarkom* had derived its power from the Second Congress of Workers' and Peasants' Deputies, which had met in Petrograd on 25 October 1917, and this same Congress had elected an All-Russian Central Executive Committee (which in turn chose its own Presidium, headed until his death in March 1919 by Iakov Sverdlov). A precise demarcation of functions was never achieved. It was never even seriously attempted. For some months, furthermore, there was the theoretical possibility that the entire constitutional basis of the state would be redefined by the Constituent Assembly. Lenin had not wanted to hold elections for the Assembly since he foresaw that the Bolsheviks would not win them. But he was overruled by other members of the Bolshevik Central Committee. The elections took place as promised in mid-November. The Bolsheviks lost, gaining only a quarter of the popular vote. At last Lenin got his way and the Bolsheviks and Left SRs forcibly closed down the Constituent Assembly on 6 January 1918. The subsequent Third Congress of Soviets definitively proclaimed the establishment of *Sovnarkom* as the government of the revolutionary state.

Yet the Constituent Assembly's dissolution did nothing to clarify relations between *Sovnarkom* and the All-Russian Central Executive Committee. This did not matter much in practical politics. Lenin and Sverdlov had a close, amicable working relationship and passed important documents to each other for co-signature. The fact that Sverdlov simultaneously worked as the Bolshevik Central Committee Secretary was an additional lubricant to the wheels of the general engine of administration. As many other leading Bolsheviks were appointed to posts in the Red Army in the second half of 1918, so these two men concentrated massive day-to-day authority in their hands.

But they had their critics. Many Bolsheviks in the localities felt that a more clearly articulated state order was essential; they stood for centralist, authoritarian principles and urged that Lenin and Sverdlov should set about drastic organizational reform. Needless to emphasize, both Lenin and Sverdlov found much in these ideas quite congenial. They, too, wanted an effectively centralized state – and they had the skill and ruthlessness to impose it. Thus central and local Bolsheviks leaders agreed on the cardinal priority of institutional transformation. And, after a patchy debate in the second half of 1918 and the first quarter of 1919, they moved towards the consolidation of the Russian Communist Party (Bolsheviks) as the supreme institution of the Soviet state in everything but name. Their thinking was highly practical. The party alone – they believed – had the vision, the ideology, the achievements in revolutionary struggle and the personnel to impose a degree of order on the chaos. The party also had an operational organization. Thus it came about within a couple of years of the October revolution that a one-party state emerged, a one-party state over which the party wielded real and concentrated power.

At the centre this meant that most vital decisions were no longer taken by the *Sovnarkom* or the All-Russian Central Executive Committee. Instead it was the Bolshevik Central Committee which supplied the state's governing core. Or rather it was the Central Committee's inner sub-committee, the Politburo, which deliberated and laid down the line on the great matters of state. For only a few of the Central Committee's members could remain in Moscow for the duration of the civil war. Most of them were badly needed to head civilian state bodies in the regions or to serve as leading political commissars in the Red Army, and could not be spared for day-to-day work in the capital. Even the Politburo was seldom able to meet in full conclave. Its early members after Sverdlov's death from Spanish influenza in March 1919 were Lenin, Trotsky, Stalin, L. B. Kamenev and N. N. Krestinskii. Trotsky and Stalin were frequently absent and the custom was for their opinion to be solicited by telegrams. In this improvised fashion the Politburo asserted itself as the dominant institution in the party immediately after having been brought into regular life in January 1919.

And so the Politburo was widely trusted by the absentee leaders, and these leaders themselves held great autonomous power in the various agencies which they headed. The examples are numerous. Trotsky chaired the Revolutionary-Military Council of the Republic. Kamenev ran the Moscow Soviet; N. I. Bukharin edited *Pravda*; F. E. Dzerzhinskii led the Cheka. Meanwhile G. E. Zinoviev led the Executive Committee of the Third (Communist) International. Many other major jobs were handled by Stalin, who was the Politburo's trouble-shooter for all kinds of emergencies. In mid-1918 he was the centre's main political commissar on the southern front while remaining the People's Commissar for Nationality Affairs; in 1919 he was appointed to the Politburo and the Orgburo (the Central Committee's Organizational Bureau); and in the following year he became the first chairman of the Workers' and Peasants' Inspectorate (*Rabkrin*) shortly before being appointed as a political commissar in the Red Army that drove the Polish armed forces out of Ukraine in mid-1920 and pursued them to Warsaw. All these major leaders were encouraged to operate in their respective posts with the maximum of initiative in pursuit of the general objectives set by the Politburo.

None of them were shrinking violets. The exercise of authority came easily to them all, and by and large they succeeded in burying their jealousies for the good of the common cause. Rivalry with Trotsky was widespread; certainly Stalin, Zinoviev and Kamenev found it exceptionally difficult to cooperate with him. But the Bolshevik central leadership had little choice but to yield to Lenin's demand that they work as a team. Otherwise the party's entire future would have been ruined by internal dissension.

Disputes were diminished by the freedom given to the political leaders to get on with their respective jobs. In any case, no Bolshevik aimed at a revolutionary campaign characterized by constitutional proceduralism. Centralism, hierarchy and discipline were aims, but they were aims underpinned by an irresistible commitment to action, action, action. Sverdlov at his office in the Bolshevik Central Committee in the first weeks after the October revolution summarized his attitude as follows: 'You understand, comrade, that it is difficult to give you instructions any more concrete than "All Power to the Soviets!" This is apparently all that can be said, except to add that it is of supreme importance to take charge of the post and telegraph offices and also the railways.' These words derived in part from a desire that there ought to be a 'revolution from below' as well as a centrally imposed revolution. It also reflected a recognition that the centre could not supply all the human and material resources required by the localities. But it came, too, from a persistent, basic antagonism to the inhibitions of rules, regulations, laws and constitutions. Bolsheviks expected their draconian legislation to be applied unchallengeably to others, namely to their enemies. They themselves refused to be bound by them.

Thus, at the deepest level, the Soviet state was the embodiment of constitutional and legal nihilism. The early decrees of *Sovnarkom*, as Lenin frankly declared, were not meant as formulations satisfactory to professors of jurisprudence. They were designed to inspire, to excite and to instigate. Popular participation was required for the process of revolutionary transformation. So far from being annoyed by rampaging workers and soldiers who committed 'excesses', several Bolsheviks leaders – Lenin and Stalin were notable examples – praised their zeal. If decrees were sometimes implemented in a fashion at variance with *Sovnarkom*'s detailed wishes, then this was a price the Bolsheviks were willing to pay in quest of political mobilization.

This approach did not entirely disappear in the civil war. To be sure, the central agencies of the regime acted to curtail overt institutional disorder. Indeed, the elevation of a newly centralized party to the position of supreme state agency in 1918–19 was a deliberate discouragement to the utopianism of 1917. The campaign to secure a disciplined administrative hierarchy was relentless; even the various internal party oppositions went along with the slogans of centralist control. Furthermore, the favour shown to the workers, peasants and soldiers was increasingly paralleled by substantial limitations on their latitude for independent collective activity. The trade unions were used to bring the factory-workshop committees to heel, and the party and government exerted strenuous control over the trade unions. Soldiers' committees were simply abolished. District and village soviets were established to rival the peasant land communes; the urban authorities also laid down quotas, from mid-1918, for the delivery of grain, hay, conscripts and labour from the countryside.

Nevertheless, it deserves emphasis that, despite all such changes, there remained much space for local administrative bodies to display a great deal of initiative within the framework of policy set by the central state authorities. The Weberian model of a settled, rule-bound administration did not come close to being accepted by the Bolshevik Party. Occasionally Trotsky came close to advocating it; but even he supported action at the expense of rules and procedures. Marxist-Leninist theory was hostile to proceduralist principles, and the civil war made it essential on practical grounds that the state allowed and stimulated its functionaries in the localities to improvise whatever measures came to hand in order to deal with wartime emergencies.

Thus the provinces had to cope as best they could. Local Bolshevik leaders became mini-Lenins. They headed and guided not only party committees but also the various soviet bodies of their locality. For example, Lazar' Kaganovich in Nizhnii Novgorod in 1917 was both chairman of the provincial party committee and chairman of the provincial soviet executive committee. And the local leaders made their own laws and issued their own daily decrees. Due legal process, which had begun to emerge in the last decade of tsarism, was shunted into oblivion. Until spring 1918 the People's Commissariat of Justice had a certain restraining influence on infringements of constitutional order, but this was mainly because of the activity of the Left SRs, who belonged to *Sovnarkom* at the time. Once the Left SRs had split from the Bolsheviks, the People's Commissariat virtually ceased to exist until after the end of the civil war. The protection of the Soviet citizen before the law was nugatory. Arbitrary administrative dispensations became the norm.

This was no accidental phenomenon. As Marxists, the Bolsheviks had always insisted that the will to separate legislative, executive and judicial powers within the state was a 'bourgeois' con trick. In reality, they insisted, the middle classes always organized only a facade of demarcation. After the October revolution, the Bolsheviks had no intention of dispersing their own newly seized power by means of any serious functional division. Regularly they took decisions in which they were decision-makers, practical executives and judges. At the centre, for instance, this meant that the Politburo in 1922 not only decided how to persecute the Russian Orthodox Church, but also relayed its administrative instructions down the hierarchy of party, soviets and political police and even specified the exact penal sentences to be meted out to the arrested ecclesiastical authorities. The point is that each provincial town's leading party functionaries acted in the same fashion at the local level.

Inevitably the regulation of inter-institutional disagreements was more efficient in Moscow and Petrograd than elsewhere. The movement of the military fronts in the civil war had the consequence that no local leader could run local affairs totally without interruption. Several factors were bound to disturb him (and indeed nearly all of them were male). First, he could not keep a permanent hold on his staff: conscriptions were too deep and too frequent. In the second place, there was the fact that contingents of various armed forces might enter the locality: these might include not only the Red Army but also armed units of the Cheka or of the People's Commissariat of Food Supplies. In such an environment there were recurrent upsets to whatever orderliness had been obtained.

Orderliness was also impeded by the political and social composition of the Soviet regime at the lower levels. At the centre it was easy enough to stipulate that only tried and trusted Bolsheviks should occupy the leading posts of state. There were exceedingly few exceptions. G. V. Chicherin, People's Commissar for Foreign Affairs in succession to Trotsky from 1918, was an ex-Menshevik who joined the Bolsheviks only after the October revolution. But only slightly lower down the administrative hierarchy there were plenty of non-Bolsheviks. It could hardly be otherwise. The Bolsheviks had only a handful of thousands of members at the moment of the Romanov monarchy's collapse in February 1917 and, fast though the party grew during 1917, they were obliged to have recourse to employing functionaries inherited from the tsarist regime. The bulk of officials in the People's Commissariats had to be constituted by such persons. There remained much sensitivity about the composition of the agencies of coercion, and the People's Commissariat of Internal Affairs was purged of its previous leaders. The Provisional Government had already taken steps in this direction; but for the Bolsheviks, who were delivering open threats to the regime's declared enemies and their supporters, it was a matter of urgency. The party was determined to avoid being overthrown by internal revolt.

At the same time the party stimulated the recruitment of workers and others of the lower social orders to administrative responsibility. This occurred on an impressive scale in the state economic institutions in particular. Workers became directors and foremen – and some undertook training that enabled them to be promoted to political office in the 1920s and especially in the 1930s.

And yet the 'dictatorship of the proletariat' was very far from being the most apposite description of reality. From secret statistics, the central political leaders knew very well that a sizeable proportion of state personnel recruited came from persons who disguised their true background. Literate and administratively experienced functionaries among the working class were at a premium; but there were plenty of them available elsewhere. Both clerks in bankrupt large factories and former owners of shops and small businesses were ready and willing to take up governmental employment in order to survive physically. And if survival was one motive, ambition was another. The Bolsheviks – like the Provisional Government before them – seemed to offer a career for talented individuals. Several thousands of thrusting young civilian administrators and army officers were attracted to this apparently meritocratic regime. In the middle of the civil war, 60,000 former Imperial Army officers were serving in the Red Army. There were also thousands of professional experts in the People's Commissariats who had found it difficult to establish themselves in the old tsarist ministries. The result was that a tiny group of Bolsheviks straddled a great state structure which contained an administrative corps who knew nothing of Bolshevism.

This in turn made the institutions of state less responsive than they otherwise might have been to the party's current policies. Bolshevik attempts at intensive indoctrination were largely confined to party members and were anyway pretty unsuccessful, especially during the years of military conflict. Indeed, there were many observers who took the view that the political, social and cultural composition of the Soviet state's personnel would sooner or later have an impact on the nature of state policies. A group of *émigrés* under Nikolai Ustrialov in Harbin expressed these ideas in a collection of articles called *Change of Landmarks* (1921). Their basic analysis was that the Soviet leadership was steadily de-Bolshevizing itself and shifting across to aims congruent with those of Russian imperialism and economic and cultural modernization. Thus the internationalist, class-based utopianism – according to Ustrialov – would eventually give way to a more realistic appraisal of the country's long-term interests and contemporary needs.

There were certainly some grounds for viewing the Bolsheviks in such a perspective; and the fact that so many lowly officials, who were detached from central party influences, behaved in consonance with the *Change of Landmarks* agenda confirms that there really were possibilities that the regime might gradually undergo such a transformation. But leading Bolsheviks were already alert to this prognosis and were determined that it should not be realized. They always looked for precedents in what they regarded as the degeneration of the French revolution into the Bonapartist dictatorship. And many of them saw Trotsky as a potential Soviet Bonaparte. Trotsky had flagrantly promoted non-Bolsheviks to high office not only in the Red Army but also in the Revolutionary-Military Council of the Republic. Trotsky himself had been an anti-Bolshevik before 1917. In Russia, as in revolutionary France, there were acute tensions both inside the state and between the state and various social groups, tensions which the Bolshevik one-party state did not eradicate. The fear of many leading Bolsheviks at the centre and in the provinces was that a military resolution might be attempted by a charismatic man of overweening ambition. And Trotsky appeared to be such a man.

There were several reasons, however, why things would not automatically take the French path. In the first place, the discussion of precedents was widespread and continual. Moreover, Trotsky himself was not minded to follow Napoleon Bonaparte's example, at least in the sense of aspiring to blunt the social and economic edge to the October revolution. Nor, after 1920, was he prominent among those few Bolsheviks who desired to spread the October revolution at the point of a bayonet.

Furthermore, Ustrialov and his fellow nationalists vastly underestimated the enduring internationalist objectives of the regime at home and abroad. This was a result of socialist ideology in general and Marxism in particular. It also stemmed from the nature of the collective background of leading

Bolsheviks. Of the membership of the Politburo elected after March 1919 only Lenin could justifiably sign questionnaires claiming to be an ethnic Russian – and even he had other ethnic elements in his family's background. The strength of this non-Russian background was not limited to the Politburo or even to the Central Committee and *Sovnarkom*. Nor was it glimpsed only in the Soviet republics outside the RSFSR. In 1919 there were attempts to found internal republics within the RSFSR based on the ethnic principle – and several internal republics were installed in the 1920s. And in each such republic much attention was paid to the priority of promoting the local non-Russian to high office. Increased respect was also shown to the religious beliefs and cultural traditions of Ukrainians, Georgians and other peoples. The USSR, while refusing to offer national plebiscites on secession, made unprecedented concessions to the wishes of those citizens who spoke no Russian and wished to have nothing to do with Russian culture. And most officials had little positive inclination towards either Russian or non-Russian nationalism.

This is not to deny that there were other ways in which the Soviet state, in all its successive forms, displayed many of the traditional characteristics of the Russian empire. Indeed, it was riddled with the worst features of the tsarist administration. Venality was rampant and officials were indolent, self-satisfied and hostile to the just demands of citizens.

Moreover, the technology of administration was weak and had become weaker since 1917. And officials, once given a job in the local agencies of the People's Commissariats, were rarely subject to the discipline of being sacked for infringing higher commands. The notorious complacency of tsarist ministries did not disappear but was strengthened. At the same time, the space for autonomous civil activity was drastically reduced. The economy's industrial sector was almost wholly nationalized by the middle of the civil war. The commercial sector was heavily regulated and agriculture was subject to continual state depredation. The inception of the New Economic Policy in 1921 lessened but did not remove the state's dominance in the economy. Cultural activities, too, were deeply affected by state interference and a formal structure of pre-publication censorship was introduced in 1922 in the form of *Glavlit*. And the individual citizen's access to employment, housing, food and healthcare was in the gift of party and governmental officialdom. The administrative machinery remained ramshackle and yet the intrusion of the state into the life of society grew ever deeper. The unavoidable result was the development of a civic culture based upon the all-important practical need of citizens to stand in queues to persuade or bribe officials to grant them what theoretically should have already been theirs by legal right.

The question arises whether any of this was unavoidable. Some would suggest that factors outside the party's control – such as the country's economic backwardness or the foreign military intervention – precluded a less authoritarian outcome. Others contend that, if only the principles of

Leninism had been maintained, then the bureaucratic Leviathan would never have been created. Both such types of apologetics are unconvincing even though it must be admitted that the party confronted massive objective difficulties and had a residual commitment to enhancing the general conditions of life and work for most people. The bureaucratic Leviathan surely had its seeds in the kind of seizure of power that took place in the October revolution. Authoritarianism was not an accidental side-product of Leninism. It was at its core and was cultivated further by the series of ruthless reactions to the circumstances which developed in 1917–20. These circumstances included not only the campaigns by the White armies but also peasant revolts, workers' strikes and mutinies in the Red armed forces. And the inception of the one-party state consolidated the process.

The logic of this historical development was unbreakable until such time as a Communist Party leadership challenged the basis of the October revolution. This happened only at the end of the 1980s, and even then the import of his actions was but dimly perceived at the time by Mikhail Gorbachev. In the intervening seven decades a terrible form of state, economy and society had been induced into existence.

Further reading

Carr E. H.,*The Bolshevik Revolution*, vol. 2 (London, Macmillan, 1952).

Figes O., *Peasant Russia, Civil War: The Volga Countryside in Revolution (1917–1921)* (Oxford, Clarendon Press, 1989).

Koenker D. P., Rosenberg W. G. and Suny, R. G. (eds.), *Party, State and Society in the Russian Civil War* (Bloomington, Indiana University Press, 1989).

Pipes R., *The Formation of the Soviet Union: Communism and Nationalism, 1917–1923* (New York, Atheneum, 1968).

Poliakov I. A., *Perekhod k NEPu i sovetskoe krest'ianstvo* (Moscow, Nauka, 1987).

Sakwa R., *Soviet Communists in Power: A Study of Moscow during the Civil War, 1918–1921* (London, Macmillan, 1988).

Service R., *Lenin: A Political Life*, vol. 3: *The Iron Ring* (London, Macmillan, 1995).

The Cheka

ALTER L. LITVIN

The Cheka, or All-Russian Extraordinary Commission to Combat Counterrevolution, Speculation and Administrative Crimes (before August 1918, 'to Combat Counterrevolution and Sabotage') operated from 7 December 1917 until 6 February 1922. It was run by a board consisting of Bolsheviks, although from 8 January until 6 July 1918 the board also contained some Left SRs. Its chairman was F. E. Dzerzhinskii, except for a brief period from 8 July to 21 August 1918 when it was chaired by Ia. Kh. Peters.

The history of the Cheka remains to be written, even though it has been the subject of innumerable books, articles and novels. Soviet historiography produced apologias for the activities of the Chekists, based exclusively on the assessments of Lenin, Dzerzhinskii, M. Ia. Latsis, Peters and other state and Cheka leaders, who believed the institution to have been essential to the victory of the revolution. The documents that have been published have described successful Cheka operations and certain items of evidence concerning the suppression of various 'counterrevolutionary activities'. In these works, as in the monographs, history has been replaced by stories of the heroic deeds of the Chekists. They lent support to the legend of the 1930s that 'the organs are always right', romanticized the work of the Chekists, and even presented the 'Red Terror' as a grim necessity brought about by the activities of the enemy. The literature which was published outside the USSR in the 1920s concentrated on descriptions of the Cheka's torture chambers and the terror. Many of the books which were published outside the USSR in the 1970s and 1980s adopted basically this same approach.

Soviet and non-Soviet works have differed not only in their assessments of the Cheka. Unlike Soviet historians, George Leggett has examined official documents critically, and this approach has enabled him to revise many established notions and to conclude that in reality the Council of People's Commissars (*Sovnarkom*) was not in control of the Cheka's activities. Christopher Andrew and Oleg Gordievsky have also drawn attention to the Cheka's operations abroad.

The major obstacle to writing a history of the Cheka and to understanding this feature of the Russian state is the fact that most of the primary material remains secret. Another difficulty for researchers is that the published laws passed at the time were supplemented by many secret official directives. This 'dual' approach to legislation, along with the construction of the state on the basis of a 'revolutionary legal consciousness', complicates the problem still further.

The decree of 7 December 1917 passed by the *Sovnarkom* gave the Cheka the task of combating sabotage and counterrevolution by carrying out preliminary investigations and handing the culprits over to revolutionary tribunals. Originally the Cheka apparatus consisted of three main departments: for information, organization and combating counterrevolution. On 11 December 1917 a department for combating speculation was created, and on 20 March 1918 a department to combat administrative crimes was set up. The number employed by the central apparatus was small: 23 in Petrograd, and 120 by the time it transferred to Moscow in March 1918. From 14 January the Cheka began to form armed detachments. These were reorganized in June into 35 battalions of up to 40,000 men, spread around the central gubernias of European Russia. In August, 38 gubernia Chekas and 75 uezd Chekas were operating in the Soviet part of the country. The August 1918 census showed that 52.2 per cent of the employees in the Cheka central apparatus were Communists, and that its social composition was 10.6 per cent of working-class origin, 38 per cent white-collar, 36.7 per cent from the military, and 14.7 per cent from the peasantry and the intelligentsia. The Cheka had a greater proportion of Communists than the other People's Commissariats, especially Communists whose party membership preceded the October revolution. Many of these had been recommended by the RKP (Bolshevik) Central Committee and the Soviet VTsIK. The Cheka had fewer employees inherited from its pre-revolutionary counterpart than any other Soviet institution – just two persons, one of whom was the former chief of the special gendarmerie, General V. F. Dzhunkovskii, who was invited at the beginning of 1918 to act as consultant in the creation of the Cheka's intelligence network.

The decree which established the Cheka was signed by Lenin 42 days after the Bolsheviks seized power. Soviet historiography has laid responsibility for the formation of the Cheka on the 'counterrevolution', which did not submit to infringements of its civil rights, and resisted the abolition of its property rights and the regime's 'expropriation of the expropriators'. Having realized the extent of the resistance, Lenin began to dream of a Russian Fouquier Tinville, and approved Dzerzhinskii's speech at a session of the *Sovnarkom* which demanded that justice be set aside, and that the 'agents of counterrevolution' be dealt with 'in a revolutionary fashion'. By seizing power in Russia, the Bolshevik leadership had created an extreme situation, and they saw a way out in the organization of a powerful extraordinary punitive institution, capable of terrifying and terrorizing the population. This was why Lenin, and after him the Chekists, called the Cheka the main defender of Soviet power. A powerful secret service was created, unconstrained by legal restrictions, which could crush any opposition to the regime.

Decisions of the RKP(b) CC and the *Sovnarkom* rapidly transformed the Cheka into the main organ of coercion, and underpinned its legal status by decree. On 21 February 1918 the *Sovnarkom* produced a document, part decree, part appeal, entitled 'The Socialist Fatherland is in Danger!' It gave the Cheka the right to deal with 'enemy agents, profiteers, marauders, hooligans, counterrevolutionary agitators and German spies'. without going through the courts. One day later the list was extended to include 'saboteurs and other parasites', whom the Cheka was to 'shoot on the spot'. Dzerzhinsky admitted that at that time the Cheka had only 'general instructions to wage a merciless struggle', and that there were no guidelines specifying with whom, and for what crimes, the Cheka was expected to deal. 'Other parasites' could include any citizen, and this opened the way to Cheka arbitrariness. The presence of the Left SRs in the Cheka did nothing to lessen the terror. An examination of the minutes of the Cheka Presidium between January and June 1918 shows that the Bolsheviks and Left SRs were unanimous in their decisions. V. A. Aleksandrovich, a Left SR, was the First Deputy Chairman of the Cheka, a member of the 'troika' with Dzerzhinsky and Peters which initially formed the operative leadership of the Cheka. On 15 June the first Cheka 'troika' with the right to order immediate execution was formed, consisting of Dzerzhinsky, Latsis and Aleksandrovich, with Peters, V. V. Fomin, and I. I. Il'in as deputies. The Cheka board determined that 'anybody proved to be involved in a conspiracy against Soviet power and the republic shall be shot. The troika's verdict must be unanimous.' By then the Cheka was making widespread use of intelligence methods, surveillance, secret agents recruited from among the arrestees and members of 'counterrevolutionary organizations', interception of domestic and foreign correspondence and so forth. At the same time the first instructions appeared detailing precisely who was to be shot. The list included former gendarmes and police officers who carried weapons without permission or false papers, and active members of the Kadet, Octobrist and SR (right or centre) parties. In judging this sort of case it was 'obligatory that a representative of the RKP(b) be present'. At a local level the representative had to be a member of the gubernia or uezd RKP(b) committee. An active member of a 'counterrevolutionary party' was considered to be any member of a committee, central or local, and any member of an armed detachment. Summary execution was encouraged by the *Sovnarkom*, which on 10 June, in view of the Czechoslovak troops' uprising, called for 'officers involved in conspiracy, traitors, and associates of Skoropadskii, Krasnov and the Siberian Colonel Ivanov' to be exterminated without mercy.

The First All-Russian Conference of Chekists took place in Moscow on 11–14 June 1918, with 86 delegates representing 43 Cheka organizations. It declared the Cheka to be the 'bastion of defence of Soviet power', called for the execution of 'obvious and unmasked counterrevolutionaries', and for close watch to be kept over the commanders of the Red Army. The Chekists proposed that punishments be made more severe, and that they should be able to carry them out unhindered. From February 1918 onwards the Cheka grew without interruption, both in size and in the range of its activities. In the summer of 1918 the Cheka was based in the Hotel Select on the Lubianka in Moscow, from which it expanded into the neighbouring building, the offices of the 'Rossiia' insurance company. There were 12 Cheka departments based in these buildings, and the entire territory of Soviet Russia was covered by a network of local Chekas and their military units. On 6 July two Cheka agents, the Left SRs Ia. G. Bliumkin and Nikolai Andreev assassinated Count Mirbach, the German ambassador in Moscow. One Cheka detachment, commanded by the Left SR D. I. Popov, became a centre of armed resistance to the Bolsheviks, who in their turn were struggling to finish off their political opponents and to establish a one-party system in Russia. The Bolsheviks crushed the Left SR resistance, executed 13 Chekists including Aleksandrovich, abolished the previous Cheka board and declared that greater care would be exercised in selecting Chekists. A new Cheka board was formed on 21 August, consisting of 11 Communists: Dzerzhinsky, Peters, Fomin, Latsis, I. K. Ksenofontov, V. N. Iakovleva, M. S. Kedrov, V. V. Kamenshchikov, N. A. Skrypnik, I. N. Polukarov and Ianushevskii.

By the autumn of 1918 economic, moral and political terror existed in Russia. This can be seen in the decrees of the *Sovnarkom* and the Constitution of the RSFSR. Some opponents of the authorities were physically liquidated. The Cheka was organizationally and morally prepared to institute state-decreed total terror. On 5 September the *Sovnarkom* distributed instructions on the introduction of the Red Terror, signed by the People's Commissars of Justice and of Internal Affairs, and the *Sovnarkom* Business Manager (D. I. Kurskii, G. I. Petrovskii and V. D. Bonch-Bruevich). It was not signed by Lenin, Ia. M. Sverdlov or Dzerzhinsky, presumably because of the everyday nature of these punitive measures.

The introduction of the Red Terror as state policy led to demands from Chekists for the 'mass liquidation of the bourgeoisie', the use of torture and so on. The introduction of war communism from the summer of 1918 involved the regulation of every aspect of Russian society, and in practice there were no boundaries to distinguish revolutionary order from lawlessness. The nobility and the Cossacks faced annihilation, whilst some peasants were threatened with a decision adopted by the *Sovnarkom* on 15 February 1919 'to take hostages from among the peasants, and to shoot them if the snow-clearing is not carried out'. Dzerzhinsky warned workers that all those who are dissatisfied with workers' power should be regarded as 'non-workers' and as 'not pure proletarians' infected with petty-bourgeois ideology, and that the concentration camp is a 'school of labour'.

The leadership of the Cheka issued detailed instructions on arrests, execution and the taking of hostages: 'Shoot all counterrevolutionaries. Let the regional organizations execute on their own account . . . Take hostages like owners of large factories from among the bourgeoisie and its allies. Make it known that no appeals on behalf of those arrested will be accepted. The regional organizations shall determine whom to take hostage . . . Small local concentration camps shall be established . . . Obvious counterrevolutionaries should be shot . . . Measures should be taken to ensure that the corpses do not fall into the wrong hands.'

The Red Terror claimed at least 10,000 victims. This led some politicians to discuss curtailing the powers of the Cheka. However, since the Cheka was carrying out the wishes of the elite of the ruling party, its powers were not limited, and torture of those arrested became the rule rather than the exception. Moreover, a decision of the RKP(b) CC on 12 December 1918 forbade criticism of the Cheka on the grounds that it was an organ which was 'working under exceptionally difficult conditions'. In order to assuage public opinion in March 1919 the RKP(b) CC instructed I. V. Stalin to oversee the activities of the Cheka, and shortly thereafter N. I. Bukharin was appointed to the Cheka board 'with the right of veto'. By its official participation in the work of the Cheka the Bolshevik leadership sanctified an orgy of terror: executions, concentration camps, hostage-taking, torture and contempt for individual rights.

Both the composition of the Cheka board and the leaders of its departments changed according to the circumstances. In 1920 the *Sovnarkom* confirmed the following Cheka board: Dzerzhinsky, Ksenofontov, Latsis, Peters, V. A. Avanesov, N. N. Zimin, F. D. Medved', M. S. Kedrov, V. S. Kornev, V. R. Menzhinskii, V. N. Mantsev, S. A. Messing and G. G. Iagoda. By then there were 86 oblast' and republican Chekas, 16 special departments in the army, as well as Chekas for rail and water transport. The national breakdown was as follows: 77.3 per cent Russians, 9.1 per cent Jews, 3.5 per cent Latvians, 3.1 per cent Ukrainians, 0.5 per cent Belorussians, 0.5 per cent Muslims, 0.2 per cent Armenians, 0.1 per cent Georgians. The 'Chekist International' was supplemented by 315 Germans, 46 Finns, 25 Czechs, 13 Chinese, three Swedes, two Britons and a Frenchman. This disproves the thesis of those Russian ultra-patriots who claim that the viciousness of the Cheka was a result of the dominance of 'aliens'. Russians accounted for 52 out of 86 of the chairmen of gubernia and republican Chekas. Among the Chekists in 1920 just 513 (1.03 per cent) had higher education, whilst the majority, 28,647 (57.3 per cent), had only an elementary education.

A combination of military success and economic failure induced the VTsIK on 17 January 1920 to abolish the right of the Cheka and of local Chekas to carry out death sentences. Officially the ban on Cheka executions lasted until 28 May 1920, when they were resumed in connection with the Soviet-Polish war. Sixteen gubernia Chekas had the right to execute restored to them, and a further eight were granted the right if they received the sanction of the All-Russian Cheka. On 4 November 1920 the VTsIK affirmed that in the official war zones the Cheka had the right to execute. An examination of the minutes of the All-Russian Cheka troika and of the presidiums of individual gubernia Chekas shows that summary executions never ceased in 1920, although there were significantly fewer of them in the first half of that year than in the second.

One of the most barbaric Cheka actions of 1920 was the Crimean tragedy which followed the evacuation of General Wrangel's troops. The lack of adequate documentation makes it impossible to check the numbers of executions cited by different sources, which range between 25,000 and 125,000. But the documents which do exist confirm that the extent of the shootings was unprecedented. *Izvestiia Vremennogo Sevastopol'skogo Revkoma* ('News of the Sevastopol Provisional Revolutionary Committee') on 28 November 1920 announced the execution of 1,634 persons, including 278 women. The same newspaper two days later announced the shooting of 1,202 persons, including 88 women. When E. G. Evdokimov, in charge of the special department on the southern front, received his decoration it was stressed that the men under his leadership had shot around 12,000 persons, including 30 governors, 50 generals, more than 300 colonels and so on. On 2 January 1921 the Crimean oblast' committee of the RKP(b) agreed to the Chekists' suggestion that the special department, having carried out a death sentence, should simultaneously expel the victim's family from the Crimea. By the summer of 1921 more than 100,000 persons had been expelled.

The victorious end to the armed struggle did not lead to any diminution of the role of the punitive organs. A report on the activities of the Cheka stated that around 7 billion roubles had been spent on financing the institution between 1918 and 1920, excluding expenses of a 'secret character', and that in 1921 the peasant uprisings, the Kronstadt revolt, workers' strikes and increasing activity by the opposition showed that 'the work of the Cheka is more necessary than ever'.

Dzerzhinsky remained chairman of the Cheka in 1921, although the practical work of the organization was run by his deputy I. S. Unshlikht. A secret operations department of the Cheka was created in January 1921, with departments for counterespionage in the army, combating opposition parties and the clergy, running secret agents and gathering intelligence, and preparing political trials. At various times of the year, depending on circumstances, up to 200,000 Red Army men were placed under Cheka command. With the introduction of the New Economic Policy there arose the question of curtailing the powers of the Cheka, of depriving it of the right to execute without trial, and of subordinating it to the People's Commissariat of Justice. However, the arrests and executions continued.

The reorganization of the Cheka in 1921 had a cosmetic character, as the Chekists objected to any limitation of their powers. The Chekists who were laid off were held in reserve and enlisted at their place of residence in Special Purpose Units (ChON) and other militarized detachments and institutions connected with the Cheka. As before, the Cheka was primarily engaged in political investigations and running agents.

In Soviet historiography, the reorganization of the Cheka has been explained in terms of the new situation which existed in the country after the end of the civil war and the introduction of NEP. However, there were other motives, including the realization that the Cheka was no longer in a position to avert peasant armed uprisings and army mutinies, or the open dissatisfaction of the bulk of the population. The Cheka was no longer able to preserve a system which had led people to detest it and had led the economy to catastrophe. It had become essential to rename the Cheka the State Political Administration (GPU), as the original name had become too firmly associated in people's minds with the horrors of extraordinary measures.

Following a fairly protracted discussion between November 1921 and January 1922 in the RKP(b) Politburo and the Cheka board, the VTsIK decided to abolish the Cheka on 6 February 1922, and all the cases of those arrested were passed over to revolutionary tribunals and courts. The GPU was set up within the apparatus of the People's Commissariat for Internal Affairs (NKVD), and its functions included combating espionage and banditry, and guarding the state borders, railways and waterways. It retained the Cheka's cadres and troops, and the right to search, to arrest and to receive secret information. Formally, its functions were limited to espionage and counterespionage. In reality, the range of the GPU's functions grew throughout 1922. In October the border troops were placed under its control. Military and political censorship became the responsibility of the Department of Political Control of the Secret-Operative Administration. The number of informers was increased, and powers to deal with people without going through the courts reappeared. These included the right to order administrative exile to distant parts of the country and abroad, the right to conduct investigations, the right of the GPU board to pass sentence on GPU employees without going through the courts, introduced on 16 October 1922, and so forth.

In April 1922 there were 99 departments of the GPU in operation, subdivided into categories, depending on their size and political importance. In addition to special sections for the Moscow, Petrograd, Ukrainian and Central GPUs, there were 20 in the first category (such as the Crimean, Tatar and Irkutsk GPUs); 36 in the second category (Briansk, Voronezh, etc.); and 39 in the third category (Vladimir, Mari, Chuvash, etc.). The size of the staff and the rates of pay depended on the category. The size of GPUs of the first category was set at 236 employees, including 21 in the secret department and 35 agents. The respective figures for the second category were 136, 7 and 10, and for the third category 87, 5 and 2. Rates of pay in the GPU ranged from 3,731 roubles to 18,657 roubles. GPU schools were set up, where students learned how to carry out different types of surveillance, recruit agents, maintain communications, record evidence, conduct interrogations and so on.

The Cheka continued with its executions right up to its abolition on 6 February 1922. In January 1922 the troika of Unshlikht, Menzhinskii and G. I. Blagonravov examined the cases of 100 arrestees, and sentenced 42 of them to be shot. On 6 February, 28 cases were examined, and 18 people were sentenced to death. Thereafter, there is no mention of summary executions in the minutes of GPU meetings until the autumn. Later on, all the Cheka's 'rights' were restored to its successor.

The Cheka was the armed secret service of the elite of the Bolshevik Party, and Dzerzhinsky was accountable only to the Chairman of the *Sovnarkom*. Along with the RKP(b) and the army, the Extraordinary Commission was the foundation of the Soviet state. It was the model of Russian totalitarianism. Its activities combined successful espionage and counterespionage with the implementation of criminal orders, the organization of falsified trials, provocations and arbitrary behaviour. The abolition of the Cheka and its reorganization first into the GPU, then into the Unified State Political Administration (OGPU) of the *Sovnarkom* in November 1923, did little to alter the nature of its activities in combating dissent and in preserving and strengthening the Soviet regime. It was an extraordinary, but certainly not temporary institution, operating in a country in which 'extraordinary measures' were a normal, not an exceptional phenomenon.

Further reading

Andrew C. M. and Gordievsky O., *KGB: The Inside Story of its Foreign Operations from Lenin to Gorbachev* (London, Hodder and Stoughton, 1990).

CHEKA. *Materialy po deiatel'nosti chrezvychainykh komissii* (Berlin, izdatel'stvo Tsentral'nogo biuro Partii sotsialistov-revoliutsionerov, 1922).

Dziak J. J., *Chekisty: A History of the KGB* (Lexington MA, Lexington Books, 1988).

Goncharov A. K., Doroshenko I. A., Kozichev M. A. and Pavlovich N. N., compilers, *Iz istorii Vserossiiskoi Chrezvychainoi komissii 1917–1921* (Moscow, Gosudarstvennoe izdatel'stvo politicheskoi literatury, 1958).

Gul' R. B., *Dzerzhinskii: Nachalo terrora* (New York, Most, 1974).

Knight A. W., *The KGB: Police and Politics in the Soviet Union* (London, Allen and Unwin, 1988).

Leggett G., *The Cheka: Lenin's Political Police* (Oxford, Oxford University Press, 1981).

Litvin A. L., 'VChK v sovetskoi istoricheskoi literature', *Voprosy istorii* 5 (1986), pp. 96–103.

Makintsiian I., ed., *Krasnaia kniga VChK*, vols. 1 and 2 (Moscow, Gosizdat, 1920–2; republished Moscow, 1989).

Mel'gunov S. P., *Krasnyi terror v Rossii 1918–1923* (Berlin, Vataga, 1924).

Obrazovanie i deiatel'nost' mestnykh chrezvychainykh komissii 1917–1921 (Moscow, 1961).

Organizatsionnyi otchet VChK za 4 goda ee deiatel'nosti (Moscow, 1921).

Portnov V. P., *VChK 1917–1922* (Moscow, Iuridicheskaia literatura, 1987).

Prikazy VChK za 1919–1922 gg. (Moscow, 1918–22).

Rocca R. G. and Dziak J. J., *Bibliography on Soviet ·Intelligence and Security Services* (Boulder CO, Westview Press, 1985).

Sofinov P. G., *Ocherki istorii Vserossiiskoi chrezvychainoi komissii (1917–1922)* (Moscow, Gosudarstvennoe izdatel'stvo politicheskoi literatury, 1960).

The Constituent Assembly

NIKOLAI N. SMIRNOV

A constituent assembly is a representative institution, a gathering of people's deputies empowered to devise the basic laws and constitution of a state. Its ideological roots go back to the French Enlightenment and the ideas of 'popular sovereignty' and a 'social contract'. The idea of a constituent assembly was cherished by the European revolutionary movement from the end of the eighteenth century onward.

In Russia the demand for a constituent assembly was contained in the programmes of virtually all political parties and movements, each of which interpreted its value and form in accordance with its particular programmatic and tactical goals and methods of struggle. From the RSDRP, through the SRs, to the Popular Socialist (NS) Party, each called for the convocation of a popularly elected constituent assembly with far-reaching powers. At the Foundation Congress of the Constitutional Democratic Party (Kadets) in October 1905, a resolution was passed with the same demand, although the Kadets accepted the right of the monarch to call the assembly because they considered it essential that he retain supreme power in the transitional period.

Despite all this, until 1917 the idea found firm social support only among the democratic intelligentsia. This narrow basis reflected a lack of parliamentary traditions and weak agitational work by the political parties themselves.

In February 1917 the demand for a constituent assembly remained in the background, owing to the inclination of the party leaders to leave the problem of state power to the Duma's Progressive Bloc. It was only at the beginning of March that the demand for elections to a constituent assembly on the basis of universal suffrage featured in the discussions between the leaders of the Executive Committee of the Petrograd Soviet and the members of the Provisional Committee of the State Duma. On the night of 2 March these leaders set out the juridical status of the Constituent Assembly. This included the principles on which free elections ('the will of the people') would be organized. In the course of its work the Assembly was to decide on the main questions of state life – first and foremost, the structure of the state and government – and would independently decide upon the areas and limits of its competence. In its declaration of 2 March, the Provisional Government called for immediate preparation for the Assembly's election by equal, secret and direct ballot. The Assembly was to establish Russia's permanent form of government and write its constitution.

In March and April the idea of the Constituent Assembly enjoyed an unprecedented surge in popularity. Scholars such as O. N. Znamenskii have attributed this to a number of circumstances. A long-standing agitational demand had become a practical state goal, recognized by both the Soviet and the Provisional Government. Political parties could now freely disseminate previously forbidden slogans. There was also a distinctive 'March mood' among the population: joy at the victory of the revolution, naïvely romantic hopes of unity among all sections of society, and so forth. In the opinion of L. G. Protasov, for a certain time the prospect of a Constituent Assembly guaranteed stability in the country. By the end of April the Kadets, NSs, SRs and Mensheviks had between them published no less than 22 pamphlets on the Constituent Assembly.

The Russian version of the Constituent Assembly differed from its foreign counterparts in that at the same time that its convocation was being planned, its traditional task was being completed. When the monarchy was abolished, a democratic republic with unprecedented political freedoms was, in fact, established. However, the Provisional Government was hampered by a desire not to 'pre-empt' the Assembly. Decisions on many questions of political reform, which required immediate solution, were deferred to the Constituent Assembly for many months before it was finally convened. As Protasov has observed, the weight of unresolved problems multiplied catastrophically every day the Assembly was postponed, and this facilitated Russia's slide into general crisis and civil war.

Initially, the leaders of the political parties thought that the preparatory work should take between three and four months. But in practice it was over eight months before the elections took place and over ten before the Assembly met. There were several reasons for the delay. For one thing, in its declaration of 2 March the Provisional Government did not commit itself to any clear timetable. For another, despite the complexities involved – from drafting an electoral law to compiling an electoral register and organizing the nomination of candidates – the Provisional Government failed to combine its efforts with those of the soviets, the local authorities, and political parties and organizations, and decided instead to entrust most of the work to the organs of local government. Since these were themselves first to be re-elected on the basis of universal suffrage, it would not have been possible to convene the Constituent Assembly before August or September.

In fact, as early as March, the leaders of various political parties argued against haste. The SRs, basing themselves on the opinions of their local party organizations, proposed fixing the date for the autumn, since before then the peasants, the bulk of the electorate, would be occupied in the fields. The Mensheviks and NSs, in view of the complexity of devising an electoral law, of organizing and holding elections and so forth, recommended a date no earlier than September. And in general the coalition parties thought that an election campaign would only be feasible once the front had quietened down, which could not be before October or November. The Bolsheviks, in contrast, argued for the speediest possible organization of elections, but at the same time they tried to convince the masses that only the soviets could realize the hopes of the exploited people.

By May the political parties had worked out general principles for organizing and carrying out the elections. They were to be on the basis of a general, equal, direct and secret ballot and the military, including the units at the front, were to take part. Detailed preparations were to be made by the zemstvos and urban dumas once they had been duly re-elected on the basis of universal suffrage – a point to which the Bolsheviks gave only conditional support, preferring to see the soviets organize the elections. There was to be a proportional voting system, and electoral districts were to coincide with administrative districts. The interests of minorities were to be guaranteed, but the question of the minimum voting age caused controversy. The Bolsheviks proposed the age of 18, the SRs and Mensheviks favoured 20 or 21, while the Kadets were firmly against persons under 21 having the vote.

The electoral laws were being drafted both by a Commission on the Constituent Assembly of the Legislative Department of the Executive Committee of the Petrograd Soviet, and by the Provisional Government's Special Council for Preparing the Draft Statute on the Elections to the Constituent Assembly. In the Soviet Commission, created at the end of March, most of the jurists belonged to the SRs, Mensheviks, Trudoviks and NSs, whereas in the government's Special Council, most of them belonged to the Kadets. By mid-April the advantages of pooling their efforts were clear and the Provisional Government expanded the Special Council, inviting the Petrograd Soviet and a range of public organizations to nominate representatives – eight from soviets of workers' and soldiers' deputies, six from peasant soviets, two from every minority-national organization, and two for the trade unions.

In due course, the number and boundaries of the electoral districts were established (73 civilian districts and eight army districts), and the size of the Assembly was set at 800 members. The minimum voting age was set at 21, electoral rights were granted to serving soldiers, and restrictions based on property, domicile, literacy and so on were abolished. The democratic nature of the Statutes on the Elections to the All-Russian Constituent Assembly prepared by the Special Council were undisputed and they strengthened Russia's reputation as the most democratic state in the world. But the protracted preparatory work on the Constituent Assembly undermined its popularity. True, the democratic intelligentsia consistently supported it, and enthusiastically inflated the role it could play. But, as the prominent SR O. S. Minor observed, the mood among the masses changed: 'As the initial honeymoon period of the revolution faded, its banner, the Constituent Assembly, became tarnished. People ... still demanded the Assembly, but without enthusiasm, no longer believing in it.'

The July Days showed the increasing demand for all power to be transferred to the soviets, and this prompted the Provisional Government on 14 July to announce that the convocation of the Constituent Assembly was being accelerated. The elections were set for 17 September and the Assembly was scheduled to open on 30 September. The press published the materials of the Special Council, and parties and public organizations began their pre-electoral preparations.

On 17 July the gubernia and oblast commissars received instructions from the Minister of Internal Affairs, I. G. Tsereteli, requesting that every effort be made to implement the government's decision. But at the same time, in the course of negotiations between the government, the Soviet Central Executive Committee (TsIK) and the candidate ministers for the new coalition government, the socialist ministers gave their opponents the chance to 'convince them' that it would be expedient to postpone the elections. Thus, on 9 August the government officially declared that the elections would be postponed until 12 November, and the Constituent Assembly would open on 28 November.

Two days previously, on 7 August, the first meeting of the All-Russian Commission on Elections to the Constituent Assembly (*Vsevybory*) had taken place. It contained 16 representatives from six political parties, but the decisive role was played by the Kadets, who controlled it completely and who provided both the nominal (though frequently absent) chairman, N. N. Avinov, and its effective head, V. D. Nabokov. In August and September *Vsevybory* set up local electoral commissions charged with various tasks including establishing polling stations, preparing publicity materials and, along with the executives of the urban dumas and zemstvos, drawing up the electoral registers for the elections. After the Kornilov revolt, the Provisional Government, *Vsevybory*, and the local electoral commissions desperately sought to hold out until the Constituent Assembly could meet and they could at last break out of the vicious circle of 'not preempting its will'.

By September and October it had also become clear which questions were to be decided by the Assembly. As Znamenskii, Protasov and I have shown, for the middle classes the most important of these questions was the creation of a legal state and the resolution of the crisis in Russia in a reliable, peaceful and reformist fashion. The lower classes were keen above all to have their social needs met, and were little concerned about exactly how these were to be satisfied. The majority naïvely believed that the very fact of the Assembly meeting would solve the whole complex of social, economic and political problems. Even the incomplete data assembled by *Vsevybory* show that over 60 groupings put up candidates. For example, in the Volynia electoral district there were 30 lists declared, and in the Samara district there were 95. A family with five or six adult members would have been able to paper the walls of their house with the lists they received.

After the overthrow of the Provisional Government by the Bolsheviks, the Council of People's Commissars (*Sovnarkom*) which replaced it resolved on 27 October to keep to the existing timetable and hold the elections on 12 November. It is significant that the first, most important decrees of Soviet power contained the qualification that they remained in force 'until the Constituent Assembly'. However, the Bolsheviks now allotted a limited role to the Assembly in 'formalizing' the changes which had occurred in society, and did not recognize its right to decide on social or political questions.

The electoral statute laid it down that the elections should take place over three days. Exceptions were made for the active units of the army. According to *Vsevybory* voting began on time and was completed by 15 November in 46 out of 81 electoral districts. Elsewhere, it did not prove possible to stick to the timetable. In 20 districts the elections were to begin either on 15 or on 26 November, and in a further 12 districts the polls were set for December 1917 or January 1918. *Vsevybory* apparently had no information on the remaining three districts (the Crimea, Russian troops in France, and Russian troops on the Balkan peninsula).

The formal results of the elections were as follows: the 'petty bourgeois' parties (including nationalists) received 62 per cent of the votes, 'bourgeois and landowner' parties (including nationalists) won 13 per cent, and the Bolsheviks got 25 per cent. The Bolsheviks gained greatest support in Petrograd and Moscow, on the fronts closest to the capitals, in many gubernia towns and in the north-west and central industrial districts. Protasov's examination of the results, which, although not exhaustive, is the most complete, shows that more than 47 million people out of a total electorate of 80 million voted – a turnout of between 62 and 63 per cent. Considering the difficult political situation then obtaining in Russia this can be considered a high turnout. The most striking paradox of the elections was the absenteeism of the intelligentsia, who had initiated the demand for the Constituent Assembly, and the participation of rural voters, who supported the SRs. The peasants clearly believed that the SRs expressed their interests, whereas the soldiers and the urban workers preferred the Bolsheviks.

According to the incomplete data available, 715 deputies were elected. The Bolsheviks gained 175 deputies, the SRs 370, the Left SRs 40, the Mensheviks 16, the NSs two, and the Kadets 17. One deputy declared no party affiliation, and there were 86 deputies from various national groupings. There is no information about the remaining eight deputies. The elections were held in conformity with rules which had been worked out long before the Bolsheviks had come to power, and the electorate voted for united lists of the Menshevik and SR parties, despite the fact that both parties had since split. Although the Bolsheviks were clearly defeated at the polls, Protasov argues that the majority of the electorate was none the less close to them in spirit and in the way the party set about achieving its ends.

As the appointed day for the opening of the Constituent Assembly (28 November) drew nearer, the right SRs, supported by the Mensheviks and, in part, by the Kadets, intensified their pro-Assembly campaign. Their newspapers called for 28 November to be turned into a 'national holiday' and for people to 'unite around this organ of democracy'. At the same time the political opponents of the Bolsheviks began to prepare armed detachments to defend the Assembly.

The Bolsheviks adopted counter-measures. On 21 November the Soviet VTsIK approved the resolution 'On the Right to Recall Delegates', granting soviets the right to recall 'awkward' (*neudobnye*) deputies from all representative institutions, including the Constituent Assembly, and also to organize elections to replace them. On 26 November the *Sovnarkom* issued a decree, confirmed five days later by the VTsIK, 'On the Opening of the Constituent Assembly' insisting that at least half the deputies had to be present before the Assembly could open and that even with a quorum present, it could only be opened by a person 'empowered by the *Sovnarkom* to do so'.

By 28 November only 172 deputies had gathered in Petrograd. Nevertheless, deputies from the right-wing socialist parties, with Kadet support, attempted to open the Assembly on their own account. Anti-Bolshevik demonstrations were arranged for that day in Petrograd and Moscow, and the organizers had high hopes of the provinces. However, as one of the SR leaders B. F. Sokolov admitted, even at that time a gulf had opened between the masses and the Assembly: 'the people were certainly not as convinced of the Constituent Assembly's power of salvation' as its supporters had reckoned. An examination of the letters sent to the *Sovnarkom*, the local administration department of the Commissariat of Internal Affairs (NKVD), and the offices of the Constituent Assembly shows that a significant portion of workers, peasants and soldiers was inclined to recognize the Assembly only if it were in close contact with the *Sovnarkom*.

The Bolsheviks took firm measures to abort the attempt to open the Assembly independently. That same evening, the *Sovnarkom* passed a decree 'On the Arrest of the Leaders of the Civil War Against the Revolution', which declared that 'members of the leading committees of the Kadet Party, as a party of enemies of the people, are to be arrested and handed over to revolutionary tribunals'. On 1 December the VTsIK approved the decree, and on this basis Countess S. V. Panina, F. F. Kokoshkin, A. I. Shingarev and Prince P. D. Dolgorukov, members of the Kadet Central Committee, were arrested.

On 29 November, *Vsevybory* was reorganized, and M. S. Uritskii was put in charge. Members of *Vsevybory* who refused to collaborate with the Bolsheviks were relieved of their positions. Credentials issued by the old *Vsevybory* were declared to be invalid and the deputies to the Assembly who had gathered in Petrograd were obliged to register and receive provisional credentials at the office in the Tauride Palace of the Commissar of the new *Vsevybory*.

The Fourth Congress of the SR party, from 26 November to 5 December, resolved that the struggle for the Constituent Assembly was its main task. The right SRs issued leaflets and pamphlets, and worked out plans for the Assembly's armed defence. In the Menshevik camp a split threatened. Their Extraordinary Congress from 30 November to 7 December adopted a resolution which condemned 'Blanquist' methods of struggle, and called both for a Constituent Assembly with full powers, and for a 'homogeneous socialist government' from the NSs to the Bolsheviks. Some of the delegates, on the other hand, called for active participation in the 'Union for the Defence of the Constituent Assembly' and for intensification of the anti-Bolshevik campaign. The First Congress of the Left SR Party, from 19 to 28 November, called for the Assembly to implement 'the basic decisions of the Second Congress of Soviets', but also expressed the hope that it would enshrine workers' and peasants' power in the constitution. Even though they joined the Bolsheviks in the *Sovnarkom*, the Left SRs retained the hope that they would be able to reach a compromise with the right SRs in the chamber of the Constituent Assembly.

Some Bolsheviks, such as L. B. Kamenev, G. E. Zinoviev, A. I. Rykov and D. B. Riazanov, advanced the idea of turning the Constituent Assembly into some kind of 'revolutionary convention'. They believed that once they had expelled the Kadets, the Bolsheviks and Left SRs would enjoy a 'colossal majority'. Members of the provisional bureau of the Bolshevik Constituent Assembly fraction saw the convocation of the Assembly as the culmination of the revolution, and called on the Bolshevik CC and the *Sovnarkom* not to try to control its convocation and work. On 11 December a session of the Bolshevik CC, on Lenin's initiative, declared these members of the Bolshevik Assembly fraction to be 'capitulationists' and replaced them. The next day the CC adopted Lenin's theses on the Constituent Assembly in which, in view of the constitutional illusions of a significant part of the population, the Assembly was offered a 'last chance'. This was 'for the people to exercise as broadly and as rapidly as possible the right to elect the members of the Constituent Assembly anew, and for the Constituent Assembly to accept the law of the Central Executive Committee on these new elections, to proclaim that it unreservedly recognizes Soviet power, the Soviet revolution and its policy on the questions of peace, land and workers' control, and resolutely to join the camp of the enemies of the Kadet–Kaledin counterrevolution'. In other words, the Bolsheviks reduced the role of the Constituent Assembly to affirming the legitimacy of all the actions of the new state authorities.

On 20 December the *Sovnarkom* set the opening session of the Assembly for 5 January 1918 if there was a quorum – that is, not less than 400 deputies who had registered with the new *Vsevybory* beforehand. The same session of the *Sovnarkom* decided to call an ordinary congress of workers', soldiers' and peasants' soviets. The newspaper *Petrogradskii golos* ('Petrograd Voice') on 24 December explained the need for this in the following terms: 'The Council of People's Commissars . . . intends to express its attitude to the current composition of the Constituent Assembly, which is characterized as an institution which does not correspond to the will of the working and peasant masses.' At a plenary session of the VTsIK on 22 December it was argued that 'the Constituent Assembly in its present composition lags a whole epoch behind the development of events, and to a far greater extent reflects the bourgeois revolution than the workers' and peasants' October revolution'. The Bolsheviks who spoke at this session suggested that the VTsIK declare firmly that it would only recognize a Constituent Assembly which 'decisively and unconditionally stands on the side of the labouring classes against the landowners and bourgeoisie, strengthens Soviet power, confirms the decrees on land, workers' control, and the nationalization of the banks, recognizes the right of all the peoples of Russia to self-determination and supports the foreign policy of the Soviets, which aims for the most rapid conclusion of a democratic peace'.

The following day, *Pravda* published a leading article warning that 'the enemies of the people want to tear power away from the Soviets, the class organs of the working people. This is the essence of all the noise that is being made about the Constituent Assembly.' In this way the Soviet government let it be known that it had reliable information about preparations by anti-Soviet forces to take 'defensive measures'. The 'Union for the Defence of the Constituent Assembly' intended to organize a demonstration on the day the Assembly opened, and the military organization of the SRs was preparing an armed uprising. Counter-measures were taken: Petrograd was declared to be under a state of siege; an Extraordinary Commission for the Protection of the City and a military council were appointed including Ia. M. Sverdlov, V. D. Bonch-Bruevich, N. I. Podvoiskii, P. P. Prosh'ian and M. S. Uritskii; sailors from the cruiser *Avrora* and the battleship *Respublika* were detailed to guard the Tauride Palace; and on 3 January 1918 the Petrograd Soviet appealed to the population not to take part in meetings and demonstrations. By 5 January the Tauride Palace was fully prepared to receive the deputies and was closely guarded by sailors, Red Guards and soldiers.

That morning demonstrators gathered at nine assembly points. Most of them were state employees, intellectuals, students and high-school pupils, along with a few workers and soldiers. According to eyewitness accounts, the demonstrators did not look as if they were about to stage a revolt. As Sokolov wrote later, 'they gathered listlessly and rather diffidently, without any noticeable enthusiasm . . . Their dissatisfaction was passive and malicious.' The columns of demonstrators crossed the Field of Mars and went up Liteinyi Prospekt towards the Tauride Palace, where they were stopped by revolutionary troops. There were a number of armed clashes with some casualties. By the middle of the day the groups of demonstrators had been dispersed.

In the Tauride Palace the Assembly's first session had not opened at the allotted time, and members of the different fractions were holding separate meetings. The SRs (with at least 237 deputies), the Bolsheviks (with 110–120), the Left SRs (30–35), the Mensheviks (16), the representatives of national parties and organizations (more than 80) and the NSs (two) agreed to postpone the opening until the evening and await the outcome of the demonstrations. At around four o'clock the doors of the White Hall opened and at least 410 deputies took their seats. The left-hand side was taken by the Bolsheviks and Left SRs, while the centre and the right-hand side were taken by the right SRs, the Mensheviks and representatives of other groups. The upper circle was taken by 400 ticket-holders from the general public.

Representatives from camps of mortal enemies had gathered in the Tauride Palace. The session and its outcome were characterized by the psychology and logic of uncompromising struggle. The proceedings were accompanied throughout by approving or outraged catcalls, whistles, foot-stamping and applause.

The SRs tried unsuccessfully to use the late arrival of Sverdlov, the chairman of the VTsIK, to open the session themselves. Once he had read out the 'Declaration of the Rights of the Working and Exploited People', Sverdlov, on behalf of the highest representative organ of the Soviet republic, declared the session open and proposed it elect a chairman. V. M. Chernov, the leader of the SRs, won this position by 244 votes to 151. The SR deputy N. P. Oganovskii wrote in his diary of Chernov's speech: 'The chairman's speech got us into such a deep mess that we will never get out of it.'

The speech of the Menshevik leader, Tsereteli, left no doubt that the majority of the deputies would not recognize the Bolshevik revolution. Having rejected the Bolshevik proposal that they begin by considering Sverdlov's 'Declaration of Rights', the deputies voted by 237 to 146 in favour of the agenda proposed by the SRs. At the top of this agenda were the questions of peace and land, and only after resolving these would they consider a 'Declaration of the Forms of State Structure in Russia'. In protest, the Bolsheviks and Left SRs demanded a break for fractional meetings.

The Bolshevik fraction decided to use the podium of the Assembly to read out a final declaration drafted by Lenin and then to leave the Tauride Palace, which sealed the fate of the 'master of the land of Russia'. The Constituent Assembly lost the necessary quorum on which its powers depended. After vacillating briefly, the Left SRs supported the Bolsheviks and around four o'clock on the morning of 6 January they, too, announced they were leaving the Assembly. Just over 200 deputies remained in the White Hall.

The head of the guard at the Tauride Palace, A. G. Zhelezniakov, requested that the chairman, Chernov, close the session. The latter quickly read out the introductory points of the SR 'Law on the Land', one of the points of the decree declaring Russia to be a democratic federal republic, and an appeal to the Allied powers to define the precise conditions for a democratic peace. At 4.40 a.m. on 6 January, having set the time for the next session at 5 p.m. the same day, Chernov declared the session closed.

On the evening of 6 January an expanded session of the VTsIK approved a decree proposed by the *Sovnarkom* on the dissolution of the Constituent Assembly. The VTsIK members greeted its words with stormy applause: 'The people wanted the Constituent Assembly to be convened, and we convened it. But now it can see what this notorious Constituent Assembly really is. So now we have fulfilled the will of the people, a will which calls for "all power to the soviets".' As Protasov has observed, the Bolsheviks overthrew an assembly of elected people's representatives which was absolutely legitimate even from the point of view of 'revolutionary legality'. Thus all hopes for Russia's constitutional development were dashed.

That same evening, the SRs and their allies attempted to continue the session. When the commandant of the Tauride Palace refused to admit the deputies, they gathered in the Gurevich High School, and gloomily considered where the Constituent Assembly should now work. There followed a number of secret sessions under strict conspiratorial conditions. Delegates first decided to move to Kiev, and launch the struggle for the Constituent Assembly from there. However, on 15 January the forces of the Ukrainian Rada were pushed out of Kiev, so the remnants of the Constituent Assembly moved to Samara, where on 8 June they formed the 'Committee of Members of the Constituent Assembly' (*Komuch*). After Soviet troops took Samara on 7 October 1918, *Komuch* moved to Ufa under the banner of the 'Congress of Members of the Constituent Assembly'. In December 1918 some of its members were shot by White forces in Omsk. The remainder emigrated. Thirty-three former members of the Assembly met in Paris in 1921 and created an executive committee of P. N. Miliukov, A. I. Konovalov, N. D. Avksent'ev and Kerensky, but its activities came to nought.

The story of the Russian Constituent Assembly is a tragic one. Immediately after its dispersal more demonstrators' blood was shed in Moscow, Petrograd, Novgorod and elsewhere in Russia. The liquidation of the Constituent Assembly in fact rolled back the democratic changes of the February revolution. The inevitable consequences were the one-party monopoly of power, the total state control of all social life and Russia's self-isolation from the rest of the world. The resultant system which developed acquired a completely closed character and proved incapable of renewing itself. The fate of the Constituent Assembly showed the incompatibility of the two methods of transforming society – violently, by means of armed struggle, and peacefully, by expressions of the people's will.

Further reading

Malchevskii I. S., ed., *Vserossiiskoe Uchreditel'noe sobranie. Sbornik dokumentov i materialov* (Moscow and Leningrad, Gosudarstvennoe izdatel'stvo, 1930).

Protasov L. G., 'Vserossiiskoe Uchreditel'noe sobranie i demọkraticheskaia al'ternativa', in V. Iu. Cherniaev, ed., *Anatomiia revoliutsii. 1917 god v Rossii: massy, partii, vlast'* (St Petersburg, Glagol, 1994), pp. 134–48.

Radkey O. H., *Russia Goes to the Polls: The Elections to the All-Russian Constituent Assembly, 1917*, updated edition (Ithaca, Cornell University Press, 1989).

Rubinshtein N. L., *K istorii Uchreditel'nogo sobraniia* (Moscow and Leningrad, Gosudarstvennoe sotsial'no-ekonomicheskoe izdatel'stvo, 1931).

Smirnov N. N., *Tretii Vserossiiskii s"ezd Sovetov: istoriia sozyva, sostav, rabota* (Leningrad, Nauka, 1988).

Sokolov B. F., 'Zashchita Vserossiiskogo Uchreditel'nogo sobraniia', *Arkhiv russkoi revoliutsii* 13 (Berlin, 1924).

Sviatitskii N. V., *Itogi vyborov vo Vserossiiskoe Uchreditel'noe sobranie* (Moscow, Gosizdat, 1918).

Vishniak M. V., *Vserossiiskoe Uchreditel'noe sobranie* (Paris, Sovremennye zapiski, 1932).

Znamenskii O. N., *Vserossiiskoe Uchreditel'noe sobranie: istoriia sozyva i politicheskogo krusheniia* (Leningrad, Nauka, 1976).

Education, Schools and Student Life

ALEKSEI R. MARKOV

The leading centres for Soviet studies in the USA, Britain, Germany and France have produced several books and numerous dissertations and articles over the last 25 years on the Bolsheviks' 'cultural policies'. The fashion was started by Sheila Fitzpatrick's book *The Commissariat of Enlightenment*, which appeared in 1970. This flow of publications was to a certain extent connected with the sharp rise in the number of studies on the first few years of Soviet cultural policy which appeared in the USSR from the late 1950s up to the 1980s. It is a curious fact that at the same time as interest in the question grew, Western historians invariably claimed that the 'cultural front' was a question of second- or third-rate importance for the Bolshevik leaders.

It is probably quite natural that the 1960s' generation of scholars, who were influenced by sociology and created the 'new social history' of the Russian revolution, paid most attention to structures and institutions, models of administration and regionalism. It is also not surprising that the themes covered in Western discussions and studies had much in common with the Soviet literature. These included various aspects of the structure, operation and place in the administrative system of the People's Commissariat of Education (*Narkompros*); the question of the formation of the Soviet intelligentsia and the proletarianization of higher education; and the Bolshevik 'project' for education in the context of the post-revolutionary social and economic situation. Until very recently neither Western nor Russian historians had paid much attention to the teachers, students or professors, or examined their sub-culture, mentality and discourse. Only in the last few years have authors like James McClelland and Larry Holmes begun to deal with these matters. The reason for this apparent delay in investigating the 'spiritual world' of the subjects and 'objects' of Soviet educational policy lies in the relatively late development of the 'new cultural history' within social history. None the less, this is the standpoint from which the history of Soviet education will be written in the next few years – a prediction based on the fundamental shift in present-day Slavonic studies clearly identified in the recent article by Michael Holquist.

Although Soviet historiography was 'ideologized', in the sense that it had to adopt the formalized official 'Marxism' of the 1960s–1980s, it examined the same disputed questions as its Western counterpart, albeit in its own way. These questions include the extent to which *Narkompros*'s plans for reorganizing schools were realistic; the minimal practical results of *Narkompros*'s constructive efforts; regional contradictions between Moscow, Petrograd and the Ukraine; the German theoretical sources of many educational innovations; the aims and the realities of the policy of proletarianizing higher education; and the causes, scale and consequences of the conflicts between lecturers and students and the state.

There has only been one attempt to write a complete history of education between 1917 and 1921, that undertaken by F. F. Korolev in his two monographs of the 1950s. The author's approach was typical of his time. It was necessary to present a positive overall picture of unprecedented revolutionary changes in the education system, while assessing these changes far more cautiously and critically in the small print. The main points made by Korolev were as follows: the attempts by *Narkompros* to lay the foundations of a polytechnical education did not meet with any significant success and by the beginning of the 1920s the supporters of professionalized schooling were clearly regaining their positions. Higher secondary schools in many respects resembled the former gymnasia. Teaching was done using the old pre-revolutionary coursebooks and syllabuses. The utopian attempts to do away with marks and exams ended in failure. The policies of the Petrograd and Moscow education authorities differed fundamentally from one another and from the programmes advanced by A. V. Lunacharsky and N. K. Krupskaia – the Petrograd approach was highly conservative both in words and deeds, whereas Moscow, with its 'labour processes', was ultra-revolutionary in its plans but very inclined to compromise with the lecturers in practice. The ground for post-revolutionary experiments in schooling had been prepared by pre-revolutionary experiments such as those of S. T. Shatskii, and were based on more or less modern, mainly German, educational theories like Lay's illustrative school. *Narkompros*'s centralizing urge to bring all types of educational establishment under one roof constantly met with opposition from the economic authorities. In addition, the conflict between *Narkompros* and the teachers, professors and students was presented as before as narrowly political, a part of the struggle between the Bolsheviks and the Kadets and moderate socialists.

Most of Korolev's points were incorporated into the Soviet historical literature of the 1960s–1980s with virtually no changes, although a recent monograph by a contributor to this volume, N. N. Smirnov, on the teaching profession in 1917–18, argues the exact opposite – that the teachers' conflict with the Soviets was fundamentally a professional one. Many aspects of the traditional view have also been echoed by Western historians, particularly

Fitzpatrick. However, Western historians make a different assessment of the ideological bases of Lunacharsky's and Krupskaia's pedagogical theories – it was an obligatory ritual for Soviet researchers to stress their profoundly Marxist or, at least, Russian revolutionary-democratic origins. On the above-mentioned conflict of the lecturers and students with the Soviet authorities, Western historians have focused their attention on the Bolsheviks' encroachments on educational autonomy (a fundamental value of the intelligentsia), and on the economic and financial background to the eventual conciliation. It is noteworthy that almost nobody has examined the question of the corporate sub-cultures of students, professors and secondary school teachers, and the way that Bolshevik encroachments deepened the crisis in relations between them and the government. Incidentally, secondary school teachers were a very diverse category. The gulf between a teacher at an elementary school and a lecturer at a gymnasium was almost as wide as that between a *raznochinets* and an aristocrat. In the final analysis, the historiography of the 1950s to the 1980s revolved around the problem of continuity versus discontinuity in the structures and functions of educational institutions. Soviet researchers obviously inflated the depth and scale of the break with the past overall, whilst in the individual, concrete aspects of the picture they painted their conclusions were quite the opposite. Anglo-American and French historiography, which was not bound by the official ideology, stressed the continuity in the overall picture as well.

Schools

The most important events in education following the February revolution were the recreation of the All-Russian Teachers' Union (VUS) in April 1917 and the formation of the State Committee on Education (GKNO) in May. The first of these events was particularly significant, re-establishing as it did a professional and political association of the Russian teaching profession, banned since the first Russian revolution (1905), with important implications for its post-October history. The language of the union's programme documents is examined below. The work of the GKNO, which has now been analysed in detail by Smirnov, provides an example of an attempt to elaborate a school reform relying mainly on the interested corporate bodies – particularly representatives of the teachers' union. Later on, many of the ideas of GKNO were used by *Narkompros*, which reworked them to fit the project of a Soviet civilization.

On 29 October 1917 Lunacharsky, the People's Commissar for Education, issued an appeal 'To Students' in which he wrote: 'The proletariat and peasantry, having recently secured their victory, call on your teachers to start as soon as possible on renewing our and your stagnant schools.' The Bolsheviks' project for education was to renew it on the basis of rationalization (by making it polytechnical), and profound democratization (or 'proletarianization').

This is not to say that *Narkompros* had any detailed programme for reorganizing education before the summer or autumn of 1918. However, Krupskaia's interest in modern educational ideas, which was well known in party circles, points to a theoretical trend based on the ideas of German educationalists from around the turn of the century, such as Kerschensteiner, Seidel and Lay. This took the German projects for labour schools and social education and reworked them in a Marxist fashion. The German theorists, some of whom were also themselves teachers, were continuing and developing the ideas of the Enlightenment, of Pestalozzi and Rousseau. In this respect the Bolsheviks themselves were continuing the Enlightenment tradition, and their polytechnical schools should have given Russia a modern European character. In common with all the Russian liberal intelligentsia, the leaders of *Narkompros* had a highly critical attitude towards the education system of the old regime, and rejected its elitism, authoritarian organization and lack of relevance to real life. At the same time, they regarded educational institutions as 'factories' for producing the Soviet 'new man', who was seen on the one hand as a self-motivated, socially active subject, and on the other as having been consciously indoctrinated with communist ideology. The contradiction between these two tasks of the new school system was one cause of the fluctuations in post-October educational policy.

In the midst of the rigid centralization of the war-communism period, the educational reformers L. G. Shapiro and V. N. Shul'gin argued that it was not necessary to have a common curriculum for secondary schools. Indeed, until 1921 there was no such curriculum. On 31 May 1918, *Narkompros* abolished the grading system, and on 30 September the VTsIK approved a 'Decree on the Single Labour School', article 19 of which forbade examinations. Thus schools no longer had any differentiated accounting system for the learning process. At the same time the Education Commissariat of the Northern Commune issued a circular obliging teachers to run courses on the Soviet constitution of 1918. However, even in this sphere the extent of uniformity and centralization should not be exaggerated – the Commissariat's instructions permitted a 'creative approach' in teaching ideological subjects. In this respect it is useful to speak of an attempt to create a Soviet school community. State indoctrination was seen as a temporary surrogate, in Russian conditions, for a civil society in the Soviet style. The school system, which, to use Gail Warshofsky Lapidus's phrase, was a 'microcosm of the larger social universe', also had to pass through that phase. There were various attempts made to create a new community of teachers and students between 1917 and 1920. One of these sought to destroy the system of class subjects and move to a system of labour processes and labour tasks. This was the Moscow perspective, which was adopted in the decisions of the First All-Russian Congress on Education and in the Declaration of the State Commission on Education entitled 'Basic Principles of the Single Labour School'. The outcome of this process would have been that the teachers and students together would have constituted something akin to a work collective. Another idea was to bring the wider community onto the governing bodies of schools. This was reflected in the plan for Councils of People's Education advanced by Lunacharsky in January 1918, in which two-thirds of the places would be allocated to 'toilers', and in the election of representatives of party groups, factories and other institutions to school councils in Petrograd and some gubernias in 1920, and so on. A third idea was for a broad development of students' self-management. This was the so-called 'choir principle' contained in the 'Basic Principles of the Single Labour School'. It was realized in various forms. These included student committees; bringing students onto school committees; the formation of 'student gubernia executive committees' in Kostroma; the creation of students' political organizations like the 'Children's Communist Party' in 1919–20; and organizations of Young Communists. The pinnacle of this movement was the First All-Russian Congress of Communist School Students in April 1919, attended by 200 delegates representing 8,000 secondary school students in 37 gubernias. One of its sessions was addressed by Lenin.

The most dramatic results were obtained by the experiment to 'prepare' a new teaching community within the Union of Internationalist Teachers (SUI), which split from the All-Russian Teachers' Union (VUS). *Narkompros* had come into conflict with VUS, the State Committee on Education (GKNO) and some regional teachers' organizations. There was a whole range of reasons for this. Ideologically, Russian liberal opinion, shared by the most politically and professionally active groups of teachers, did not accept the October coup. On the professional and corporate level, the groups in question had elaborated a school reform programme on their own account, and were not about to surrender their leading roles either to the Provisional Government's Ministry of Education, or to the Bolsheviks' State Commission on Enlightenment. A psychological reason was that the Bolsheviks were regarded as dangerous extremists, and Lunacharsky himself was seen as a splitter who had only recently been taking part in the GKNO. This conflict was deepened and intensified precisely as a result of the attempts to counterpose another trade union to the VUS – the SUI, composed of former VUS members. Like any new sect, the SUI leadership took an extreme position towards its parent organization. In this respect it is important to distinguish between them and the leading figures in *Narkompros* – particularly Lunacharsky and Krupskaia – and their policies. It was also quite natural for the SUI to look for support among the most numerous and at the same time most marginal group of teachers – those in the elementary schools. Although *Narkompros* offered consistent support to the SUI, it realized the sectarian narrowness of the organization and worked towards forming a trade union which would have more of a mass base and at the same time be more loyal to the Bolsheviks. There is no shortage of examples of this from the summer of 1918 onwards: the First All-Russian Congress on Popular Education in August, the organization in Petrograd of the Union of Workers in Educational and Cultural-Enlightenment Institutions from the end of September to the middle of December, and the Foundation Congress of the Union of Workers in Education and Socialist Culture in July 1919. The dissolution of the VUS in December 1918 and a compromise reached in January 1919 with the SUI leaders made it possible to induce many teachers, including former VUS activists, to collaborate with *Narkompros* and take part in the new teachers' union.

It is very instructive to compare the underlying philosophies contained in the documents of the two teachers' unions in 1917 and 1918. The stress on apoliticism and the profoundly 'professional' character of the VUS programme, with its clearly expressed 'liberal' pathos, contrasted sharply with the highly ideological declarations of the pro-Bolshevik union, which stood 'on the basis of the world movement for socialism'. The discourse of the liberal VUS members was characterized by an 'organic' and a related 'reformist' approach. Their programme preserved the organizational, juridical, educational and ideological diversity of pre-revolutionary schools and even accentuated it. The autonomy of secondary education was envisaged in terms of 'returning' schools to society by 'divorcing' them from the state. This belief in autonomy was all the more important in that it corresponded to the 'real' social interests of the teaching profession. The central concept in the discourse of the SUI was the logic of the 'break' – its ideologists spoke in the name of the new civilization. The leap into this 'tomorrow' necessitated, among other things, ideological compulsion. This was expressed in their project for indoctrinating school pupils, which was to start by removing divinity from the curriculum. However, the SUI programme did not reject pluralism within that 'tomorrow', and it advocated revolutionary educational experimentation. Aspects of the SUI leaders' utopia were reminiscent of that of the *Proletkul't*, which is not surprising, given Lunacharsky's own ideological evolution. In some respects it was a question of a new Enlightenment, incorporating criticisms of bourgeois society. Precisely which criticisms – the traditional Marxist ones or 'modernist' ones – remained unclear.

The important historiographical discussion about regionalism has already been mentioned. Although historians have made frequent references to this subject, the interpretation of the phenomenon itself has been limited to claiming that there were contradictions between regional elites. At least three major autonomous centres in the sphere of educational policy have been identified – Moscow, Petrograd and the Ukraine. Their regional peculiarities can be briefly summed up in the following terms: Petrograd was 'conservative', Moscow was 'ultra-radical' in its programme but 'pragmatic' in practice, and the Ukraine was 'industry-oriented'. However, this sort of classification ignores such things as the national features of the Ukraine as well as the specifically 'regional' aspects of school life in Petrograd and Moscow. An examination of Moscow's verbal radicalism should take account of the lengthy anti-Bolshevik teachers' strike and of the move of the extreme wing of *Narkompros* and of the SUI to the new capital in the spring of 1918. In Petrograd the search for a compromise began as early as May 1918, at a meeting of representatives of teachers', workers' and parents' associations with the deputies of the Vasileostrovskii regional Soviet. The synthesis of the socialist utopia of a 'single labour school' and the organic structures of the pre-revolutionary education system took place in different ways in different parts of the country, and significantly altered the utopia itself. In the Russian capitals this 'chemical reaction' occurred within the confines of the pre-existing structures. In the Ukraine the civil war had destroyed the pre-revolutionary education system, and the only successors to that tradition were the teachers themselves. The huge number of orphaned children in that republic provided favourable conditions for experiments in the socialization of childrearing, and at the same time necessitated early vocational training. The 'militancy' of the Ukrainian *Narkompros* during the discussion on polytechnical and early vocational schools was also largely the result of a powerful departmental lobby in Moscow. Finally, one should also bear in mind the very independent policies of the Ukrainian government under Khristian Rakovskii.

Higher education

The themes and problems in the historiographical discussion on the development of higher education between 1917 and 1921 show both similarities to and, necessarily, specific differences from the discussion outlined above. Historians have focused most attention on various aspects of the conflict between Bolshevik policies and university autonomy. This follows logically from the studies made of the history of the pre-revolutionary university – a belief in autonomy was a central article of faith among both professors and students, and was connected with the German orientation of Russian higher education. Close studies have been made of the Bolshevik conception of the place of universities in the new society, the internal structure and operation of the universities, as well as the attempts of *Narkompros* to realize these ideas in practice. We know far less about the consequences of these policies for the particular sub-cultures of students and professors. This question has only begun to be considered recently, by such writers as McClelland.

Narkompros's plans for the universities in the spring and summer of 1918 can only be properly understood in terms of the project for a 'new society' as a whole. The 'red professors' M. A. Reisner and M. N. Pokrovskii believed that the university as an autonomous corporate institution should be replaced by a democratic 'popular' institution consisting of two or three associations for research, study and education. The highest organ of university administration in their scheme would be a people's council, representing some kind of general social interest on both the local and the national level, through representatives from local soviets and central institutions as well as (most importantly) deputies from public organizations. Thus the 'little islands of free science' inherited from the old regime would lose their meaning and function under the 'proletarian dictatorship', the first step towards communist civilization. The hostility towards elitism and corporatism, which underlay this utopia, had its roots both in the experience of Russian intellectuals and in the spirit of new European democracy as a whole. Karl Mannheim remarked that 'the democratic ideal of knowledge is unlimited accessibility and communicability'. In many respects, as McClelland showed in *Autocrats and Academics*, this ideal ran counter to the principles elaborated by German classical philosophy, which had been partly responsible for the development of the Russian 'mysticism of science'. It was characteristic that one of the radical Russian professors, the biologist K. A. Timiriazev, who insisted on a thoroughly positivist interpretation of 'scientific', followed N. I. Pirogov in his highly suspicious attitude to the idea of corporate professorial dominance in universities. As a very old man he strongly supported the Bolsheviks' innovations. However, for most professors and students the idea of autonomy became an *idée fixe* in their discussions and struggles with *Narkompros* between 1918 and 1921. Incidentally, as Sh. Kh. Chanbarisov has shown, the policies advanced by Lunacharsky and Pokrovskii did at first include respect for this 'historical value', and it was only Lenin's intervention which led to the removal of the slogan of autonomy from *Narkompros*'s university reform programme. However, Pokrovskii's conception of autonomy had little in common with autonomy as understood by the students and professors; it was more a kind of local self-management. The latter, according to McClelland, was a fundamental principle in the initial period of Bolshevik education policy from 1917 to 1919. This was in keeping with government thinking in general in the first months after the revolution: the accent was on workers' control and decentralization, as formulated theoretically in Lenin's pamphlet *State and Revolution*. Consequently, to understand the nature of the conflict between the professors and students on the one hand, and the Bolsheviks on the other, it is important to take into account not only ideological and political disagreements about university 'freedom', but also incompatible discourses about society, which may be the major factor. In a certain sense, contrary to Frederic Lilge's opinion, the position of Lenin himself did not break with the Enlightenment project, but developed the order implicit within it. The elitist proclivities of the university corporations showed the contradictory nature of the liberal search for 'modernity' in Russia. Although I do not consider myself a completely 'post-modernist' historian, I would suggest that a discursive 'war' is connected with social conflict – it was quite natural that the old elites were not keen to give up their control over higher education and refused voluntarily to quit the scene.

Having been unable to find a common language with the professors after the failure of the second conference on university reform in September 1918, the Bolsheviks tried to find a base among the students. On the one hand, as McClelland has shown, the Soviet government counted on the social structure of the students being radically democratized. This was expected to follow the implementation of the *Sovnarkom* decree of 2 August 1918, written by Lenin, and the decisions of *Narkompros* flowing from it, which were supposed to provide as much encouragement as possible for young people from working-class and peasant backgrounds to go to university. On the other hand, the authorities shared the revolutionary myth surrounding Russian students, seen under the old regime as the 'enemy within', about which a certain 'proletarian student' reminded G. E. Zinoviev in 1919. The Bolsheviks made an important concession to the students in October 1918 when they granted some legal functions to councils of student leaders. In this way the students got a decisive voice within the university and wide-ranging corporate autonomy. Thus, until February 1919, councils of student leaders dispensed state funds allocated for the needs of university students.

However, it soon became apparent that *Narkompros* had miscalculated in both regards. The influx of students from the lower classes taken on in 1918 for the most part dissipated rapidly. They had not had the necessary preparation for university courses and the material conditions of students were very hard. As for the idea of the students as the 'enemy within', it proved to be too close to the truth for the new authorities. The student sub-culture – or, rather, sub-cultures – displayed an unexpected flexibility and adaptability to a variety of experiments over a considerably longer timespan than three to four years. In essence, the sub-culture remained closed both in its marginality – which was related to the social and economic conditions of student life – and at the same time in its elitism. The harsh deprivation which was a feature of student life long before the revolution became even more severe. Seminar rooms and libraries were frequently unheated, the rations were below physical subsistence level, and student hostels were characterized by poverty and insanitary conditions. Attempts to find a way out in communal forms of living, which also had a rich historical tradition, generally ended in fiasco. The institutions of student leadership proved equally impervious to change. The so-called 'eternal students', who spent considerably longer at university than most students and who frequently moved from faculty to faculty taking academic leave, were unrivalled in the political and social organizations within higher education. And their power increased once the councils of student leaders had been given the right to distribute state rations and regulate the economic life of university students. Moreover, again in accordance with tradition, a number of political factions operated among the student elite. The major groups were the Kadets, SRs and Mensheviks, although there were some relatively small Bolshevik groups which even had a city-wide organization in Moscow and Petrograd. However, one should not be too quick to ascribe party-political motives to any particular student action. Many observers of student life prior to 1917 noted a growing political apathy, at least towards the parties that were operating at that time.

It would also be mistaken to ignore the peculiarities of corporate psychology, as can be seen in the initial impact of the new workers' faculties (*rabfaki*). The idea of the *rabfak* arose as a result of the failure of the

Bolsheviks' attempt to flirt with the students. Those few students from lower-class backgrounds who entered university in the free intake of 1918 and managed to stay the course were quickly assimilated into the dominant student sub-culture. To make the 'new body of students' a reality, it was necessary to cultivate and support a group-consciousness among certain of its representatives. At the end of 1918 the Zamoskvorech'e district committee of the party in Moscow took a pragmatic decision to enrol a group of young workers from local enterprises at the Moscow Commercial Academy to support the Communist candidates at the elections for student leaders. This eventually led to *Narkompros* issuing a legally binding decree on 11 September 1919, attaching to universities 'autonomous educational institutions for preparing workers and peasants for higher education in the shortest possible time'. Thus the creation of a Soviet intelligentsia began to become a directed process, in much the same way as the sovietization of industry in 1918 began to replace workers' control with rigid state administration. In effect the *rabfak* students constituted, at first, a third corporation within the university. The strained relations between the students from the first *rabfaki* in 1919 and the so-called 'mainstream' students who studied in the old faculties, can to a considerable extent be seen as a conflict of sub-cultures. In fact, at first the appearance of a small number of *rabfak* students hardly changed the traditional practices of student social life. This continued with its familiar meetings, *zemliachestva* (associations of students from the same region) and councils of leaders, even though *Narkompros* had formally dissolved the councils on 10 July 1919.

In many respects McClelland is right to point to 1920 as marking a particular stage in the policies of *Narkompros* and its committee dealing with professional and technical education. It was at that time that the attempt to militarize higher education came to the fore, particularly in medicine and engineering. However, as he recognizes, once again these goals were not attained, a fact that was later admitted by such *Narkompros* leaders as Lunacharsky. Indeed, this new course had even less effect on the way of life of the students and professors. It is typical that in 1920, the Petrograd leadership in the person of Zinoviev tried to reach a compromise with the students on the basis of an anti-Polish platform – it was at that time that the Soviet–Polish war was breaking out. At a conference of Petrograd students in June, Zinoviev laid great stress on patriotic attitudes and made a number of tempting proposals, such as wider freedom of speech, albeit within Soviet confines. At the same time, he once again referred to the revolutionary traditions of Russian students. Most of the delegates accepted the proposed terms of this social contract. The militarization of higher education, which took the form of speedier graduation, mobilized status and military rations for engineering and medical students, was from the outset very much a temporary measure dictated by circumstances, as is shown by the 'de-ideologization' of syllabuses noted by McClelland.

The reforms of 1921, set out in the first Soviet university statute, promised a serious and profound change both in the policies of *Narkompros* and in the functioning of the university community. The statute, adopted by *Sovnarkom* on 2 September 1921, introduced strict centralization into the running of higher education. The administrations of these institutions were appointed from above and were completely subordinate to the Chief Administration of Professional and Technical Schools and Institutions of Higher Education. This latter body was a separate structure within *Narkompros* – from 20 January until 11 February 1920 called 'Chief Committee on Professional and Technical Education'. At the same time the partially elected university councils allowed the authorities to keep open a channel for exchanging opinions with the students and professors. It has been noted that the degree of state control established by the 1921 decree exceeded even the 'reactionary' university statutes of 1884. The administration enjoyed full power within higher education institutions, under the overall supervision of the authorities. When the authorities returned the post of rector to the professors as a body in 1922, the limitations on their administrative power posed by student representation were removed. Lenin, who was personally involved in formulating education policy during the transition to NEP, considered this structure to be optimal for involving the scientific elite in restoring the country and sovietizing the universities. Within higher education the new line led, at first, to a sharpening of the developing conflict between the rival sub-cultures of the 'old' and 'new' bodies of students. At the end of 1921 and the beginning of 1922, it also resulted in a 'war' between the professors and *Narkompros*'s professional and higher education structures for better terms in their 'contract'.

Overall, Bolshevik policy on secondary and higher education between 1917 and 1921 showed a strategic shift from the utopian vision of the 'spontaneous' emergence of a Soviet community of 'teachers and taught', towards centralized state administration and the active cultivation of Soviet schools and universities. At the same time, the authorities were obliged to recognize the reality of pre-existing stable sub-cultures within the educational community, and to seek some kind of sensible compromise, at least with the teachers. Such compromises were reached with university teachers around the start of NEP, and with school teachers somewhat earlier. There is a pressing need for historians to study the problem of these sub-cultures, and more work remains to be done on the question of communist discourse on education.

Further reading

Anweiler O., *Geschichte der Schule und Pädagogik in Russland vom Ende des Zarenreiches bis zum Beginn der Stalin-Ära* (Berlin, Osteuropa-Institut, 1978).

Bérélowitch W., *La soviétisation de l'école russe (1917–1931)* (Paris, L'Age de L'Homme, 1990).

Chanbarisov Sh. Kh., *Formirovanie sovetskoi universitetskoi sistemy* (Moscow, Vysshaia Shkola, 1988).

Fitzpatrick S., *The Commissariat of Enlightenment: Soviet Organization of Education and the Arts under Lunacharsky, October 1917–1921* (Cambridge, Cambridge University Press, 1970).

Holmes L. E., *The Kremlin and the Schoolhouse: Reforming Education in Soviet Russia 1917–1931* (Bloomington, Indiana University Press, 1991).

Holquist M., 'Ten Theses on the Relevance of Cultural Criticism for Russian Studies (History, Myth, Biography)', *New Formations* 22 (Spring 1994), pp. 4–13.

Korolev F. F., *Ocherki po istorii sovetskoi shkoly i pedagogiki 1917–1920 gg.* (Moscow, APN, 1958).

Lapidus G. W., 'Educational Strategies and Cultural Revolution: The Politics of Soviet Development', in S. Fitzpatrick, ed., *Cultural Revolution in Russia 1928–1931* (Bloomington, Indiana University Press, 1978), pp. 78–104.

Lilge F., 'Lenin and the Politics of Education', *Slavic Review* 27, 2 (June 1968), pp. 230–57.

McClelland J. C., 'Bolshevik Approaches to Higher Education 1917–1921', *Slavic Review* 30, 4 (December 1971), pp. 818–31.

McClelland J. C., *Autocrats and Academics: Education, Culture and Society in Tsarist Russia* (Bloomington, Indiana University Press, 1979).

Smirnov N. N., *Rossiiskoe uchitel'stvo nakanune i v dni revolivtsii 1917 goda* (St Petersburg, Nauka, 1994).

Factory Committees

STEVE SMITH

The origins of the factory committees

The overthrow of the Romanov dynasty in February 1917 was seen by workers as a signal to dismantle the autocratic regime in the workplace and to replace it with a 'constitutional' order. They began by expelling the most hated foremen and administrators and tearing up the old factory regulations, and proceeded to establish committees to represent their interests *vis-à-vis* management. The speed and spontaneity with which factory committees were created can be explained in part by the fact that they had a long prehistory. As far back as 1820 workers at the Frianovo textile mill had asked that their elders (*starosty*) be allowed to oversee the implementation of factory regulations and payment of wages. And from the 1870s the demand for permanent elected representatives began to appear in strikes. In 1903, as an extension of the 'police unions' sponsored by Colonel Zubatov, head of the Moscow Okhrana, the government passed a law which permitted workers to nominate candidates from whom the management would choose elders. Inspired by a desire to discourage the development of independent organizations, the law was unpopular with workers, not least because elders enjoyed no legal immunity and could not summon meetings of the whole workforce, but it was also disliked by employers, who resented concessions to the principle of permanent representation.

With the outbreak of revolution in 1905, the movement to establish elected bodies of permanent representatives took off. The petition which workers carried to the Winter Palace on 'Bloody Sunday' contained a demand to this effect, but it was the decision to set up an official commission under Senator N. V. Shidlovskii to investigate the causes of worker disaffection which catalysed the movement. On 1 February he invited workers to elect representatives, from whom 50 would be chosen to sit on a commission, and in spite of opposition from the more militant plants in the capital, 145,259 workers in 209 state and private enterprises elected

372 representatives. After the disbandment of the commission, many of these representatives transformed themselves into the nuclei of factory commissions (*zavodskie komissii*) or councils of elders (*sovety starost*). The latter were so named in order to take advantage of the 1903 law, but they were seldom bound by its restrictions. The committees grew most rapidly in the large metal plants, where they gained *de facto* recognition from management. In some cases, they justified themselves in the fashionable language of constitutionalism. At the Patronnyi plant the factory commission was known as the 'works duma' and at the large Cheshire textile mill the commission drew up a 'workers' constitution' which codified its right to look into complaints, rewrite the rules of internal order and be consulted over dismissals. This encroachment on employers' 'right to manage' went furthest in the printing industry, where by the second half of 1906 the printers' union had persuaded employers to accept 'autonomous rules' which sanctioned the participation of commissions in matters of hiring and firing, changes in rates of pay and work practices. Generally, however, employers resisted the intervention of committees in the running of the workplace and, with the onset of unemployment in 1906 and political reaction in 1907, the committees fell into disarray. A few, such as those at the Sestroretsk armaments works and the Nevskii ship-building works in the capital, survived for several years, but unlike the trade unions, they did not re-emerge in the strike wave of 1912–14. During the war the Workers' Groups of the War Industries Committees pressed unsuccessfully to revive factory elders. After the postponement of the opening of the Duma on 12 January 1917 the now revolutionary-minded Central Workers' Group called on workers to elect factory committees, and its call was heeded a month later when mass strikes precipitated the overthrow of the autocracy.

The first phase of factory committee activity

The committees re-established themselves most quickly in the ten enterprises run by the Artillery Administration (*Glavnoe Artilleriiskoe Upravlenie*) and the five run by the Naval Ministry (*Morskoe Vedomstvo*), which together employed around a third of the factory workforce of the capital. The strength of the committees in the state-owned sector may reflect the efforts by the government in 1905 and 1906 to extend the law on elders to state-owned plants, but it was more probably due to the fact that many of the army and naval officers who ran these plants fled during the turmoil of the February revolution. Left without a management, the factory committees, led mainly by SRs and Mensheviks, struggled to keep production going for the war effort, but linked this concern to a vision of a democratized system of industrial relations. As early as 13 March a conference of artillery enterprises called for 'full democracy and collegiality' in the running of production and claimed rights to oversee supplies, orders and the execution of tasks; to demand access to company records and documentation; to object to appointments of managerial and technical personnel; and to determine the internal rules of the enterprise. At the conference of workers in state enterprises on 15 April a resolution, possibly authored by P. A. Voronkov, an SR member of the Petrograd Soviet and evidently a worker at the New Arsenal, defended 'preliminary' control of production, under which committees had a consultative voice in all organs of administration and access to all papers and documentation, but rejected the idea of committees taking responsibility for production. This distinction between 'responsible' and 'preliminary' control was to become central to the movement of workers' control of production and distribution, in which *kontrol'* had the sense of supervising and checking, rather than of taking charge.

In the private sector factory committees acted, initially, as surrogate trade unions, since it took a couple of months for the trade unions to re-establish themselves. The committees demanded the eight-hour day, large wage increases to compensate for wartime inflation, a minimum wage, controls on overtime working, and an end to piece rates. Yet here, too, the committees asserted a modicum of *kontrol'*, in so far as they protected premises, sought out supplies of fuel and raw materials and, above all, insisted on the right to be consulted on matters of hiring and firing. Indeed, the committees extended their activities beyond the sphere of production, involving themselves in food supply, policing and education.

Prior to the revolution the Petrograd Society of Factory and Mill Owners (*Petrogradskoe Obshchestvo Fabrikantov i Zavodchikov*, PSFMO) had been one of the most politically supine sectors of capital, since it relied heavily on state orders. As soon as the autocracy was overthrown, however, it adopted a programme similar to that advocated by the Progressist industrialists of Moscow. On 10 March it signed an agreement with the Executive Committee of the Petrograd Soviet recognizing the eight-hour day as a norm; it agreed to the setting up of concilation boards in each enterprise, comprising equal numbers of worker and management representatives, to resolve disputes; and it backed the law, promulgated on 23 April, which legalized factory committees as the workers' representative organs. Outside Petrograd employers tended to be less convinced that the future lay in such a 'Western' model of industrial relations, kept their distance from the factory committees and temporized over implementing the eight-hour day.

The law on factory committees galvanized their formation across the former empire. Metalworkers, especially those in large enterprises, were particularly energetic, but their lead was eagerly followed by railway workers, who formed line committees, and miners, who formed mine committees. These committees took on a huge array of functions. At the Nevskii shipyard in Petrograd the works committee had a militia commission, a food commission, a commission of culture and enlightenment, a technical-economic commission, responsible for wages, safety, first aid and internal order, a reception commission, responsible for hiring and firing, and a commission to deal with correspondence. At the Metal Works no fewer than 28 commissions existed, involving some 200 workers, not counting the 60 *starosty* elected from the workshops. Soon efforts were made to coordinate the activities of factory committees on a territorial basis. In the capital a council representing 34 factory committees in Nevskii district was set up in May, though only four such district councils were successfully established. Much more influential was the Petrograd Central Council of Factory Committees (CCFC), created by the First Conference of Petrograd Factory Committees (30 May–5 June), which soon acquired national significance. After the First All-Russian Conference of Factory Committees (17–22 October), it was reorganized into the All-Russian Council of Factory Committees. Initially, the council concerned itself with wage disputes and with averting factory closures, but it quickly became heavily involved in organizing supplies of fuel, raw materials and food, and in coordinating workers' control of production on a city-wide and national scale. By October it employed 80 people full-time in its various sections.

In passing the law on factory committees, the Provisional Government was careful not to formalize a right of workers' control, since employers were deeply sensitive to any encroachment on their authority. Yet we should be wary of assuming that workers' control automatically spelt doom to the project of consolidating a bourgeois-democratic capitalist order. Vladimir Cherniaev argues that there was a potential for 'social partnership' between factory committees and management during the period of dual power, and that workers' control could serve as a 'shock absorber' of industrial conflict. There are well-documented cases where factory committees did perform this function and, more pertinently, their efforts to improve labour productivity were much appreciated by employers. As late as 9 August the works committees of the Admiralty shipyard, the New Admiralty and the Okhta shell section met with directors, technicians and foremen and agreed to transfer to piece rates to boost productivity. Yet by this stage, the economic and political conditions were hardly conducive to 'social partnership', if ever they had been. As the economy slid into crisis, workers lambasted the employers for putting profits before jobs, and employers, in the words of the director of the Obukhov works, condemned the factory committees for 'introducing the artel' [team or association of workers] principle with respect to the capital of others'.

The radicalization of workers' control of production

From the early summer a mounting crisis in the economy became evident, the chief symptoms of which were severe shortages of fuel, raw materials and food. Coal production in the Donbass dropped from 157 million *pudy* to 131 million between January and May, and the coal that was produced failed to reach the industrial centres as a result of the growing paralysis of the railway system. Shortages, spiralling costs, declining productivity and an increasingly combative workforce made industrialists start to lay off employees, convincing workers that the crisis was deliberately being engineered by the employers. Faced with the prospect of mass unemployment, factory committees expanded the scope of workers' control in order to preserve jobs and to combat capitalist 'sabotage'. 'Fixers' (*tolkachi*) were sent in search of oil and coal; stocks of raw materials were monitored; access to order books and company accounts was demanded. Employers did not oppose all such activities. In May the Vyborg District section of the PSFMO agreed that factory committees could seek out raw materials but refused to give premises to or pay members of their control-economic commissions. They particularly objected to the call by the First Conference of Factory Committees for an end to commercial secrecy. At the Langenzippen works the committee attempted to stop the payment of dividends to shareholders, pending an enquiry, but in general it proved difficult for committees to extend control into the sphere of company finances. Even in the Urals, where the scope of control was far-reaching, only a few committees, such those at the Kaslinskii metallurgical works in the Kyshtynskii district and the Nadezhdinskii works in the Bogoslovskii district succeeded in gaining access to accounts and order books.

The aggressive challenge to the 'right to manage' made employers ever more intransigent. The PSFMO demanded that M. I. Skobelev, the Menshevik Minister of Labour, take action to curb the committees. On 23 August he issued a circular affirming that the right to hire and fire belonged exclusively to the employers, and five days later, he issued a second circular forbidding the committees to meet during working hours. The circulars provoked uproar in the labour movement, not least because they appeared around the time of the Kornilov rebellion. From now on, the two sides of industry were at open war. In September and October well over 1.2 million workers went on strike, including 700,000 railway workers and 300,000 textile workers in Ivanovo-Kineshma. Industrial conflict was probably most acute in the Donbass where, by the beginning of September, almost 200 mines had closed and nearly 100,000 were out of work. The Bolshevik-led mine committees responded to mass lay-offs by organizing occupations of the mines. In some instances the committees placed mine owners and managers under arrest, as at the Iasinovskii mine and the South Russian mining company, and there were instances of beatings and even murder. In late September the government sent in Cossacks to try to end the mine occupations.

In a few instances factory committees sought to prevent closures by placing enterprises under workers' management. Such incidents have been seen by some historians, such as Paul Avrich, as evidence of widespread anarcho-syndicalism within the factory committee movement. In fact such acts were fairly rare. One calculation suggests that of 2,094 acts of worker control between July and October, only 4.3 per cent involved factory committees taking over enterprises. Although anarcho-syndicalism did increase in popularity after October, most such takeovers were motivated not by a utopian desire to set up producers' communes but by the hope of forcing the government to take financial responsibility for the enterprise by appointing an official, or board, to run it (so-called 'sequestration'). This was true, for instance, of the few cases of workers' management in Moscow (at the Dinamo machine-construction works, the Benno-Rontaller button factory and the Ganzen wood factory). Only in the Ukraine did the fevered tempo of class conflict, combined with appalling levels of closure, lead to significant numbers of worker takeovers. In Khar'kov committees took charge of the Gel'ferikh-Sade agricultural-machinery plant, the Steam-Engine and the General Electric Works. In general, however, factory committees were under few illusions about the difficulty of running factories in the absence of orders, operating capital and technical and financial expertise.

Against this background of 'excesses', the Mensheviks and SRs stepped up their criticism of workers' control of production, arguing that spontaneous initiatives by atomized groups of workers could only aggravate the crisis. They insisted that only planned, centralized and all-embracing control by the state could restore order to the economy. And they maintained that this was politically preferable, since it would allow the entire 'revolutionary democracy', according to the Mensheviks, or 'toiling people', according to the SRs, and not just the working class, to participate in the massive effort of control. Some of the moderate socialists went so far as to accuse the Bolsheviks of deliberately seeking to wreck the economy for political ends, a charge that has been echoed by some historians. The Menshevik Solomon Schwarz, for example, made this charge against the Council of Factory Committees, yet the range and vigour of its practical activities hardly bear him out. Certainly, council leaders were determined to break the power of capital at the point of production, but they did not subscribe to the view that the worse the crisis got, the nearer they were drawing to socialism (it is true that during the period of war communism, some, such as Bukharin, did advocate such a view). Whether in practice workers' control did make the economic crisis worse is a difficult question that merits further research. Again the assertion is frequently made by historians, yet the evidence points in different directions. Whilst there were 'excesses' committed by some factory committees, such as physical attacks on technical and managerial personnel or hoarding of scarce materials, the great majority struggled to alleviate shortages and to keep production going.

The politics of workers' control

The protocols of factory committees which have been published demonstrate that they concerned themselves with practical matters and rarely discussed politics. Nevertheless, members of committees took a broadly political approach to their work, and from early on tended to be elected on party slates (illustrating how much more the labour movement in 1917 was subject to party political differentiation than in 1905). In the spring and early summer, especially in the metal industries, Mensheviks and SRs tended to dominate the factory committees. But as the institutions closest to the rank-and-file, they soon began to register the radicalization that was taking place in popular political attitudes. By the time of the First Conference at the beginning of June, the majority of delegates backed Bolshevik resolutions, although it is doubtful that the Bolsheviks formed majorities in most factory committees at this stage. Even in Petrograd it was not until the Kornilov rebellion that Bolsheviks came to dominate most factory committees. At the Lessner works in September the Bolsheviks won 471 votes, non-party candidates 186, the SRs 155 and the Mensheviks 23 in new elections to the committee. At the Pipe Works the Bolsheviks had won 36 per cent of the vote in elections in June, but won 62 per cent in October. In Moscow Bolshevik influence was much less than in the capital. The Moscow Conference of Factory Committees, which opened on 23 July, said nothing about workers' control in its resolution on the economy. Here, too, however, by the time of the Second Conference (12–17 October), three-quarters of delegates were Bolsheviks.

The First Conference of Petrograd Factory Committees was followed by three further conferences of Petrograd factory committees between August and early October, and then by the All-Russian Conference, which opened on 17 October. Bolshevik perspectives on the economic crisis and workers' control were endorsed by all these conferences. Indeed, no less a Bolshevik than Lenin drafted the resolution, 'Measures to Combat Disruption in the Economy', that was passed by the First Conference. This called for a state-wide system of workers' control of production and distribution, to be achieved by assigning workers' representatives two-thirds of the places in all institutions of economic regulation. This 'official' activity was to be complemented by workers' control at the point of production, especially of the financial and banking operations of enterprises. Lenin at this time believed in the importance of 'accounting and inspection' (*uchet i kontrol'*) by workers, as a means of combating bureaucratism in the state organization of the economy. But his resolution had little to say on the functions of the factory committees, making only a passing reference to their role in implementing 'real' control, a task he saw them sharing with the trade unions and soviets. Significantly, this is Lenin's sole reference to factory committees in four volumes of writings published between February and October, an astonishing silence, given their extraordinary importance. The leaders of the CCFC endorsed Lenin's perspective of 'state workers' control', yet they placed a higher value on workers' control, not merely as a prophylactic against capitalist sabotage but as a preparation for ultimate workers' self-management. This accent on democracy in production was not shared by Lenin. For him the transformation of capitalist relations of production was to be achieved at state, not enterprise, level; and progress to socialism was to be guaranteed by the proletarian nature of the state rather than by the degree of power exercised by workers on the shop floor. Nevertheless, the significance of such differences was not yet widely appreciated: so far as rank-and-file workers were concerned, the Bolsheviks were the only party prepared to support workers' control and that was what mattered.

The relationship of the factory committees to the trade unions

The building of trade unions proved to be slower than building factory committees, yet by the time of the Third All-Russian Trade Union Conference (21–28 June 1917) there were 976 unions with a membership of 1.4 million, and by October as many as 2,000 unions with a membership of over two million. The coexistence of trade unions and factory committees led to clashes concerning their respective spheres of competence. At the First Conference of Factory Committees a majority voted in favour of the committees being separate from the unions, on the ground that their job – that of controlling production – was different from that of the trade unions. A minority of trade-union representatives, however, countered that there was no room for two organizations, and that the committees should become the basic cells of the unions. The setting up of the CCFC, alongside the Petrograd Council of Trade Unions, further ruffled trade-union feathers, and on 11 June the central board of the metalworkers' union called unequivocally for the strict subordination of the committees to the unions. The Second Conference of Factory Committees affirmed that the trade unions had the job of defending wages and conditions and of ensuring the implementation of labour legislation, and that the committees had the job of regulating production. At the All-Russian Conference in October trade-union representatives accused the committees of being parochial organizations unsuited to the broad tasks of reconstructing the national economy. Nevertheless, in spite of continuing rivary, there is evidence that the committees were slowly shifting towards acceptance of a merger with the trade unions in the long term. Moreover, outside the capital and the metalworking industry, relations were much smoother. In the textile industry, for instance, the factory committees became *de facto* cells of the trade unions even before October, thus adumbrating the relationship which was to come about in January 1918 at the First All-Russian Trade Union Congress.

Workers' militias and Red Guards

From the first, factory committees were active in setting up workers' militias to protect factory premises and maintain order in working-class districts.

After a civil militia was established by the new municipal authorities in Petrograd, the Executive Committee of the Soviet pressed the workers' militias to disband, but the latter were mistrustful of a professional militia answerable to a 'bourgeois' authority. After the April Days, as the unpopularity of the Provisional Government grew, armed detachments of workers were created, which took the name of Red Guards. These had a more political character than the militias, being concerned to defend the revolution against the threat from the right. The Red Guards had the backing of the factory committees and more radical district soviets, as well as of the Bolsheviks. Badly battered in the reaction which set in after the July Days, they received a new lease of life with the Kornilov rebellion. In Moscow at this time factory committees sent 209 envoys to the soviet to demand the formation of a unified Red Guard and weapons to arm it. By October there may have been as many as 200,000 Red Guards throughout Russia. Most were fierce supporters of the Bolshevik Party, but in their ranks there were also Left SRs and anarchists. Attempts by the Bolsheviks to give the Red Guards a more centralized structure came to little, and this, together with their low level of military training and experience, meant that the party relied principally on the soldiers of the Petrograd garrison in the October revolution. However, at least 20,000 Red Guards in Petrograd, of whom 18,000 were armed, took part in the uprising under the command of the Military-Revolutionary Committee. They were active in securing bridges and other key points on 24 October, and played a subsidiary role the following day in capturing the Winter Palace. The Red Guards really proved their mettle in combating the various outbreaks of armed resistance to the Bolsheviks, especially in the Ukraine in February 1918. The formation of the hostile Volunteer Army, however, confirmed Trotsky in his view that these decentralized and democratic formations would have to give way to a conventional army.

The Bolsheviks in power

One of the first measures enacted by the Bolshevik government was the Decree on Workers' Control, published on 14 November 1917. This affirmed the right of workers in all enterprises to set up control commissions to monitor all aspects of production, have access to all spheres of administration and, crucially, to make their decisions binding on employers. It also set up a hierarchy of control organs topped by an All-Russian Council of Workers' Control, on which trades unions, soviets and technical personnel, as well as factory committees, were represented. The drafting of the decree evidently caused contention between moderate Bolsheviks, such as V. P. Miliutin and Iu. Larin, who were fundamentally unsympathetic to workers' control *in situ* and favoured comprehensive state regulation of the economy, and members of the CCFC who wished to see rapid progress towards nationalized industry under workers' management. The opening of the archives in the former Soviet Union should allow us, finally, to determine how far the decree reflected Lenin's views, and to clarify the reasons why at this stage he backed the factory committees against the trade unions. The decree did not spell out the nature of workers' control in any detail and this proved to be a bone of contention between the CCFC and the short-lived All-Russian Council of Workers' Control. The CCFC insisted that workers' control now meant active intervention in production, whereas trade unionists and moderate Bolsheviks defined it as accounting and inspection and insisted that enterprise control commissions be subordinate to the control-distribution commissions of the relevant trade unions and to central organs in general.

As early as 26 October, the CCFC discussed with Lenin and trade-union representatives its plans for the creation of a Provisional All-Russian Council of National Economy (VSNKh) to carry out state regulation of industry. Lenin gave his support to this proposal and the commission which drafted a decree on 15 November broadly followed the ideas of the CCFC. On 1 December a decree was promulgated which established VSNKh with a remit to organize the national economy and state finance; to work out a plan for the regulation of economic life and the coordination of the various organs of economic regulation; and to confiscate, requisition or forcibly syndicate industrial enterprises where necessary. The leaders of the CCFC were well represented at its first meeting on 5 December, when N. A. Skrypnik was in the chair, and N. K. Antipov was one of two secretaries. Subsequently, as the structure of VSNKh was formalized, CCFC representation became less evident. The CCFC was also instrumental in setting up a *Sovnarkhoz* (economic council) of the Northern Region. This had its first session on 19 January and was to prove as influential as VSNKh during the next year. Because the CCFC played so signal a part in the creation of a centralized apparatus of economic regulation, some historians, such as Gennady Shkliarevsky, have argued that factory committee leaders were always predominantly apparatchiks in embryo, rather than genuine representatives of rank-and-file workers. It is true that some CCFC leaders, such as V. Ia. Chubar', N. I. Derbyshev or A.M. Kaktyn', went on to hold influential positions in Soviet administration, but this was not true of the great majority of activists.

At the grass roots the rapidly deteriorating economic situation, together with severe conflict between workers and employers, encouraged factory committees to intensify workers' control. Where employers abandoned or sought to close down their enterprises, control organs did not hesitate to take them over. Anarcho-syndicalist sentiment increased at this time and may have encouraged committees to run things independently of central authorlty, especially in the mines and on the railways. At the factories belonging to former minister A. I. Konovalov, in Boniachka and Kamenka in Ivanovo-Voznesensk province, workers backed the proposal of the anarcho-communist, Romanov, to take the factories 'into their own hands' (a widely used formula, and one often indicative of anarchist sentiment). The local Bolsheviks sent the provincial commissar of labour, A. N. Asatkin, to dissuade them and on 12 January the workers agreed that 'all the property of Konovalov should be confiscated for the benefit of the state'. Yet despite increasing anarchist influence, most takeovers remained motivated by a desire to protect jobs. In Petrograd province between November 1917 and March 1918, only 27 factories were taken over, and in nearly all cases this was viewed as a temporary measure pending the transfer of the enterprise into state ownership.

Trade-union leaders may have looked askance at 'syndicalist' excesses, but were equally critical of what they termed *mestnichestvo* (parochialism) – a tendency on the part of factory committees to collude with employers to protect supplies of fuel and raw materials and to foil attempts by local supply organs to regulate the distribution of scarce resources. This seems to have been one of the key arguments which persuaded the party leadership to back the trade unions against the factory committees, despite the fact that Bolshevik influence within the unions was less secure than in the factory committees. They came to the view, however, that only the trade unions, as organizations embracing entire branches of industry, had the organizational and ideological wherewithal to tackle the mammoth problems of economic regulation. At the First All-Russian Congress of Trade Unions (7–14 January 1918) the Bolshevik D. B. Riazanov called on the factory committees to 'choose that form of suicide which would be most useful to the labour movement as a whole'. His resolution stated that the 'parallel existence of two forms of economic organization in the working class with overlapping functions can only complicate the process of concentrating the forces of the proletariat', and called for the committees to become the basic cells of the trade unions in the workplace.

If the factory committees lost out to the trade unions at an institutional level, they may have comforted themselves with the thought that one of their chief aspirations was realized far sooner than they had dared hope. From October the CCFC had urged the government to move rapidly towards full-scale nationalization of industry as well as state regulation of the economy, but Lenin was unenthusiastic, preferring to retain a private sector under government supervision and workers' control. In response to the breakdown of industry, however, factory committees, local soviets and regional economic councils (*sovnarkhozy*) took it upon themselves to 'nationalize' enterprises threatened by closure, and pressured VSNKh to take them into state ownership. The result was that the party moved much more rapidly than it had intended towards taking industry into state ownership. The factory committees, however, had hoped that nationalization would mean workers' management, yet the government proved less willing to support this. The First Congress of *Sovnarkhozy* (25 May–4 June 1918) decided that only one-third, rather than the proposed two-thirds, of members of management boards of nationalized enterprises should be elected by workers, the rest being appointed by VSNKh or its regional councils. Even this was unacceptable to Lenin who, appalled by the plummeting levels of labour productivity, now called for the restoration of one-person management. Although the crisis in railway transportation led others to support this proposal, resistance from the factory committees and trade unions ensured that there was little progress towards it prior to 1920.

By the end of the civil war the whole of industry was nationalized, though some small plants were still run by their former owners. The worker-dominated board had given way to one-person management. The factory committees, though still capable of displaying a surprising degree of auto-nomy, were now integrated into the trade-union apparatus. The decree on factory committees issued by the All-Russian Central Council of Trade Unions and the People's Commissariat of Labour in 1920 laid down that it was their job to maintain labour discipline and increase labour productivity and it categorically forbade them to interfere in management orders. The idea of workers' control continued in an attenuated form, but it was now deemed to be the job of the workers' inspectorates, trade-union bodies responsible for monitoring affairs in critical sectors such as rail transport and food supply, and the state control organs, responsible for auditing the affairs of government departments. The ideal of workers' management had been consigned to oblivion. In 1919 only 10.8 per cent of enterprises, for which there is information, had been run by individual directors, but by the autumn of 1920 this had risen to 82 per cent. How far this outcome was determined by the terrifying problems thrown up by the imploding economy and how far by the Bolsheviks' deep-seated preference for centralization and technical expertise remains contentious.

Further reading

Avrich P. H., 'The Bolshevik Revolution and Workers' Control in Russian Industry', *Slavic Review* 22, 1 (1963), pp. 47–63.

Cherniaev V. I., 'Rabochii kontrol' i al'ternativy ego razvitiia v 1917 g.', in *Rabochie i rossiiskoe obshchestvo: vtoraia polovina XIX–nachalo XX veka* (St Petersburg, Glagol, 1994).

Itkin M. L., *Rabochii kontrol' nakanune Oktiabria* (Moscow, Vysshaia shkola, 1984).

Mikhailov N. V., 'Samoorganizatsiia trudovykh kollektivov i psikhologiia rossiiskikh rabochikh v nachale XX veka', in *Rabochie i intelligentsiia v Rossii v kontse 19-ogo veka i v nachale 20-ogo veka* (St Petersburg, Glagol, 1996).

Mints I. I., *Fabrichno-zavodskie komitety Petrograda v 1917g.: protokoly*, 2 vols. (Moscow, Nauka, 1979 and 1982).

Shkliarevsky G., *Labor in the Russian Revolution: Factory Committees and Trade Unions, 1917–1918* (New York, St Martin's Press, 1993).

Smith S. A., *Red Petrograd: Revolution in the Factories, 1917–1918* (Cambridge, Cambridge University Press, 1983).

Smith S. A., ed. and annot., *Oktiabr'skaia revoliutsiia i fabzavkomy*, 2 vols. (New York, Kraus International, 1983).

Startsev V. M., *Ocherki po istorii Petrogradskoi krasnoi gvardii i rabochei militsii* (Moscow, Nauka, 1965).

Wade R. A., *Red Guards and Workers' Militias in the Russian Revolution* (Stanford, Stanford University Press, 1984).

Family, Marriage and Relations Between the Sexes

ELIZABETH WATERS

The family was regarded by both supporters and opponents of the regime in pre-revolutionary Russia as the state in microcosm. The tsar was the father of his people, and relationships of duty and obedience in the domestic household mirrored those of the wider society. While in establishment ideology this symmetry was held to be divinely ordained, for the radical intelligentsia the patriarchal principle was unequal and oppressive, and liberation from the grip of the family a necessary parallel to liberation from political inequality and oppression.

Critics of tsarism from the 1840s onward took the dependence of women within the family as a major theme. In *What Is To Be Done?*, published in 1863, N. G. Chernyshevskii gave as much weight to his heroine's efforts to achieve emotional and psychological autonomy as to her public project of a cooperative sewing workshop. The phenomenal success enjoyed by the novel suggests the importance nihilist and populist generations paid to the private sphere and balance between lifestyle and political commitment. By the early twentieth century there was less unanimity on such matters. The failure of 1905 produced cultural and philosophical currents that decentred the struggle for the good of the people and fostered a different sense of self, less austerely utilitarian. The revolutionaries for their part remained loyal to the earlier traditions of the intelligentsia and attacked bourgeois culture for its decadence and self-indulgence, but they invested their faith in the proletariat and the mass party and no longer regarded the family as political touchstone or priority. While both F. Engels's classic, *The Origin of the Family*, and A. Bebel's *Woman and Socialism* went through several Russian editions before the revolution, neither had much impact on the day-to-day outlook of militants, who saw the factory and the class struggle as the place and mode of their activity.

Bolshevik theory and policy on the family

After the Bolsheviks took power socialist critiques of the family assumed a higher profile. The proletarian victory brought into the line of vision things previously seen as secondary or predicated on changes in the economic base. Moreover, the enormous strain of the war years on families inevitably increased their political importance. By the spring of 1917 more than 14 million men had been mobilized, an estimated 36 per cent of the male population of working age; the wives of conscripts, the *soldatki*, struggled alone in a bleak economic climate to keep their families together, often unsuccessfully as the number of waifs (*besprizornye*) bore witness.

The party spoke in vague terms of the better life that the overthrow of the old regime would bring; more specifically there were references to a new form of family based on mutual consent in which women would be free and illegitimate children have rights. In deference to the strong sense of kinship retained by workers as well as peasants, mass propaganda rarely went further than this. To the narrower audience of men and women within the party, a Marxist analysis was expounded in more or less simplified terms. The link between family and private property was demonstrated; the connection between the reform of these institutions and female emancipation was emphasized. By abolishing private property and introducing sexual equality the revolution promised to create conditions for a new type of family, to provide men and women with the opportunity to arrange their personal lives as they saw fit, no longer constrained by material considerations or hobbled by psychological hierarchies. Substitution of state institutions for family ones in the near future was often implied. This was a consequence in part of the pedagogical purpose and formulaic style of Bolshevik publishing at this time, in part of the conviction, inspired by the success of the October coup, that a fundamental restructuring of the fabric of society was possible as long as revolutionary will did not slacken. The break-up of families and the breakdown of kinship welfare patterns encouraged the view that events themselves were quickening the pace of social processes and irreversibly pushing domestic and affective relationships into the era of communism.

The Soviet government responded to the acute food shortages of the civil war by introducing rations and setting up public canteens which by 1920 were feeding over 300,000 urban families. A series of decrees introduced free meals and other benefits for young children whose health and welfare could no longer be guaranteed by parents and families. A further rise in the number of *besprizornye* was met by a rapid expansion of the system of state-run homes: by 1920–21 there were 260,637 children in care, a tenfold increase on 1917. The predictions of the socialist classics concerning private housekeeping (it would be 'transformed into a social industry') and the education of children (it was to become 'a public affair') were apparently confirmed in practice.

This was certainly the conclusion drawn by the *Zhenotdel*, the women's department of the party, which from its inception had marked transformation of the family as a key concern. Papers presented at the First All-Russian Conference of Working and Peasant Women in 1918 expressed confidence that communal solutions to the individual domestic stove and family nursery could be found. Public services would make possible the separation of kitchen and marriage and relieve women of the 'cross of motherhood'. N. I. Bukharin and E. A. Preobrazhenskii in *The ABC of Communism* (1919) drew a similar picture of the revolution transforming beyond recognition the domestic household, a throw-back to the distant past, and they looked with satisfaction to its disappearance along with a whole range of social institutions of similar genesis and function. House communes, central laundries and social education would serve the generations to come.

It is not difficult to locate statements of iconoclastic expectation. Nor is it difficult to point to sections of the social pyramid, from the politically conscious elite to the broad masses, with whom such statements cut no ice. Marxist theory was thinly spread even among the party faithful and mass movements bent on undermining the traditional family were not an ingredient of the Russian revolution. To determine the relative weight of thoughts and feelings for and against the domestic *status quo* and the influence of these thoughts and feelings on people and events is less simple. Activists in the women's department and radical theorists did not speak for all Communists, yet they were far from isolated or ineffectual. The party programme adopted in 1919 looked forward to the 'creation of a network of pre-school institutions, creches, kindergartens, hearths etc. aimed at improving social upbringing and emancipating women'. Eagerness for reform varied between departments and commissariats according to the professional ethos of the staff and the type of work in which they were engaged. Faith in the superiority of social institutions was strong in the Commissariats of Education and Welfare whose decision-makers drew on Western liberal theories of child development and social security as well as socialist doctrine. Delegates to the First All-Russian Congress for the Protection of Childhood talked in a libertarian manner of the evil of the bourgeoisie and the need to free children from parents. A. V. Lunacharsky, Commissar of Enlightenment, thought it right and beneficial to 'remove children from the family setting and its petty-bourgeois structure'. The Department for the Protection of Motherhood and Infancy, *Okhmatmlad*, set up in 1918 to assume responsibility for creches, children's homes and maternal-welfare clinics, was more inclined to rank medical imperatives above social ones. 'Open' institutions which complemented family care were observed to give children a better chance of survival and favoured for this reason even if their fit with socialist theory was less satisfactory. Yet the commitment of the department to a family in which women were equal and had the possibility of combining work with maternity was never in question. Those in charge of *prodrazverstka* (grain requisitioning) and food distribution were less ideologically inclined and saw their work in terms of crisis management, not revolutionary transformation of the domestic household.

Policies of family reform invariably lagged behind expressed intention. It was suggested by the *Zhenotdel* that there was an element of prejudice in this, an unwillingness to make the necessary sacrifices or to understand the crucial leverage of the family in society. For the most part discrepancies between theory and practice were more simply explained by poverty and overwhelming demand. A. D. Kalinina, commissar of the Moscow Provincial Department of Social Welfare, and a believer in substituting 'social upbringing' for the family, noted sadly the inadequacy of the buildings used for children's homes, the lack of equipment, and the inexperience of personnel. The steep rise in the number of children in care made it all but impossible, others lamented, 'to realize the tasks of communist education'.

As the passage of the civil war blunted hopes for the immediate construction of communist society so the urge to enumerate its delights declined. Socialized eating and upbringing had less appeal when food was consistently unappetizing, canteens unsanitary, and the mortality rates in overcrowded children's homes relentlessly high. The reluctance of the masses to endorse communal solutions except as a survival measure undoubtedly also weakened maximalist confidence, though by no means extinguished hopes for social justice through social engineering.

Marriage and divorce

The reform of marriage and divorce illustrates well the tug between liberal ideas and Russian social realities. Tsarist law encoded the subordination of women in family and society, requiring the wife to obey her husband, take his name, and follow his place of residence. Social-democratic critique of such legislation was long established and an alternative Bolshevik programme, at least in broad outline, was not controversial. Two of the early decrees of the Soviet regime introduced the principle of civil registration and of individual freedom of action in initiating and ending marital relationships. The decree on marriage passed on 20 December 1917 was superseded the following October by a Family Code, which covered the same terrain in greater detail: marriage was by mutual consent and could be entered into by all but the closest relatives; neither religious difference nor membership of a monastic order was recognized as an impediment; couples were no longer obliged to undergo a church ceremony, in fact henceforth only civil registrations had legal force. The changes in divorce law were even more far-reaching. Previously divorce had been under the jurisdiction of the Holy Synod, and virtually unobtainable; the decree on divorce of 19 December 1917 made it freely available at the request of both or one of the parties in a simple civil process. The 1918 Code set out procedures for application to the local courts in cases of disagreement between the spouses and made provision for appeals against rulings. The assumption of the law-makers was that when marriages went wrong they could be dissolved, and that the role of the court should be limited to mediation in unresolved conflicts of interest between spouses and protection of the rights and welfare of children.

With these reforms Soviet Russia not only caught up but overtook the modern family legislation of other Western countries. A. G. Goikhbarg, an ex-Menshevik lawyer who played a key role in drawing up the new laws, characterized them as 'almost entirely free of male egoism' and believed they would ensure equality and independence within marriage. Ease of divorce, and the explicit rejection of adoption and of community of property in marriage were unprecedented and demonstrated a willingness to undermine the pillars of the traditional family. At the same time, the law enumerated in considerable detail the mutual rights and duties of family members. Not only were parents legally obliged to care for and educate their offspring – illegitimate as well as legitimate – but children had to provide for needy parents and relatives who were not in receipt of state aid. Husbands were obliged by the decree of 1917 to pay maintenance to divorced wives, and the 1918 Code made both spouses equally responsible for the support of a divorced partner who was unable to work. The Bolsheviks may have looked to the state to provide for individual security in the society of the future but while welfare benefits were piecemeal and inadequate marriage remained a social contract .

It was one thing to pass laws, another to broadcast them and ensure compliance. The obstacles created by poor communications and low literacy rates were compounded by the chaos and disruption of civil war, although conscription did offer some effective ways and means of instruction. The young, handsome and politically literate Red Army soldier, successfully seeking the hand of a peasant girl and leading her not to the altar but to the registry office (ZAGS), was a propaganda cliché, and one which lingered on into the mid-twenties in publications such as 'Two Weddings', a short story that contrasts the traditional wedding and hard wifehood of the mother with her daughter's post-revolutionary marriage to a commissar, celebrated in a ZAGS with every expectation of living happily ever after. That the message of greater freedom of marriage and divorce was heard even in the countryside is evident from the reports of widespread dissatisfaction at the threat it posed to the integrity of the peasant household. This dissidence led in 1922 to a legal amendment prohibiting the division of landholdings for purposes other than establishing new agricultural communities. A divorcee was obliged to accept monetary compensation.

Data on marriage and divorce in the years immediately following the new legislation are patchy and unreliable. In 1921 the marriage rate, low since 1914, soared as the upheavals of war and revolution came to an end; it reached 9.8 per 1,000 of the population in 1925 and 10.6 in 1926 (the 1913 figure was 8.5). The number of married girls in the 16–19 age group rose from 18.7 per cent in the 1914–18 period to 22.1 per cent in the years 1919 to 1923; the figures for the 20–24 and 25–29 age groups also rose from 58 per cent to 62.8 per cent and 78 per cent to 82 per cent, respectively. The number of divorces in European Russia in 1924, the first year for which official figures were published, stood at 85,547 and in 1926 reached 122,760, the increase representing a rise from 106.6 to 144.6 per 1,000 marriages.

The desirability of using law as an instrument of family change was hotly debated during the 1920s. The rising divorce rates were seen by some as the collapse of the family rather than the birth of a new one; female poverty, homeless children and an 'epidemic of abortions' were too high a price to pay for modern legislation, these critics argued. Others interpreted the apparent instability of personal relationships as a positive response to the new freedom of choice in private life and in particular to the emancipation of women. A third approach was to accept that the consequences of legislation would be both positive and negative, but to link family forms ultimately with fundamental changes in the social formation.

At the end of the nineteenth and beginning of the twentieth century, land reforms and the spread of literacy and city lifestyles were accompanied in European Russia by an increase in the number of peasant households. The urban imbalance in the sex ratio, pronounced in the early period of industrialization, was evening out by 1914 and continued to close very rapidly in the post-revolutionary period as the working-class family became a more common phenomenon. In Moscow by 1926, 51 per cent of women were married as compared with 44 per cent in 1897, and the percentage of widows had fallen from 22 at the end of the nineteenth century to 16.7. The ratio of men to women – an even more telling index – fell between 1897 and 1926 from 132:100 to 95:100. Family and household in European Russia were steadily becoming synonymous – and also smaller, as the birth-rate, which rose sharply in the wake of the civil war, fell again and continued its downward curve.

In non-European Russia no such trends towards smaller families were discernible and post-revolutionary reform took a different course. In these regions the tsarist regime had left local custom alone, recognizing in the tight weave of religion and patriarchy systems that paralleled if not exactly replicated its own model. The Bolsheviks declared the Muslim practices of bride price (*kalym*) and polygamy symbolic of women's subordination in marriage and the family, and the party published the marriage laws of the RSFSR in the newspapers of non-Russian areas as it gained political hold. In 1920 a decree banning *kalym* and polygamy was passed in Kirgizia, in 1921 similar legislation was enacted in Turkmenistan and the First All-Kazakh Congress of Soviets expressed its intention to follow suit. Enthusiasm for family reform, however, was weak among the native Bolshevik cadres, and not until the regime had consolidated its control over Central Asia in the mid-1920s did campaigning begin in earnest. The ban on *kalym* and polygamy challenged religious doctrine and core cultural norms, and enforcement provoked a violent retaliation from male kin who felt themselves and their families dishonoured.

Relations between the sexes

Socialists had traditionally played down sexual antagonisms, considering them imaginary, or at most secondary to those based on class. The Marxist classics had described women as the proletarians of the family and this did give a tentative legitimacy to female marital rebellion. One delegate at the 1918 women's conference announced that she had come against her husband's will, in fact had 'thrown off his yoke'. A leaflet produced in Ivanovo-Vosnesensk province for International Women's Day (8 March) 1919 ranked family and husband alongside capital as instruments of oppression. In his popular novel, *Cement*, F. V. Gladkov traced against the backdrop of the revolution the political transformation of a working-class woman and her re-evaluation of family roles, conjugal as well as maternal. Other novelists were more cautious in their appraisal of women's capacity to appreciate social change or to command public respect. In the stories of I. E. Babel' female honour is not an unknown concept and communities may on occasion be willing to defend it, but indignities and violence are the more common currency. B. A. Pil'niak refers to coercive sex in passing, a phenomenon apparently too common to require elaboration.

The Bolsheviks were divided in retrospect over the immediate impact of the revolution on relations between the sexes. A survey carried out in the 1920s which asked whether the revolution had heightened or weakened the power of sexual feelings found a third of respondents felt the latter to be the case; in 1927 a Komsomol (Communist Youth League) newspaper expressed its conviction that the revolution had swept away all interest in pornography; a collection of short stories published in the mid-1920s recalled how personal life had faded in importance during the civil war. A medical specialist, L. M. Vasilevskii, on the other hand, considered sexual licence the 'brother of standing armies and the barrack system'. Women were said to have acted 'unnaturally' – that is promiscuously – during the civil war. Zhenia, the notorious young communist in A. M. Kollontai's short story *Three Generations* published in 1923, practised 'free love' at the front and subsequently had an affair with her stepfather who may or may not be the father of her child. E. M. Iaroslavskii related the non-fictional case of a woman who lost her party membership because she had sexual relations with two men but was reinstated when it became known she had been at the front during the civil war. Revolutionary behaviour, whether it was remembered as chaste or licentious, was understood not as a socialist prototype but as a temporary response to social stress. The revolution in sexual relationships was expected to take time and was in the 1920s still largely spoken of in the future tense.

In 1917 the 'sexual question' was not an item on conference agendas and few leading Bolsheviks commented on the matter. Clara Zetkin has left record of a conversation with Lenin in 1920 in which he is said to have made an unflattering assessment of contemporary morality and attacked the 'glass of water theory' that sex was a physical reflex of the same order as thirst. It should be borne in mind that Zetkin was setting down her reminiscences after Lenin's death when his authority was ritually invoked by Communists, and although several of the views she attributes to him are corroborated from other sources – sexuality was a diversion from the class struggle and bourgeois morality was corrupt – the fierce attacks she documents on 'hypertrophy in sexual matters' and the mores of the young appear to have more to do with her concerns in 1924 than with Lenin's during the civil war. Kollontai was the only Bolshevik to have written at any length before 1917 on love and sex and her essays were republished shortly after the revolution. Her aim was, first, to rescue the subject from relegation to the trivial by presenting it in the context of a Marxist analysis of society and change, and second, to demonstrate the subtle and far-reaching influence of concepts of power and possession on emotions and relationships. By the early twenties she was erroneously but firmly identified with the 'glass of water theory', and dismissed as an extremist, incorrect and un-Leninist. This should not obscure the fact that during the revolutionary period many of her ideas were considered rather mainstream: belief in the perfectibility of human nature, or at least the potential for its considerable improvement was widely shared, and the class nature of morality was a commonplace.

A provincial pamphlet on prostitution published in 1920, for example, explained how prostitution was based on exploitation and would disappear along with oppression, and how it could not involve working-class men because the decadence characteristic of the ruling class was not found amongst the proletariat. The authors did not anticipate large-scale prostitution in the new Soviet state. In fact, contemporaries had noticed a decline in organized prostitution earlier, at the outbreak of war in 1914. The exodus of men to the front reduced the client pool and many brothels closed. In Saratov on 5 April 1917 a meeting of prostitutes, presumably inspired by revolutionary example, voted to disband and take up honest work, though apparently before long many of them, unable to make a living, were regretting their decision. In the chaotic barter economy of the revolution and civil war organized prostitution did not recover, but many women were forced to exchange sex for food, shelter and protection. As a result of these encounters sexually transmitted diseases spread and it was this that forced the Bolsheviks to recognize the persistence of the problem and to set up, at the end of 1919, an interdepartmental commission on prostitution under the Commissariat of Health.

The February revolution had abolished tsarist regulations requiring prostitutes to undergo regular medical check-ups and surrender their internal passports in exchange for the incriminating 'yellow ticket'. Asked by the Soviet government to comment on further legal options, the commission rejected the criminalization of prostitution, favoured by some as a way to contain venereal diseases, on the grounds that the sentencing of women and not their clients was unfair discrimination, and that the exchange of sexual favours for economic benefits was anyway the very principle that underlay traditional marriage. This was very much along the lines of decades of European socialist writing on the subject. In the same spirit, the 'struggle' against prostitution was interpreted very broadly, the commission organizing lectures on sexual education, the family and morality. One of its members, I. Gel'man, spoke of his hope for the 'liberation of the human soul from the vice-like grip of the past'. Such hopeful liberalism notwithstanding, the commission ruled that full-time prostitutes be categorized along with beggars and vagrants as deserters from the labour front and sent to camps, a clear case of socialist orthodoxy giving way to the ideologies of regimentation characteristic of the civil war period.

This intervention in private life proved, however, the exception rather than the rule. Measures to regulate marriage and reproduction were discussed – given the prevalence of venereal diseases ought not a medical to be compulsory for bride and bridegroom? given the loss of life in war and revolution ought not abortion to be a criminal offence? – but they were not introduced. A medical before marriage was deemed impractical, since couples might avoid it simply by choosing a *de facto* relationship. V. P. Lebedeva, head of *Okhmatmlad*, used a similar argument to counter the views of Professor N. K. Kol'tsov, an eminent scientist of radical sympathies who took the platform at the first conference on the protection of motherhood and infancy to explain why abortion was not desirable from the eugenics point of view and why the state should fight the 'egoism' that drove women to terminate pregnancies. Repressive laws, she said, did not work.

The tsarist laws which made abortion a criminal offence had been a focus of critical discussion before the revolution for liberal and radical doctors and lawyers alike. Socialists, including Lenin, were on record as supporting the principle of birth control, but they did not seek actively to promote it. The punitive abortion laws shared the fate of the rest of the tsarist code in October 1917, and discussions began soon after within the Commissariats of Justice and Health on what if anything should replace them. In private doctors expressed alarm at the prospect of legal abortion and official questionnaires sent to local medical authorities elicited some strong objections. The debate was taken into the public arena by the Bolshevik doctor, N. A. Semashko, who in the pages of *Izvestiia* defended legal abortion while specifically dismissing freedom of choice as its rationale: the question, he argued, should be viewed not from the point of view of the rights of women, 'but from the point of view of the interest of the whole of society (the collective) for which abortion is undoubtedly harmful'. Though this was not a statement of party position – there was no official theory or policy – it was probably more representative and influential than the counterview that women's interests and Marxism were compatible, even necessarily synonymous, and abortion a right that could be exercised even against the interests of the state. The government decree of November 1920 which finally legalised hospital abortion declared that since the state was unable to provide for all children it must come to women's aid. Untroubled motherhood rather than untrammelled sex was the object. Government and people were agreed that childbearing was woman's natural estate and unless circumstances were acutely adverse she would not want to terminate a pregnancy.

Motherhood, a central icon of tsarist Russia, did undergo a brief revolutionary metamorphosis. Maxim Gorky pictured women mothering husbands, lovers and even men in general; he looked forward to the time when women would 'smile the smile of the Madonna' and press to their breasts the 'new-born man of Russia'. 'Marriage' of the people and the revolution was one popular motif in the political culture of 1917; revolution as Russia's child was another. Metaphors from private life did not long survive the onset of the civil war which promoted images that were exclusively masculine and non-familial.

The extent to which the Bolsheviks were prepared to use the family as an instrument of social engineering has been an issue for anti-communists, socialists, feminists and historians, though attention has focused on the 1920s and 1930s rather than the revolution. Western historians have cleared the regime of 'silly' charges of nationalizing women or preaching 'community of wives' and underlined the revolution's modernizing intentions, though it is doubtful that this emphasis will be universally accepted and likely that evaluations of Bolshevik theory and practice will continue to generate debate and disagreement.

Much of the scholarly research on Soviet marriage and family is recent, a response to the rise of social history and the development of women's and gender studies. Bolshevik ideologies, laws and party policies furnished early topics as sources were more easily available. Greater access to a wider range of material – archival, regional and statistical – is beginning to place this pioneering work in broader context. The questions of interconnections between long-term social processes and the immediate impact of war and revolution in the making of private life can now be productively posed.

Further reading

Bystrianskii V., *Kommunizm, brak i sem'ia* (Petrograd, 1921).
Kollontai A., *Novaia moral' i rabochii klass* (Moscow, VTsIK, 1918).
Kollontai A., *Sem'ia i kommunisticheskoe gosudarstvo* (Moscow, Gosizdat, 1920).
Kollontai A., *Love of Worker Bees* (London, Virago, 1977).

Lapidus G., *Women in Soviet Society: Equality, Development and Social Change* (Berkeley, University of California Press, 1978).

Schlesinger R., *Changing Attitudes in Soviet Russia: The Family* (London, Routledge and Kegan Paul, 1949), pp. 81–168.

Stites R., *The Women's Liberation Movement: Russian Feminism, Nihilism and Bolshevism, 1860–1930* (Princeton, Princeton University Press, 1978).

Peasant Armies

ORLANDO FIGES

Introduction

Until recently the history of the civil war was written as a conflict between the Reds and the Whites. But the opening up of the Soviet archives has revealed that behind the main battle lines there was also a whole series of hidden civil wars between peasant armies and both the two main sides. The most important peasant wars were in western Siberia, the south-east Ukraine, the Don, the northern Caucasus, the middle Volga region, and Tambov province in central Russia. But throughout the country there were smaller revolts as the peasants took up arms to defend their villages against the conscriptions and the requisitionings of both Reds and Whites.

The Soviet establishment concealed these peasant wars. Local peasant armies that fought against the Whites were mislabelled 'Red partisans', even though they usually had their own independent ideals and organization. Peasant armies that fought against the Reds were meanwhile dismissed as 'kulak counterrevolutions', stage-managed by the SRs or the Whites. Documents about them were locked up in the archives, and made available only to the most trusted Communist historians. Russian *émigré* and Western historians, such as Mikhail Frenkin and Oliver Radkey, who tried to write about these revolts objectively, were limited to fragments of frequently misleading information from the contemporary Soviet press.

It took another revolution to reveal the real extent of these peasant wars. Today, with the archives almost fully open, historians are constantly discovering important documents about unknown rebellions. The first collection of these documents (on the peasant war in Tambov province) was published in 1994, and further collections are due to appear. In time it will become possible for historians to compare all the various insurrections and to draw conclusions from them about the peasantry – their hopes and fears and limitations – in the revolution and civil war. What follows below is intended as a digest of what we know so far, and as a framework for future research.

Peasant armies against the Whites

All the White armies were plagued by peasant revolts in the rear. It was a reflection of the problems they encountered in trying to conscript soldiers and requisition foodstuffs from a peasantry that was largely hostile to their counterrevolutionary intentions. The Whites tended to counteract this problem with increasing repression, but this merely strengthened the peasantry's resistance and drove many of them to form motley armies – armed as much with pitchforks as with rusty hunting guns – to defend their villages against the Whites.

Some of these peasant armies fought as partisans alongside the Red Army and later became regular units of it. The village army of Domashki in Novouzensk district, Samara province, formed in 1918 to fight Ataman Dutov's Cossacks, was a classic example. It became the nucleus of the 219th Domashki Rifle Division, a regular detachment of the Fourth Red Army. The Pugachev, Novouzensk, Krasnokutsk and Kurilovo regiments were all set up in a similar way. All the soldiers were relatives and neighbours. In the Kurilovo Regiment there was a father with six sons. Their cohesion was unmatched by any other fighting force in the civil war, with the exception of the Cossack detachments formed by individual stanitsas, which were similar in many ways.

But most peasant armies fought against the Whites independently of the Bolsheviks. This was true of the two main regions of peasant war: in Siberia against Admiral Kolchak's forces; and in the Ukraine against General Denikin's.

From the start of its military campaign, Kolchak's army was forced to deal with numerous peasant revolts in the rear – notably in Slavgorod, south-east of Omsk, and in Minusinsk on the Enisei. This was not so much a Red partisan movement, as Soviet historians described it, although Bolshevik activists, usually in a united front with the anarchists and Left SRs, often played a major role in the organization of the movement. It was, rather, a vast peasant war to defend the revolution in the villages against the Omsk regime. A good example of its ideology is to be found at the First Peasant Congress of Insurgents from Kansk, Krasnoyarsk and Achinsk districts in April 1919. The congress proposed a whole 'constitution of peasant power', with a 'peasant government', communal taxes, and the 'distribution of the riches of the land among the toiling peasantry'. It even passed a 'peasant code' which set sentences of community service for those found guilty of drunken brawls, gambling, catching spawning fish, and – an act evidently seen by the peasant delegates on a par with these – rape.

The partisan movement was strongest in those regions – Tomsk and Enisei provinces in central Siberia, the Altai and Semipalatinsk in the south, and the Amur valley in the east – where the most recent Russian immigrants were concentrated. These were generally the poorer peasants, many of whom had to supplement their income by working on the railways and down the mines. But the movement also spread to the richer farming regions as the repressions of the Omsk regime increased. Peasant deserters from Kolchak's army played a leading role in the partisan bands. They had that little extra knowledge of the outside world which can be enough in a peasant community to catapult a young man into power. The peasant bands fought by guerrilla methods, to which the wild and remote forest regions of the taiga were so well adapted. Sometimes they joined forces with the Red Army units which had been hiding in the taiga since the Bolsheviks had been forced out of Siberia during the summer of 1918. The partisans' destruction of miles of track and their constant ambushes of the trains virtually halted the transportation of vital supplies along the Trans-Siberian Railway to Kolchak's armies for much of the offensive. Thousands of his soldiers had to be withdrawn from the front against the Reds in order to deal with the partisans. They waged a ruthless war of terror against them, shooting hundreds of hostages and setting fire to dozens of villages in the partisan strongholds of Kansk and Achinsk, where the wooded and hilly terrain was perfect for holding up the trains. This largely succeeded in pushing the insurgents away from the railway, but since the terror was also unleashed on villages unconnected with the partisans it merely fanned the flames of peasant war. As Kolchak's army retreated eastwards, it found itself increasingly surrounded by hostile partisans. Mutinies and desertion spread through its ranks as the peasant conscripts from Siberia neared their villages. Future research on this topic will show if the Whites were defeated by the Reds or if they collapsed as a result of their problems with the peasantry in the rear.

The south-eastern Ukraine, where Nestor Makhno's peasant partisans were largely in control throughout the civil war, was a major thorn in the side of Denikin's army. Nestor Makhno was the Pancho Villa of the Russian revolution. He was born in 1889 in Huliai Pole, the centre of his peasant insurrection. In 1905 he had joined the anarchists and, after seven years in the Butyrka Prison, returned to Huliai Pole in 1917, where he formed the Peasant Union – later reformed as a soviet – and organized a brigade, which carried out the seizure of the local gentry's estates. During the civil war Makhno's partisans fought almost everyone: the Rada forces; General Kaledin's Cossacks; the Germans and the Hetmanates; Petliura's Ukrainian nationalists; the rival bands of Grigoriev and countless other warlords; the Whites; and the Reds. The strength of his guerrilla army lay in the quality and the speed of its cavalry, in the support it received from the peasantry, in its intimate knowledge of the local terrain, and in the fierce loyalty of its men. Makhno's alleged exploits, which included drinking bouts of superhuman length, gave him a legendary status among the local peasants (they called him 'Batko', meaning 'father'). It was not unlike the seventeenth-century peasant myth of Stenka Razin as a champion of truth and justice blessed with supernatural powers. Under the black flag of the anarchists, Makhno stood for a stateless peasant revolution based on the local self-rule of the free and autonomous soviets which had emerged in the countryside during 1917. When the Whites advanced into the Ukraine Makhno put his 15,000 men at the disposal of the Reds. In exchange for arms from Moscow, his troops became part of the Third Division under P. E. Dybenko, although they retained their own internal partisan organization. Trotsky made a point of blaming their lack of discipline for the Red defeats. In June he ordered the arrest of Makhno as a 'counterrevolutionary' – his anarchist conception of a local peasant revolution was inimical to the proletarian dictatorship – and had several of his followers shot. Makhno's partisans fled to the forests and turned their guns against the Reds. Most of the peasants in the south-east Ukraine supported his revolt.

Peasant armies against the Reds

During 1918–19 there were several hundred peasant revolts behind the Red lines. But with one or two notable exceptions, such as the 'War of the Chapany' on the Volga during the spring of 1919, these were largely local protests against the excesses of the Reds, and did not result in the organization of large-scale peasant armies comparable to those against the Whites. Full-scale peasant war against the Bolsheviks did not really take off until the summer of 1920 – by which time the defeat of the Whites had been assured. However much the peasants disliked the Reds, they feared a counterrevolution even more.

The spread of peasant wars during 1920 was not just due to the defeat of the Whites. Three years of Bolshevik requisitioning had brought much of the countryside to the brink of famine. The violence of the requisitioning brigades, the widespread corruption and petty despotism of the local Soviet and party officials, had made many peasants hate the new regime.

By the autumn of 1920 the whole of the country was inflamed with peasant wars. Makhno's peasant army, still up to 15,000 strong after Wrangel's defeat, roamed across the Ukrainian steppe and, together with countless other local bands, succeeded in paralysing much of the rural Soviet infrastructure until the summer of 1921. In the central Russian province of Tambov the Antonov rebellion was supported by virtually the entire peasant population: Soviet power ceased to exist there between the autumn of 1920 and the summer of 1921. In Voronezh, Saratov, Samara, Simbirsk and Penza provinces there were smaller but no less destructive peasant rebel armies which caused havoc for the Bolsheviks and effectively limited their power to the towns. Hundreds of small-scale bandit armies controlled the steppelands between Ufa and the Caspian Sea. In the Don and the Kuban

the Cossacks and the peasants were at last united by their common hatred
of the Bolsheviks. The rebel armies of the Caucasian mountains numbered
well over 30,000 fighters. In Belorussia the nationalist-led peasants took
over most of the countryside and forced the Soviets of Minsk and Smolensk
to be evacuated. By far the biggest (though least studied) of the peasant
revolts broke out in western Siberia: the whole of the Tiumen', Omsk,
Cheliabinsk, Tobolsk, Ekaterinburg and Tomsk regions, complete with
most of the major towns, fell into the hands of the peasant rebels, up to
60,000 of them under arms, and virtually the whole of the Soviet infrastructure remained paralysed during the first six months of 1921. And yet
throughout Russia the same thing was happening on a smaller scale: angry
peasants were taking up arms and chasing the Bolsheviks out of the village.
Less than 50 miles from the Kremlin there were villages where it was dangerous for a Bolshevik to go.

What is remarkable about these peasant wars is that they shared so many
common features, despite the huge distances between them and the different
contexts in which they took place.

Most of the larger rebellions had started out in 1920 as small-scale peasant revolts against the requisitioning of food which, as a result of their
incompetent and often brutal handling by the local Communists, soon
became inflamed and spread into full-scale peasant wars. The Tambov
rebellion was typical. It had started in August 1920 in the village of
Kamenka when a food brigade arrived to collect its share of the new grain
levy. At over 11 million *pudy*, the levy for the province had clearly been set
much too high. The 1920 harvest had been very poor and if the peasants
had paid the levy in full they would have been left with only one *pud* of
grain per person, barely 10 per cent of their normal requirements for food,
seed and fodder. Already in October there were hunger riots. By January, in
the words of the Bolshevik V. A. Antonov-Ovseenko who was sent in to
help put down the revolt, 'half the peasantry was starving'. The peasants of
Kamenka were relatively wealthy – which meant they starved more slowly
than the rest – and an extra levy was imposed on them. They refused to pay
the extra levy, killed several members of the requisitioning brigade, and
armed themselves with guns and pitchforks to fight off the Soviet reinforcements sent in from Tambov to put their revolt down. Neighbouring villages
joined the uprising and a rudimentary peasant army was soon organized. It
fought under the Red flag – reclaiming the symbols of the revolution was an
important aspect of these people's uprisings – and was led by the local peasant SR hero, Grigorii Pluzhnikov, who had organized the war against the
gentry estates in 1905 and 1917. Meanwhile, a network of Peasant Unions
(STKs) began to emerge in the villages – often they were organized by the
local SRs – which replaced the soviets and helped to supply the insurgent
army. Over 50 Communists were shot. The speed with which the revolt
spread caught the Bolsheviks in Tambov unprepared. The Soviet and the
party apparatus in the province had become extremely weak. People had

been leaving the party in droves – many of them ex-SRs who soon joined the rebels – as industrial strikes and corruption scandals had made belonging to it both a source of danger and a source of embarrassment. Because of the war against Poland there were only 3,000 Red Army troops, most of them extremely unreliable, in the provincial garrison. They had only one machine-gun for the whole of the insurgent district of Kirsanov. The rebels took advantage of this weakness and marched on the provincial capital. Thousands of peasants joined them as they approached Tambov. The Bolsheviks were thrown into panic. When reinforcements arrived they forced the rebels back and unleashed a campaign of terror in the villages. Several rebel strongholds were burned to the ground, whole herds of cattle were confiscated, and hundreds of peasants were executed. Yet this merely fanned the flames of peasant war. 'The whole population took to the woods in fright and joined the rebels', reported one local Communist. 'Even peasants once loyal to us had nothing left to lose and threw in their lot with the revolt.' From Kirsanov the rebellion soon spread throughout the southern half of Tambov province and parts of neighbouring Saratov, Voronezh and Penza. It was at this point that the Left SR Aleksandr Antonov took over the leadership of the revolt, building it up by the end of 1920 into what Lenin himself later acknowledged was the greatest threat his regime had ever had to face.

Soviet propaganda portrayed the peasant rebels as 'kulaks'. But the evidence suggests, on the contrary, that these were general peasant revolts. The rebel armies were basically made up of ordinary peasants, as suggested by their agricultural weapons, pitchforks, axes, pikes and hoes, although deserters from the civil-war armies also joined their ranks and often played a leading role. In Tambov province there were 110,000 deserters, 60,000 of them in the woodland districts around Kirsanov, on the eve of the revolt. Many of the rebels were destitute youths – mostly under the age of 25. F. Popov's peasant army in Saratov province was described as 'dressed in rags', although some wore stolen suits. The bands of the Orenburg steppe were, in the words of the party organization of the Buguruslan district, made up of

> people who have been completely displaced through poverty and hunger. The kulaks help the bandits materially but themselves take up arms only very rarely indeed. The bands find it very easy to enlist supporters. The slogan 'Kill the Communists! Smash the Collective Farms!' is very popular among the most backward and downtrodden strata of the peasantry.

Inevitably, given the general breakdown of order, criminal elements also attached themselves to the peasant armies, looting property, raping women and perpetrating pogroms against the Jews. Recent historians, inclined to idealize the peasant armies, have ignored their darker side.

The strength of the rebel armies derived from their close ties with the village: it was this that enabled them to carry out the guerrilla-type operations that so confounded the Red Army commanders. What the Americans later learned in Vietnam – that conventional armies, however well armed, are ill-equipped to fight a well-supported peasant army – the Russians discovered in 1921 (and rediscovered 60 years later in Afghanistan). The rebel armies were organized on a partisan basis with each village responsible for mobilizing, feeding and equipping its own troops. In Tambov and parts of western Siberia the STKs, which were closely connected to the village communes, performed these functions. Elsewhere it was the communes themselves. The Church and the local SRs, especially those on the left of the party, also helped to organize the revolt in some regions, although the precise role of the SR leadership is still clouded in mystery.

With the support of the local population the rebel armies were, in the words of Antonov-Ovseenko, 'scarcely vulnerable, extraordinarily invisible, and so to speak ubiquitous'. Peasants could become soldiers, and soldiers peasants, at a moment's notice. The villagers were the ears and eyes of the rebel armies – women, children, even beggars served as spies – and everywhere the Reds were vulnerable to ambush. Yet the rebels, when pursued by the Reds, would suddenly vanish – either by merging with the local population, or with fresh horses supplied by the peasants, far outstripping the pursuing Reds. Where the Reds could travel 30 miles a day the rebels could travel up to 100 miles. Their intimate knowledge of the local terrain, moreover, enabled them to move around and launch assaults at night. This supreme mobility easily compensated for their lack of artillery. They literally ran circles around the Reds, whose commanders complained they were 'everywhere'. Instead of engaging the Reds in the open, the rebels stuck to the remote hills and forests (hence the peasant bands were often called the 'greens') waiting for the right moment to launch a surprise attack before retreating out of sight. Their strategy was purely defensive: they aimed not to march on Moscow – nor even for the most part to attack the local towns – but to cut themselves off from its influence. They blew up bridges, cut down telegraph poles and pulled up railway tracks to paralyse the Reds. It was difficult to cope with such tactics, especially since none of the Red commanders had ever come across anything like them before. The first small units sent to fight the rebels were nearly all defeated – M. N. Tukhachevskii said their 'only purpose was to arm the rebels' – and they soon became demoralized. Many Reds even joined the rebels.

The aims and ideology of the revolts were strikingly uniform – and this reflects the common aspirations of the peasant revolution throughout Russia and the Ukraine. All the revolts sought to re-establish the peasant self-rule of 1917–18. Most expressed this in the slogan 'Soviet Power without the Communists!' or some variation on this theme. The same basic idea was sometimes expressed in the rather confused slogans: 'Long Live Lenin! Down with Trotsky!', or 'Long Live the Bolsheviks! Death to the Communists!' Many peasants were under the illusion that the Bolsheviks and the Communists were two separate parties: the party's change of name in February 1918 had yet to be communicated to the remote villages. The peasants believed that 'Lenin' and the 'Bolsheviks' had brought them peace, that they had allowed them to seize the gentry's land, to sell their foodstuffs freely on the market, and to regulate their local communities through their own elected soviets. On the other hand, they believed that 'Trotsky' and the 'Communists' had brought civil war, had taken away the gentry's land and used it for collective farms, had stamped out free trade with requisitioning, and had usurped their local soviets.

With the slogan of 'Soviet Power', the peasant rebels were no doubt partly seeking to give their protest a 'legitimate' form. They sometimes called their rebel organs 'soviets'. None the less, their commitment to the democratic ideal of the revolution was no less genuine for this pretence. All the peasant movements were hostile to the Whites. Many of the rebel leaders (e.g. Makhno, A. P. Sapozhkov, P. Mironov, I. Serov, K. T. Vakhulin, Maslakov and S. I. Kolesov) had fought with the Reds, and often with distinction, against the Whites. Others had served as Soviet officials. Antonov had been the Soviet Chief of Police in the Kirsanov district until the summer of 1918, when, like the rest of the Left SRs, he had broken with the Bolsheviks and turned that same region into a bastion of revolt. Sapozhkov, who led a rebel peasant army in the Novouzensk district of Samara during the summer of 1920, had formerly been the Chairman of the Novouzensk Soviet, a hero of its defence against the Cossacks, and a leader of the Bolshevik underground in Samara against the *Komuch*. G. Piatakov, a peasant rebel leader in the neighbouring Saratov province, had been a Soviet Provisions Commissar. N. V. Voronovich, one of the rebel leaders in the Caucasus, had been the chairman of the Luga Soviet in 1917. He had even taken part in the defence of Petrograd against Kornilov.

The peasants often called their revolts a 'revolution' – and that is just what they aimed for them to be. As in 1917, much of the rural state infrastructure was swept aside by a great tidal wave of peasant anger and destruction. This was a savage war of vengeance against the Communist regime. Thousands of Bolsheviks were brutally murdered. Many were the victims of gruesome (and symbolic) tortures: ears, tongues and eyes were cut out; limbs, heads and genitals were cut off; stomachs were sliced open and stuffed with wheat; crosses were branded on foreheads and torsos; Communists were nailed to trees, burned alive, drowned under ice, buried up to their necks and eaten by dogs or rats, while crowds of peasants watched and shouted. Party and Soviet offices were turned upside down. Police stations and rural courts were burned to the ground. Soviet schools and propaganda centres were vandalized. As for the collective farms, the vast majority of them were destroyed and their tools and livestock redistributed among the local peasants. The same thing happened to the Soviet grain-collecting stations, mills, distilleries, beer factories and bread shops. Once the rebel forces had seized the installation 'huge crowds of peasants' would follow in their wake removing piecemeal the requisitioned grain and carting it back to their villages. This

reclamation of the 'people's property' – in effect a new 'looting of the loot-
ers' – helped the rebel armies to consolidate the support of the local population. But not all the rebels were such Robin Hoods. Simple banditry also
played a role. Most of the rebel armies held up trains. In the Donbass region
such hold-ups were said to be 'almost a daily occurrence' during the spring
of 1921. Raids on the local towns, and sometimes the peasants, were another
common source of livelihood. The appearance of these rebel forces, with their
vast herds of stolen livestock and their long caravans of military hardware,
liquor barrels, and bags of grain must have been very colourful. Antonov's
partisans made off from Kniazeva in the Serdobsk district with the entire
contents of the costumes and props department of the local theatre, complete with magic lanterns, dummies and bustles.

By March 1921 Soviet power in much of the countryside had virtually
ceased to exist. Provincial Bolshevik organizations sent desparate telegrams
to Moscow claiming they were powerless to resist the rebels and calling for
immediate reinforcements. The consignment of grain to the cities had been
brought to a virtual halt within the rebel strongholds. As the urban food crisis deepened and more and more workers went on strike, it became clear
that the Bolsheviks were facing a revolutionary situation. Lenin was thrown
into absolute panic: every day he bombarded the local Red commanders
with violent demands for the swiftest possible suppression of the revolts by
whatever means. 'We are barely holding on', he acknowledged in March.
The peasant wars, he told the opening session of the Tenth Party Congress
on 8 March, were 'far more dangerous than all the Denikins, Iudeniches and
Kolchaks put together'. Together with the strikes and the Kronstadt mutiny
of March, they would finally force that congress to abandon the widely
hated policies of war communism and restore free trade under NEP.

This concession apart, it was military might and ruthless terror that held
the key to the suppression of the major peasant revolts, although in some
places, such as the Volga famine region, hunger and exhaustion did the job
instead. The turning point came in the early summer, when the Bolsheviks
re-thought their military strategy: instead of sending in small detachments
to fight the rebels they swamped the rebel areas with troops and unleashed
a campaign of mass terror against those villages that supported them whilst
trying to wean away the others through propaganda. The new strategy was
first applied in Tambov province, where M. N. Tukhachevskii, fresh from
his success against Kronstadt, was sent in April to crush the Antonov revolt.
At the height of the operation in June the insurgent areas were occupied by
a force of over 100,000 men, most of them crack troops from the elite
Communist security units and the Komsomol, together with several hundred heavy guns and armoured cars. Aeroplanes were used to track the
movement of the bands and to drop bombs and propaganda onto their
strongholds. Poison gas was also used to 'smoke the bands out of the
forests'. Through paid informers the rebels and their families were singled
out for arrest as hostages and imprisoned in specially constructed concen-

tration camps: by the end of June there were 50,000 peasants in the Tambov camps, including over 1,000 children. It was not unusual for the whole village population to be interned and later shot or deported to the Arctic Circle if the rebels did not surrender. Sometimes the rebel villages were simply burned to the ground. In just one volost of the Tambov district – and it was not even particularly noted as a rebel stronghold – 154 peasants were shot, 227 families were taken hostage, 17 houses were burned down, and 46 were torn down or transferred to informers. It has been estimated that 100,000 people were imprisoned or deported and 15,000 people shot during the suppression of the revolt.

Along with the big stick there was also a small carrot to induce the peasants to abandon their support for the rebels. Villages that passed a resolution condemning the 'bandits' were rewarded from a special fund of salt and manufactured goods. The Bolsheviks were counting on the rebels, once they had heard of these resolutions, to take reprisals against the treacherous villages so that they could drive a wedge between them and undermine the rebels' social base. There was also an amnesty for the rebels, although those who were foolish enough to surrender, about 6,000 in all, were nearly all imprisoned or shot. Finally, there was a barrage of propaganda about the benefits of the NEP, although its rather questionable efficacy hardly warrants the claims later made for it by the Bolsheviks. Many peasants, even in the Moscow region, had never heard of the tax in kind, while most of those who had, as Tukhachevskii acknowledged at the time, were 'definitely not inclined to believe in the sincerity of the decree'.

By the late summer of 1921, when much of the countryside was struck down with famine, most of the peasant revolts had been defeated in the military sense. Antonov's army was destroyed in June, although he escaped and with smaller guerrilla forces continued to make life difficult for the Soviet regime in the Tambov countryside until the following summer, when he was finally hunted down and killed by the Cheka. In western Siberia, the Don and the Kuban all but the smallest peasant bands had been destroyed by the end of July, although peasant resistance to the Soviet regime continued on a smaller scale – and in more passive ways – until 1923. As for Makhno, he gave up the struggle in August 1921 and fled with his last remaining followers to Romania, although his stronghold in the south-east Ukraine continued to be a rebellious region for several years to come. To many Ukrainians Makhno remained a folk hero (songs were sung about him at weddings and parties as late as the 1950s) but to others he was a bogey man. 'Batko Makhno will get you if you don't sleep', Soviet mothers told their children.

Further reading

Antonovshchina: Krest'ianskoe vosstanie v Tambovskoi gubernii v 1919–1921 gg. Dokumenty i materialy (Tambov, 1994).

Brovkin V., *Behind the Front Lines of the Civil War: Political Parties and Social Movements in Russia, 1918–1922* (Princeton, Princeton University Press, 1994).

Esikov S. and Protasov L., '"Antonovshchina": novye podkhody', *Voprosy istorii* 6/7 (1992).

Figes O., *Peasant Russia, Civil War: The Volga Countryside in Revolution (1917–1921)* (Oxford, Clarendon Press, 1989).

Figes O., 'The Red Army and Mass Mobilization during the Russian Civil War', *Past and Present* 129 (1990), pp. 168–211.

Frenkin M., *Tragediia krest'ianskikh vosstanii v Rossii 1918–1921 gg.* (Jerusalem, Izdatel'stvo 'Leksikon', 1987).

Malet M., *Nestor Makhno in the Russian Civil War* (London, Macmillan, 1982).

Radkey O. H., *The Unknown Civil War in Soviet Russia* (Stanford, Hoover Institution Press, Stanford University, 1976).

The Press and the Revolution

BORIS I. KOLONITSKII

It is as impossible to imagine the Russian revolution of 1917 without mass publications – newspapers, leaflets and pamphlets – as it is to imagine it without cars and trains. This was the period in which the press played a particularly significant role in political struggles: radio had not yet become an important mass medium, but the telegraph and rotary presses made it possible to disseminate news quickly.

It is true that newspapers were always very late in reaching the more far-flung army divisions and remote villages, and that the greater part of the population was illiterate. However, the fate of the revolution was decided in the towns, and the level of literacy in the army and among urban males (the most politicized sections of the population) was significantly higher than the average for the country as a whole.

The major printing centres were Petrograd, which had over 300 print-works, and Moscow, which had 250. The printers were one of the best organized groups of workers – in 1917 their trade union had 81,000 members, 26,000 of them in Petrograd and over 16,000 in Moscow. By the time of the revolution there was a very wide variety of publications in Russia. The most popular daily paper was the liberal Moscow *Russkoe slovo*, published by I. D. Sytin. In 1917 its circulation fluctuated between 670,000 and 910,000. More 'popular' papers like *Gazeta-Kopeika* also enjoyed a wide circulation. In 1916 its print run varied between 100,000 and 160,000, and in 1917 between 55,000 and 120,000. However, in Russia the ratio of newspaper titles to the total population was 1:64,500, whereas in France it was 1:5,900, and in the USA 1:4,100.

During the February revolution in Petrograd the printers joined the general strike and refused to resume the production of any title without the sanction of the Petrograd Soviet. This real control over the press was an important factor in establishing the system of 'dual power'. On 27 February 1917 only the information sheet *Izvestiia*, written by a committee of Duma journalists, was produced with the Soviet's sanction. The following day, the

Izvestiia of the Petrograd Soviet began to appear, printed at the Kopeika printworks which had been occupied 'by revolutionary right'. At the same time the Soviet did not permit the old newspapers to resume publication until the socialist parties had started to produce theirs. Representatives of these parties were sent to various state printworks and began to bring out their papers, using the stocks of paper they found there. Thereafter the pre-revolutionary papers were allowed to reappear, and on 5 March the major titles were again on sale in Petrograd. The Bolsheviks' *Pravda* also appeared on that day. It was produced at the printworks of the government paper *Sel'skii vestnik*, and its print run fluctuated between 42,000 and 100,000. On 7 March the same printworks began to produce the Mensheviks' *Rabochaia gazeta*, with a print run of between 25,000 and 96,000. The Socialist Revolutionaries produced their publications at the printshops of the Ministry of Internal Affairs, the Senate, the Synod and the Petrograd City Governor's office. The print run of the central SR organ *Delo naroda*, which appeared from 15 March, was between 58,000 and 78,000. On 10 March the Executive Committee of the Petrograd Soviet declared that any publication was free to appear without its sanction. This system of granting permission was not adopted by the Moscow Soviet. Nevertheless, both in the capitals and in the provinces certain right-wing publications ceased to appear, and this was usually as a result of the actions of the new authorities. On 5 March the Executive Committee of the Petrograd Soviet banned the publication of the Black Hundred papers *Zemshchina*, *Golos Rusi* and *Russkoe znamia*, which had in fact already closed. Certain provincial right-wing papers such as *Golos Samary* (Samara), *Russkoe slovo* (Makeevka), *Rostovskii listok* (Rostov) and *Dvuglavyi orel* (Kiev) were also shut down.

In spite of the shortages of paper and printing equipment and the general economic difficulties following the February revolution, many new publishers and periodicals sprang up. There were a number of reasons for this. In the first place, in a declaration of 3 March the Provisional Government proclaimed full freedom of the press, and subsequently the legal provisions for this were worked out and enacted. On 8 March a special commission was set up on liquidating the Main Administration on Press Affairs – the censor's office. On 15 March the Provisional Government decreed that certain materials were to be submitted to the military censor prior to publication. Theoretically, in certain circumstances this would have made it possible to control the press, but in fact this decree was never implemented. On 27 April the government adopted a decree 'On Institutions on Press Affairs', which stated that both the press and the distribution of publications were free from administrative interference. Meanwhile, many soviets and soldiers' committees followed the example of the Petrograd Soviet and took control of the printshops of state and local government institutions, monasteries and right-wing publications, along with their stocks of paper. This facilitated the rapid development of the socialist press. Finally, with the mass politicization of the population, there was an enormous demand for political publications of all types. Stocks of old pamphlets left over from the time of the first Russian revolution sold out overnight. In these circumstances both commercial publishers and the propaganda departments of political parties tried to expand their activities.

Most prominent among the new publishing houses, papers and journals were those of the socialist parties, soviets and other committees. Certain soviets, particularly those of Helsingfors, Kazan, Moscow and Odessa, established relatively large-scale publishing operations. The SR party was the most active in producing propaganda pamphlets and books. Its central publishing commission alone brought out 87 titles with a total print run of 8.3 million. (All the figures cited in this article refer only to Russian-language materials.) The Menshevik *Rabochaia biblioteka* produced 33 titles with a print run of 1.8 million. Overall, in Petrograd alone the moderate socialists published no less than 500 different pamphlets with a total run of 27 million. The total output of moderate socialist publications in Petrograd for June was almost 700,000 copies, and by the autumn it was 550,000 to 580,000 copies. *Priboi*, the central publishing house of the Bolsheviks, produced around 50 titles with a total print run of about one million. In June the Bolsheviks had two newspapers in Petrograd, the print run of which fluctuated from 90,000 to 175,000 per day. By October they had four papers, with a total daily run not exceeding 200,000.

At the same time, the liberals were also extending their publishing activities as they tried to arrange the production of materials for a mass readership. In Petrograd the Constitutional Democrats (Kadets) founded the newspapers *Svobodnyi narod* and *Zemlia*. They acquired printshops both in the capitals and the provinces. The main Kadet publishing house produced 54 pamphlets with a total print run of 3.2 million. The Provisional Committee of the State Duma founded a large publishing concern *Osvobozhdennaia Rossiia*, in which liberals and moderate socialist defencists collaborated. It produced 28 pamphlets with a print run of 5.2 million. A smaller publishing house of a similar political orientation was founded by the Central War Industries Committee. The Committee for Military-Technical Aid produced leaflets, and later the Central Committee for Social and Political Education was founded on the basis of this operation. Initially the liberal and conservative (so-called 'bourgeois') publishing concerns produced significantly greater quantities of material than their political opponents. However, early in 1917 many publishers of that persuasion began to curtail book production. This was for political reasons – they clearly realized that this form of propaganda was not effective. Nevertheless, 'bourgeois' publishers in Petrograd produced more than 250 pamphlets with a total print run of 11 million. And it was newspapers of that orientation which predominated in the capital – in June their total daily print run exceeded 1.6 million, and in October it was still more than 1.4 million.

After February, parties to the right of the Kadets had in effect lost all their influence, and in this situation certain newspapers fulfilled the role of centres of political organization. A 'Republican Union' was formed around the newspaper *Russkaia volia*, which tried to carry on propaganda work. Then A. A. Suvorin's popular paper *Malenkaia gazeta* appeared, which enjoyed unprecedented popularity among the lower strata of the urban population. The paper's political line was distinguished by a clever combination of chauvinism and social demagogy – it called itself 'the paper of non-party socialists'. The right-wing extremist Military League established links with this paper. V. V. Shul'gin's *Kievlianin* continued to act as a centre for Russian nationalists in the Ukraine.

Russia became the scene of the greatest propaganda battle of World War I. Germany and its allies flooded the Russian trenches with their publications, hoping to encourage the disintegration of their enemy's army. First of all they used papers produced for prisoners of war – the Berlin *Russkii vestnik* and the Vienna *Nedelia*. They later organized the production of leaflets and special publications for the front, such as the newspaper *Tovarishch* published in Vilnius. Initially these publications were dropped from balloons and aircraft, or were fired from mortars. Later they were handed over in the course of 'fraternization'.

The Russian command and military committees attempted to engage in counter-propaganda, and the Allied missions also took appropriate measures. They sent in their own literature, organized information agencies and publishers and provided support to 'friendly' enterprises. The Petrograd publishing house *Demokraticheskaia Rossiia*, the largest producer of leaflets in the country, was established with considerable Allied financial support. In the autumn of 1917 the American Red Cross mission provided significant subsidies to the right SRs grouped around the paper *Volia naroda*.

Of course, press freedom was not absolute. Post office officials and army officers hindered the flow of socialist publications to the provinces and in particular to the front. However, at this stage there was also a threat to press freedom from the left. At times of political crisis the question of control over the press became sharper. Anarchists in Petrograd attempted to seize the well-equipped printworks of *Russkaia volia* and Suvorin's *Novoe vremia*. At the same time soviets and their committees sometimes censored the publications of their opponents. An all-Russian meeting of the organization of editors of daily papers complained that 'from the very first days of the revolution . . . [the soviets] completely failed to understand the meaning of press freedom'. This sort of activity worried the Provisional Government, and on 28 March it declared that cases of banning and impounding periodicals by soviet representatives were acts of 'impermissible arbitrariness'. However, in March, April and especially May 1917 attempts to hinder the publication and distribution of conservative and liberal papers were made by soviets in Kazan, Odessa, Nikolaev, Rybinsk, Nizhnii Novgorod, Khar'kov, Mogilev, Kurgan, Sukhumi and elsewhere.

The surge in this sort of activity by the soviets can be related to the peculiarities of a deteriorating political situation. The April Crisis was preceded by a growing campaign by the right-wing, conservative and liberal press against the Bolsheviks, then against workers and soviets in general. In reaction to this, increasing numbers of resolutions were passed, primarily by workers, condemning the 'bourgeois press' and frequently calling for a boycott of that press. In this situation many soviets and committees in turn adopted radical resolutions, and several soviets did not limit themselves to resolutions. None the less, these 'closed' titles generally resumed publication.

At the same time, in the early period of the revolution, some soviets controlled by Mensheviks and SRs also took repressive measures against the Bolshevik press. Thus the Military Section of the Ekaterinodar Garrison resolved in May to close *Prikubanskaia pravda* and to arrest its publishers. The paper subsequently resumed publication. Several soviets placed restrictions on the printing and distribution of Bolshevik literature.

The July Crisis led to certain restrictions on press freedom. On 5 July a detachment of government troops occupied the offices of *Pravda*, and the next day the Bolshevik printworks and the offices of their Priboi publishing concern were sacked. The publication of *Pravda* and *Soldatskaia pravda* was stopped and some provincial Bolshevik publications were closed. The Bolsheviks themselves estimated in September that 17 of their publications had been suppressed. However, most of these papers soon reappeared under new names.

The laws governing the press were also changed. On 7 July the Minister of War prohibited the distribution of *Pravda, Soldatskaia pravda* and *Okopnaia pravda* among serving soldiers. On 13 July the Provisional Government adopted a temporary measure giving the Minister of War and the Minister of Internal Affairs the right to close down newspapers and magazines which opposed the policies of the government and the military authorities, and to bring their managing editors before the courts. It was proposed to tighten military censorship, and B. V. Savinkov, the Assistant War Minister, signed a new set of 'Temporary Regulations on the Special Military Censorship of the Press'. In these conditions the military authorities sometimes tried to close publications of soviets and committees controlled by moderate socialists as well. However, in this case, too, 'closed' titles quickly resumed publication. On 2 September the popular internationalist social-democratic paper *Novaia zhizn'* was banned. For a few days it appeared under the title *Svobodnaia zhizn'*, and within days the ban was lifted.

The soviets' control over the press was one of the most striking manifestations of dual power. They continued to strike blows against hostile papers after the July events. Soviet pressure in Petrograd led to the closure of the extreme right-wing *Malenkaia gazeta*, although shortly thereafter it resumed publication as *Narodnaia gazeta*. The Kronstadt Soviet closed the local authority's paper *Kronshtadt*. In Tsaritsyn the paper *Respublikanets*, which the local soviet's executive bureau considered 'evidently counter-revolutionary', was closed down. These examples show that even at that time local soviets continued to behave like organs of power.

General L. G. Kornilov's rebellion led to stronger and stricter soviet control over the press. The explosion of political activity during the revolt produced numerous resolutions condemning the rebels and demanding the closure of the counterrevolutionary ('Kornilovite') press. Calls to adopt these measures were frequently addressed to soviets at all levels. Similar resolutions were adopted by the soviets of Helsingfors, Ivanovo-Voznesensk, Vladimir, Kineshma, Saratov, Tula and a host of other towns and villages. In many places extraordinary organs of power (revolutionary committees, committees for the defence of the revolution, revolutionary headquarters and so on) were formed either by the soviets directly or with their participation. Sometimes they were specially charged with investigating the press and closing and confiscating 'bourgeois' papers. In Petrograd, the Committee of People's Struggle Against Counterrevolution suggested that printers should carefully examine the texts they were setting, and if they saw anything suspicious they were to inform the committee. At a session of the Petrograd Soviet on 31 August, it was reported that the committee had shut down four titles. Incidentally, the Political Department of the War Ministry stated that the closure of *Slovo, Novoe vremia* and *Novaia Rus'* had been undertaken on the orders of the Military Governor-General rather than the Committee of People's Struggle Against Counterrevolution. On 6 September, when the paper *Novoe slovo* appeared in place of *Zhivoe slovo*, the committee appealed to the printers' union and the typesetters refused to set the second issue. Papers considered by the soviets and revolutionary committees to be counterrevolutionary were also shut down in Bezhitsa, Borisoglebsk, Kiev, Kovrov, Kozlov, Nizhnii Novgorod, Odessa, Ostrogorsk, Syzran', Vladivostok and Zhizdra. In some towns, such as Rostov-on-Don and Yalta, individual numbers of local papers were confiscated, and in others, such as Gomel' and Odessa, certain issues of papers published elsewhere were seized. Soviets and other committees introduced press censorship in Gomel', Ekaterinoslav, Kazan, Kiev, Morshansk, Odessa, Poltava, Rostov, Rybinsk, Tambov, Tsaritsyn, Vitebsk, Zhitomir and elsewhere. In several cases they established complete control over the printworks, thereby extending censorship to all printed material. It was also not uncommon for control to be extended to the telegraph, thus subjecting press telegrams to censorship. There were protests against the local censorship of the telegrams of the Petrograd Telegraph Agency from Ekaterinoslav, Khar'kov, Novgorod, Novocherkassk, Polotsk, Tambov and other towns.

Occasionally the suppression of hostile publications went way beyond the struggle against the Kornilov rebellion. The soviet of the Vyborg District in Petrograd issued a ban on the sale of all non-socialist newspapers in its area. News-vendors who disobeyed this prohibition had the papers confiscated by the local militia, making the purchase of non-socialist papers practically impossible. Similar measures were taken in some other workers' districts. However, an inter-district meeting of soviets recognized that such a ruling was unlawful, and proposed that it be rescinded. From 6 September all papers were again on sale in the working-class districts of Petrograd.

This mass suppression of hostile publications using extraordinary measures and extraordinary organs constituted a kind of dress rehearsal for those blows against the press which followed the October revolution.

Once the Kornilov rebellion had been put down, soviet control of the press relaxed, and many soviets and committees officially announced that they had revoked their censorship. However, this relaxation did not mean a simple return to the *status quo ante*; many soviets continued to impose important limitations on press freedom, and in such places as Buguruslan and Samara they closed the papers of their opponents. In certain places pre-publication censorship was introduced. At the same time the control exercised by the typesetters over the contents of newspapers increased considerably, and they sometimes refused to print materials hostile to socialist parties. However, the most striking manifestation of soviet control over the press in those days was the restriction on the sale of papers; in some small towns and workers' settlements it was forbidden to bring in 'bourgeois papers'. Many soviets, in Ekaterinodar, Kineshma, Kyshtym, Voronezh and elsewhere, continued to pass resolutions demanding the closure of the 'counterrevolutionary', if not the entire 'bourgeois' press. These sorts of demands, along with the practical actions outlined above, were a symptom of the Bolshevization of the soviets. However, some non-Bolshevized soviets were also calling at that time for the suppression of hostile titles. This was a consequence of the social polarization and confrontation brought about by the Kornilov revolt. In the atmosphere of those days all opponents had consciously placed themselves 'outside the law', and the principle of press freedom did not extend to hostile publications. Some collectives, which had only recently been passing resolutions demanding the restoration of press freedom when it was the left press that was being suppressed, now demanded the immediate prohibition of the counter-revolutionary press. Sometimes these two demands were found side by side in one resolution.

The Provisional Government and its representatives also moved against right-wing publications which criticized the policies of Kerensky. Between August and October in Petrograd these successive titles published by Suvorin were closed, or rather, suspended: *Narodnaia gazeta* (*Rus'*, *Novaia Rus'*), *Zhivoe slovo* (*Slovo*), *Novoe vremia*, *Obshchee delo* (*Vseobshchee delo*). Just like the left-wing titles, they resumed publication under different names.

By the autumn of 1917 the former interest in political pamphlets and newspapers had given way to indifference. Many bookstores and dispatch offices were overstocked, and even publications distributed free of charge could not find readers. This was a reflection of the growing apoliticism which was an important aspect of the situation on the eve of October.

In making their preparations for the October uprising the Bolsheviks paid a great deal of attention to the control of information. Consequently, in the course of their seizure of power the Petrograd Telegraph Agency, as well as some editorial offices and printworks were occupied by armed detachments. Some of these printworks and their paper stocks were given to various Bolshevik and allied organizations. On 26 October the Petrograd Military-Revolutionary Committee passed a resolution to close a number of papers and to arrest their staff. In Moscow *Russkoe slovo*, *Utro Rossii* and *Russkie vedomosti* were shut down. In other towns the seizure of power was attended by the closure of the papers of political opponents. In October and November this occurred in Buguruslan, Ekaterinburg, Helsingfors, Kungur, Nizhnii Novgorod, Revel', Samara, Syzran' and elsewhere. At times preliminary censorship was brought in. Printshops and paper stocks were frequently confiscated. By the end of 1917, 30 printworks had been requisitioned; by July 1918 this number had increased to 70, and by the end of 1918 to 90. In Kiev the Central Rada stopped the publication of the paper *Voin svobodnoi Rossii*. The Rada had earlier seized the printing equipment of the Pochaev lavra and certain other monasteries.

On 27 October the *Sovnarkom* adopted a 'Decree on the Press', which set out the ground rules for its struggle with the press. The new government acquired the right to combat publications which carried appeals to resist or not to recognize the new authorities, and thereby declared war on the entire opposition press. On 4 November this decree was considered at a session of the All-Russian Central Executive Committee of Soviets (VTsIK). Although its supporters were able to ensure they had a majority, it led to a serious political crisis. Some prominent Bolsheviks resigned their government posts in protest, and the Left SRs also opposed the decree.

Nevertheless, further pressure was brought to bear. On 7 November a decree was adopted establishing a state monopoly on advertising, aimed at weakening the financial basis of the opposition press. Special commissariats were established to ensure government control of the press, and at the end of 1917 a special Revolutionary Tribunal on Press Matters was set up, which had its first session in January 1918. In May it was merged with the general system of revolutionary tribunals. At the same time, other organs were also involved in suppressing the opposition press – soviets, revolutionary committees and the Cheka. According to the calculations of A. Z. Okorokov, 122 papers were shut down between October and December 1917, 216 between January and March, and 234 between April and July 1918.

The Bolsheviks' repressive policy towards their opponents' press was at the centre of the political struggle. Many prominent cultural figures protested against it. So too did a significant proportion of the printworkers, among them the Mensheviks, who had won a majority at the second All-Russian Conference of Printers' Unions in December 1917, were very influential. There were also economic motivations for the printworkers' protest – the suppression of newspapers and confiscation of printworks led to lower wages and unemployment for printers. Moreover, policies towards the opposition press varied from place to place. In certain towns control over the press was regarded as a temporary measure. In Moscow it became much stricter after the seat of government had been transferred there.

At first the Bolsheviks' repressive measures appeared to be no more effective than those of the Provisional Government – newspapers supposedly closed 'for ever' continued to appear under different names. However, the confiscation of printing works, combined with the general policy of repression, led to many titles really ceasing publication. And after the Left SRs' uprising in July 1918, the opposition press as such ceased to exist on the territory controlled by the Bolsheviks, although from time to time attempts were made to bring out individual editions.

From October 1917 onwards the party-state propaganda system of the new authorities began to take shape, and became an important part of the regime's power structure. The takeover of large, modern printworks led to a considerable increase in the scale of specifically party propaganda. The Bolshevization of the soviets led to a Bolshevization of their propaganda structures. Thus the VTsIK's publishing house became the most important producer of political literature, and in 1918 it brought out 168 book titles with a total print run of 18 million. It is a telling fact that its first publication was a biography of V. I. Lenin.

Further reading

Grigor'iants T. S., *et al.*, *Periodicheskaia pechat' v Rossii v 1917 godu: Bibliograficheskii ukazatel'*, in 3 parts (Leningrad, Gosudarstvennaia publichnaia biblioteka imeni M. E. Saltykova-Shchedrina, 1987).

Kel'ner V. E., 'Iz istorii obshchestvenno-politicheskoi knigi v Rossii v 1917 g.', in I. I. Frolova, ed., *V. I. Lenin i problemy izucheniia knizhnogo dela v Rossii vtoroi poloviny XIX i nachala XX vv.: Sbornik nauchnykh trudov* (Leningrad, Gosudarstvennaia publichnaia biblioteka imeni M. E. Saltykova-Shchedrina, 1979), pp. 69–105.

Kenez P., *The Birth of the Propaganda State: Soviet Methods of Mass Mobilization, 1917–1929* (Cambridge, Cambridge University Press, 1985).

Kolonitskii B. I., 'Sovety i kontrol' nad pechat'iu (mart–oktiabr' 1917 goda)', in S. I. Polotov, ed., *Rabochie i rossiiskoe obshchestvo: Vtoraia polovina XIX–nachalo XX veka (Sbornik statei i materialov, posviashchennykh pamiati O. N. Znamenskogo)* (St Petersburg, Glagol, 1994), pp. 151–63.

Okorokov A. Z., *Oktiabr' i krakh russkoi burzhuaznoi pressy* (Moscow, Mysl', 1970): a list of papers closed down by organs of Soviet power between 1917 and 1918 is on pp. 343–76.

Pethybridge R. W., *The Spread of the Russian Revolution: Essays on 1917* (New York, St Martin's Press, 1972).

Posadskov A. L., *Sibirskaia kniga i revoliutsiia, 1917–1918* (Novosibirsk, Nauka, 1977).

The Provisional Government

HOWARD WHITE

On 27 February 1917 leading figures in the State Duma met to consider how to respond to the mutiny of the Petrograd garrison and to Nicholas II's dissolution edict. By the end of the day they had decided to take power. They sent commissars to take over ministries and other important state institutions, and set about the creation of a new government. During 1 and 2 March, the membership of this Provisional Government was agreed and the backing of the army command and the Petrograd Soviet obtained. A delegation was sent to Nicholas II to demand his abdication, and a message proclaiming the end of imperial rule was telegraphed across the empire. Over the next few days, the authority of the Provisional Government was formally recognized by the army, state and public institutions, and by Russia's allies.

Despite this endorsement, the Provisional Government soon began to lose the confidence of important elites and of the population as a whole. In the space of six months it was reorganized four times. In August it survived what was widely interpreted as an attempted coup by the army command, but on the night of 25–26 October it was overthrown by forces mobilized by the Bolshevik Party. The following day the Second Congress of Soviets created a new government. Unable to raise armed support to mount a serious challenge, the Provisional Goverment effectively ceased to exist.

The failure of the Provisional Government has naturally been central to any history of the Russian revolution. It is not difficult to explain why the government lost support; argument instead has turned upon whether this was a matter of misfortune and miscalculation or whether it was inevitable. This requires judgements to be made about the nature of the government and of the revolutionary process as a whole. Soviet historians generally depicted the government as defending (at times by force) 'bourgeois' values and interests, particularly concerning private property. Most modern Western historians have agreed that the government could not have resolved social problems and won public confidence without abandoning its own values, in particular a conception of the national interest which required vigorous prosecution of the war and preservation of the unity of the empire. In this interpretation the government is assumed to represent 'middle-class' Russia which, whether defined narrowly as industry, commerce and landownership or more broadly as 'propertied society', was a social constituency lacking size and cohesion. An alternative interpretation is advanced by writers who identify competing groupings inside the government and argue that there were opportunities to ward off political challenges and to either contain or resolve social problems.

Although much has been written about the period between the February and October revolutions, the activity and inner politics of the Provisional Government have attracted relatively little attention. Those who feel that October was the logical, even inevitable outcome of February have been disinclined to spend time rifling the dustbin of history. In the USSR the dominant intellectual paradigm precluded serious study for many years. Nor is it easy to find out what went on inside the government. Its records consist mostly of correspondence and administrative paperwork: there are relatively few briefing papers or policy documents. There are no formal records of cabinet discussions: only a note of attendance and reports made or decisions reached. Transcripts of some sessions exist, although their origin is uncertain. The press was not able to report the detail of debates. Several ministers wrote memoirs, as did a number of lesser figures who were close to the government, but most are attempts to write the history of the revolution and are more concerned with general issues than with the activity of the government. Eagerness to assign credit and blame has resulted in portraits of individual politicians which are often entertaining but not necessarily reliable.

The collapse of the Soviet system, however, reopened debate about the 'inevitability' of Bolshevism and the possibility of an alternative political tradition. Events in Russia in the late 1980s and early 1990s focused attention on the importance of political leadership and timing, reinforcing a more general trend in Western social thought to assert the autonomy of the political sphere. Interest in the Provisional Government has revived.

The list of ministers agreed on 1 March had been under secret discussion for two years. All but two of the 11 were leading members of the State Duma, the exceptions being Prince G. E. L'vov, head of a major public organization, and M. I. Tereshchenko, a senior figure in another. Prince L'vov was designated Prime Minister because it was felt important to broaden the government symbolically and because he was not a party leader. The best-known ministers were the leaders of two important liberal parties, P. N. Miliukov and A. I. Guchkov, and the socialist lawyer A. F. Kerensky. Two of the ministers, Tereshchenko and A. I. Konovalov, were owners of factories; Konovalov shared the views of a particular section of Russia's business community, but it cannot be said that either business or landowning elites were truly represented in the government. It included a doctor, a lawyer and three academics – but they are all best thought of as professional politicians with expertise in particular fields: Miliukov in international relations, Guchkov in military affairs, N. V. Nekrasov in transport, etc.

The government reflected the broad coalition which had emerged in the Duma during 1915–16 under Miliukov's leadership. (The Social Democrats were also offered a seat, but declined.) The parliamentary opposition had expected to take power – but not as the result of a revolution; their government was intended to be a 'ministry of confidence' which would bring the ethos and energy of the public organizations to the imperial state machine and undertake two tasks: a more effective pursuit of the war and a gradual transformation of Imperial Russia into a parliamentary democracy like Britain or France. Such a controlled liberalization would never have been easy, particularly in view of the financial and economic crisis resulting from three years of war, but the situation on 3 March was altogether more complex. Tsarist civil administration had collapsed, with the police disarmed and the huge rear garrisons and naval bases in violent or symbolic mutiny. The myths which supported tsarist rule, particularly the mystique of autocracy, had already eroded and were now being physically destroyed as imperial portraits and eagles were torn down and epaulettes were ripped from officers' shoulders; in Moscow even the police dogs were adorned with red ribbons. Ordinary people began to feel that, as a revolution had happened, their aspirations for a better society should be met: an eight-hour working day, the transfer of land to those who worked it, the right of ordinary people not merely to speak and vote but to be treated as citizens and to organize their own immediate social and working environment. A third task thus confronted the new government: getting the population back to work and dealing with their aspirations for a new order. Although outwardly an 'official optimism' was the order of the day, many ministers probably would have agreed with the moderate socialist V. B. Stankevich: 'In our hearts we felt captives of a hostile, anarchic force.'

The Provisional Government was not immediately well placed to command the confidence of this much broader public. The Duma had been elected on a very narrow franchise. When a heckler asked Miliukov 'Who elected you?' he could only reply 'The revolution', and acknowledge that the government represented propertied people: 'only they can organize the country'. The government faced several difficulties in its claim to represent the revolution. Its image was patrician: Kerensky was the only minister with whom ordinary people found it easy to identify. It could not dissociate itself from the officer corps, which had lost the confidence of the soldiers. The Soviet commanded the allegiance of most of the population of the city. On the other hand, particularly outside Petrograd, there was considerable euphoria and goodwill; the revolution had been relatively non-violent; and in the person of Kerensky the government possessed the most popular individual politician in the country. The cause did not seem lost.

The terms under which the new government was to operate were established in a series of negotiations between 1 and 3 March. The first question to arise was the government's relationship to the Duma: the Kadet leader Miliukov insisted that the government should not be formally accountable to it and should be invested, in effect, with absolute power. The second question was the government's relationship to the Petrograd Soviet. Here Miliukov succeeded in securing a promise of support at the price of a programme which did not significantly bind the government's hands. The dominant figures in the Soviet, Iu. M. Steklov, N. N. Sukhanov and N. S. Chkheidze, were determined not to tie themselves to what they saw as a 'bourgeois' government. (Kerensky made a dramatic appearance before the Soviet in which he claimed, to great applause, the role of its representative in the government, but the Soviet leaders ignored this and Kerensky made little effort to build a role for himself in the Soviet.) However, this was only a partial victory: the Soviet proceeded to declare that its support for the government was conditional (its formula 'in so far as' clearly implying mistrust) and to make clear that it had every intention of acting as intermediary between the government and the garrison and working population of the city. The image of a 'dual power', in which the government's authority was counterbalanced by and dependent upon the Soviet, quickly spread. On a third question, the fate of the monarchy, Miliukov suffered defeat: Nicholas II abdicated on behalf of his son and the tsar's brother declined the throne. Miliukov and Guchkov tried to resign but were dissuaded.

In the course of these negotiations two distinct groupings, cutting across party lines, became evident inside the cabinet. Miliukov was the dominant figure in the first; the second, which consistently took a more radical position, centred around Kerensky, Nekrasov and Tereshchenko. The influence of the first group was boosted by the presence of like-minded people, primarily experts from the Kadet Party, in the second echelon of the government: the cabinet secretary, members of the Juridical Conference created to advise on legislation, many of the assistant ministers, and those chosen to chair important commissions such as that charged with planning the Constituent Assembly.

The government's programme was published on 3 March. Some of the points, notably an amnesty, civil rights and elected local government, had long been part of the liberal agenda and were quickly implemented; the others, including a people's militia to replace the police, guarantees to the Petrograd garrison and the rapid summoning of a Constituent Assembly, may have caused misgivings but were impossible to resist. The programme contained no reference either to the pursuit of the war effort or of social reform, because the Soviet leaders sensed that these issues could not be easily resolved. This left the government some freedom of manoeuvre, but the question of how to restore order remained.

It was answered almost immediately. Kerensky describes how, on 4 March, Prince L'vov arrived for a meeting of the government in some panic, as it was becoming apparent that all over the country various Committees of Public Organizations had seized power: someone pointed out that this was more or less what had happened in Petrograd, and the appropriate course of action was to welcome and encourage local initiative. On 6 March, Guchkov set up a commission to 'democratize' the armed forces by recognizing and regulating the soldiers' committees set up during the revolution. This swiftly became the hallmark of the government's strategy: the way to get the country fed and back to work or barracks was to involve people, to encourage representatives of all strata of society to reach agreement, to persuade rather than coerce. Through this, it was hoped, the population would be drawn into participatory frameworks that could be institutionalized in liberal democratic forms: elected representative bodies, political parties and interest group structures which would permit elites to bargain on behalf of their constituents. This was more than a reluctant acceptance of necessity: it combined the romantic populist tradition of trust in the people with the more cautious liberal tradition of educating and guiding the people. It was applied almost immediately to food supply, local government, and most strikingly in the armed forces; the 'committeefication' of the revolution was then extended as the solution to the problems of industrial relations and disputes over agrarian relations and land use. The government hoped by this strategy not so much to pre-empt the Constituent Assembly as to channel it into an acceptable framework: they feared that, as in the French revolution, it might otherwise produce terror and chaos instead of a new constitution. The strategy was not easy to operate because of the tension within it between accommodation and channelling of initiatives and demands from below. The Miliukov group was keen to regularize, institutionalize and limit participation, while delaying the Constituent Assembly to allow the process time to operate; fears that the Constituent Assembly would disrupt the war effort also encouraged delay.

At first the strategy was successful. Order was restored in the garrisons, the supply situation improved rapidly, agreements were reached between employers and industrial workers. A state monopoly in grain was accepted by producers and traders. Relations with the Soviet improved with the creation of a Contact Commission to resolve disagreements before they became public and with the return from exile of I. G. Tsereteli, who brought a less confrontational attitude to the Soviet leadership. However, the country as a whole gradually became aware of the Soviet's reservations about the government and began to sense an ambivalence in the government about the revolution. The local Committees of Public Organizations found that the Ministry of Internal Affairs seemed suspicious and keen to introduce appointed commissars to run local affairs. The most unpopular minister was A. A. Manuilov, whose cautious approach to educational reform was angrily attacked by teachers and university leaders.

Behind the scenes, the government began to suffer from its internal divisions, which reinforced a tendency for each minister (and even assistant minister) to pursue his own policy. The sheer volume of business made strategic thinking difficult: Kerensky complained about the 'vermicelli' of petty matters brought before the cabinet. (The government spent three hours discussing whether to abolish the Corps of Pages and was asked to grant permission for an Orthodox peasant to convert to Islam.) A routine was established of cabinet meetings every day, with minor matters handled in the afternoon in the presence of assistant ministers and interested parties, and major policy issues debated in closed session far into the night. The Prime Minister sought consensus on every issue (the decision not to take full minutes of debates was designed to encourage this) and it is likely that underlying disagreements were not resolved. The multiplication of committees and conferences inherent in the government's strategy compounded the confusion: the committees set up to oversee land use, for example, came into conflict with those concerned with food supply. Most ministers were exhausted.

Yet it was not social protest but a political issue which brought matters to a head: the Soviet leadership, followed by Kerensky, decided to force the government to confront the issue of war aims. The resulting crisis saw the first anti-government demonstrations. The Miliukov group sought to force the Soviet into giving the government proper support. The result was the reorganization of the government to include representatives of the Soviet leadership. This, it was hoped, would put an end to 'dual power'. Guchkov and Miliukov resigned, but four of Miliukov's supporters remained in the government in order to counter any attempt to shift it to the left.

The new cabinet of 16 ministers announced on 5 May included six socialists. Two were representatives of minor socialist parties who were experts in particular fields; they quickly affiliated with the Kerensky group. However, the addition of SR V. M. Chernov (Agriculture) and Mensheviks Tsereteli and M. I. Skobelev created a new grouping inside the government, and a rivalry with Kerensky which was both political and personal. The new cabinet issued a declaration the same day which contained, along with assurances on war aims, local government reform and the Constituent Assembly, the first clear address to social issues. The liberals conceded economic regulation, labour protection, taxation of the wealthy and preparation of land reform. The socialists for their part accepted that the war would be prosecuted with increased vigour and that land reform must await the Constituent Assembly. Despite the general welcome given to the new government, both the Soviet leaders and the remaining members of the Miliukov group were reluctant participants in a coalition, and the tensions inside the government increased. Within a few weeks Konovalov had resigned in protest over economic regulation, although his replacement was a Kadet with similar views. The result was that the Ministry of Trade and Industry and the Ministry of Labour pursued contradictory policies. Conflict between the Ministries of Agriculture and Interior intensified as Chernov began to prepare aggressively for land reform – ordering, without cabinet approval, a moratorium on land lease and sale, which he was forced to retract.

Although the government began to talk openly of the threat of anarchy, it remained reluctant to use force and placed its hopes on the simultaneous extension of committee structures and the creation of elected local governments. Kerensky was made Minister of War and Navy in the hope that his energy and popularity would help avert the disintegration of the armed forces. Convinced that a 'democratized' army was the key to the restoration of order, on 8 May he authorized a Declaration of Soldiers' Rights which transferred disciplinary powers from officers to unit courts.

During May and June social tensions began to intensify, partly as a result of economic breakdown. Government authority began to be defied – the Kronstadt naval base repudiated its authority, a peasant congress in Kazan decided to proceed with land redistribution, anarchists occupied buildings in Petrograd. Individuals began to feel insecure as crime and rural unrest began to increase. The army command began to rotate garrison units to the front amidst talk of a new offensive: most eventually complied, but under considerable protest and there were often ugly incidents. The army, factory and land committees became increasingly militant, instead of a moderating force. There were serious disturbances in Tomsk and in the Black Sea fleet. As they had feared, the socialist ministers were placed in the position of having to reject the demands of ordinary people; the Bolsheviks were beginning to score their first victories in meetings and elections inside and outside the capital. Meanwhile right-wing views began to be expressed openly; many Kadets were alarmed at their poor performance in local elections around the country and increasingly sceptical of the government's strategy. A new challenge presented itself in the form of Finnish and Ukrainian demands for autonomy. Matters came to a head in late June, as the military offensive began to collapse in ignominy: the remaining Miliukovites in the government resigned as the 'July Days' of mass protest broke out in Petrograd.

Everyone sensed that this was a turning point. For the Miliukovites, the time had come to call a halt to the revolution, reverse democratization (especially in the armed forces) and restore order by force. In the next weeks similar views were expressed by representatives of the business community and senior army commanders. General Kornilov was appointed commander in chief partly because he seemed less hostile than other generals, but rumours spread that he too had presented demands to the government. The Soviet leaders also spoke of 'firm authority' but insisted it must be coupled with a much more determined pursuit of an end to the war, regulation of the economy and social reform. On 7 July Prince L'vov resigned in favour of Kerensky, criticizing the Soviet leaders (particularly Chernov) for trying to force a socialist programme onto the government and encouraging lawlessness; he confided to a friend that he could not bring himself to give the order to fire on the crowd, but hoped Kerensky would do so. The remaining ministers published on 8 July a declaration accepting the principle of the transfer of land to the tiller and promising to call a conference of Russia's allies to discuss the war. At this point the Soviet leaders seriously considered attempting to create a government without the Miliukovites. By now SRs and Mensheviks controlled most newly elected local governments as well as most local soviets and even provided many of the government's own local commissars. But the Kerensky group were opposed and the issue was not forced.

The rump cabinet did take action against those held responsible for the July disturbances: arrests were made, newspapers suppressed, rebellious army units disbanded or transferred, and the death penalty was restored at the front. Tsereteli took over as Minister of Internal Affairs and ordered government commissars to assert their authority; he even clashed with Chernov over illegal actions by land committees. A sort of order was restored; military expeditions were sent, with some success, to pacify the Bolshevik strongholds of Tsaritsyn and Krasnoiarsk. The Miliukovites, however, refused to rejoin the government unless the 8 July declaration was withdrawn – and prevented other Kadets from doing so. Kerensky forced a resolution of the crisis on 21 July by resigning. A meeting of party leaders reluctantly agreed to allow him to choose a cabinet, in which ministers would be considered individuals rather than party representatives.

The second coalition cabinet consisted of 15 ministers, nine of whom were socialists. Tsereteli withdrew but the Soviet leadership was still represented by Chernov and Skobelev, together with a number of lesser figures, such as the Menshevik A. M. Nikitin and the SR N. D. Avksentiev; four Miliukovites agreed to serve. This reproduced the tripartite split which had characterized the first coalition, with the difference that Kerensky had now the upper hand. He was an effective Prime Minister, in that he kept good order in the cabinet, but he increasingly surrounded himself with a personal entourage of aides and advisers. Many of the ministers were past or present associates: Nikitin had worked with him on the Lena goldfields case in 1912. The others grew increasingly distrustful: his reliance upon the former terrorist B. V. Savinkov to run the Ministry of War was felt to be particularly undesirable. Although Kadet experts survived in the second echelon of the government, a new grouping was emerging which V. I. Startsev has labelled 'an SR *nomenklatura*' loyal to Kerensky.

The new cabinet continued to pursue social agreement, striking a deal with the Ukrainian Rada, although there was a general tendency to assert influence over committee structures by increasing reliance on commissars; one of the sources of Kerensky's power was his control of a network of army commissars. The government was increasingly preoccupied with economic crisis. Towards the end of August it was forced to double grain prices and to print more paper money, introducing new banknotes which quickly acquired the mocking title 'Kerenki'. The Moscow State Conference merely reinforced the impression that there was no common ground between liberals and socialists. It was against this background that General Kornilov began to prepare a coup, possibly in the belief that Kerensky would support it. When the coup began, Kerensky denounced it and sought dictatorial powers from the government: the cabinet resigned on 27 August to give him a free hand.

After the defeat of Kornilov, Kerensky sought to rebuild a coalition government. However, the Soviet leaders were no longer prepared to tolerate the participation of Kadets, whom they believed were implicated in the Kornilov affair, and began to question Kerensky's own role. They decided that a conference of 'democratic' organizations should be charged with creating a new government. To counter this, Kerensky set up a five-man Directory as an interim cabinet (himself, Tereshchenko, Nikitin, and two senior military figures whom he trusted, General Verkhovskii and Admiral Verderevskii) and began to try to recruit a team from amongst the minor socialist parties and Kadets who had broken with Miliukov. Eventually this proved successful, since the Democratic Conference could not reach agreement, but the result was a cabinet of second-rank people who, in most cases, did not really represent their parties. Its membership was finally agreed at a meeting of party leaders on 22 September, at which Tereshchenko observed that the Provisional Government had now spent 56 of its 197 days without a proper cabinet.

The new cabinet had 17 members, the majority being socialists from the minor parties. Their declaration of 25 September promised greater and more effective state intervention to solve the economic crisis, the transfer of all land to the jurisdiction of the land committees, concessions to minority nationalities, and the continued pursuit of a 'democratic' solution to the problem of military discipline – all major concessions by the Kadets. A Provisional Council of the Republic was to act as an interim parliament with the right to propose legislation and question ministers.

This was very much Kerensky's government, nothing of substance being decided in his absence. Now residing in the Winter Palace, he is described by contemporaries as aloof, weary and strangely calm. He had broken off virtually all contact with the Soviet leaders. The cabinet was much less divided than in the past but lacked a clear sense of direction: most members felt they could do little to influence events and hoped merely to survive until the Constituent Assembly. No serious effort was made to implement the 25 September programme. There was some attempt at strategic planning, which focused on reorganizing and cutting the armed forces and evacuating institutions from Petrograd in the hope of both easing the economic situation and weakening political opponents. Plans were made for the systematic use of troops for internal policing. But the government lacked the nerve to pursue these policies in the face of hostility from the army command and the more militant socialists. Only General Verkhovskii was prepared to contemplate drastic action: he got the cabinet to discuss the idea of peace, but nothing came of it. The general mood was one of helplessness.

Restoring the government's authority after the Kornilov affair was difficult. In most cities the soviets had set up 'revolutionary committees' with emergency powers which were reluctant to disband; most of them excluded

Kadet representatives on principle and demanded the dismissal of Kadet commissars and officials. There were serious uprisings in Tashkent and Tambov in September and Kaluga in October. As before, a sort of order was restored in the cities, but there was much less success in containing rural unrest. The economic situation deteriorated. Moves to call a second Congress of Soviets, likely to be much more radical than the first, were soon followed by rumours of plans by the Bolsheviks to seize power. As tensions increased, mutual hostility between the Miliukovites and the Soviet leaders paralysed the Council of the Republic. Verkhovskii's bid to break the dead-lock by calling openly for Russia to make peace was unsuccessful. On 24 October Kerensky came to demand support from the Council for forcible suppression of any Bolshevik uprising: the Soviet leadership demanded that land be transferred to the land committees and peace negotiations be opened, finally abandoning – but too late – the search for consensus.

If the account of the Provisional Government given above is correct, it should be evident that it deserves to be treated as an actor in the drama. It should also be evident that there were a number of distinct groupings within it. If the government represented anything, it was an attempt to find con-sensus across the political divide between liberals and socialists, and to use this to bridge the social divide between propertied Russia and the mass of the population. This was a 'liberal democratic' ambition, but pursued by a government which was not democratic (in the sense of representing the population) and was increasingly seen (less fairly, given its record on civil and political liberties) as not particularly liberal either. There were members of the first cabinet who were sceptical of this attempt and who made some effort to defend the liberal and propertied interest against popular socialism, but they were soon marginalized – as later was the one socialist, Chernov, who was reluctant to make concessions. It was Kerensky, rather than Miliukov, who came to personify the government.

The search for consensus faced serious obstacles. The presence of Miliukov and Guchkov in the first cabinet, and of Kadet experts behind the scenes, was not conducive to it. Yet attempts to find a surrogate for Kadet participation in the government foundered: no-one else could credibly rep-resent propertied Russia. The policies pursued by Steklov on behalf of the Petrograd Soviet, and by Chernov later, were also very damaging. Much of the Soviet leadership remained suspicious of the liberals and unwilling to take power. Kerensky too, for all his pursuit of coalition, was resentful of other politicians and convinced of his own special mission.

Was this inevitable? Those who say it was tend to stress the social divide between 'propertied society' and 'the democracy'. Had the Soviet leadership had been more supportive of the government, they would have lost the con-fidence of ordinary people all the sooner. On the other hand, it can be argued that the government's strategy was not entirely implausible: seeking elite consensus and channelling and limiting participation are now routinely recommended to democratizers. Social issues only began to dominate the agenda in May and June. Moreover, there is some evidence that a social base for consensus existed in the form of the 'committee class' (the educated junior officers and men who staffed the army committees and their civil equivalents) and perhaps the lower urban middle strata more generally. A more determined pursuit of consensus, a better-organized government, a more cautious military policy and an early Constituent Assembly might have made a difference.

Were there other alternatives? Miliukov came to reject the strategy of consensus and incorporation and to argue that the Provisional Government had been too weak, singling out Prince L'vov for foolish idealism in refusing to resort to force and Kerensky for personal ambition in preventing the restoration of order sought by Kornilov. But if it is accepted that the administrative and ideological structures of the tsarist state were destroyed in February, there could be no question of using the old machinery to stop the revolution. A restoration of order could only come through building a new state machine – mobilizing a key group of supporters in an armed bid to monopolize the use of force. This implies both consent and coercion: the problem for the Miliukovites lay not so much in finding a key group of supporters (the officer corps, cadets and Cossacks proving more than sufficient to form the nucleus of White armies later) but in being prepared to contemplate civil war at the same time as world war.

The third possibility, more realistic in terms of the actual membership of the Provisional Government and its associated structures, is that a government should have been formed which was able to proceed with land reform and democratization. It would not have been impossible to recruit a few non-socialists to such a government in an effort to defuse resistance; it might even have been possible to harness Kerensky's extraordinary energy and popularity. Whether such a government could have ruled primarily by consent depends, again, upon the interpretation made of the revolutionary process as a whole. Some historians have argued that the institutions and practices of 'the democracy' were a sufficient basis for a new political order; others regard them as incapable of either resolving basic conflicts between town and village or of effective day-to-day administration, and conclude that some form of authoritarian and coercive rule was the only way to reassert the state interest over individual and group interests. It might not, however, have proven as ambitious or as long-lasting as that of the Bolsheviks.

Further reading

Browder R. P. and Kerensky A. F., eds, *The Russian Provisional Government 1917: Documents*, 3 vols. (Stanford, Stanford University Press, 1961).

Gerasimenko G., *Narod i vlast' (1917)* (Moscow, Voskresen'e, 1995).

Ignat'ev A. V., *Vneshniaia politika Vremennogo pravitel'stva* (Moscow, Nauka, 1974).

Kerensky A. F., *Russia and History's Turning Point* (New York, Duell, Sloane and Pearce, 1965).

Miliukov P. N., *Istoriia vtoroi russkoi revoliutsii* (Sofia, Rossiisko-bolgarskoe knigoizdatel'stvo, 1921–4), translated as *The Russian Revolution* (Gulf Breeze, FL, Academic International Press, 1978–87).

Nabokov V., 'Vremennoe pravitel'stvo', *Arkhiv russkoi revoliutsii*, tom 1 (Berlin, I. V. Gessen, 1922), translated as *V. D. Nabokov and the Russian Provisional Government* (New Haven, Yale University Press, 1976).

Rosenberg W. G., *Liberals in the Russian Revolution: The Constitutional Democratic Party, 1917–1921* (Princeton, Princeton University Press, 1974).

Schapiro L., 'The Political Thought of the First Provisional Government', in Richard Pipes, ed., *Revolutionary Russia* (London, Oxford University Press, 1968).

Startsev V. I., *Revoliutsiia i vlast': Petrogradskii Sovet i Vremennoe pravitel'stvo v marte–aprele 1917g* (Moscow, Mysl', 1978); *Vnutrenniaia politika Vremennogo pravitel'stva (pervogo sostava)* (Leningrad, Nauka, 1990); *Krakh Kerenshchiny* (Leningrad, Nauka, 1982).

Volobuev P. V., *Ekonomicheskaia politika Vremennogo pravitel'stva* (Moscow, Izd-vo Akademii nauk SSR, 1962).

The Red Army

FRANCESCO BENVENUTI

Early Bolshevik military performance

The dissolution of the Russian army, and the Red Guard

In November and December 1917, the defence of the revolutionary order was provided by a number of small armed volunteer units, the 'Red Guard', mainly organized earlier in urban and industrial centres. Recruited on a limited scale (within single factories and the industrial regions of major cities) and made dependent on the authority of the local soviets, the units of the Guard were predominantly manned by Bolshevik Party members and those elements of the population most influenced by the party's appeal. Although poorly trained, these were enthusiastic and highly politicized groups with a strong *esprit de corps*. As for the millions of soldiers mustered into the tsarist army, their capacity for combat had definitely disappeared by the time that the Soviet government signed an armistice with the Central Powers on 2 December. The success of the revolutionary coup launched by the Bolsheviks on 25 October was largely secured by the anti-war mood predominant among ordinary peasant-soldiers.

On 9 November a Bolshevik NCO, N. V. Krylenko, one of the leading military figures in the first revolutionary government, was appointed commander in chief of the Imperial Army. His predecessor, General N. N. Dukhonin, fell victim to a mob of rioting soldiers. On the day after, the new Bolshevik rulers attempted to implement their traditional anti-war slogans by beginning the general demobilization of the Russian armed forces. During November and early December they decreed a process of 'democratization' within the old army. The elected soldiers' committees, established by the Petrograd Soviet on 2 March 1917 (in its Order Number One), were granted sweeping powers over every aspect of life in the unit. Officers were now to be elected by their own soldiers, or by the soldiers' committees of the larger units. Ranks, titles and insignias were abolished. Demobilization and formal democratization were the final blow to the old Imperial Army, one of the most powerful acts of the October revolution, and one which provided the new government with a strong sense of popular legitimacy.

Alternative military models

None the less, in the second half of December, anxious about the possible resumption of military activities by Germany, the Bolshevik leaders strove to ascertain whether at least part of the old army could be salvaged for the defence of the new regime. Lenin's conclusion was that it could not. There was, furthermore, the risk that efforts to revitalize the Imperial Army might encourage counterrevolutionary attempts by tsarist generals. In any case, the Bolsheviks were politically bound by the radical programme which Lenin had put forward for the Russian revolution. One of the points of his 'April Theses' was that a 'general arming of the people' should replace the 'standing army' of the traditional continental type. Here was the pre-war socialist idea of a popular, democratic and essentially peaceful 'militia', based upon short periods of military training and a continual alternation between productive work and service at arms. Commanders would be elected by their troops, or at least carefully selected and con-trolled by civilian organs. By contrast, with its class-based caste of profes-sional officers, its long-term training in barracks secluded from a normal social environment and from the political life of the country, the standing or regular army had long been seen by most European socialists as a sym-bol and source of aggressive nationalism abroad and social repression at home.

The militia sphinx

The notion of a militia army remained rather confused in Russia during the first years of the revolution. Bolshevik supporters of the militia idea were fond of tracing it back to a number of historical precedents that were often hardly comparable: the guerrilla detachments that had fought Napoleon's armies in Tyrol and Spain; Garibaldi's corps of 'Red Shirts'; the Swiss mil-itary system; the Boer army in the Transvaal War. In a typically romantic vein, the Bolshevik military leader N. I. Podvoiskii would even compare the future Red Army to the ancient hordes of the Huns. In practice, in the Bolsheviks' eyes, the Red Guard itself largely embodied the essential traits of an authentic socialist militia.

The origins of the Red Army

The volunteer Red Army

It was only in the first half of January 1918 that the supreme political organs of revolutionary Russia took the decision to build up a new, 'socialist' army: the 'Red Army of Workers and Peasants', as it was described in a decree of 15 January. The new-born army was initially conceived of as a select corps of volunteers led by an elected body of improvised commanders. Enlistment was permitted only after the political loyalty and the social background of the recruits had been tested. For the moment, more realistic Bolsheviks were satisfied with this approach. They were afraid of sparking a wave of popular discontent against the new power by taking more energetic measures to compel Russians to shoulder yet again the burden of a military obligation, whatever the novelty of its form. The volunteer army also suited the tastes of the more ideologically committed members of the party. Their ideal was a non-hierarchical, strongly motivated, and purely 'proletarian' fighting force, restricted in size and composed of small and largely autonomous detachments rooted in the localities. This second group of revolutionaries (which included some of the Bolsheviks' early allies in government, the Left Socialist Revolutionaries) championed guerrilla and 'partisan' methods. They saw these combining the necessary flexibility in tactics with the basically active, 'offensive' orientation that corresponded with the spirit of the revolution, unlike the ingrained inclination of 'bourgeois' armies for essentially static and 'defensive' strategies.

In January and February 1918 the volunteer Red Army grew out of a heterogeneous and unstable merger between Red Guard battalions and some surviving units of the former Imperial Army in the north-west. Command was provided by party men with some military experience (such as Podvoiskii, the main supporter of a purely militia system, and E. M. Sklianskii, whose role in building the Soviet military system would grow under Trotsky's leadership); and by a number of former high-ranking officers (such as General M. D. Bonch-Bruevich, General P. P. Lebedev, Admiral V. M. Al'tfater and Lieutenant Colonel A. I. Egorov), whose abrupt change of political allegiance was made easier by the persistent threat posed by the Austro-German army.

Towards a peace treaty

These forces were soon put to the test. On 28 January Trotsky, the first Soviet Commissar of Foreign Affairs and the head of the Soviet delegation negotiating peace with the Central Powers at Brest-Litovsk, rejected an onerous German ultimatum. On 18 February, 700,000 enemy troops resumed hostilities along the entire length of Russia's western front, where there were only some 50–60,000 Soviet fighters capable of effective combat. Scattered episodes of heroism could not halt the German forces. In the fighting around Narva the ill-trained and poorly disciplined Red units panicked and retreated in confusion. Petrograd was directly exposed.

In the face of the exceptionally harsh peace terms put forward by the Germans, the Bolshevik Central Committee (CC) hesitated for some days, weighing the alternative possibility of declaring a 'revolutionary war'. To Lenin's profound indignation (he threatened the CC with resignation, should the German offer be refused), N. I. Bukharin suggested that war be resumed in the form of guerrilla operations conducted in the enemy's rear. Deliberately ignoring the sacrifice of national territory that prosecution of the war would demand, Bukharin's proposal rested mainly on the wishful expectation of an imminent continent-wide European revolution. In the end Lenin's opinion prevailed. A peace treaty was signed at Brest on 3 March 1918. The Bolshevik heirs of the Russian empire were forced to renounce the Baltic provinces, a large part of Belorussia and the whole of the Ukraine.

Learning from defeat

This did not prevent the Soviets learning from the irresistible German military advance and the failure of an international revolution to materialize. As in the time of Peter the Great and Alexander II, military defeat prompted a thorough military reform, with vast implications for the civilian administration of the country as well.

Reorganization of the Red Army was begun the day after the Brest Treaty was signed, when Trotsky was given full authority as War Commissar. On the same day, the military command of the Soviet Republic was reconstituted as a Supreme Military Council (VVS). 'Screens' of military units were deployed along the western front in order to check any infringement of the peace by the Central Powers. Lenin now stated that the short-term aim of Soviet power was an army of one million men. The Soviets were enjoined to 'learn how to wage war from the Germans'. In April, 'military commissariats' were established in the main regions of the country, soon to be entrusted with the military training of the male population between 18 and 40 years of age. Training courses for a new generation of officers of plebeian origin were set up, the old military colleges were reopened and adequately staffed. The government also began to pay attention to the condition and needs of the navy and air force. Efforts devoted to the deployment of a respectable fleet of small battleships to patrol the country's lakes and rivers would prove to be particularly useful during the civil war. Years later, the Red Army would also include a substantial number of 'national' units, recruited among the native population of the republics and autonomous regions of the USSR. But for the time being the Bolsheviks feared that the formation of such units could stimulate the growth of 'counterrevolutionary nationalism'.

The choice of the 'regular' army

Recruiting the ex-tsarist officers

On 21 March the election of officers within the Red Army was abolished. At the end of the month, the CC decided in favour of recruiting former tsarist officers into the new army, in an attempt to make use of their specialized knowledge and experience. This was a controversial decision which deeply divided the party. Krylenko had resigned as commander in chief earlier in March, unwilling to accept the changes in the party's military policy. Between May and July, after the outbreak of civil war in the Urals region, three high-ranking military leaders held the post in succession, though their tasks were limited to this new eastern front: M. A. Murav'ev, a Socialist Revolutionary, who went over to the enemy in early July and was killed by local Bolsheviks shortly thereafter; A. F. Miasnikov, an old party member with some military experience; and I. I. Vācietis, a former colonel of the tsarist army, who since October had placed his division of Latvian riflemen under the banner of Soviet power.

In his article 'The Immediate Tasks of Soviet Power', published on 28 April, Lenin explained that the recruitment of former tsarist officers was part of a more general policy. For the sake of work discipline and economic efficiency, the authority of managers and the remaining high technical-administrative staff in the factories was to be restored at the expense of the revolutionary collectives. Lenin appealed to a combination of the traditional principle of 'one-man command' in management (*edinonachalie*) and the 'revolutionary enthusiasm of the masses'.

Initially, militia training methods were resorted to on a wide scale in the rear, coupled with training and quartering in barracks. Moreover, the chaotic conditions of the emerging civil war often made it impossible for Red Army units to employ any forms of warfare other than scattered 'partisan' actions. Yet the military model outlined in the measures taken by the central authorities in the spring of 1918 was of a predominantly 'regular army' type. A decree adopted on 29 May 1918 completed the first stage of transformation of the volunteer Red Army by re-establishing general and compulsory military service (the original term of service being limited to six months). In June, mobilization (limited according to the social origin of the recruits) was declared over large areas of Central Russia. This first call to arms was prompted by the news that, in the Volga region, armed units of former Czechoslovak POWs, experienced veterans of World War I, were revolting against Soviet power. Substantial anti-Bolshevik forces of all shades from central, eastern and northern Russia quickly rallied around them. During these same days, in the south, former tsarist General A. I. Denikin ordered a compulsory anti-Bolshevik mobilization among the Cossacks of the Don region.

The 'military commissars'

Thousands of former officers had spontaneously joined the Red Army in the days of the German advance in late February, and had been assigned to new commands. The problem for the Bolsheviks was how recruits from the old officer corps would react in the event of war against an internal enemy, that is, in the event of civil war. In order to control the political loyalty of the 'military specialists' (the ostensibly neutral designation of former tsarist officers), to prevent treason and desertion, and to establish the necessary degree of confidence between them and their troops, one or more 'political/ military commissar' was attached to every commander from the regimental level upwards. Trained and assigned by a special administration in the War Commissariat, initially the military commissars were not necessarily members of the Bolshevik Party (they became a compact Communist body only during 1919). To become operational, every military order needed to be signed by the commander and countersigned by the commissar.

The commissar's right of control over the commander obviously weakened the principle of 'one-man command' and sanctioned a somewhat confused form of 'dual command'. However, this contradiction was deemed inevitable by the Bolsheviks for the time being. If the military leader was a 'Red commander' (i.e., a party member, or a tested sympathizer of Soviet power; and at the same time a war veteran, or a factory worker more or less hastily graduated from one of the newly established military courses), the commissar's role was mainly that of legitimizing and strengthening his partner's purely military authority among the troops. The commissar was the living guarantee that his unit was indisputably acting under the aegis of Soviet power, and a symbolic compensation for the abolition of the election of commanders.

Early opposition

The dramatic turns in military policy during the spring of 1918 were greeted by an outburst of criticism. Mensheviks and Socialist Revolutionaries fiercely objected to the alleged abandonment of the ideal of a socialist militia. They denounced the exclusive social character of the Red Army rank-and-file (the Bolsheviks relied mainly on factory workers and 'poor peasants'), which they contrasted with the Jacobin and socialist slogan of the 'nation in arms'. In the mutual understanding which was being established between former tsarist officers and the Soviet military authorities, these critics saw the traditional danger of 'Bonapartism' as well as an unprecedented threat of 'Red militarism'.

Among the Bolsheviks, outright condemnation of the turn to the 'regular' army was mainly articulated by the Left Communist group. Originally brought together by opposition to the Treaty of Brest-Litovsk, this group quickly expanded the range of its dissent, objecting to the empowerment of 'bourgeois specialists' in both the economic and military fields. Reflecting a characteristic variant of the revolutionary mentality of the time, the group assumed that, in the 'class wars' of the future, 'politics will have first place, while technique will play a secondary role ... A weak class army is better than a strong non-class army.' Former tsarist officers could be tolerated only as military instructors and advisers.

Civil war

The first challenge

The outbreak of civil war on a large scale in the late spring of 1918 placed the Soviet Republic in a precarious situation. On paper the Red Army was now more than 300,000 strong, but only a small proportion was combat-ready. In early August 1918 Kazan fell into the hands of anti-Bolshevik forces. These included the Czech Legion, a large number of 'White' tsarist officers with newly recruited troops, and a portion of the former socialist and liberal deputies to the Constituent Assembly.

The battle for Kazan (August–September 1918) was the Valmy of the Bolshevik revolution. Trotsky personally organized the counter-offensive. Victory at Kazan was made possible by resorting to traditional and ruthless disciplinary methods. Machine-guns positioned behind the lines made it impossible for Red soldiers to retreat. Summary executions and the decimation of units were applied in cases of mass flight, irrespective of party membership: 'first the commissar, and then the commander', as one of Trotsky's orders reads. At the same time, tireless propaganda was carried on within the ranks. Small but compact groups of convinced and enthusiastic party members were attached to wavering units. Subsequently, the Red command made the harsh repressive methods tested at Kazan, combined with a heroic and epic inspiration, into a powerful disciplinary mechanism.

The battle for Kazan overlapped with decisive efforts by the authorities to build up a clear and consistent chain of command throughout the military administration, reaching down to the army in the field. On 2 September, a new Revolutionary-Military Council of the Republic (RVSR) was charged with presiding over all field operations. Trotsky became its chairman. On 6 September, Vācietis was appointed commander in chief. His powers were

generously defined at the end of the month, along with those conferred upon
the commanders of 'armies' (groups of divisions) and of 'fronts' (army
groups). Every division, army and front was under the command of a local
Revolutionary-Military Council, staffed with the commander and two or
more commissars.

Learning from victory

A new military mystique quickly spread, first and foremost within the
Communist Party itself. It produced both a new political profile for party
members and a new type of party organization. In November 1918 the
Soviet Republic was declared a 'single military camp' and a newly established Council for Labour and Defence (STO) was endowed with extraordinary powers. The Commissariats of War, Transport and Supplies,
coordinated by a handful of high officials, came to monopolize the country's
resources in manpower and commodities, all of which were subordinated to
the needs of the military. Factories and civil service bureaucracies were 'militarized' *en masse*, and subjected to 'iron discipline' (though they were also
supplied with frontline food rations). The severe and visionary period of
what was later dubbed 'war communism' had begun.

Stalin versus Trotsky

Soon after the victory at Kazan, active and not merely verbal opposition
arose within the Red Army. In the town of Tsaritsyn (later Stalingrad), on
the lower Volga, party and military leaders of the southern front rejected the
appointment by Vācietis of the former tsarist general P. P. Sytin as new front
commander. The rebels were Stalin, K. E. Voroshilov (after November
1925, War Commissar of the USSR) and S. K. Minin (the Chairman of the
Tsaritsyn Soviet). The Tsaritsyn group claimed to be the only competent
military leadership on the spot, and flatly asserted its disagreement with
Trotsky's (and Lenin's) policy of staffing the Red Army with former tsarist
officers. They were soon obliged to give in. On 5 October 1918 the
Tsaritsyn group was deprived of command of the southern front and Stalin
was recalled to Moscow. The Tsaritsyn affair helped to establish a long-
lasting personal and political rivalry between Stalin and Trotsky, but there
was more to it. In the weeks before the episode described above, Stalin,
Voroshilov and Minin had styled themselves as the bards of a rather self-
promoting epic, the leitmotif of which was the heroic defence of the
'besieged fortress', a casting of Tsaritsyn as the 'Red Verdun'. Years later,
this powerful myth of military origin would be extended to the whole of
Soviet Russia, and it would become one of the driving forces of Stalinist
ideology.

The party and the military

Reorganization of the party

In the autumn, the central military authorities completed the reorganization of the Red Army by initiating a profound reform of the military party organizations. After March 1918, the soldiers' elective committees (which the volunteer army had inherited from the Imperial Army) had been largely replaced by committees elected by party members, a system which Trotsky came to label 'military syndicalism'. In October 1918 party committees were abolished by the CC, and only the appointment of weaker party bureaux was allowed. At the same time, the CC outlined a new political hierarchy in the army. Party cells lost their independence and were subordinated to the 'political departments' (organs, already existing as part of the units' commanding staffs) and to the ranking military commissars. This was set out in a CC instruction on 10 January 1919, the fruit of the labours of Stalin, Ia. M. Sverdlov, K. K. Iurenev and I. N. Smirnov (the last two being trusted collaborators of Trotsky within the War Commissariat). Finally, at the end of 1918 the all-Russian general staff (*Vseroglavshtab*) published the rules of military service and a code of discipline. Badges designating different military specialities were also restored (though new hierarchical ranks for Red Army commanders would only be created in September 1935).

The Eighth Party Congress

At the end of December 1918, the capture of Perm in the Urals by 'White' General A. V. Kolchak laid Trotsky and Vācietis open to criticism. A particularly malicious, but not totally unsound, critique was voiced by joint reports presented to the CC by Stalin and F. E. Dzerzhinskii (the head of the Cheka). In February, Trotsky and the RVSR were induced to recognize the independence of the Cheka's security organs and of its special fighting units within the Red Army.

By the time that the Eighth Party Congress gathered in Moscow on 18–23 March 1919, the newly dubbed 'Military Opposition' had gained remarkable strength. Trotsky, absorbed by the situation on the eastern front, could not attend. His only contribution to the discussion was a written document in which he depicted the 'regular' Red Army as a tough but entirely provisional military device, which in due course would be replaced by a proper militia system with elected commanders. In his absence, he was defended by G. Ia. Sokol'nikov, who presented the official report on military affairs.

Behind the closed doors of a special 'military commission' made up of delegates from the army, the opposition received majority support for many of its proposed military reforms, and issued a verdict blaming Trotsky's conduct of military affairs. At this point Lenin himself came to Trotsky's rescue. He criticized both Voroshilov and V. M. Smirnov, the main speaker for the Military Opposition at the congress and a former Left Communist (not to be confused with the aforementioned I. N. Smirnov). A mending of the rift was made possible by Sokol'nikov's willingness to compromise behind the scenes, if not in public, and by disagreements within the opposition.

The birth of the political-military apparatus

The main point on which Smirnov and the Military Opposition had to yield was the request that the purely military authority of the 'military specialists' be shared by the commissars (the principle of 'collective command'). On the other hand, the congress did decide to extend the administrative and political powers of the corps of military commissars and, as Stalin had advocated with particular energy, to strengthen the entire organization of the party within the army. The military cells, the commissars and the political departments were fused into a single Political Administration of the RVSR (PUR). In a sense, the opposition dropped its original demands for a democratization of the structure of the party in the army in exchange for a strengthening of the status of the party's military organizations.

To Trotsky's relief, however, the PUR's first leader was I. T. Smil'ga, a convinced supporter of 'one-man command'. Indeed, Smil'ga was more confident than Trotsky and the high command that the growing political reliability of the Soviet officer corps would soon render the commissars' control superfluous.

The Red Army overreaches itself

Changes in the high command

Some of the consequences of the compromise reached at the Eighth Congress surfaced in May–July 1919 in Petrograd, then under threat from the White armies of General N. N. Iudenich. Taking advantage of the mood of suspicion that prevailed among the local Red troops, and backed by Petrograd party secretary G. E. Zinoviev, Stalin resumed his 'anti-specialist' agitation. He and Zinoviev persuaded the CC to remove Trotsky's key lieutenants from the theatre of operations, and without scruple sought to implicate the commander in chief himself in an obscure case of treason. In these confused circumstances, Vācietis's military plan for an attack on the southern front was voted down by the CC. In its place, the Bolshevik leadership adopted the strategy worked out by the brilliant Red commanders of the eastern front. On 3–4 July, the CC appointed one of these men, S. S.

Kamenev (not to be confused with L. B. Kamenev, a CC member and close associate of Zinoviev), a former tsarist general and the commander of the front, to replace Vācietis as the new commander in chief. In protest, Trotsky handed in his resignation as War Commissar, but withdrew it after receiving a formal expression of confidence from the CC itself.

The labour armies

For a few months after the victory over Kolchak, Iudenich and Denikin, in autumn–winter 1919, the Red Army had no important armed adversary to confront. Yet demobilization was not proclaimed. The Bolshevik leaders had come to the conclusion that the military methods of leadership and organization, which had proved successful at the front, could also be used to restore the country's badly shaken economy.

In early January 1920, Lenin and Trotsky hailed with enthusiasm local experiments intended to convert non-fighting units into 'labour armies' of soldier–workers, engaged in repairing roads, restoring coal-pits and searching out fuel. The Soviet leadership was irresistibly tempted by a vision of 'fusing' the army and the economy into a single, all-embracing military-economic body, directed by an integrated hierarchy of officer-managers, whose functions were perceived, by Trotsky in particular, as fully interchangeable. At the Ninth Party Congress in March 1920, the War Commissar revived once again the idea of an imminent transition to a militia system. The Red commanders, however, with their increasingly strong professional orientation, were distinctly cool towards the idea, probably fearing that its implementation would minimize their own specific military role.

Expansion, victory and defeat

At the height of its expansion, in 1920, the Red Army numbered more than five million men; one out of every six or seven soldiers was still a volunteer. The officer corps numbered more than 230,000. Of these, more than one third were 'military specialists' who had served the old regime. Between March 1918 and March 1920 party membership in the ranks had risen from 45,000 to 300,000 (excluding casualties), and the number of party cells from 3,000 at the end of 1918 to 7,000 in mid-1920. During the civil war some two million soldiers failed to answer the call-up, or deserted from their quarters (mainly during the agricultural seasons), or during operations. Many of them returned to their units soon afterwards, in which case they were not punished. Desertion was a particularly worrying phenomenon during the early stages of the civil war and again during the Russo-Polish war (April–August 1920). Whereas war with Poland attracted many former tsarist officers into the Red Army, the rank and file were severely disappointed by this attempt of their high command to transform a 'defensive' war into a revolutionary, 'offensive' campaign aimed at conquering Warsaw and carrying the revolution into Central Europe.

Defeat in the war with Poland did much to dispel the grand plans for an integrated industrial-military complex. Moreover, military failure, followed by the routing of the last White general, P. N. Wrangel, at the end of 1920, proved to be the starting point for a rapid disintegration of the system of war communism, which was suddenly deprived of its legitimation – ensuring military efficiency in time of war. In the winter of 1920–21, important rural and industrial areas of Central Russia rose in revolt. Repression by special Red Army units followed.

Peace

The civilians' counter-offensive

With the beginning of demobilization in mid-January 1921, the Red Army became and for some years remained the Cinderella of the Soviet state. Resources were diverted to the civilian sector, along with a considerable part of the military, technical and political personnel. Confusion accompanied by destitution began to affect the everyday life of the surviving regular units. Their living conditions came largely to depend on the goodwill of the civilian authorities in the localities of their quarters. These harsh conditions helped to 'democratize' the internal life of the army and to weaken discipline. This process had been underway since the Ninth Party Conference in September 1920, and was encouraged by fears that excessive severity in time of peace would exasperate the soldiers. The political apparatus of the Red Army was induced to comply with the demands both of the ordinary soldier-party members and of the territorial party organizations, which were traditionally resentful of the army's political self-sufficiency.

Again: militia or regular army?

In these conditions, the supporters of the 'regular' military model had no choice but to maintain a defensive stance, whereas the supporters of a militia system tried to use the opportunity to push through their long-cherished plans. Stormy military debates continued in the period from the Tenth to the Eleventh Party Congress (March 1921–April 1922). In the end, the champions of the 'regular' army (including the talented M. N. Tukhachevskii, the ill-starred hero of the 'March on Warsaw' and a future Marshal of the Soviet Union), reaped a resounding, if largely predictable, victory of principle. The problem of the final shape of the Red Army was not yet entirely settled. For the moment, a 'mixed' model was adopted. A small but expandable, 'permanent' armed core was maintained in case of emergency, while a larger number of citizens were trained and periodically called up according to the territorial militia system. But it was openly acknowledged that the main reason for the predominance of the militia units was a matter of mere expediency, not principle. Simply put, the Soviet state could not afford the financial burden of keeping an adequate force permanently under arms. In this last revival of the militia-vs.-regular-army question, Trotsky displayed a rather detached attitude. After the end of the civil war, the War Commissar lost interest in military affairs and was increasingly absorbed by problems of economic reconstruction and international politics.

Further reading

Benvenuti F., *The Bolsheviks and the Red Army, 1918–1922* (Cambridge, Cambridge University Press, 1988).

Erickson J., *The Soviet High Command: A Military Political History, 1918–1914* (London, Macmillan, 1961).

Erickson J., 'Some Military and Political Aspects of the "Militia Army" Controversy, 1919–1920', in C. Abramsky, ed., *Essays in Honour of E. H. Carr* (London, Macmillan, 1974).

Hagen M. von, *Soldiers in the Proletarian Dictatorship: The Red Army and the Soviet Socialist State, 1917–1930* (Ithaca and London, Cornell University Press, 1990).

Kliatskin S. M., *Na zashchite Oktiabria* (Moscow, Nauka, 1965).

Kolychev V. G., *Partiino-politicheskaia rabota v Krasnoi Armii v gody grazhdanskoi voiny, 1918–1920* (Moscow, Nauka, 1979).

Korablev Iu. I., *V. I. Lenin i zashchita zavoevanii Velikogo Oktiabria* (Moscow, Nauka, 1979).

Meijer J. M., *The Trotsky Papers, 1917–1922*, 2 vols. (The Hague and Paris, Mouton, 1971).

Nation R. C., *War on War: Lenin, the Zimmerwald Left, and the Origins of Communist Internationalism* (Ithaca and London, Duke University Press, 1989).

Nenarokov A. P., ed., *Revvoensovet Respubliki (6 sent. 1918 g.–28 avg. 1923 g.)* (Moscow, Politizdat, 1991).

Procacci G., *Il partito nell'Unione Sovietica, 1917–1945* (Bari, Laterza, 1974).

The Russian Orthodox Church

MIKHAIL V. SHKAROVSKII

At the outbreak of revolution in 1917, the Russian Orthodox Church was undergoing a profound internal crisis. On the surface, it appeared to be an impressive force. It had between 115 and 125 million adherents (about 70 per cent of the population), around 120,000 priests, deacons and other clergy, 130 bishops, 78,000 churches, 1,253 monasteries, 57 seminaries and four ecclesiastical academies. None the less, the authority and influence of this powerful organization had been considerably eroded over the two previous centuries. The abolition of the patriarchate at the beginning of the eighteenth century, and the introduction of the Synod system subordinating the Church to the state, deprived it of its independent voice in society. Parish priests had become akin to police officers. They swore allegiance to the secular authorities and reported on the political attitudes of their congregations. The autocracy even interfered in theological discussions. As the official church, the Russian Orthodox Church also shared responsibility for the autocracy's policies and the social injustices it created. Consequently, from the end of the nineteenth century attitudes in Russian society towards the values of Orthodoxy cooled noticeably, and the importance of the Church within other social institutions declined. Anti-clerical attitudes spread from the intelligentsia to the rest of the people. During the revolution of 1905–07, some priests were driven out and even killed, and priests' houses were ransacked.

From 1905 the greater part of the clergy, including the episcopate, showed dissatisfaction with the policies of the Holy Synod and with the existing church system. Signs of renewal appeared, including movements for church reform, parish brotherhoods, religious-moral circles and societies. Orthodox journals were published and evangelism restarted. However, the autocracy prevented the Church from gaining the independence it desired and from convoking a Church Council (*Pomestnyi Sobor*). During World War I the Synod was dominated by the nominees of Grigorii Rasputin, and anti-clericalism increased. The crisis in the Church, its dependence on the state and the fall in its spiritual authority meant that it could not provide any moral barrier to extreme methods of political struggle.

From February to October 1917

The February revolution involved some anti-clerical activity, including the arrest of bishops on the orders of local soviets. However, it was at the same time a religious revolution, unique in the history of Orthodoxy. In March and April 1917 extraordinary diocesan congresses of clergy and laity removed ten discredited bishops. Elected diocesan councils placed significant limitations on the power of bishops. Electoral procedures were introduced for all offices within the Church, along with a collegiate and representative form of church administration, and parish life was democratized. These changes were in keeping with the projects for church reform developed in 1905–07.

The crisis of the autocracy had awakened hopes in the episcopate for a change in the relationship between Church and state. Members of the Synod had refused on 26 February 1917 to issue an appeal to the people to support the monarchy, and on 6 March the Synod called for support for the Provisional Government. V. N. L'vov, a long-standing proponent of church reform, was made Chief Procurator by the Provisional Government. All these developments made the old Synod seem anachronistic. It refused to approve the changes in diocesan and parish work, thus risking anarchy within the Church. In mid-April, on the initiative of L'vov, the government changed the composition of the Synod. New, mainly liberal, members were chosen.

By July the Synod had confirmed the right of diocesan congresses to elect bishops; it had made the parish the basic self-governing democratic unit of the Church with a wide role for the laity; and it had established a Preparatory Council to prepare for an All-Russian Sobor. For the first time in the history of Russian Orthodoxy free elections for bishops, including the Metropolitans of Moscow and Petrograd, took place in a number of dioceses.

Throughout 1917 the Orthodox clergy displayed significant social stratification and a wide range of political sympathies. In some churches they continued to mention the Emperor Nicholas II in their prayers, but some priests joined socialist parties. On 7 March the 'All-Russian Union of Democratic Orthodox Clergy and Laity', the most active of the left groupings, was founded in Petrograd. With the assistance of L'vov it took control of the main Synod publication *Tserkovno-obshchestvennyi vestnik* ('Church and Society Messenger'), demanded wide-ranging reforms within the Church and, with its slogan 'Christianity is on the side of labour, not on the side of violence and exploitation', positioned itself close to the socialists. However, radical groups of this type were only a small extreme tendency.

The main bulk of the clergy remained apolitical and, although favouring democratic changes within the Church, did not advocate the separation of Church and state as demanded in all socialist programmes.

The All-Russian Congress of Clergy and Laity, held in Moscow on 1–10 June, formulated demands and suggestions on the basic points of church reform. The congress welcomed the revolution, but expressed the wish that the Church continue to receive the legal and material support of the state, that divinity continue to be an obligatory subject in school, and that the Orthodox Church retain its schools. Consequently, a conflict soon broke out with the government. The Synod protested against the law of 20 June which transferred the parish church schools to the Ministry of Education. A similar clash occurred over the intention to exclude divinity from the list of compulsory subjects. The decrees of the Provisional Government 'On the Abolition of Religious and National Restrictions' (20 March), and 'On Freedom of Conscience' (14 June) did much to confirm real religious freedom. At the same time the government recognized the colossal role of religion in the spiritual and moral aspects of people's lives. Although it gained a certain *de facto* independence, the Church did not gain *de jure* freedom, as the Provisional Government remained its highest authority. The Chief Procurator of the Synod had to be a member of the government. On 5 August L'vov was replaced as Chief Procurator by the Minister for Religions, A. V. Kartashev, who retained all his rights and responsibilities. Just before the Sobor opened, a decree was issued stating that the draft law on the Russian Church's new form of self-administration, on which the Sobor was working, would have to be confirmed by the government.

The All-Russian Sobor opened in Moscow on 15 August. Its members were elected by free and secret ballot. Women took part for the first time at the parish level. Of the 564 deputies more than one half – 299 – were laity. There were open disagreements among the Sobor's participants, particularly over the question of restoring the patriarchate. This idea had already been rejected at the Preparatory Council by a majority led by Archbishop Sergii (Stragorodskii), and the left wing of the Sobor proposed a democratic-collegial system of administration instead of a patriarchate, with equal voting rights for parish priests and bishops.

The impact of October

This attitude began to change after October 1917 as the political crisis developed. It was increasingly felt that the advance of anti-religious forces needed to be opposed by a church headed by a spiritual leader, and whereas it had been doubted whether the Provisional Government would have been willing to approve the introduction of a patriarchate, this was no longer relevant. On 30 October, by a large majority, the Sobor resolved to reintroduce the post of Head of the Church, and on 5 November the Metropolitan of Moscow, Tikhon (Belavin), was elected Patriarch. In accordance with church law, a Holy Synod consisting of bishops, and a Supreme Church Council of parish clergy and laity were established, attached to the patriarchate. In view of the political situation in Russia, the Sobor also took an unprecedented decision to allow the Patriarch to designate a number of successors to the position of Patriarch in the event of his illness, death or similar eventuality. Their names were to be kept secret. This decision was to play a major role in the subsequent history of the Russian Church.

The Sobor held three sessions between 15 August 1917 and 20 September 1918. Thereafter it was compelled to cease operating, even though it had not completed its work. It had taken decisions on giving women a more active role in the life of the Church, on fraternities of learned monks, and on evangelism. It was able to issue new rules on the synod structure of the Church, which were based on broad participation and the elective principle at all levels – from the patriarchate to self-governing parishes. These finally gave legal status to the changes brought about by the revolution in the Church of 1917. Without them Russian Orthodoxy would have found it much more difficult to survive the atheist state's attacks upon it.

The tragic conflict between the Church and the new authorities began to develop immediately after the October revolution. The election of the Patriarch was taking place at the same time as the churches within the Moscow Kremlin were being damaged by fierce fighting. The main blame for the deterioration of relations with the patriarchate lay with the Council of People's Commissars (*Sovnarkom*), which proceeded from the premise that a Marxist world view was incompatible with religious belief, and regarded the Church as an ally of tsarism and exploitation. Religious organizations were therefore increasingly excluded from the political, economic and cultural life of Russia.

Conversely, the bulk of the church leaders and the clergy were hostile to the Bolsheviks' seizure of state power. However, the Orthodox Church did not align itself with any of the opposing forces, and instead urged an end to social and party conflict and to the incipient civil war. On 2 November, at the time of the armed clashes in Moscow, the Sobor called on both sides to halt the bloodshed and to refrain from exacting revenge. On 11 November the Sobor decided to hold a funeral service for all those who had fallen, and appealed to the victors not to besmirch their cause by shedding the blood of their brothers. The Orthodox Church held to this line in subsequent years.

The very first decrees of the new Soviet government impinged on most of the Church's areas of activity. The 'Decree on the Land' passed at the Second Congress of Soviets, and the subsequent 'Decree on Land Committees' of 4 December included the land which belonged to churches and monasteries. The nationalization of the banks resulted in the loss of the accounts held by the clergy. Decrees passed in December transferred all educational institutions, including theological ones, to the Commissariat of

Education, while the registration of births, deaths and marriages became the exclusive preserve of state institutions.

On 2 December the Sobor, which had still not lost all hope of regularizing church–state relations, approved a 'Decision on the Legal Situation of the Russian Orthodox Church'. It affirmed the 'independence of the Church from the state', but preserved for Orthodoxy 'primacy among religious denominations', listing many pre-existing rights and privileges. In the circumstances of the time, however, this 'Decision' stood no chance of being implemented.

At the end of December 1917 and during January 1918 there was a wave of anti-religious actions, which anticipated the law which had been drafted separating Church and state. Some churches in palaces, institutions and residential buildings were closed, and the Synod printing-house was confiscated. The authorities tried forcibly to take over the living quarters at the Aleksandr Nevskii Monastery in Petrograd. On 19 January there were clashes between Red Guards and the faithful at the monastery. The monastery was successfully defended, despite some casualties. At the instigation of the Petrograd Metropolitan Veniamin, a crusade of half a million believers marched in defence of the Church on 21 January. In an appeal issued on 19 January, Patriarch Tikhon denounced and anathematized the enemies of Christ's truth, who had been engaging in bloodshed and fratricidal strife across the country and thereby promoting the 'cause of Satan'. The Bolsheviks interpreted his appeal as counterrevolutionary.

The *Sovnarkom* adopted a 'Decree on the Separation of the Church from the State and of Schools from the Church' on 20 January, and published it three days later. It set out the future status of the Church, which lost its former rights, although the decree also contained a number of democratic aspects, such as the right freely to profess any religion. The decree prohibited religious societies from owning property, deprived them of juridical status, and nationalized church property.

This law was ill-received by the clergy and the faithful. On 27 January the Sobor approved an appeal 'To the Orthodox People', calling on the laity to unite under the banner of the Church in defence of all they held sacred. Numerous religious processions, some of which were fired upon, took place in the towns; services in defence of the patriarchate were held in public places and petitions were sent to the government. There followed a mass religious upsurge in Russia. From 1918, thousands of new converts, including some prominent intellectuals, joined the now persecuted Orthodox Church. An 'All-Russian Union of United Orthodox Parishes' was also formed.

The *Sovnarkom* had expected its decree to be implemented quickly and relatively painlessly, but this was prevented first and foremost by the opposition of millions of peasants, who supported the expropriation of church and monastic property but were against making births, marriages and deaths a purely civil affair, depriving parishes of their property rights, and dropping divinity from the school curriculum. Peasants thus resisted Bolshevik efforts to break the 'unshakable traditions' of 'a life of faith' in the Russian countryside. The implementation of the law was also hindered by the lack of suitable officials to carry it out, and by the inconsistency of the local authorities' understanding of the law.

On 18 March Patriarch Tikhon wrote his only openly political appeal, condemning the Treaty of Brest-Litovsk. However, around the same time he refused to give his blessing to the White movement. A delegation from the Sobor visited the *Sovnarkom* on 27 March, in order to express its disagreement with the January Decree. In the course of the discussions the delegation was given to understand that the *Sovnarkom* might supplement that decree with a new, more liberal one. The *Sovnarkom* secretary, V. D. Bonch-Bruevich, promised to involve ministers of religion in the preparation of a law on religious cults, but this promise was never kept. The discussions did not produce any tangible results.

After the discussions broke down, more active measures were taken against the Church. On 8 May the Commissariat of Justice created the 'Eighth (later Fifth) Department' under P. A. Krasikov to implement the Decree. The Constitution of the RSFSR, approved by the Fifth Congress of Soviets on 10 July, restricted the political rights of the clergy. In response to a decision of the Sobor 'On Measures Brought About by the Current Persecution of the Orthodox Church', the *Sovnarkom* on 30 July adopted a decree making anyone using church bells to summon the population liable to be handed over to a tribunal court. On 24 August the Commissariat of Justice issued further guidance on the decree separating Church and state, hardened the position of the authorities, and insisted on full implementation within two months, which was clearly impossible. In fact, even by 1921 it had not been completed in some gubernias of Russia.

The civil war period

Hundreds of priests, monks and bishops were among those shot during the 'Red Terror'. In September 1918 the brotherhoods of parish councils were liquidated, most of the church press was closed down, and the authorities compelled the Sobor to cease its work.

Had the Sobor continued into 1919, the Church would undoubtedly have continued on the path of reform, and would have become more of a living, dynamic organism. The October revolution put a stop to the process of church renaissance, and gradually liquidated the democratic changes in church life. In the 1920s, it discredited the very idea of reform by sponsoring the 'renovation' or 'Living Church' movement. Essentially, the October revolution represented a kind of religious counterrevolution. The main ideologists of transformation within the Church, the liberal church intelligentsia, moved increasingly to more conservative positions. The actions of the *Sovnarkom*, with their evidently anti-religious intent, and the heavy blows suffered by the Orthodox Church in the first year of Soviet power ensured the failure of the patriarchate's peace overtures. The actions against the Church had a most powerful effect on the consciousness of all the major social groups and helped increase the ferocity of the civil war. In response to this persecution, Patriarch Tikhon sent his sharpest message to the *Sovnarkom* on 26 October 1918, in which he wrote: 'You have divided the whole people into warring camps, and plunged them into a fratricide of unprecedented ferocity . . . And there is no end in sight to the war you have started, since you are trying to use the workers and peasants to bring victory to the spectre of world revolution.' One month later, on 24 November, the Patriarch was placed under house arrest for the first time.

The spread of civil war was accompanied by a hardening of Bolshevik anti-religious policies. The RKP(b) anticipated that religious faith and the Church would soon die away completely, and that with a 'purposeful education system' and 'revolutionary action', including the use of force, they could be overcome fairly quickly. At a later stage Soviet atheist literature referred to this period as '*Sturm und Drang*'. In the programme adopted at the Eighth RKP(b) Congress in March 1919, the party proposed a total assault on religion, and talked of the coming 'complete disappearance of religious prejudices'.

In order to attain this goal the authorities brought in ever-increasing restrictions. On 3 April 1919 the Commissariat of Justice decreed that voluntary monetary collections among the faithful were permissible 'only for the needs of a particular church building'. At the beginning of 1919 a complete ban was introduced on religious instruction for anybody under the age of 18. Existing monasteries were only permitted to function if they turned themselves into labour communes or workshops. The closure of cloisters began at the end of 1918. By 1921, 722 monasteries had been nationalized, over half of those existing in Russia. From the summer of 1918 the authorities waged a campaign to destroy 'holy relics'. This offended the faithful and was a crude intervention in the affairs of the Church, an attempt to regulate its way of life and worship. In the spring of 1919 these actions became widespread, and became a means of conducting anti-religious propaganda by deeds. On 14 March the Commissariat of Justice decreed that they should be welcomed. The authorities also looked upon the Church as a ready source of additional state funds. In 1919 they began a speculative trade in valuable artefacts, including items which they had seized from churches.

Within the RKP(b) leadership a group of 'irreconcilables' believed that the entire clergy was reactionary, and that it was necessary to fight relentlessly against the Church until it was completely destroyed. The 'statists' considered that it would be expedient to foment a split in the patriarchate, to separate the 'progressive' section of the clergy, and, by giving this section certain privileges, to use it for their own ends. The Commissariat of Internal

Affairs (NKVD) and the Cheka had their own ideas on 'church policy', and from 1918 they aimed to destroy the patriarchate from within. Various such attempts were made in the course of the civil war. An 'Executive Committee of Clergy' was created in Moscow, and a 'People's Church' operated in Penza. There was the *Iliodorovshchina* at Tsaritsyn, when the monk Iliodor, formerly an associate of Rasputin and a prominent anti-semite, spoke in praise of Soviet power to a large crowd at the cathedral. All these attempts ended in failure. The majority of the clergy and the faithful remained loyal to the Patriarch.

In the course of 1919 and 1920, the Patriarch and his advisors adopted the tactic of recognizing the new power whilst defending the independence of the Church, making use of the principle of the separation of Church and state. In a message of 8 October 1919, Patriarch Tikhon called on the clergy to 'refrain from participation in political parties and demonstrations', and to submit to the 'orders' of the Soviet authorities. Despite all the obstacles placed in its way, the Orthodox Church was able to conserve its structure during the civil war. Thousands of small churches which were supposed to have been closed down, even in the capitals, continued to function, as did religious schools. Charitable works continued, and religious processions took place, until the autumn of 1921 in Petrograd.

A very small number of priests served in the Red Army. The right-wing section of the clergy was active in its support of the White cause. In the course of the war those dioceses which had been torn away from the patriarchate became self-governing, and organized local centres. From November 1918 a 'Provisional Higher Religious Administration' operated in Siberia and the Urals, and a similar organ arose in the south of Russia in May 1919. They were often dragged into political struggles. Military chaplains served with the White armies – Kolchak had around 2,000, Denikin had more than 1,000, and Wrangel had over 500. All this provided further ammunition for the Bolsheviks' anti-clerical campaign. During 1920 state bodies continued the tactic of excluding religion from all aspects of life. A circular issued by the People's Commissariat of Justice on 18 May resulted in almost all the diocesan councils being liquidated in Russia. A further 58 holy relics were uncovered by the summer. On 29 July the *Sovnarkom* approved a proposal from the justice commissariat 'On the Countrywide Liquidation of Relics'. However, the authority of the Church prevented this proposal from being carried out in full. Eight months later, on 1 April 1921, a secret circular issued by the commissariat admitted defeat on this score. By the autumn of 1920 the nationalization of church property had been completed. A report produced by the Eighth Department of the Commissariat of Justice stated that 7,150 million roubles, 828,000 *desiatiny* of church lands, and 1,112 buildings for rent had been expropriated by the state.

The first wave of attacks on religion had not brought the results which had been expected by such Bolshevik theorists as N. I. Bukharin. The majority of the population of Russia remained religious, for all the barbaric methods which had been tried to tear people away from the Church. The patriarchate also emerged from the civil war undefeated.

The RKP(b) leadership gradually came to realize the need to change its tactics. In August 1920 an agitation and propaganda department was organized by the RKP(b) Central Committee. On 12 November *Sovnarkom* passed a decree creating a Chief Political Education Committee (*Glavpolitprosvet*), headed by N. K. Krupskaia. Anti-religious seminars were held by gubernia committees of the party to train propagandists and others for this work. In the spring of 1921 Lenin called on his supporters 'definitely to avoid offending religious sensibilities'. The first 'cavalry attack' on the Church was halted. There were, however, even more difficult times ahead.

Historiography

The treatment of this period in Soviet historiography is extremely tendentious, portraying the Church as a reactionary, anti-popular institution. The same can be said, with a number of qualifications, of the historical works of the ideologists of renovation in the 1920s, such as A. I. Vvedenskii, B. V. Titlinov and Dmitri Adamov. Another current is represented by the works of the clergy and laity of the Moscow patriarchate, most of which remain unpublished manuscripts in the libraries of Russian ecclesiastical academies. These works take a very negative attitude towards all left-wing, reformist tendencies and towards the founders of the Russian Church Abroad, while providing an apologia for the position of the leaders of the patriarchate and its attitude towards Soviet power.

The greatest contribution has been made by foreign (English- and German-language) and Russian *émigré* literature, which has, overall, presented a realistic picture of Soviet state policies towards the Church and the harsh anti-religious actions of the authorities. However, the influence of various group loyalties among these scholars can be clearly discerned, and there is little use of Russian archival materials.

From the end of the 1980s new Russian treatments began to emerge, generally taking an intermediate position on a number of disputed points. Initially, Russian historians such as V. A. Alekseev, M. I. Odintsov and Iu. Babinov held to conceptions which painted the church policy of the RKP(b) in a positive light, but, as they became better acquainted with declassified documents, their views became more objective. In the most recent period there have been some highly innovative works by a new generation of Russian specialists, such as O. Iu. Vasil'ev and P. N. Knyshevskaia.

So far as the pre-revolutionary period is concerned, until the 1980s both Soviet historiography and works published abroad, such as those by Richard Pipes, Harrison Salisbury and Alexander Solzhenitsyn, depicted the Church as isolated from what was happening in society, a true ally of tsarism, lacking independence and in fact a dying institution. J. Cunningham's monograph was therefore an important landmark, in that it convincingly showed that at the beginning of the twentieth century the Church was not closed in on itself, nor was it intolerant of other churches, or moribund. Cunningham described the mass movement among the clergy for reforms during the first Russian revolution, although he concluded that by 1908 the hope that the Church could be revitalized had proved unfounded. The recent works of D. Pospielovsky and the German scholar G. Schulz contain an examination of that genuine renaissance of Russian Orthodoxy in 1917 and 1918 which had such unique potential. None the less, the question of the religious revolution of the spring and summer of 1917 remains unexplored.

Schulz's work shows that the Sobor, far from interrupting the church revolution, in many respects gave legal recognition to its achievements and continued the development of its ideas in new conditions. Indeed, he argues that the second millennium of the Russian Orthodox Church began with the Sobor, rather than on the formal anniversary date of 1988, and that in some respects it led the whole of Christendom. The papers on the Sobor, which have recently been declassified and made available in the Russian State Historical Archive, give a very clear picture both of its exceptional importance and of the genuine revitalization of the Church's parish, evangelical and missionary work at the end of 1917 and in the first half of 1918. These papers refute both the Soviet view, that the basic aim of the Sobor was to struggle against the revolution, and the view of the ideologists of the renovation, supported by the dissident writers of the 1960s, A. E. Levitin and V. M. Shavrov, that the Sobor was an interruption of the reform movements of 1905 and 1917. As foreign historians like J. Chrysostomus, N. Struve and A. A. Bogolepov correctly argue, the activity of the Sobor was directed in the first instance towards an examination of church questions, even though it frequently had to react to political problems as they arose.

This question is closely related to discussion about the overall political position of the Russian Orthodox Church during the civil war. Soviet historiography stressed that the Church acted as an independent anti-Soviet force which strove to lead all the other forces of counterrevolution. The anti-Soviet orientation of the patriarchate has been exaggerated by many foreign scholars as well. W. Fletcher, for example, has argued that it was the Soviet system which reactivated the Church and provoked it to offer active political resistance. However, the work of Lev Regel'son has demonstrated convincingly that the patriarchate adopted a neutral, conciliatory position.

There are also varying assessments of the evolution of the attitude of individual church leaders to the Soviet authorities. Patriarch Tikhon is presented as an opportunist time-server by many writers, ranging from the anti-religious to his right-wing critics. However, as Pospielovsky correctly observed, Tikhon's message of 8 October 1919 urging submission to the Soviet authorities was issued at the time of Denikin's initially successful push towards Moscow. Under such conditions there could be no question of 'time-serving' of any kind. The head of the Church realized the inevitability of Bolshevism, and believed that salvation from it could be found only in religion, not in bloodshed and war. The documents from the Holy Synod and Patriarch Tikhon's office which are now available show that at times the position of Soviet power looked far from secure. For example, at the beginning of March 1918 attempts were made to preserve the Petrograd Synod office because a German occupation of the capital seemed 'certain' to the higher Church administration. However, as early as 6 December 1918 the Patriarch wrote to the *Sovnarkom* that he had done nothing to oppose Soviet power, and nor did he intend to do so, even though he was out of sympathy with many of the government's policies, because 'it is not our business to judge the governments of this world'. The evolution in the Church's attitude to Soviet power began earlier and was more consistent than has previously been thought. Recently declassified documents show that the Russian historian Odintsov's claim that the Patriarch 'betrayed the political course of the Church' in order not to lose his millions of followers is quite untrue.

Pospielovsky has developed his argument by showing the continuity between the views of Tikhon and those of subsequent heads of the Russian Church. He has stressed that, although Tikhon's successor Patriarch Sergii made significantly more concessions, the idea of compromising as far as possible with the authorities in the civil sphere whilst preserving the inviolability of theological and liturgical matters was followed from 1919. The opposite viewpoint, expressed by Mikhail Pol'skii, Regel'son, and Deacon Vladimir Stepanov (Rusak), that Sergii betrayed the cause of his predecessor, is unfounded.

The religious policies of the Soviet state and the RKP(b) remain one of the most controversial questions. Soviet historians, asserting that all works about the persecution of the Church were 'reactionary lies', justified cases of priests being arrested in terms of a struggle against their counterrevolutionary activity. Conversely, P. Anderson and many other foreign scholars have claimed that anti-religious propaganda immediately took 'the physical form of a vengeful and fierce attack by militant atheism upon the faithful'. It has also been claimed by Struve that in 1918 Soviet law aimed to make it impossible for religious cults and services to operate. However, for all the anti-clericalism in the church policy of the *Sovnarkom*, its direction was not predetermined from the outset. There were various points of view among the RKP(b) leadership on the place of the Church in the new state, and the general line was subject to fluctuation. Many anti-religious acts were the result of concrete historical circumstances. For example, the archives show that in April 1918 there were plans to establish an inter-confessional commission to work out a decree on the separation of Church and state. There were discussions in the Commissariat of Justice in May 1918 about the withdrawal of the status of a juridical person from religious organizations, and almost everyone regarded this measure as temporary. It is another matter that the subsequent proposal made by certain leading Soviet figures, to 'democratize' the provisions of the decree separating Church and state, never materialized. Church interests were greatly affected by a range of general laws which were not specifically directed against it. The state's desire to replenish its almost empty coffers at the Church's expense also played an important role.

Foreign historiography has paid insufficient attention to the objective basis of the persecution of religious organizations – the anti-clericalism of significant sections of the population, without which widescale persecution would hardly have been possible. For example, the leading theologian J. Meyendorff argued that in Russia the leadership and intelligentsia had abandoned religion, whilst the mass of the people were devoted to the Church. Solzhenitsyn has also argued that there was no intense anti-clerical feeling among the Russian people. However, there are a mass of facts which show that by October 1917 anti-clerical attitudes were widespread. In addition, social groups with some very primitive ideas gradually improved their status, and these people could only understand the new revolutionary ideology in a quasi-religious and dogmatic fashion. Millions of newly-converted 'Marxists' could not accept that a church could continue to operate and propagate a 'reactionary ideology'. They required complete uniformity as soon as possible.

Although the majority of the documents which were previously kept under lock and key in Russian archives have become accessible, the Cheka materials kept in the storage rooms of the Russian Security Service, and the materials of the top party bodies held in the Presidential Archive, remain beyond the reach of researchers.

Further reading

Alekseev V. A., *Illiuzii i dogmy* (Moscow, Politizdat, 1991).

Bogolepov A. A., trans. Moorehouse A. E., *Church Reforms in Russia 1905–1918* (Bridgeport, CT., Russian Orthodox Church of America, 1966).

Chrysostomus J., *Kirchengeschichte Russlands der neuesten Zeit. Band I. Patriarch Tichon 1917–1925* (Munich, Anton Pustet, 1965).

Cunningham J., *The Vanguished Hope: The Movement for Church Renewal in Russia, 1905–1906* (Crestwood. New York, St Vladimir's Seminary Press, 1981).

Fletcher W., *The Russian Orthodox Church Underground 1917–1970* (Oxford, Oxford University Press, 1971).

Kartashev A. A., *Revoliutsiia i Sobor 1917–1918 gg. Nabroski dlia istorii Russkoi tserkvi nashikh dnei* (Paris, Bogoslovskaia mysl' – Trudy Pravoslavnogo Bogoslovskogo instituta v Parizhe, 1942).

Levitin A. and Shavrov V., *Ocherki po istorii Russkoi tserkovnoi smuty*, 3 vols. (Küsnacht, Institut Glaube in der 2 Welt, 1978).

Metropolitan Manuil (Lemishevskii), *Russkie Pravoslavnye ierarkhi perioda s 1893 po 1965 gody (vkliuchitel'no)*, 6 vols. (Erlangen, Fairy v. Lilienfeld, 1979–89).

Odintsov M. I., *Gosudarstvo i tserkov' (Istoriia vzaimootnoshenii 1917–1938 gg.)* (Moscow, Znanie, 1991).

Pospielovsky D., *The Russian Orthodox Church under the Soviet Regime 1917–1982* (New York, St Vladimir's Seminary Press, 1984).

Regel'son L., *Tragediia Russkoi tserkvi 1917–1945* (Paris, Imka-press, 1977).

Rössler R., *Kirche und Revolution in Russland. Patriarch Tichon und der Sowjetstaat*, (Cologne and Vienna, 1969).

Schulz G., 'Begann für die russische Orthodoxe Kirche das dritte Jahrtausend im Jahre 1917?', *Kirchen im Kontext unterschiedlicher Kulturen. Auf dem Weg ins dritte Jahrtausend* (Göttingen, Vandenhoeck und Ruprecht, 1991).

Struve N., *Christians in Contemporary Russia* (London, Harvill Press, 1967).

Titlinov B. V., *Tserkov' vo vremia revoliutsii* (Petrograd, Byloe, 1924).

Valentinov A., *Chernaia kniga ('Shturm nebes')* (Paris, Russkoe natsional'noe studencheskoe ob"edinenie, 1925).

Vvedenskii A. I., *Tserkov' i gosudarstvo (Ocherk vzaimootnoshenii tserkvi i gosudarstva v Rossii 1918–1922 gg.)* (Moscow, Gosizdat, 1923).

The Soviets

NIKOLAI N. SMIRNOV

During the revolutionary months of 1917, soviets (councils) were elective political organizations which evolved rapidly from being organs of revolutionary democracy into organs of state power and local government.

On 27 February 1917 Mensheviks and Socialist Revolutionaries (SRs) called a meeting in the Tauride Palace of accredited workers' representatives from Petrograd factories, which created the Petrograd Soviet of Workers' and Soldiers' Deputies. The experience of the 1905 Russian revolution made it possible to set up the Petrograd Soviet, and to define its short- and long-term aims, remarkably quickly. At the first session of the Petrograd Soviet, the best-known and most authoritative leaders of the labour movement and its political organizations among the participants were given the status of 'deputy' and constituted its leading organ, the Executive Committee. The preponderance of SRs and Mensheviks reflected their influence among the workers and soldiers on the eve of the overthrow of the autocracy.

The Petrograd Telegraph Agency broadcast the news of the formation of the Soviet and the appeal of its Executive Committee to create soviets in other regions. By the end of March there were already more than 600 soviets of workers', soldiers', sailors', peasants' and Cossacks' deputies in operation. The sovietization of Russia continued over the following months. The most widespread types of soviets were of workers' deputies, of workers' and soldiers' deputies, of peasants' deputies (created along the lines of the soviets of workers' deputies – peasants' committees and other peasant organizations also appeared at this time), of sailors' deputies (at the military naval bases at Sevastopol and Helsingfors, etc.), of Muslim workers' deputies (in Central Asia), as well as unified soviets of workers', soldiers' and peasants' deputies.

The speed at which the new organs of revolutionary democracy were created was due both to the experience of the 1905–07 revolution and to a desire to replicate the Petrograd experience. This accounts for the uniformity in their structure, and in the way they operated.

The original declared aim of the Petrograd Soviet leaders was to protect the interests of the workers and the exploited masses against encroachment from capitalists and landowners. Within days, however, they began to assume the functions of state and political leadership. And as the Bolsheviks became more active, there was mounting tension between the two power structures, the soviets and the government. The entry of Mensheviks and SRs into the Provisional Government did not put an end to this dual power. Instead, under increasing Bolshevik criticism, it led to the more moderate socialists being 'flushed out' of the soviets. The creation of a Republic of Soviets, demanded at the Seventh (April) Conference of the RSDRP (Bolsheviks), came to be regarded by the masses as the culmination of the struggle of the oppressed against their oppressors.

As early as March, having agreed to the formula *postol'ku–poskol'ku* (that the soviets would recognize the Provisional Government *to the extent that* the Provisional Government recognized the soviets), the government lost the ability to introduce 'unpopular' measures. Its attempts to normalize industrial production by limiting wages and introducing direct militarization of labour, and any suggestion that it might try to increase the level of military activity, led to waves of political crisis in April, June and July, and to changes in the composition of the government. At meetings and demonstrations, the slogan 'All Power to the Soviets' gradually displaced the idea that the 'master of the Russian lands', the Constituent Assembly, should be convened as quickly as possible.

Deputies to the soviets were democratically elected: collectives of workers, peasants or soldiers numbering as few as ten or as many as 100 or more would elect one of their number as deputy without restrictions based on property status, domicile, nationality, party membership or religious belief. The deputy was answerable to his electors, remained in constant contact with them and was mandated. He could be recalled from the soviet at any moment. In the election of deputies such factors as honesty and good character, lack of political ambitions and so forth were very important.

However, the leading positions in the soviets were taken by politicians experienced in mass work. The Mensheviks Fedor Dan and Iraklii Tsereteli took the helm of the Petrograd Soviet. The majority of ordinary delegates merely played the role of political extras, the 'swamp'. In many respects this resembled the situation in the Convention in the great French revolution. The Bolsheviks and their political opponents fought for influence in the 'swamp', and this determined what political decisions were taken.

During the early months of 1917 the Petrograd Soviet of Workers' and Soldiers' Deputies also functioned as the central organ of the local soviets. The latter oriented themselves towards the Petrograd Soviet and followed its lead. In June the First All-Russian Congress of Soviets of Workers' and Soldiers' Deputies and the First All-Russian Congress of Soviets of Peasants' Deputies created the Central Executive Committee (VTsIK) of the Soviets of Workers' and Soldiers' Deputies and the Executive Committee of the Soviets of Peasants' Deputies respectively. Until November 1917 these two leading soviet organs operated separately. The formation of these central soviet organs, whose recommendations guided local soviets in their practical work was, in practice, the beginning of the creation of a new type of state apparatus. Its claim to all the power in Russia would inevitably lead to a clash with the Provisional Government and to an end to the system of dual power.

The economic chaos, the military failures, and the impoverishment of most of the urban and rural population which characterized the summer and autumn of 1917 impelled the local soviets towards taking over the functions of local government from the zemstvos and the urban dumas. The structure of the soviets changed. Their executive committees created commissions, departments and committees to deal with economic and financial questions, and with the organization of education and health services. Representatives from local government, cooperatives, and various types of unions and organizations became actively involved in the day-to-day life of the soviets. At the highest level, ministers and their deputies, regional commissars (who had replaced the tsarist governors), and the leaders of urban dumas and zemstvos were more and more often making reports to plenary sessions of soviet congresses and participating in their work. Similarly, in army divisions the decisions of soviets of soldiers' deputies and of military committees were more likely to be acted upon than were the orders of the military command.

The growth and increasing strength of the soviets as organs of power inevitably placed constraints upon the organs of the Provisional Government, as well as guaranteeing freedom of speech, assembly and the press.

From February to October 1917 the soviets passed through three main stages of development. The first stage, from February to June, was one of dual power, in which the soviets could have assumed power peacefully. However, the SR and Menshevik leadership of the soviets believed the Russian revolution could not go beyond the bounds of a bourgeois revolution, and regarded the soviets as temporary organizations, necessary only until the Constituent Assembly was convened. From April, the Bolsheviks, who were trying to take control of the soviets themselves, argued that the soviets should become the sole institutions of power, with full responsibility for revolutionary social transformations.

The second stage, from the July Days until the Kornilov affair in August, represented a temporary retreat from the principles of dual power. The moderate socialist leadership of the Soviet Central Executive Committee granted the Provisional Government a certain freedom of action against the Bolsheviks, which in its turn led to a fall in the authority of the SRs and Mensheviks. The soviets were effectively transformed into powerless institutions. Only in places where the Bolsheviks were strong did they continue to behave like organs of power. The decision of the Sixth RSDRP (Bolsheviks) Congress in July/August temporarily to

withdraw the slogan 'All Power to the Soviets' was not directed so much at
the workers and peasants of Russia, as at Bolshevik deputies and propagandists. In fact, this decision marked the beginning of the struggle to drive
the SRs and Mensheviks out of the soviets. It was no accident that this decision did not meet with unanimous approval even in the Bolshevik leadership. The bulk of the soviets continued to be led by opponents of the
Bolsheviks and were generally supported by a non-political populace. Even
the Russian intelligentsia was seized by the idea of soviets. Prior to the July
events there had been just one or two soviets of working intellectuals,
whereas from July to September they could be counted in dozens.

The third stage started with the revolutionary upsurge against the
Kornilov revolt in August, and culminated in the October armed uprising
and the transfer of all power to the soviets. This stage was marked by an
increasing Bolshevization of the soviets and by ever more persistent
demands that all power be transferred to them through their All-Russian
Congress. From the autumn most local soviets relied upon the armed force
of the Red Guard and revolutionary soldiers, although their freedom of
action was still restricted by the Provisional Government and by the 'bourgeois' local government structures. By September 126 local soviets were
demanding the transfer of all power in Russia to the Soviets of Workers' and
Soldiers' Deputies. This demand was supported by most of the regional
soviet congresses held in October. The rapid Bolshevization of the soviets in
the autumn of 1917 made it possible for them to become organs of revolutionary power.

According to the incomplete data available, by October 1917 there were
1,429 soviets functioning in Russia. Of these, 706 involved workers and soldiers, 235 were united soviets of workers, soldiers and peasants, 455 were
peasant, and 33 were soldiers' soviets. By that time the overwhelming bulk
of the soviets in the major industrial centres had already realized the slogan
'All Power to the Soviets' *de facto*, whereas soviets in the non-industrial
regions tended to support 'Power to the Democracy', or 'Power to the
Coalition'.

The victory of the October armed uprising overthrew the Provisional
Government and transferred its power to the soviets of workers', soldiers'
and peasants' deputies. This process received its legal sanction from the
Second All-Russian Congress of Soviets of Workers' and Soldiers' Deputies,
which took place in Petrograd from 25 to 27 October. The All-Russian
Central Executive Committee (VTsIK) was declared to be the highest organ
of state power, whilst the highest executive organ of power (the government, answerable to the VTsIK) was to be the Council of People's
Commissars (*Sovnarkom*), created by the congress.

Workers' and soldiers' soviets then initiated a process of unification with
the peasant soviets. As a rule, these mergers were effected by peasant congresses electing representatives to the executive committees of workers' and
soldiers' soviets, thereby creating single organs of workers' and peasants'

power. This process was accompanied by the removal of the right SRs and Mensheviks from the soviets and an increase in the influence of the Bolsheviks. The mergers developed most rapidly in regions adjacent to major industrial centres. The number of unified soviets also grew in non-industrial gubernias, where the victory of the October armed uprising was followed by a noticeable growth in Bolshevik influence.

The merger process accelerated considerably after the Extraordinary Peasant Congress of November 1917 took the decision to unite the Executive Committee of the Soviets of Peasants' Deputies with the VTsIK. At the same time this congress approved the transfer of power at the local level to soviets of workers', soldiers' and peasants' deputies. The Second All-Russian Peasant Congress of Soviets, also in November 1917, confirmed the decision of the Extraordinary Peasant Congress. In Lenin's view, this decision 'secured the victory of soviet power' (*Polnoe sobranie sochinenii*, vol. 35, p. 167). By March 1918 the process of merging the soviets was more or less complete.

In November and December 1917 the SRs and Mensheviks tried without success to regain the initiative from the Bolsheviks. By the time of the Third All-Russian Congress of Soviets in January 1918, there had been qualitative changes in the party allegiances of the deputies, and in the types of soviets. This can be seen from Tables 1 and 2. Table 1 is based on the congress questionnaires completed by the delegates; the figures in the final column show the number of completed questionnaires against the total number of delegates at the congresses.

The majority of the soviets operating by January 1918 had been elected in the period leading up to and immediately following the October armed uprising, and the largest single category was that of united workers', soldiers' and peasants' soviets.

In the first few months of Soviet power the state structure of the dictatorship of the proletariat was in the process of formation. On 15 January, at the Third All-Russian Congress of Soviets a resolution was adopted 'On the Federal Institutions of the Russian Republic', which defined this structure as follows: (1) The All-Russian Congress of Soviets of Workers', Soldiers' and Peasants' Deputies; (2) the All-Russian Central Executive Committee (VTsIK) elected by the congress, the highest organ of power in the period between congresses; (3) the Council of People's Commissars, the government elected by the VTsIK. All local matters were entrusted to local soviets. The top power structures had the right to regulate relations between soviets and resolve disputes between them, and to deal with matters of state which did not impinge upon the rights of the national republics which comprised the federation. The decree 'On the Removal from Decrees and Laws of All References to the Constituent Assembly' of 18 January abolished the 'provisional' status of the new power, as operating 'until the convocation of the Constituent Assembly'. In this way the Bolsheviks finished with what they called 'parliamentary illusions'.

Table 1 Party allegiance of congress deputies

Congress	Bolsheviks	LSRs	SR Maxi-malists	Cent/Rt SRs	Trudoviki and NSs	Non-faction-SDs	Men-vik Internats	Cent/Rt Men-viks	Anarchists	National Groups	Non-party	Total[1]
First	105 (13%)	–	–	285 (34.5%)	8 (0.9%)	70 (7.5%)	32 (4%)	276 (33%)	1 (0.1%)	–	47 (6%)	824 (1,090)
Second	338 (52%)	98 (15%)	–	88 (13%)	1 (0.1%)	4 (0.6%)	45 (7%)	47 (7%)	1 (0.1%)	4 (0.6%)	23 (4%)	648 (859)
Third	602 (53%)	239 (21%)	19 (1.7%)	37 (3.2%)	2 (0.1%)	–	18 (1.6%)	24 (2.1%)	9 (0.7%)	5 (0.4%)	175 (15%)	1,130 (1,798)

[1] The first figures in this column refer to the number of delegates who completed the conference questionnaire; the figures in brackets give the total number of delegates at the congress.

Table 2 Types of soviets represented at congresses

Congress[1]	Total	United	no. of each type of representative			
			Workers' and Soldiers'	Workers'	Soldiers'	Peasant
First	305	75	173	24	17	15
Second	402	119	195	46	22	20
Third	619	255	160	27	17	160

[1] The figures for the first and second congresses are cited from E. N. Gorodetskii, *Rozhdenie Sovetskogo gosudarstva 1917–1918*, 1987, although these figures are incomplete and the structure of 15 soviets is unclear. I have derived the figures for the Third Congress from questionnaires and mandates in the Russian State Historical Archive.

The Constitution of the Russian Soviet Federative Socialist Republic (RSFSR), adopted by the Fifth All-Russian Congress of Soviets (4–10 July 1918) confirmed the system of soviets that had developed. With the formation of autonomous republics and regions within the RSFSR, their local soviets were being brought together through regional soviet congresses. For those areas such as the Ukraine and Belorussia, which had the status of sovereign Soviet republics when and where they were under Soviet control, the highest bodies of the soviet system were the republican soviet congresses, which elected the TsIKs of the republics. The soviet system guaranteed broadly based participation by the working population of all nationalities in state administration, through the direct election of deputies to town and village soviets. The system of representation was changed: in towns and villages with less than 10,000 inhabitants it was one deputy per 100 inhabitants (but not less than three or more than 50 per town or village); in towns and cities it was one deputy per 1,000 inhabitants (but not less than 50 or more than 1,000 deputies). Urban voters were given proportionally greater representation than rural inhabitants at all-Russian and regional soviet congresses, while at the level of the town soviets, the workplace-based system of elections gave workers proportionally greater representation than other urban inhabitants, such as white-collar workers, students or housewives. The right to elect and to be elected irrespective of religious belief, nationality, domicile or education was enjoyed by citizens of the RSFSR of both sexes who had reached the age of 18, provided they were either engaged in socially useful work, were soldiers or sailors, or were unable to work. Electoral rights were denied to people with unearned incomes (private traders, ministers of religion and so forth), to former employees and agents of the police, gendarmerie and secret police, and to the mentally ill and those convicted of various crimes. Delegates to soviet congresses were not chosen directly by the voters, but were elected by the deputies of the soviets concerned.

For their day-to-day work, soviet congresses at all levels, as well as village and town soviets, elected executive committees. In the summer of 1918 all the old local government institutions (*upravy*, zemstvos and dumas) were abolished, and their functions were transferred to the appropriate executive committees.

On 14 June 1918 the VTsIK excluded all the Mensheviks and centre and right SRs from its ranks, on the grounds that they were hostile to soviet power, and it encouraged all soviet bodies to follow this example. Following the Left SR revolt of 6 July 1918, all the Left SR delegates who supported their Central Committee's policy were expelled. This effectively made the soviets single-party institutions. In 1919 the party composition of soviets was as follows. For soviets in gubernia towns: Communists and their sympathizers, 76 per cent; non-party, 12.2 per cent; representatives of 'petty-bourgeois' parties, 2.2 per cent; affiliation unknown, 9.6 per cent. For village soviets: Communists and their sympathizers, 5.2 per cent; non-party, 94.8 per cent; representatives of 'petty-bourgeois' parties, less than 0.1 per cent. In 29 gubernias of central Russia at the end of 1918, 724 out of 874 members of gubernia executive committees were Communists, as were 2,625 out of 4,046 members of uezd executive committees.

During the civil war (1918–22), the soviets were responsible for mobilization and conscription into the Red Army, caring for wounded Red Army men and the families of those who had died, the struggles against counter-revolution and epidemics, food requisitioning, organizing the economy, and cultural work. In this period the constitutional provisions concerning the soviets were violated. In the war zones, soviets were replaced by Revolutionary Committees, many town soviets were liquidated, and the administrative system became extremely centralized.

Although the soviets had originally arisen as revolutionary, mass, creative organs, after the Bolsheviks took power they became bureaucratized and strictly centralized organs. They continued in this form for more than seven decades.

There is a large quantity of source material, both published and archival, on the history of the soviets. The published material includes such items as the *Decrees of Soviet Power*, works on the 'triumphal march of soviet power' at the local level, and so forth. Among the primary source material there are the holdings of the Russian State Historical Archive, which include the questionnaires completed by soviet congress delegates and by the soviets represented at the congresses. The holdings of local historical archives reveal the internal dynamics of the soviets' development and of the popular movement organized by the soviets to make them the sole organs of power. Materials on the history of the creation of the VTsIK and the *Sovnarkom*, well represented both in archival and in published sources, allow one to examine the peculiarities of the new state system, such as the combination in the soviets of both legislative and executive functions.

The current state of historical literature in Russia and elsewhere requires us to rethink many established ideas about the formation and evolution of the soviets as organs of state power and administration. First and foremost, we need to reject the one-sided and subjective approaches to the problem taken by certain works on the history of the Russian revolution and the formation of the soviet state. We need a thorough examination of the difficulties involved in creating soviets both centrally and locally, the mistakes made in soviet construction in the first years of the workers' and peasants' state, the contradictions of the real historical process and the role of the masses and of political parties.

Further reading

Andreev A. M., *Sovety rabochikh i soldatskikh deputatov nakanune Oktiabria* (Moscow, Nauka, 1967).

Anweiler O., *The Soviets: The Russian Workers' Soldiers' and Peasants' Councils 1905–1921* (New York, Pantheon, 1974).

Bol'shevistskoe rukovodstvo gosudarstvennymi i obshchestvennymi organi-zatsiiami trudiashchikhsia (oktiabr' 1917–1920 gg.) (Petrozavodsk, RIO Petrozavodskogo gosudarstvennogo universiteta imeni O. V. Kuusinena, 1984).

Gimpel'son E. G., *Iz istorii stroitel'stva Sovetov (noiabr' 1917 g. – iiul' 1918 g.)* (Moscow, Gosudarstvennoe izdatel'stvo iuridicheskoi literatury, 1958).

Gorodetskii E. N., *Rozhdenie Sovetskogo gosudarstva 1917–1918* (Moscow, Nauka, 1987).

Ionkina T. D., *Vserossiiskie s"ezdy sovetov v pervye gody proletarskoi dik-tatury* (Moscow, Nauka, 1974).

Lenin V. I., *Polnoe sobranie sochinenii*, 55 vols. (Moscow, Izdatel'stvo Politicheskoi Literatury, 1958–65).

Razgon A. I., *VTsIK Sovetov v pervye mesiatsy diktatury proletariata* (Moscow, Nauka, 1977).

Smirnov N. N., *Tretii Vserossiiskii s"ezd Sovetov: istoriia sozyva, sostav, rabota* (Leningrad, Nauka, 1988).

Town and City Government

NIKOLAI N. SMIRNOV

Imperial Russia

Before the February revolution there were five categories of towns and cities in the Russian empire. In the first rank were the 'capital' cities; the other towns and cities were placed in ranks two to five. Second-rank towns were gubernia towns with populations exceeding 100,000; third-rank towns were other gubernia towns and uezd towns of comparable size; fourth-rank towns comprised other uezd and non-uezd towns; and fifth-rank towns had a simplified system of local government. Urban local authorities were formed and run in accordance with the Town Statute of 11 June 1892, which applied to all towns of the Russian empire, apart from those in Poland, Turkestan, the Transcaspian Oblast', and a number of towns in the Caucasus which had their own forms of local government. The statute regulated elections to the town's organs of local government, determined their organizational structure and functions, and defined the limits of their autonomy and their subordination to the administrative authorities. The administrative organ of local government was the duma, elected every four years. The number of duma councillors (*glasnye*) varied from 30 to 72, depending on the population of the town or city, while Moscow had 180 councillors, and St Petersburg had 250. The councillors elected an executive organ, the *uprava*, and its chairman, the mayor (*gorodskoi golova*).

The competence of local authorities was limited to the boundaries of the town and any other territories allotted to it. Local-government organs were concerned exclusively with the local economy: the organization of services and amenities (water supply and sewage, street-cleaning, town planning, etc.); food supplies (markets), fire prevention and emergency services; healthcare and public welfare (the foundation and maintenance of charitable institutions, hospitals, and public health measures); the development of education and culture (developing the school system, libraries, museums, theatres, etc.); and local trade and industry, commodity exchanges, credit institutions and so forth.

The Town Statute granted autonomy to local government within the bounds of its allotted powers. However, on questions of elections, budgets and the administrative powers of dumas the law set firm limits on this autonomy. The mayor could only commence his duties once he had been approved by the governor in an uezd town, the Minister of Internal Affairs in a gubernia town, or the tsar in one of the capitals. In contravention of the basic principle of any kind of self-government – the election of public bodies – the law permitted the local representatives of the central administration to appoint both leading officials and duma councillors. Apart from elected councillors, voting rights in the dumas were also enjoyed by the chairman of the zemstvo *uprava* and a representative of the ecclesiastical authorities.

If the Minister of Internal Affairs or the governor did not find it possible to approve the persons elected by the duma, new elections were held. If their outcome was unacceptable, the positions remained vacant until they were filled by people appointed by the Minister of Internal Affairs in the capitals, gubernia or oblast' towns, or by the governor in other towns.

The mayor, his assistants and their deputies, and all the other members of the *uprava* were servants of the state; they were appointed and dismissed by the government, and could only take up their jobs with the permission of the gubernia authorities. Any official of the town *uprava* could be punished by the courts or by the administration. Officials of the local authorities had ranks of state servants conferred upon them. According to an interpretation made by the Minister of Internal Affairs in 1893, town *upravy* were government institutions, and were subordinate to the administrative authorities.

The town duma's independence of action was very limited, and every step was supervised by the administration. The mayor had to present to the governor a list of the questions which had been discussed at duma sessions, together with a copy of all its decisions, and the latter only came into effect two weeks later, provided the governor did not block them. The governor could do so at any time – indeed, he could block even those which did not require his approval. The administration did not need to conclude that a duma decision was illegal before annulling it; the decision could be deemed 'incorrect', 'not in accordance with state interests and needs', 'evidently contrary to the interests of the local population', and so forth. Thus, the law gave the administration wide powers to interfere in the affairs of town institutions.

The high property qualifications for voters stipulated in the local government electoral law guaranteed an electorate which would produce political leaders who could ensure that town dumas worked effectively, and were loyal to the autocracy. The property qualifications differed according to the rank of the town. For the capitals it was 3,000 roubles, for gubernia towns with over 100,000 inhabitants and for Odessa it was 1,500 roubles, for other gubernia, oblast' and the most important uezd towns it was 1,000 roubles, for the rest it was 300 roubles. In the lowest rank towns with the simplified form of administration, the property qualification was just 100 roubles. Electoral rights were also accorded to government, charitable, educational and scientific institutions, and to persons, societies and companies owning trading or industrial enterprises. In the capitals this was limited to merchants of the first guild and in other towns to those of the first and second guilds.

Elections to town dumas were conducted either at one single electoral meeting or, if there were a large number of electors, in sections. The elections were deemed valid if the number of votes cast exceeded the number of posts available and candidates for them. Every elector also had the right to be elected. To be included in the ballot one had either to express the desire to stand, or to be nominated by no fewer than five electors. The law did not provide for any special election meetings to propose candidates for the dumas. The ballot was secret, and used balls for voting. To be elected as a duma councillor one had to gain an absolute majority of the votes. The governor was responsible for organizing and conducting the elections.

The higher authorities (the Senate, the State Council, the Council of Ministers, the State Duma and so on) could take up to three months before ruling on complaints and suggestions from town dumas. The executive organ was subordinate to the administrative one, but if a majority at the town *uprava* deemed a duma decision to be unlawful, and it was not possible to reach agreement, the *uprava* would pass the matter to the governor.

The Town Statute brought in a range of restrictions designed to prevent local government officials abusing their positions for their own advantage. Officials were banned from acting as contractors or suppliers to local government, and from purchasing municipal property when they were responsible for organizing its sale.

The town dumas had a number of negative features. The most important of these were that the executive and administrative organs were headed by one and the same person; that the dumas had no power of coercion; that the right to vote was denied to those in rented accommodation; and that contacts between dumas in different towns were prohibited. During World War I, however, this last limitation was frequently overcome following the creation of the All-Russian Union of Towns.

The 1892 Statute established that there would be two forms of urban local government: full, and simplified. These were determined on the basis of population size, the state of municipal finances, the occupations of the bulk of the townspeople, and the level of development of trade and industry. The simplified form of local government did not extend to gubernia towns or other towns with a comparable electorate. According to the 'Rules on Simplified Local Government' the duma was replaced by a 'Council of Town Representatives' consisting of between 12 and 15 people, elected from among local property owners at a meeting of local householders. The council elected a town *starosta* and one or two assistants at the governor's discretion. Despite certain advantages (a wider electorate and fewer officials to maintain) towns with simplified local government were deprived of the right to produce 'obligatory resolutions', engage in town planning, control the liquor trade and so on. This had implications for both the income and expenditure sides of the municipal budget.

Municipal incomes were comprised of 'normal incomes' (from property and rents, from municipal and suchlike enterprises), various taxes (on property values, on trade and industry, special taxes on householders, on privately owned horses and carriages, on dogs, hospital taxes, duties and the like), and 'extraordinary incomes' (grants from the treasury and zemstvo councils, profits from municipal banks, municipal loans, etc.). On the expenditure side, money was spent on public amenities (government institutions, maintaining the organs of local government, organizing military service and billeting, the maintenance of the police and the fire brigade, the upkeep of bridges, pavements, embankments and so forth, street lighting and establishing new public amenities), and on municipal enterprises (water and sewage, tramways, abattoirs). Other expenditures included education, institutions for the poor, medical, veterinary and sanitary services, public buildings, upkeep of monuments and other municipal property, payments on loans, transfers to the municipal capital fund and other municipal needs. There were few sources of credit. The number of towns which enjoyed the right to raise loans from the state treasury and from public town banks was very limited. Usually local government bodies had to resort to credit from private institutions and individuals on very unfavourable terms. Such long-term municipal credit as was raised took the form of local bonds, but their use was not very widespread. Consequently, Russian towns, with the exceptions of St Petersburg and Moscow, were not well funded, and as a result the municipal economy was poorly developed. In their overwhelming majority, towns in the Russian empire were dirty, badly lit, and lacked reliable water supplies, sewage systems and public transport. Even in the capitals and the major centres of trade and industry, where there was a rapid growth of income and fairly wide opportunities to raise money through credit and loans, the local authorities proved incapable of dealing with many vital problems.

Conditions in the imperial capital were more favourable. The 1903 'Statute on Local Government in St Petersburg' gave voting rights to tenants, divided the chairmanships of the duma and the *uprava*, reduced the number of questions which had to be referred to the minister for approval, and established that petitions from the duma should be ruled upon within one month.

Under the Provisional Government

The overthrow of the autocracy created a basis for transforming local government organs. The Provisional Government abolished the posts of governor-general, governor, town governor (*gradonachal'nik*), chief of police (*politsmeister*), and district police officer (*ispravnik*), along with their respective offices. It also abolished the police administrations, committees on press affairs, gendarme administrations and secret police (*okhranka*) departments. Responsibilities were taken on by the gubernia, town and uezd commissars of the Provisional Government and their offices or, in the interim, the chairmen of the gubernia and uezd zemstvo *upravy* and the mayors.

Provisional 'committees of public organizations' were also elected in many places, made up of local councillors, representatives from various public organizations, liberal officials and other prominent local figures. These committees declared themselves to be provisional local authorities and replaced the governors and other officials of the old regime, created new militia organs, and recommended or elected the oblast', gubernia or uezd commissars of the Provisional Government.

In the first months of the revolution municipal authorities expanded their spheres of competence. Some also expanded territorially into surrounding regions, especially in Siberia and the Semirechensk, Akmolinsk, Arkhangel'sk, and Astrakhan gubernias. A law of 15 April 1917 established district dumas and *upravy* in towns with a population exceeding 150,000. A council of dumas coordinated their work within the town.

The militia was established to replace the police by a law of 17 April. Towns were sub-divided into districts, and the districts into areas served by one militia station with cells for arrestees. The maintenance and administration of the militia were placed in the hands of the local authorities, who chose the chiefs of the town, district and area militias and their assistants.

Under the Provisional Government the role of the courts was circumscribed to a certain extent. Courts with representatives of the estates (*sosloviia*) were abolished, and jury courts became widely used. The jurisdiction of district courts was extended significantly. A Provisional Government decree of 4 May reorganized the local courts and gave greater powers to justices of the peace. A law of 30 May created the administrative court, and in gubernia and oblast' towns special administrative departments were established at the district courts to consider conflicts between state organs, Provisional Government commissars and local authorities.

The gubernia, uezd and town food committees, which had arisen spontaneously in March, were made formal institutions and integrated into the Ministry of Agriculture by a law of 2 April. Their allotted tasks included combating speculation, operating the grain monopoly, compulsory purchase of grain, and dealing with anything that caused disturbances among the hungry masses.

On 9 June the Provisional Government passed a resolution 'On Changing the Existing Town Statute'. The functions of the local authorities were declared to be 'matters of local administration and economy, along with other matters entrusted to them by particular laws'. The powers of the town dumas were increased. They were able to elect officials (the mayor and his assistants, members of the town *uprava*, the duma chairman) and confirm them in office. Dumas were granted the right to pass obligatory resolutions on 33 matters of municipal administration. These included town planning regulations, the maintenance of cleanliness and order, the administration of the militia, provision of medical and legal services, the running of educational institutions, and supply of foodstuffs and essential items. Town dumas were 'independent' in their actions, although they were obliged to inform the government commissar about their 'obligatory resolutions', and the commissar would inform the duma within two weeks of his agreement or disagreement. This provision, article 73 of the new statute, was criticized for turning duma independence into a fiction.

The Petrograd City Duma was to have no fewer than 12 sessions a year. Its chairman was to be elected by the councillors for one year. City councillors were not permitted to take paid jobs as officials of the city administration. Councillors were paid out of city funds for all sessions of the duma they attended. The duma would decide the salaries of the mayor and his assistants and of *uprava* members. Duma councillors had the right to relinquish their positions, which would then be taken by one of the candidates on the electoral list.

For day-to-day administration and for dealings with government and other institutions the duma elected a town *uprava* headed by the mayor. At the request of the *uprava* the duma could elect special commissions or individual persons to run various branches of the town administration and the municipal economy. These persons could be duma councillors or anybody with the legal right to be elected to the town duma.

The Provisional Government and the parties which supported it believed that a complete reform of local government would only be possible after the convocation of the Constituent Assembly. Until then, they decided to limit themselves to half measures. One of these was the immediate re-election of local authorities on the basis of the new electoral law.

On 15 April the Provisional Government passed a resolution 'On the Conduct of Elections for Town Duma Councillors and on District Municipal Administration', which arose in part from a proposal by the Ministry of Internal Affairs. Henceforth, councillors were to be elected on a system of proportional representation, on the basis of an equal, direct and secret ballot of citizens over 20 years of age, including those in the armed forces. The government intended to conduct municipal elections in accordance with these new rules around the end of May and the beginning of June 1917, but the course of political events in Russia and the worsening economic crisis meant that the elections were postponed until later in the summer.

Over most of Russia the elections took place between 30 July and 20 August. The majority of votes went to representatives of liberal-bourgeois and moderate socialist parties. In 50 gubernia towns, the Bolsheviks received on average 7.5 per cent of the poll. In the uezd towns they received just 2.2 per cent. In Moscow, the Bolsheviks took 23 seats in the City Duma, while the SRs took 116, the Kadets 34, the Mensheviks 24 and the Popular Socialists (NS) three. In the elections to the Petrograd City Duma on 20 August, the Bolshevik vote reached 33.5 per cent, while around 20 per cent voted for the Kadets.

By the autumn of 1917, the local state apparatus had become a complex mosaic. Beside the new officials and institutions there remained many old judicial, financial, economic and military bodies. However, the importance of local authority bodies grew, and they became genuine organs of self-government. Alongside the dumas, committees of public organizations and military-industrial committees played a large role in local administration. Following the Kornilov revolt, in both the centre and the localities the soviets of workers' and soldiers' deputies began to intervene more often in the economic affairs of the towns, operating through their representatives in the dumas and in other public organizations. The Bolshevization of the soviets led to increasingly frequent conflicts with the local authorities, which did not help the latter fulfil their statutory responsibilities.

After October

The political positions and the activities of the duma majorities during the October uprising made the municipal administrations bastions of anti-Bolshevism. Virtually everywhere the town dumas associated themselves with the local branches of the Committee to Save the Country and the Revolution, participated in the organization of resistance to the Bolsheviks, and worked to remove them from power, which made it quite impossible to work together with the Bolshevized soviets. Therefore the Council of People's Commissars decided to dissolve those dumas which did not recognize it. The Petrograd City Duma was dissolved in November 1917, and in fresh elections the Bolsheviks took the majority of seats. In Moscow, following a fierce armed struggle the Military-Revolutionary Committee dispersed the duma and the city *uprava*. A general meeting of Moscow district councillors who recognized Soviet power elected a soviet of district dumas to organize the city economy. Events in the provinces unfolded in a similar fashion.

In December 1917 the Commissariat for Local Government prepared the transfer of the basic administrative and economic functions of the town dumas and *upravy* to the local soviets. On 4 January 1918 the main committees of the All-Russian Union of Towns were abolished and their property was transferred to the Supreme Council of the National Economy. On 24 January 1918 the People's Commissariat of Internal Affairs published a statute 'On the Replacement of Zemstvo and Town Local Authorities by Soviets'. It decreed the dissolution of those dumas that had resisted Soviet power, and proposed that those which had collaborated with Soviet power be merged with the soviets.

The liquidation of the former system of local government proceeded by stages throughout 1918, as the soviets became able to take on the work which had previously been performed by the town dumas and *upravy*. The functions of the town dumas went to the deputies of the soviets, and the functions of the *upravy* went to the soviet executive committees.

Further reading

Diakin V. S., *et al.*, eds., *Reformy ili revoliutsiia? Rossiia 1861–1917* (St Petersburg, Nauka, 1992).

Eroshkin N. P., Kulikov Iu. V. and Chernov A. V., *Istoriia Gosudarstvennykh uchrezhdenii Rossii do Velikoi Oktiabr'skoi sotsialisticheskoi revoliutsii* (Moscow, Ministerstvo vysshego i srednego spetsial'nogo obrazovanie RSFSR, 1965).

Gorodetskii E. N., 'Oktiabr'skaia revoliutsiia i starye organy samoupravleniia', *Vestnik MGU*, 11 (1947).

Grunt A. Ia., 'Munitsipial'naia kampaniia v Moskve letom 1917 g.', *Istoriia SSSR 5* (1973).

Kruchkovskaia V. M., *Tsentral'naia gorodskaia Duma Petrograda v 1917 g.* (Leningrad, Nauka, 1986).

Mil'chik I. I., 'Petrogradskaia Tsentral'naia Gorodskaia Duma v fevrale-oktiabre 1917 g.', *Krasnaia letopis'* 2, 23 (1927).

Nardova V. A., *Samoderzhavie i gorodskie dumy v Rossii v kontse XIX–nachale XX veka* (St Petersburg, Nauka, 1994).

The Trade Unions

DIANE P. KOENKER

Trade unions as a legal form of worker organization emerged in Russia only in the aftermath of the 1905 revolution. The revolutionary conditions of their origin and the repressive political climate soon forced unions underground, and tied them to a far more explicitly political agenda than their counterparts in Western Europe. This close association of trade unions with revolutionary, Social-Democratic politics in turn shaped the role that Russian trade unions would play in the revolutionary transformations of 1917–21.

Trade-union traditions

Extremely limited workers' trade organizations before 1905 and Social-Democratic experience imported from Western Europe provided the context for the first flowering of Russian trade unions in the aftermath of the 1905 revolution. Legalized by the law of 4 March 1906, workers' trade unions (*professional'nye soiuzy*) quickly formed and spread in Russia's major economic centres. These first unions attracted young, skilled, and male urban workers in small, craft-based industries; they never achieved mass membership levels, least of all in large-scale industry, but some of the smaller trades recruited as many as half of their workers into their organizations. Trade unions were still in the process of formation and self-definition when their growth was abruptly cut short by the period of reaction launched by Prime Minister P. A. Stolypin's *coup d'état* of 3 June 1907. Unions and other forms of labour organization were banned, and individuals who engaged in organizational activity, including strikes and other kinds of collective behaviour, were subject to arrest and imprisonment. Membership fell dramatically, although efforts to revive and maintain rudimentary union structures persisted. After peaking at 250,000 in January 1907, by 1910 the number of workers belonging to legally sanctioned unions stood at only 60,000. Individual unions also preserved their identities by episodic publications and through various organizational meetings, either underground or abroad.

Through the years óf reaction from 1907 to 1912, and continuing during a rise of labour unrest between 1912 and 1914, Russian trade-union leaders and practitioners professed strict loyalty to a Marxist, Social-Democratic world view. This identification between trade unionism and Social-Democratic politics provoked numerous clashes among the leaders of the Social-Democratic Party wings, Bolsheviks and Mensheviks, over the appropriate and necessary degree of autonomy or subordination of the union movement *vis-à-vis* the parties. Although an increasing number of union activists and members favoured Bolshevik politics of revolutionary activism over Menshevik gradualism in the years just before the 1917 revolution, even Bolshevik trade unionists frequently disagreed with their party leadership over the degree to which union goals should be subordinated to party political goals.

The trade-union movement that existed on the eve of the February revolution reflected the ideology and features that would characterize union organization in the pre- and post-October revolutionary periods. The goal of trade unions, to organize and mobilize the mass of Russia's working class, required unity of all workers, regardless of differing political viewpoints. At the same time, the close historical links between the trade unions and the Social-Democratic parties meant that party considerations and conflicts over policy would assume extreme importance. These contradictory goals led to a recurring conflict in the union movement between those who pushed for the subordination of the unions to revolutionary goals, and those who believed in the autonomy of trade unions within the revolutionary state. At the same time, the relative weakness of Russia's trade unions before 1917 – their narrow, politicized appeal to skilled, male workers who had been willing to risk tsarist repression – meant that in 1917 unions would appear as a novel form of organization for most Russian workers, and would come to compete with other forms of worker organization for legitimacy and authority among workers themselves.

Trade unions in 1917

No law sanctioned the creation of trade unions after the fall of the tsarist regime in February. Returning political exiles and veterans of the trade-union movement simply set to work to charter trade unions and to recruit members. The newly formed soviets of workers' deputies in many locations encouraged union organization, and local councils, or bureaux, of trade unions also spearheaded the organizational effort city by city. By the middle of June 1917, 1,733 trade unions had organized 1.8 million workers in 30 industries ranging from textiles (38 unions with 346,000 members) to metals (200 unions with 285,000 members), medical services (100 unions with 66,000 members) and mining (two unions with 32,000 members).

At the same time, union activists (particularly those from the Menshevik Party) began to prepare for Russia's first all-Russian congress of trade unions, which would set the agenda for the newly independent trade-union movement. Such a congress was first proposed in 1906, but the subsequent political reaction had annulled plans for the constitutive meeting of an all-Russian trade union organization. The turbulent conditions of 1917 also made organizing difficult, and activists settled for calling a trade-union conference for 20–28 June. A conference by definition was less author-itative than a congress, but this gathering, labelled the Third All-Russian Conference of Trade Unions, managed to debate a number of key tasks of trade-union mobilization. The watchword of the conference was 'unity': broad, class-based organizations of workers were essential for defending the interests and political goals of workers in newly liberated Russia. But the theme of unity merely patched over deeper conflicts in the movement between those with a trade-union agenda (most Mensheviks and some Bolsheviks) and those who wished to subordinate trade-union goals to the immediate goals of the revolution. In general, Menshevik union activists envisioned that the union struggle would be carried out in a democratic capitalist system, and their goal was to position Russian trade unions as well as possible to conduct this struggle. Bolshevik activists (a minority at this conference) had already set their sights on a more radical socialist revolution, in which socialist trade unions would become partners of a socialist state. The conference debated and adopted a series of resolutions on some key principles of trade-union practice. On the important issue of independence, the conference voted that unions would be 'class-based', that is, Marxist, but independent of specific political parties. The conference addressed the perpetual structural conflict between sectional, craft organ-izational principles, and industry-wide organization, and voted solidly for industrial unions that would be linked into regional and national union structures. Among the tasks of trade unions, one of the most controversial was strike leadership. The conference firmly adopted a principle endorsed by both Mensheviks and Bolsheviks, that the strike was a tactic of 'last resort', and that 'proletarian discipline' should be used instead of strikes to bargain through political and arbitration structures for workers' demands. At its conclusion, the conference elected a provisional All-Russian Central Council of Trade Unions (*Vserossiiskii tsentral'nyi sovet professional'nykh soiuzov* – VTsSPS), whose task would be to continue to consolidate the trade-union movement and to organize the first congress of Russian trade unions in the near future.

Individual unions also began to organize national central committees during the course of this conference, and the centralized structural model of Russian trade unionism received its affirmation here: the VTsSPS served as the organizational and political centre for trade-union activities. In individual cities, central bureaux of trade unions would serve an analogous local role. Trade unions organized by industry would be linked horizontally with these central bureaux and vertically through provincial committees to national central committees for each industrial union. The official structure was thus centralized and hierarchical in theory, although in practice central discipline was difficult to enforce.

Trade-union leaders often had very clear ideas about what role their organizations should play in the new society, but the union rank-and-file had much less experience and familiarity with trade-union practices and prospects. The 1917 revolution had produced other institutions which represented working-class interests, and which competed in practice for workers' allegiance. Soviets of workers' deputies were created as political organs, but they assumed many functions analogous to those of trade unions, including strike mediation, labour placement, and organization of trades. Factory committees emerged initially to organize workers within individual factories, but as trade unions failed to organize quickly enough to deal with problems of wages, hours, control and regulation, factory committees began to join together in city-wide conferences to deal with many of the problems that trade unions were meant to handle.

The relationship of trade unions to the increasing number of strikes illustrates some of these problems of multiple authorities in the workers' revolution. The trade-union movement officially discouraged strikes, and viewed strikes in individual factories or sections of industries as damaging to proletarian solidarity. None the less, in so far as workers insisted on striking to bargain for their demands, trade unions in practice often took the lead in organizing these protests, in formulating grievances, and in negotiating outcomes. Unions were particularly active in coordinating strikes in the first four months of the revolution, a time of active union growth: victorious strikes certainly helped add prestige to the union leaderships that led them. Toward the end of the summer and into the autumn, however, trade unions more actively discouraged strike activity as economically and politically counterproductive, and a large number of strikes proceeded without union approval in this period.

The fundamental contradiction between the trade union's role as the defender of wage workers' interests within the *status quo* and its role as an agent of revolution continued to plague the movement. Political differences between Mensheviks and Bolsheviks crystallized around these two positions, and the VTsSPS and other central trade-union organs became arenas, alongside the soviets, for the party political struggle. The Bolsheviks claimed to score a major political victory when the Moscow Central Bureau of Trade Unions, up until now dominated by moderate Menshevik trade unionists, responded to the Bolsheviks' call on 9 August to declare a general strike to protest against the impending gathering in Moscow of a State Conference. When the delegates to this conference, called by Kerensky to shore up the Provisional Government against the socialist threat, arrived in Moscow, they found the city at a standstill, and some had to walk from the railway stations to their accommodation in the centre of town. At the same time, increasing numbers of Russian workers signed up as members of trade unions. Although the major spurt in union growth occurred between March and June 1917, by December 1917, another 900,000 workers had joined the movement, which then totalled 2,753,300 workers in over 2,000 unions.

The history of Russian trade unions in 1917 has been a top-heavy one, and has viewed trade unions primarily as participants in the political, revolutionary struggle for state power. Soviet historiography has contributed to this exclusively political perspective by concentrating on trade unions as an indicator of the Bolshevik conquest of the working masses, paying little attention to divisions and fractures within the organized labour movement. For example, most Soviet studies of 1917 regard trade unions and factory committees as seamless parts of the same organizational whole. This is a result of reading back into the historical record the decisions taken by the First All-Russian Trade Union Congress in 1918, which declared that factory committees were but local units of trade unions. This was not the case in 1917: factory committees and trade unions were as often rivals as partners, regardless of shared political sympathies. The emphasis on structure and politics, however, has not been confined to Soviet historiography, and this approach leaves a number of unasked questions about the nature and extent of the role played by unions in the everyday lives of their 2.7 million members. Only further research on local unions in individual industries can provide the answers. How did the unions of 1917 reach out from their small pre-1917 base among skilled, urban and male workers? What was the impact on workers' own organizational culture of their relative unfamiliarity with trade-union practices? Was the union idea for them a 'natural' one, or did other forms of organization more closely address their needs, experience and interests? Although wage-earning women played a very small role in union leadership, they were clearly drawn into union organizations. The agency of Russian women workers in trade-union and other kinds of labour activism in 1917 remains a blank spot in the history of the revolution.

Trade unions under Communist rule

The position of trade unions in Russian society changed dramatically with the Bolshevik declaration of socialist power on 25 October 1917. In a socialist state, the government was expected to provide and guarantee the benefits that trade unions in capitalist societies had to fight for. Hence, the coming of socialism in Russia defined new tasks for the still infant trade-union movement. These tasks were codified at the First All-Russian Congress of Trade Unions in January 1918, and were amplified in subsequent all-Russian congresses in January 1919 and in April 1920. As official organs of state power, trade unions in Soviet Russia should organize industrial workers for state

goals. In the economic *débâcle* of revolution and civil war, the overriding
state goal had become the revival and promotion of production. Therefore,
trade unions should work closely with state economic agencies (led by the
Supreme Economic Council, VSNKh) and with the Commissariat of Labour.
Communists (as the Bolsheviks had renamed themselves in March 1918) still
disagreed in 1918 and 1919 whether this 'statization' of trade unions implied
that workers' organizations would be subordinated to those of economic
management, or whether management itself would be carried out by
workers' organizations. In fact, most Communists refused to recognize that
a conflict existed between these two positions. To facilitate the smooth coordination between state agencies (and policies) and the trade unions, these
successive congresses also approved a strictly centralized and hierarchical
structure for trade unions. Annual congresses would elect the VTsSPS, whose
decisions functioned as law on trade-union matters. Provincial councils of
trade unions served as their local representatives. Individual trade unions
would also be organized by province and nationally; their policies were subordinate to those of the central council. Factory committees would function
as local and subordinate units of the trade unions; this last decision was
meant to rein in decisively the anarchic and independent movement of factory committees that had developed during 1917. The first chairman of the
VTsSPS was G. E. Zinoviev, elected in January 1918. Overburdened with
other party responsibilities, he was replaced in March 1918 by M. P.
Tomskii, who would lead the Soviet trade-union movement until his political defeat in 1929. Other major players in trade-union leadership were S. A.
Lozovskii, a political maverick who left the Bolsheviks immediately after the
October revolution and rejoined them in 1920, and Communists G. N.
Mel'nichanskii, N. I. Derbyshev and Ia. E. Rudzutak.

A dissenting view of the role of trade unions was defended by Menshevik
Party leaders Iu. O. Martov and I. M. Maiskii and their trade-unionist members. Socialism had not yet matured in Russia, they argued, and workers still
needed union organizations that were independent of the state, and whose
primary task was to defend the interests of workers as against that state and
its economic managers. At the Trade-Union Congress in January 1918, 66
of 416 delegates supported this Menshevik position. At the Second Congress
a year later, only 30 delegates supported the principle of independence and
by 1920, 'independent' opposition to the majority position was negligible.
These votes at the centrally controlled congresses cannot be used to gauge
the opinion of rank-and-file workers, whose political loyalties, priorities and
affiliations remained fluid. Certainly, at the end of 1917 the majority of
industrial workers embraced Bolshevik solutions to the crises of the economy and of power. Individual unions of printers and of chemical workers
attempted to resist government pressures to adopt the productivist position;
dissidence and resistance in these unions were crushed by the use of the centralized principle of union structure, by manipulative democratic measures,
by imposition of economic pressures on rank-and-file 'independents', and by

outright repression – the arrests of union leaders and members who opposed the Communist Party line. In addition, every trade-union leadership organ, from the local factory committee to the VTsSPS, possessed a 'shadow' executive committee composed of the Communist Party members in those organs: these party factions always met prior to meetings of the particular collective, transmitting policy decisions from central party organizations, and sending information to higher levels through party rather than through trade-union channels. To understand the workings of the trade unions in the post-October period, one needs to read not only the record in the trade-union press and archive, but also the parallel party record.

Communist leaders boasted that despite the collapse of industrial production during the civil-war years, trade-union membership continued to climb: from 1.5 million in mid-1917, to 2.6 million in early 1918 to 3.5 million by January 1919. The VTsSPS met regularly, publishing a newspaper that discussed trade-union issues of the day, *Professional'noe dvizhenie* ('Trade-Union Movement'). Individual union leaders moved back and forth from their union jobs to managerial responsibilities. How meaningful these trade unions were for their rank-and-file members is more difficult to determine: research at the local levels confirms a blurring of lines between union and managerial personnel. Less is known about how workers on the shop floor related to the centrally determined tasks of the unions, and about the extent to which trade unions as an institution could claim any authority in their eyes. Factory committees retained substantial authority and independence during this period, as did local factory managements.

Trade-union aspirations for independence and autonomy from state tutelage were defeated in 1918–20 by labelling these aspirations 'Menshevik' and 'counterrevolutionary'. The experience of the union of printers, where Menshevik viewpoints held out the longest, illustrates this process. The largest local printers' union, the Moscow branch, persisted in supporting the Menshevik, independent position on trade unions, but Communist activists managed to win control of the union's central committee by splitting the union and calling their own congress in May 1919, which the VTsSPS then labelled authoritative. The independent Moscow branch was henceforth an 'outlaw' because it did not obey the dictates of the union centre. Meetings to protest these union policies were construed, in the context of civil war, as threats to the state itself, and the subsequent arrest of the leaders of the independent printers was justified in the name of revolutionary survival.

But fundamental conflicts remained between the role of trade unions as representative of workers' interests and as representatives of state interests. Communist leaders and even the historian E. H. Carr believed that there could be no real conflict of interest between genuine workers and the workers' state, and that resistance to state policies among workers and trade unions must be blamed on the effect of peasant dilution of the workforce. Further empirical research into workers' identities can test such propositions; the 'peasantness' of Russia's workforce was frequently invoked to explain away anti-Communist behaviour as a manifestation of 'false consciousness'. (The 'aristocratic' nature of printing was used to explain away the urbanized printers' opposition to Communist policies.) It is clear, however, that Communists also disagreed among themselves on the proper role of trade unions. Trotsky proposed the complete subordination of the unions to the needs of production, and began to implement this view through a policy of the militarization of labour, first applied to the railway union. His replacement of the independently minded railway central committee with a productivist leadership, *Tsektran*, was a response to the collapse of industrial production and of labour discipline, and especially to the failure of transport, so critical both for production and for the war effort. Parallel institutions (trade unions and economic agencies) were seen to be inefficient; trade unions, Trotsky felt, were becoming nests of bureaucratic cronyism rather than executive centres for production. But the problems that statization were meant to resolve arose from the fundamental social and economic collapse in Russia in this period, and the institutional, centralized reorganization that *Tsektran* represented was no more successful in resolving them than had been the relatively decentralized railway union before it. The heavy-handed methods invoked by *Tsektran* and the apparent privileging of managerial interests over workers' interests provoked fierce debate and criticism within the party, which spilled over into the public press between January and March 1921. This trade-union debate recapitulated the familiar and insoluble dilemmas of trade-union organization in a socialist state: should the unions' main job be to stimulate production or to defend the immediate and sectional interests of their members? Should labour be voluntary or compulsory? Should unions take orders from the state or be independent? Trotsky took the extreme statist viewpoint, supported by N. I. Bukharin. Tomskii defended the independence of trade unions, the old Menshevik position. A dissident position coalescing around the so-called Workers' Opposition also rejected Trotsky's formulation. The debate came to a head at the Tenth Party Congress in March 1921, in the throes of widespread opposition to the Communist regime, including the revolt of sailors at the Kronstadt naval fortress. Ultimately, Lenin and a group of centrists forced a compromise which acknowledged that workers had felt ill-served by their statized unions, but the compromise did little to answer the underlying question of the role of the trade union in a socialist state, a question that would recur in practice after the implementation of the New Economic Policy.

Trade unions outside Communist rule

Trade-union fortunes in Russian territory not under Communist control during the civil war also reflected the historical weakness of Russian trade-union traditions and the strength of statist traditions of labour policy. The experience of trade unions under White rule ranged from limited toleration to outright repression. In the Ukraine, the German authorities permitted trade unions to exist during their occupation in 1918: the first all-Ukrainian conference of trade unions assembled in Kiev in May 1918, dominated by Mensheviks, who would constitute the leadership of the embattled trade unions in most of the territories under White control. The Menshevik approach was based on the uncertainty of the outcome of the revolution and civil war; their goal, therefore, was to preserve trade-union structures and to defend workers' interests first, and to work for socialist politics second.

Trade-union freedom in Siberia was tolerated under the rule of the Socialist Revolutionaries, but fell victim to the rightward move of the Siberian government in late 1918. A trade-union congress and other workers' organizations were suppressed, and following the November 1918 coup by Admiral A. V. Kolchak, trade-union leaders were arrested and imprisoned without charges. Military authorities warned striking printers in Tomsk that pickets would be shot. By early 1919, the socialist press reported that trade unions in Siberia were moribund.

In South Russia, even after the withdrawal of German troops from the Ukraine, trade-union activity remained officially legal and sometimes tolerated under White governments. The most powerful union organ, the Council of Southern Trade Unions, or *Iugprof*, cooperated at first with the White governments and White armies; led by Menshevik trade unionists, this Kharkov-based organization focused on protecting the immediate interests of workers. An anti-semitic, nationalist union movement developed in Kiev in 1919, under the leadership of K. F. Kirsta, which fought the Menshevik-led unions as much as employers. Meanwhile, the Special Conference of the Commander in Chief of the Volunteer Army approved regulations in November 1919 that allowed workers to form trade unions in defence of their occupational interests. As under the tsarist regime, union leaders had to register with local authorities, and the right to strike was not granted. Whites never attempted to repress unions completely, but they and their armies harassed organized labour, arresting labour leaders without cause, closing down newspapers, searching union offices, dispersing meetings, and intimidating workers. When the White General P. N. Krasnov, for example, captured the industrial town of Iuzovka on 10 November 1918, he ordered all workers with revolutionary sympathies to be hanged in full view of the public. Such widespread repression made organization of effective trade unions as difficult as it had been under tsarism. In the Donbass, as in central Russia, despite the presence of trade-union structures for miners and metalworkers, workers sought to advance their interests individually, submitting petitions to their management rather than working through labour organization. Russian trade unions thus found themselves institutionally marginalized, for different reasons, in both the Red and the White arenas of the civil war.

Conclusions

Although the formation of industrial working classes has almost universally been accompanied by the creation of trade-union-like structures, the experience of Russian trade unions warns against the adoption of any universal law of working-class formation. Because of the conditions of tsarist repression and the primacy of politics over economics among Russia's revolutionary leaders, trade unions in Russia had not developed deep institutional roots within workers' own experience by the time of the socialist revolution of October 1917. They were as much the creature of socialist leaders, who borrowed heavily from German experience in deciding what trade unions ought to be, as of worker self-organization or the local struggle between workers and their employers. Thus trade unions competed structurally and functionally with numerous other institutions that claimed to represent workers' interests, from soviets and factory committees in 1917 to state economic agencies under Soviet power.

Moreover, the Communists' own discourse rendered trade unions problematic as authentic and indigenous worker organizations. Lenin had condemned 'trade union consciousness' as second-class and even harmful to the main agenda of revolutionary politics in his 1902 tract, *What Is To Be Done?*. For many Communists (especially those not directly involved in union organization), the trade unions were simply an instrument for the penetration, disciplining and leadership of the mass of workers. Trade unions in the 1920s became a 'school of socialism', a training ground in organizational practice, rather than an authentic forum for workers' interests.

As a result of this history, ideas and policies about trade unions have commanded more interest among historians than have actual union practices. Documentation of central party discussions and debates – stenographic reports of all-Russian congresses – has also been much more readily available than evidence of how and whether these debates affected and were shaped by activities on the shop floor. The link in question between leaders and rank and file is not just organizational, but linguistic. Research into the local and particular experience of trade unions in the revolutionary period should look for the ways in which policies were articulated and formulated, the ways in which trade-union structures, practices and language helped workers to construct their own ideas about the meaning of the revolution, the role of wage workers in that revolution, the meaning of class, and the very identity of 'worker'. The particular history of Russian trade unions – their origins as small, illegal organizations of skilled male workers, their subordination to political goals, their failure to achieve hegemony within the labour movement in 1917 – must condition the questions that are asked. None the less, historians should note that however 'artificial' trade unions may have been in terms of their place in worker consciousness, unions became the primary vehicle for recording the experience of workers in the

Soviet Union, and these records offer extremely rich opportunities for the exploration of any number of issues concerning labour relations and working-class experience in the Russian revolution.

Further reading

Anskii A., ed., *Professional'noe dvizhenie v Petrograde v 1917 g.* (Leningrad, 1928).

Bonnell V. E., *Roots of Rebellion: Workers' Politics and Organizations in St Petersburg and Moscow, 1900–1914* (Berkeley, University of California Press, 1983).

Brovkin V. N., *Behind the Lines of the Civil War: Political Parties and Social Movements in Russia, 1918–1922* (Princeton, Princeton University Press, 1994).

Egorova A. G., *Partiia i profsoiuzy v oktiabr'skoi revoliutsii* (Moscow, Mysl', 1970).

Friedgut T. H., *Iuzovka and Revolution: Politics and Revolution in Russia's Donbass, 1869–1924* (Princeton, Princeton University Press, 1994).

Hogan H., *Forging Revolution* (Bloomington, Indiana University Press, 1993).

Koenker D., *Moscow Workers and the 1917 Revolution* (Princeton, Princeton University Press, 1981).

Koenker D. P., 'Labor Relations in Socialist Russia: Class Values and Production Values in the Printers' Union, 1917–1921', in L. H. Siegelbaum and R. G. Suny, eds., *Making Workers Soviet: Power, Class, and Identity* (Ithaca, Cornell University Press, 1994).

Koenker D. P. and Rosenberg W. G., *Strikes and Revolution in Russia, 1917* (Princeton, Princeton University Press, 1989).

Kolesnikov B., *Professional'noe dvizhenie i kontr-revoliutsiia* (Khar'kov, Gosudarstvennoe izdatel'stvo Ukrainy, 1923).

Pervyi vserossiiskii s"ezd professional'nykh soiuzov, 1918 (Moscow, 1918).

Rosenberg W. G., 'The Social Background to Tsektran', in D. P. Koenker, W. G. Rosenberg, and R. G. Suny, eds., *Party, State, and Society in the Russian Civil War* (Bloomington, Indiana University Press, 1989).

Smith S. A. *Red Petrograd: Revolution in the Factories, 1917–1918* (Cambridge, Cambridge University Press, 1983).

Sorenson J. B., *The Life and Death of Soviet Trade Unions* (New York, Atherton, 1969).

Swain G., *Russian Social Democracy and the Legal Labour Movement, 1906–1914* (London, Macmillan, 1983).

Tret'ya vserossiiskaya konferentsiya professional'nykh soyuzov, 1917: stenograficheskii otchet, ed. D. P. Koenker (London, Kraus International, 1982; reprint of 1927 edition).

The Village Commune and Rural Government

ORLANDO FIGES

Introduction: the commune and the problem of rural government

The under-government of the countryside was the crucial weakness of the Russian state between 1900 and 1930. Both the tsarist and the Soviet regimes depended on squeezing out resources from the agricultural sector; both were committed to modernizing the peasant economy, to educating the peasants and integrating them into the national culture; yet neither had the means to extend its influence to the remote villages in which the peasants, 80 per cent of the population, lived.

Russia's vast size and its general backwardness – its small tax-base and poor communications – largely account for this under-government. The state lacked the manpower or the financial means to appoint officials in the countryside. The legacy of serfdom also played a part. Until 1861 the serfs had been under the jurisdiction of their noble owners and, provided they paid their taxes, the state did not intervene in the relations between them. Only after the Emancipation – and then very slowly – did the tsarist government come round to the problem of how to extend its influence to its new peasant 'citizens'. But the main reason for the state's failure to penetrate the village was the strength and resilience of the *mir*, or village commune, which enclosed the peasants in a separate world, with its own moral codes and legal customs, in hostile opposition to the state. The word *mir* in Russian also has the meaning of 'world' and 'universe'.

The *mir* was governed by an assembly of peasant elders (*skhod*) which, alongside the land commune (*obshchina*), regulated virtually every aspect of village and agrarian life. In most cases the *mir* and the *obshchina* covered the same village, although where the villages were small it was known for the *obshchina* to control the land of several village communes. The commune's powers of self-government had been considerably broadened by the Emancipation, when it took over most of the administrative, police and judicial functions of the landlords and became the basic unit of rural administration (*obshchestvo*) subordinate to the rudimentary organs of state administration in the volost township. It controlled the land transferred to the peasants from the landlords during the Emancipation and was made collectively responsible for the payment of redemption dues on the land. In most parts of Russia the arable land was kept in communal tenure – hereditary tenure was found mainly in the western Ukraine, and in the Polish and Baltic lands – and every few years the *mir* would redistribute the hundreds of arable strips between the peasant households according to the number of workers or 'eaters' in each. The commune also set the common patterns of cultivation and grazing on the stubble necessitated by the open-field system of strip-farming; managed the woods and pasture lands; hired village watchmen and shepherds; collected taxes; carried out the recruitment of soldiers; saw to the repair of roads, bridges and communal buildings; established charity and other welfare schemes; organized public holidays; arbitrated disputes; and administered village justice in accordance with local custom.

The *mir* could engender strong feelings of communal solidarity among the peasants, bound as they were by their common ties to the village and its land. This was reflected in many folk sayings: 'What one man can't bear, the *mir* can'; 'No one is greater than the *mir*'; and so on. Such solidarity bears witness not so much to the 'natural collectivism' of the Russian people, so idealized by the romantic Slavophiles and Populists, as to the peasants' need for self-organization in their struggle for survival against the harsh climate and the domination of external enemies, such as the landlords and the state. Indeed, as the growing Western literature on the social life of the peasantry has shown, the village was a hotbed of vendettas, greed, dishonesty and sometimes gruesome acts of violence by one peasant neighbour against another; it was not the haven of communal harmony that intellectuals from the city imagined it to be. But the difficulties of small-scale peasant farming, which in the vast majority of households was carried out with only one horse and a tiny store of primitive tools, meant that simple forms of neighbourly cooperation or communal projects, such as clearing woods and building dams, were often in the best interests of individual peasants.

This solidarity was enforced by the patriarchal elders of the commune. Voting at the *skhod* was always open, either by shouting or standing in groups, and all resolutions had to be unanimous. There was a strict conformity in the material life and mores of the village, with dissident behaviour often bringing upon its perpetrators brutal punishments. And yet at the heart of this collectivism was a common set of values and beliefs that united the village – and in times of revolution the whole peasantry – against the rest of the social order. The commune stood for the basic peasant principles of family ownership of household property, and of the exclusive rights of labour to the land. This made it hostile to the efforts of the tsarist regime to extend the principles of private inheritable property to the peasantry before 1917; and to the efforts of the Soviet regime to socialize the peasants' household property by pooling tools and livestock in collective farms.

Rural government under the old regime

The weakness of rural officialdom

Contrary to the revolutionaries' mythic image of an all-powerful 'old regime', the tsarist state was in fact extremely weak in the rural regions. For every 1,000 inhabitants of the Russian empire there were only four state officials at the turn of the century, compared with 7.3 in England and Wales, 12.6 in Germany, and 17.6 in France. The effective power of the imperial government stopped at the 89 provincial capitals where the governors had their offices. Below that there was no real state administration to speak of. Neither the uezd or district towns nor the volost or rural townships had any standing government officials. There was only a series of magistrates and captains who would appear from time to time on some specific mission, usually to collect taxes or sort out a local conflict, and then disappear once again.

The 2,000 land captains (*zemskie nachal'niki*) appointed mainly from the gentry as part of Alexander III's 'counter-reforms' in 1889 remained the main agents of the tsarist regime in the countryside until 1917. Until the 1900s, when their powers were gradually diluted, they were given almost complete executive and judicial power over the peasants, including the right to overturn the resolutions of their villages, to discharge their elected officials, and to have them flogged for minor misdemeanours. Known by the peasants as 'little tsars', the land captains reinforced the fear and hatred of authority accumulated over centuries of serfdom.

The regular police was also very small by European standards. The average rural police sergeant, who often did not even have a horse and cart, was responsible for maintaining order among 50,000 people in several dozen settlements. The government used the police as a sort of catch-all executive organ in the countryside. Apart from the maintenance of law and order, the police were put in charge of collecting taxes, implementing orders and decrees, enforcing health and safety regulations, inspecting public buildings, carrying out statistical surveys, and generally supervising 'public morals' (e.g. making sure the peasants washed their beards).

The Stolypin reforms

At the time of the Emancipation the tsarist government had assumed that under the domination of its patriarchal elders the commune would continue to uphold the established social order. But in fact the commune was set to become the main organizing force of the peasant revolution in both 1905 and 1917. The peasant war against the manors was concentrated in areas of communal land tenure. After 1905 this persuaded landowners and government officials that such violence followed from the commune's practices: the periodic redistribution of the land between its household members on the basis of their family size gave the peasants little incentive to improve their allotments or to produce anything other than babies (the birth-rate in Russia was nearly twice the European average), which resulted in a growing shortage and exhaustion of the land, as well as the depletion of livestock herds, as peasants brought more pasture lands under the plough.

In 1906 Prime Minister Stolypin proposed a series of reforms to counteract the revolutionary tendencies of the commune. In the field of land and property relations these reforms gave individual peasants – and whole villages where a two-thirds majority of household heads voted for it – the right to convert their communal allotments into private property on fully enclosed farms outside the village (*khutora*) or consolidated holdings within it (*otruba*). Further legislation followed to accelerate the process of land reorganization and to help the 'separators' purchase additional land from the gentry and the state with low-interest credit from the Peasant Land Bank. Stolypin's aim was to undermine the commune by creating a new class of peasant landowners, who might respect the gentry's property and support the established order. This was his famous 'wager on the strong'. The whole strategy was closely linked – and historians have often overlooked this – to a series of political and judicial reforms which would give the peasants, as landowners, equal rights to the nobility: through the creation of a volost zemstvo, elected on a small property franchise, they would gain a real stake in local government; and through the abolition of the peasant courts, which operated on the basis of local custom, they would at last be brought as equal citizens into the system of civil law.

In the past liberal Western historians tended to assume (often more on the basis of their own ideological prejudices than empirical evidence) that Stolypin's reforms 'must have been succeeding' – only to be swept away by the First World War. Peasant Russia, they claimed, was being stabilized on the Western model and, if it had not been for the war, a social revolution might have been averted. But recent research has tended to stress that the thrust of the reforms had already been brought to a halt before 1914 – and hence that it was only a question of time before there was another revolution on the land.

Initially, the land reforms did have some success. The most entrepreneurial peasants – and those most eager to sell up their land and move into the cities – rushed to consolidate their communal plots as private property. They found an ally in the local gentry, who accepted the reforms as the only real alternative to the revolutionary confiscation of their land. But by 1910, when the immediate threat of revolution had been lifted, most of the squires had come to see the creation of a new class of peasant landowners, with full political and legal rights, as a threat to their own domination of the countryside. Through the United Nobility, whose members dominated the State Council, they blocked the introduction of the volost zemstvo; and through the land captains they helped to bring the land enclosures to a virtual halt. Meanwhile, the communes were increasingly opposed to the land reforms. They mistrusted change and did not like the invasion of agronomists, charged with redrawing the commune's boundaries. Above all, the peasants were afraid that if some peasants were allowed to own part of the communal land, others would be deprived of access to it for their livelihood. This fear was strongest amongst the younger sons and daughters of the peasant family, for once a household consolidated its land as private property the customs of family ownership ceased to function and the land became the property of the household elder, who could bequeath it to his eldest son.

The village revolution of 1917

News of the February revolution filtered down unevenly to the countryside. Some of the more remote villages did not learn about it until the end of March, and in some places, such as Kazan and Mogilev provinces, where the tsarist forces remained dominant, not until April. Many of the peasants were at first confused by the downfall of the tsar, who had always had the status of a god, and for a while they spoke in muted voices about the revolution. But as the weeks went by and they grew in confidence the peasants voiced their opposition to the tsarist order and assumed control of rural government.

The democratization of rural government began with the removal of the detested land captains and their henchmen, the police, during the month of March. Most of them fled the countryside – some to re-emerge in the White armies of the civil war – but others stayed and sometimes even got themselves elected (along with the landowners and the clergy) to the temporary volost committees established by the Provisional Government on 20 March. Charged with upholding the existing order, the committees were supposed to be made up of 'all the intellectual forces' in the countryside. But they were soon transformed into peasant organs, and passed their own 'laws' to legitimize the seizures of the gentry's land, although other villagers (e.g. landless labourers, craftsmen, teachers and the clergy) were allowed to join them if they went along with their revolutionary aims. The same thing happened with the volost land committees, established during March. The government had intended these to protect the gentry's property rights, while regulating all agrarian relations until the Constituent Assembly. But they were taken over by the local peasantry and transformed into revolutionary organs, helping to impose fixed rents on the gentry's land, to account for it, and eventually to redistribute it among the peasantry. In an effort to prevent this subversion of the land committees, the Provisional Government cut its grants to them; but the peasant communes merely filled the gap, financing the committees through self-taxation, and the committees continued to expand.

At the heart of this peasant revolution was the village commune, which emerged revitalized in 1917. Most of Stolypin's peasant pioneers had not fared very well and, with the prospect of sharing in the spoils of the commune's war against the manors, voluntarily broke up their private allotments. Only the small minority of fully enclosed farms (*khutora*) had to be brought back into the commune by force. Meanwhile, the commune itself was democratized. Although this complex process has yet to be researched by historians, its basic contours appear to be as follows. First, the voice of the younger peasants was becoming more important at the *skhod* because the household partitions of previous years had increased the number of younger household heads and because the prestige of the younger peasants had increased as a result of their service in the army and the growing need for literate village leaders after the collapse of the old regime and the flight of the intelligentsia from the countryside. Second, it may be that women were appearing for the first time at the *skhod* – as the heads of households in the absence of their husbands in the army. Finally, it seems that the general village and volost assemblies, where not just the peasants but all adult residents were present, became the main forum of rural government, and took over many of the commune's basic tasks, after the collapse of the old administration in the volost.

The village commune was the organizing force of the revolution on the land. It served as the link – stretching back to serfdom – between the peasants and their landlord's estate. It was on this basis that the peasants justified their moral and historic right to confiscate his property: 'Ours was the lord, ours is the land.' During the seizure of the gentry estates the members of the commune displayed a remarkable degree of solidarity and organization. It was common for the village assembly to pass a resolution compelling all the members of the commune to take part in the march on the manor, or in other forms of peasant resistance, such as rent strikes and boycotts, on the threat of expulsion from the commune. It was a matter of safety in numbers. Contrary to the old Soviet myth, there were very few conflicts within the village between the richer and poorer peasants. But there were a great many conflicts between neighbouring communes, sometimes ending in little village wars, over the control of the estates.

The 1917 revolution in the countryside essentially amounted to the emergence of the peasantry as an autonomous and hegemonic force in its own political environment. It realized the *volia* – the direct self-rule of the villages free from the intervention of the gentry or the state – which the peasants had dreamed of for centuries. All the main political organs of the revolution in the countryside – the various *ad hoc* village committees, the peasant unions and the village soviets – were really no more than the commune in a more revolutionary form. The soviet assembly was indistinguishable from an open gathering of the village or the commune; and the peasants often failed to differentiate between them in their protocols – i.e. it was recorded that the resolutions of the soviet had been passed by a 'general meeting of village A' (*obshchee sobranie A – oi derevni*) or by a 'village *assembly* of communes B and C' (*sel'skii skhod B- oi i V- oi obshchin*). Conversely, any organ imposed from above or made up of largely non-peasant elements was either boycotted or subverted by the peasantry. This was the case with the volost zemstvos, whose long-awaited establishment was the liberals' main hope in the countryside. The election of these new organs during August was usually met by silence or violence from the peasants, who had already set up their own volost committees and sometimes even their own soviets.

The peasant soviets and the emergence of the Bolshevik dictatorship

The first peasant soviets were general peasant organs elected directly by the village and communal assemblies, and were mostly made up of local farming peasants, albeit often in uniform. Established in the autumn and winter of 1917, the soviets soon took over full power in the countryside, either removing the volost zemstvo by force or, more frequently, simply replacing it after a vote at a general assembly of the volost. The soviets saw their task as the defence of the interests of the local peasantry. They helped the communes to distribute the gentry's land and property; regulated trade in the interests of the peasants; and addressed the famine crisis that affected many regions in the spring by preventing grain exports from the volost and, if necessary, sending delegations to buy up stocks of flour from the fertile south and Siberia. The local soviets often behaved like (and even called themselves) autonomous republics, paying scant regard to the orders of the higher authorities. Many of them employed their own police forces and set up their own courts, while some even had their own flags and emblems. Nearly all of them had their own volunteer militia, or Red Guard, organized by the younger peasants straight out of the army to defend the revolutionary village and its borders.

The Bolsheviks left the countryside alone during the first six months of their regime. They lacked the means to control the rural soviets, most of which were non-party or led by SRs, and in any case the localist perspective of the soviets was in their interests in so far as it neutralized the peasants during the struggle for power in the cities. Having completed their own local revolutions through the soviets, most of the peasants were indifferent to the Bolsheviks' closure of the Constituent Assembly, even though they had voted by a large majority for the SRs to represent them there. As one SR put it, the peasants thought of the Assembly as a distant parliament, they associated it with the State Duma, whereas the soviets were 'near and dear to them, reminding them of their own village assemblies'.

By May 1918, however, the Bolsheviks were no longer prepared to tolerate the localist tendencies of the soviets. There was a chronic food shortage in the cities, thousands of workers were on strike, and the civil war was entering a new phase. If their fragile regime was to survive, it would have to impose its control on the village to extract foodstuffs and soldiers from the peasants. The Bolsheviks now blamed the urban crisis on the fact that the peasant soviets were dominated by the 'kulaks', who were hoarding grain and conspiring with the SRs to starve the revolution out of existence; and as a part of their 'battle for grain' they called upon the poor peasants to unite with the workers against them.

The Committees of the Rural Poor (*kombedy*) were to stir this 'class war' in the village. Lenin heralded their institution, on 11 June, as the moment when the countryside embarked upon the socialist revolution. This was to be the peasants' October, when the 'rural proletariat' would join in the 'class struggle' against the 'rural bourgeoisie'. In reality, it was the moment when Marxist dogma collapsed under the weight of peasant reality. Most villages thought of themselves as farming communities of equal members related by kin – they often called themselves a 'peasant family' – and as such were hostile to the idea of a separate body for the poor. They either failed to elect a *kombed*, leaving it to outside agitators, or else set up one which every peasant joined on the grounds that all the villagers were poor. In this case, the *kombed* was indistinguishable from the soviet. The peasants of Kiselevo-Chemizovka in the Atkarsk District, for example, resolved that a *kombed* was not needed, 'since the peasants are almost equal, and the poor ones are already in the soviet. The organization of a separate *kombed* would only lead to unnecessary tensions between citizens of the same commune.' Bolshevik agitators were quite unable to split the peasants on class lines. The poor peasants were simply not aware of themselves as 'proletarians'. Nor did they think of their richer neighbours as a 'bourgeoisie'. They all thought of themselves as fellow villagers and looked at the efforts of the Bolsheviks to split them with suspicion and hostility.

Consequently, most of the *kombedy* were set up by elements from outside the commune. These were not the poor peasant farmers but immigrant townsmen and soldiers, landless craftsmen, and labourers excluded from the land commune. A study of 800 *kombedy* in Tambov province found that less than half their members at the volost level had ever farmed the land; 30 per cent of them had been soldiers in the war. In the semi-industrial villages of the north these social types may well have been 'insiders'; but in the agricultural south they were mainly 'outsiders' to the village. Disconnected from the peasant commune, upon which all rural government depended, they were unable to carry out their tasks without resort to violence. They requisitioned private property, made illegal arrests, vandalized churches and generally terrorized the peasants. It was more like a local mafia than an organ of the Soviet state. In one Saratov volost, for example, the *kombed* was run by the Druzhaev brothers in alliance with the chief of the regional police, Comrade Varlamov. They went around the villages extorting money, guns and vodka from the terrified peasants. Livestock was also confiscated and handed over to their henchman among the 'village poor'. One peasant who could not pay was forced to watch them rape his wife. This state of terror lasted for six months. The villagers petitioned 'Comrade Lenin' in the hope of ending it. As one of them put it: 'The people are beginning to say that life was better under the Tsar.'

After a series of peasant uprisings, the Soviet regime abolished the *kombedy* in November 1918. Although these uprisings were condemned as 'kulak revolts' in the press, privately the Bolshevik leaders acknowledged that they amounted to protest by the peasantry as a whole. The regime's state-building efforts in the countryside were henceforth focused on the volost soviets, which it sought to fill with the new party members recruited in such large numbers from the countryside. And the key to this was the soviet re-elections of 1919.

By the end of 1918, the peasant revolution had, for the most part, been completed and the volost soviets had become organs of taxation. The result was a growing peasant apathy towards the soviet assemblies – less than 30 per cent of the electorate bothered to vote in the volost soviet elections of 1919 – which virtually ensured the electoral success of the Bolsheviks. As the only legal party faction in the soviets, they alone could meet to coordinate their electoral tactics; and with the power of the Cheka and the Red Army behind them, they could easily intimidate the peasant voters. According to a study of the Vólga region, 71 per cent of the volost soviet executives had at least one Bolshevik member (and this was nearly always its chairman) by the autumn of 1919, compared with 38 per cent in the previous spring. Two-thirds of all the executive members were registered as Bolsheviks. This gave them a crucial bureaucratic foothold in the volost township, something which the tsarist regime had never had. Once under the domination of the party, the volost soviet executives soon became transformed from democratic organs of peasant revolution into bureaucratic organs of the party-state. Soviet assemblies were seldom called and, in their absence, the executives ruled with their permanent departmental staffs, which were appointed in each policy area. And whereas in 1917–18 the soviet executives had been largely made up of smallholding peasants, they were now increasingly made up of full-time professional bureaucrats paid by the party-state and only seldom re-elected. Plough-pushers were giving way to pen-pushers.

The key to this process of Bolshevik state-building was the support of that young and literate class of peasants who had left the village in the war. In the Volga region 60 per cent of the members of the volost soviet executives were aged between 18 and 35 (compared with 31 per cent of the electorate) and 66 per cent were literate (compared with 41 per cent). This was the generation that had benefited from the boom in rural schooling at the turn of the century and had been mobilized during the war. In 1918 they had returned to their villages newly skilled in military techniques and conversant with the two great ideologies of the urban world, socialism and atheism. The peasants were often inclined to view them as their natural leaders during the revolution on the land. The old peasant patriarchs were generally not literate enough to cope with the complex tasks of administration now that the gentry and the rural intelligentsia were no longer there to guide them. To many of these peasant-soldiers, whose aspirations had been broadened by their absence from the village, the prospect of working in the soviet appeared as a chance to go up in the world. After the excitement of the army it could often seem a depressing prospect to have to return to the drudgery of peasant farming and to the 'dark' world of the village. By working in the soviet and joining the party they could enhance their own prestige and power. They could get a nice clean office job, with all its perks and privileges, and an entry ticket into the new urban-dominated civilization of the Soviet regime. Throughout the peasant world Communist regimes have been built on the fact that it is the ambition of every literate peasant son to become a clerk.

The unsolved problem of rural government

Having lost control of the volost soviet, the reaction of the peasant smallholders was to turn their backs on it and retreat to their communes. The growing conflict between the peasantry and the party-state, which erupted in a series of large-scale peasant wars in 1920–21, was thus fought on the same battle-lines – with the villages on one side and the volost township on the other – as the earlier conflict had been fought between the peasantry and the gentry-state.

In many ways, indeed, the 1920s saw the re-emergence of the old relationship between state and peasantry. Beyond the volost townships, the new state, like the old, had no real power in the countryside. The world of the village remained unconquered and largely unknown to the state. Very few Bolsheviks lived in the villages or had any real ties with the peasantry. Only 15 per cent of the rural party members were engaged in farming; while less than 10 per cent came from the region in which they ruled. The village soviets, although technically subordinated to the volost, were very rarely willing to go against the communes, upon which they depended for their budgets. The Bolsheviks responded by centralizing power and closing down a large number of village soviets; but this merely increased their isolation. By 1929 only every ninth village had a soviet. Taxes could not be collected properly, Soviet laws could not be enforced.

The longer NEP went on the greater the disjunction became between the ambitions of the Soviet regime and its bureaucratic impotence in the countryside. Militant Bolsheviks were increasingly afraid that the revolution would degenerate, that it would sink in the 'kulak' mud, unless a new civil war was launched to subjugate the village and its commune to the town. Here were the roots of Stalin's civil war against the village, the civil war of collectivization. Without the means to govern the village, let alone transform it on socialist lines, the Bolsheviks sought to abolish it instead.

Further reading

Atkinson D., *The End of the Russian Land Commune, 1905–1930* (Stanford, Stanford University Press, 1983).

Danilov V. P., 'The Commune in the Life of the Soviet Countryside before Collectivization', in R. Bartlett, ed., *Land Commune and Peasant Community in Peasant Russia: Communal Forms in Imperial and Early Soviet Society* (Basingstoke, Macmillan, 1990).

Figes O., 'The Village and *Volost'* Soviet Elections of 1919', *Soviet Studies* 40, 1 (1988).

Figes O., *Peasant Russia, Civil War: The Volga Countryside in Revolution (1917–1921)* (Oxford, Clarendon Press, 1989).

Figes O., 'The Russian Peasant Community in the Agrarian Revolution, 1917–1918', in R. Bartlett, ed., *Land Commune and Peasant Community in Peasant Russia: Communal Forms in Imperial and Early Soviet Society* (Basingstoke, Macmillan, 1990).

Kabanov V. V., 'Oktiabr'skaia revoliutsiia i krest'ianskaia obshchina', *Istoricheskie zapiski* 111 (Moscow 1984).

Mironov B., 'The Russian Peasant Commune After the Reforms of the 1860s', *Slavic Review* 44 (1985).

Weissman N., *Reform in Tsarist Russia: The State Bureaucracy and Local Government 1900–09* (New Brunswick, Rutgers University Press, 1981).

Weissman N., 'Policing the NEP Countryside', in S. Fitzpatrick, A. Rabinowitch and R. Stites, eds., *Russia in the Era of NEP: Explorations in Soviet Society and Culture* (Bloomington, Indiana University Press, 1991).

The White Armies

EVAN MAWDSLEY

Introduction

Historians have defined 'the Whites' in various ways. The term could be applied to all armed and organized Russian anti-Bolshevik forces; the Soviets often used the term 'White Guard' (*belogvardeets*) in this sense. A distinction, however, needs be made between, for example, Denikin's Volunteer Army and an SR-organized force like the *Komuch* People's Army; the latter was opposed both to the Bolsheviks *and* to the conservative generals. The Cossack forces, with their distinct social base, also need to be dealt with separately. In this essay 'Whites' refers to the conservative, Russian nationalist, military officers who dominated the organized anti-Communist struggle from the end of 1918.

The Volunteer Army and the Armed Forces of South Russia

The 'Volunteer Army' was the most outstanding of the White armies in virtually all respects. In the chaos that followed the collapse of the Kornilov action and the October 1917 revolution key figures in the army command looked for suitable bases for the survival of 'healthy' elements and for resistance both to the Bolshevik government and to the Central Powers. The Don and Kuban Cossack regions in south-east European Russia offered distance from Petrograd and a supportive Cossack leadership. After October General A. M. Kaledin, the Don ataman (chieftain), had openly declared his opposition to the new order. The fact that the Cossack lands were on the Black Sea coast was incidental in 1917, but would yield advantages 12 months later after the defeat of Turkey and the opening of the Straits to Allied shipping. With hindsight, however, this choice of a counterrevolutionary *place d'armes* contained the seeds of many of the Whites' future problems. It was a long march – 600 miles – from the Don back to the centre of power. And Great Russian centralizers found themselves in a peculiar provincial region with dreams of self-rule.

In any event, General M. V. Alekseev, the former Supreme commander in chief, arrived at Novocherkassk, the Don capital, and was joined by the commanders who had been interned with General Kornilov. The 'Alekseev Organization' became the Volunteer Army, with Kornilov and Alekseev dividing military and political responsibilities. A number of young officers arrived to support them. The new force could not hold out against Bolshevik Red Guards from the centre. The rank-and-file Cossacks, coming home radicalized from the World War front, were not prepared to back their conservative leaders. At the end of February 1918 the Don cities fell to the Reds. Kaledin committed suicide, and the 4,000-man Volunteer 'Army' set out on the legendary 'Ice March', a trek across the empty and frozen Kuban steppe. The 'First Kuban Campaign', as it was later called, was harrowing. Kornilov himself was killed in April during an attack on the Red-held Kuban Cossack capital, Ekaterinodar (later Krasnodar).

What saved the Volunteers was the collapse of Soviet power in southern Russia. This stemmed in part from Cossack resistance to the new local Soviet government, which was based on non-Cossack 'outlanders' (*inogorodnye*). The Don Cossacks, now under Ataman P. N. Krasnov, a tsarist general, retook the main centres of their host territory. It was also true that – ironically – the pro-Allied (or at least anti-German) Volunteers were saved in part by the advance of the Central Powers across the Ukraine. From Novocherkassk Krasnov developed warm relations with German and Austrian forces further west in the Ukraine and the Donbass. The Volunteers were now able to regroup on the Don and march south again for a 'Second Kuban Campaign'. This gave them Ekaterinodar in August 1918 and the rest of the north Caucasus almost as far as Astrakhan by February 1919, wiping out an entire Red 'army group'. They now had a firm territorial base that they would hold until March 1920. By September 1918 the Volunteer Army had 35,000–40,000 men in three divisions. It now had to rely on conscription, but the conscripts raised in the Kuban region were motivated and effective fighters.

By this time, the Volunteers were identified with General A. I. Denikin, because of the death from illness of Alekseev and the battlefield deaths of other senior commanders. Denikin, who was of humble origins, naturally used a military model (unified, centralized command) for his administration, although an auxiliary civilian 'Special Council' was also active. His 1918 'Programme' stressed national unity before everything else, including social reform. This was what he and his 'constituency', disgruntled army officers, wanted. The opinions of the Cossacks were less and less to be taken into account. The Don Cossacks were now in an embattled front line under the main assault of the Red Army from the north. They were outnumbered three to one so, although Krasnov and his colleagues may have detested the arrogance of the 'all-Russian' Volunteers, they had little alternative. As the first Allied emissaries arrived on the Black Sea coast, Krasnov was also compromised by his pro-German 'orientation'. In early January 1919 the Don Cossacks accepted operational unity of the Don and Volunteer Armies under General Denikin within the 'Armed Forces of South Russia' (AFSR), and in February Krasnov stepped down, to be replaced as ataman by the pro-Denikin General A. P. Bogaevskii.

Having established its base, the Volunteer Army continued the chain of successes that had begun in August 1918 and ended only in November 1919. Fifteen months of offensive success was unparalleled in the civil war. Admiral Kolchak would only hold the initiative in the east for two or three months, and for other anti-Bolshevik armies the period of success lasted only a month or two. One thing that made the Volunteer Army, and the AFSR after it, so much more successful in military terms was a pool of 'national' military commanders, a substantial reserve of trained manpower, above all motivated junior officer veterans and the Cossack cavalry, and a reasonably secure base. Despite constant numerical inferiority the southern Whites were able to secure their base, drive off Red attacks, and launch a great offensive north and west. General V. Z. Mai-Maevskii, who took over the Volunteer Army in May 1919 (Denikin was 'main commander in chief' of the whole AFSR) had already conducted a brilliant defence of the encircled Donbass and would now lead a general offensive to the north, taking Kharkov in June. General P. N. Wrangel, commanding the so-called Caucasus Army, took the 'Red Verdun' of Tsaritsyn in the same month. In contrast to the situation in Siberia and North Russia, these important early advances were achieved without any major involvement of Allied infantry. The British did provide lavish *matériel* aid later in 1919 – 198,000 rifles, 6,200 machine guns, 1,121 artillery pieces and even 60 tanks – but much of this arrived too late be absorbed by the AFSR.

Denikin's general 'Moscow Offensive' was launched in July 1919. The Volunteer Army's I Corps, the 'Kornilov', 'Markov' and 'Drozdovskii' Divisions, formed an elite spearhead that drove north up the Kharkov–Kursk–Orel–Tula–Moscow railway. They took Orel and then were smashed back in October–November by two improvised and uncoordinated Red counter-strokes, the second of which was the onslaught of Budennyi's Red cavalry. Denikin has been accused of both military and political mistakes, most notably by his successor, Wrangel. Perhaps Denikin should either have gone for Moscow *or* tried generally to expand his territorial base. He actually tried to do both, and in the shortest possible time. It may have been, also, that Denikin had lost control of the AFSR's four armies. Wrangel felt his Caucasus Army could have been included in the Volunteer spearhead, rather than being kept at Tsaritsyn, and it is conceivable that this might have allowed greater success.

Denikin also lacked a consolidated rear, and as the Volunteers began to fall back the bubble burst. An uprising by the partisan leader Nestor

Makhno was only the most striking sign of the military and political vacuum. The zone between the southern Don host territory and the central Russian provinces had changed hands repeatedly in 1917–19 and had no settled administration. There had been an element of 'carpetbagging' with landowners returning to their estates. The AFSR had also not developed an effective military supply organization. The Whites had had to rely on 'self-supply', and looting certainly did not create a stable situation. There was no effective attempt at propaganda. A lack of civilian administrators stemmed partly from the speed of the advance, and partly from White distrust of everyone to the left of the Kadets. Denikin made gestures to broaden his base once his army really began to retreat, replacing his Special Council with more broadly based institutions, but by this time it was much too late for these concessions to have any effect.

The decisive fact, however, was probably that the pool of dedicated manpower was fixed. As the AFSR expanded to 100,000, overall quality plummeted – some were POWs captured from the Reds. Denikin himself estimated that his forces held a territory with over 40 million people. This certainly made him the most successful of the counterrevolutionary leaders. But he only controlled this level of population for a few months in the summer of 1919. The real base was the North Caucasus and the Don Region with a population of eight–nine million, of which the Cossacks numbered three million.

In any event the destruction of the AFSR was now rapid and was assisted by the spread of disease. The appearance of effective massed Red cavalry was also a major factor; conflict with and between the Cossacks made it impossible to create a counter-force. After a ghastly winter campaign the AFSR survivors embarked at Novorossiisk in March 1920. Some 34,000 people, mostly Volunteers and Don Cossacks were taken off; most of the rest were captured.

The Russian Army of General Wrangel

White Crimea had survived the Red winter offensive thanks to geography (the Perekop isthmus), Red inattention, and a sturdy local defence. It provided a haven for the remnants of the AFSR. Denikin himself could not survive the *débâcle* and a council of war chose General Wrangel, one of Denikin's ablest subordinates but also one of his severest critics, to replace him.

The Wrangel government was different from the AFSR in a number of respects. Wrangel was probably more conservative than Denikin (unlike Denikin he was a genuine aristocrat), but he saw the importance of a functioning civil administration ('leftist policies with rightist hands'). The core of his small army, 35,000 strong, were Denikin's elite units, but Wrangel had not been one of the original Volunteers, and he dropped the 'Volunteer' title, which had become discredited, in favour of the 'Russian Army'. He also stressed the restoration of firm discipline.

In June 1920 Wrangel broke out of the Crimea and took the grain area of the north Tauride. But he had no chance of general success. He only agreed to take power after obtaining a waiver from his fellow commanders – to the effect that his object was not victory but the extraction of the army. The Crimea was only one of 50 provinces in European Russia, and had a total population of about three million. In contrast to 1919 there were no other major White Russian armies in the field. This was called in Stalinist historiography the 'Third Entente Campaign', but Wrangel had been disavowed by the British. The French, desperate to help the Poles, granted him *de facto* recognition but no troops and little equipment – although he does seem to have been able to incorporate British equipment already 'in the pipeline' for Denikin. Wrangel may have avoided Denikin's disputes with Cossack politicians, but that was because he had lost his vital Cossack base; a desperate seaborne landing was attempted in the Kuban in August 1920 but this failed to raise the Cossack Vendée again.

Ironically what Wrangel had on his side was the Soviet-Polish war. There was a double irony here. Wrangel the conservative all-Russian nationalist only survived because of the attack on 'Russian' territory by the hated Poles. And the Poles only attacked when they did because they thought Wrangel was too weak to recreate Great Russia. In any event, once the Polish front had stabilized, overwhelming Red power was turned against the Crimea. The Red offensive began on 28 October 1920. Wrangel did not try to hold the Perekop isthmus but effected a huge seaborne evacuation. Some 146,000 soldiers and civilians left the Crimean ports, nearly five times the number evacuated from Novorossiisk by Denikin. This time, however, the destination was Turkey; Wrangel was the liquidator of the White movement in Europe.

The Russian Army of Admiral Kolchak

The Siberian pattern was different from that in South Russia. Denikin's AFSR began its existence as an army headquarters; Kolchak inherited a regional civil government. The short-lived 'Provisional All-Russian Government' (PA-RG) had been formed in late September 1918, and was effectively centred on Omsk in Western Siberia. The right and left could find no common ground. In November 1918 a military coup, organized by right-wing Kadets and carried out by young officers and the local Cossacks – and with a debatable degree of blessing by local Allied authorities – resulted in the arrest of SR leaders and the installation of a military dictator.

The Supreme Ruler (*Verkhovnyi pravitel'*) was Admiral A. V. Kolchak. Nationally known as a senior and successful World War commander (of the Black Sea Fleet) and an opponent of the democratization of the armed forces, Kolchak was an accidental figurehead, a sailor marooned on his way – he hoped – to join the armies in South Russia. He had arrived in Omsk in mid-October 1918 and served as War Minister for two weeks. Politically he delivered what the coup-plotters wanted, an 'apolitical' government focused on 'law and order' and war on the Bolsheviks, brooking no compromise with the detested SRs.

Even with a military dictator, the military potential of the Siberian Whites was much inferior to that in South Russia. The successes of 1918 had been based on the Czechoslovak Legion. There was no pool of motivated 'volunteer' officers comparable to the 'eaglets' who flocked to the Don, despite the fact that the Academy of the General Staff had been evacuated to Ekaterinburg (later Sverdlovsk). There was nothing like the Don and Kuban Cossack hosts to supply trained and mobile manpower. The Cossacks in Siberia were scattered and few in number. The Ural and Orenburg Cossacks were soon cut off, and the Cossacks in central Siberia, remote from the Urals battlefields, devoted themselves to milking Kolchak's supply route along the Trans-Siberian Railway.

In contrast to Denikin, Kolchak's military success was short-lived. The 'Ufa offensive' of March 1919 took his Western Army halfway from the Urals to the Volga. Thereafter the attack was stalled by the spring thaw. The Red Army rapidly shifted reserves east, and in May it counterattacked. In early June the Reds re-took Ufa and pushed Kolchak back to his starting point.

Kolchak concentrated on military affairs and his government was dominated by a cabinet of very youthful Kadet advisers. Land hunger was not a big factor in Siberia, and in fact there had been no big gentry estates in the region. Little was developed in the way of civilian policies aimed at consolidating the Siberian hinterland or attracting support on the other side of the front. Kolchak did in the end try to broaden his political base, agreeing to a National Zemstvo Congress, but like Denikin he did this when his armies had been broken. Kolchak did not have to worry about large minorities as Denikin and Iudenich did (although the defection of the Bashkir Corps in February 1919 was a blow). He did not have Denikin's squabbles with the Cossacks, although this was a net weakness, as he had few Cossacks to squabble with. Economically, Kolchak failed to make use of the gold reserve he held. It is debatable, however, how any government could have dealt with fragments of the old economy, cut off in the Urals from the Russian hinterland.

Even in his chosen sphere of the military, he showed little talent in planning operations or choosing subordinates. There was no-one in the command of his 'Russian (*Rossiiskaia*) Army' of the talent or status of Alekseev, Kolchak, Denikin, Wrangel or Mai-Maevskii. D. A. Lebedev, Kolchak's chief of staff – *de facto* responsible for land operations – was a wartime colonel in his thirties, as was his War Minister, N. A. Stepanov; worse still, Lebedev and Stepanov could not agree on the joint activities of front and rear. M. K. Diterikhs, a 'real' general, took over as front commander in the early summer of 1919, but he was ignored by his subordinates and this led to the fall of the Urals line. Kolchak received a substantial amount of Allied military equipment as early as the end of 1918. There were 600,000 rifles from the British, and uniforms for 200,000 men (but less artillery and equipment than Denikin received). There were few frontline Cossacks with the main army, and hence little White cavalry. In March 1919 Kolchak appears to have built up a peak frontline force of 110,000, with perhaps twice as many non-combatants. On paper, this was larger than the AFSR in October 1919. In fact, conscripts were held back from the front until too late; they arrived only in time for the autumn 1919 retreat, when they melted away. Red combat troops took some time to build up, but by May 1919 the Red Eastern Army Group had reached a total strength of 360,000.

If the Volunteer Army was remarkable for spending 15 months on the offensive, Kolchak probably carried out the longest retreat in military history. From April 1919 to the spring of 1920, the Siberian armies were constantly on the retreat, only halting 300 miles east of Lake Baikal at Chita. Kolchak gave up the Urals in the summer of 1919, held briefly some river lines in Western Siberia, and in November 1919 had to give up Omsk itself. By this time his army and command structure were in complete disorder. They could not hold the great – frozen – Siberian rivers. Like the Volunteers, Kolchak's veteran unit of General V. O. Kappel' had an 'Ice March', but theirs (around Krasnoiarsk) was at the end rather than the beginning of the campaign. In January 1920 the Siberian cities along the railway line began to revolt, led by the SRs. Kolchak was handed over by his Czechoslovak protectors to one such SR government, at Irkutsk near Lake Baikal, which became a Communist-led Military-Revolutionary Committee. The Admiral was tried and shot in February 1920, at the moment Denikin's AFSR was fighting its last desperate battles in the Kuban.

The smaller White armies

The North-western army

The White army nearest to a vital centre of Soviet Russia was, ironically, one of the weakest. In May 1919 as the 'Northern Corps' (actually a brigade-strength force of 6,000 men) it crossed into Soviet territory. Although the corps caused panic in the 'cradle of the revolution', all it secured was a 'Russian' base in a sparsely inhabited wedge of territory in Petrograd province; it became the North-western Army. The leaders were General A. P. Rodzianko and later General N. N. Iudenich, an elderly hero of the World War. Iudenich did not take over active command until October 1919 and did not get on with his subordinates. At its maximum strength the North-western Army's manpower was only 14,000, many of them POWs, and its supplies were limited. The Allies – in practice the British – had little time for the army, which had been originally set up by the Germans and to which they had no moral commitment. Politically the Baltic Whites had nothing to offer, and a 'North-western Government' had to be cobbled together under pressure by a British general. The all-Russian pretensions of the Whites and Kolchak's refusal to grant independence led to acute conflict with the Estonians, upon whom the North-western Army was dependent.

Despite all these shortcomings, Iudenich did launch his major attack against Petrograd in October 1919, in support of Denikin's Moscow campaign. This was actually an impressive piece of White grand-strategic coordination, and Iudenich forced the Reds to transfer vital reserves away from the southern front. But Iudenich's chances of success were slim; the defending Reds had an advantage of 5:1 in manpower. The North-western Army – which, unlike the other White forces, had no strategic depth – was thrown back across the Estonian border and interned.

Arkhangel'sk and Murmansk

The northern White governments have been especially 'visible' in histories of the civil war because of the presence of substantial Allied forces. In addition, General E. K. Miller, who was the last head of the Arkhangel'sk government, succeeded the 'South Russian' Generals Wrangel and Kutepov as head of the *émigré* White movement. However, the Murmansk and Arkhangel'sk governments were atypical. These were in 1917–20 remote, backward, and largely rural districts – the total population of the region was perhaps 600,000 in an area the size of France but covered with forests and swamps, and cursed with severe weather. The Allies committed few troops, despite the fact that their first 'intervention' was here in the spring of 1918. The biggest operation, down the Dvina from Arkhangel'sk in August 1919, involved 3,000 British troops and 1,000 Whites, and it was really a preparation for evacuation in September–October 1919.

Miller arrived to take over the Provisional Government of the Northern Region in January 1919. Arkhangel'sk had had the first civilian government to come under attack from the military; although the Allied representatives had intervened to prevent the worst excesses they made sure that the restored government had a smaller SR element. It was not a particularly severe government, but it had little control of the vast territory it nominally held. Unlike South Russia or even Siberia there were no Cossacks and few officers. The Finns might have made more of a contribution, especially along the Murmansk Railway, but Kolchak refused to recognize the Helsinki government. When the Red Army finally began its advance up the northern Dvina there was little to stop them, and Arkhangel'sk fell in February 1920 followed by Murmansk in March.

Eastern Siberia

The Whites operating in Eastern Siberia paid more attention to the Japanese than to their nominal centre, the far-away Omsk government. The best-known leader was Grigorii Semenov, a subaltern from the Transbaikal Cossack Host. Eastern Siberia only came into its own again after Kolchak's collapse, with its centre in Chita. There were similarities with Wrangel's succession to Denikin, but Semenov had a very weak military and population base and was never able to open active campaigning against the Reds in 1920 the way that Wrangel did. The refugee troops of Kolchak's army disliked Semenov and had no intention of fighting for him. Semenov's seems to have been the most terroristic of the White governments. He also had no support in other parts of Siberia, and when the Japanese decided to pull back to the coast he had to give up Chita, which fell in October 1920. The last stand was around Vladivostok, which was still controlled by the Japanese. The right, supported by veterans of Kappel''s army, took power in May 1921, and held on for 15 months. The last 'ruler', from June 1922, was the mystic General Diterikhs, but the only thing that kept the Reds out of the Primorskaia Region and Vladivostok was the Japanese garrison. In October 1922 it finally withdrew, and the last White government collapsed.

Conclusion

There was a Red Army, but no such thing as a single White Army. It was not so much a question of personalities or petty rivalries: the various White armies were separated by geography, and their base regions were different one from the others. For the same reason it is almost impossible to speak of White 'grand strategy', because coordination was virtually impossible. Kolchak and Denikin, the two personifications of the White cause, never met each other.

And yet, after November 1918, the organized counterrevolutionary movement did have much in common. What was similar were all-Russian pretensions, conservative politics and military rule. The last invites comparisons between Russian and other nineteenth- and twentieth-century military governments, especially in South America and Africa. Like Kolchak, many soldiers have come to power through *coups d'état*. The important difference is that military governments elsewhere were built on peacetime armies, with an intact officer corps and a rank-and-file prepared to obey orders; in some countries there were also traditions of military intervention. None of this held true for Russia.

The Whites were conservative, but seeing them in crude class terms is no longer satisfactory, especially for Russian historians. A recent analysis of 71 veterans of the Volunteer Army's 'First Kuban Campaign' noted that only five had landed estates, and many were of non-noble status. Kornilov, Alekseev and Denikin were all of humble origins, and even Wrangel and Kolchak were technocrats by education. The nature of 'the White cause', the *Beloe delo*, was inextricably linked with the First World War and the passions aroused by that national humiliation. The White leaders saw themselves as the embodiment of 'Russia'. This reaction is easier to understand from the perspective of the 1990s. It is also easier from a modern perspective to understand the difficulties of the political 'middle way'. The Whites did not understand modern pluralistic politics, just as 75 years later many politicians in post-Communist Russia do not understand them. Iudenich's slogan, 'Against the Bolsheviks, without politics', sums up accurately the consciously 'non-political politics' of his movement. But unless Bolshevism had fallen apart from within, this world outlook would never have brought the Whites to power.

There is much more to be learned about the White movement. In the West the most interesting new work on the civil war has been on popular opposition within the territory nominally controlled by the Communists. The anti-Communist governments are less fashionable, although Norman Pereira and John Smele's accounts of Kolchak's Siberia have been added to Peter Kenez's work on South Russia. In addition to the American and French records, and the main body of the Russian archives, the material from the *émigré* Russian Foreign Historical Archive (RZIA) in Prague is now accessible in Moscow (in GARF and elsewhere). Much of the Russian effort since glasnost has been re-publication of banned memoirs. *Voprosy istorii* ('Questions of History') has been including a section of Denikin's memoirs in nearly every issue since early 1990. Russian historians, 75 years after the events, no longer demonize the Whites although some – taking the old SR views – see the Whites as the 'Bolsheviks of the right'. Meanwhile on the nationalist right there is an uncritical nostalgia for the ideals and methods of the Whites. To the extent that mainstream Russian historians now see one side as no better than the other they are approaching the Western consensus. What is needed now is more detailed analysis of the social and political policies of the Whites. Even their military efforts require an archivally based analysis to ascertain how the Whites achieved so much with so little.

Further reading

Bortnevski V., 'White Intelligence and Counter-Intelligence during the Russian Civil War' (Carl Beck Papers in Russian and East European Studies, University of Pittsburgh, 1995).

Collins D. and Smele J., *Kolchak i Sibir': Dokumenty i issledovaniia, 1919–1926* (White Plains, Kraus International, 1988).

Denikin A. I., *Ocherki Russkoi smuty*, 5 vols. (Paris, J. Polovozky et Cie, 1921–6).

Drokov S. V., ed., 'Podlinnye protokoly doprosov A. V. Kolchaka i A. V. Timirevoi', *Otechestvennye arkhivy* 5–6 (1994).

Goldin V. I., *Interventsiia i antibol'shevistskoe dvizhenie na Russkom severe* (Moscow, Izdatel'stvo Moskovskogo universiteta, 1993).

Kenez P., *Civil War in South Russia, 1918: The First Year of the Volunteer Army* (Berkeley, University of California Press, 1971).

Kenez P., *Civil War in South Russia, 1919–1920: The Defeat of the Whites* (Berkeley, University of California Press, 1977).

Lazarski C., 'White Propaganda Efforts in the South during the Russian Civil War, 1918–19 (the Alekseev–Denikin Period)', *Slavonic and East European Review* 70, 4 (1992).

Lehovich D. V., *White against Red: The Life of General Anton Denikin* (New York, Norton, 1974).

Lincoln W. B., *Red Victory: A History of the Russian Civil War* (New York, Simon and Schuster, 1989).

Mawdsley E., *The Russian Civil War* (Boston, Allen and Unwin, 1987).

Pavlov T. F., 'Russkii zagranichnyi istoricheskii arkhiv v Prage', *Voprosy istorii* 11 (1990).

Pereira N. G. O., *White Siberia: The Politics of the Civil War* (Montreal, McGill-Queen's, 1996).

Poliakov Iu. A. and Igritskii Iu. I., eds., *Grazhdanskaia voina v Rossii: Perekrestok mnenii* (Moscow, Nauka, 1994).

Ross N., *Wrangel' v Krymu* (Frankfurt/Main, Posev, 1982).

Smele J. D. *Civil War in Siberia: The Anti-Bolshevik Government of Admiral Kolchak 1918–1920* (Cambridge, Cambridge University Press, 1996).

Trukan G. A., *Put' k totalitarizmu: 1917–1929 gg.* (Moscow, Nauka, 1994).

Ushakov A. I., *Istoriia grazhdanskoi voiny v literature russkogo zarubezh'ia* (Moscow, ITsRM, 1993).

Voinov V. G., 'Ofitserskii korpus belykh armii na vostoke strany (1918–1920 gg.)', *Otechestvennaia istoriia* 6 (1994).

SOCIAL GROUPS, IDENTITIES, CULTURES AND THE QUESTION OF CONSCIOUSNESS

The Aristocracy and Gentry

DOMINIC LIEVEN

According to the 1897 census just over 1.2 million subjects of the Russian emperor were hereditary nobles. This comprised approximately one out of every 100 Russian subjects, a figure considerably higher than in most of the German states, rather lower than in pre-revolutionary France (1.5 per cent), and much lower than in nineteenth-century Hungary (4 per cent in 1820) or in pre-partition Poland (8 per cent). In the Russian case the nobility's importance was enhanced by the relative weakness of middle-class groups. Until the reign of Nicholas I (1825–55), almost all business fortunes ended in aristocratic hands either through ennoblement or through the marriage of non-noble heiresses into the aristocracy. The nobility also creamed off the elite of the professional middle class, a very large proportion of which was in the state's service. Even in 1897 there were two-thirds as many hereditary nobles as there were members of the non-noble professional, clerical and merchant estates combined.

The hereditary nobility was extremely heterogeneous. By 1905 only 30 per cent of noble families owned land. Ninety-two per cent of properties were of less than 1,000 *desiatiny*, though in a number of cases individuals owned more than one estate. Nevertheless, most Russian noble landowners in 1900 could not hope to sustain a European gentlemanly lifestyle from their farms and forests alone. Ever since the reign of Peter I (1682–1725), entry to the nobility through service in the armed forces and bureaucracy had been easy by European standards. Although the military and civil ranks required before receiving ennoblement were considerably raised in the nineteenth century, this was more than offset by the huge expansion in the army and bureaucracy. Between 1875 and 1895, for instance, 37,000 individuals acquired hereditary noble status, almost double the number between 1825 and 1845.

It was one of the traditional strengths of the Russian empire that the Russian aristocracy had intermarried willingly with the elites of the non-Russian provinces, and that these elites had been accepted *en masse* into the

imperial ruling class. A key example of this was the incorporation of the raw
Cossack officer class of the Ukrainian Hetmanate into the Russian nobility
during the eighteenth century, which contributed both to the Russianization
of most of the Ukrainian landed elite and to early nineteenth-century
Ukraine's relatively painless integration into the empire's Slav core. Other
nobilities tended in general to retain their ethnic identity, which by no
means precluded loyal service to the Russian emperor. The German nobility
of the Baltic provinces, though numerically small, played a uniquely important role in Russian government, especially before the last quarter of the
nineteenth century. In 1897 there were 70,972 native nobles from the
Caucasus, most but by no means all of whom were Georgians. By far the
largest and least trusted group of non-Russian nobles were the Poles, who
made up 28.6 per cent of the empire's hereditary nobility in 1897. Though
Polish nobles were never remotely as prominent in the imperial service as
Baltic Germans, even in the twentieth century they made an important
impact in technical non-political jobs in the Russian provincial bureaucracy.

The core of the imperial nobility were the families which descended from
the pre-Petrine Russian aristocracy and gentry, and from eighteenth-century
political and military leaders, some of whom had been granted vast estates.
Although some eighteenth-century favourites were of very humble origin,
most were nobles and would not otherwise have come within range of imperial benevolence. Common wealth, culture and service, together with
political alliance-building and intermarriage within ruling families, created
a relatively homogeneous aristocratic elite in the eighteenth century which
survived until the empire's demise in 1917. As elsewhere in Europe, Russian
aristocratic magnates were better armoured against the pressures of a capitalist economy than was the case with the bulk of the landowning gentry.
Between 1900 and 1914, for instance, the 155 individuals who owned over
50,000 *desiatiny* sold only 3 per cent of their land, the nobility as a whole
over 20 per cent. Roughly half of these individuals were titled aristocrats
and most came from old noble families. If aristocratic magnates no longer
dominated the machinery of government in eighteenth-century style, their
influence on the Romanov family and in the upper echelons of the administration remained great. Moreover, many less wealthy members of old
gentry families occupied top posts in the government. Of the 215 men
appointed to the State Council, for instance, between 1894 and 1914, most
of whom had previously filled the senior ranks of the bureaucracy and
armed forces, one third belonged to the pre-Petrine Russian nobility, and
most of these men were considerable landowners. The great majority of
Nicholas II's ministers of foreign and internal affairs came from old gentry
families, P. A. Stolypin standing out because of his ability and lack of previous experience in Petersburg, not because of his traditional upper-class
background or landed wealth. Detailed study of the ancestry both of great
landowners and of key figures in government during Nicholas II's reign suggests that the old Russian nobility had retained considerably greater

importance than many historians, beginning with A. Romanovich-Slavatinskii, have supposed.

The hereditary nobility as a whole was too large and heterogeneous to share a common identity or interest. It lacked even an equivalent of the French 'de' or German 'von' to distinguish it from the rest of mankind. Before 1861 by far the greatest of the nobility's legal privileges was its monopoly on serf ownership. When this disappeared with Emancipation (1861), noble privilege and status were largely empty. Catherine II's charter of 1785 had guaranteed nobles a number of civil and political rights but these were not always honoured by her successors and fell far short of the corporate privileges inherited by many European nobilities from the feudal era. In late imperial Russia noble status provided no legal barrier against arbitrary arrest and administrative exile for political activity, and the security police were well capable of opening the private correspondence not only of aristocrats but even of members of the Romanov family. Though the district and provincial noble assemblies and marshals did provide some institutional means whereby the landed elite could choose leaders and express its opinions to the ruler, the government usually ensured that these assemblies' sphere of activity was kept very narrow. Not until after the 1905 revolution were nobles allowed any form of all-imperial autonomous organization, let alone any representative body through which they might participate in central government and legislation. In local rural government, however, the elected noble marshals and the gentry-dominated zemstvo boards and assemblies did play a vital role. Though their autonomy was circumscribed, it provided an institutional base for the landowning class, without whose support the government was incapable of effective administration and modernization of the Russian provinces. The zemstvos were a key base for noble opposition to the government in the run-up to the 1905 revolution. Subsequently the regime put much effort into attempting to bridge the gap between itself and the provincial nobility.

Before the mid-nineteenth century nobles dominated most aspects of Russian economic activity. This meant not merely market-oriented agriculture and the agricultural processing industries but also textiles and metallurgy. After 1861 there began a process of seemingly inexorable economic decline of the nobility. By the 1890s Russian metallurgy was dominated by the non-noble entrepreneurs of southern Ukraine. Noble textile factories had disappeared. The nobility retained a foothold only in industries related to agriculture, forestry and mining: even here noble-owned factories were a minority. Only about 10 per cent of sawmills and paper factories were owned by nobles in 1900. Even as regards flour mills and sugar refineries, where some aristocrats did still play a major role, their enterprises were usually smaller than those of their leading non-noble competitors.

In agriculture decline seemed equally apparent. The 1861 settlement divided the nobles' estates between the landlords and peasants, in many ways following the basic programme put forward by the radical wing of the

Decembrist movement in the 1820s. In 1862 nobles owned 87 million *desiatiny*, by 1905 only 51 million, a decline of 43 per cent. Between 1905 and 1914 a further one-fifth of noble land was sold, mainly to peasants. Depressingly for the Russian nobility, landlords seemed to do best in regions where they were least Russian. The German nobles of the Baltic provinces still owned 44 per cent of the total land fund in 1905, the predominantly Polish nobles of Belorussia and Lithuania 40.4 per cent and 36.5 per cent respectively. By contrast, even in strongholds of Russian noble landowning such as the Central Agricultural region and the Southern Steppe the aristocracy and gentry owned just over one-fifth of the land. In the mid-Volga region the figure was 15.9 per cent and in the Central Industrial region it was 13.7 per cent. Like their counterparts in continental Europe, Russian landlords after the abolition of serfdom often found that their forests were their most valuable remaining possessions. Steeply rising prices for wood offered many opportunities for profit to the nobles, who owned more than half of all the forests in 28 of 49 provinces of Russia, Belorussia and the Ukraine. Even in 1914, however, Russian nobles were in general well behind their German peers as regards the efficient exploitation and preservation of forests. The result was the unnecessary devastation of much woodland and the loss to nobles of potentially very valuable long-term assets.

Many reasons exist for the apparent failure of the Russian nobility in the economic sphere after 1861. Neither by ethos nor training was the traditional Russian noble landowner an entrepreneur or a careful calculator of profit and loss. Under serfdom landlords enjoyed seemingly free use of peasant labour, animals and tools. Few developed techniques of management and accountancy appropriate to a free market. After Emancipation the investments required to fence off noble demesne land from surrounding peasant farms, let alone to build up the animals, machinery and salaried personnel to exploit this demesne in capitalist fashion, were generally very steep. Capital was scarce, especially given the huge scale of the magnates' properties. Though nobles in 1861 were compensated for the loss of their land, and to a limited and unofficial extent also for that of their serf labour, most of this compensation was either claimed back by the state to cover past debts or lost by the need to realize redemption bonds at below par before they became due. As regards noble industrial enterprises, the sudden and uncompensated loss of serf labour together with their enterprises' small-scale, remote rural location and backward technology made most factories uncompetitive after 1861.

The familiar and depressing catalogue of Russian nobles' failure needs, however, to be strongly qualified by an awareness both of Russian economic realities and of similar trends in the rest of Europe. The two decades of agricultural depression which began in the late 1870s hit European nobles hard. In East Anglia, for example, traditional home of big estates using advanced agricultural techniques, the gentry never recovered from the collapse of grain prices in these decades. Russian nobles, whose profits derived largely from exports, could not follow the Prussian Junkers' path of salvation through protection. The Russian nobles' loss of control over their country's industry mirrored a universal European pattern. Only in Silesia did a section of the aristocracy still dominate the industry of one of Europe's major economic regions by 1914. But although the Urals' aristocratic industrialists had fallen on hard times by 1900, their long-term prospects were quite bright. The Urals had far greater iron ore deposits than the Ukraine, and coal existed in abundance in western Siberia. By 1914 new railway lines were promising to link these coal and iron deposits and to end the Urals' isolation: Petersburg capital was flowing in to finance the region's industrial restructuring. Meanwhile, given the costs and risks of direct ownership of modern industry, the strategy of many Russian nobles of investing their capital in stocks and bonds made excellent sense and was in line with the behaviour of the European aristocracy as a whole. By 1914 some Russian magnates had huge portfolios and in 1910, of the 137,825 nobles residing in Petersburg, 49 per cent lived on income from securities. In the century before 1914 the incomes of Russian magnates had failed to keep pace with those of their English and German peers, not at all surprising given the generally more backward state of the Russian economy. Nevertheless, even in 1914 the richest Russian aristocrats still had incomes of between £100,000 and £200,000 per annum, which were immense sums in those days even by English and German standards. On the whole, the ratio of debt to income among Russian magnates in 1914 was much healthier than had been the case a century before. Some aristocrats were making large incomes from urban property and there was good reason to believe that the rapid development of Russia's economy would have the same long-term effect on the Russian aristocracy as on its English and German counterparts. Those aristocratic magnates with substantial urban property, big share portfolios or widely diverse assets would see their incomes rocket and would become the core of a new plutocracy. A growing gulf would exist between these families and less fortunate aristocrats more wholly dependent on agriculture, a group to which almost all members of the landowning gentry belonged.

Even as regards Russian noble agriculture the situation was not as bad and the nobles not as culpable as is generally imagined. Climate, soil, communications and overheads made it very difficult for big estates in most Russian regions to compete on the international grain market with New World producers. In the domestic market peasant farmers could often outcompete the great estates, with their big outlays on management, labour and machinery. Nor were the costs of attempting to run large estates in a capitalist manner purely economic. Bringing previously rented land into direct cultivation and enforcing rigorous capitalist principles in the exploitation of one's fields and forests often made the improving landlord deeply unpopular with the surrounding peasantry, as 1905 proved. There were therefore both political and economic incentives to let one's land to peasants or alternatively to sell it and maintain the safer and more comfortable life of an urban *rentier* living on a secure and largely invisible income. The enormous increase in land prices between 1862 and 1912 encouraged this trend: in these five decades noble land had increased in value by 443 per cent while diminishing in extent by more than half. Of course by pursuing this strategy the Russian nobility undermined their position as a ruling class rooted in rural society. But since in the modern capitalist world there is no place for such a rural hereditary ruling class, the willingness of much of the nobility to merge into a broader, largely urban, professional and *rentier* world was a thoroughly positive phenomenon. The main problem in 1914, a political rather than an economic one, was that this trend had not yet had time to develop fully and that in some regions sharp conflict between the peasantry and a weakened but still considerable landowning class was a threat to political stability and social order.

The political traditions of the Russian nobility differed significantly from those of most of Europe. The autocratic regime allowed nobles only weak civil and corporate rights. On the other hand, the Russian autocracy proved a formidable mechanism for military power and territorial expansion, from which the nobility, as the polity's largest shareholders, derived both pride and profit. After Peter I's death, eighteenth-century Russia evolved into a semi-aristocratic polity whose monarch's power was severely constrained by aristocratic factions in court and administration, and by the state's dependence on the rural nobility for taxation, public order and military conscription. The development of the nineteenth-century bureaucracy altered this balance, however, and created a polity much less firmly rooted in the social elite than had previously been the case. There developed an increasingly large, autonomous and intrusive administration over which, unlike in almost any other European society, Russian elites exercised no parliamentary scrutiny or control. On the one hand, this enhanced the state's ability to pursue policies such as the 1861 Emancipation and the rapid industrialization of the 1880s and 1890s against the wishes and interests of most of the social elite. On the other hand, the partial alienation of the state even from its traditional aristocratic and gentry allies increased the regime's isolation and vulnerability.

In the decade before 1905, this isolation reached unprecedented levels and the gentry-led zemstvo movement played a crucial role in the onset of the 1905 revolution and the regime's forced concession of a semi-constitutional regime. But the events of 1905–06 revealed the basic dilemma facing the Russian landed nobility. As twentieth-century Europeans many of them resented and even despised the often blundering and anachronistic dynastic police state. On the other hand, as peasant behaviour in 1905–06 revealed, they relied on that police state for their survival. Without the tsarist regime to stop them, peasants would either destroy the nobles' estates by riot and arson or vote them out of existence in democratic elections, as they tried to do through the First and Second Dumas.

In the winter of 1905–06 both some landowners and the regime itself toyed with the idea of trying to buy off peasant opposition by partial expropriation of the estates. Such a policy might whet peasant appetites rather than satisfying them, however. Very often the intensively exploited and most productive capitalist estates were precisely those most resented by local peasants, which ruled out a policy based on alienation of only rented land. Since in early twentieth-century Europe the expropriatión of private (let alone noble) property without full compensation was unthinkable, a treasury already bankrupted by the Japanese War would have been burdened by new, formidable and economically unproductive expenditure. European experience tended to suggest that as the emancipation process and the conflicts it aroused faded into memory, and as peasant prosperity and respect for property developed, the rural social order would become more stable: this happened, for instance, in France and in southern and western Germany after the rural revolutions of 1789 and 1848 respectively.

The immediate effect of the 1905 revolution was to push the regime and the landowning nobility back into close alliance and greatly to enhance the nobles' political power. For the first time the provincial noble assemblies were allowed to create a central umbrella organization, known informally as the United Nobility. Its lobbying activity at court, in the ministries and in parliament became an important factor in Russian politics. The United Nobility's influence was great partly because many of its leaders were elected to the newly established Council for the Affairs of the Local Economy, and to the State Duma and State Council, the new parliament's two houses. As in Prussia after the 1848 revolution, the creation of a moderate and timid constitutional order resulted in a parliament strongly influenced by landowning nobles, who for the first time were able to articulate programmes, unite to defend their group interests, and choose their own leaders. In time the Prussian agrarians became a formidable conservative force and a thorn in the side of the Berlin government. Their Russian equivalents also strongly circumscribed Stolypin's reformist strategy.

On the whole, government and parliament could agree on policies designed to restore Russia's military power and international standing. There was consensus too on the defence of private property and a considerable degree of agreement on the main planks of Stolypin's agrarian reforms. But when the Premier attempted to reform the archaic and inefficient system of provincial and district (i.e. uezd) government he ran into immense noble opposition, and was forced to withdraw. The landed nobility disliked bureaucracy only marginally less than democracy, and Stolypin's attempts to widen the zemstvo franchise while strengthening bureaucratic power and inter-agency coordination at district level aroused their deep resentment. The power of noble landowners in both houses of parliament contributed to the blocking of much reformist legislation and thereby increased the frustration of other sections of society with the new semi-constitutional order. On the other hand, some of the more liberal gentry members of the

Octobrist Party in the Duma themselves became increasingly frustrated both by the conservatism of the upper house and by the government's continuing use of emergency powers to subvert the civil rights promised in the October 1905 manifesto and the Fundamental Laws of April 1906.

Lack of party discipline, especially among the Octobrists, together with constant battles between the two houses of parliament and the growth of inter-ministerial conflict after Stolypin's death (1911) all contributed to a growing sense of disillusion and malaise within the politically active sections of the nobility by 1914. In the landowning class and the zemstvos, however, the anti-government mood was much less strong than before 1905 and, with memories of that year still fresh, there was no chance of noble support for a renewed Liberation Movement. Nor was there anything in 1914 to warrant fears of renewed peasant violence in the near future. But Stolypin's rather optimistic statement that 20 years of peaceful development would transform Russia betrayed an awareness that in the intervening period the state and the social elites it sustained would remain vulnerable .

European comparisons suggest that in 1914 the Russian landowning nobility was both not powerful enough and too powerful for its own good. In nineteenth-century England 7,000 individuals, almost all of them from the aristocracy and gentry, owned over 80 per cent of the land. Prussian landowning was never this aristocratic but in some provinces the big estates covered more than half the land. Both upper classes controlled rural society with little difficulty. In the English tenant farmer and the Prussian 'big' peasant the nobles also had powerful allies in the defence of property and order, and in opposition to the radicalism of the rural poor. In 1848–49 the Prussian nobles could play off peasant and landless labourers in a way that was impossible for Russian landowners faced with the much more homogeneous communal peasantry. On the other hand, however, the Russian nobles had not yet succeeded in marginalizing themselves in the manner of the west and south German nobilities. By 1914 the latter very seldom owned more than 5 per cent of the land in any province and were therefore barely a worthwhile target for expropriation. In any case, the growing power of urban and industrial lobbies had tended to create a common agrarian front, which in Catholic areas enjoyed the powerful support of the Church.

After 1905 there were some indications that the Russian nobility might be moving along the healthy road to west German-style marginalization but the extent of its remaining landholdings in many provinces meant that this process could not occur overnight. A less happy parallel, however, is offered by the experience of the aristocracy of southern Spain, where class tensions between landowner and rural proletarian in the 1930s were at least as bitter as in the Russian countryside in 1917. Franco saved the Andalucian magnates from extinction at the price of civil war and almost four decades of authoritarian rule. During the latter period the modernization of Spain's economy and society ended Andalucia's class war through mechanization of the latifundia and the emigration of most of the region's rural masses to the factories of Madrid and Catalonia. In these changed circumstances even the Spanish aristocracy could accept democracy with few qualms.

When the monarchy collapsed in 1917, the Russian landowning nobility had enjoyed not even Stolypin's two decades of peace, let alone the four granted to their Spanish counterparts by Franco. The Union of Landowners, actually established in late 1916, became the main institution through which the nobles (and other big landlords) sought to preserve their property. Desperate and by no means always unsuccessful efforts were made to mobilize support for the union among Stolypin's 'splitters' (peasants who had 'split' off from communal landownership) and other peasants who owned private land. Most provinces and one-third of all districts in European Russia had branches of the union. But the pressure of the communal peasantry, sometimes abetted by rebellious soldiers from local garrisons, was overwhelming. By July 1917 the Union's leadership was committed unequivocally to counterrevolution and would certainly have supported a military regime had it come to power by *coup d'état*. In reality only such a regime offered any chance of saving the nobles' estates, which would have been lost without compensation through the votes of a democratically elected constituent assembly just as surely as actually occurred through Bolshevik decrees and the peasants' *jacqueries*. No Russian equivalent of General Franco or Admiral Horthy emerged, however, to save the Russian aristocracy and gentry from extinction.

Further reading

Becker S., *Nobility and Privilege in Late Imperial Russia* (DeKalb, IL, North Illinois University Press, 1985).

Korelin A. P., *Dvorianstvo v poreformennoi Rossii, 1861–1914* (Moscow, Nauka, 1979).

Lieven D., *The Aristocracy in Europe, 1815–1914* (Basingstoke, Macmillan, 1992).

Manning R., *The Crisis of the Old Regime in Russia: Gentry and Government* (Princeton, Princeton University Press, 1982).

Roosevelt P., *Life on the Russian Country Estate: A Social and Cultural History* (New Haven, Yale University Press, 1995).

Bolshevik Cultural Policy

CHRISTOPHER READ

Despite being rooted in the gritty empiricism of *Das Kapital*, Marxism had a utopian dimension. Unlike many previous revolutionary movements, Marxism aimed not only at altering the balance of power and ownership in society but also at transforming human nature, at moving from what Marx had called the 'pre-history of human society' or making the leap, in Engels's words, 'from the realm of necessity into the realm of freedom'. Russian revolutionaries were particularly aware of such wider aims, not least because, even before Marxism took hold, the idea of cultural transformation was familiar to them. Above all, N. G. Chernyshevskii's novel *What Is To Be Done?* (1863), significantly subtitled *Stories of New People*, provided role models of new human types which exerted wide influence over several generations of revolutionaries. Although in 1917, immediate, practical problems commanded most attention, the long-term aims of the revolution already began to assert themselves with increasing force. No definition of aims could overlook the central importance of cultural revolution. In the long run, the success or failure of the Bolshevik enterprise depended at least as much on its ability to create and propagate its new values as it did on the more practical issues of raising working-class and poor peasant living standards. From this crucial perspective, the revolution was a struggle between the ultimately utopian revolutionary values of the Bolsheviks and the existing values of intelligentsia, peasant and working-class Russia. The final collapse of communism was in no small part attributable to its failure to win the population over to its deeper values.

Related to this was a second set of more immediately practical cultural aspirations. Naturally enough, given that the mass media had begun to develop in the form of the press and film, the issue of propaganda was prominent in the revolution and ensuing civil war. It also followed that literacy and a new form of schooling were integral parts of the revolutionary project. But these were connected to two more specifically Bolshevik reasons for paying attention to culture, the issues of 'consciousness' and 'productionism'.

The question of consciousness had been a deeply rooted theme in Lenin's thought from at least the turn of the century. Starting from Marx's view that an individual's reflections on his or her role in society led to that person becoming aware of his or her social and economic position in general and of his or her class position in particular, Lenin developed an increasingly elaborate theory of the importance of consciousness for the revolution. He largely attributed the non-appearance of the revolution Marxists had expected to the failure of the working class to develop its own, pure class-consciousness. Left to itself, he argued, it could develop only 'trade-union consciousness', by which he meant an awareness of the task of improving its immediate circumstances such as wages and working conditions, without naturally evolving (as Marx had argued it would) to an awareness that only a revolutionary transformation in property relations could provide a lasting solution to the problems of working people. The fundamental task of creating this 'revolutionary consciousness' among workers had an obvious cultural component – of education and propaganda above all. The result was Lenin's major contribution to Marxist theory, the need for a party composed of people with the required 'higher' levels of consciousness. From this point of view, Lenin's whole concept of the party and the essence of the party's project – to instil revolutionary consciousness in the Russian and, eventually, the world proletariat – were very much rooted in considerations of culture. In addition, it was assumed that the oppression inherent in the exploitative capitalist economic system prevented the mass of people from fulfilling their human potential. The revolution, it was confidently believed, would unleash enormous creative powers among the formerly oppressed classes and they would realize their full humanity. Lenin himself, in the midst of the October revolution, announced that the time had come to give 'complete creative freedom' to the masses.

'Productionism' was a much less abstract but, none the less, vital element of Bolshevism which emerged as the Bolsheviks struggled with the practical problems of running the broken-down economy of Russia. Productionism meant sparing no effort to maximize economic output, especially of industry, and subordinating all other issues to this, so that economic growth became the immediate *raison d'être* of party and state. The focus on productionism had a cultural root in the ideological drive to strengthen the working class, a drive made particularly urgent by the need to overcome Russia's 'backwardness', which had left it with a very small urban working class, largely of rural origin. Productionism also had cultural implications, notably the need to raise the skill levels of workers as well as to recruit them to the Bolshevik project.

A final element which raised the importance of cultural policy must also be taken into account – the cultural component of tsarist ideology. Tsarism itself had cultural pretensions associated, above all, with the Orthodox Church. In the early twentieth century even non-revolutionary intellectuals had realized that the struggle against tsarism was not only political but also spiritual, that is, it possessed a cultural dimension. It was almost an axiom that the left was as atheist, scientific and rational as tsarism was religious, obscurantist and irrational.

Although leading Bolshevik Party members, including Lenin, had shown considerable interest in these cultural questions for a decade or so prior to 1917, in the immediate aftermath of October practical problems absorbed much of their attention. Culture was something of an afterthought, but certain issues did present themselves. In particular, steps had to be taken to deal with the educational system. From October 1917 to the end of the academic year in summer 1918 schools and universities, like most cultural institutions, continued as normally as possible under the prevailing conditions. It appears that only in summer 1918 did the party and state leadership, represented by A. V. Lunacharsky, the historian M. N. Pokrovskii and others in the Commissariat of Education (*Narkompros*) realize that, if they did not act quickly, the largely unreformed tsarist education system would grind on for another year. In order to prevent this the first major cultural interventions – in schools and universities – were discussed. Debates among the elite were bitter and soon highlighted a crucial division within the leadership about approaches to culture, between those who might be labelled 'pragmatists' and 'utopians'. The latter called for radical reforms in the direction of various revolutionary blueprints, the former realized that, for the time being, only partial reform was on the agenda, not least because of the lack of sympathy for the Bolshevik project on the part of the vast majority of the personnel in schools and colleges and the lack of human and material resources to fuel revolutionary change in education.

There was no precedent for creating a national education system built on socialist principles. *Narkompros* set out to build one in a few months using the meagre resources of the collapsing and inadequate tsarist education system. Some aspects were not controversial – notably that it should break with the 'bourgeois' principles of the past, including religion, give priority to the working class and also embrace the peasantry. All were agreed, as the name Unified Labour School suggests, that the theory and practice of work would be at the centre of the curriculum. But the ensuing debate about how to apply such principles was highly illustrative of the evolution of Bolshevik policy in general. In this case the more ideological group wanted a more radical transformation of the school day, the school week (to seven days) and the school year (abolition of vacations). Classroom study in all areas would set out from Marxist principles. The social sciences and history, for example, would explain how control of the labour process led to class divisions and that Marxism was a liberating philosophy which would overthrow class society and build communism. Opponents did not so much oppose these principles as ask how they could be applied without committed teachers, appropriate textbooks, financial resources and amidst a general atmosphere of chaos, de-proletarianization and falling output in all sectors. Instead, they proposed a less radical modification of the existing academic curriculum and the gradual introduction of schemes linking older pupils to local workplaces for more immediately practical purposes. The latter set of propositions, which was railroaded through, smacked of the all-pervasive principles of productionism which were consuming radical policies in many vital areas.

While the party leadership succeeded, at least in theory, in implementing its school policy, although it is unlikely that most schools were fully aware of the new directions, the higher education system put up a resolute defence of traditional liberal values of university autonomy, academic standards and academic freedom. In the short term, this prevented a state takeover at the first attempt in 1918. Even reforms which the universities did accept, like elections of rectors and certain professors, rebounded because electors almost invariably took them as an opportunity to throw out party candidates in favour of more respected scholars. Universities even extracted the right to maintain their own presses. The triumphs of 1918 were, however, short-lived. Those in charge of university policy at *Narkompros*, like Otto Shmidt, learned that direct confrontation would not work and that salami tactics of introducing reform little by little should be adopted. In the end university autonomy was curtailed in 1922 and new statutes, prominently featuring the values of productionism, preferential treatment for proletarians and their allies, and the question of raising consciousness, were introduced. There was an accompanying purge of university teachers, particularly in subjects like philosophy and theology. Over 200 were expelled from Russia at short notice in summer 1922, including some of the most prominent academics who had stayed on, like the philosopher Nikolai Berdiaev and the historian S. P. Mel'gunov. Scientists and engineers were largely spared such treatment because their specialized skills were at a premium. The venerable Academy of Sciences also remained relatively unscathed and continued its traditional activities, including the extremely un-Bolshevik subjects of theology and ancient oriental languages, until the late 1920s.

It was not only within the traditional education system that practical policies on culture were being implemented. What were, essentially, new and specifically Bolshevik areas of policy-making began to appear. In September 1920 the Central Committee set up a section dealing with agitation and propaganda (*agitprop*) charged with spreading the Bolshevik gospel. Prior to this there had been a proliferation of propaganda organizations responsible to *Narkompros*, the trade unions or soviets. Under their aegis a vast range of activities evolved. From humble reading rooms to vast street theatres, by the written word and the moving image, the message of Bolshevism was spread throughout the land. Some of Russia's greatest painters, poets, film-makers and novelists took part and there was an explosion of artistic and cultural experimentation which can still inspire today. They produced posters, decorated streets for festivals, pioneered newsreels, put on plays, built monuments and planned the architectural transformation of homes, workplaces and leisure facilities. Marc Chagall was artistic commissar for his home town of Vitebsk. The poet and artist Vladimir Maiakovskii produced propagandistic cartoon strips for the Russian Telegraph Agency. Even 'bourgeois' writers such as Andrei Belyi and V. F. Khodasevich lectured to groups of workers seeking to become writers themselves. Specially commissioned trains and riverboats took teams to the provinces to lecture, put on dramas and show what were, for many people, the first movies they had ever seen. By such means the themes of struggle against the counterrevolution and the aim of achieving a better world for the ordinary population were spread.

However, the party's attitude was ambiguous, not least because many of those involved were not Bolsheviks. Rather, they were imbued with the older populist mentality according to which the duty of the intellectual was to serve the people. They were working for the revolution in the broad sense rather than for the Bolsheviks in the narrow sense. For the time being, a certain amount of pluralism was tolerated because, without the help of many talented people who were later to be branded as heretics and counterrevolutionaries, the new authorities would not have had the resources to mount such a campaign.

But it was not just the country that had to be imbued with the new ideals. The party itself had to be turned into a more reliable cultural instrument. With this in view, the grim time of the civil war also saw the boldest attempt by the party leadership to define itself by means of a new party programme adopted in March 1919. A textbook called the *ABC of Communism*, written by two leading figures on the more visionary left of the party, Evgenii Preobrazhenskii and Nikolai Bukharin, attempted to popularize its themes. In the forefront was the special role of the working class in the overthrow of capitalism, the impending world revolution, and the superiority of the scientific and rational outlook over traditional religion. The authors portrayed a future world, freed from exploitation and money, in which a culturally transformed humanity would cooperate harmoniously. Social divisions, selfishness and criminality, they argued, would be things of the past. Reading groups were set up in factories and other institutions so that party members could familiarize themselves with the new ideas and pass them on to the workforce at large.

At the same time, a system of political commissars was set up in the Red Army with the twin tasks of maintaining political control, especially over the 15–20,000 former tsarist officers serving in its ranks, and of spreading the principles of communism to the ordinary rank-and-file, many of whom were peasants who in turn, it was hoped, would spread the new ideas throughout Russia's innumerable and otherwise unreachable villages. Clearly activity of this kind was a natural extension of Lenin's prerevolutionary struggle to raise consciousness.

However, there were problems. The details of what party policy should be continued to be contested. In particular, the Proletarian Cultural-Educational Association (*Proletkul't*) challenged the assumptions of the party leadership. The debate focused on two issues, the nature of proletarian culture and *Proletkul't*'s claim to autonomy. Both issues were related to the theories of *Proletkul't*'s chief inspiration, A. A. Bogdanov.

Long before the revolution, Bogdanov had attempted to find a solution to what he saw as a crucial problem for the revolution – how should proletarian culture be nurtured? Marx, he pointed out, had argued that new historical stages (feudal, bourgeois, etc.) had gestated in the womb of the societies they were destined to replace. This applied as much as anything to their cultural evolution. Bogdanov pointed, for example, to the role of the Renaissance in developing the sense of individualism which was to be essential to the development of a bourgeois, capitalist society and its associated values of bourgeois individualism. In other words, bourgeois culture had been in the process of being formed for centuries before it actually triumphed. Could the same be said of proletarian culture? Bogdanov assumed a victorious proletariat would need its own values to be fully developed before its revolution could succeed. But the reality was that a proletarian political revolution had occurred before a truly proletarian culture had crystallized. In such circumstances, Bogdanov saw his task to be twofold: to help define the values of proletarian culture and to help nurture those values among the proletariat.

It was to realize this vision that *Proletkul't* was set up in October 1917 as an amalgamation of various local, soviet-based, cultural organizations. Its early history was stormy and confused but, as far as Bogdanov and his associates were concerned, its tasks were clear. In the terminology of the time, *Proletkul't* groups were to be 'laboratories of proletarian culture' defining and spreading proletarian values. The definition of values was relatively straightforward. In place of the bourgeois values of individualism, competition, money, personal acquisition of profit, philosophical idealism, authoritarianism and the manipulation of religion to ensure social tranquillity, Bogdanov and his associates proposed proletarian values of collectivism, cooperation, production for need not profit, philosophical materialism, science, rationalism and democracy. Their 'experiments' in their 'laboratories' were sometimes bizarre – for instance, non-competitive sports in which no score was kept, collectively written poems and stories, industrial machines used as musical instruments – but some of them were taken up by radical intellectuals in the 1920s and were even incorporated as part of 'socialist realism', the cultural orthodoxy established in the 1930s.

However, it was not so much what the organization and its members did which attracted opposition, but rather its claim to independence. For Bogdanov, it was imperative that, as far as possible, the workers should be left to develop their culture for themselves. Intervention by intellectuals such as himself and, even more emphatically, the party, should be kept to a minimum and, ideally, only be occasioned by requests from workers. The growing insistence that *Proletkul't* should be independent of the party threatened its survival. Until 1920, *Proletkul't* received a certain amount of protection from Bogdanov's brother-in-law, Lunacharsky, but when Lenin himself intervened Lunacharsky could do no more. While the main charge brought against *Proletkul't* was that, like the Futurists, it wanted to destroy existing art treasures and cultural values in a rapid, violent fashion, it was above all its desire to be independent of the party which caused Lenin's attack. The autonomy of *Proletkul't* was greatly circumscribed in December 1920, although it continued to function in rudimentary form for more than another decade.

The decree on *Proletkul't* was also a sign of the emergence of a more active cultural policy on the part of the party leadership. As the emergency of the civil war receded, neglected issues like culture became a priority. The main direction of party policy was to control wider areas of culture and to limit broad, speculative approaches such as that of Bogdanov and concentrate instead on bread-and-butter issues of literacy and party propaganda and, as we have seen, turning the educational system into the servant of productionism. Other landmarks in the evolution of party control over culture had begun with the banning of opposition newspapers, which had been initiated in the first days of the revolution and had resulted in a party monopoly of the press by summer 1918. This was followed by the nationalization of printing establishments and publishing houses and the expansion of the role of the State Publishing House (*Gosizdat*), which had originally been set up in December 1917. By 1919, it exercised a virtual state monopoly over publishing, not least by means of its censorship committee which supervised the output of all publishers. A separate censorship apparatus (*Glavlit*) was set up in 1922. From 1923 theatre and music censorship were brought together in *Glavrepertkom*. The permanent establishment in 1922 of a secret police, the GPU, which was directly descended from the 'temporary' Cheka set up in December 1917, had important cultural implications since it was already heavily involved in press surveillance and internal security including political imprisonment for opposition intellectuals and organizing the mass expulsion of intellectuals in summer 1922.

One other factor had, almost inadvertently, helped to strengthen the authorities' hold on culture. In addition to deliberate policies of intervention, the cultural world had been utterly transformed by the social and economic changes of 1917–22. The flight of the elite, the disintegration of the unified economy of the fallen empire and the collapse of market relationships and the money economy had devastated cultural production. There were hardly any regular sources of income for creative intellectuals. Some held on as lecturers and teachers and a few selected figures qualified for official rations during the civil war but, in general, the economic relationships on which high culture depended had been shattered. There were no journals, no non-party newspapers, no art market, no rich patrons, no independent schools. By default, the state had become the only surviving source of major patronage and this added immensely to its power. For the time being competing groups of intellectuals believed they could colonize the state institutions and control them in the interests of their own *groupuscule* (mini group), a feature of intellectual life which persisted beyond the mid-1920s, but the state administrators were steadily increasing their power at the same time, not least by pitting cultural factions against one another.

By the end of the civil war cultural control had become a matter of course. Nothing could show more clearly that Lenin's proposed 'complete creative freedom for the masses' of 26 October 1917 had not produced the hoped-for results: there had been no explosion of revolutionary consciousness of a kind acceptable to the Bolshevik leadership. In its continuing absence, party guidance along the rocky path of rising consciousness was the only way to advance. While the 1920s certainly became a 'golden age' for acceptable strands of revolutionary culture and great achievements in literature, film and fine arts were recorded, a multitude of unacceptable trends were marginalized by refusal of access to publication or public exhibition by means of censorship and the imprisonment or expulsion of many unorthodox writers, thinkers and artists.

The culmination of such processes, however, lay in the future. In 1921, in the cultural field as elsewhere, the Soviet state was a curious amalgam of strength – in that it was no longer endangered by internal resistance – and weakness – in that its values were alien not only to the vast number of peasants but also to the majority of intellectuals and workers. As far as popular culture is concerned, with the exception of the attack on religion and the abolition of the popular/yellow press, the new authorities had made little headway. *Rabfaki* (workers' faculties) in higher education were only just getting off the ground and Bolshevik initiatives, like monuments, street festivals celebrating the new revolutionary holidays, workers' clubs, reading rooms and prototype palaces of culture, were up against formidable opposition presented by vodka and tradition.

Even though in 1923 Trotsky was still arguing, in apocalyptic fashion, that the revolution would release such immense creative energy that the average human would reach the heights of Shakespeare or Goethe, in practice, Soviet culture was already embarking on the process whereby it was to become a byword for the preservation of 'conservative' cultural values (realist fine arts; traditional symphony orchestras; ballet; chess; conventional competitive sports, etc.) at the expense of revolutionary experimentation. In 1921, the outcome was not entirely predetermined. Although spontaneous cultural life was beginning to be made to flow in acceptable channels, final decisions about the dimensions of those channels still lay in the future. However, steady expansion of the cultural apparatus was underway and the principles of productionism and consciousness-raising, on which future decisions were to be based, were already making themselves felt. By 1921–22 the balance of power in culture had begun to swing away from creativity towards order imposed by party officials.

Further reading

Claudin-Urondo C., *Lenin and the Cultural Revolution* (Hassocks, Sussex, Harvester Press, 1977).

Fitzpatrick S., *The Commissariat of Enlightenment: Soviet Organization of Education and the Arts under Lunacharsky (1917–21)* (Cambridge, Cambridge University Press, 1970).

Gleason A., Kenez P. and Stites R., eds., *Bolshevik Culture* (Bloomington and London, Indiana University Press, 1985).

Gorzka G., *Bogdanov und der russische Proletkult. Theorie und Praxis einer sozialistischen Kulturrevolution* (Frankfurt and New York, Campus Verlag, 1980).

Kenez P., *The Birth of the Propaganda State: Soviet Methods of Mass Mobilization, 1917–1929* (Cambridge, Cambridge University Press, 1985).

Lapshin V. P., *Khudozhestvennaia zhizn' Moskvy i Petrograda v 1917 godu* (Moscow, Sovetskii khudozhnik, 1983).

Lenin V. I., *O literature i iskusstve*, 7th edn (Moscow, Khudozhestvennaia Literatura, 1986).

Mally L., *Culture of the Future: The Proletkul't Movement in Revolutionary Russia* (Berkeley, University of California Press, 1990).

Paris-Moscou 1900–1930: Catalogue de l'Exposition (Paris, 1979).

Read C., *Culture and Power in Revolutionary Russia: The Intelligentsia and the Transition from Tsarism to Communism* (London, Macmillan Press, 1990).

Rosenberg W. G., ed., *Bolshevik Visions: First Phase of the Cultural Revolution in Soviet Russia*, second edn, 2 vols. (Ann Arbor, University of Michigan Press, 1990).

Stites R., *Revolutionary Dreams: Utopian Vision and Experimental Life in the Russian Revolution* (New York, Oxford, Oxford University Press, 1989).

The Cossacks

SHANE O'ROURKE

From the outbreak of strikes in Petrograd in February 1917 until the evacuation of the last anti-Bolshevik forces from the Crimea in November 1920 the Cossacks played a momentous role in the Russian revolution and civil war. That role was complex and defies simple categorization. Cossacks fought on all sides in the conflict: for the independence of their homelands; as part of the wider anti-Bolshevik struggle; as supporters of the Bolshevik regime. Often the same Cossacks participated in all three struggles at different times. Attempts to characterize this by simplistic divisions into Red and White or by slightly more sophisticated tripartite divisions of Cossack society into kulak, middle and poor strata rapidly lose most, if not all, of their explanatory power when they are applied to the course of the revolution and civil war in the Cossack areas. Explanations of Cossack behaviour have to be sought in the distinctiveness of their traditions, the long-term structural tensions that existed within the Cossack territories and the immediate experience of World War, revolution and civil war.

The Cossack tradition

The Cossacks were a military caste that had been created by fugitives from serfdom. Arising in the early sixteenth century, they settled on the frontiers of the Muscovite state along the Don and Dnepr Rivers. During the seventeenth and eighteenth centuries the Cossack states were slowly incorporated into Muscovy and then the empire. In the process they lost their former status as the embodiments of popular freedom and became the most feared defenders of the autocracy. However, this process was never completed and the Cossacks retained much of their earlier distinctiveness to the end of the old regime. Their military tradition, their local democracy and their system of communal landholding remained intact. These gave the Cossacks a highly developed sense of their identity and the means to articulate that identity after the collapse of the imperial state.

The Cossack *voiska* in 1914

By 1914 there were eleven Cossack *voiska* stretching from the River Don in the west to the River Amur in the east. The largest and most important of the Cossack *voiska* were the Don and the Kuban and it was these that were of decisive significance in the revolution.

The issue that more than any other single factor would determine the course of the civil war in the Cossack territories was already apparent by 1914. In the space of a few decades the Cossacks had gone from being an absolute majority of the population to a minority whose relative significance was continuing to decline. The rest of the population was made up largely of peasants although there was a small but significant proletariat in a few of the larger towns, particularly Rostov, Taganrog and Ekaterinodar.

Caste barriers between the Cossacks and the peasantry created animosity but what poisoned relations was the distribution of land. The Cossack minority owned most of the land, while the peasants had to make do with much smaller and poorer allotments. The Cossacks were uncomfortably aware of the acute landhunger of the peasantry whose relative dominance of the population was continuing to grow. For the peasantry, Cossack land-holdings were almost as iniquitous as those of the nobility and Church. Cossack determination to hold on to their land and peasant determination to redistribute was the fundamental cause of conflict in the Cossack *voiska*.

Conflict within the Cossack areas was not, though, a simple split between Cossack and non-Cossack. Between the ordinary Cossacks and the Cossack elite there was a depth of suspicion and resentment not much less than that between the peasantry and nobility. In contrast to this, the Cossack communities based around their *stanitsas* remained remarkably cohesive. Despite some differentiation, there is no evidence to suggest these communities were disintegrating into kulak, middle and poor layers. There were fault lines in Cossack society which could be exploited but they were not the ones of the standard Leninist interpretation.

The attitude of the Cossacks to the outside world was undergoing a transformation in the early twentieth century. Despite the assiduous efforts of the government to promote the idea of a unique bond between the Cossacks and the throne, dissatisfaction was growing. The primary reason for this was the rising cost of military service which was creating an intolerable burden for large numbers of Cossacks. In addition to this, the Cossacks were no longer willing to carry out repression unquestioningly. There had been clear indications of this in the 1905 revolution even though the Cossacks had been the main instrument of repression.

The Cossack *frontoviki*

The *frontoviki*, i.e. those who fought at the front, did not exist as a distinct group before the First World War. Thousands of Cossacks had fought in previous wars but none of them were as alienated as the Cossacks who were frontline soldiers in the First World War. The attitudes and beliefs these Cossacks brought home with them in the early part of 1918 were very different from the ones they had left with in 1914.

The Cossacks were the most intensively mobilized section of the population. They were called up earlier and, proportionally, in greater numbers than any other section of society. The experience of war forged a common bond between the Cossack *frontoviki* and the other regiments that fought alongside them in the trenches. The caste barriers that had divided Cossack and peasant were severely undermined among those who shared the suffering at the front. Simultaneously the *frontoviki*, along with millions of other soldiers, felt deeply alienated from the societies that they had left behind. Thoroughly war-weary after almost three years of war, Cossack regiments were called upon to suppress the disorders that had broken out in Petrograd in February 1917.

There were two Don Cossack regiments stationed in Petrograd, the First and Fourth, both recently withdrawn from the front. A third regiment, the Fourteenth, was just across the border in Finland. It was in the First and Fourth regiments that the first tremors of the impending political earthquake were felt. These regiments displayed marked sympathy for the striking workers, refusing to disperse them and attacking police who were prepared to open fire on the crowds. The reluctance of the Cossacks to assist the police exposed the crisis of tsarist power.

Between February and October the Cossack regiments remained an unknown quantity for both supporters of the revolution and its opponents. Despite the understanding that had existed between the Cossacks and the revolutionary crowds in the first days of the revolution, all the 'revolutionary democracy' regarded the Cossacks with suspicion. This was primarily because of their long association with repression but also because Cossack regiments remained coherent military formations throughout this period in contrast to most other sections of the army. The Cossack tradition and the retention of military discipline appeared to indicate that the Cossack regiments were still willing to carry out their time-honoured role as the upholders of state authority. Those on the right reached the same conclusion, although obviously regarding it as something to be welcomed rather than feared. The use of the Cossacks to put down the unrest of the July Days seemingly confirmed both sides' assumptions about the Cossacks.

Both left and right failed to appreciate the transformation that was taking place among the *frontoviki*. They were as influenced by the revolution as other units, although it took longer for this to become apparent. The lack of desertions, the retention of officers, and the maintenance of military discipline did not signify continuing Cossack appetite for repression but rather the exceptionally close ties that existed within the Cossack regiments. Although the Cossack regiments did not disintegrate, they slowly went over *en masse* to the revolution. In July the All Cossack Conference of the South-West Front, which met in Kiev, reflected unambiguously the influence not only of the Soviets in general on the *frontoviki*, but of the Bolsheviks in particular.

The decision of General A. M. Kaledin, the leader or ataman, of the Don Cossacks to form an electoral alliance with the Kadets further alienated the *frontoviki,* but it was the Kornilov coup at the end of August that finally severed any remaining sense of loyalty they may have had to the Cossack authorities in their home area. The attempt to use Cossack troops against the Petrograd Soviet and Kaledin's role in the conspiracy confirmed to the *frontoviki* that Kaledin and all the Cossack authorities had aligned themselves against the people.

When the *frontoviki* returned home in early 1918, they dispelled any illusions that might have lingered as to where their political loyalties lay. The majority had an attitude of benevolent neutrality to the Soviet regime while a significant minority was prepared to fight to establish Soviet power in the Cossack *voiska*. Together with other pro-Soviet forces, they deposed the old Cossack authorities and proclaimed Soviet power within the Cossack *voiska*.

The experience of Bolshevik rule and the bitter land war with the peasantry led many, but not all, *frontoviki* to reconsider their attitude to Soviet power particularly as far as their own territories were concerned. *Frontoviki* were prominent in the revolts against the Bolsheviks that broke out in early spring 1918 and they participated in the heavy fighting to clear their homelands of Bolsheviks. In the Don, Cossacks served in their own army while in the Kuban they fought mainly in the Volunteer Army. However, there was much less enthusiasm to take the fight beyond the border of their own *voiska*, as General Denikin bitterly noted. Many *frontoviki* retained a residual sympathy for the Soviet regime even if they were no longer so keen to be a part of it.

The struggle for Cossack autonomy

The fall of the dynasty elicited no response from the Cossack areas. There was no outcry, no call for the tsar to be restored. The revolution did, however, open up the question of the relationship of the Cossack *voiska* to the central authority to a degree not seen since the great Cossack revolts of the seventeenth and eighteenth centuries.

The tsarist state had never quite succeeded in eradicating the memory of independent Cossack republics. This historical memory was given concrete expression within days of the February revolution. In the most important

Cossack *voiska* the institutions of independent statehood were created even if the *voiska* did not immediately lay claim to this status. These elementary forms of statehood and the widespread, if fluctuating, Cossack support for them made the Cossack areas the most formidable opponents of the Bolshevik regime once the majority of Cossacks rejected Soviet power within their own *voiska*.

Fear of peasant designs on Cossack land provided the spur to Cossack organization. The assemblies through which Cossack sovereignty had been exercised, on the Don the Krug, in the Kuban and the Terek the Rada, were recreated nearly two centuries after their suppression. The Don Krug elected General Kaledin as ataman and he became the most influential of all Cossack leaders until his suicide in January 1918.

None of the Cossack institutions succeeded in creating a stable system of government. Elected exclusively by the Cossacks, they were rejected by the peasantry, the working class and the large non-Cossack garrisons in the major towns. These set up rival authorities in the form of soviets. Attempts by the Cossack authorities to broaden the base of their support failed because neither side was prepared to compromise on the central issue dividing them: land. The Cossacks were willing to allow the redistribution of noble and church property but they adamantly refused to include their own land in any such redistribution. The failure to establish any understanding between the two sections of the population before the October revolution made a violent solution to the land question increasingly likely.

Initially none of the Cossack *voiska* expressed a desire for independence. Under the leadership of General Kaledin, they each recognized the Provisional Government as the sole legitimate authority and firmly supported its policy of war until final victory. But the failure of the Provisional Government to halt the disintegration of the state and the army soured relations between it and the Cossack authorities to the point where Kaledin threw in his lot with the conspiracy to overthrow the government and replace it with a military dictatorship under General Kornilov.

The worsening relations between the Cossack *voiska* and the Provisional Government intensified the momentum towards full independence. Tentative steps were taken to create a 'Union of All the Cossack Voiska' but nothing substantial had been achieved by October. The Bolshevik coup overcame any remaining doubts. The Don, the Kuban and the Terek all announced their secession from Russia.

The frailty of Cossack independence was cruelly exposed over the next three months. The *frontoviki* were openly hostile while even the more conservative sections of Cossack society preferred to adopt a temporizing attitude to the new government. This left the Cossack governments without any significant armed support. Under pressure internally and externally, all the Cossack *voiska* collapsed in early 1918 to be replaced by Soviet republics. Yet within weeks newly invigorated Cossack states again emerged which took the Bolsheviks two years of heavy fighting to destroy.

The new states that arose as a result of anti-Bolshevik feeling were openly committed to a policy of independence. In contrast to the earlier attempt, the Cossack governments could now count on the firm support of large sections of the Cossack population. A general mobilization was proclaimed to which the Cossacks responded enthusiastically. However, while most Cossacks were determined to expel the Bolsheviks from their territories, few had much interest in the wider anti-Bolshevik struggle. It was also clear from the policies pursued by General Krasnov, the new Don ataman, and those of the Kuban Rada that the Cossack states wanted independence regardless of who ruled in Moscow. This precluded any possibility of a good working relationship between the Cossack states and the Volunteer Army.

Two other fundamental problems also remained. One was the rejection of the new Cossack states by all the non-Cossack population, i.e. over half of the total; the other was the continued susceptibility of sections of the Cossack population to Bolshevik propaganda. The constant military pressure to which these states were subjected exacerbated these weaknesses and led to the collapse of the Cossack *voiska* in 1920.

The Cossacks and the Bolshevik regime

Apart from the *frontoviki*, most Cossacks initially adopted a cautious attitude to the Bolshevik regime. For its part the new regime, conscious of the potential threat from the Cossacks, went out of its way to assure them that it had no interest in the land of ordinary 'toiling' Cossacks. At the same time, however, the Bolsheviks were telling the peasants that they were the only rightful owners of the land and urged them to seize it immediately.

Before long, however, the reality of Bolshevik occupation forced the Cossacks to accept that there was no place for them in the new order. Immediately the Soviet republics were established in the Cossack *voiska*, the land war with the peasantry entered a new and very violent phase. The peasantry began to seize Cossack lands and loot Cossack property. This was accompanied by a wild and uncontrolled eruption of terror by the new authorities. Hundreds of Cossacks were shot in an arbitrary and haphazard settling of accounts with the people so long identified as the ruthless defenders of the old order.

This reactivated the anti-Bolshevik struggle that had failed so dismally only a few weeks earlier. The revolt began in the Don among Cossacks of the southern *stanitsas*. Revolts followed in the Kuban and the Terek which succeeded in expelling the Bolsheviks from all the Cossack *voiska*. The military experience of the Cossacks and the existence of a state structure to provide coordination ensured that there would be no more easy Bolshevik victories in the Cossack areas as long as the Cossacks themselves retained the willingness to fight.

It was this willingness that the Bolsheviks now attempted to undermine through propaganda. Again they played on the latent resentments of ordinary Cossacks against their own elite, emphasizing that Bolshevik quarrels were with the Cossack elite not the Cossacks in general. The Cossacks were much more amenable to this propaganda when they were fighting outside their own *voisko*. By late autumn 1918, Cossacks fighting in the Upper Don and at Tsaritsyn started to return home, opening the Cossack heartland to the Bolsheviks once more. In early 1919 the Cossack *voiska* neared collapse for the second time.

What Bolshevik propaganda had skilfully won, Bolshevik administration immediately lost. The decision was taken in the Central Committee to end once and for all the Cossack threat. All the upper strata of Cossack society were to be exterminated as was any Cossack who had participated in the anti-Bolshevik struggle at any time. Unlike the earlier policy of terror, this one was systematically implemented. Instead of pacifying the Cossacks it provoked a new revolt which again expelled the Bolsheviks and provided the base for the culmination of the efforts to overthrow the Bolshevik regime later on in 1919.

The failure of General Denikin's march on Moscow in October 1919 marked the beginning of the end of the anti-Bolshevik struggle. The Cossacks now had few illusions about what Soviet rule meant for them and months of bitter fighting followed before Soviet power was definitively established in the Cossack *voiska*. Although ruthless in their consolidation of power the Bolsheviks treated the Cossacks with more circumspection having no wish to provoke a third Cossack rebellion.

Conclusion

The Cossack tradition came to an end with Bolshevik victory in the civil war. In the course of that conflict the Bolsheviks had learnt to their cost what formidable enemies the Cossacks could be. No other community fought so stubbornly in defence of its way of life. Even so, Cossack behaviour was not one-dimensional but reflected the tensions that existed among them and in the wider society. Caste loyalty underpinned Cossack identity but the experience of World War led to a large and influential section of Cossack society rejecting that identity for a time. The land war with the peasantry created unity of interest between the ordinary Cossacks and the Cossack elite but it did not eradicate mutual resentment. Bolshevik propaganda exploited the divisions within Cossack society yet the reality of Bolshevik rule reunited it. A determination to drive the Bolsheviks out of their *voiska* was countered by an equal reluctance to take the fight beyond those borders. These shifting currents defined the complex flow of events in the Cossack *voiska* throughout the revolutionary period.

Further reading

Donskaia letopis': Sbornik materialov po noveishei istorii donskogo kazachestva so vremeni russkoi revoliutsii 1917 goda, 3 vols. (Belgrade, izdatel'stvo Donskoi istoricheskoi komissii, 1923).

Ermolin A. P., *Revoliutsiia i kazachestvo* (Moscow, Mysl', 1982).

Kirienko Iu. K., *Revoliutsiia i donskoe kazachestvo, fevral'–oktiabr' 1917 g.* (Rostov-na-Donu, izdatel'stvo Rostovskogo universiteta, 1988).

Longworth P., *The Cossacks* (London, Macmillan, 1969).

McNeal R., *Tsar and Cossack* (London, Macmillan, 1987).

O'Rourke S., 'Warriors and Peasants: The Contradictions of Cossack Culture 1861–1914' (D.Phil. dissertation, University of Oxford, 1994).

Sholokhov M., *And Quiet Flows the Don,* trans. S. Garry (Harmondsworth, Penguin, 1967).

Sholokhov M., *The Don Flows Home to the Sea,* trans. S. Garry (Harmondsworth, Penguin, 1970).

The Emigration

ROBERT C. WILLIAMS

The terms 'Russian emigration', 'Russian diaspora', or 'Russia abroad' (*Zagranichnaia Rossiia*) usually denote the several million individuals forced to flee the Russian empire after its collapse in revolution and civil war between 1917 and 1921. In fact, emigration had been a fact of Russian life for centuries. The post-revolutionary exodus was a massive and specific form of a traditional phenomenon in Russian history, as well as a part of the aftermath of World War I. The Russian emigration was also a sequel to earlier European political emigrations that followed the revolutions of 1688, 1789, 1830, 1848 and 1905.

It is important to distinguish exiles, *émigrés*, and refugees, although these terms are often used interchangeably. Traditionally, Russians sought *exile* in Western Europe on a temporary basis to conduct political and cultural activity forbidden at home. In the nineteenth century, virtually every major European city had its colony of Russian artists, students, writers, journalists and revolutionaries. These political exiles were joined in the 1880s by a massive out-migration of *émigrés*, largely Jewish, seeking to escape persecution, tsarist military conscription and economic hardship. Several million *émigrés* left Russia between 1881 and 1914, mainly for the United States, and Russia became a country of net emigration rather than net immigration. Finally, Russian *refugees* were involuntarily displaced persons driven from their homeland by the events of war, revolution and civil war.

The Russian emigration that followed the 1917 Russian revolution and subsequent civil war contained all three of these elements, although the refugees far outnumbered the more traditional exiles and *émigrés*, in so far as these could be distinguished. Although estimates vary, there were probably two or three million refugees from the Russian empire abroad in the 1920s, mainly young males who had fought in the White armies against Soviet forces during the Russian civil war. These refugees were concentrated in Germany, Czechoslovakia, the Balkans, Poland, the Baltic states and China, especially in the large cities of Berlin, Prague, Paris, Sofia, Warsaw, Riga and

Harbin. There were some 70,000 refugees in Berlin by late 1919, and as many as 500,000 in Germany by 1923, which was often a transit station for other destinations. The majority were not ethnic Russians, but Poles, Jews and Germans. Many other refugees from the Russian empire identified themselves not as Russian but as Armenian, Georgian, Ukrainian, Finnish or other non-Russian nationality. Until 1923, Berlin housed the largest concentration of Russian *émigrés*, succeeded by Paris and then New York City, but every capital city had its Russian colony in the interwar period.

Exodus

The revolutionary emigration began as a massive exodus from the war zones of the Russian civil war, beginning with the German withdrawal from the Baltic and the Ukraine in the winter of 1918–19 following the Armistice. Russian troops from the White armies of Generals N. N. Iudenich, A. I. Denikin, P. N. Krasnov and P. N. Wrangel were evacuated from the ports of Novorossiisk (Sea of Azov), the Crimea and Georgia (Black Sea), and the Baltic. In November 1920, over 100 ships conveyed General Wrangel and his troops from Sevastopol to Constantinople, from which they subsequently transferred to temporary camps in Turkey, and finally to the Balkans and Western Europe. White soldiers and their families from the Baltic and north Russia more often migrated through Poland to Germany. In the far east, they went through Harbin to China, Japan and the United States, although Harbin, a major town on the Trans-Siberian Railway, remained a major Russian *émigré* centre into the 1930s.

Settling the homeless

As hundreds of thousands of refugees poured into Europe, foreign cities took on their own specific characteristics. Paris in 1919 became the political centre of the Russian emigration, in part because of the Paris Peace Conference. Berlin became the focus of book publishing. Warsaw, Riga and Istanbul were way stations, Sofia a gathering point for veterans, Prague a scholarly and literary centre, and so on.

New institutions quickly sprang up to help massive numbers of homeless and displaced persons. The wartime Union of Zemstvos and Towns, *Zemgor*, administered refugee affairs from Paris. The Council of Ambassadors (*Soveshchanie poslov*), headed by M. N. Giers, utilized the old network of Russian embassies and consulates abroad to look out for the legal rights of refugees and their passports. The Russian Red Cross, the Young Men's Christian Association, and the American Relief Agency all provided food, clothing and books. The Russian Military Mission in Berlin ministered to former prisoners of war, the Russian Veterans' Union (ROVS) aided former soldiers, and the Orthodox Church assisted the faithful. Organizations such as the Union of Russian Emigré Students (Prague, 1922), Russian National University, and the YMCA provided educational assistance.

The League of Nations, through its High Commissioner for Refugee Affairs, the Norwegian Arctic explorer Fridjof Nansen, established a new system of passports for so-called 'stateless persons', to provide international identity papers for refugees after the war. These papers became vital after 1921, when the new Soviet government deprived all *émigrés* of Soviet citizenship. Following German recognition of Soviet Russia at the Treaty of Rapallo (16 April 1922), the legal status of *émigrés* became increasingly problematic and confusing.

Life abroad

Although Russian *émigré* cultural life attracted most attention, the lives of ordinary Russians thrust abroad was far more tragic and commonplace. Obtaining visas was very difficult. With the 6 May 1921 treaty between Germany and Soviet Russia, Soviet representatives began issuing visas and passports in Berlin. By December, the Soviet government had published decrees depriving of their citizenship all individuals who had left the country without a visa after 7 November 1917, and all who had lived abroad more than five years without à Soviet passport. Many subsequently became stateless persons moving from one country to another and living on Nansen passports.

Few *émigrés* could easily find employment or education. Many had lost their life savings. Their credentials from Russia meant nothing in a new society. Poverty and downward mobility were normal. Many wealthy Russians and even royalty ended up driving taxis, selling insurance, waiting on tables, running restaurants, opening dress shops, or working as hotel porters. Some found their valuable household possessions sold at auction by the Soviet government in Europe or the United States. Others simply pawned what they brought with them.

The vast majority of the Russian emigration consisted of unemployed males between 18 and 40. For the first few years, the birth-rate was low and the mortality rate high. Overall, the emigration had an above average educational level by Russian standards and was in large measure urban, educated, professionally trained and Russian Orthodox. There were very few peasants, and very few *émigrés* became naturalized citizens of the host country.

The writer Vladimir Nabokov in his many novels and stories chronicled the sad story of *émigré* struggles with a foreign language, foreign landlords, menial jobs, passport problems, disease, poor schools, and grinding poverty and rootlessness. Russian tearooms and events like the annual celebration of

Russian culture on Pushkin's birthday (8 June) or a 'Miss Russia' beauty contest masked the difficult reality of *émigré* life.

Politics

Russian *émigré* politics was by and large a continuation of old quarrels in new forms. The traditional political spectrum of pre-revolutionary Russia – from the Union of Russian People on the right through the Octobrists and Constitutional Democrats in the centre, to the left-wing Socialist Revolutionaries, Social Democrats (Mensheviks), and anarchists – persisted in emigration. In addition, there were the former officials of the Imperial and Provisional Governments, followers of various political-military groupings and generals from the civil war, delegates of the non-Russian nationalities, and monarchists supporting various Romanov pretenders, notably the Grand Dukes Nikolai Nikolaevich and Kirill Vladimirovich. The belief that substantial 'Romanov treasure' existed in foreign bank accounts stimulated the appearance of several 'Anastasias' and other claimants to the Romanov throne. The Soviet government soon began to take advantage of the situation by funding fellow-travelling organizations, encouraging *émigrés* to return home and, on one occasion, even establishing a bogus monarchist organization, the Trust.

The Russian monarchists were initially concentrated in Bavaria, where they held a conference at Bad Reichenhall in May–June, 1921. Right-wing Germans from Russia's former Baltic provinces, such as Max Erwin von Scheubner-Richter and Alfred Rosenberg, popularized anti-semitism and the spurious *Protocols of the Elders of Zion* among their German sympathizers, including the Nazis. They portrayed the Russian revolution as an Asiatic-Jewish plot against Western civilization. Peter Struve moved his Kadet-oriented journal *Russkaia mysl'* ('Russian Thought') to Sofia (1921), Prague and Berlin (1922–4), and finally Paris (1927). The peasant-centred Socialist Revolutionaries settled in Prague, where they established their journal *Volia Rossii* ('Russian Freedom'). The Mensheviks, led by Iu. O. Martov, settled in Berlin, where they published *Sotsialisticheskii vestnik* ('Socialist Messenger') (1921–63), which subsequently moved to Paris and New York.

While a few groups and individuals established contacts with political parties in the host country (the Mensheviks and the Independent Socialists (USPD) in Germany), they were mainly isolated factions in exile conducting politics in the Russian language and in uncompromising opposition to the new Soviet regime. The condition of emigration more often deepened old political disputes than created new ones. A tragic example was the March 1922 murder in Berlin of the Kadet politician Vladimir Nabokov, father of the novelist, by two Russian fascists seeking to kill his fellow Kadet, P. N. Miliukov.

Intellectual and cultural life

The Russian emigration spawned a rich intellectual and cultural life even in the midst of homelessness and poverty. Most *émigrés* saw the emigration as the true bearer of Russian culture history, and literature; the new Soviet Russia in their view had no claim on these traditions. Russian literature and culture became for the *émigrés*, in the words of the writer Dmitri Merezhkovsky, 'our final homeland'.

Again, art, music and literature, like politics, often echoed the ideas and influences of the pre-revolutionary Silver Age (1890–1914) in Russia. Russian *émigré* publishing houses produced books, journals and daily newspapers in abundance. The dailies included the Kadet *Rul'* ('The Rudder') in Berlin; Alexander Kerensky's *Dni* ('Days') in Berlin, and after 1926, Paris; *Segodnia* ('Today') in Riga; *Novoe vremia* ('New Times') in Belgrade; and the *Poslednie novosti* ('Latest News') (1920–40), edited by Miliukov in Paris. The publishing houses of Z. I. Grzhebin (1869–1929) and Ivan Ladyzhnikov produced more books in the early 1920s than did their counterparts in Moscow and Petrograd. The Berlin houses of Petropolis, Epokha and Skify dominated the Russian market throughout the interwar period.

The literary 'thick journal' *Sovremennye zapiski* ('Contemporary Notes', 1920–40) in Paris published a wide range of *émigré* authors, including Vladimir Nabokov (under the pseudonym Sirin), the Nobel Prize winner Ivan Bunin, Zinaida Hippius, Aleksei Remizov, Marina Tsvetaeva, Mark Aldanov, Konstantin Balmont, Viacheslav Ivanov, and Merezhkovsky. So did the famous YMCA Press, established in Prague in 1921 and moved later to Berlin (1923) and Paris (1925).

The emigration was, in addition, a repository of history. Historians such as Miliukov, Mikhail Karpovich and George Vernadsky became well known in the West, as did the sociologists Pitirim Sorokin and Georges Gurvitch. In Belgrade, the Yugoslav Academy of Sciences published a 'Russian Library' of *émigré* contributions. In Prague, the Russian Historical Archive and Library, established with the support of the Czech Ministry of Foreign Affairs, served as a depository for *émigré* papers and correspondence. And in Paris, too, the Turgenev Library was a magnet for Russian readers.

Intellectuals in emigration stressed the cataclysmic nature of history, the non-Western elements in Russian culture, and the general decline of the West. The religious philosopher N. A. Berdiaev produced a series of books arguing the eschatological nature of 'the Russian idea' and calling for a Christian renewal out of the 'new middle ages' of the present. The so-called Eurasian scholars published a collection entitled *Iskhod k vostoku* ('The Way Out to the East', Sofia, 1921) where they argued for the Iranian, Mongol and Turkic roots of modern Russian culture. The *Smena Vekh* ('Change of Landmarks') circle, founded in Prague in 1921 and responding to the pre-war critique of the Russian radical intelligentsia, *Vekhi*

('Landmarks') (1909), wrote for the Berlin journal *Nakanune* ('On the Eve'), and called for reconciliation with the new Soviet regime as the logical continuer of Russian national traditions in the struggle against the Poles and other Western armies of intervention. The so-called Scythians, a group of poets emphasizing Russia's eastern roots, organized a journal in Berlin with the Left Socialist Revolutionaries.

Cultural life was enlivened by the forced expulsion from Soviet Russia of hundreds of well-known Russian intellectuals in late 1922: Berdiaev, the philosophers S. L. Frank and N. O. Lossky, F. A. Stepun, the economist S. N. Prokopovich, the historian A. A. Kizevetter, and the jurist P. I. Novgorodtsev among them. In September 1922, the philosopher V. V. Zenkovsky organized the Russian Philosophical Society in Berlin. Two months later, Berdiaev, with funding from the YMCA, opened the Religious Philosophical Academy and launched a series of lectures and classes by eminent scholars.

Many *émigré* artists were familiar with Europe from their pre-war studies and travel. Vasily Kandinsky, who had lived in Munich before 1914, moved quickly into the front rank of German abstract expressionist painters. Marc Chagall left his native Vitebsk for the studios of Paris he knew so well. The rayonnist painters Mikhail Larionov and Natalia Goncharova also returned to Paris to live. In Berlin, the painter El Lissitzky and his journal *Veshch* ('Object') served as a meeting place for *émigré* and Soviet artists with their European modernist counterparts. The Berlin Van Diemen Gallery art exhibit of 1922 was another point of contact. Other artists sought a reputation in the United States: the futurist David Burliuk, Sergei Sudeikin, Boris Anisfeld and Boris Grigoriev among them. The World of Art painter Nicholas Roerich migrated to America where his mystical paintings of the Himalayan Mountains made him the centre of a religious cult. Icons, jewellery, and paintings soon flooded the Western market in the wake of the emigration, pawned by desperate *émigrés* or sold by the Soviet government to earn hard currency.

Russian music was another *émigré* export. Igor Stravinsky and Sergei Rachmaninoff became composers in exile, the bass Fedor Chaliapin continued to sing to Parisian audiences, and the conductor Serge Koussevitsky achieved new fame with the Boston Symphony Orchestra. Sergei Jaroff's Don Cossack choir sang for enthusiastic audiences around the world. The Ballet Russe de Monte Carlo continued the dazzling productions of Sergei Diaghilev with the dancing of Vaslav Nijinsky and Anna Pavlova. Sergei Prokofiev composed his music in America for a time before returning home in 1932.

Religion was a major unifying factor in emigration. The Russian Church hierarchies abroad, often centred in the old parish churches attached to the imperial embassies, were divided after 1921 between the Bishops Synod of Sremtski-Karlovci (Serbia) and the supporters of Metropolitan Evlogii in Europe, both at odds with the Patriarch in Moscow. This division was compounded by the pro-Soviet 'Living Church' established to woo support for the new regime. Those who wished to improve the intellectual life of the church gathered in the Russian Theological Academy in Paris (1925) (Berdiaev, Sergei Bulgakov, George Florovsky, George Fedotov) and around the journal *Put'* ('The Way') (1925–40). The Russian Student Christian Movement was active and supported by the YMCA. Ecumenical ties to the Anglican Church were fostered by the Fellowship of St Albans and St Sergius (1928), in which Fathers Bulgakov and Florovsky were especially active. Much of the rich legacy of Russian Orthodoxy was portrayed in Florovsky's *Puti russkogo bogosloviia* (Belgrade, 1938).

Although *émigré* intellectual life was diverse and difficult to characterize, *émigré* writers and thinkers generally tended to oppose the regime from which they had fled and to see in the Russian revolution some kind of apocalypse, catastrophe or return to a more primitive time of troubles. Some refused to adopt in their writings the new orthography established by the Soviet regime in 1918. Many associated Russia with the East rather than the West. In general, *émigré* thought continued pre-revolutionary discussion and debate, rather than breaking new ground.

Returnism

In time, the *émigrés* faced a number of difficult questions: how should they respond to Western recognition of the Soviet government? Should they seek naturalization in a new country? Should they assimilate? Should they resign themselves to a lifelong experience of wandering abroad as stateless persons? A small number of Russian *émigrés* ultimately decided to return home after the civil war. A movement known as returnism (*vozvrashchenstvo*) in the 1920s and sponsored by the Soviet government encouraged this, but with little success. The best-known returnees in the 1920s were Maksim Gorky, Boris Pasternak and Aleksei Tolstoi, who were followed home in the 1930s by Sergei Prokofiev (1932), and the writers Aleksandr Kuprin (1937) and Marina Tsvetaeva (1939).

Relatively few *émigrés* returned, however. Most oscillated between their native culture and their new homeland. Some assimilated in Europe, others moved on to the United States. By the 1930s, new generations of exile children were finding their own way, shaped as much by the events of the Great Depression and the rise of fascism as by the inheritance of their parents. The Russian emigration lived on not in its politics, but in its culture.

The Russian emigration was a consequence of the social, political and cultural upheaval that followed World War I and the Russian revolution. Yet it had no clear chronological beginning or end. Exile and emigration were part of the long *durée* of Russian history and the post-1917 emigration ultimately lost its social and geographical identity as individuals assimilated, died, became citizens of other countries or returned home. The 1917–21 period was a violent time of troubles which saw the great exodus of millions of tragic victims of war, revolution and civil war from the territory of the Russian empire. But emigration long pre-dated 1917 and would continue throughout the twentieth century. The 1920s were but one chapter in a long saga.

The Russian emigration was also a major social group created in part by the Russian revolution and located abroad. Most *émigrés* tried to sustain their Russian identity, and remained conscious of their vital role in preserving Russian history, culture and language.

The Russian emigration has remained a difficult subject because of its lack of definition and the passions involved. As a social phenomenon, the emigration is not easily limited chronologically or geographically. Most individual *émigrés* knew only their own small circle and lacked an overview of the emigration as a whole. The quantity of historical source material on the emigration is enormous but scattered around the world. Soviet scholarship was virtually non-existent: the very topic was politically off limits. The *émigrés* themselves tended to focus on topics other than their own situation: Russian history and culture, the political past or current events. Access to the Prague Archive and other materials in Russia may open up new vistas for a history of the Russian emigration that has yet to be written.

Further reading

Hardeman H., *Coming to Terms with the Soviet Regime: The 'Changing Signposts' Movement among Russian Emigrés in the early 1920s* (De Kalb, Illinois, Northern IL, University Press, 1994).

Johnston R. H., *New Mecca, New Babylon: Paris and the Russian Exiles, 1920–1945* (Kingston, Montreal, McGill-Queens University Press, 1988).

Raeff M., *Russia Abroad: A Cultural History of the Russian Emigration, 1919–1939* (Oxford, Oxford University Press, 1990).

Stephan J. J., *The Russian Fascists: Tragedy and Farce in Exile, 1925–1945* (New York, Harper and Row, 1978).

Struve G., *Russkaia literatura v izgnanii*, 2nd edn (Paris, YMCA Press, 1984).

Volkmann H. E., *Die russische Emigration in Deutschland, 1919–1929* (Würzburg, Holzner, 1966).

Williams R. C., *Culture in Exile: Russian Emigrés in Germany, 1881–1941* (Ithaca, Cornell University Press, 1972).

The Intelligentsia

JANE BURBANK

Without the Russian revolution, the category 'intelligentsia' might not have
entered the vocabulary of international social science and politics. The concept was not firmly established in European academic discourse in the nineteenth century, and in Russia the intelligentsia as a coherent group was
threatened with extinction in the years before World War I. The revolution
of 1917, however, gave urgent significance to the idea of a social group
defined by its anti-state, progressive values; in addition, the Bolsheviks'
seizure of the state provided the basis for the reformation of an intelligentsia
around oppositional principles in the Soviet Union. Both these intelli-
gentsias – one associated with the making of the Bolshevik revolution, and
a second identified by its opposition to Soviet power – became familiar concepts in world politics. In Russia, however, the intelligentsia was never a
fixed or homogeneous category. This article focuses on controversies in
Russia around the definition of the intelligentsia, the intelligentsia's complex relationship to the revolution of 1917, and the shifting trajectory of
intelligentsia identity in modern Russian history.

Controversies over definitions

There could be no more vibrant example of the constructed nature of social
identity than the protracted struggles to define the intelligentsia in the two
decades before the revolution in Russia. Writers at this time took certain
features of the intelligentsia for granted. First, the intelligentsia was a collective entity; second, this group existed in Russia; third, the intelligentsia
had a history; and fourth, this history was connected to furthering the cause
of freedom and justice. But how did one define who was in the intelligentsia
group and who was out? How was the role of the intelligentsia to be
assessed? These were critical questions for people who sought to change
Russian history.

The challenge of bourgeois society

Two developments gave inquiries into the nature of the intelligentsia salience in the decade before 1917. The first was the expansion and diversification of 'society'; by the turn of the century it became evident that educated people in the professions, arts and civic life were not united in their ideas about political change, if they cared about it at all. Confronted with the disarray of elite concerns, people who claimed the mantle of intelligentsia tradition strove to set themselves apart from the rest of society.

This exercise in self-definition took shape in histories of the intelligentsia movement, such as P. N. Miliukov's *From the History of the Russian Intelligentsia* (1902), Iu. O. Martov's *Social and Intellectual Currents in Russia from 1870 to 1905* (1910), and R. V. Ivanov-Razumnik's *History of Russian Social Thought* (1906). Each investigation reflected a particular vision of progress, but the common implication of these works was that the intelligentsia had a well-established past and that real *intelligenty* would orient themselves towards this tradition.

Ivanov-Razumnik's study made explicit the threat to the intelligentsia posed by the transformation of society in Russia. A major argument of his *History* was that not every educated person could be considered an *intelligent*. The 'other' against which the intelligentsia could measure itself was *meshchanstvo*, a social group characterized by its absorption in the petty materialism of ordinary life. *Meshchanstvo* was defined by a series of lacks – the 'absence of clear individuality, ... the narrowness and triviality of its world view', the 'absence of creativity, absence of energy'. Ivanov-Razumnik ascribed an absolute divide between intelligentsia and *meshchanstvo*: they were 'two irreconcilably hostile forces'.

This antagonism enhanced the self-depiction of the intelligentsia as admirably spiritual and self-sacrificing. According to Ivanov-Razumnik's requirements, the intelligentsia was an 'ethically anti-*meshchanskii*, sociologically non-estate, non-class historically continuous group, characterized by the creation of new forms and ideals and putting these into practice in a tendency towards physical and mental, social and individual liberation of the personality'. The notion that the history of the intelligentsia was coterminous with the history of Russian social thought followed from this choice of values, not class, as the terrain of differentiation.

Despite efforts to distinguish the intelligentsia from other members of society, early twentieth-century commentators retained organic notions of the Russian polity: the thinking intelligentsia was the 'head' of the Russian social organism. By defining what was progress and how to get there, the intelligentsia claimed to represent the 'whole people'. Lenin offered a Marxist variant of this authority in *What Is To Be Done?* (1902), by declaring that the theory of socialism was developed by intellectuals and had to be imparted to the proletariat.

The intelligentsia's assertion of its moral leadership of the nation was in clear contradiction with another organic ideology – the idea of autocracy, according to which the well-being of the populace was the tsar's responsibility. This challenge to the *raison d'être* of autocracy was exalted by *intelligenty*, but they remained impervious to the arrogance of their own claim to represent all the empire's people. The intelligentsia's unexamined assumption of the mantle of popular sovereignty went largely unremarked in autocratic Russia, although it was to have enormous consequences for Russia's future.

The revolution of 1905 and Vekhi

The questions of who the intelligentsia was and what it was good for became acute in the aftermath of the 1905 revolution. The upheaval both strengthened the association of the intelligentsia with the cause of revolution and called this politics into question. The debate over the intelligentsia exploded in 1909 with the publication of *Vekhi* ('Landmarks'). In this widely read manifesto, N. A. Berdiaev, P. B. Struve, S. N. Bulgakov and four other prominent intellectuals attacked the intelligentsia at its most vulnerable point – its self-image. The *vekhovtsy* (the authors of *Vekhi*) castigated the intelligentsia for ignorance; blind materialism; lack of respect for the state, law, and religion; egoism; and wilful rejection of practical, small-scale reforms. This characteristic 'maximalism' had led to disaster in 1905.

Many left and liberal intellectuals published rebuttals to *Vekhi*. The massive response indicated that the book had hit its target in a sensitive spot, but that the intelligentsia, as a category defined through discourse, would not disappear soon. This was fortunate, for the revolution of 1917 gave the intelligentsia's self-assigned tasks of critical thought and articulation of national goals new vitality in response to Bolshevik power.

The intelligentsia and the revolution of 1917

The Bolsheviks' transformation into leaders of the state opened up a new division within the post-revolutionary intelligentsia – a divide between the rulers and the ruled. Bolshevik intellectuals could assert their version of entitled leadership through control of state institutions and of public discourse. *Intelligenty* who remained outside the state did not hand over their moral mission to the new governors, but instead revived their culture of speaking for the nation.

The rebirth of the intelligentsia was enhanced, unintentionally, by the Bolsheviks' removal of one pre-revolutionary threat to intelligentsia identity. The eradication of the bourgeoisie, bourgeois society, bourgeois press and market economy ensured that the intelligentsia's opposition would be driven into clandestine, but familiar moleways. In the nurturing haven – for

ideas – of persecution and illegality, Russian *intelligenty* formulated a broad
array of perspectives on Bolshevism, the revolution's origins, and its consequences for Russia.

Marxist intelligenty *confront the Bolshevik revolution*

The revolution was a radical shock to most socialists' assumptions about
the trajectory of Russian history. Russian Social Democrats generally did
not imagine that socialism could be achieved before capitalist production
and bourgeois political structures had prepared the way for a society of
equality and well-being. For this reason, many Menshevik intellectuals were
appalled in 1917 by the 'maximalism' of the Bolsheviks' promises of 'immediate socialism'.

MARTOV PROTESTS THE COMMISSAROCRACY

The apparent success of the Bolsheviks' claim to be leading the proletariat
against the bourgeoisie paralysed Menshevik leaders after October 1917.
For Martov, the head of the Menshevik Central Committee, it seemed
impossible to lead his party into active opposition to the Bolshevik government when this would mean aiding the 'counterrevolution'. But neither
could Martov bring himself to join the Bolshevik government, whose violence, inhumanity, dictatorial politics and 'barracks' manners were alien to
his sense of what socialism was supposed to be. Martov retreated into a
position of loyal, but critical opposition in the form of sophisticated, ironic
and increasingly bitter commentaries on the 'commissarocrats' and their
betrayal of socialism.

Martov's writings and those of other Menshevik intellectuals demonstrate that the association of Bolshevism with socialism was contested by
socialists from the moment of the seizure of power. The key element in the
moderate socialists' criticism was dictatorship; from their perspective, the
Bolsheviks' single-party state, directed personally by Lenin and Trotsky,
was a revival of tsarist autocracy and a radical distortion of Marxist theory.
The blame for this treachery and for the long shadow it cast on the
prospects of any future 'real' socialism Martov placed squarely on Lenin's
disregard for historical conditions and his attempt to build socialism
through sheer will and power.

A second focus of Martov's interpretation of the revolution was his analysis of Bolshevik economic policy, and in particular the idea of integrating
the trade unions into the state apparatus. Only a highly industrialized,
highly productive economy based on the labour of a skilled, numerous and
conscious proletariat would create the conditions of plenty under which 'no

one would have to purchase an improvement in his life at the price of another's'. A socialist state in a poor country would end up addressing the deficits of production by turning proletarians into 'cogs' of the new state machine. Martov's articulation of the problematic outcomes of premature socialism defined a dilemma that was to plague Soviet development for years to come.

THE FOUNDERS OF RUSSIAN SOCIAL DEMOCRACY REJECT BOLSHEVISM

The intellectual founders of Russian social democracy – G. V. Plekhanov, A. N. Potresov, V. I. Zasulich, and P. B. Aksel'rod – all took stands harshly critical of Bolshevik-style revolution. In Plekhanov's last published article, from January 1918, he denied that the Bolsheviks' dictatorship had 'anything to do with socialism or Marxism'. Zasulich refused to condone the Bolsheviks' politics and especially their eradication of the democratic political institutions so badly needed by the country. They were a 'new autocracy' that was destroying the industrial base vital to Russia's future and to the proletariat.

Potresov railed against both Bolshevik treachery and peasant anarchy in his underground newspaper *Den'* ('The Day'). Like Martov, he regarded Russia's poverty as fundamental to the outcome of the revolution but, unlike Martov, Potresov took his conclusions to their logical end and called for an alliance between the proletariat and the bourgeoisie to make 'poor, indigent, backward Russia rich'. He joined the liberal Union for the Regeneration of Russia while continuing his work with the St Petersburg 'workers' intelligentsia', actions that were anathema to both Bolsheviks and the post-October Mensheviks.

Aksel'rod devoted the last years of his life to destroying Western illusions about the Russian revolution and to organizing international socialist intervention in Russia. In 1919 he published a major essay on the revolution, entitled *Who Betrayed Socialism? Bolshevism and Social Democracy in Russia*. His answers were Lenin and the primitive traditions of the early Russian revolutionary movement. Bakuninism – the glorification of destruction in the cause of liberation – and the terrorist tactics of the revolutionary intelligentsia had served as models for Lenin, who after 1917 had constructed a 'dictatorship over the proletariat'.

Despite deep differences over how to respond to Bolshevism, these social-democratic *intelligenty* shared certain views of the revolution. First, Russian socialists were acutely aware of the threat to socialism posed by dictatorship. Second, as Marxists they were sensitive to the impossibility of building a just society on an inadequate economic base in a country where the proletariat was a minority. Third, they made strong distinctions between Russia and Europe, and criticized Lenin for rejecting a European path to socialism. Fourth, Marxist intellectuals sensed that the possibility of achieving 'real' socialism had been set back by the Russian revolution, with its basis in conspiracy, terror, dictatorship and poverty.

Communitarian intellectuals in revolutionary Russia

Marxists were not the only socialists in Russia. The most popular party in Russia, according to the elections to the Constituent Assembly, was the Socialist-Revolutionary Party. The Socialist Revolutionaries' concept of the working class included both peasants and industrial workers, and explicitly recognized the intelligentsia's role as 'conscious fighters for peace and justice'.

SOCIALIST REVOLUTIONARIES IN CONFLICT WITH BOLSHEVISM

Despite their victory in the elections to the Constituent Assembly, the Socialist Revolutionaries fared just as badly as the Mensheviks in their efforts to change the course of revolutionary politics. The SRs' policies were ratified by the Constituent Assembly, and then ignored when the Assembly was locked out on 6 January 1918. With the Mensheviks, the SRs were expelled from the soviets on 14 June 1918. Socialist Revolutionaries took part in various actions against Bolshevik power – the July 1918 rebellion in Moscow, *Komuch* (Committee of Members of the Constituent Assembly), underground publishing and agitation. In 1922, the party's leaders in Russia were put on trial for treason and sent to the GULAG.

The Socialist Revolutionaries' inclusive attitudes towards the peasantry meant that they were sensitive to the Bolsheviks' anti-rural policies and condemned Bolshevism as a 'dictatorship of the city over the country'. Bolshevism meant 'new Soviet labour service' (*barshchina*) and 'serfdom' for the country's peasants. Like the Social Democrats, the SRs introduced the theme of Russian backwardness into their analyses of the revolution: Russia did not have the 'material or social-psychological preconditions' for socialism; the country was 'impoverished and uncivilized'. In addition, the SR leader Viktor Chernov condemned the Bolsheviks for substituting 'plebianization for democratization'. The 'monstrous universalized bureaucratization of everything – of the state, the national, and the popular economy' pre-empted real democratization of government.

VISHNIAK ON THE INTELLIGENTSIA AND DEMOCRACY

Another Socialist Revolutionary, Mark Vishniak, responded to the experience of the revolution with an extensive critique of both Bolshevism and the intelligentsia's own traditions. It was clear that Lenin wanted to destroy the Constituent Assembly, but Vishniak felt that the whole intelligentsia was at fault as well. While *intelligenty* had on many occasions been willing to sacrifice themselves *for* the people, they had never concerned themselves with the people's right to determine their own government. The Constituent Assembly had been only an 'idol' for the 'freedom-loving but rootless and doctrinaire Russian intelligentsia'.

In *Le régime soviétiste* (1920), Vishniak set out to analyse the theory and practice of Bolshevik government. He noted that the Bolsheviks' founding declarations constituted a break with European law; the constitution rejected parliamentary government, the separation of powers, and the concept of universal rights and duties. But he rejected Lenin's claim that these principles represented a new and 'higher' democracy. What was new in 'Soviet democracy' in fact was old: Bolshevik principles represented a regression to absolutism, based on distinctions between social estates. In support of this analysis, Vishniak observed that the Soviet constitution prescribed the unequal distribution of privilege on the grounds of class: the working class was granted freedom of conscience, speech, assembly and access to education, while 'exploiters' were assigned only duties. But in reality, some rights were denied everyone – the right to strike for example – and some were highly differentiated. The rationing system allotted bread in four categories according to 'utility to the Soviet government'. One urban worker's vote counted five times as much as a rural vote, and those who did not engage in 'productive and socially useful work' were disenfranchised.

Le régime soviétiste also described the centralized, top-down, rule-breaking behaviour of the Bolshevik leaders: elections were not held as scheduled; parties were excluded from the soviets; the secret ballot was eliminated as a 'bourgeois prejudice'. Despite the abolition of the death penalty, it was used extensively by the Cheka. The 'normal' practices of autocratic rule – secret police, bureaucratization, nepotism, peculation – all these were back in Bolshevik clothing. The real government was the personal dictatorship of Lenin and his companions in the Central Committee of the Bolshevik Party.

Vishniak stands out among Russian *intelligenty* for his defence of formal democracy. To him, democracy had to be constructed by democratic means, and that meant consulting the 'people' through elections about what they wanted. Regularized and observed electoral procedures, and an equal voice for each citizen were the essence of a real break with autocratic government. This concern for the structures of representational government was not shared by most intellectuals who, as Vishniak observed, evaluated state policies according to their consequences, rather than their legitimacy.

KROPOTKIN'S CRITIQUE OF STATE COMMUNISM

The world-famous anarchist P. A. Kropotkin spent his last years in Bolshevik Russia, exiled from the capitals by the Bolsheviks. In his 1917 pamphlet, *Communism and Anarchy*, Kropotkin contrasted 'state' or 'bossist' (*nachal'nicheskii*) communism with anarchist communism. The state with its power to compel deprived the individual of freedom, and without freedom cooperation was impossible. From this perspective, the Bolshevik state was an example of 'how communism cannot be introduced'. The Bolshevik government had increased the 'natural evils of State communism ... tenfold', Kropotkin wrote in 1920. The destruction of the free press and of free elections combined with the enormous bureaucratization of every detail of life destroyed the possibility of constructive work.

Kropotkin condemned the Bolsheviks for returning to the past – for ruling by way of 'old deformities, of unlimited and omnivorous authority' – and he worried that as a result of the revolution, 'the very word "socialism" will become a curse'. He felt that the Russian revolution, unlike the English or the French, lacked a 'lofty, inspiring ideal'. The emancipatory traditions of French communism had been displaced by a revolution based on economic materialism and the 'unleashing of individual desires'. In this judgement, Kropotkin appealed explicitly to the humanistic values that animated, implicitly, other socialists' outrage at the Bolsheviks' betrayal of their goals.

Russian liberals

On the day after the Bolshevik seizure of power, the liberal press was shut down; this was the beginning of a long war between liberal intellectuals who thought they had been empowered by the overthrow of tsarism and the Bolshevik leaders who stepped into their place at the head of state. Liberal *intelligenty* assisted the Volunteer Army, tried to convince European powers to put their might behind the opposition to Bolshevism and, concurrently, produced several significant analyses of the revolution.

MILIUKOV AND STRUVE INTERPRET THE LESSONS OF THE REVOLUTION

Miliukov's 850-page *History of the Second Russian Revolution* (1918) explained the Bolsheviks' success in October as a consequence of the political ineptitude of liberals and socialists in the Provisional Government. Several long-term factors had generated the revolutionary crisis – society's hostility towards the state, the absence of a bourgeoisie, the 'utopianism' of the intelligentsia, the anarchism of the masses, the autocracy's unwillingness to enact a real reform. The major actors in 1917, however, had been the army, the moderate intellectuals and the Bolsheviks. The Bolsheviks had won the army and the masses over to their side through their effective repetition of 'attractive' slogans.

Struve also noted the popularity of the Bolsheviks' slogans and identified long-term causes of the revolutionary crisis. In *The Historical Meaning of the Russian Revolution and National Tasks* (1918), Struve wrote:

the Russian revolution is explained by the coincidence of the distorted ideological education of the Russian intelligentsia . . . with the action of the world war upon the popular masses: the war put the people in conditions that made them especially receptive to the demoralizing propaganda of intelligentsia ideas.

Struve held the intelligentsia responsible for their 'renegade spirit', but it was the autocracy's refusal to include the gentry and the intelligentsia in state politics that had produced this rebellious mentality.

Struve was preoccupied with what he saw as the contradictions of social-ism: it attempted to realize two incompatible principles – egalitarianism and national organization of production. The transfer of property to the state was the legal expression of socialism's egalitarian ideal – the only ideal that appealed to the masses – but the state, once in control of the economic mechanism, found itself unable to produce goods to distribute. Struve asserted: 'The Russian experience has shown with full clarity, at the cost of terrible suffering . . . the living tragedy of socialism.'

INTERNATIONAL CONSEQUENCES AND NATIONAL TASKS

In 1920, Miliukov published in London an early work of anti-Bolshevik propaganda: *Bolshevism: An International Danger*. Designed to influence the European powers, the book described Bolshevism as a pragmatic, revolutionary ideology that had dispensed with socialist theory. Miliukov complained that European socialists were being outflanked by the Bolsheviks' revolutionary mystique. Within European socialism, Miliukov warned, 'the Bolsheviks were winning not so much by their own strength as by the weakness and inconsistency of their antagonists'. He warned that the Bolsheviks' goal was now world revolution, and that they would pursue their ends by any means – negotiation, using any allies, organizing revolu-tion in the East where conditions were less hostile to communist success.

Struve's observation that the revolution served as the 'experimental refutation of socialism' did not leave him confident that the lesson would be learned. The experience of the revolution was proof for him of the fallacies of positivism – of seeing progress as inevitable in world history. He hoped that the Russian emigration could play a role in a revitalization of Russian patriotism. The 'significance' of the emigration, he wrote in 1922, was 'almost exclusively spiritual and as such it will count in Russia in the future'.

The nation redefined

In 1918, several idealist intellectuals joined Struve in the publication of a symposium on the revolution. *From the Depths* contained articles by *vekhovtsy* and others who shared Struve's view of the revolution as a national and spiritual tragedy. Of the contributors, Berdiaev offered the most provocative psychological interpretation of the revolution.

BERDIAEV'S THEORIES OF MORAL ILLNESS

Bolshevism, in Berdiaev's perspective, was only a symptom of the general crisis in the Russian national character. The ugly anarchy released in 1917 expressed the 'moral illnesses' of Russia. Culture, Christianity and individual freedom meant nothing to the Russian people. Berdiaev buttressed this harsh indictment with evidence from Gogol, Dostoevsky and Tolstoy. Gogol, with his 'exceptional ... sense for evil', had captured the normal vices of Russian people – greed, pomposity, deceit, malice, despotism – in petty, not tragic forms. *The Inspector General* displayed Russians' deep fear of getting caught in their own lies by a higher, but not necessarily better, authority, and foretold the dread of counterrevolution. Dostoevsky, in Berdiaev's account, was the expert on the Russian intelligentsia. If Russian people had a low opinion of themselves and others, the intelligentsia was all too ready to believe in human perfectibility. The revolution had only brought to life Gogol's people and Dostoevsky's 'boys' – the Russian intelligentsia. As for Tolstoy, Berdiaev thought that the writer most admired by the intelligentsia had himself fallen prey to the diseases of the 'Russian moral consciousness' with its 'denial of personal moral responsibility and personal moral discipline'. Tolstoy's theory of art and his denial of the value of institutions – Church, state, and nation – expressed a Russian hostility to cultural achievement.

In his *Philosophy of Inequality* (1918), Berdiaev found the Russians' 'Eastern' frame of mind, as well as a 'false relationship between the male and female principles' in their psyche, at fault for their losses in the war and revolution. Berdiaev's Nietzschean values meant that a nation had to be led by a worthy elite. He objected to the 'compulsory brotherhood' of socialist theory, because Christian love had to be given in freedom. Later, in European exile, Berdiaev linked his interpretation of the revolution to the pessimism of O. Spengler's *Decline of the West*. He came to see the revolution as the culmination of European modernity, which had destroyed the creative, Christian spirit of the Renaissance. Berdiaev's revised version of the revolution assigned Russian intellectuals a creative role; they were to mediate between East and West, and to bring spiritual culture to the world.

EURASIANISM

The role of the 'East' in Russian culture was central to Eurasianism – a social philosophy produced by Russian *émigrés* in the early 1920s. The linguist N. S. Trubetskoi placed the revolution in a relativist frame in his provocative book, *Europe and Humanity* (1920), written from his refuge in Sofia.

Europe and Humanity amounted to a full-scale attack on European 'civilization'. Trubetskoi denounced the pretentious universalism of the 'Romano-Germans'. The imposition of values peculiar to Europe had been harmful for 'humanity' – i.e., the non-Europeans. Borrowing from Europe led to the decline of patriotism, to national fragmentation, to impossible attempts to overcome 'backwardness'. Trubetskoi suggested that the real humanity – Slavs, Chinese, Indians, Arabs, Negroes, and all others subjected to the yoke of European exploitation – had a common enemy. His book ended with a call for intellectuals to liberate their consciousness from European domination.

Trubetskoi's cause was joined by other *intelligenty* in the first manifesto of the Eurasian movement, *Exodus to the East*, published in 1921. Trubetskoi's contribution represented ancient Slavs as cultural intermediaries between Indo-Europeans and Proto-Iranians, a legacy betrayed by the Russian elite when it adopted a Western orientation in the time of Peter the Great. In the second Eurasian collection, *On Our Way* (1922), Trubetskoi predicted that the destruction of Russia's economy in the revolution would result in new exploitation by Europeans, but that sooner or later Russia would become the 'leader of the liberation of the colonial world from the Romano-Germanic yoke'. Bolshevism would be welcomed in the colonies as the expression of the 'idea of national liberation'.

Trubetskoi at some times stressed Russia's Orthodox piety, at others its Asian essence, or its daring rebelliousness, or its mediation between East and West. What was consistent – and anathema to the left and liberal intelligentsia – was the attack on European culture. Universalism, progress, reason – these were all dismissed as Eurocentric egoism. After the revolution, the Eurasians brought back the old question of Russia's relationship to Europe; this time, the prize for breaking with the Romano-Germans was leadership of the anti-colonial nations.

USTRIALOV AND THE 'CHANGE OF LANDMARKS' MOVEMENT

The *smenovekhovtsy*, adherents of the 'Change of Landmarks' movement, celebrated the potential of the revolution to remake Russia as a great power. The outstanding intellectual of *smenovekhovstvo* was N. V. Ustrialov, a Kadet Party member at the time of the revolution and later a director of the Russian Press Bureau for Kolchak's Siberian army. After the defeat of Kolchak's forces, Ustrialov switched sides. The 'will of history' had expressed itself in the Bolsheviks' victories, he felt, and *intelligenty* should support the Bolsheviks in the interests of the 'unification and resurrection of our homeland, her power in the international arena'.

Empire and world power were the goals that Ustrialov set for Russia. He delighted in the Bolsheviks' ability to frighten European leaders with their threats of class warfare, and he was confident that the Soviet government would quickly bring the 'pygmy states' on Russia's borders back into the fold. Size was the most essential component of state power; a great national culture could only be built on a physically large scale. While Ustrialov rejected socialism as an economic system, he supported the Bolshevik leadership for its willingess to use tough measures to rebuild the state.

In 1921, Ustrialov and his circle of like-thinkers published their manifesto, *Smena vekh* ('Change of Landmarks'), in Prague. The title was a deliberate affront to the contributors to *Vekhi*. The *smenovekhovtsy* attacked the *émigré* intelligentsia for lack of patriotism: the intelligentsia should join the Bolsheviks in rebuilding the state. Ustrialov incorporated the revolution into a narrative of Russian national expression: the revolution had begun with anarchic violence typical of the Russian masses; it had been inspired by 'revolutionary romanticism' typical of the Russian intelligentsia; and it would be controlled by the Bolsheviks who understood the people's yearning for strong authority (*nachal'stvo*). The revolution had thus 'brought Russia to the fore of the world stage', and its ultimate result would be a new 'cultural-state type'.

Continuities and discontinuities in the intelligentsia tradition

From Ustrialov's perspective, the revolution had put an end to the old opposition to the state upon which the intelligentsia had built its identity. In the interests of Russian power, the intellectuals should renounce their hostility to Bolshevism and rejoin the nation. Their function should be service – practical endeavours, not critical thought. Some *smenovekhovtsy* tried to take this course, but for most leaders of the intelligentsia joining the post-revolutionary state was both reprehensible and impossible. As the civil war came to a close, harsh repression was the Bolsheviks' response to their former rivals.

Smena vekh did mark a shifting of boundaries in the history of the Russian intelligentsia, however. The Soviet state attempted to redefine the intelligentsia according to function: *intelligenty* were the mental workers of the new society. Most educated people who remained in Russia after the civil war performed this role; they became teachers, administrators, engineers, scientists, artists – the professionals of Soviet development. They thus realized one aspiration of the pre-revolutionary *intelligenty*: collectively, they achieved a position of tutelage over the nation.

Intellectuals in the emigration preserved their commitment to the intelligentsia's traditional function of critical thought and, over time, a moral opposition grew within the Soviet Union. These new oppositional *intelligenty* also displayed strong continuities with their predecessors in the revolutionary period and before. First, they regarded themselves as bearers of a historical tradition, and thus fortified *preemstvennost'* (historical succession) as a criterion of intelligentsia self-consciousness. Second, they shared with the 'insider' managers of the new state the culture of guardianship and representation of the nation. Third, this autocratic mentality continued to nurture strongly individualized creativity and to inhibit political formations based on compromise and unity.

In one fundamental respect, the intelligentsia in Soviet times gradually shifted its vision of Russian society. Most leaders of the pre-revolutionary intelligentsia remained convinced through all their trials of the virtues of the Russian masses (even Berdiaev slowly moved towards this view); the people were assumed to be supportive of each intellectual's ideas. With time, this populist trust eroded. The Soviet intelligentsia's loss of confidence in the people constitutes a major break with the democratic illusions of the past.

The intelligentsia has been both praised and blamed for giving birth to a new form of state in Russia after 1917. Many intellectuals at the time of the revolution argued that intelligentsia habits – a deep hostility to state power, a willingness to tolerate and even encourage destructive violence, a disregard for democracy, narrow-minded dogmatism, utopianism and impracticality – were responsible, at least in part, for the catastrophic consequences of the old regime's collapse and for the values that informed the new dictatorship. But as the *Vekhi* debate illustrated, it was possible to belong to the intelligentsia and still criticize it. The great achievement of Russian *intelligenty* during the revolution was to carry on the mission of independent thought. This courageous activism allowed the intelligentsia to survive the revolution, not intact, but as a site of critical reasoning and aspiration.

Further reading

Aksel'rod P. B., *Kto izmenil sotsializmu? Bol'shevizm i sotsial'naia demokratiia v Rossii* (New York, Narodopravstvo, 1919).

Berdiaev N. A., *Filosofiia neravenstva: Pis'ma k nedrugam po sotsial'noi filosofii*, 2nd edn (Paris, YMCA Press, 1970).

Burbank J., *Intelligentsia and Revolution: Russian Views of Bolshevism, 1917–1921* (Oxford, Oxford University Press, 1986).

Iskhod k vostoku: Predchuvstviia i sverzheniia: Utverzhdenie evraziitsev (Sofia, n.p., 1921).

Ivanov-Razumnik R. V., *Istoriia russkoi obshchestvennoi mysli*, 2 vols., 3rd edn (St Petersburg, Tipografiia M. M. Stasiulevicha, 1911).

Iz glubiny: Sbornik statei o russkoi revoliutsii, 2nd edn (Paris, YMCA Press, 1967).

Konrad G. and Szelenyi I., *The Intellectuals on the Road to Class Power: A Sociological Study of the Role of the Intelligentsia in Socialism* (Brighton, Harvester Press, 1979).

Kropotkin P. A., *Etika* (Petersburg and Moscow, Golos truda, 1922).

Miliukov P. N., *Bolshevism: An International Danger* (London, George Allen and Unwin, 1920).

Miliukov P. N., *Istoriia vtoroi russkoi revoliutsii*, 3 vols. (Sofia, Rossiisko-bolgarskoe knigoizdatel'stvo, 1921–4).

Na putiakh: Utverzhdenie evrasiitsev, book 2 (Moscow-Berlin, Gelikon, 1922).

Pipes R., ed., *The Russian Intelligentsia* (New York, Columbia University Press, 1969).

Plekhanov G. V., *God na rodine* (Paris, J. Povolozky, 1921).

Potresov A. N., *Posmertnyi sbornik proizvedenii* (Paris, n.p., 1937).

Read C., *Religion, Revolution, and the Russian Intelligentsia: The 'Vekhi' Debate and its Intellectual Background, 1900–1912* (London, Macmillan, 1979).

Smena vekh: Sbornik statei (Prague, n.p., 1921).

Struve P. B., *Collected Works*, ed. R. Pipes, 15 vols. (Ann Arbor, University Microfilms, 1970).

Trubetskoi N. S., *Evropa i chelovechestvo* (Sofia, Rossiisko-bolgarskoe izdatel'stvo, 1920).

Ustrialov N. V., *V bor'be za Rossiiu* (Harbin, Okno, 1920).

Ustrialov N. V., *Pod znakom revoliutsii (Sbornik statei)* (Harbin, Izdatel'stvo 'Russkaia zhizn'', 1925).

Vekhi – Intelligentsiia v Rossii – Sbornik statei 1909–1910 (Moscow, Molodaia gvardiia, 1991).

Vishniak M. V., *Le régime soviétiste* (Paris, Union, 1920).

The Lower Middle Strata in 1917

DANIEL ORLOVSKY

The revolutions of 1917 and indeed the early years of Soviet power were marked by powerful social movements that shaped politics even as the policies of successive governments shaped them. Neither the histories nor the contemporary discourse of 1917 excludes such categories as workers, peasants, the bourgeoisie, soldiers, sailors and now the nationalities. The master narratives of 1917 have exclusively been written about them and in their terms. Yet in the years leading up to 1917 and during the revolution itself there existed also a powerful movement of white-collar employees (*sluzhashchie*), technical, managerial and professional personnel, largely hidden from view by the accepted narratives and discourses. These groups were the dynamic product of late imperial Russian economic and social development and formed part of what might be termed a layered society organized along occupational and professional lines. Anywhere one cared to look across the 1917 landscape, it was these groups with their professional associations and congresses that provided the infrastructure of so-called public and state institutions alike – zemstvos and urban dumas, committees of public organizations, the cooperatives, the War Industries Committees, all manner of land and food supply and volost committees in the countryside, the organized movements for national, ethnic, religious or regional autonomy and even the soviets themselves. All had significant white-collar or lower middle strata membership and, taken together, all had a profound impact on the course of revolutionary state-building in 1917 and under the Soviet regime.

On the eve of World War I, the layering of society in the Russian empire and masking of occupations behind official *soslovie* categories was already far advanced. Census data from St Petersburg and Moscow in 1910 and 1912 respectively reveal growing numbers of white-collar employees, 'proto-professionals', clerks and service personnel of all sorts. In St Petersburg, for example, there were over 100,000 white-collar employees, not counting those gratuitously included within the category of 'worker', or various other categories of state, low-level professional and other service personnel. Moscow could boast of at least 200,000 employees, a figure that easily equalled, and probably exceeded, the number of true blue-collar factory workers. In the provinces could be found the growing army of 'third element' zemstvo and urban duma employees and growing numbers of such professionals as teachers, agronomists, statisticians, doctors and feldshers, judicial administrators and various technicians.

Many of these so-called professions were themselves stratified, with the higher ranking occupations, such as doctors, holding sway and status over their lower ranked and less privileged types, in this case the feldshers. In general lower wages, often frozen by the war and combined with galloping inflation and cost of living increases, plus the search for new status both within and outside the occupations/professions, and ideological commitments to the state-building project, motivated the lower middle strata to organize and press before, but especially during, 1917 for 'democratization'. Most often, especially for all layers below the lofty status heights of, say, the attorneys and professors, this meant radical forms of democratization rather than the more legalistic, 'civil society' and rule-of-law-oriented version of democracy sponsored by the Kadets and other liberals. It sometimes meant full active participation in the politics of the left and alignments with or membership within the Socialist-Revolutionary, Menshevik and even Bolshevik parties.

The lower middle strata were also very well ensconced in the interstitial parties of the left – for example the Labour Group (Trudoviks) and the Popular Socialists (NSs)– as well as in right and centre factions of the parties mentioned above. Their primary power base, however, remained linked to their occupations and professions, and this lent a strange and perhaps unexpected cast to the fledgling Russian democracy of 1917. For the lower middle strata were more often than not pursuing their aims and throwing about their considerable weight, which derived from sheer size and knowledge and control of the empire's considerable infrastructure, through professional congresses and organizations, unions, cooperatives, and state-sanctioned public committees that often pressed the primacy of their interests over those of parties or even the projected and much mythologized Constituent Assembly. The cooperative employees, for example, consistently maintained an anti-party line at their congresses and attempted to the bitter end to elect their own representatives to the Democratic Conference in September and later to the Constituent Assembly. Similarly, lower middle strata *intelligenty* created a Soviet of the Labouring Intelligentsia in Moscow which attempted to provide for that group what the soviets of workers' and soldiers' deputies had given to their constituents: namely, forceful and prominent defence of their interests and strong political clout.

What the role of the lower middle strata in 1917 does reveal with great clarity is the deep alienation of many of these groups from both the 'bourgeoisie' and its parties and, as 1917 wore on, from the Provisional

Government itself. Unions and professional organizations and the above-named soviets all began to see the Provisional Government, which through its policies and a wide range of decrees had in fact thrown its weight behind the movement of the lower middle strata, as increasingly bureaucratic and unresponsive to their needs and interests. Such was the case with the very powerful All-Russian Union of Railway Workers and Employees and the Union of Post and Telegraph Employees. Initial state-sponsored democratization driven by the aspirations of the rank-and-file employees soon deteriorated in the face of a variety of bureaucratic roadblocks and the state's failure to deliver promised wage increases and radical reorganization of workplace authority.

Several examples here will suffice. The Provisional Government on 25 March declared a food monopoly with fixed prices on grain. At the same time it created a Main Food Committee with subordinate committees at the provincial, district and volost levels. This entire apparatus was staffed by lower middle strata experts and political activists. But even more important was the government's declared intention to cut the commercial classes out of the grain trade (as wholesalers, suppliers, etc.) and substitute for them the cooperatives. The situation made nobody happy as the government failed to give consistent directives to its new apparatus (the same was true in the area of land relations with the advent of the land committees) and the lower level organs began to take matters into their own hands with their own brand of revolutionary legality.

Commercial and industrial employees were also quick to organize into unions. In July these unions held an all-Russian congress. Congress resolutions expressed much solidarity with the proletariat (indeed, they defined themselves as part of the proletariat) and with the soviets of workers' and soldiers' deputies. Union goals were to improve the economic and legal status of employees as well as to 'give full attention to the spread of socialist ideas among their members'. This was especially important given that 'the specific milieu of commercial and industrial employees makes them more receptive to bourgeois [more accurately lower middle-class – *meshchanskaia*] ideology'. The congress also called for government intervention in the economy and obligatory syndication of the distribution of manufactured goods. These attitudes resulted in a growing number of strikes and unresolved labour disputes. It was clear that the Provisional Government could not count on the support of the organized employees. Other occupational groups associated with banking, industry and other capitalist enterprises also organized and very often saw the revolution as a means to establish their own claims as state-builders and makers of a 'new order'.

The Provisional Government and the lower middle strata lost their respective chances to join forces and take power as a 'unified socialist government' (*odnorodnoe sotsialisticheskoe pravitel'stvo*) at the Democratic Conference in September, 1917. The Menshevik-Internationalist Iu. O. Martov was on record in August claiming that it was crucial for the left to wean the 'petty bourgeoisie' (by which he meant the many occupations discussed here) away from the Bolsheviks and that they were obviously a crucial part of the democracy's social base. Similarly, Lenin saw the value of employee radicalism for his own cause. Despite great hostility from the Bolshevik and SR left that was growing in strength in the wake of the Kornilov affair and the deepening economic, social and political crisis, the organized lower middle strata might have carried the day and pressured Kerensky into forming a new government without representatives of the 'propertied classes'. But the thinking and the subsequent vote were muddled, with delegates voting at first for coalition, but without the Kadets (the only possible coalition partner), and then later for yet another coalition that only served to dissipate their political influence. Kerensky took the conference mandate to form his last fatally flawed coalition government propped up by the weak Council of the Republic or Preparliament.

The irony is that the lower middle strata far outlived the Kerensky government. The advent of Soviet power after October brought new challenges and new opportunities to these occupational groups. Lenin supported the use of 'bourgeois specialists', meaning professionals and experts with higher education. For many in these professions and proto-professions, Soviet state-building and indeed much of the Soviet project with its utopianism and excessive rationalism provided an arena and state support for the realization of their own professional agendas. This was certainly true in areas such as engineering, public health and medicine, academic life, economics, management and the like. But the lower strata of employees and technically trained personnel also found a home in the new Soviet state and society. They formed what I term a 'hidden' class – white-collar workers and others who were instrumental in using their knowledge of the existing infrastructure to help create the apparatuses and vast bureaucracies of the new socialist state. They were hidden in the sense that they were mediators who could not be called workers or peasants in the world's first official workers' and peasants' state and society. They could not fit easily into the official discourse or mythologies of the new order and yet they were indispensable to its daily life and to the realization of its project, and, as the 1920s drew on, they were everywhere and in ever greater numbers.

The party expended considerable energy attempting to halt their growth, to proletarianize the apparatus, to restore and maintain class purity. But the party's actions were futile. If we ask how the new Soviet regime managed to maintain and build its authority during the tumultuous civil-war years (1917–21), one of the answers has to be the presence and active participation of the lower middle strata. Their dynamism, skills and adaptability deeply influenced the events and processes of 1917 and then went on to shape the Soviet state and indeed Soviet society far beyond the accepted temporal borders of the revolution. It is a legacy that remained embedded in the Soviet system to its very end.

Further reading

Cherniaev V. Iu., ed., *Anatomiia revoliutsii: 1917 god v Rossii: massy, partii, vlast'* (St Petersburg, Glagol, 1994).

Izmeneniia sotsial'noi struktury Sovetskogo obshchestva oktiabr' 1917–1920 (Moscow, Mysl', 1976).

Koenker D. P., Rosenberg W. G. and Suny R. G., eds., *Party, State, and Society in the Russian Civil War: Explorations in Social History* (Bloomington, Indiana University Press, 1989).

Remington T. F., *Building Socialism in Bolshevik Russia* (Pittsburgh, University of Pittsburgh Press, 1984).

Officers

PETER KENEZ

The history of the revolution is best understood as a crisis in authority. By October 1917 it became clear that the liberals and moderate socialists, like the tsarist regime before them, had failed to provide the country with a functioning government. The democrats may have had electoral support, but they were incapable of turning that support into a military force and an administration. The alternatives open to the peoples of the Russian empire were Bolshevism and military counterrevolution.

The officers were virtually predestined to lead that counterrevolution. They knew how to organize armies and fight battles; their military careers had taught them the importance of organization; their *esprit de corps* and common experience gave them the mutual trust necessary for this dangerous venture. Without knowing who these officers were and how they saw their task it is impossible to understand the nature of the revolution and civil war. Unfortunately, historians have elucidated the thoughts and motivations of the officers far less well than the mentality of the Bolsheviks. The reasons are easy to understand. The generals were not intellectuals and they did not systematically summarize their goals and beliefs.

The social background of the tsarist officer corps was heterogeneous. While during the second half of the nineteenth century many non-nobles received commissions in, for example, the German and French armies, this same process of increasing social heterogeneity went even further in Russia. By the time of World War I approximately half of the officers came from non-noble families. This great influx changed the character of the officer corps. While in Germany and France the newcomers were quickly absorbed and middle-class young men were assimilated into military society by their aristocratic colleagues, the Russian corps became fragmented. The scions of ancient noble families served in Guards regiments, where they enjoyed many privileges: they advanced quickly through the ranks and participated in the pleasures of the social life of the capital. By contrast, the average non-noble officer was likely to serve in the infantry stationed in an outlying district, and to receive such a meagre salary that he could hardly support his wife and children. As nineteenth-century Russian literature amply illustrates, such a man enjoyed little social prestige. Yet, for many ambitious young men of peasant families who could not afford an education, the military school was an avenue of social mobility. While the great majority of these men never rose very high in the military hierarchy, there was room for the talented and ambitious.

Those who survived the competitive examinations for admission to the Academy of the General Staff and then did well there could reach the highest command posts in the army. During World War I sons and grandsons of serfs often commanded armies. Later some of these generals came to play major roles in the White movement. The fathers of Generals M. V. Alekseev and A. I. Denikin were born serfs and the father of General L. G. Kornilov was a poor Cossack. The social background of the leaders of the White movement could have had political significance if the leaders had chosen to emphasize it. By pointing to their own background they could have defended themselves against the charge that their movement was merely fighting for class interests. The Whites, however, lacked the necessary political acumen. In any case, it is clear that the vulgar Marxist notion, according to which the political views of the White generals can be explained by reference to narrow self-interest, can be dismissed out of hand.

Although in social background, career pattern and lifestyle there was an enormous variety within the pre-revolutionary officer corps, there were also unifying ideas and political views. Like their continental colleagues, the Russian officers were conservative and anti-intellectual, distrusted technology and placed their faith in *élan* as a key to victory. For example D. N. Garlinskii, a military journalist writing in 1911, trying to evaluate the causes of defeat in the war with Japan, blamed the intelligentsia, serf liberation and the spread of education. In his view, education had undermined the national will. He recommended increased censorship to counter the ideas of equality and social justice which had fatally weakened the army. In Russian military circles, as elsewhere in Europe, a vulgarized form of Nietzscheanism was widespread. Articles in military journals extolled the ennobling aspects of war, deplored the 'peaceful character of the Russian people', and asserted that everything valuable, such as statecraft, technology and even art was born of war. The same writers warned of the dangers of eternal peace, which would ultimately destroy the 'spiritual side' of man. They contrasted 'decadent peoples, who wanted to avoid fighting and collect money' with the virile young nations to whom the future belonged.

The Russian political, social and intellectual environment, of course, deeply influenced the thinking of the officers. First of all, the educational system in general, and military education in particular, was backward. In their schools the officer cadets did not acquire a love of learning. As a consequence, later in life the officers read very few books and had almost no intellectual interests. Anti-intellectualism is often associated with conservatism and indeed the officers were profoundly conservative. This was largely the result of self-selection: those young men who chose a military career chose to fight for the Russian state as it was constituted. The officers' conservatism was instinctive and unreasoning. In military schools the students received no lessons in contemporary government, and indoctrination hardly went further than a ritual repetition of the formula: 'For Faith, Tsar and Fatherland'. Those who taught the future officers limited themselves to prophylactic measures and were content to keep the young away from subversive influences. As a result, rather significantly, military schools did not teach modern Russian literature because only pre-nineteenth-century works could be considered completely safe. Although the officers accepted the political and social *status quo* without question, they did not regard themselves as conservatives. They repeated *ad nauseam* the doctrine according to which the army stood above politics. This was an article of faith. The officers without hesitation carried out orders to suppress revolutionaries, rebellious peasants and striking workers, but to protect the tsar from his internal enemies did not seem to them a political act. In the Russian political environment conservatism meant the acceptance of autocracy and a rejection of 'politics'. The officers had a narrow definition of politics. They imagined it to be nothing more than participating in party activities, elections and giving speeches in the Duma. They saw those who chose a political career as troublemakers and enemies of the tsar.

The intelligentsia had little interest in military values. Unlike their European colleagues, who at this time were deeply permeated with nationalist passions, the majority of Russian thinkers were interested either in the problems of their own society or in the salvation of their souls. Under the circumstances it is understandable that the officers who in contemporary literature saw only caricatures of themselves, and in the writings of leading intellectuals found only attacks on values in which they deeply believed, felt misunderstood and responded with a bitter hostility.

Anti-semitism was widespread in all segments of Russian society and the officer corps was far from immune. Nevertheless, at the turn of the century it was still possible for a Jew, once converted, to become an officer. By the time of World War I, however, anti-semitism had taken a more modern form, becoming racial instead of religious. In officer cadet schools during the war, students were occasionally asked to prove that they had no Jewish ancestors. Although Jews could not become officers, they were, of course, called up. Officers rarely interfered to stop mistreatment of Jewish soldiers, for they assumed Jews to be guilty. The officers saw Jews as people who could never become good soldiers and who were congenital troublemakers, responsible for the spread of various subversive ideologies.

Although the fundamentals of the Whites' world view were formed in the late nineteenth-century Imperial Army, the experiences of the officers during the traumatic years from 1904 to 1917 obviously greatly influenced their perceptions. In this period the officers suffered one humiliation after another. During the unsuccessful war against Japan, for the first time they encountered a powerful revolutionary wave. They had to explain to themselves not only the causes of the defeat by a foreign enemy, but also the intense dissatisfaction of their fellow Russians. The military men learned something from the defeat, and after the war some necessary reforms were introduced into the army, though these reforms were not nearly far-reaching enough. However, the political lessons to be drawn from the revolution were much more ambiguous. In one respect there was a volte-face on the part of the tsarist regime: while in the past the government had been satisfied with keeping the officers out of politics, during the 1905 revolution the War Ministry ordered them to explain to their soldiers both 'the errors in the demands of the extremists' and the October Manifesto. Since there was nothing in their past which would have prepared them for this task, the officers either ignored the order, or carried it out so poorly that they gained few converts for the government. However, the 1905 revolution was defeated and the tsarist regime succeeded in consolidating itself. This meant that the officers did not have to take an independent political position, but once again could rally round the autocracy. Next time they would not be so fortunate.

The military men were not warmongers: they did not desire a war against Germany in 1914 any more than other Russians did. In fact, the leading generals, conscious of the weakness of the country, warned the government of the consequences. However, once the war began, the officers did not merely share in the general, though short-lived, patriotic enthusiasm, but were carried away by it. Soon the workers and peasants lost interest in the outcome of the war, but the officers, on the contrary, came to believe in the decisive importance of the great struggle for the future of the nation. Many, General Denikin for example, conceived a hatred for Germans which they never lost. It is easy to understand that the war seemed very important to them: they had had to convince themselves that this was so in order to sacrifice themselves and millions of their countrymen with such desperate abandon. But they could not help realizing that the Russian people did not share their notion of patriotism. The consequences of this realization for the future were far-reaching. The officers' distrust of the common people further increased.

In 1914 and 1915 the officer corps suffered drastic losses. At the outbreak of the war the War Ministry had mobilized reserve officers, but there were not nearly enough of them. Under the circumstances the army was forced to train officers in an intensive course for 4–8 months. These men, mostly ex-non-commissioned officers from peasant families, and the reserve officers, largely from the intelligentsia, differed greatly in outlook from the professional officers. The officer corps, which had already become socially heterogeneous, now lost its political unity. It became even more unlikely that during the revolutionary year of 1917 the officer corps could take a united and successful stance. Few of the reserve officers joined the anti-Bolshevik armies and none of them received important command posts. Understandably, during the war the high command was entirely in the hands of professional officers, and the same men set the tone and defined the ideological position of the counterrevolutionary armies.

From the point of view of the officers, the February revolution was a more important turning point than the Bolshevik takeover. The great majority watched events with dismay. They had sworn allegiance to the tsar and had absolutely no desire for a change in the form of government. They expected little from the liberal leaders of the Provisional Government and even less from the socialists in the soviets. However, they did nothing. They saw that resisting the revolution would have undermined the country's ability to fight a foreign foe and consequently accepted the sacrifice of the tsar as a necessary price to pay for the successful continuation of the war. Their conscience was greatly eased by the abdication manifesto of the tsar, in which the deposed ruler instructed his followers to carry out the orders of the new government.

They were further discouraged from acting in February 1917 because taking part in politics, as opposed to simply carrying out orders, was against their training and deepest beliefs. They did not know how to assert their influence effectively. It soon became clear that the overthrow of the tsarist regime had not only failed to improve Russia's chances of victory, as some optimistic politicians had hoped on the basis of mistaken analogies with the French revolution, but had actually created disorganization and a disastrous collapse of all authority. Nobody could prevent the soldiers from disobeying and defecting.

The officers once again felt cheated and betrayed. It is not surprising that they blamed the politicians, who did not seem to know how to use their newly acquired powers. This condemnation deepened into hatred which soon completely clouded the officers' judgement. They could no longer see how much they had in common with the liberal politicians. Like the officers, the members of the Provisional Government had no desire for social revolution and were anxious to continue the war. Kerensky, the new Prime Minister, chose a young general, L. G. Kornilov, as his commander in chief, precisely because Kornilov proposed to use draconian methods to reimpose discipline in the army. But Kornilov and like-minded generals responded by organizing a mutiny, ostensibly against the soviets, but in fact also against the Provisional Government. This irresponsible act contributed to the spread of anarchy and to the Bolshevik seizure of power.

The immediate consequence of the officers' unreasoning antipathy towards liberals and socialists was that it immobilized them at the time of the Bolshevik takeover. This was certainly one of the missed opportunities. When one considers the courage and determination with which many officers fought the Bolshevik enemy during a long and bloody civil war, it is amazing that the very same officers had done nothing in October 1917. There were many reasons for this seeming paradox. Those who commanded the soldiers must have realized that not many of them would have carried out orders; the officers had no reason to know who the Bolsheviks were and what kind of regime they would establish; they could hope that a regime founded on outlandish doctrines would soon collapse on its own; and they were loath to abandon the front against the Germans. These important 'reasons', however, in most cases boiled down to the more fundamental fact that the majority of officers simply could not bring themselves to fight for Kerensky.

Another consequence of the officers' bitterness against politicians became evident during the civil war: the White armies never learned to use the services of civilians. When the most important task was to establish a functioning administration, the generals turned to discredited bureaucrats of the tsarist regime or, worse still, employed brutally tactless officers to administer villages, towns and provinces. The Whites' failure to extend their rule over the conquered population and to build a competent administrative machinery was the most important reason for their ultimate defeat.

Following their victory, the rule of the Bolsheviks remained so insecure that their enemies, however weak, could organize almost with impunity. Socialist and non-socialist politicians put together a number of abortive schemes. In the long run, among the many domestic enemies of the Bolsheviks only the ex-officers of the Imperial Army proved to be dangerous. The first, the best organized and longest lasting of these armies, the so-called Volunteer Army, began in the south on Cossack territories. Generals Alekseev and Kornilov, who in 1918 were among the best-known figures of the defunct Imperial Army, initiated the organization. After Kornilov's death in April 1918 General Denikin took charge, and he led the army in the decisive campaigns of 1918 and 1919. The last leader of the Whites was General Wrangel, who struggled against insurmountable odds in 1920.

In the east, moderate socialists and liberals organized a rickety anti-Bolshevik government, which did not last long. In November 1918 rightists organized a coup and military men, under the leadership of Admiral Kolchak, took charge. The Siberian counterrevolution at first achieved impressive victories, but then the White armies fell back and the movement disintegrated.

Those who fought in the White armies did not represent a cross-section of the old officer corps. Those who did not succumb to the attraction of the line of least resistance and decided to fight the new regime at a time when the struggle did not seem very promising were an unrepresentative minority. They were usually young, many of them still students in military schools, and they were the most conservative. By and large these were men who had been most embittered by the sufferings imposed on them by the revolution. Moderates and fathers of families as a general rule preferred to stay at home. Most ex-officers wanted to stay out of the fighting, to the disgust of the anti-Bolshevik leaders.

A remarkable number ended up by serving in the newly created Red Army. Historians have attempted various explanations for this curious phenomenon. Some have argued that it was the officers' patriotism which drove them into the arms of the Bolsheviks. Lenin, after all, headed the *de facto* government of the country, when, in spite of his efforts, the war still continued. Others have stressed the officers' professionalism in explaining their behaviour. They understood that the new leaders, whatever their political and social philosophy, were determined men who would not vacillate the way the Provisional Government had done, and consequently would have a better appreciation of the needs of the military. However, it is most likely that the great majority of the officers accepted service because they feared the consequences of their refusal for themselves and their families. Some of these defected at crucial moments, inflicting great harm on the Bolshevik cause which they served unwillingly. Nevertheless, however imperfectly, it was the White movement which represented the mentality and interests of the old Russian officer corps.

One way to establish the political profile of the officer corps is by looking at the manifestos issued by the White armies. One is struck not by the political views expressed in the public statements of the generals, but by their obvious political ineptitude. Instead of developing an attractive political and social programme, the generals agonized over the twin issues of legitimacy and popular sovereignty. As far as legitimacy was concerned, the source of the problem for the Whites was that it was not clear when legal continuity had ended. Obviously, the Bolsheviks were usurpers, but the White movement split on the question of whether the legislation of the Provisional Government should be recognized. The rightists, such as Hetman Skoropadskii, the German puppet ruler of the Ukraine, and Ataman Krasnov of the Don Cossacks, insisted that the legal continuity of the Russian state ended in February 1917. The Volunteer Army, on the contrary, in its constitution of October 1918, recognized the laws passed by the Provisional Government with some specified exceptions. This paragraph of the constitution shows more explicitly than any other proclamation of the Volunteer Army that it cannot be said to have advocated a simple return to the past.

Undoubtedly, the vast majority of the officer corps would have liked to bring back the Romanov monarchy. The leaders of the movement, Denikin, Wrangel and Kolchak, however, resisted monarchist pressure because they understood that an open espousal of the Romanov cause would be political suicide. The leaders vacillated on the issue of how to decide what form the state should take in the future, and what 'popular sovereignty' meant. At times when the Whites were doing well on the battlefield their pronouncements sounded less democratic than on occasions when the cause seemed in danger.

In fact, the Russian people formed its image of the army not so much on the basis of manifestos as on the basis of the kind of people the Whites attracted to their service. The Headquarters remained faithful to the dogma that the army stood above politics. What this meant in the context of the civil war was that Denikin did not include among his advisers, on the one hand, any socialists and, on the other, those who had been compromised either by having too conspicuous a position in the imperial regime or by past cooperation with the Germans. Denikin was and remained suspicious of all politicians, political parties and party platforms, and repeatedly dissociated his movement from any political group.

Denikin's closest civilian advisers were largely from the liberal Constitutional Democratic (Kadet) Party. Many of these, such as K. N. Sokolov and V. A. Stepanov, lost all trace of their former liberalism as a result of their experience in the revolution. The situation was far worse in the provinces, where reactionary officers chose to install their own men. The army badly needed administrators and the military men were obviously ineffectual in these unaccustomed roles. As a general rule the Whites turned to tsarist functionaries for help. Under the circumstances the peasants were not convinced by Denikin's conciliatory proclamations. What they saw was that the same men who had been chased out by the revolutionaries returned to their posts with the aid of the Volunteer Army and continued to act in the same spirit as before the abdication of the tsar.

Just as the leaders of the movement asserted dogmatically and with great frequency that the army stood above politics, they also proclaimed that the army stood above classes and that it was not fighting for narrow class interests. As the first principle was absurd, for participation in a civil war is an eminently political act, so was the second. The army's touted neutrality was biased in favour of the rich and powerful, even if some leaders, such as General Denikin, did not realize this. The issue which concerned the peasants most was, of course, land reform. It did not require great political insight to understand that peasant attitudes in the civil conflict would be determined to a large extent on the resolution of this issue. The Whites, expecting the early demise of the Bolshevik government, hoped that they could simply wait and avoid controversy. As the struggle continued, Denikin understood that his movement had to take a stand. The handling of this question more than any other showed the political ineptitude of the generals. Months were spent on fruitless committee meetings. Not until the summer of 1920 was the first, and extremely conservative, land reform law introduced by General Wrangel, and by then it was much too late.

The workers received even less than the peasants from the Whites. The Volunteer Army repressed autonomous workers' organizations and pursued an economic policy which caused great hardship for the urban poor. A commission working on labour legislation drew up a draft, but it was unacceptable to the representatives of the workers and it made little difference to the life of the factories.

When the White leaders were pressed as to why they were fighting, they invariably answered 'for Russia'. An inflated sense of patriotism and nationalism filled all the public statements of the White leaders. That nationalism became the cornerstone of the White programme should not be surprising. The military men had always prided themselves on their patriotism and the years of fighting a dangerous foreign enemy further heightened this emotion. But, perhaps more importantly, they fastened instinctively onto nationalism because they lacked any other rallying point. Logically speaking, it made little sense to say that they were fighting for 'Russia' because, obviously, so were the Bolsheviks. What the Whites had in mind was that Russia could exist only on the basis of certain social and political principles, congruent with its history. Consequently those who wanted to change the social and political order in a fundamental way were against Russia. Thus nationalism and conservatism reinforced one another. The fact that the Bolsheviks proudly advertised themselves as internationalists made it easier for the Whites to present themselves as the only true nationalists.

However, nationalism turned out to be an inadequate ideology for winning the civil war. The peasants proved impervious to patriotic appeals. The generals saw with disgust that the majority of the people cared more about tangible gains, such as land, than about the future boundaries of the country. Nor were many interested in the question of whether the formerly subjugated peoples of the empire would remain under Russian rule. Only those who had been partisans of the White cause were moved by nationalist slogans; otherwise the proclamations fell on deaf ears.

Further reading

Jones D. R., 'The Officers and the October Revolution', *Soviet Studies* 28, 2 (1976), pp. 207–23.

Kenez P., *Civil War in South Russia, 1918: The First Year of the Volunteer Army* (Berkeley, University of California Press, 1971).

Kenez P., *Civil War in South Russia, 1919–1920: The Defeat of the Whites* (Berkeley, University of California Press, 1977).

Mawdsley E., *The Russian Civil War* (Boston, Allen and Unwin, 1987).

Mayzel M., *Generals and Revolutionaries: The Russian General Staff During the Revolution* (Osnabruck, Biblio-Verlag, 1979).

Wildman A., *The End of the Russian Imperial Army: The Old Army and the Soldiers' Revolt (March–April 1917)* (Princeton, Princeton University Press, 1980).

[This article is based on research that was first published in *Soviet Studies* 32, 1 (1980). Copyright 1980, University of Glasgow Press. All rights reserved.]

The Peasantry

ORLANDO FIGES

Introduction

Russia was still a peasant country at the turn of the twentieth century: 80 per cent of the population were classified as belonging to the peasantry; and most of the rest traced their roots back to it. Russia's towns and cities all remained essentially 'peasant' in their social composition and character. Most of the workers were either immigrants from the countryside, or the children of such immigrants; and many still returned to their farms for harvest or sent money back to their villages. Only a few miles from any city centre it was already the remote countryside.

When the nineteenth-century Russian revolutionaries talked about 'the people' (*narod*) what they really meant was the peasantry. As an intellectual tradition, the social revolution was about the liberation of the peasants. The 'peasant question' – how to overcome the poverty and ignorance in which most of the rural population lived – was the starting point of all the major theories of the social revolution.

All the more surprising, then, that the peasantry has been so little studied and so poorly understood by historians of the revolution. Compared to the workers, the study of the peasantry is still in its infancy. The old Soviet historiography was flawed by its rigid Leninist dogma and, in particular, by its misguided attempt to divide the peasants into two hostile classes – the rural proletariat and bourgeoisie (the 'kulaks') – which hardly existed in reality. From the 1930s, when the murderous collectivization of peasant agriculture was carried out, it was also marked by a deep animosity towards the old peasant way of life, which was always portrayed as 'dark' and anti-socialist. Western historians, meanwhile, were also often guilty of creating peasant stereotypes. They claimed that 'the peasants' wanted this or that, as if 140 million people living in three-quarters of a million settlements scattered across one-sixth of the surface of the globe could be treated as a homogeneous group.

It was only from the 1960s that a more sophisticated approach to the peasantry began to appear in the historical literature. In the Soviet Union this was first apparent in the works of historians such as V. P. Danilov and A. M. Anfimov, who, in so far as the establishment would let them, approached the peasant household and society in terms of their own internal organization rather than in the class terms defined by Marx and Lenin. Meanwhile, in the West it was as a result of three related trends – the rise of social history, the growing influence of social anthropology, and the rediscovery of A. V. Chaianov and his theory of the peasant economy – that Russian peasant studies became more refined. Historians began to stress the influence of regional, ethnic, demographic and cultural factors, in addition to economic ones, on the identity of the peasantry.

With the opening up of the Soviet archives, we can look forward to detailed local studies of the revolution in the countryside. The first appeared in 1989. It is only when we know the regions separately that we can reach any meaningful conclusions about the peasantry as a whole. We also need to study particular sub-groups – the peasant elders and village youth, soldiers and their wives, craftsmen, traders, landless labourers and part-time officials – within the village community. For while all these were 'peasants', not all of them identified themselves as such; and the rural revolution was defined as much by the striving of certain types to break with the old life of the peasantry as it was by the efforts of others to defend it.

The peasantry on the eve of the revolution

Social and cultural developments

Diverse social trends were apparent in the countryside at the turn of the twentieth century. Many of these could be termed as the side-effects of 'modernization'. The revolution among the peasantry was in part a result of these trends and in part a reaction against them.

In the central agricultural regions of Russia, much of the Ukraine and Siberia, the village still retained many of the features of what anthropologists would call a 'traditional society'. It was largely an oral culture, in which the customs of the past served as a model for the collective actions and mores of the village, and in which the elders, as the guardians of these traditions, were the most important people. This was by and large a conservative culture. There was an inbred mistrust of any ideas from the world outside the peasants' own experience, a strict conformity in the housing, the furniture, the clothing, the personal habits and the morality of the villagers, and a built-in bias towards the past. The 'old way of life' was naturally deemed better than the new.

And yet at the same time there were broader forces leading to the decline of this patriarchal world. The money economy was slowly penetrating into rural areas and drawing peasant sons into seasonal wage labour, giving them a greater sense of individual worth. Fed up with the tyranny of their household elder, many broke away from the old extended family to set up new farms of their own. This constant sub-division of the peasant households, although detrimental economically, shifted power from the older to the younger peasants at the communal assembly of household heads. So too did the spread of rural literacy. The young and literate peasant was much better equipped than his father to deal with the new agricultural technologies; with the accounting methods of the money system; with written contracts, land deeds and loan agreements; and with the whole new world of administration – from the simple recording of clock-time and dates, to the reading of official documents and the formulation of village resolutions and petitions to the higher authorities – into which they entered after the Emancipation of 1861. The status of the young and literate peasant rose as the market and bureaucracy filtered down to the village and the peasant community relied more upon leaders with the skills demanded by this new society. Not surprisingly, the leaders of the village during 1917 were drawn mainly from the young and literate.

The peasant economy

The economic position of the peasantry before 1917 has long been a subject of intense debate. Some historians paint a picture of impoverishment as a result of overpopulation, soil exhaustion and increasing taxation by the state. But others point to improving harvest yields and increased peasant spending on consumer goods. The situation was in fact quite complex, with marked differences in the living standards not just of the major regions but of neighbouring villages and even households.

The highest living standards were to be found in a circular band of regions around the periphery of central Russia where commercial farming had taken root in the nineteenth century (parts of the Baltic, the western Ukraine, the fertile regions of south Russia, the Kuban and western Siberia). There was little land shortage in these regions, largely because the land was intensively farmed and not subject to communal repartition. In central Russia, by contrast, the backward farming methods of the communal peasants and the domination of the landed gentry made it very hard for many peasant households to support themselves from, on average, a seven-acre plot; and not surprisingly it was here that the war against the manors was concentrated in 1905–07 and 1917–18. Many peasants responded by falling into debt, or by sending sons and daughters to work in the towns. Others tried to bring more land under the plough, either by renting it at more and more expensive rates from the landowners, or by reducing their fallow acreage, the result of which was that livestock herds declined and, without manure, the soil became exhausted. In this situation the slightest misfortune, such as a fire or the sudden death of an adult worker, could make all the difference between the survival and the collapse of a peasant household. And yet even here there were enterprising peasants, who by dint of hard work and sobriety, or by some handicraft or farming innovation, managed to achieve a basic comfort for themselves: they had huts with wooden floors instead of mud, two cows in the courtyard instead of one, and shoes for their sons to go to school.

The peasants' revolutionary ideology

It is mistaken to suppose that the Russian peasantry had no moral order or ideology to substitute for the tsarist state. Many historians portray the peasantry as primitive and ignorant people who could only play a destructive role in the revolution and who were thus ripe for manipulation by the Bolsheviks. Yet during 1917–18 the peasants quickly restructured the whole of rural society, from the system of land relations and local trade to education, justice and social welfare, and in so doing they often revealed a remarkable political sophistication, which did not come from a moral vacuum. The ideals of the peasant revolution had their roots in a long tradition of peasant dreaming and utopian philosophy. Through peasant proverbs, myths, tales, songs and customary law, a distinctive ideology emerges which expressed itself in the peasants' actions throughout the revolutionary years.

Two ideas were central to the peasant revolution: land and liberty. Everywhere in Russia rights of land use were defined by the labour principle. The peasants often said that the land belonged to God but that every family had a right to support itself from it through its own labour. This was the basic principle of the peasant land commune, which in most regions redistributed the land between the households in accordance with the number of 'eaters' in each, and which carried out the revolution on the land. The peasants believed with a religious fervour that since the land should belong to those who tilled it, the squires did not own it rightfully and the hungry peasants had a moral right to take it from them. Peasants who had enclosed communal plots of land and had turned them into private property under the Stolypin land reforms (1906–11) also had them taken from them by the communes in 1917.

The peasants' concept of liberty (*volia*) meant the freedom of the village from all external powers – the tsarist state, the gentry and the Church – and the peasants' right to rule themselves according to their own moral norms. This in effect is what the peasants gained when the state collapsed in 1905 and even more so in 1917. The peasant communities were extremely quick to fill the vacuum with their own institutions – a fact which illustrates the extent to which the commune had always been an unofficial government in waiting as well as the extent to which the peasant organizations of 1905, the peasant unions and cooperatives, as well as the primary Socialist-Revolutionary (SR) organizations, had taken root in the countryside.

The peasant revolution, 1917–18

The revolution on the land

The peasant 'war against the manors' picked up momentum during the course of 1917. The main forms of struggle during the spring stopped short of the confiscation of the gentry's land. The peasants demanded lower land rents; enforced sales of grain, tools and livestock to the communes at prices deemed 'fair' by the peasantry; and took away the prisoners of war employed by the gentry on their estates. It was only later, from the start of the summer agricultural season, that the peasants began to confiscate the land, starting with the meadows at the time of mowing (May) and ending with the ploughed fields from the harvest time (September–October).

This early caution may be explained by the fact that the peasants were afraid to attack the gentry's estates before it was clear that the old regime would not be restored, as it had been after 1905, with the mass repressions of the peasants which had followed. During March and April there were still many remnants of the old regime in the countryside (land captains, priests and police constables) who found their way into the newly elected volost committees. The Provisional. Government, moreover, had forbidden any change in property relations; and for the moment the peasants waited patiently for a new land law, just as they had waited for a Golden Manifesto from the tsar transferring all privately owned land to the peasantry.

During May, however, three things happened to change the situation. First, the SR Viktor Chernov was appointed Minister for Agriculture in the First Coalition Government. The peasants took this as a green light for their own confiscations of the gentry's land – especially after Chernov's appearance at the First All-Russian Peasant Congress, where he conspicuously failed to warn the local peasant land committees not to take the law into their own hands. Second, the revolution on the land received a pseudo-legal endorsement from a series of provincial peasant congresses where the appeals of the SR party activists for patience were drowned by the angry voices of the delegates. The resolutions passed by these assemblies in favour of the confiscation of the land were understood as 'laws' by the local peasantry. Finally, from Easter huge numbers of peasant-soldiers returned from the army, either on leave or as deserters, and this had much to do with the increase of peasant militancy. The peasant-soldiers often took the lead in the march on the manors. With their guns and their military know-how, they were the natural leaders of the village armies that were formed to seize the gentry's land and property, and to defend them against other villages. They also tended to encourage acts of violence and vandalism against the landowners and their estates; and such acts increased as time went on. The peasants burned the manors to drive the squires out; smashed agricultural machinery (which in recent years had removed much of the need for hired peasant labour); carried away the contents of the barns on their carts; and destroyed anything, like paintings, books or sculptures, that smacked of excessive wealth.

There was a marked regional variation in the level of peasant violence. Most of the destruction of the gentry's property was confined (as it was in 1905–06) to a circular band of provinces around the southern edge of the central agricultural zone (from Samara and Saratov in the south-east, through Tambov, Voronezh, Kursk, Kharkov, Chernigov, Ekaterinoslav, Kherson and Poltava, as far as Kiev and Podolia in the south-west). These were regions of overpopulation and large-scale land ownership by the gentry: land rents were high and wages low. They were also regions where the fertile soil and the long growing season had encouraged the gentry to farm commercially, cultivating land they had once leased to the peasants, who depended on this land to feed their families, or renting it to them under increasingly exploitative conditions. Here the peasant revolution was a life-or-death struggle for the land.

Peasant politics

The Provisional Government was a government of persuasion: it lacked the will, let alone the power, to enforce its policies by coercion. Its main response to the national crisis it inherited was to call on the people to fulfil their patriotic duty as free citizens. And its first call was on the peasantry, upon whom it relied for soldiers and foodstuffs. But here was the rub: for its call on the peasants fell on deaf ears.

Everything was working against the government. For one thing, the urban political language it employed was largely alien to the peasants: words such as 'democracy', 'state', and 'republic' were misunderstood and mispronounced by them. Peasant delegates at provincial assemblies frequently complained that they could not understand what their party leaders were talking about. The most pressing problem for the government was how to couch the concept of the state. In the minds of many peasants the term *gosudarstvo* (state) was inextricably linked to the term *gosudar'* (tsar) – so the problem was to forge a sense of civic obligation without reinforcing the old monarchical psychology, the fear and reverence of personal authority which remained so strong among the peasantry. The fate of the democracy depended on this mission. For although the tsar himself was politically dead for the vast majority, there were many confused peasants who spoke, for example, of the need for 'a new elected tsar at the head of the republic', or even for a 'democratic autocracy', meaning a strong man to take control. The urban propagandists went about their task by talking of the state in terms familiar to the peasants (e.g. as a household or a family). Yet, as far as one can tell from preliminary study, they failed to get across their message to the peasants, who were unconvinced they had an obligation to the people beyond their own community.

Politically, the peasant revolution was expressed as a war against the towns. In the Ukraine, the Baltic lands and the Caucasus, where the native peasantry was ruled or dominated by a foreign elite in the capital, this was also a war of national liberation. Centuries of tsarism had bred in the peasants a fundamental mistrust of all state authority, expressed in their desire for *volia*. There was a general breakdown of central power in the provinces during 1917. Peasant assemblies passed their own revolutionary 'laws' in defiance of the Provisional Government and its provincial commissars. Villages and volosts declared themselves 'autonomous republics' – zones free from the higher authorities. And in just about every village the government's decrees were used by the peasants for cigarette paper. Lenin had the foresight to order his officials to despatch the October Decree on Land with old calendars in the hope that these would go up in smoke first!

From the viewpoint of the government's survival, the most damaging aspect of this peasant 'localism' was the refusal to supply food to the towns. The growing shortage of consumer goods – and their inflated prices – gave the peasants no incentive to sell their grain at the low prices fixed by the Provisional Government in March. The peasants withdrew from the market, preferring to store their grain or turn it into vodka, or else sold their foodstuffs to black-marketeers. In the towns, where this contributed to the chronic breakdown of supplies, the peasant action was called a 'grain strike', and among the poorest workers, in particular, it reinforced an old mistrust and hatred of the peasants which the Bolsheviks exploited. And yet as the peasants themselves saw it, they were fighting a just war against the towns, which for years had been a source of economic exploitation and oppression.

The first six months of Soviet rule were the climax of this peasant revolt against the influence of the central state. The first peasant soviets were, for the most part, democratic organs elected directly by the village communes and implementing their own local revolutions in accordance with the peasants' own notions of social justice. They set up their own organs of self-government, organized militias, elected judges, regulated local trade, and with the endorsement of the Decree on Land redivided the land confiscated from the squires and the peasant landowners created by Stolypin between the households in the commune. The land redivisions were mostly carried out on the old labour principle of the peasantry: every household, including the squire in his manor, was allotted land so long as it was willing – and considered able by the rest of the peasants – to farm it. The amount of land which each household got was usually dependent on how many mouths (or 'eaters') it had to feed, although the poorest peasants and those getting land for the first time were often forced to make do with a share of the estate's land furthest from the village and the most vulnerable to re-confiscation in the event of a counterrevolution.

With the completion of this local revolution, the peasants had very little need for the democratic institutions of a central state. True, the peasants turned out in very large numbers to vote – mainly for the SRs – in the elections to the Constituent Assembly. But it would be mistaken to conclude from this that the peasants shared that party's veneration for the assembly. Most of the villagers had cast their votes as a single bloc, either on the instructions of their elders (who often had close links with the SR apparatus) or else on the basis of a village resolution to vote for one party and maintain unity. For most of the peasants – and even more so for the peasant women voting for the first time in a national election – this was largely a symbolic act. Very few were prepared to fight the SRs' battle for the restoration of the assembly after it was closed down by the Bolsheviks, as the dismal failure of the *Komuch* proved. To the vast mass of the peasants, whose political outlook was confined to their own village and its fields, the assembly was a remote parliament dominated by the 'chiefs' of the urban parties. They associated it with the State Duma and felt no need of its sanction for their revolution on the land.

The peasantry in the civil war

The war against the village

Few people expected the Bolsheviks to last when they first took power. The industrial cities and the northern armed forces, where the Bolsheviks had their main bases of support, were all starved of food; and without supporters in the countryside, there seemed very little that the Bolsheviks could do to prevent hunger from turning into disaffection and opposition. During their first six months in power the Bolsheviks were forced by their own impotence to leave the countryside well alone, allowing the peasants to organize their own free trade with the towns and cities. But by the spring they found that this was causing chaos as thousands of workers left their factories every day to barter with the peasants, bringing industry to a virtual halt and creating huge problems for the railways. If they were to cope with the military crisis caused by the revolt of the Czech Legion, and in their minds perhaps more importantly, if they were to save their tiny island-bases in the cities from being drowned in the sea of petty peasant capitalism, they would have to seize control of the food supply.

In May Lenin launched a 'battle for grain', sending armed detachments of workers to the villages to buy up at fixed prices or seize by force the surplus grain which he claimed the 'kulaks' had been hoarding to speculate on the hunger of the towns. In a series of extraordinarily violent speeches and articles during the summer he called on the workers to kill all the 'kulaks', whom he accused of conspiring with the SRs and all the other 'petty-bourgeois parties' to starve the Soviet regime out of existence. The armed brigades were to be assisted by Committees of the Poor (*kombedy*), whose task was to point out the 'kulaks' in the village. But these proved extremely ineffective and the armed brigades, without village accounts of the harvest surpluses, usually assumed that any empty barn, even if it belonged to a starving peasant, was a sure sign that its owner was a 'kulak grain hoarder'. The campaign thus broke down into violent and indiscriminate requisitioning of the peasants' property – a civil war against the village that grew ever fiercer in the two succeeding years.

After a series of peasant uprisings – condemned as 'kulak revolts' in the press but privately acknowledged by the Bolshevik leaders to be a protest by the peasants as a whole – the Soviet government abolished the *kombedy* in November 1918. Lenin announced a new accord with the middle peasants, the overwhelming majority of the rural population, whom his regime needed to man the Red Army against the Whites. But there was no let up in the 'battle for grain'. From January 1919, under the *prodrazverstka* or food quota system, the brigades were instructed to requisition set amounts of foodstuffs from the villages, regardless of whether or not these foodstuffs were surplus to the peasants' basic needs. The brigades and commissars went about their business with a violent ruthlessness – often copying the worst torture methods of the tsarist regime and then inventing some – that can only lead one to conclude that many of the Bolshevik rank-and-file, especially those who came from poor peasant backgrounds, were driven by a hatred of the peasantry.

Meanwhile, the peasants responded to this onslaught with the traditional 'weapons of the weak': they hid their foodstuffs underground or sold them to the 'bagmen' who, despite the bans on passenger transport, still came from the towns to buy up stocks of food; they reduced their production to subsistence levels or switched it towards the needs of rural industry (e.g. by growing hemp or oil-producing seeds); and while stopping short of a full-scale peasant war, they frequently attacked the Soviet supply apparatus in village-based revolts. It was only later, in 1920, when the Whites had been defeated in the civil war and in many regions the Bolsheviks were taking the last vital stocks of seed, that the peasants rose up in a nationwide revolt. But it came too late: the 1920 campaigns of requisitioning left the peasants too weak to survive the harvest failure of 1921, which ended in a famine crisis throughout the south-east; and it left them too weak to resist the Bolsheviks.

The war against the Whites

However much the peasants disliked the Bolsheviks with their bossy commissars and their violent requisitions, they feared the White armies even more. A White victory would reverse the peasant revolution on the land.

Indeed, that was the main aim of the White officers, most of whom were the gentry's sons fighting to regain their lost inheritance. The White leaders did their best to appear democratic but their hands were tied on the land question. The most Denikin could offer to the peasants was a vague promise that at some time in the future they would be allowed to buy some of the gentry's land (at prices set by gentry-dominated committees); but in the meantime they would have to return the land they had seized in 1917. It was not until 1920, when the Whites were on the verge of total defeat, that Wrangel passed a land law that was remotely acceptable to the mass of the peasants. By his own admission the law was meant only for propaganda.

As long as the Soviet regime stood between the Whites and their own revolution on the land, the peasants would rally to its defence whenever the Whites threatened to break through. This is suggested by the fact that in October 1919, when Denikin's forces had advanced as far as Orel, less than 200 miles from Moscow, a quarter of a million peasant deserters returned voluntarily to the Red Army from the two military districts of Moscow and Orel. These were regions where the peasantry had made substantial land gains in the revolution. But even where the peasants had not gained any land, such as in gentry-free Siberia, the tsarist-like behaviour of Kolchak's officials, who requisitioned food and soldiers with even more violence than the Bolsheviks, was enough to turn vast tracts of the countryside into hotbeds of resistance against the Whites.

The peasant Brest-Litovsk

By March 1921, with the countryside engulfed in peasant wars and a famine crisis looming large, Lenin finally gave in to the arguments for a tax in kind to replace the food requisitionings. As he told the Tenth Party Congress, the dictatorship of the proletariat needed to stabilize its relations with the peasantry if it was to survive, and this temporary concession to the peasants, allowing them to sell their surplus food on the free market, was the price it had to pay. It was a peasant Brest-Litovsk.

Lenin and his closest followers came to believe that the New Economic Policy was not just a retreat but the only way forward to socialism in a peasant society such as Russia without the support of the advanced industrial economies. The experience of war communism had proved that it was impossible to stamp out the market; yet as long as the state controlled the 'commanding heights' of the economy, it could effect the transition to socialism by taxing and socializing the peasant sector.

This was a hard lesson for the Bolshevik rank-and-file to learn, however, and throughout the short existence of NEP there was a deep hostility towards it within the Soviet apparatus. Many of the party's rank-and-file were the sons of peasants who had had to leave the village for the towns, or who had rejected the old village way of life, despising it as 'dark' and 'backward', often after their horizons had been broadened by military service. They had identified with the Bolsheviks as a party of the *workers* promising to sweep away the old peasant Russia. Yet during the 1920s they had to stand by and watch as the peasants flourished. Food shops in the towns were filled with supplies; but their prices were too high for the mass of workers and the growing numbers of the unemployed. The NEP, in short, appeared to these comrades as a betrayal of the revolution's egalitarian principles – its promise to destroy the rotten capitalist world – and in Stalin's renewed war against the peasantry they saw a new way forward.

Further reading

Danilov V. P., *Rural Russia Under the New Regime*, trans. with an introduction by O. Figes (London, Hutchinson, 1988).

Figes O., *Peasant Russia, Civil War: The Volga Countryside in Revolution (1917–1921)* (Oxford, Clarendon Press, 1989).

Figes O., 'The Red Army and Mass Mobilization during the Russian Civil War', *Past and Present* 129 (1990), pp. 168–211.

Figes O., 'The Russian Revolution of 1917 and its Language in the Village', *Russian Review* 56 (1997).

Gill G. J., *Peasants and Government in the Russian Revolution* (New York, Barnes and Noble, 1979).

Kabanov V. V., *Krest'ianskoe khoziaistvo v usloviiakh 'voennogo kommunizma'* (Moscow, Nauka, 1988).

Kingston-Mann E. and Mixter T., eds., *Peasant Economy, Culture, and Politics of European Russia, 1800–1921* (Princeton, Princeton University Press, 1991).

Lewin M., *Russian Peasants and Soviet Power: A Study of Collectivization* (London, Allen and Unwin, 1968).

Shanin T., *The Awkward Class: Political Sociology of Peasantry in a Developing Society, Russia, 1910–1925* (Oxford, Clarendon Press, 1972).

Refugees in the Russian Empire, 1914–1917

Population Displacement and Social Identity

PETER GATRELL

The social history of the Russian revolution has concentrated upon organized social forces, whose leaders left behind compelling accounts of political struggle and whose actions impinged directly on the existing forms of state power. Dominant historical narratives have found little room for social groups or actions that cannot readily be accommodated within the framework of conventional political organization. The neglect of social groups that are not easily subsumed within the customary categories of historical inquiry is nowhere more apparent than in respect of refugees in the war-torn Russian empire. The refugee population reached 2.6 million by the end of 1915, and continued to rise thereafter, to a recorded total of 4.9 million in January 1917 (around twice as many Soviet citizens were displaced following the German invasion of 1941). In all likelihood, these figures should be inflated by at least 10 per cent to take account of unregistered refugees. The consequences of population displacement on this scale were profound, and not just because the large refugee population made nonsense of official attempts to maintain the fiction of social cohesion in wartime. In the first instance, it created a social category that breached the conventional typologies of social stratification in tsarist Russia. The established framework of social description was subverted and redefined. This process formed part of broader political struggles in the final years of the old regime. The constitution of what may be termed 'refugeedom' helped not only to undermine established notions of social status and control, but also to give fresh meaning to the civic impulses that had begun to emerge before 1914 and that crystallized in wartime around the new 'public organizations' (obshchestvennye organizatsii).

The implications of population displacement in wartime extend beyond issues of classification, political representation and statistics. They include refugees' sense of self. Did they regard themselves as marginal, as victims of war, as suspended subjects waiting to be restored to their pre-war condition? My argument is that refugees not only became aware of their predicament, and of the humanitarian impulses that turned them into objects of pity and charitable relief, but also that they began to become conscious of their rights. We ought, therefore, to go beyond an analysis of the process of displacement and resettlement, to uncover the causes of attempts by refugees to escape from the categories imposed on them – to understand, in other words, how refugees sought to realign themselves, to break free of the designations they were allotted, and to transcend refugeedom.

In wartime Russia, refugees were and remained subjects of the tsar. They did not cross an internationally recognized border, but there was no doubting their status. Refugees had been forced to leave their homes by the threat of violence. In official parlance, 'refugees [*bezhentsy*] are those persons who have abandoned localities threatened or already occupied by the enemy, or who have been evacuated by order of the military or civil authority from the zone of military operations; also natives of states hostile to Russia'. The official definition allowed for the inclusion of Poles, Jews, Latvians, Lithuanians and Russians, all of whom fled from the zone of military action; it included refugees who were subjects of other rulers, notably Ruthenians from Austrian-ruled Galicia, and the relatively small number of Armenians who escaped Ottoman genocide in 1915. Officials thus granted the existence of a new category of subjects, but in extending the tsarist lexicon they had yet to come to terms with the attendant conceptual and administrative difficulties.

Imperial Russia had a long tradition of administrative intervention in population movement, including the forced relocation of entire categories of people to distant parts of the empire. The state also asserted its right of administrative surveillance, and of ascription of the tsar's subjects to specific estates (*sosloviia*). Even after the 1905 revolution, many administrative powers over population settlement remained intact. Special regulations applied to huge swathes of the empire. 'Foreigners' (*inorodtsy*), a category that included all Jews, along with the indigenous population of Siberia, Central Asia and the Caucasus, were not entitled to an internal passport. Without this document, even short-distance journeys were extremely difficult. Prior to 1906, the land commune monitored peasant movement, lest individual peasants shirk responsibility to pay their share of the combined tax levy by moving out of the village for good. None of these regulations prevented migration, but they reminded the population that spatial movement was a privilege rather than a right. The most striking administrative attempt to specify residential requirements affected the Jewish population of the Russian empire. The Fundamental Laws of 1906 conceded the principle that the tsar's subjects could live where they pleased, but simultaneously declared that such rights were limited by special laws. The Pale of Settlement survived unscathed, and was justified on the grounds that Jews, if allowed to settle freely in the empire, would 'expropriate' Russian peasants and undermine public order. This approach distinguished government policies towards the Jews from those it pursued towards other minorities.

Not for nothing did Aleksandr Kerensky speak of the Pale of Settlement as 'the geographical expression of another boundary line, a circle of moral untouchability' that surrounded each Jew in the Russian empire.

War and population displacement

World War I unleashed new kinds of movement, new forms of public action and new fears about the consequences of the loss of control over population settlement. During the initial phase of the war, between August and December 1914, the German army pushed back the invading armies in east Prussia and prepared to advance on Warsaw. When the Russian army invaded Galicia, tens of thousands of Jews, Russians, Poles, Latvians, Ukrainians and others were forced, either by the advancing German army or by the actions of the tsarist general staff, to leave their homes. Worse was to come in the spring and summer of 1915, as the German army moved north-east to occupy all of Poland, Lithuania and part of Belorussia. The Austrian army reconquered Galicia and joined up with the Germans in Russia's south-west. Many of the Ruthenian peasants under Austrian rule followed in the wake of the retreating Russian troops. By the end of 1915 around 400,000 refugees had passed through the border province of Volynia alone. Many of the decisions to uproot entire villages were taken not by the settlers themselves but by the Russian army. The negative association between Jews and frontier security was deeply ingrained in military consciousness ever since Nicholas I had decreed that they could not live within 50 km of the western frontier. Local army commanders accused Jews of spying for the enemy: even well-meaning outside observers betrayed a deep-seated prejudice, suggesting that Jews were so poor that they would stop at nothing, even treachery, in order to obtain additional cash. Such perceptions underpinned widespread attacks on Jewish persons and property, encouraging what the Minister of the Interior described as 'a pogrom mood' in the army. Not all refugees were dispersed without protest. The governor of Volynia reported that many refugees were 'angry and indignant at having been forced to move. They panicked during the retreat from Galicia, attacking and destroying property, and inflicting many losses on the local population.' Local police and village authorities were powerless to prevent refugees from roaming the countryside and, apparently, looting at will.

The crude and desperate measures employed by the Russian army were not confined to the Jewish and Polish population of the Russian empire. Ordinary German farmers in Russia's south-western provinces were forced to leave their holdings. General Ianushkevich, chief of staff, regarded the expropriation of the property of German settlers as a golden opportunity to reward Russian soldiers who had distinguished themselves in battle, and to provide an incentive for those who might be tempted to surrender. The Caucasian front presented an equally disturbed picture. Refugees of

Armenian origin scrambled across the battle zone, seeking to escape the outrages inflicted by Ottoman military and government officials. By the end of 1916 there were at least 300,000 ex-Ottoman Armenian refugees in Erevan alone.

Much of what has been said so far tends to underline the haste with which established communities were wrenched apart, dispersed and – in Turkish-ruled Armenia – decimated. Government ministers privately denounced the crude and arbitrary displacement of civilians, and bemoaned the political consequences. A. V. Krivoshein, Minister of Agriculture, told his colleagues that 'it is doubtful that refugees feel goodwill towards an authority that permits actions which are incomprehensible, and not just to simple people'. In more apocalyptic vein, he argued that 'curses, sickness, misery, and poverty are spreading all over Russia'. This rhetoric was commonplace. But, beyond Armenia at least, further reflection prompts us to modify the catastrophist version of events. First, although the physical and psychological condition of many refugees left much to be desired, one should not ignore the degree to which moments of upheaval generated measures of self-help that counteracted the natural tendency to despair. Some refugees were devastated by the experience of enforced departure; for others the war was an opportunity to reconstitute communities in new locations. The second qualification to the 'victimological' perspective is that abrupt physical displacement had an uneven impact. In a crucial sense the war liberated Russian Jewry by forcing the tsarist government to recognize that it could no longer continue to sustain the Pale of Settlement. Third, the war created an opportunity for critics of the old regime to exploit population displacement in order to forge a powerful weapon in their struggle against tsarist autocracy. In particular, the representatives of 'educated society' were able to manufacture a 'refugee problem' in order to condemn the central government and the army leadership for their incompetence, cruelty and lack of foresight. The contacts that the Union of Zemstvos had earlier forged with the commanders on the south-western front, when it played an active part in the relief of wounded soldiers, promoted a good working relationship when the refugee issue came to the fore. But a bureaucratic reaction to the claims advanced by the zemstvos and municipalities was not long in coming. In August 1915, the tsar approved the formation of a Special Council for Refugees, under the chairmanship of the Minister of the Interior. The new body disbursed funds for refugee relief, oversaw the registration and relocation of refugees, and planned to 'return them to the place of their permanent settlement, to restore their business [*khoziaistvo*], and to make arrangements for their future wellbeing'.

Refugee resettlement and relief

Refugees who had survived the journey from the front faced all manner of immediate difficulties, to which local authorities responded as best they could.

Zemstvos provided underwear, shoes and other items for refugees. Emergency accommodation was found in railway stations, empty factories, hotels, bathhouses and monasteries. Ordinary residents, as opposed to local professionals and some municipal leaders, took a rather different view of the strangers in their midst. Many cities and towns were already inundated with wounded soldiers. Initial sympathy and hospitality rapidly evaporated as urban neighbours realized that refugees had no money to pay for accommodation or food. There was also a class element in the response of local people towards refugees. Well-dressed newcomers provoked envy. In Iaroslavl', it was reported that 'intellectual and better-off refugees suffer many tribulations, because many local householders refuse to lease their apartments, or else stipulate draconian rents'. Direct evidence on peasant attitudes towards refugees is hard to find. As strangers, refugees were given hospitality; they were certainly treated more favourably than peasant villagers who had made themselves 'outsiders' by privatizing their plots under the Stolypin land reform. Peasants appear to have been more tolerant towards outsiders who found themselves billeted in the village through no fault of their own, particularly when they could make a net contribution to the family economy.

Refugees and the 'humanitarian narrative'

The basic tasks of providing emergency relief and then attempting to resettle refugees were implemented by a range of agencies in the public and the voluntary sector. But it was one thing to begin to arrange for material assistance, by providing food, clothes, shelter and fuel. How could this effort be maintained, once the first charitable impulses had been dissipated? What kinds of stories did Russians tell one another in order to justify the sustained forms of assistance that would inevitably lead to an increased burden on the public purse or a more extensive voluntary commitment? As one observer wrote, 'only those who have actually seen the flight of the Russian population can in any way conceive the horrors that attended it'. It was imperative to shape the experience of eyewitnesses into a form that could readily be understood by those who had not been present at the moment of expulsion. Newspaper accounts of the conditions experienced by refugees (especially orphaned refugees) played a crucial role in forming public opinion. Graphic photographs of refugees reinforced the culture of humanitarianism.

The most common image conveyed, as well as the most dramatic, was that of the sick refugee. This quickly supplanted images of the unfortunate yet stoic victim of war. Accounts of illness also extended to a preoccupation with the psyche of refugees. The Kiev refugee relief committee expressed concern that 'the horrors experienced by refugees have produced an epidemic of psychiatric abnormalities'. Powerful stories were told of deranged women who had dug graves for their dead husbands and had thrown in their children as well.

At the heart of the humanitarian initiative was the desire to protect and wherever possible restore the family, whose breakdown was believed by many educated Russians to be associated with crime. However, the desire to maintain family integrity frequently conflicted with public health imperatives. A clear tension emerged where families sought to remain together but medical authorities wished to isolate infected individuals.

Refugees and gender

The constitution of refugeedom also brought issues of gender to centre stage. In the first place, educated women claimed a particular responsibility for the welfare of refugee women and children. This expertise enhanced the civic profile of Russian women, already raised by their entry into the sphere of military nursing. Second, images of refugee suffering and need took on a gendered aspect. The English nurse, Violetta Thurstan, was at pains to draw such distinctions: 'the old men can be made content with a little tobacco and the company of their old cronies; perhaps, too, they are a little more used to travelling and mixing with the outside world than the women, who seem to miss terribly their accustomed seat near the stove among their familiar household goods'. It was vital to restore a sense of purpose amongst female refugees, by giving them domestic tasks. They were given tiny allowances to enable them to buy food for their dependants; what mattered was not the amount or the fact that food could have been prepared more efficiently by communal kitchens, but rather the retention of female dignity.

Female refugees also attracted special concern by virtue of the peculiar risks to which they were believed to be exposed. Thurstan applauded the intervention of female students in Petrograd who 'have done admirable work in keeping the young girls straight and out of temptation'. The main task for the guardians of young married refugee women was to improve their mothering abilities. Refugeedom created opportunities to address the vexed issue of infant mortality, for so long a matter of concern to zemstvo doctors. Pregnant women were offered places at schools for mothers where they received instruction in childcare, in the hope that they would learn the need for proper neo-natal care to ensure the survival of Russia's next generation. In this way, refugee relief was harnessed to self-improvement and eugenics.

The 'rights' of refugees: outsiders or insiders?

Except in rare instances, refugees were not perceived as fellow citizens (or citizens-in-waiting), but rather as the hapless victims of war. Marked by a specific kind of misfortune, the refugee was an unlikely candidate for assimilation, although assimilation might be a by-product of the refugee's relocation amidst a settled population. A report from Stavropol concluded that, thanks to organized relief, 'all refugees are living in virtually the same conditions as the local population'. But refugees could easily become an object of contempt, since they disturbed and threatened the prevailing public space. Furthermore, as diseased bodies, refugees were often liable to be incarcerated in special barracks or hospitals where they could be isolated from the local population. By labelling them as refugees, voluntary organizations and official agencies drew attention to their peculiar calamity and helplessness, and thus to the need to distinguish them from other groups.

The assertion of rights entailed access to legal advice across a range of issues, particularly those relating to the seizure of personal property. Liberal lawyers engaged by the public organizations were not only able to reaffirm the outrageous behaviour of army commanders and unaccountable officials, but also to underline the need to treat the refugee as a deserving supplicant, whose personal dignity was affronted and whose property had been violated.

Missing from official histories, however, is the evidence that refugees themselves succeeded in asserting their right to decent and humane treatment. Sometimes this took the form of a refusal to accept the destination that had been stipulated by government or other public agencies for refugee relief. A determined group from Vitebsk rejected outright the offer of a transfer to a remote village. Refugees also demonstrated a capacity to organize in support of claims for better conditions. Nor were individual refugees bereft of support when their personal circumstances became difficult or even dangerous. Far from being isolated, individuals might draw upon local liberal opinion to defend their rights. Provincial newspapers played an important role in this regard. In Iaroslavl', for instance, the highly-regarded newspaper *Golos* ('The Voice') maintained a vigorous and successful campaign when a local police official was found to have assaulted a refugee.

The unforeseen flight from their homes that refugees had been forced to endure was mirrored in their refusal subsequently to bow to official demands that they stay put in their new location for the duration of the war. Many instances came to light during 1916 of refugees seeking to return to their homes in the western borderlands, even though military commanders argued that this spontaneous drift would play havoc with troop transport and supply trains and feared the potential for refugees to spread disease in the mobile theatre of war. This was an ironic reversal of fortune, and deserves to be read as a sign of popular assertiveness. By the later stages of the war, few refugees were prepared to submit once again to military will.

Refugees and the construction of 'national' identity

The enforced resettlement of population during World War I from areas threatened by the enemy was also, as Alfred Knox put it, 'a national migration'. Many of the displaced were ethnically non-Russian, a veritable 'mixture of racial types' (*raznoplemennaia pestrota*), in the words of the governor of Akmolinsk province. The war enhanced their visibility and exposed the need for state action to accommodate the increasingly vociferous demands of those on the empire's periphery. By compelling them to resettle, the war evoked expressions of concern amongst Russians about the welfare of non-Russian nationalities. Voluntary organizations that catered for refugee relief very quickly acquired a national complexion. The war empowered existing national organizations, or created them for the first time. Societies for the relief of Polish refugees sprang up virtually overnight. When the government established the Special Council for Refugees it named seven separate committees from which one representative was to be chosen: Polish, Armenian, Jewish, Muslim, Latvian, Lithuanian and Georgian. These had numerous counterparts in provincial towns.

At the local level, refugees did not always form ghettos. Sometimes, as in Vologda, refugees were housed according to nationality, where special schools catered for Latvian speakers. But many ethnic minorities integrated themselves more fully into local communities. In Riazan, Polish refugees made use of local medical services, learned Russian at local schools, and worshipped at the local Catholic church. Many refugees found quarters in Russian neighbourhoods. Officials who toured provincial towns expecting to find refugees in tight-knit groups complained that they had to look hard in order to contact national minorities. Amidst the welter of ethnically specific canteens, clubs, schools and orphanages – Jewish refugees tended to live a more self-contained existence – one should not lose sight of this phenomenon.

Although there does not appear to be any direct evidence that Polish, Latvian or Lithuanian refugees were at the forefront of moves to establish greater national autonomy, nevertheless their presence in the Russian interior was significant in several respects. First, the mere fact of their displacement forced the existence of minorities on the attention of Russian peasants and townspeople who might never have stopped to think of the multinational character of the Russian empire. What rights they should enjoy and what respect should be accorded individual national cultures were questions that could not easily be avoided. Second, national relief committees conferred legitimacy on established movements in support of greater cultural freedom and political autonomy. They were able to tap a deep well of genuine suffering amongst refugees that readily assumed a 'national' form. But refugees displayed a range of political viewpoints and there is little to be gained by attempting to identify the common currency of debate. The point is that nationality became at key moments an important attribute, not that it was the sole determinant of refugee activism.

Refugees after revolution

The revolution of 1917 found many refugees installed in places of relative safety. Some had already begun to return to the homes they had abandoned in 1915. Those who stayed on were inevitably caught up in the dramatic social changes that took place when the Bolsheviks came to power. Their numbers were swelled by hundreds of thousands of demobilized soldiers who returned to their villages in order to take part in the redistribution of land. Although the new agrarian legislation entitled refugees and other in-migrants to a share in the resources now at the disposal of the peasantry, most peasants parcelled out the privately owned land among themselves. Refugees who plied a useful trade were allowed to stay on; others were encouraged to leave. Those who remained behind found themselves in desperate straits. Villagers no longer had need of their labour. The fact that privately owned land could legitimately be expropriated and added to the stock of peasant allotments prompted the village community to turn inward. There remained a clear dividing-line between peasant and refugee.

Concluding remarks

Tsarist officials insisted on the validity of *soslovie* and continued to ascribe individuals to specific categories. From the state's point of view, this formal categorization reminded the tsar's subjects of their rights and obligations. *Soslovie* may have failed to capture the emergence of new social groups such as the working class, industrialists, the creative intelligentsia and educated professionals. Nevertheless, it still had the capacity to mobilize particular groups, such as the landed gentry, clergy, and some members of the merchantry who felt threatened by economic modernization. By contrast, much of what we now know of the political behaviour of organized groups of workers indicates that they had established an alternative identity and had begun to think in class terms. The revolution of 1917 intensified this sense of class polarization. But the sharp edge of class conflict was quickly blunted during the civil war, when industrial production collapsed and mass de-urbanization took place, leaving behind a diverse group of petty traders, artisans and day-labourers who struggled to survive. Many of the leaders of the working-class revolution in 1917 moved into positions of administrative authority in party and state bodies. Russian society by 1920 comprised millions of peasant households as well as a motley group of urban survivors, characterized by Victor Serge as 'a grey crowd of thousands of people who are neither workers nor rich nor poor nor revolutionaries nor absolutely ignorant nor truly educated'. Needing, however, to identify both their enemies and their supporters, the Bolsheviks adopted class labels which were crude and inappropriate instruments of social categorization.

Refugees in wartime Russia tested the validity of the officially sanctioned categories of *soslovie*. But the peculiar status of refugees also challenged more modern kinds of group affiliation such as those that attached to occupation and class. To be a refugee was to stand outside established boundaries of society, to be waiting on the margins of social life in the hope that one's status would be resolved, and to become accustomed to new structures of space. From this point of view, refugees mocked modernity no less than they ridiculed tsarist social stereotypes. Their liminality challenged traditional categories and confused those who anticipated an orderly shift to modern forms of social organization.

Recent work on social theory invites us to challenge essentialist approaches to social identity, and to reflect on the ways in which the subject is constructed. From this perspective, it cannot be taken for granted what it 'means' to be a refugee, as if there were some irreducible characteristic that underpinned the status of refugee. This is not to overlook attempts that were or are made to universalize the refugee, but it does alert us to the suggestion that refugeedom conceals multiple differences of ethnicity, gender, age, occupation and social status. The historical record is replete with the significance that attaches to such distinctions. The refugee intelligentsia were found superior accommodation. Young refugee women were afforded special protection lest they fall into the trap of vice. It cannot be assumed that the attribute of displacement automatically conferred a sense of common experience, let alone that it triggered joint action. The construction of a 'shared narrative' that had the capacity to inscribe – or invent – a common emotional awareness, and perhaps to prompt collective endeavour, proceeded most obviously at the level of ethnicity.

At the same time, we also need to take into account the susceptibility of individuals to the organizing, surveillance and information-gathering capacities of external authorities, whether of the state, locality or professional agents, with their tendency to create refugee subjects. Refugees were counted, described, organized, confined (for their 'protection' and that of local residents), and even put on display for the benefit of visiting dignitaries and well-wishers. There is much to learn in this regard from the work of Michel Foucault, specifically the possibility of being able to trace the emergence of an entirely new discourse, a 'rupture' in prior ways of thinking about the individual and the group in early twentieth-century Russia, and the creation of new taxonomies of social order. Yet, if the category of refugee is more problematic than often appears to be the case – if our knowledge of refugees is discursively organized – what role is there for the study of the impact of formal political structures on refugee status and organization? As has often been pointed out, Foucault argued that power should be distinguished from the exercise of domination by the state. Rather, in his view, power must be related to the process of knowledge accumulation and classification. At this point the historian confronts a genuine difficulty, since there were identifiable interests in Russian society which articulated their own claims by fixing on particular forms of knowledge or defining social problems in particular *political* ways. In wartime Russia professional groups, municipalities, national committees and peasant communities were involved in the process of constructing subjects, and they did so for an unconcealed political purpose. Perhaps this is compatible with Foucault's project, which was intended to challenge prevailing assumptions about the primacy of class, economic interest and state power. But attempts to privilege a de-politicized discourse must make the historian of population displacement in wartime Russia pause, in the face of pervasive political struggles. Social identities were at stake, but so too was the political future of Russia.

Further reading

Calhoun C., ed., _Social Theory and the Politics of Identity_ (Oxford, Blackwell, 1994).

Cherniavsky M., ed., _Prologue to Revolution: Notes of A. N. Iakhontov on the Secret Meetings of the Council of Ministers, 1915_ (Englewood Cliffs, NJ, Prentice-Hall, 1967).

Fitzpatrick S., 'Ascribing Class: The Construction of Social Identity in Soviet Russia', _Journal of Modern History_ 65 (1993), pp. 745–70.

Freeze G., 'The _Soslovie_ (Estate) Paradigm and Russian Social History', _American Historical Review_ 91 (1986), pp. 11–36.

Kulischer E. M., _Europe on the Move: War and Population Changes, 1917–1947_ (New York, Columbia University Press, 1948).

Neuberger J., _Hooliganism: Crime, Culture and Power in St Petersburg, 1900–1914_ (Berkeley, University of California Press, 1993).

Polner T., _Russian Local Government during the War_ (New Haven, Yale University Press, 1930).

Thurstan V., _The People Who Run: Being the Tragedy of the Refugees in Russia_ (London and New York, G. P. Putnam's Sons, 1916).

Zolberg A., et al., _Escape from Violence: Conflict and the Refugee Crisis in the Developing World_ (Oxford, Oxford University Press, 1989).

The Role of Ritual and Symbols

RICHARD STITES

Before the revolution

Major human shake-ups – wars, revolutions, religious revivals, social movements and cultural awakenings – have generally produced symbols: visual, auditory and even tactile texts designed to arouse collective emotions. Signs invested with meaning – easily legible like the Christian cross, or encoded like the graffiti of modern urban youth – form a paralanguage. When embedded in a public ceremony such as a festival, parade or spectacle, the symbols are combined with' gestures and words to flesh out the social drama. It is rarely difficult to trace the origins of particular elements of the spectacle back to pagan, classical, folk or various local traditions. The revolutionary rituals of modern times were of course 'invented traditions' built in turn on earlier traditions that were also invented. But the historical genealogy of signs and choreographed movements (mass song, marches) alone cannot tell us much about the meanings intended and received at the moment of invention, presentation or performance. Ritual 'texts' must be analysed within the larger political frame.

Like all revolutions, the Russian revolution of 1917, and its continuation during the civil war of 1917–21, drew its symbolic language largely from inherited forms which were adapted to the purpose at hand. The deepest layer of derivation was pre-Christian Russian cyclical and seasonal ceremonies and their rituals which included magic incantation, cathartic destruction of devils, and wild release in song, dance and feasting. All these passed into Russian Orthodox Christianity which crystallized into outdoor processions and indoor sacramental solemnities combining hierarchical order, sacred images, music, stationary worship and luxurious displays of vestments and ornament. The ecclesiastical affects of this tradition were partly retained by the Provisional Government in 1917 and wholly abandoned by the Bolshevik regime that succeeded it. On city streets or at fairs, the most widespread popular form of gathering for performance was the folk festival or funfair, with its dazzling array of foods, games, amusements and carnival shows – a perfect vehicle for later revolutionary holiday celebrations.

The Petersburg or imperial era of Russian history (1703–1917) was marked by the prominence of imported European ritual forms that transformed a crucial portion of interior and exterior space: parade, court ceremony and ball. The military review, established in the eighteenth century, was neither religious nor popular in any sense: it was a sign of state power, not so much of combat preparedness but of order commanded from the top. From about the mid-eighteenth to the mid-nineteenth century, the parade dominated the appearance of almost every Russian town. The highly elaborate uniforms were meant to flaunt power and dazzle viewers; the visible ranking and command structure to reinforce hierarchy and obedience; the geometrical and mechanical forms to impose an urban diurnal clock. One could measure time of day more accurately by the changing of a guard detail than by the ringing of church bells. Revolutionaries could dispense with the court ceremony, coronation festivity and gentry ball, but not with the parade, since soldiers played such a great role in the presentation of the revolution on the streets of Petrograd. It was relatively easy to 'proletarianize' military parades even before the Bolsheviks took power because army uniforms had gradually been simplified in the later nineteenth century and fancily attired officers were no longer in evidence. Breaches of the new parade 'etiquette' in 1917 – the funeral of Cossacks killed in the July street fighting and General Lavr Kornilov's public appearances – were seen as jarring throwbacks to pre-revolutionary ritual forms and interpreted by hostile observers as counter-revolutionary.

A later development in public ceremonial life of the tsarist era was the patriotic pageant. Begun by Panslav enthusiasts in the 1860s and 1870s, it was meant to celebrate 'popular' wars – particularly the Russo-Turkish War of 1877 and World War I. The Panslav affairs were marked by large public indoor benefit meetings, featuring speeches, songs and musical performances; religious services in solidarity with the South Slavs; and the creation of heraldic banners that were sent to the front. In World War I, patriots revived the genre. M. I. Dolina, a dedicated monarchist and reactionary propagandist, gave hundreds of patriotic benefit concerts that offered folk songs, balalaika bands, martial wind ensembles, regimental choirs, songs set to the words of the famous Bessarabian anti-semite publicist Pavel Krushevan, texts provided by the Russian right, and readings of official edicts. An interesting, though not original, device used by Dolina was the patriotic *tableau vivant* – actors dressed as Suvorov, Kutuzov and other national-military heroes, frozen alongside common people for the visual contemplation of the audiences. The juxtaposition of genres and the staged mixture of social orders was designed to promote a picture of all-Russian solidarity and loyalty.

The most immediately relevant form of pre-revolutionary ritual – that of the radical sub-culture – was of course wholly illegal in tsarist times. It developed underground, in secret meetings in the woods or in protest demonstrations – the word *demonstratsiia* becoming a synonym for parade or march in the revolution and in Soviet times. Beginning in the 1890s, meetings were held to celebrate the newly proclaimed international holiday, 1 May; speeches were framed by a singing of the *Internationale*, the hymn of the Second or Socialist International, founded in 1889. Protest marches and funerals of fallen comrades became more common during the revolution of 1905. Red banners, songs – including revolutionary funeral dirges – were the bare accompaniment of these moving texts but the visual austerity was more than compensated for by the emotional texture and quasi-religious aura.

The February revolution

The first days following the fall of the monarchy in March 1917 were marked more by spontaneity than by ritual – which implies rules, textual continuity and repetition. Parallel actions in many cities were too close in time for this to have been social mimicry. They included large crowds of all classes assembling in the main squares or boulevards or in front of public buildings where new authorities had set up shop – self-appointed municipal leaders or soviets. The crowds cheered 'free Russia' in a spirit of generalized joy and social solidarity; and they honoured recently freed political prisoners or veteran radicals. In Petrograd, the celebratory pattern culminated in the first public collective gesture: the burial of those killed in the February overthrow. In almost every one of its components, the interment spoke of social harmony and peace. Planning was jointly done by a largely middle-upper-class Provisional Government and the Petrograd Soviet – also middle-class in leadership, but with a lower-class base; the crowds were socially heterogeneous; and the theme was harmony at the dawn of a new era. Marching columns, their assembly at the Field of Mars – the burial ground – banners and slogans, red-draped buildings, severe dress, and revolutionary funeral hymns were the chief ingredients. Hardly noted in eyewitness accounts was the absence of church participation – a thoroughly novel development in public solemnities.

The next major city-wide celebration displayed a different visual and kinetic face. This was the burial of the seven Cossacks killed defending the Provisional Government during the July Days. It combined the church procession and military review of bygone days: the traditional pomp of the armed forces and a requiem mass at St Isaac's Cathedral, one of the holiest shrines of the capital whose history was closely connected with the monarchy. This funeral was literally a sign of the times, a semiotic counterrevolution reflecting perfectly the aspirations of the more conservative elements in the Provisional Government and those further to their right. Between the

burials of the first and second sets of martyrs, public rituals and performances still spoke of relative social and national solidarity – political evenings
and 'revolutionary concerts' featuring *tableaux vivants* and the presentation
of old radical veterans in the majestic setting of the imperial theatres. But
the political division of the city and the country as a whole had grown
tremendously. The differences between the Provisional Government and the
Petrograd Soviet over war, army life, social reforms and revolutionary
change were matched in the very style of proceedings of the two bodies
housed in the same building, the Tauride Palace.

One could hardly imagine two assemblies more different in appearance
and manners. The buttoned-down lawyers, professors and industrialists of
the Provisional Government in one wing of the Palace tried to conduct business in an orderly legalistic manner adhering to the old rules of the Duma.
In the Petrograd Soviet in the other wing, mass participation was taken
literally, as several thousand roughly-dressed factory hands, recruits and
frontline veterans shouted out of turn and voiced their emotions in speeches
flowery and crude. The apparent chaos of the Soviet meetings – resembling
those of a village *mir* – was misleading: positions were advanced, votes were
held, measures were taken. Bespectacled socialist intellectuals stumbled over
sleeping sergeants with rifles in hand and were choked by the smell of
makhorka, the cheap tobacco of the common folk. Some were repelled; but
most of them were thrilled to be rubbing shoulders with 'the people'. The
extraordinary juxtaposition of these two bodies and their outward appearance and gestural language were as much a key to the deep gulf dividing
Russian society as were their political agendas. Their symbolic and political
worlds continued to diverge up to the Bolshevik takeover in October 1917.

Soviet symbols

The Provisional Government had taken as its seal and currency motif a
modified double-headed eagle of the Romanovs, visually domesticated with
folded wings, and minus the accoutrements of autocracy – orb and sceptre.
The French Republic's *Marseillaise* with Russian lyrics had served as an
unofficial anthem. When the Bolsheviks took power, their new Soviet
regime donned a different symbolic attire to create an identity around its
social base and its aspiration to create a new world. This was accomplished
by replacing the old seal, flag and anthem. The national seal caused the most
excitement and controversy. Lenin and Anatoly Lunacharsky, the
Commissar of Enlightenment, held a competition among artists whose
entries provided a dazzling and even amusing array of motifs including
futuristic squares and wedges. The one chosen as most likely for adoption
contained three implements meant to symbolize the classes who made the
revolution or for whom it was made: the sickle for the peasantry, the industrial hammer for the proletariat, and a short sword for the army. Lenin

objected strenuously to the sword's militaristic associations. This was winter–spring 1918 in the midst of peace negotiations with the Germans at Brest-Litovsk. Lenin, bending over backwards to present Soviet Russia as a nation of peace, argued against it in committee for weeks until the offensive weapon was removed.

The remaining hammer and sickle (both frequently used in old provincial heraldry) was framed by a reassuring wreath adorned with classical elements, including the Roman fasces – a bundle of rods wrapped around an axe. The fasces was later removed, possibly in response to its adoption by the fascist regime in Italy. The first official appearance of the new Soviet emblem was on the cover of the first constitution of the RSFSR in summer 1918. The hammer and sickle was then planted on the corner of the new red flag. The name 'hammer and sickle' was widely used thereafter for factories, communes, schools, and other institutions.

The arrangement of the hammer and the sickle (in Russian the word order is always 'sickle-and-hammer' – *serp i molot*) on flag and seal makes no statement about a superordinate–subordinate relationship between the two signs and what they stand for. But when poster artists began incorporating them into their art, they almost invariably depicted a man holding the hammer and a woman with the sickle. In later readings, this meant associating man with industry, machine, city, power and the future; women with agriculture, rural backwardness, nurture and fertility. Here, where art history and political history – so often segregated from each other – intersect, it is important to distinguish between intention, function and reception. We can rarely know the intentions of artists at the time of creation and there is no way of discovering what symbol makers and poster artists 'meant' when they gendered the pictures mentioned above. It is reasonable to suppose that they simply copied forms from the life they knew – particularly in the recent war years when men in factories and women in the fields were very much a national norm. Similarly there are no clues about what viewers thought or felt when they looked at visual gendering. Therefore, in interrogating the 'function' of this kind of motif, historians have no evidence that it was intended to identify women with agriculture and men with industry as an ideological position or cultural statement. The real function of the material, then, is not so much as a 'sign' of the regime's thinking, but rather as a signal for historians to start looking for real evidence of the gendering of town and country, a search that might not have occurred to them without close examination of the iconography of the time. To do more than this is to engage in ahistorical theorizing.

Reconstructing a new public face for the revolution also required renaming and replacing public signs of the old regime. During World War I, students had gone around the capital replacing German with Russian names on street signs. The city itself was renamed from St Petersburg to Petrograd. For self-protection during a rage of anti-'German' pogroms in Moscow, Russians of German, Latvian, Jewish or Scandinavian descent rushed to adopt Slavic-sounding patriotic names like Romanov or Serbsky (Serbian). Hammer became Molotov, Berg became Gorskii, Taube became Golubev, Schwartz became Chernov, Schmidt become Kuznetsov, and Eiche became Dubnov. In 1918, Bolshevik renaming of streets and squares began and later spread to the renaming of cities – Petrograd into Leningrad after Lenin's death in 1924 being one of the first. Tsarist emblems and monuments were torn down. Lunacharsky ensured that some of the more artistic statues remained untouched, but most monuments to tsars and tsarist heroes were pulled down in ceremonial acts. To replace them, Lenin presented a plan of 'monumental propaganda' – public unveiling of hero figures.

These visual ornaments received great fanfare in the early years of revolution. The objects of statuary art chosen by political leaders were of cultural and radical figures of European and Russian history. The cultural set was presumably meant to tie the revolution to canonized tradition, and the political set to establish a revolutionary genealogy from Spartacus through the French revolution, the utopian socialists, the European Marxists and – paralleling it – the Russian radical tradition from Radishchev and the Decembrists to 1917. Lenin, believing in the inborn passivity of a mass audience, ordered that the unveiling of the statues be accompanied by lectures indicating the precise significance of the monuments. The figures were unveiled during special holidays at key points in the city, with talks by such important political orators as G. E. Zinoviev and A. V. Lunacharsky. Thus the faces of great socialists, writers and former state criminals now replaced the massive equestrian replicas of monarchical Russia.

Soviet festivals

The great festivals and holiday celebrations swirling around the unveiled statuary were not as spontaneous as those of the February revolution; and they soon hardened into highly organized and ritualized performances. From 1918 to the end of the civil war, Petrograd, Moscow, and other towns within the Bolshevik-controlled heartland came alive on May Day, Revolution Day (7 November) or for special congresses, with colourful floats, parades, wall decorations, fireworks and lights, and a variety of out-door theatricals. Some of the most talented artists of the day splashed their glowing paints over public places to create a carnival appearance. These earliest celebrations tried to blend tradition with modernity. In a created festive atmosphere, the barkers, puppeteers, marchers, and speech-makers mocked the enemies of the revolution and burned straw figures of White and Interventionist leaders. Big outdoor theatricals deployed thousands of performers and technicians in the staging of battles, *tableaux vivants*, mystery plays and historical revolutionary epics. By the end of the civil war, the Soviet festival style was largely in place, surrounded by stylized slogans and symbols that had emerged from the revolutionary years.

Further reading

von Geldern J., *Bolshevik Festivals, 1917–1920* (Berkeley, University of California Press, 1993).

German M., *Art of the October Revolution* (New York, Avrora, 1980).

Kenez P., *The Birth of the Propaganda State: Soviet Methods of Mass Mobilization, 1917–1929* (Cambridge, Cambridge University Press, 1985).

Lane C., *Rites of Rulers* (Cambridge, Cambridge University Press, 1981).

Mally L., *Culture of the Future: The Proletkult Movement in Revolutionary Russia* (Berkeley, University of California Press, 1990).

Mazaev A. I., *Prazdnik kak sotsialno-khudozhestvennoe iavlenie* (Moscow, Nauka, 1978).

Stites R., 'Adorning the Russian Revolution: The Primary Symbols of Bolshevism, 1917–1918', *Sbornik* (Leeds, England) 10 (Summer 1984).

Stites R., *Revolutionary Dreams: Utopian Vision and Experimental Life in the Russian Revolution* (New York, Oxford University Press, 1989). See pp. 270–3 for sources and literature in Russian.

Tumarkin N., *Lenin Lives!* (Cambridge, MA, Harvard University Press, 1983).

Verner A., 'What's in a Name? Of Dog-Killers, Jews, and Rasputin', *Slavic Review* 53, 4 (Winter, 1994), pp. 1046–70.

Wortman R., *Scenarios of Power* (Princeton, Princeton University Press, 1994).

Russian Industrialists and Revolution

PETER GATRELL

Our knowledge of the business elite in revolutionary Russia remains far inferior to that of the organized industrial working class, nor is there any mystery about the reasons for this neglect. The balance cannot be redressed by focusing exclusively on business leaders' opinions, actions and organization. Important though it is to be better informed about these issues, they must be related to the changing economic and political context within which industrialists operated.* This makes it imperative that we have the kind of detailed studies of individual industries that are common in the economic historiography of Germany, France, Britain and the United States, which will make it possible for historians to compare the economic power, political influence and social status of Russian industrialists with that of their counterparts elsewhere.

The pre-war decades

During the last quarter of the nineteenth century, industry throughout continental Europe was buffeted by foreign trade rivalries and, later, by restrictions on the availability of credit. In Germany, the economic challenge was met by industrial reorganization (that is, mergers and cartelization), carried out with the assistance of powerful joint-stock banks and with government blessing. Some of the more dynamic economies – Germany was again the pioneer – succeeded in exploiting innovative technologies to create new industrial sectors, such as chemicals and electrical engineering. Tariff

---

*Numerically, the business elite was very small, no more than 200,000 individuals by 1910–12, according to Gindin, including family members. Together they presided over 3,500 major industrial enterprises employing more than 200 workers, and 10,000 large wholesale firms, and were closely linked with leading Russian financiers through interlocking directorships. A further 22,000 businesses employed between 16 and 20 workers.

protection in France and Germany shielded traditional iron and steel trades from the worst effects of foreign competition. In Russia, rapid industrial growth after 1885 was associated with macroeconomic policies designed to encourage foreign direct investment in basic industries, including metallurgy, coal and oil. The rate of joint-stock company formation increased. The revival of commercial confidence in Europe after 1900 was boosted by the recovery of domestic and export demand for manufactured goods. The upturn in Russian heavy industry was slower to occur than in Western Europe. When it eventually came, after 1910, it relied heavily on the traditional instruments of tsarist industrialization – government contracts, tariff protection and foreign finance – although an enhanced role was also played by domestic banks. Established firms reorganized themselves, integrated production, and secured their position by forming syndicates; new conglomerates in the steel and engineering trades commanded the same kind of market power as their equivalents in Germany.

These economic realignments generated fierce protests from domestic interests that felt threatened by big business and institutional finance. In Germany, medium manufacturers attempted with some success to mobilize consumers, shopkeepers and white-collar workers. In Russia, the protest against monopoly was masked by broader social and political struggles, but here too the iron and coal syndicates were charged with economic exploitation of the consumer. No less significant, these developments exposed divisions amongst European businessmen: between suppliers of raw materials and manufacturers of finished or semi-finished goods, between export-oriented firms and those working primarily for the home market, as well as between large and small firms. Intra-industry divisions persisted throughout the period, and in Germany, as Geoff Eley and David Blackbourn point out, 'when the bourgeoisie acted on the larger, national political stage, very real sectional, regional, and religious divisions became apparent and were magnified'. In Russia, too, what Tim McDaniel terms the 'congenital weakness' of the business community was compounded by internal fragmentation. In part, this reflected the size and diversity of the Russian empire. As Alfred Rieber and Thomas Owen have shown, the older generation of Moscow's mercantile elite was at home in the hierarchical world of corporate estates (*sosloviia*), whereas the newcomers who spearheaded the introduction of heavy industry from their base in St Petersburg adopted a more cosmopolitan and modern view of social organization and economic ambition. The cleavage was complicated by the fact that younger Moscow businessmen rejected both the political timidity displayed by their elders and the links with government maintained by the emerging oligarchy in the capital. The Association of Industry and Trade, formed in 1906 and by 1914 representing 251 industrial firms, 34 banks and insurance companies, 11 transport companies and 19 trading houses, never overcame these rifts.

Regional and ethnic differences were not unique to Russia, and an equivalent contrast between the family firms of Moscow and the corporate enterprises based in St Petersburg can be seen in France and Germany. In Britain, too, historians have made much of the gulf between city 'gentlemen' and business 'players', to say nothing of the separate worlds inhabited by Jewish and Quaker financiers and industrialists. Yet common assumptions and beliefs were capable of overriding differences of status, ethnicity and sectoral activity amongst industrialists, except in Russia, where such differences prevented the establishment of a common bourgeois-industrial culture. Whether these jealousies and rivalries actually made a difference to the longer-term viability of private enterprise in Russia, or undermined its capacity to unite in the face of challenges to its legitimacy,.is something to which we shall return. But business fragmentation alone cannot account for the eventual failure of corporate enterprise in Russia.

By 1900 the broad cultural and ideological hegemony of the European bourgeoisie appeared to be secure. Again, the consensus is that Russia was exceptional, because the process of industrialization went hand in hand with state supervision and intervention, preventing the consolidation of a secure bourgeois ethos. McDaniel argues that 'autocratic modernization' exposed the tensions inherent in the promotion of capitalist industrialization by an unreformed polity. Corporate capitalism lacked legitimacy in tsarist Russia. *Parvenu* industrialists were attacked by the nobility, by the cultural intelligentsia, and by professionals. State-sponsored industrialization was accompanied by bureaucratic suspicion that government contractors and financiers simply lined their pockets with public money. This oligarchy constantly argued that they deserved long-term financial support and public confidence. Russia's big businessmen never boasted the close contacts that the Centralverband deutscher Industriellen maintained with the German bureaucracy or the Comité des Forges enjoyed with the French government. Both associations helped to shape social and commercial legislation. Although individual Russian firms secured government patronage (some leading company directors had themselves occupied government posts), the tsarist state had the capacity to undermine the private sector, by threatening to transfer contracts to government enterprises, cutting subsidies and tariffs, restricting the activities of ethnic minorities (Jews especially), or simply spreading stories of private greed and the neglect of workers' interests. The best that Russian industrialists could hope for was the state's willingness to clamp down on labour militancy. Nor did Russian businessmen and financiers establish significant contact with the aristocracy, in contrast to the situation in Western Europe, where the two groups (especially in France and Britain) frequented the same clubs, lived in the same neighbourhoods and intermarried (again, this applies more to the financial than the manufacturing elite). Close contact between a member of the Russian landed nobility and an industrialist or banker brought shame and even scandal on the former's family.

However, Russian industrialists were not alone in feeling insecure about their political leverage and social position. In the early twentieth century, it was still unusual for European industrialists to occupy government posts. Between 1870 and 1914 the proportion of businessmen in parliament declined in Britain, France and Germany. Clearly, the growing importance of manufacturing and finance was not reflected in the significance its spokesmen attached to parliamentary representation. Instead, they confined themselves to careful political lobbying. A more worrying symptom of changing political conditions was the growth of the labour movement, whether in the form of organized trade unions or socialist political parties. In Germany, big business counted on non-socialist parties to check the impact of parliamentary socialism and on government social reforms to dent the appeal of trade unionism. Leading firms also championed 'yellow' or non-socialist unions. Even so, German big business did not always breathe easily. The challenge of labour was paralleled by the attacks on large corporations launched by the growing *Mittelstand*, as well as by an increasingly unsympathetic landed elite.

In Russia, the political paralysis of the industrial elite was largely self-induced, although it was not helped by the broad anti-enterprise culture referred to earlier. Business leaders (like the gentry and professional middle class) were divided over their attitudes to autocracy. Attempts to form business parties foundered, and industrialists – many of whom had taken a broadly liberal stance during 1905 – renounced parliamentary politics when it became clear that they enjoyed limited electoral support. Instead, industrialists pinned their hopes on a continuation of past practice, that is, lobbying the tsarist government over selected issues, such as tariff protection or the reform of company law (the Association of Industry and Trade was formed precisely to pursue this strategy). But, unlike the entrepreneurs and bankers of the Rhineland who retreated into political passivity after the 1848 revolution with a guarantee of economic and legal freedoms, Russian industrialists abandoned liberal politics without any promises or concessions from the old regime. What survived was a genuine fear of a revived revolution that would unleash more powerful anti-capitalist forces in Russian society.

Liberal-minded industrialists responded to revolution in 1905–06 with something other than asinine faith in the ability of the tsarist government to repress the working class. But they were in a minority in advocating labour and welfare reforms, which most employers resisted. In the most dynamic sectors of industry, such as engineering, industrialists introduced more modern techniques of factory organization, in the expectation that workers would come to appreciate the link between improved labour productivity and personal reward. But this strategy was not typical of Russian industry as a whole, where the old doctrine of '*Herr im Haus*' exercised considerable sway.

Industrialists and war

In Russia, as in Germany and France, big business made impressive 'positional gains' during the First World War, including access to government agencies responsible for the regulation of the war economy. The state assumed the risks of constructing new plant for munitions production and of creating entirely new sectors, whilst allowing the private sector to retain substantial profits. By joining government-sponsored war boards or associations, entrepreneurs obtained contracts, inputs and information. In France, the powerful Comité des Forges singlehandedly organized the supply of war materials, and had a virtually free hand to determine the price of finished products. In Germany, too, in Jürgen Kocka's words, 'negotiations and compromises between various directors of enterprises on the one hand, and between them and the state's representatives on the other, replaced the regulatory function of the capitalist market to a previously unknown degree'. However, the relationship between business and the state remained uneasy, particularly when government and military officials broached plans for more extensive state control.

The outbreak of war opened up fresh opportunities for Russian heavy industry. Leading government contractors hurriedly concluded fresh contracts for munitions with the procurement agencies. Other firms in the private sector that had hitherto concentrated on civilian work also joined the headlong rush to manufacture armaments. The main responsibility fell on metalworking and machine-building firms in Petrograd and the surrounding region. But the critical situation with munitions supply made the government anxious to broaden the manufacturing base, as well as to extend its apparatus of control over production and distribution. The flow of orders during 1915 prompted some government officials to express their concern that many large firms had swallowed huge sums of money, without making sufficient efforts to improve productivity. Business leaders complained about fresh plans to extend state ownership, about projects for compulsory amalgamation, and about the excess profits tax. The pages of the industrial press were filled with soul-searching editorials and heartfelt denunciations of ministerial machinations. How much the editorials reflected genuine entrepreneurial anxiety, and how much they were simply a smokescreen erected to mask the wartime profitability of big business, is difficult to tell and can only be answered by considering industrialists' behaviour and strategies in different sectors of the economy. Spokesmen for the engineering industry, for instance, attacked proposals for state enterprises to develop new products (such as machine tools) for the post-war market. The engineering employers' association, established early in 1916 in response to the planned sequestration of the giant Putilov works, led the campaign against the excess profits tax during 1916, arguing that profits were ploughed back into the enterprise in order to finance the acquisition of new capital. They demanded increased depreciation allowances to set against tax liabilities. Their efforts met with only limited success. By contrast, regulation of the vital iron and steel industry allowed the leading syndicate (*Prodamet*) to contribute to the allocation of orders and to play the leading role in negotiations on product prices. Steel producers could also afford to be more relaxed about their prospects, because their plant could quickly be re-adapted to civilian production, whereas manufacturers who had converted to military production needed to write off their wartime investments.

In the late summer of 1915 the government established a Special Council for State Defence (*Osoboe soveshchanie po oborone gosudarstva*). Major Russian industrialists, closely involved in its short-lived predecessor commission, lost the right to participate in its deliberations. They complained that, though the new body included many worthy figures, very few of them were actually industrialists, still less did they represent the largest enterprises working for defence. The jibe was directed at members of the new 'War Industry Committees' (WICs), which included many of the medium and small manufacturers who sought a share of lucrative government contracts. But the anger was superfluous; major employers were regularly being invited during 1916 to take part in its deliberations. The lack of formal institutional representation for big business did not silence its voice or deprive it of economic power, just as the access granted the WICs did not accord them any privileges in industrial production, where their role was marginal.

However, changes in economic administration opened up other wounds. The WICs protested that neither the state nor big business had sufficient grasp of the scale or type of industrial mobilization that the war necessitated. Complaints were made that the directors of the largest firms in engineering and metallurgy enjoyed too close an association with government officials. The WICs hoped to shatter this cosy relationship. They quickly established themselves in provincial towns and cities, and dedicated themselves not simply to the production of uniforms and munitions for the war effort, but also to the principle of a morally superior form of enterprise that need not disappear with the cessation of hostilities. The political implications of this configuration of industrial mobilization were enormous, because the WICs rejected the apolitical stance of the Association of Industry and Trade and, like the Progressist Party with which they were linked, challenged the regulation of the war economy by a government that lacked public accountability. As Rieber points out, the WICs also gave vent to the Great Russian chauvinism characteristic of the Moscow merchantry. No patriotic Russian could fail to see the need for political change.

The other main consequence of the European war was to compel national governments to rethink their attitudes towards organized labour. 'Total war' required that serious attention be given to the rewards that might be offered to labour in return for its cooperation in the operation of an efficient war economy. This re-evaluation was helped by the willingness of most national labour leaders to adopt a patriotic stance at the outbreak of war and to speak of capital in less confrontational terms than hitherto. In France, Britain and Germany employers made crucial concessions. The French government promoted a new industrial relations policy, imposed compulsory arbitration on employers and workers (in January 1917), and stipulated a minimum wage throughout French industry. In Germany, trade unions were consulted from the outset and involved in key decisions relating to labour policy. A shotgun marriage between workers and employers was arranged under the Auxiliary Service Law. Labour exchanges and workers' committees were legalized, in return for which workers agreed to restrictions on job mobility. German employers eventually (in November 1918) accepted collective bargaining and the eight-hour day. The war thus conferred legitimacy on organized labour.

The issue of labour representation proved particularly explosive in Russia. Aleksandr Guchkov, chairman of the Central War Industry Committee and an industrialist who had grown disillusioned with parliamentary politics, espoused the doctrine of 'social peace' and advocated an English-style *rapprochement* between labour and capital. In similar vein, his deputy, Aleksandr Konovalov, maintained that the organized working class 'represented the element on which depends ultimate victory over the enemy'. According to this perspective, capital should collaborate with labour in modern economic life. The government not surprisingly rejected such a radical view of industrial relations, and found leading industrialists willing to toe the official line. The engineering employers' association was the chief source of opposition to 'workers' groups' and conciliation procedures, its members articulating a more technocratic view of labour as a production input, rather than as one half of a dynamic partnership in industry. But many liberal employers were themselves lukewarm about Konovalov's radical vision of industrial relations.

Industrialists and revolution

The dramatic collapse of the tsarist state in February 1917 unleashed a powerful working-class movement in favour of better treatment, improved pay and conditions of work and the right to monitor the decisions taken by employers. In Rieber's words, the revolution 'swept away their defences against the working class, and they were incapable of rebuilding them alone'. Most industrial associations exercised little influence over their members, let alone over the government: 'factory owners are poorly organized [lamented one distraught employer] compared to the superbly well organized workers'. The political reconfiguration prompted progressive members of the Petrograd oligarchy to articulate a vision of class cooperation. The Petrograd Society of Factory and Mill Owners (PSFMO) maintained that 'free citizen-employers and free citizen-workers can find a common language'. Urged on by Konovalov, newly installed as Minister of Trade and Industry, the PSFMO abandoned its previous intransigence and conceded wage increases and a reduction in hours, whilst urging that fresh wage demands could only be considered if the government offered financial support. Konovalov was also able to obtain industrialists' agreement to participate in arbitration and conciliation procedures. But these arrangements did not survive the deepening economic crisis: the rhetoric of particularist class conflict quickly replaced the 'common language' of citizenship.

Early concessions made in Petrograd (and copied by southern iron and steel producers) did little to heal the rifts amongst Russian industrialists. Those behind the formation of a new All-Russian Confederation of Trade and Industry sought to wrest the leadership of the business community from the hands of the Petrograd-dominated Association of Industry and Trade, derided by P. P. Riabushinskii, the prominent Moscow industrialist and banker, as an 'industrial bureaucracy'. The new body included numerous stock-exchange committees and merchant associations, which it was intended to organize into a national union equivalent to those established by other professional groups and by workers. Riabushinskii condemned Russia's dependence on international capital and called for a strong government, free from the influence of 'soviets and committees'. However, Riabushinskii kept his distance during the Kornilov plot, whereas members of the Petrograd oligarchy contributed to Kornilov's funds, in the hope that he could resurrect the business-government axis on a firm anti-socialist basis.

The conduct of industrial strategy and the future form of industrial organization also generated fierce inter-firm rivalries within the same branch of industry. The engineers' association did its best to maintain a degree of solidarity amongst its members, but the besetting problems of financial insolvency, falling productivity, supply breakdowns and labour militancy induced a mentality of *sauve qui peut*. The association's executive favoured some rationalization of production; given that raw materials and fuel were in short supply, work should be allocated to ensure that a smaller number of firms were kept fully occupied. But they insisted that any amalgamation of enterprises should be carried out under their control. They resolutely opposed proposals for compulsory amalgamation, which – like price controls – were perceived as a 'state socialist' project to restrict commercial freedom in the post-war period, and were seen to indicate a worrying trend in government economic policy.

The militancy of labour prompted employers to demand 'moral' as well as financial support from the government. Ministers were urged to remind workers to renounce excessive claims on employers or otherwise 'disorganize' production. Industrialists berated labour leaders for threatening the entire basis of private enterprise, by making intolerable demands for access to company records; such demands, they insisted, were not grounded in law and if they were would lead to the complete destruction of factory life. The issue at stake was the very principle of private ownership of capital. The Special Council lent its support, demanding 'exceptional measures' against workers whose presence was not conducive to defence production. But the Provisional Government refused to accede to this pressure – had it not done enough, by attempting to curb the factory committees in August? – and shifted responsibility for the maintenance of production on to employers.

By the end of September, the engineering employers' association adopted a more conciliatory note, resolving to 'encourage by all possible means the creation of good relations between employers, workers and white-collar staff' and to take steps 'to eliminate all kinds of misunderstandings which arise concerning the agreements made between employers and workers'. Such phrases might have inspired confidence six months earlier, but now the accompanying proposals seemed pitiful: participation in arbitration courts, the creation of funds to aid workers who suffered poor health, the establishment of labour exchanges in the engineering industry. To resurrect ideas in the autumn of 1917 that had been commonplace amongst liberal employers since the turn of the century, and to expect them to appeal to militant workers, merely revealed how deep employers' heads had hitherto been buried in the sand. Individual members drafted draconian measures to deal with the financial and political crisis, in some cases by preparing to dismiss between one-third and one-half of the workforce. At the Nikolaev shipyards, workers arrested the managers of the shipyards; elsewhere, several managers suffered physical assaults. The Provisional Government came to an end amidst a breakdown of law and order in individual enterprises, and against a background of entrepreneurial disunity.

Industrialists and the Soviet state

Whether industrialists could salvage anything from the wreckage depended in part upon the creation of some kind of *modus vivendi* with the new Soviet state. But employers were again divided. Some felt that the new regime, though not kindly disposed towards capitalist proprietors, might nevertheless establish discipline in the factories. Favouring a pragmatic approach, some businessmen agreed to work with the new Supreme Council for the National Economy (VSNKh); others remained sceptical. In January 1918 the engineering association endorsed the view that 'the idea of workers' control is entirely acceptable, but only of course on condition that control does not amount to interference in the organization of production, because such interference from that quarter will simply scare off capital'. But more assertive action by organized labour undermined this strategy.

Some leading entrepreneurs signalled their intention to collaborate with the new state. Warning that the revolution was likely to promote a flight of capital, A. P. Meshcherskii entered into negotiations with VSNKh; so, too, did the leaders of the influential Stakheev trust. Iu. Larin, a member of VSNKh's presidium, initially sought to reassure the entrepreneurs, by supporting calls for guaranteed long-term government orders and endorsing the view that 'workers' control' should merely 'inform': 'the organization of entrepreneurs and the organization of workers', he said, 'are two sides of the same coin and both are under the overall control of the state'. Here, perhaps, was the basis of a solution to the entrepreneurial dilemma: a strong central authority could provide financial stability, security of input supply, labour discipline, security of assets – in other words, the conditions that employers had hoped to extract from the Provisional Government. But Meshcherskii alienated the powerful Metalworkers' Union and influential sections of the Bolshevik Party, and his erstwhile colleagues amongst the entrepreneurial elite left him isolated.

Privately owned firms in heavy industry passed into the hands of the state during the first half of 1918; the joint-stock banks had already been nationalized in October 1917. Stories of grass-roots nationalization reached the headquarters of employers' associations. Few businessmen showed the persistence of Meshcherskii in seeking to retain some control of the levers of economic power. Some remained on Russian soil and helped fund the ephemeral anti-Bolshevik groupings that survived until the end of 1918. Most of the industrial and financial elite emigrated, sustaining organizations devoted to the 'economic regeneration' of Russia. Having lost their assets, and lacking access to foreign governments, this activity was futile.

Conclusions

Some characteristics of Russian industry and industrialists were common to those in Germany and France. A handful of large firms dominated the production of strategically important commodities and enjoyed a close commercial relationship with government. But most branches of industry were not linked directly to the state, except in wartime. In each country, industrialists displayed deeply divided opinions and strategies, reflecting entrenched cultural and geographic variations, as well as sectoral differences. These were probably more profound in Russia, although Heiko Haumann suggests that the traditional contrast between the economic activities of entrepreneurs in Moscow and Petrograd diminished as textile magnates diversified into other industrial activities. Basic differences between Russia and Western Europe were the result of closer state intervention in the process of industrialization and the persistence of a bureaucratic and public culture that was suspicious of corporate private enterprise. This deprived big business of a secure grip on the administration of economic mobilization, such as occurred in France. Large firms did exercise significant influence over defence production, in contrast to medium manufacturers. But the political pretensions of the latter, expressed in the WICs, helped to reinforce a public antipathy to big business that was not reproduced elsewhere to the same extent. The WICs also represented a challenge to government direction of the war effort. Late in 1916, Riabushinskii and his followers called for the overthrow of the old regime. Popular hostility to big business and to tsarist rule was compounded by the failure to adopt a strategy of industrial mobilization that incorporated organized labour. This strategy had been adopted in Germany and France. In Russia, nothing was further from the minds of government bureaucrats or the industrial oligarchy.

After the February revolution, an attempt was made by big business to negotiate with organized labour, but this was frustrated by the deteriorating economic crisis. Employers were exposed to the wrath of workers. Some employers sought to align themselves with the government, but the Provisional Government favoured increased regulation, rather than its abandonment and – as in Germany – big business resisted this strategy. Eventually, relations between industrialists and workers became sharply polarized, the former wishing to maintain the economic power of capital and achieve ideological hegemony, the latter seeking to expropriate privately owned assets on the grounds that private enterprise had lost whatever legitimacy it possessed. By the autumn, these conflicts were being played out at the level of the state, moving it (in William Rosenberg's words) 'from a place of mediation to a source of partisan outcomes'.

Important issues remain unclear in the history of Russia's industrialists before and during 1917. Two may be singled out. We still know little about the personal fortunes of Russian business leaders. By the early twentieth century, Western European financiers and (to a lesser extent) industrialists commanded huge wealth, having supplanted large landowners as the owners of spectacular fortunes. What of the corresponding situation in Russia, and how did Russia's business elite dispose of its wealth?

Second, historians have concentrated upon the broad conflict between capital and labour. But this has been at the neglect of interaction between industrialists, financiers and technical specialists. The industrial entrepreneur had to deal with managers, scientists and engineers, company accountants, and lawyers, who possessed professional training and claimed the right to advise on business strategy. How rarefied a sphere did the business elite inhabit? Were employers aware of their potential vulnerability to these competing sources of expertise and authority, which could claim a 'disinterested' stake in the development of industry?

Further reading

Berlin P. A., *Russkaia burzhuaziia v staroe i novoe vremia* (Moscow, Kniga, 1922).

Bokhanov A. N., *Delovaia elita Rossii 1914 g.* (Moscow, Institut rossiiskoi istorii RAN, 1994).

Diakin V. S., *Russkaia burzhuaziia i tsarizm v gody pervoi mirovoi voiny, 1914–1917* (Leningrad, Nauka, 1967).

Eley G. and Blackbourn D., *The Peculiarities of German History: Bourgeois Society and Politics in Nineteenth Century Germany* (Oxford, Oxford University Press, 1984).

Feldman G. D., *Army, Industry and Labor in Germany, 1914–1918* (Princeton, Princeton University Press, 1966).

Fridenson P., ed., *The French Home Front, 1914–1918* (Providence, Berg, 1992).

Galili Z., 'Commercial-Industrial Circles in Revolution: The failure of "Industrial Progressivism"', in E. R. Frankel *et al.*, eds., *Revolution in Russia: Reassessments of 1917* (Cambridge, Cambridge University Press, 1992), pp. 188–216.

Gindin I. F., 'Russkaia burzhuaziia v period kapitalizma, ee razvitie i osobennosti', *Istoriia SSSR* 2 (1962), pp. 57–80, and 3 (1962), pp. 37–60.

Haumann H., *Kapitalismus im zaristischen Staat, 1900–1917* (Königstein, Hain, 1980).

Kocka J., *Facing Total War: German Society, 1914–1918*, English edn. (Leamington Spa, Berg, 1984).

Laverychev V. Ia., *Po tu storonu barrikad: iz istorii bor'by moskovskoi burzhuazii s revoliutsiei* (Moscow, Mysl', 1967).

McDaniel T., *Autocracy, Capitalism and Revolution in Russia* (Berkeley, University of California Press, 1988).

Owen T. C., 'Impediments to a Bourgeois Consciousness in Russia, 1880–1905: Estate Structure, Ethnic Diversity, and Economic Regionalism', in E. W. Clowes *et al.*, eds., *Between Tsar and People: Educated Society and the Quest for Public Identity in Late Imperial Russia* (Princeton, Princeton University Press, 1991).

Rieber A. J., *Merchants and Entrepreneurs in Imperial Russia* (Chapel Hill, University of North Carolina Press, 1982).

Roosa R. A., 'Russian Industrialists during World War I', in G. Guroff and F. V. Carstensen, eds., *Entrepreneurship in Imperial Russia and the Soviet Union* (Princeton, Princeton University Press, 1983), pp. 159–87.

Rosenberg W. G., 'Social Mediation and State Construction(s) in Revolutionary Russia', *Social History* 19 (1994), pp. 169–88.

Shepelev L. E., *Tsarizm i burzhuaziia v 1904–1914 gg.* (Leningrad, Nauka, 1987).

Siegelbaum L. H., *The Politics of Industrial Mobilization in Russia, 1914–1917: A Study of the War-Industries Committees* (London, Macmillan, 1983).

Volobuev P. V., *Proletariat i burzhuaziia Rossii v 1917 godu* (Moscow, Nauka, 1964).

Soldiers and Sailors

EVAN MAWDSLEY

World War and revolution

'One can say, without any exaggeration, that there has never in world history been another revolution and civil war in which the "military factor" played such a decisive role as it did in Russia in 1917–1922.' It is in fact hard to disagree with this argument – made in a 1993 'round table' by the Russian historian L. M. Gavrilov. The Russian revolution, an extraordinary event, took place in an equally extraordinary context. It began in the thirty-first month of the Great War, during which the imperial government mobilized no fewer than 15.5 million men.

On the eve of 1914 the 'Russian steamroller', with a peacetime (pre-mobilization) strength of 1,400,000, could be relied on as a defender of the autocracy against external and internal threats. The army had saved the autocracy in 1905–06. This regular army no longer existed in 1917, and arguably the fate of the autocracy – and even of the 1917 Provisional Government – was decided in 1914–15 on the battlefields of East Prussia and Poland. In the 17 months up to December 1915 the army lost 320,000 killed and mortally wounded and another 1,550,000 captured or missing. The best junior officers and NCOs were lost, along with those age cohorts who had been most effectively socialized into service life. Elite Guards and Cossack units also suffered especially badly. After 1915 an army still existed, indeed a much larger force, but its effectiveness and reliability were in almost inverse proportion to its size.

By November 1916 the active army – the four army groups (*fronty*) on the German–Austrian front, plus the Caucasus Army Group – had expanded to an astonishing, and unsupportable, 6,960,000 men. A further 2,265,000 were in the rear-echelon, the 12 internal military districts (*voennye okruga*) with their hundreds of garrisons. Although this strength had been achieved partly by calling up the younger annual 'classes' as they came of age, the bulk were older men. Even the trained reservists called up in

1914–15 could have completed their three years of active service over a decade previously (the effective period of reserve liability period was 15 years). Much worse were the untrained second-line reserve, the *ratniki*, who had not been balloted for pre-war service or who had had exemptions. The worst were the so-called 'second-category' *ratniki* – untrained men with family responsibilities. By the autumn of 1916 even the older members of this category, aged from 32 to 41, were being called up, a mass of 1,070,000 men who were neither effective fighters nor defenders of the *status quo*. Russia was not unique in the dilution of its pre-war army; indeed, as a proportion of total population Germany mobilized for active service more than twice – and France three times – as many men. Russia was, however, less able politically and economically to take the strain.

The February 1917 revolution was not initiated by the army, less still by the anti-war sentiment of the soldiers, but the inability of the Petrograd garrison to contain the civilian street disturbances was critical. Not only was the swollen garrison of 180,000 unwilling to act, but this garrison did not have any first-class units. The unique features of the wartime situation also included the absence of the emperor, 400 miles away at the Mogilev GHQ (*Stavka*), and the support by the army high command for a change in the person of the ruler. However, even more important than the contribution of the soldiers to the revolution was the impact which the first, localized, revolution had on the army. The collapse of the autocracy was central, more because it undermined authority in general than because of any specific act of the tsar's successors. Order Number One of the Petrograd Soviet, for example, authorized committee control, but changes took place spontaneously at regimental level. Nor was the upheaval the product of agitation among the troops by the Bolsheviks and other radical groups; they had at the outset few supporters and virtually no members in the active forces. Likewise a German policy of subversion can be ruled out as a major factor.

Various general explanations for developments in the army have been put forward. Allan Wildman's magisterial two-volume work, *The End of the Russian Imperial Army*, is the starting point for any understanding of what happened among the soldiers. He stressed the almost 'elemental', spontaneous nature of the crisis that was going on, the schism in Russian society, and the alienation of the mass of peasant conscripts, not just from the autocracy, but from 'cultured' Russia in general. (Recently Leopold Haimson has also made much of peasant hatred of 'superordinate' bodies.) Most original is Wildman's depiction of those men from the intelligentsia and the peasantry who found an identity in the war, and who formed a 'committee class' staffing the upper echelons of the newly elected committees. In contrast, Mikhail Frenkin's two Russian-language works stressed the importance of Bolshevik manipulation. What is certain is that all along the front, and deep in the rear, there ensued a spontaneous disintegration, itself a result of the wartime watering down of the army. It is useful to distinguish between 'democratization' (organizing units on a non-hierarchical principle, e.g.

committee control) and 'politicization' (the larger development of an interest in national political issues, with the penetration of the soldiers' milieu by civilian political activists – usually socialist or nationalist). One followed the other. The army command, and to a degree the Provisional Government, placed their hopes in an offensive to restore a commitment to the war, but the June 1917 offensive failed in both military and political terms. Meanwhile the rear garrisons slipped increasingly outside anyone's control. The July Days in Petrograd were only the most dramatic of a series of confrontations. The failure of General Kornilov's attempted 'action' in August 1917, moving reliable troops to Petrograd to destroy the influence of the Soviet, was trebly important: it finally broke the authority of the *Stavka*, it demonstrated the lack of support for the Provisional Government among the soldiers, and it further alienated them.

The sailors played a highly visible part, but the navy was unlike the army and its radicalization had a different source. The argument about the army is that it was transformed, 'diluted' and potentially 'revolutionized' by high casualties and wartime expansion. Ironically, the navy had suffered only slight losses in the World War. But the battle fleet and training detachments – at Kronstadt – were demoralized by inactivity. It was also important that the sailors tended to come from a working-class background. Looking at the broad picture, what emerges is that the relatively small number of sailors proved so significant because the Russian capital happened to be a sea port; they were also less politically 'neutral' than the soldiers, more mobile and more concentrated.

By October 1917 the Russian armed forces were apparently incapable of large-scale combat operations, and they could not be used to implement the will of the government. There is some debate about how 'revolutionary' the soldiers were – although in the Constituent Assembly elections they voted for radical parties. In major formations like the Northern and Western Army Groups the Bolsheviks received much the largest share of the vote – 470,000 out of 840,000 in the former and 650,000 out of 980,000 in the latter. In the Baltic Fleet the Bolsheviks won 43,000 out of 69,000. The pattern in the rear was also striking. In the vote in gubernia towns (i.e. province capitals) the urban garrisons were often much more likely to vote for – and support – the Bolsheviks than were the town's civilians, not to mention the gubernia's rural hinterland. But the army was also clearly not a police force for *whoever* was in power. Governments would have to fend off challenges by political means, or they would go under, and that is what happened to Kerensky.

The civil war

The overthrow of the Provisional Government did not mean that Russian soldiers ceased to be an important political force. Indeed, in the three years that followed October the Red Army was the largest and most successful institution in Soviet Russia; it was the favoured child of the government and came to serve as a model for other institutions.

The peacetime Imperial Army was destroyed in 1914–15. The swollen wartime horde which succeeded it was destroyed in the winter of 1917–18, and indeed its demobilization was a condition of Brest-Litovsk. The impact of the return of radicalized servicemen to their home communities during that winter was great; on the other hand, the evaporation of the army, especially in the rear garrisons, reduced the Bolsheviks' base of armed support, and explains the acute difficulties which they faced from the spring of 1918.

The events of late 1917 and early 1918 had completely smashed the structure of the old army; with the sole exception of the Latvian rifle regiments, the Soviet government carried no units over from the old army. In a sense, this whole process, which remains to be studied in detail, made the creation of new armies in 1918 more difficult. Tradition and the military mystique had been ground away for most of the army in 1914–15, and were finished off by the democratization of 1917. On the other hand, the raising of forces was made easier by the militarization of the First World War. The early Red Army, even when organized on the 'volunteer' principle in the spring and summer of 1918, evidently contained a high proportion of veterans. Once general conscription began in late 1918 it concentrated on the six age classes (1893–98) called up from October 1914 to February 1917 for the World War. Wartime equipment and uniforms were available to supply this smaller force, and commanders with some training were available in the form of cadre and wartime officers.

The Red Army became the largest institution in the new Soviet state. Although smaller than the wartime Imperial Army, it exceeded in size the pre-1914 standing army and the armed forces of most other countries. It is often suggested that the Red Army expansion followed from the loss of Kazan in August 1918, but the expansion also had much to do with the opportunities and threats of a world where the Central Powers had been defeated. The Red Army was, like its Imperial predecessor, a peasant army. Initial expectation of a class-based proletarian army was discarded as soon as the numbers began to grow at the end of 1918. Orlando Figes has stressed the 'extensive recruitment' for this army, recruiting as large a slice of the rural population as possible in order to cope with loss from desertion. To this might be added a more general notion, held both by the Imperial and Red commands, that victory could be won by overwhelming weight of numbers. That was probably a correct approach. In any event the army swelled from 370,000 in July 1918, to 2,320,000 in July 1919, and to 4,400,000 in July 1920. Of these only about a third to a half were in the 'active forces', i.e. 1,310,000 in July 1919 and 1,540,000 in June 1920. In contrast, the number of workers in state-controlled industry was only about 1,250,000. The Russian Communist Party itself numbered only 600–700,000, at least half of whom were involved in the army.

The Red Army was badly supplied and riddled with sickness. Orlando Figes has estimated that there were 3,710,000 deserters in the 1918–20 period. Even though perhaps 90 per cent of these were only absent from their units or depots for a few weeks, it was a vast number. Sickness was a much more serious factor in the civil war than in the World War, with 6,240,000 soldiers recorded as being taken ill, and it presumably accounted for a large proportion of the 620,000 who died of 'wounds and sickness'; 280,000 Red Army soldiers died from typhus alone in 1918–20. Compared to this, only 160,000 soldiers were recorded as having died from sickness in the World War, out of a much larger strength. Vladimir Brovkin has drawn attention to a number of military mutinies during the civil war, especially in the depots. But the soldiers stopped short of general mutiny, and there did not ensue even the general chaos that had prevailed in the army under the Provisional Government. Above all the Soviet government succeeded where the Provisional Government had not: it created a fighting army.

The Kronstadt uprising of March 1921 was the exception that proved the rule. This was an armed uprising that took place at the naval base off Petrograd. Aside from being the last, it was also the most important anti-Communist mutiny in the Red armed forces. It involved a big garrison – 26,000 men – and was at least partly political (the mutineers adopted an anti-Communist manifesto). It appears to have occurred spontaneously, triggered by the massive strike wave in Petrograd in February 1921, but there is some evidence for the involvement of an anti-Soviet underground. Over 2,100 men were sentenced to death after the revolt was put down by a frontal assault across the ice, and one source gives Red losses in the Petrograd Military District as 1,900 killed and missing and 1,200 wounded and sick. In January 1994 a Presidential Commission exonerated the Kronstadt rebels.

It was important that, even after Kronstadt, Red soldiers still could be relied on to put down the peasant disorders in 1921–22, along with other paramilitary detachments. The army was substantially reduced, with the ground forces at 1,200,000 in January 1922 (down from 3,880,000 in June 1920, and below the level of the pre-war standing army). There was substantial fighting in this period, less, to be sure, than in the 'conventional' fighting of 1918–20, but it still brought 10,000 killed in battle and 12,000 wounded. Deserters numbered 230,000 in 1921, of whom 30,000 were in units fighting anti-Soviet uprisings; total deserters in 1922 were still 110,000.

Conclusion

Of all the social groups in the Russian revolution and civil war the soldiers and sailors are still among the most neglected by historians. This is partly because of the nature of the sources. It is also partly because such *déclassé* elements do not fall into neat categories; both social historians and 'official' Soviet historians have felt more comfortable with industrial workers and – to a lesser degree – peasants. Koenker *et al.*'s *Party, State, and Society in the Russian Civil War: Explorations in Social History* (1989) had 16 specialist articles, not one of them devoted to fighting men. The experience of 1914 to 1922 indicates that the soldiers and sailors were far from an undifferentiated mass of alienated peasants, and much more research is required to understand their political and combat motivation.

Why did soldiers and sailors behave differently at different times? Popular psychology was an important dimension. John Bushnell has stressed the importance of the tsar myth, rooted in peasant psychology, in explaining the fluctuation of 'mutiny' *in* the army and 'repression' *by* the army in 1905–06. Clearly the perception of authority was important a decade later; the abdication (and murder) of Nicholas II were also critical, both in 1917 and – for the Whites – in the civil war. The Provisional Government could not, by definition, establish such authority, and the White dictatorships were no substitute. The Soviet government for all its faults and weaknesses claimed permanence and had a historic base in Moscow.

All things being equal, motivation to fight for and support a government is easier if there is a cause to fight for. Most Russian soldiers were patriotic, but Russia's positive objectives in the World War were not clear. Although they had occupied Poland, the Central Powers were not threatening the existence of Russia and its population (as the Axis would 25 years later). The authorities' situation in 1917 was not helped by the enemy's canny tactic of restraint from offensive operations; the soldiers could not easily be rallied around a 'fatherland in danger' policy, especially as some elements of the Provisional Government were pinning their hopes on a peace reached by democratic-diplomatic means. On the other hand, a simple sense of national peril was not enough, as the abortive Soviet attempt in February 1918 to organize a defence against the German advance would show. In the civil war, Communist propaganda made much of the external danger, but the threatened restoration of landowners and the recapture of 'Russian' territory provided a more tangible cause. Figes says that the White danger was a key factor making the peasants of central Russia rally around the Soviet cause. To be fair, the enemies of the Soviet 'cause' were less substantial than those of its tsarist predecessor: lightly equipped White armies of at most 100,000 need to be compared to Austro-German forces numbering – in 1916 – 1,600,000 frontline troops. The strength of authority and identity with a cause could, of course, be 'artificially' stimulated. Not enough is yet known about patriotic propaganda in 1914–16, but Kerensky's speaking tours of the front in 1917 proved insufficient. The Communists, for their part, devoted many more resources to influencing the mood of their soldiers.

Effective armies are not simply armed hordes. Successful (and loyal) armies also benefit from core elites. The old elites were lost in the first stages of the war. The tsarist and Provisional governments did get some support from the wartime officers (*praporshchiki*) but this was not enough to provide a backbone, and neither were the so-called 'battalions of death'. From the Provisional Government's point of view, elite units were not to be trusted, and the Kornilov action justified that suspicion. The most successful White army, that of General Denikin and later of General Wrangel, relied on elite officer units and larger formations built around veterans of the early civil war campaigns. The Red Army benefited from the Latvian riflemen in the first stages of the civil war, and the First Cavalry Army in the later stages, but Communists provided an important backbone throughout.

Discipline structures – and democratization – are also important. The orthodox discipline of the Imperial Army was effective. Authority was much watered down in the army of 1915–16, but that army still functioned. Committee control after February 1917 was corrosive of both military effectiveness and political reliability. 'Conscious discipline' of a patriotic or class-based kind was ineffective. The advocates of conscious discipline were dominant in 1917; fortunately for the Communists they were defeated in the intra-party debate of 1919 between Trotsky and the 'Military Opposition'. To be sure, the Soviets still took great pains to distance themselves from the mentality of the old regime. The army was the 'Workers' and Peasants' Red Army' (RKKA). The term *soldat*, at that time seen as a term of abuse, was replaced by 'Red Army man' (*krasnoarmeets*). But the stress was on discipline. Lenin eventually backed Trotsky: 'If you say that this is an autocratic feudal system and protest against saluting, then you will not get an army in which the middle peasant will fight.' The Communists in fact created a double or treble structure in the form of the ex-officer (*voenspets*), the commissar, and 'special' control (the OO and *osobistskaia rabota*). It also created for the Reds a body of men and women whose notion of what Mark von Hagen has called 'militarized socialism' would have an important impact on the later Soviet state. The Whites relied more on traditional discipline and a motivated elite. Both the Reds and the Whites were able to keep units together – although this did not prevent indiscipline against outsiders.

The Russian revolution was no more praetorian than it was proletarian, but without the presence of the soldiers and sailors the events of 1917 would have been very different. Furthermore, the motivation and organization of fighting men were crucial to the outcome of the struggle that followed over the next five years.

Further reading

Beskrovnyi L. G., *Armiia i flot Rossii v nachale XX v.: Ocherki voenno-ekonomicheskogo potentsiala* (Moscow, Nauka, 1986).

Brovkin V., *Behind the Front Lines of the Civil War: Political Parties and Social Movements in Russia, 1918–1922* (Princeton, Princeton University Press, 1994).

Bushnell J., *Mutiny amid Repression: Russian Soldiers in the Revolution of 1905* (Bloomington, University of Indiana Press, 1985).

Cherniaev V. Iu., ed., *Anatomiia revoliutsii. 1917 god v Rossii: massy, partii, vlast'* (St Petersburg, Glagol, 1994).

Ferro M., 'The Russian Soldier in 1917: Undisciplined, Patriotic, and Revolutionary', *Slavic Review* 30 (1971).

Figes O., 'The Red Army and Mass Mobilization during the Russian Civil War, 1918–1920', *Past and Present* 129 (1990).

Frenkin M., *Russkaia armiia i revoliutsiia: 1917–1918* (Munich, Logos, 1978).

von Hagen M., *Soldiers in the Proletarian Dictatorship: The Red Army and the Soviet Socialist State, 1917–1930* (Ithaca, Cornell University Press, 1990).

Haimson L., 'The Problem of Social Identities in Early Twentieth Century Russia', *Slavic Review* 47, 1 (1988), pp. 1–20.

Koenker D. P., Rosenberg, W. G. and Suny R. G., eds., *Party, State and Society in The Russian Civil War* (Bloomington, Indiana University Press, 1989).

'Kronshtadtskaia tragediia 1921 goda', *Voprosy Istorii* 4–7 (1994).

Mawdsley E., *The Russian Revolution and the Baltic Fleet* (London, Macmillan, 1978).

Mawdsley E., 'Soldiers and Sailors', in Robert Service, ed., *Society and Politics in the Russian Revolution* (Basingstoke, Macmillan, 1992).

Saul N., *Sailors in Revolt: The Russian Baltic Fleet in 1917* (Lawrence, Regents Press of Kansas, 1978).

Shchetinov Iu. A., 'Za kulisami Kronshtadtskogo vosstaniia 1921 goda', *Vestnik Moskovskogo universiteta: Istoriia* 2–3 (1995).

'VIII s"ezd RKP(b): Stenogramma zasedanii voennoi sektsii s"ezda 20 i 21 marta 1919 goda i zakrytogo zasedaniia s"ezda 21 marta 1919 goda', *Izvestiia TsK KPSS* 9 (1989).

White H., '1917 in the Rear Garrisons', in L. Edmondson and P. Waldron, eds., *Economy and Society in Russia and the Soviet Union, 1860–1930: Essays for Olga Crisp* (Basingstoke, Macmillan, 1992).

Wildman A. K., *The End of the Russian Imperial Army*, vol. 1: *The Old Army and the Soldiers' Revolt (March–April 1917)*; vol. 2: *The Road to Soviet Power and Peace* (Princeton, Princeton University Press, 1980, 1987).

Women and the Gender Question

BARBARA EVANS CLEMENTS

Defining the subject

'Women and the Russian revolution' is a vast subject, for more than one-half of adults in the Russian empire in 1917 were women. There is something a bit nonsensical in generalizing about the experience of so enormous an aggregation of human beings and perhaps something demeaning as well. No-one would set out to examine how 'men' experienced the Russian revolution, and yet historians today routinely treat 'women' as though this were a meaningful historical category. In fact, of course, it is, as their findings in recent decades indicate, but only if the term 'women' is carefully defined and its complexity fully understood.

In writing women's history, historians must first establish that there was a commonality in the experience of women in the Russian empire that can be profitably investigated. Women were, after all, as diverse in ethnicity, religion, social rank and place of residence as were men. They spoke different languages and worshipped different gods. Even among the ethnic Russians an enormous gulf separated the well-dressed aristocrat from the barefoot peasant. But all these women shared, across the space between them, one transcendent reality that shaped their lives as powerfully as did ethnicity or religion. That reality was patriarchy, a system of social organization that distributes power and status through hierarchies of men ranked by age and social position. Patriarchy justifies male authority by proclaiming that it is ordained by God and by nature. Women are situated in patriarchal systems according to their kinship to men; they gain power and status from seniority within their families and from those families' rank in society. Throughout the world, patriarchy has prevailed in great empires and so it was in the Russian empire in the early twentieth century. From the ancient cities of the Caucasus in the south to the fishing villages on the White Sea in the north, women lived in patriarchal societies that prescribed their subordination to men. As a consequence, there were commonalities in their experiences during the revolution that historians can explore.

There is another reason for studying the history of women that also derives from the effects of patriarchy, but here its effects are in the present rather than the past. Historians have been as affected by patriarchy as were their historical subjects. Until recently most of them accepted unquestioningly the belief, derived from patriarchal values, that women were historically insignificant. Women did not head governments (with the exception of a few, very singular, queens) and they did not overthrow governments; therefore, they did not make change. These beliefs could be sustained so long as historians concentrated their attention on political leaders, as historians of Russia were inclined to do. When women did appear in the documents of the past, the assumption that they were unimportant led historians to trivialize their activities or ignore them altogether. The result was a partial history, that is, a history with one-half of its participants left out. Studies need now be written about 'women' because women were not included in the studies that were written before.

And finally, women's history has given rise to an allied but different enterprise, the study of gender. Originally a grammatical term, gender now designates the ways in which human beings define male and female and then use those definitions to interpret much else in their world. Anthropologists, sociologists, economists, literary theorists and historians have found that gender is one of the most fundamental taxonomies in human consciousness, present in the cosmologies of all religions, in all social systems, in all definitions of the human yet documented. European culture has long associated the male with that which is rational, strong, dominant and transcendent, the female with that which is irrational, natural, nurturing and weak. These beliefs affected developments during the Russian revolution, but the study of gender as a historical category involves more than uncovering the workings of patriarchy. Analysing the multifariousness of gender understandings both complicates and expands our understanding of a host of historical phenomena, including the Russian revolution. What follows here will discuss recent findings in women's history, those on gender being still too fragmentary to consider at any length. I will conclude, however, with a few suggestions about how the study of gender should proceed.

The situation of women on the eve of the revolution

Peasant women

Before 1917 the vast majority of the female population of all the various ethnic groups in the Russian empire were peasants who lived in grinding poverty. Peasant women toiled under so many burdens that the nineteenth-century intelligentsia portrayed them as the quintessential symbols of the suffering of Russia under the tsars. Not only did they do back-breaking work for most of their lives, as did peasant men, but they also bore many babies, lost many of them to disease, and suffered abuse from the men in their communities and from the nobility. They were given very little access to formal education and had even fewer political and juridical rights than their menfolk. In the midst of all this hardship, however, there was also beauty. The lullabies and laments peasant women crooned, the stories they told of spirits that lurked in the forests, the symbols they embroidered on icon hangings, all testify to the rich culture of belief to which peasant women contributed. If they survived into middle age, they could win a place of respect in the village as senior females who wielded considerable authority over the sons, daughters and daughters-in-law of their extended families.

In the early twentieth century, peasant women still ordered their lives according to the cycles of the seasons and the traditions they had learned in childhood, despite the fact that change was flowing back and forth between the villages and the cities of the empire. Young peasant men were leaving rural areas to work as artisans or factory hands in the rapidly growing urban areas. Doctors, teachers, agronomists, and a host of other educated people intent on modernizing rural Russia were coming to the countryside. Peasant elders, male and female, eagerly bought manufactured goods – cloth, nails, cooking pots, lamps, brightly coloured pictures – but they did not welcome proposals to change the customs of the village, especially those customs that governed the position of women within the family and community. Some parents permitted their daughters to attend school for a few grades, a small number of women whose families could not provide for them migrated to find work in the cities, but most female peasants lived their lives much as their grandmothers had until the revolution.

Urban women

Meanwhile, in the cities, the situation of women was changing rapidly, in tune with similar developments throughout the European world. Women of the nobility and the middling ranks of urban society were becoming educated, entering the paid labour-force, and joining movements for reform. Recently scholars have probed much of this activity, examining the patterns of female migration to the city and the experiences of female factory and white-collar workers. They have also analysed the role of women in the intelligentsia and the crusades of Russia's feminists. This work has uncovered considerable similarities between the situation of urban women in Russia and elsewhere in Europe in the late nineteenth and early twentieth centuries. It has also revealed important differences that affected urban women's lives, particularly their efforts to improve their situation.

In the main these differences derive from Russia's history of powerful government and weak civil society. Before 1917 the recalcitrant, reactionary tsarist regime inhibited, when it did not prohibit, all social activism. The feminists and other reformers who worked in Great Britain, the United States and Scandinavia in the late nineteenth and early twentieth century drew support from an increasingly powerful commercial and professional elite. In Russia the business class was small because of the underdeveloped industrial economy. The intelligentsia, although noted for its advocacy of women's emancipation, did not have the authority of its counterparts in bourgeois democracies. Many of its members – educators, doctors, lawyers, and engineers in particular – worked for the very government that resisted reform. The intelligentsia was also split between socialists and liberals, a split that ran through the ranks of politically active women as well as men. The result was a weaker feminist movement than in Great Britain or the United States and a far greater female presence among revolutionaries. In the first decade of the twentieth century 10 to 15 per cent of the members of the Social-Democratic and Socialist-Revolutionary parties were women, the largest percentages of female membership among all of Europe's socialist organizations.

Women's participation in the revolution and the civil war

Tsarist politics climaxed in events of great significance in the history of the women of the empire, events in which women took an active part. The February revolution began with a massive demonstration led by female factory workers on 23 February, International Woman's Day. Thereafter women were often present in the crowds of demonstrators as well as on the rostrums where much of the political discussion of that momentous year took place. Contemporaries pointed to the political activism of women in 1917 as a sign of the utter bankruptcy of the regime, their unspoken assumption being that even the most passive element in Russian society had finally had enough. Others hailed women's participation as a sign that they were throwing off the bonds of poverty and patriarchy and asserting their right to be full members of the political community. Still others feared the spectacle of women marching through the streets presaged riot, disorder and anarchy. Sorting out what all the activity actually meant is one of the pressing tasks that historians of the revolution face today.

The activism of women did bespeak the depth of Russian society's disgust with tsarist rule, and it indicated as well a loosening of social controls. From February 1917 until the end of the civil war women from all walks of life became politically engaged in ways that would have been impossible under the old regime. Female revolutionaries worked within their movements, as did female Kadets (albeit in far lower numbers). Blue- and white-collar workers joined political parties, organized exclusively female trade unions and professional associations, demonstrated, attended meetings, and voted. Peasant women participated in the confiscation of the landlords' land and in village meetings where that land was repartitioned. They also asserted themselves within their families by urging their husbands to leave their parents' households in order to set up farming on their own. When the civil war began, women worked as nurses, spies and couriers for both sides, and the Bolsheviks also employed them as soldiers and political workers. In the fall of 1920, 66,000 women were serving in the Red Army, making up 2 per cent of that force. Thirty thousand women joined the Communist Party from 1917 to 1921. Jubilant at their new freedom, women across the fallen empire asserted that the revolution had done away with patriarchy once and for all.

The consequences of the revolution

Analysing the problem

The participation of women in the turmoil of 1917 to 1921 did not effect as much change in gender arrangements as its proponents hoped and its critics feared. To understand why, historians must see the revolution not as a linear sequence of actions and consequences but rather as a jumble of dissolution and reconstruction. People responded to the collapse of the old order in a variety of ways. Some seized the new, others protected the old, many tried to negotiate a middle course between radical change and blind reaction. Ordinary folk as well as revolutionaries assaulted patriarchy, but they did not dismantle it, choosing instead to jettison some of its key ideas – for example, the peasant's duty to obey the nobles – but to preserve others, chief among them the wife's duty to obey her husband.

Analytic difficulties increase when one considers that components of societies change at different speeds. People have altered political and economic structures very quickly in the last 200 years, but the same has not been true of systems of belief such as patriarchy. Patriarchy has changed, but it has done so slowly, over centuries. Some patriarchal values (e.g., the rights of monarchs) weakened long before others (e.g., the rights of fathers to control juvenile sons); the weakening of some (e.g., the power of fathers over adult sons) actually led in some places to the strengthening of others (e.g., the power of the husband within the family). In Russia, the process of adjusting traditional patriarchy to the more egalitarian ethos of the nineteenth century had begun long before the Bolsheviks took power, sometimes assisted, more often hindered by the tsarist government. The Bolsheviks declared their intent to abolish patriarchy altogether, but they stumbled up against public resistance because they were more radical than the great majority of the population, even in the cities. They were also divided in their own counsels, with their leaders espousing more change in women's situation than did their rank-and-file. The result was a complex process of interaction that multiplies analytical problems for historians.

The first step in dealing with these difficulties is to break down the category 'women' into more manageable sub-categories. The women most likely to vote, join political parties, and hold office lived in Russia's cities, where patriarchy had been challenged by notions of individual freedom and by the imperatives of an industrializing economy before 1917. Politically active women came from the European ethnic groups, and, within these groups, from the nobility, from the middling ranks of society (merchants, clerks, professionals, government workers), and, to a lesser extent, from the working class. Fifty-seven per cent of the women who became members of the Communist Party between 1917 and 1921 were from the middle and upper levels of Russian society, 37 per cent were from the proletariat, and 5 per cent were peasants. The *Bol'shevichki* became the most powerful of all the activist women of the revolution, for as members of the victorious party they went on to play a significant part in the Soviet system generally and in programmes to emancipate women in particular. In their origins, however, they were typical of the tens of thousands who had reached out for the new freedoms offered by the revolution.

Consequences for peasant women

Meanwhile, peasant women, the great majority of the female population, remained distanced from their urban sisters. Caucasian, Asian and Siberian peoples were the most removed from the revolutionary process, so among them traditional patriarchal institutions remained strong well into the Soviet period. Those who lived closer to the revolution concentrated their efforts on weakening the power of the patriarchs within the peasant family and strengthening the village itself. Peasant women were happy to confiscate the property of the landlords in 1917 and then to press for households of their own, away from the domination of their in-laws, but they were also inclined to perceive revolution and civil war as threats to their fragile security. Food was in increasingly short supply, disease ran rampant, armies called men away. To defend themselves from ever greater hardship, peasant women fought off incursions that threatened the village community, including appeals from the Bolsheviks that they emancipate themselves. They spread rumours that the Bolsheviks planned to steal babies away or 'nationalize' women and they attacked young agitators sent in by the party Women's Department (the *Zhenotdel*), because they feared losing their few remaining defences. It is not fair to charge, as the Bolsheviks did, that peasant women resisted their appeals because they were ignorant and backward. Rather, they were conservative in the purest sense of that term. They wished to conserve from further dissolution the community in which they sheltered, even if that meant conserving at the same time family values that permitted men to control women in ways the women themselves often found objectionable.

The hold of traditional society on female peasants weakened only in the 1920s when the Bolsheviks, having consolidated their power in the centre of the old empire, pushed outward to establish control over the vast hinterland and made war on peasant culture in the process. The Bolsheviks transmitted new notions about women's position in society to the countryside, challenged the structure of village authority, and then, with the collectivization of agriculture in the late 1920s, declared all-out war on that structure. Again peasant women fought back, tens of thousands of them rising up against the collectivizers, but this time they were defeated. By ruthlessly attacking uncooperative village elders and by empowering networks of government officials and the peasants who worked under them, the government destroyed the patriarchal practices that had bound older and younger men together. Clientage and patronage took the place of kinship and age as the method of distributing power among men in the countryside. The elements of patriarchy that governed gender relations lingered on, however, for within the family peasant men continued to exercise considerable control over their wives, while on the farms men ran the machinery and an even greater share of the menial labour fell to women.

Consequences for women in the cities

The Bolsheviks had a more immediate impact on urban women's situation, because they were more securely in control of the cities. Within a year of seizing power, the government had issued a new constitution decreeing political rights without gender discrimination and a family law code legalizing divorce. It had also drafted policies establishing publicly funded maternity care and regulating women's employment so as to promote their access to paid labour while protecting their reproductive health. Throughout 1918 and into 1919 a group of female Bolsheviks, led by I. F. Armand, A. M. Kollontai and K. N. Samoilova, lobbied for even more attention to be paid to women's issues. By 1919, arguing that the revolution could only succeed if the Bolsheviks made an effort to win women's support, they had secured authorization to establish the *Zhenotdel*, charged with spreading the party's message to working-class and peasant women.

The Communist Party's programme to emancipate women, formulated along with *Zhenotdel* during the civil-war years, led to major change in the lives of people in the nascent Soviet Union and later in communist-governed countries around the world. It was one of the revolution's most important products. The central components of the programme were the outlawing of gender discrimination in public institutions, the funding of social services (daycare centres, cafeterias, laundries) to alleviate housework, and the propagation of principles of women's equality. The government also made considerable efforts to draw women into the paid labour-force, establishing training programmes and, in the early 1930s, setting quotas for female employment. Soviet people seized these new opportunities enthusiastically. By 1940 over 90 per cent of urban females under the age of 50 were literate and women made up 38 per cent of the non-agricultural labour-force. Eighty-two per cent of those entering the paid labour-force for the first time in the 1930s were women. Their wages also rose, from an average of less than 50 per cent of male pay before 1917 to two-thirds that of men by 1930. To promote these changes the party disseminated in magazines, newspapers, novels, poems, radio broadcasts and films the message that women were equal members of society and deserving of respect and solicitude.

The analysis of patriarchy that underlay the party's policies played a central role in shaping the formulation and implementation of those policies. According to Marxist theory, men derived their power to oppress women from their ownership of property. Consequently, the full emancipation of women could occur only when the workers' revolution had abolished private property. Thereafter the socializing of housework and childcare would enable women to participate in the public world as men's equals. Many critics have pointed out that this economically determinist interpretation reduced patriarchy to a derivative set of values and, by so doing, enabled Marxist theoreticians to underestimate the power of patriarchy as well as to ignore its continuing influence over them. And influence them it did. Marxists, with the important exception of the small number of Marxist feminists, always assumed that the primary political actors would be men. Men would lead the revolutionary parties; male factory workers would make the revolution; then male leaders would take the steps necessary to free women. Marxist parties everywhere were overwhelmingly male in membership, as were the governments they built after they were victorious. The Russian Social Democrats honoured more fully than other Social Democrats their commitment to women's emancipation in the pre-revolutionary period, and the Bolsheviks followed through by making very substantial reforms when in power, but never did the leaders critically examine the assumption they made that men should lead. Thus they preserved the core tenet of patriarchy in their political institutions, even while proclaiming their war on patriarchy. Once women had gained access to education and to the paid labour-force in the Soviet Union, once the services to help with housework had been established, then party propagandists declared that gender equality existed. Thereafter, they blamed shortcomings on the recalcitrance of backward individuals, rather than on systemic problems resulting in part from their own inadequate understanding of patriarchy.

The limitations in the Soviet programme of women's emancipation are now as well known as its achievements. Women obtained legal rights and made considerable strides in education and employment, but they remained burdened by domestic responsibilities. When the government chose to spend its very limited funds on tanks rather than daycare centres or cafeterias, women tended the children and made the soup. Soviet women thus came to play a dual role in industrialization: they worked in the factories and they did the domestic labour that kept the factory workers fed, clothed and able to work. They also contended with the widespread assumption that men should control the public world, while women took care of their families. The party was endorsing these ideas by the mid-1930s. In so doing it renounced the egalitarian visions of such Bolshevik feminists as Kollontai to embrace instead gender ideas that prevailed throughout the industrialized European world.

The complexity of the change process

The similarity of Soviet values to those elsewhere suggests that the limited consequences of the revolution for women did not result solely from the Communist Party's failure to make good its promises. The willingness of the party to compromise its own founders' aspirations was undoubtedly responsible for the shortages of daycare centres and the unavailability of contraceptives, to name only two major difficulties with which Soviet women coped. But the persistence of modified patriarchalism resulted as well from the behaviour of millions of ordinary people who adapted old values to changed conditions. The belief that the urban woman should be a homemaker and nurturer, sustaining a refuge for the family in the midst of an alienating city, has appeared wherever industrialization has occurred in the last two centuries. It applies age-old notions that women as well as men have revered to a new world that men as well as women find unsettling. The cities of the early Soviet period were particularly unpleasant, short of all the amenities of urban life, stalked by the minions of a politically repressive regime. Soviet people who had to cope with such places did as the residents of Manchester had done a century earlier and idealized a domestic order in which women were the caretakers and men the masters. This was not Russia's old patriarchy, but a revised one based in the nuclear rather than the extended family. It reduced the powers of husbands and in-laws from what they had been in the past, while encouraging women to be educated participants in the public world. The novelist F. I. Panferov summed up the new ideal in his 1936 novel, *The Village Bruski*: 'A woman should . . . be a happy mother and create a serene home atmosphere, without, however, abandoning work for the common welfare. She should know how to combine all these things while matching her husband's performance on the job.'

The process of adapting traditional ideas about women to the circumstances of the city was not initiated by the party. Rather it had begun in the nineteenth century, a Russian current within a river of social change running through the European world. The party could speed up the changes in notions about women, divert them, even slow them down, but it was always also borne along by them. The forces that set the current flowing were those transforming societies around the world since the eighteenth century – industrialization, urbanization and the rapid international transmission of ideas. These forces made the situation in which the party did its work among women and then remade it even while the party was going about its business, with the consequence that the party was always both acting and acted upon. The 'happy mother' who 'matches her husband's performance on the job' is the creature of this complex process. That she has appeared since as an ideal for women in liberal democratic societies is yet more evidence that she is a product of far more than the machinations of an exploitative regime.

A history of the revolution's consequences for women therefore must range far beyond the chronological boundaries of 1917–21 and the policies of the leadership, notwithstanding the fact that the party and the revolutionary era were extremely important in shaping Soviet developments. Historians must also consider the actions and reactions of millions of women, taken collectively as the subjects of patriarchal restraints, but also analysed in all their diversity. They must then integrate these findings with an analysis of those major social changes associated with the transition from agrarian and rural to urban and industrialized society. Only such a complex conceptualization of women's history will do justice to the experience of so many million individuals.

Future research

The agenda for future research in this field is enormous, for bountiful archival resources are as yet unexamined and major topics have not been explored. Historians have begun to analyse the policies of the party and the work of the feminist women within it from 1917 to the Stalin period, but much more should be done. The operation of the *Zhenotdel*, the Komsomol and the trade unions at the national and local levels and the decision-making processes within the party regarding women's issues have not been studied. Nor have the effects of government programmes been examined in sufficient detail. The work of the schools, of the healthcare system, of job-training efforts are all important topics.

The huge category 'women' must be broken down by examining the experience during the revolutionary period of various groups. Among the female activists about whom very little is known are the trade unionists, the *soldatki,* the feminists, the SRs, and the Kadets. Nurses, clerks and other participants in the civil war on both sides should be examined, as should groups, for instance teachers and nuns, who attempted to weather the storm without joining Reds or Whites. In the 1920s there were all-female co-operatives and collective farms, as well as student clubs and other political, social and cultural organizations. None has yet found its historian.

There is also a pressing need to document the responses of women who were not involved in formal organizations. Historians probing the archives have uncovered evidence of extraordinary levels of female resistance to collectivization in the late 1920s. That there was similar activity during the civil war is suggested by numerous references to peasant women fighting with outsiders. Other types of collective behaviour, for example demonstrations, riots and mass migrations, should also be studied. Examining the attitudes of women towards the development of social policy in the 1920s, as evidenced for instance in debates over sexual love conducted among young people, will further illuminate women's understandings of the revolution.

Historians must analyse the ways in which responses differed according to women's ethnicity, social rank and place of residence. Generalizations that purport to cover people as remote from one another as the Siberians, Georgians, Russians and Uzbeks may be sustained by more detailed research into the history of those peoples in the revolutionary era. More probably they will be undermined by evidence that women were deeply affected by their cultures and the ways in which challenges to traditional society entered their worlds.

Only very recently has gender been considered a productive way of analysing Russian history. The society's basic understandings of male and female on the eve of the revolution have received some attention, but no major studies have analysed the shifts of gender values after 1917. There was a pervasive concern in the early 1920s that the revolution had sprung men loose from social controls, and much discussion ensued of ways to define male responsibility in a socialist society. These debates about what masculinity meant should be analysed and compared to the complementary debates over femininity. Some scholarship exists on the revised notions of femininity that had developed by the 1930s, but much more needs to be done, particularly regarding popular as opposed to officially promulgated ideas. Very fruitful cross-cultural comparisons could then be made by aligning these studies with similar work on societies elsewhere.

Studying gender involves more than examining notions of the masculine and feminine; it is a way of employing those notions to explore other values, concepts and mores. For example, the Bolsheviks' collective identity was highly masculinized from the faction's earliest days. Bolsheviks proclaimed themselves to be hard, resolute, pragmatic, rational and emotionally controlled. Did this masculinization increase during the civil war? Was there a relationship between masculinized values and autocratic behaviour? A more general, but equally promising line of inquiry would study the ways in which gendered understandings suffused the revolutionary experience, were employed by various groups for various purposes, and shifted across time.

The existence of such a wealth of unexplored topics supports the proposition with which this chapter began, that women and gender should be central analytical categories, not peripheral ones. As historians push ahead with research that examines both women's history and the workings of gender ideas in Russia's past, they will demonstrate the fruitfulness of such lines of inquiry and undermine thereby the patriarchal assumptions of male superiority that have for so long affected the writing of history itself.

Further reading

Clements B. E., *Bolshevik Feminist: The Life of Aleksandra Kollontai* (Bloomington, IN, Indiana University Press, 1979).

Clements B. E., *Daughters of Revolution: a History of Women in the USSR* (Arlington Heights, IL, Harlan Davidson, 1994).

Clements B. E., *Bolshevik Women* (Cambridge, Cambridge University Press, 1997).

Clements B. E., Engel B. A., and Worobec C. D., eds., *Russia's Women: Accommodation, Resistance, Transformation* (Berkeley, University of California Press, 1991).

Elwood R. C., *Inessa Armand, Revolutionary and Feminist* (Cambridge, Cambridge University Press, 1992).

Engelstein L., *The Keys to Happiness: Sex and the Search for Modernity in Fin-de-Siècle Russia* (Ithaca, Cornell University Press, 1992).

Farnsworth B., *Alexandra Kollontai: Socialism, Feminism and the Bolshevik Revolution* (Stanford, Stanford University Press, 1980).

Farnsworth B. and Viola L., eds., *Russian Peasant Women* (Oxford, Oxford University Press, 1992).

Goldman W., *Women, the State and Revolution: Soviet Family Policy and Social Life, 1917–1936* (Cambridge, Cambridge University Press, 1993).

Kruks S., Rapp R. and Young M. B., eds., *Promissory Notes: Women in the Transition to Socialism* (New York, Monthly Review Press, 1989).

Lapidus G. W., *Women in Soviet Society* (Berkeley, University of California Press, 1978).

Stites R., *The Women's Liberation Movement in Russia: Feminism, Nihilism, and Bolshevism 1860–1930*, 2nd edn (Princeton, Princeton University Press, 1991).

Workers

SERGEI V. IAROV

The workers are one of the political symbols of the Russian revolution, and historians of various persuasions consider them the leading force in both the anti-monarchist and the Bolshevik revolutions of 1917. Yet the political differences which existed among the workers, the weakness of their trade union and other organizations, and the indifference of a significant proportion of them to the revolution cannot be ignored.

Size, composition and the question of the peasant-worker

The data on the numbers and composition of the working class between 1917 and 1921 are incomplete. Statistical studies during the chaos and civil war of the period from 1918 to the early 1920s were necessarily very fragmentary, inaccurate and contradictory. The censuses that were taken – particularly the occupational census of 1918 and the industrial census of 1920 – were based on different methodologies and frequently did not touch upon those questions which interested statisticians in previous or subsequent years. Virtually all the aggregated figures derived from these surveys which show the dynamics and professional stratification of Russian workers during the first post-revolutionary years have been the subject of historical disputes and therefore can only be regarded as conditional. These disputes, in which B. A. Gukhman, E. G. Gimpel'son, L. S. Gaponenko, P. V. Volobuev, A. G. Rashin, V. Z. Drobizhev, A. K. Sokolov and others took part, continue to this day.

In 1917 there were between 4.2 and 4.4 million workers in Russia. In 1918 this number had fallen to 2.5 million, and in 1919 it fell still further, to 1.4 million. This very sharp decline was the result of a number of factors, including the rundown of military production, the fuel and raw materials crisis, the call-up of workers to the front, and their flight from hunger in the towns to the countryside. In 1920 there was a small rise in the number of workers to 1.5 million, but this can hardly be regarded as a sign of economic stabilization. It had more to do with compulsory labour mobilization among peasants and soldiers and the forcible attachment of workers to their enterprises. In the course of 1921 militarized labour was gradually abolished and this, coinciding with the 'concentration' (i.e. curtailment) of industry, caused a further fall in the number of workers to 1.3 million.

The process by which workers were 'flushed out' of industry did not take the same course all over the country. A characteristic feature of Russia was that the bulk of the proletariat was concentrated in the centre of the country and in Moscow and Petrograd. Over two-thirds of the workers in 34 gubernias counted in the census of 1918, were employed in the Vladimir, Ivanovo-Voznesensk, Moscow, Tver', Iaroslavl' and Tula gubernias and the two capital cities. In these areas in particular, the features of the economic disintegration in the war communism period stand out clearly. However, this disintegration manifested itself in a peculiar way, and the collapse of production during those years did not follow a simple or consistent pattern. In the centre of Russia there were mass closures of textile factories, whilst the number of employees in the metalworking industry by the end of the war communism period had hardly changed. In military factories the workforce had even grown. In the industrial gubernias of Russia the number of workers fell precipitately between 1918 and 1920, whereas in the non-industrial gubernias it actually increased.

The changes in the composition of the workforce were dependent on the peculiarities of its structure. Metalworkers and textile workers – who lost their jobs more quickly than other workers in late 1917 and early 1918 – were significantly more numerous than workers in other sectors. The food, chemical and printing industries also employed large numbers of workers. Most of the agricultural workers became self-employed peasants in the period from 1917 to 1922, although some continued to work on state farms (*sovkhozy*): in 1920 *sovkhozy* employed 145,000 people. A significant proportion of railway workers were semi-peasants, especially those employed in track maintenance, the largest group of railway employees.

The question of the extent of the peasant element in the working class has given rise to many discussions on the essential features of the Russian proletarian of the late nineteenth and early twentieth centuries. Political factors have often been involved in these discussions, as the notion that the working class was backward cannot readily be harmonized with a recognition of its 'leading role' in the revolutions. Theodore von Laue's description of the Russian proletarian as a 'peasant-worker' can only be accepted with a number of reservations, which serve more to highlight the complexity of the problem than to tip the balance one way or the other. The notion that the formation of Russian workers was incomplete rests upon the work of both zemstvo and Soviet statisticians. However, the methodology of their calculations has rarely been subjected to objective scrutiny. As Drobizhev and Sokolov have stressed, 'one should not confuse workers' links with the villages and workers' links with the peasant economy'. The 1918 census did indeed distinguish between these two phenomena. Out of 1,142,268 workers, 317,226 had 'their own land' or 'their families' land' (as the questionnaire put it), whereas 225,834 did some farming themselves or with the help of their families. It is difficult to trace how this pattern changed during the civil war, as the census of 1920 did not contain such data. Even such figures as are available have been subject to different interpretations. Some historians, with some justification, have considered them to be overstated, whereas others have argued that they testified to what Gimpel'son termed the 'cadre' industrial base of the Russian working class.

The number of workers with rural connections was certainly significant, but this alone explains little. It is not possible to distinguish the 'peasants' by their political or trade-union activity, or even by their mass psychology. The nature of the working class, its stereotypes, habits and codes of behaviour, were not perceptibly altered in the decade from 1910 by the influx from the villages. The new workers were quickly assimilated, leading to the loss of their 'peasant' characteristics. Of course, one should not ignore the 'dilution' of the established working-class milieu by alien elements. However, this question became important, particularly in Soviet historiography, partly for ideological reasons – it was necessary to explain the excesses at various enterprises between 1918 and 1922, ranging from lockouts and strikes to riots, which were difficult to square with 'workers' power'. Another important distinction between peasant and working-class milieux, and, therefore, their sub-cultures, was the level of literacy. In 1918, 79.1 per cent of male workers and 62.1 per cent of female workers were counted as literate. The qualification level of male workers, particularly metalworkers, was relatively high. On the other hand, a significant number of branches of Russian industry, notably textiles, still did not require skilled labour.

The question of 'peasant-workers' can also be regarded as one aspect of a more complex and confused problem – the 'de-classing' of workers in wartime. The term itself is inadequate, as strictly speaking it should denote the loss of professional habits or of the characteristic 'class' features of workers. However, it mainly refers to just two tendencies – the fall in the number of workers and the deterioration in their quality. The criteria for the latter concept are vague – one of them is that the workers were 'scattered', moving from large enterprises to smaller ones. However, to see this phenomenon as purely negative is dubious. It was partly a spontaneous process, but partly also a deliberate process of rationalization of industrial production, an adaptation to wartime conditions in order to maintain a specific military-industrial structural organization. Although one should not ignore the data on the movement of workers into the countryside, it is necessary also to bear in mind the system of reserved occupations for skilled workers, which protected them from being sent to the front and which made certain factories considerably more 'proletarian' than before. D. A. Baevskii, along with many other historians, is inclined to see 'a change in social outlook – a fall in class consciousness and organization' as one of the signs of the 'de-classing' of the proletariat. However, such criteria are obviously ideological concepts, and were used in equal measure by both Bolsheviks and Mensheviks, who gave them very different interpretations.

The question of class rule

The notion of the 'dictatorship without the proletariat' became widespread primarily among such Western historians as E. H. Carr, Isaac Deutscher and Moshe Lewin. Noting the workers' small numbers, fragmentation and limited professional mobility, their close links with the villages and even discrimination against them, these authors tend to regard the thesis of the 'dictatorship of the proletariat' as nothing more than a cover for the political domination of the Bolsheviks. To an extent one can agree with this, but with certain important reservations. For one thing, the Bolsheviks certainly took the aspirations of the lower levels of the proletariat into account, although they translated their day-to-day concerns into political language. Additionally, it should be borne in mind that they often corrected their political programme in response to popular attitudes. To be sure, this does not amount to the dictatorship of the proletariat, but to a certain degree and in a peculiar way the new order brought political administration within the reach of workers.

The other side of the problem is more complicated: to what extent were the workers – even if not de-classed and with the full complement of class features found in the proletariat of developed countries – able to realize their dictatorship in the conditions of 1917–20? The concept of 'class rule' needs to be approached with great caution, and is hardly able to explain the entire complex mechanism of group and individual distribution of power. But the polemic surrounding the 'dictatorship of the proletariat' has more to do with refuting an artificial ideological construction than with an attempt to develop a positive historiographical conception.

Material conditions, wage rates and rationing

The processes taking place among factory workers can only be understood in the context of the whole gamut of problems related to the workers' material security. The war years saw an increase in the workers' nominal wages – by 29 per cent in 1915, 203 per cent in 1916, and 492.5 per cent in 1917. This sort of sharp increase is incompatible with stable prices, and these figures need to be examined in conjunction with price dynamics. A number of investigators, such as K. A. Pazhitnov and B. A. Gukhman, supposed that the rise in wages outstripped the rise in prices, but this point of view was rejected by S. G. Strumilin, who estimated that real wages in 1917 had fallen to almost half their 1913 level. Despite the lack of consensus about the appropriate price index, overall the fall in real wages in the war years cannot be denied, although prior to 1917 it was not as noticeable as afterwards. With certain reservations, one can accept the figures of the census of factory production for 1913–18, which established on the basis of data from more than 2,300 industrial enterprises that workers' real wages in 1917 were less than one-quarter of their pre-war level.

By the middle of 1917 the signs of an imminent inflationary explosion were already evident. To a certain extent it was brought about by a change in the guaranteed minimum wage, which had been won first and foremost by the major trade-union organizations in Moscow and Petrograd and was introduced at that time. Another factor was the considerable increase from August 1917 in the issue of credit notes unbacked by gold. The consequences were not slow to manifest themselves. In just two months, September and October 1917, prices rose by 340 per cent in the central gubernias of Russia. This blow was only partly softened by the new wage rates, which were not brought in very quickly, and were not applied everywhere. The political anarchy and economic chaos at the end of 1917 gave a sharp impetus to the race between prices and wages. The rapidly increasing gap between them was only partially compensated for by the sale on ration cards of a limited quantity of products at fixed state prices.

Attempts to introduce a rationing system had first been made before the February revolution. From the spring of 1917 bread and sugar were put on ration, and in the summer this was extended to some other grain products and fats. At first, the difference between the 'ration-card' and market prices of these goods was not great, but the gulf between them grew with each month. The monetary component of wages still predominated in the first half of 1918, but from the end of that year the naturalization of wages accelerated. By early 1921 the 'natural' component of workers' wages exceeded 90 per cent. Money had lost any meaning. Among factory workers the demand was raised to equalize rations rather than wage rates. It was only after the adoption of the New Economic Policy (NEP) that the money component of wages began to grow again and the ration-card system for distributing foodstuffs began to fade away.

It should be remembered that money wages were frequently paid late, and that the food rations were constantly changing. It was not uncommon for no rations to be distributed for several weeks. Under such conditions the workers could only stave off starvation by selling and reselling their personal possessions, items they had produced illegally or outside of working hours, or industrial goods they had produced and been given by their enterprise in lieu of wages. This last method of payment was particularly common in the textile, footwear and tobacco industries. At that time any form of commodity exchange was called 'speculation', and the transport of goods for sale was called 'bagman trade' (*meshochnichestvo*); both these 'crimes' carried severe penalties. There were partial relaxations of the ban on trade only during the most severe food shortages – when the authorities were unable to feed the workers, they permitted workers to do it themselves. In September 1918 'bagmen' brought four times more food to the starving capitals than the state organs. But even this was not always sufficient, and in January 1920 the government began to set up free canteens for the workers, which they closed again the following year.

In 1917, labour contracts were introduced to regulate wage rates. They were regarded primarily as an instrument for limiting the rights of entrepreneurs. Therefore, from the end of 1918, by which time much of industry had been nationalized, these labour contracts lost their relevance. Wage rates began to be determined by tariff agreements worked out between the trade unions and the state. They attempted to calculate these tariffs on the basis of the quantity, quality and complexity of the labour expended by the workers. This made the tariff system extremely unwieldy, as there were more than 30 tariff categories in operation. Different sections of the workforce were allocated to different categories, and received a guaranteed wage. As the naturalization of wages proceeded, these tariff rates also lost their significance. The trade unions, which had expended considerable effort on constantly correcting the tariffs and winning certain advantages for particular branches of industry, rejected the naturalization of wages and favoured automatic linkage of the tariff rates to the price index right up to 1919. The ration system which followed copied the practices of the tariff system to a considerable extent. By 1920 there were dozens of types of rations – from 'Kremlin rations' to 'academic rations' – and this caused the same irritation among the workers as their previous division into tariff categories.

The fate of the eight-hour day

The early years of the revolution not only failed to bring the workers the promised material benefits but they lost the greater part of the benefits they had formerly enjoyed. The only real gain the workers had made from the revolution was the establishment of the eight-hour working day. It had begun to be introduced, mainly unofficially, in the spring of 1917. The Provisional Government did not object. It should be borne in mind, however, that widespread defencist sentiments among the workers made them ambivalent towards this slogan. It was partly this feeling, not just bureaucratic red tape within the Ministry of Labour and the opposition of the capitalists, which accounted for the fact that the eight-hour day had not yet been brought in at many Russian enterprises by October 1917. As soon as they had seized power, the Bolsheviks decreed its introduction in all branches of industry. However, they too had to renege on their promises in view of the economic chaos facing Russia. Overtime was preserved. A Council of Defence decree published on 23 October 1919 stated that overtime should not exceed four hours a day. The operation of this law was limited to enterprises working on urgent military orders, but, in practice, it was easy to get round these norms. The trade unions' supervision of the observance of the labour laws – the working day could not be increased at non-military enterprises without their agreement – was largely ephemeral. The abolition of overtime for women was also not implemented, since in 1918 women accounted for 43.5 per cent of the workforce, and it was not until 1920 that the figure had fallen to 27.8 per cent. There was more success in limiting the work of children and youths under 18, whose proportion in the workforce was 14 per cent in 1918, 13.2 per cent in 1919 and 8.4 per cent in 1920.

Unemployment

Unemployment virtually disappeared in the civil-war years. It had not been a serious issue in the spring of 1917, and there were no reliable statistics produced for it at that time. Some historians have since tried to estimate it by using partial data concerning the closure of enterprises and the sacking of their employees, but it is hardly justifiable to assume that all of these people should be counted among the unemployed, even if some of them did become so. From the end of summer 1917 the number of factories which closed because they were making a loss began to increase rapidly. The Provisional Government, worried by this phenomenon, produced a large-scale plan to establish labour exchanges in many Russian towns. Kerensky did not have enough time to implement the plan, nor did the Bolsheviks achieve very much in this regard at first. In January 1918 the People's Commissariat of Labour presented some figures on unemployment, which it estimated at 100,000. By April 1918, 324,000 persons were registered at the labour exchanges. This sharp contraction in employment only affected certain branches of industry and was brought about by reductions in military orders and shortages of raw materials. Almost half of those seeking work were in the Moscow and Petrograd gubernias.

From the latter half of 1918, unemployment began to fall sharply, although there was certainly no economic upturn. The three basic reasons for this were the flight of workers from the starving towns to the countryside, the total mobilization which emptied even those enterprises still in operation, and the decline in industrial labour productivity. In the autumn of 1918 it became illegal for the unemployed to refuse the services of the labour exchanges. Work books were introduced – at first for the 'bourgeoisie' and, from December 1918, for all workers. The labour exchange became an organ for compelling people to take hard, badly paid work, and fewer and fewer of them wished to avail themselves of its services. This in turn led the authorities to make their labour-allocating measures harsher and facilitated the establishment of a kind of 'serfdom' in industry and transport, which was abandoned only in 1921 under NEP.

On 3 May 1919 compulsory labour conscription was decreed. The wave of labour mobilization gathered momentum from the second half of 1919, and reached its peak in 1920. The number of workers who were 'attached' to industry grew every month. Miners, oilworkers, railway workers, river transport workers, ship repairers, chemists – these are just some of the professions that were 'mobilized' on the labour front. Even this did not help, and in 1919 and 1920 demand for labour power was significantly in excess of supply. This 'labour serfdom' led to rapidly mounting anger among the workers, which broke out during the strikes in Petrograd in the winter and spring of 1921, when the demand for 'freedom of labour' was advanced in factories everywhere. However, these restrictions on labour were rescinded not only as a result of labour unrest, but also because of the new NEP orientation of the economy. The policy of 'concentrating' production adopted in May 1921 deprived hundreds of enterprises of state support. This led to a new and rising wave of unemployment, the first signs of which were already apparent by autumn 1921.

'Workers' control'

The implementation of the idea of workers' management of the factories turned out to be highly contradictory. 'The factories to the workers' was one of the Bolsheviks' slogans, but very shortly after October 1917 they began to make a number of qualifications to it which significantly altered the slogan's initially semi-anarchist character. Historically, the first form of workers' management was so-called 'workers' control'.

In Soviet historiography the general conception of the nature, tasks and mechanisms of workers' control underwent a series of changes. The most widespread view in the 1920s was that workers' control was primarily punitive in character, and was a largely spontaneous and in some respects utopian experiment. Nobody, however, questioned its necessity. This can be seen, for example, in the works of such prominent state and trade-union figures of the period as N. Osinskii and S. A. Lozovskii. By the 1940s and early 1950s, workers' control was being presented as a well-thought-out, almost planned action, and the extent of its spread between February and October 1917 was enormously exaggerated. Later Soviet historians, notably A. A. Venediktov, V. I. Selitskii, V. P. Nasyrin and D. A. Kovalenko, took a more moderate position and helped change the historical paradigm. They were among the first in the late 1950s and the 1960s who recognized the limited scale of workers' control in the pre-October period and its contradictory nature in conditions of private enterprise.

In Western historiography there is a wider range of views about workers' control. In particular, it is seen as a tactical concession on the part of the Bolsheviks, which they rescinded once their situation had become more secure. This is the view taken, for example, by Adam Ulam, who lays great

stress on its propaganda significance. Others tend to explain the abandonment of workers' control in terms of the pragmatism of the authorities, who
were concerned above all to save the economy from chaos and who therefore broke off the workers' 'heroic experiment'. Western authors do not
consider that the Bolsheviks' 'honeymoon' with the workers lasted very
long, and all see it as being over by the time NEP was introduced.

Workers' control began to be introduced unofficially from the spring of
1917. At first it was neither systematic nor premeditated – in some places
they drove out an unpopular boss, in others they attempted to protect the
factory's stocks or premises, fearing 'sabotage'. These .were mainly the
actions of radical workers within factory committees, and although they
claimed to be acting on behalf of all the workers in the factory and presumably had their assent, their actions frequently 'deepened' the contradiction
between the managers and the managed. However, it would be unjust to
present the first steps towards workers' control as exclusively directed
against the entrepreneurs. On the contrary, there were frequent examples of
a kind of symbiosis between workers and entrepreneurs, who as well as
being in dispute with one another, also solved their enterprise's particular
problems together. A factory owner could often gain access to raw materials, credits and advances using the support of the factory committee. Even
in those areas where the interests of the employers and the factory committee clashed, they were often able to find a common language. At the
Treugol'nik factory in Petrograd at the end of 1917, for example, the management and workers jointly got a circular preventing women working
nightshifts rescinded, as this was disadvantageous to both sides. At the First
All-Russian Congress of Trade Unions in January 1918, the accusation was
even made that 'factory committees at the local level have become fixers,
organs for assisting the management'.

By the middle of 1918 the economic radicalism of Russian workers had
taken shape. Their requests for nationalization showed first and foremost
their paternalistic attitudes. State support was seen as something more reliable and solid than the 'market' manoeuvrings of the owners. The decree of
14 November 1917 on workers' control, for all its detail concerning rights
and obligations, gave workers' control neither a systematic structure, nor
any well-considered guidelines for action. In the prevailing conditions of
legal arbitrariness, workers' control became more aggressive, but not more
competent. In some places the control committee even instituted searches of
the owners' canteen. The word 'sabotage' became increasingly popular,
and, with some prompting by the government press, workers began to see
this as the reason for production stoppages and factory closures.

The trade-union leader Lozovskii, who was well acquainted with the
details of this question, regarded workers' control as a utopian idea: 'In reality, the capitalist was not going to work to teach proletarians the art of managing the enterprise, and under a proletarian dictatorship the organs of
workers' control were not going to limit themselves to supervision.'

None the less, workers' control as it was practised in 1917 and early 1918 was much more proletarian and 'mass' in its character than were the organs of the Supreme Council of the National Economy (VSNKh) – a branch of the state bureaucracy – which replaced it. Overall, the process by which workers were excluded from the management of enterprises was complex and contradictory. The slogan of workers' control was quickly forgotten after the total nationalization of factories in 1918. This seemed logical: it was supposed that from now on workers would not just supervise the management – they would comprise it themselves. 'Although it was a revolutionary slogan in the period before the October revolution, workers' control, which was proclaimed and introduced in its initial form, has now become definitely reactionary, in that it deflects the workers' consciousness from the tasks of management.' This was the epitaph to workers' control given in January 1919 at the congress of the metalworkers' union, the most influential in Russia. At the same time, attempts to confer unlimited powers on 'Red directors' in the early post-revolutionary period were not always crowned with success. The trade unions offered real resistance to one-man management in industry. But whatever else may have happened, the worker did not, generally, feel himself to be the master of the factory. The strikes and the fall in labour discipline which were endemic in 1917–1921 were one consequence of this.

Strikes and the decline in labour discipline

The political strike movement against the monarchy in February 1917 was destined to decline in the subsequent weeks. However, the number of economic strikes grew, albeit slowly. Stoppages were short and usually ended in the workers' demands being met. The disputes were generally about wages, sackings and the removal of unpopular managers or foremen. From the autumn of 1917 strikes began to acquire a political hue again. Up to October 1917 strikes were politicized by the participants adding a list of political demands to their economic ones. Such strikes can be regarded as political, although it should be borne in mind that they could usually be ended by addressing the economic questions alone.

Strikes were not uncommon after the October revolution as well, for all the 'proletarian' rhetoric of the new authorities. At first they were tolerated – they were directed against private entrepreneurs (state enterprises were still only a small minority), and although the state structures sought to end the strikes as quickly as possible, they did not view them as hostile. An exception was the printers' strike against the closure of opposition newspapers, although it is true that the slogan of 'press freedom' they advanced to a certain extent masked the economic aspect of the conflict – the printers were incensed at the loss of work and wages. After the socialization of industry in 1918, the authorities looked upon strikes as aggressive 'anti-Soviet' demonstrations, even when the strikers put forward no political slogans and the worker unrest was a result of food shortages.

Strike movements which lasted longer than the normal one or two days naturally acquired a political character. This was frequently encouraged by socialists, although the government press generally exaggerated the importance of SR and Menshevik influence on the strikers. An example of this can be seen in the strikes in Petrograd in March 1919 and especially in February and March 1921. The politicization of strikes during the civil war, as before October 1917, was achieved by bringing together political and economic demands – we see almost no purely political resolutions. The strikes usually originated in the largest enterprises and thereafter spread to a number of other, smaller factories. Strikes were only semi-legal between 1918 and 1921, although they were not officially prohibited. The half-hearted nature of these strikes is worth noting: workers refused to work the whole day, or did not work but did not leave the factory, or the strike only affected certain workshops.

The decline in labour discipline and productivity after the revolution was a particular form of economic protest. The post-October anarchy in workplaces was not of long duration, and D. A. Baevskii has even gone so far as to suggest that 'by the spring of 1918 there had been a change in the attitude of the working masses towards work and production'. However, absenteeism and covert and overt shirking increased throughout the period from 1918 to 1921. Absenteeism per worker per year in Russian industry was 22.7 days in 1917, and this had risen to 71 days in 1920. At metalworking factories between 1918 and 1920 absenteeism reached 50 per cent, and labour productivity fell to 26 per cent of the pre-war norm.

There were no effective ways to deal with loafing during the civil war. The authorities were afraid to levy fines, because this was too reminiscent of the old order. Workers paid little attention to sharp warnings from trade-union committees or to threats of sacking, both because the militarization of labour made sacking very difficult and because in practice repressive measures were rarely employed for fear of disturbances. One example of this was the attempt to stamp workers' food ration cards in Petrograd in 1921. This measure was intended to identify which workers receiving bread rations actually turned up at their factories, but it caused such a storm of protest that it was quickly abandoned. Enterprise managements often had to adopt an indulgent attitude towards shirking because they were unable to provide the workers with the necessary subsistence rations. The frequent stoppages of production caused by lack of transport, raw materials or equipment did not serve to bolster work discipline. Workers received two-thirds of their normal rations during these stoppages, and many preferred to make do with that, rather than clear snow or saw wood. It is true that there were attempts to organize unpaid 'communist' work, but it is very difficult to establish where workers took part on their own personal initiative rather than as a result of coercion from above. The voluntary nature of these unpaid *subbotniki* in 1919 and 1920 cannot be accepted unconditionally. This is a question which requires further examination.

Working-class attitudes towards the new regime

Despite the fact that the Bolsheviks described their post-October regime as 'the hegemony of the proletariat', the proletarians themselves viewed the actions of those who ruled in their name in a variety of different ways. Analyses of workers' political attitudes generally look not only at their 'words' but also at their 'deeds'. For example, many historians regard joining the Red Guards as a sign of pro-Soviet sympathies. The reality, however, is that the political and psychological meanings of the 'words' and 'deeds' of the workers are difficult to determine, since their actions can be interpreted in various ways. The desire of workers to join militarized Bolshevik detachments was often dictated by non-political considerations, such as better material rewards and the possibility of enhanced social status. A worker could do this and still remain indifferent to politics or have little notion of the political meaning of events. It is also necessary to exercise caution in assessing collective factory resolutions, which are often used to describe workers' attitudes. The way in which these documents were compiled and adopted is not always properly taken into account.

The mass political attitudes of the workers were highly changeable, and they contained a multitude of different national, regional, professional and generational colorations. Diane Koenker is right to observe that workers who supported some of the Bolshevik slogans were not always supporters of Bolshevik doctrines. Joel Carmichael has noted in this regard that the political demands of the non-party workers' movement and the Bolsheviks coincided during and after the Kornilov revolt. It should be stressed, however, that the workers' political improvisations were not uninfluenced by Bolsheviks, whose authority within the trade unions grew consistently throughout 1917.

The workers as a whole did not demonstrate tangible support for the Bolshevik coup, although, as N. N. Sukhanov recalled, the uprising in Petrograd did not require any more assistance from them than was already forthcoming. They did not hinder the uprising, nor were most of them inclined to respond to the calls of the anti-Bolshevik opposition. For the most part they were indifferent to the demand for a homogeneous socialist government as well. Although Red Guard detachments consisting primarily, but not exclusively, of workers played a certain role in the October events, one should not ignore their small numbers, the anarchic character of many of them, or their use of ideological rhetoric as a cover for group or individual interests which were far from political in nature.

On the other hand, the neutrality of the workers should not be exaggerated. They engaged in acts of opposition throughout the 1917–1921 period.

The most important of these were: the convocation of the Extraordinary Assembly of Factory Representatives (*upolnomochennye*) in Petrograd in 1918; the strike of Moscow railway workers in the summer of 1918; workers' participation in the Astrakhan' uprising, and the disturbances at the Putilov and Tula arms factories and the main Aleksandrovsk railway workshops in the spring of 1919; and the demonstrations of Moscow and Petrograd workers in February and March 1921. None the less, in the years following the revolution there was a slow, largely unconscious process of adaptation by workers to the new regime. First and foremost their language changed, they made ever more frequent use of Bolshevik political terminology to explain to themselves and to others what was happening around them. This was a language which became necessary in everyday life, a language of petition and complaint, almost a commonplace language. Its use was not so much a linguistic game as a calculated mercantile operation. People became accustomed to using this language spontaneously and internalized it, they thought and understood the world in its terms. Once this language had permeated society's thinking, it marked a change in the psychology of the masses.

As the regime became more firmly established, political protest became more petty and degenerated into catcalls at meetings and the indistinct whispers of dissenters. Another important condition for the ideological unification of the workers from around 1920 onwards was that political conflicts began to be about everyday matters such as the privileges and rations of the authorities. Thus political disputes became narrower in nature and ceased to be about matters of high principle – they did not call into question the very basis of the state. This is in no way contradicted by the fact that the death agony of war communism was marked by a sharp burst of oppositional workers' activity. Indeed, it is confirmed by the workers' disturbances in Petrograd in February and March 1921. Here was a powerful social explosion which turned out to be politically impotent – a clear demonstration of the new spiritual situation in Russian society. All the tendencies which had begun to appear in workers' actions of previous years – the self-limitation of mass protest, the peculiar way it died down, the moderation of its actions and the fact that the political slogans were obviously brought in from outside – now manifested themselves to the full.

Further reading

Baevskii D. A., *Rabochii klass v pervye gody Sovetskoi vlasti (1917–1921)* (Moscow, Nauka, 1974).

Gaponenko L. S., ed., *Istoriia Sovetskogo rabochego klassa*, tom 1 (Moscow, Nauka, 1984).

Gimpel'son E. G., *Sovetskii rabochii klass. 1918–1920 g. Sotsial'no-politicheskie izmeneniia* (Moscow, Nauka, 1974).

Koenker D., *Moscow Workers and the 1917 Revolution* (Princeton, Princeton University Press, 1981).

Koenker D. P., Rosenberg W. G. and Suny R. G., eds., *Party, State and Society in the Russian Civil War Explorations in Social History* (Bloomington and Indianapolis, Indiana University Press, 1989).

Mandel D., *The Petrograd Workers and the Soviet Seizure of Power From the July Days 1917 to July 1918* (London, Macmillan, 1984).

Remington T. F., *Building Socialism in Bolshevik Russia: Ideology and Industrial Organization 1917–1921* (Pittsburgh, University of Pittsburgh Press, 1984).

Rosenberg W. G., 'Russian Labor and Bolshevik Power After October', *Slavic Review* 44, 2 (Summer 1985).

Smith S. A., *Red Petrograd: Revolution in the Factories 1917–18* (Cambridge, Cambridge University Press, 1983).

Ulam A., *Lenin and the Bolsheviks: The Intellectual and Political History of the Triumph of Communism in Russia* (London, Secker and Warburg, 1966).

Volobuev P. V., *Proletariat i burzhuaziia v Rossii v 1917 g.* (Moscow, Nauka, 1964).

Von Laue T. M., 'Russian Labour between Field and Factory, 1892–1903', *California Slavic Studies* 3, pp. 33–65.

P A R T

VII

ECONOMIC ISSUES AND PROBLEMS OF EVERYDAY LIFE

Grain Monopoly and Agricultural Transformation

Ideals and Necessities

LARS T. LIH

Part of the drama in any revolution is the clash between the long-range ideals of transformation and the pressing necessities imposed by the task of staying in power. For the Bolsheviks, a party of proletarian revolutionaries who came to power in an overwhelmingly peasant country, this clash was caused most fundamentally by problems of town–country relations.

According to the majority of Western scholars, during the years immediately following the Bolshevik takeover in October 1917, this conflict took the form of a militant imposition of proletarian ideals in the countryside. Only after the end of the civil war in 1921, it is argued, did the Bolsheviks realize the necessity of a more gradual approach.

There is a paradoxical contrast between this image and the criticism levelled at the Bolshevik leaders by socialist critics at the time. Karl Kautsky, the most authoritative Western socialist critic of Bolshevism, argued in *The Dictatorship of the Proletariat* in 1918 that 'it would have been dangerous for the Bolsheviks to interfere even slightly with peasant private property'. Owing to the impossibility of socialist revolution in backward Russia, Bolshevik concessions would inevitably end in a dictatorship of the peasantry rather than the proletariat. Within the Bolshevik camp, the left-wing Workers' Opposition made similar charges. As Aleksandra Kollontai put it in *The Workers' Opposition*, workers, who wanted a 'rapid advance towards communism', were being held back by the party's concessions to the 'petty-bourgeois proclivities' of the peasant.

How can we explain a critique of Bolshevik policy that seems so paradoxical today? Is there any way that the image of concessions to the peasantry can be made compatible with the facts supporting our current image of what some have termed a Bolshevik 'war on the peasantry'?

Bolshevik axioms

The most informative exposition of Bolshevik goals during the first years after the revolution is still the *ABC of Communism* by Nikolai Bukharin and Evgenii Preobrazhenskii (1919). Preobrazhenskii, who wrote the chapters on agricultural and distribution policy, based his argument on what may be called the axioms of Bolshevik strategy:

- Large-scale centralized economic units are vastly more productive than scattered, small-scale ones.
- Only direct perception of material interest – not force – can induce people to adopt these higher economic forms.
- Lower economic forms should not be eliminated until higher forms are ready to replace them.
- Even in the best of circumstances, preparation of higher forms will take time, and the sacrifices imposed by the civil war have made this preparatory work even more difficult and time-consuming.
- It will therefore be necessary to rely during the foreseeable future on lower economic forms such as single-owner peasant farms and market-mediated distribution.

Given Russia's economic backwardness, compounded by the peasant seizure of the large estates, the party will face 'incredible difficulties' in convincing the peasants of the material advantages of socialist collectivism. The party must therefore devote much of its effort in the foreseeable future to improving small-scale peasant agriculture.

Preobrazhenskii's remarks on small-scale trade also deserve to be cited: 'It makes no sense for the soviet authority to simply prohibit petty trade when it is not in a position to replace that trade completely with the activity of its own organs of distribution. ... Petty trade will continue to exist until large-scale industry in the towns has been restored and the provision of basic consumer items can genuinely be carried out by state monopolies.'

To sum up: the *ABC of Communism* expresses both great confidence in the superiority of 'higher' economic forms, and (contrary to its reputation) great caution about the pace of 'liquidation' of old forms. Thus on the programmatic level the Bolsheviks had a strong sense of where they were going but also gave themselves full licence to compromise and improvise as they travelled toward their goal.

Grain monopoly

Preobrazhenskii did not apply his 'slow and steady' strategy to the grain trade, the most strategic sector of town–country trade; he put it instead into the category of large-scale trade that could be quickly nationalized. The story of the grain monopoly is partly the story of how this automatic assumption came to be viewed as a mistake.

It will be useful to introduce our discussion of policy by defining key terms. The core meaning of 'grain monopoly' is the elimination of private dealers and their replacement by a state-controlled apparatus. Even though grain monopolies had also been set up by 'bourgeois' governments such as that of Germany, a state monopoly could still be seen as a step in the direction of abolishing the private market altogether. But the mere fact of nationalization left a lot of questions unanswered: how were prices set? how flexible were they? were grain producers obligated to sell?

'Requisition' has a core meaning of forced sale, with the emphasis on 'forced'. A particular good or service is required by civil or military authority, and the owner is obligated to sell, at a price set by the state. It is an open question whether it is appropriate to extend the term 'requisition' from individual cases of forced sale to broad policies imposing an obligation (*povinnost'*) on large sections of the population. The motive for this extension seems to be to emphasize the brutal and coercive enforcement that backed up these broader policies. Much is lost, however, if we blur the distinction between a general obligation and an *ad hoc* burden placed on unlucky individuals: you must shovel snow off this railroad track because there happens to be snow there and you happen to be living nearby. Individual requisitions were widely perceived as highly unfair and open to high-handed abuse of power. Indeed, one motive for imposing general obligations was to escape the petty arbitrariness of requisition.

If the state decides to impose a general obligation, it can choose between several methods for carrying it out. One method is a 'tax', whose core meaning is assessment by rates. Unlike a requisition, where the entire burden falls on the unfortunate owner of a required good, a tax shares the burden as equitably as possible. Unfortunately, a tax is information-intensive: in order to get to an acceptable level of fairness and comprehensiveness, a great deal of knowledge is required about each individual's wealth.

In order to cut down on information costs, a *razverstka* ('assessment') can be imposed. In the case of the food-supply *razverstka* (*prodrazverstka*), an overall target was set by taking into account the needs of the state and overall harvest statistics. This overall obligation was shared out between provinces; the provinces shared out their assigned target to counties, and so on down to the individual household. This rough and ready method of sharing the burden was guaranteed to produce many inequities, but better methods may have been beyond the Bolsheviks' means.

'Sharing out' is the etymological core meaning of *razverstka*, but *razverstka* policies during the civil war were also based on the following logic: with equivalent exchange if possible and without it if necessary. Thus the *razverstka* can be identified as midway between monopoly at one end (at least a promise of compensation) and tax at the other (no compensation). As the economic collapse deepened and the Bolsheviks had fewer goods at their disposal to exchange for grain, the *razverstka* looked less like a grain monopoly and more like a tax.

Since requisitions, taxes and *razverstka* are all methods for imposing obligations on a population – methods that can be used by any type of government – they have no intrinsic connection to socialism or even the grain monopoly. If we examine the course of Bolshevik policy with these distinctions in mind, we will see a growing clash between the ideal of a grain monopoly and the methods required by the pressing necessity of collecting enough grain to stay in power and prevent complete economic collapse.

The Bolsheviks inherited the basic legislation setting up a grain monopoly from the Provisional Government, which in turn had merely completed the evolution of tsarist food-supply policy toward a state takeover of the grain trade. The monopoly legislation of March 1917 mandated fixed prices for grain, set up a network of food-supply committees, and imposed an obligation on producers to sell all their grain except for a stated norm for personal needs. The Provisional Government also recognized an obligation on its part to make industrial goods available to grain producers. A Ministry of Food Supply was established that later became the Bolshevik *Narkomprod* (People's Commissariat of Food Supply). Thus the legislation envisioned an ideal monopoly that would benefit both producer and consumer. This vision continued to inspire the Bolsheviks even though they ultimately had no more luck than the Provisional Government in putting it into practice.

The Bolsheviks also inherited the repressive consequences of the monopoly: the war against the sackmen (*meshochniki*). As the national economy continued to disintegrate and the government failed to make good its promise to provide goods, a flood of sackmen set off on long journeys to grain-producing villages to carry back a bag or two filled with food. *Meshochnichestvo* had already reached mass proportions by late summer 1917. It was a complicated phenomenon that included hungry city-dwellers, peasants from grain-deficit provinces and ex-soldiers turned full-time 'speculators'.

After the October takeover, the Bolsheviks had their hands full getting their bearings and taking full control of the state food-supply apparatus. Their first major initiative came in spring 1918: a 'food-supply dictatorship' that attempted to enforce the monopoly through class-war methods. The term 'food-supply dictatorship' was borrowed from Germany and reflected the Bolshevik conception of the monopoly as part of a pre-socialist 'state capitalism'. The Bolsheviks' enforcement strategy was two-pronged: to enlist hungry workers and peasants from grain-deficit regions in 'food-supply detachments' and to incite 'class war in the villages' by setting up Committees of the Poor (*kombedy*). The class-war strategy was justified by demonizing the 'kulaks' (better-off peasants) as saboteurs responsible for the failure of the monopoly.

The results of this strategy were meagre and the costs prohibitive. The Bolsheviks found themselves forced to compromise on both the monopoly ideal and class-war enforcement methods. The search for a more viable policy began in summer 1918: at the centre there was an effort to control the excesses caused by the class-war rhetoric of the spring, and in the localities food-supply officials experimented with more effective methods of grain collection. The result was the *razverstka* system, which took shape by early 1919 and remained in place for the duration of the civil war.

The *razverstka* method was also an inheritance from the past: it was first used by the tsarist Minister of Agriculture, A. A. Rittikh, in late 1916. (The origin of the term '*razverstka*' in tsarist bureaucratic practice would seem to exclude the possibility that the Bolsheviks equated it with socialism in any way.) A genuine monopoly required a detailed accounting (*uchet*) of the grain held on each farm; the *razverstka* was a recognition that this information was unavailable and that cruder methods had to be used. A genuine monopoly was also supposed to provide a full economic equivalent for grain, whereas the best the *razverstka* could promise was to distribute whatever goods were available. The *razverstka* system also represented a compromise on the class-war enforcement strategy: the Committees of the Poor were disbanded, efforts were made to bring the food-supply detachments under better control, and village assemblies had more say in making assessments. Although the Bolsheviks compromised on both the monopoly ideal and class-war enforcement, they certainly did not repudiate either one.

From early 1919, the fate of the *razverstka* system can be traced on two curves, one ascending and the other descending. On the ascending curve there was a gradual improvement of the food-supply organization from totally unacceptable to barely tolerable. This curve continued past the civil war, since the food-supply tax of the early 1920s was collected by the same apparatus. The descending curve tracked the deterioration of the economy, which increased the relative burden of grain assessments and decreased the amount of material compensation the Bolsheviks could provide. As Aleksandr Tsiurupa, head of *Narkomprod*, said at the Tenth Party Congress in March 1921, the quantity of nails now being received by the village was less than the quantity of castor oil received before the war. Agriculture was so weakened by the burdens placed on it that a drought in the Volga region in 1921 turned into a devastating famine.

Ever since the end of the civil war, there have been attempts to come up with a statistical expression of the burden borne by the peasants. The effort to wring hard conclusions out of the shaky statistics of the period should not obscure two basic but contradictory realities. One reality is that the relative burden caused by the *razverstka* went up as the economy as a whole shrank and this led to fierce peasant resistance. The other reality is that something like half of the food received in the cities came there via the black market and the sackmen, which implies that the Bolsheviks collected nowhere near the full surplus (even without taking into account other voluntary uses for grain such as home-brewed liquor).

The glaring inadequacies of the food-supply organization were never denied even by the Bolsheviks. In order to collect the grain and enforce the prohibition against private trade, violence against both the grain producers and the sackmen was required and liberally applied. Huge wastefulness in storage, transport and retail distribution made *Narkomprod* almost as unpopular with consumers as it was with producers. Lack of proper inform-ation led to inequities in individual grain assessments that infuriated both peasants and state officials. Finally, abuse of power by local food-supply officials was endemic.

How we evaluate these facts depends on our view of the constraints fac-ing the Bolsheviks (and their enemies in the civil war as well). If we believe that the Bolsheviks had the option of relying on a trained professional bureaucracy, adequate information, or fully equivalent exchange, then we are bound to condemn them for choosing the worse way. Some such reas-oning seems to be the majority view among Western scholars. If we believe that the *razverstka* system was not itself the cause of these basic realities but rather an adjustment to them, then we are bound to condemn it less severely.

The end of the *razverstka* system

The *razverstka* system came to an end when the Bolsheviks decriminalized the private grain trade in spring 1921. We still have no fully adequate account of the timing and significance of this crucial decision. One barrier to a full explanation is a number of widespread misconceptions. It is often asserted, for example, that the Bolsheviks thought they had achieved their ideal monopoly in 1920 and that this ideal consisted of taking grain from the peasants without providing economic incentives. Readers are also com-monly informed that the Bolsheviks were living in a dream world in 1920, unaware of the immense economic and political danger caused by their unrelenting pressure on the grain producer.

As sometimes happens, Soviet historians have contributed to this Western consensus about Bolshevik blindness, although for different motives. The overriding aim of Soviet monographs about the end of the *razverstka* system seems to have been to reveal the insight of the great Lenin. In order to make their case, Soviet historians willingly emphasized the shortsightedness of everyone else, particularly the unpopular food-supply officials.

These misconceptions have been allowed to stand partly because of the genuine ambiguity of the *razverstka* system, which by 1920 confused even the food-supply officials who operated it. The debate among officials during that year can be summarized by the question: was the *razverstka* system best thought of as a monopoly on crutches or a tax on crutches? A monopoly needs crutches if it does not have a substantial fund of industrial exchange items; a tax needs crutches if it does not have information about individual farms. The *razverstka* system was designed to collect grain in the absence of both requirements. As the economy began its long climb from near collapse, thus creating the opportunity for real improvements in collection methods, the question of the identity of the *razverstka* system became a vital one, since the answer would determine the direction of reforms.

In spring 1921, the decision was finally taken to improve the *razverstka* by turning it into a tax and to find other methods of moving towards an effective grain monopoly. Historians have traditionally been severe about the timing of the decision, judging it to be much too late. After the civil war wound down in early 1920, it is argued, the costs of continuing the *razverstka* system and the benefits of ending it should have been obvious to any rational person. Since the Bolsheviks waited for a full year to take the plunge, they must have been blinded by an irrational ideology.

In order to evaluate this argument, we have to examine more carefully the constraints under which the Bolsheviks at least thought they were operating. The party leadership had to answer three questions: do we need to collect a substantial amount of grain for centralized distribution? If so, can we afford to take the risk of changing methods? If we can relax our grip and make a significant cut in our grain collection targets, what changes should we make?

The answer to the first question was that the state needed grain under central control in order to distribute it to workers in industry and soldiers in the Red Army. The Bolsheviks judged that given the economic imbalance between industry and agriculture, it would be ruinous to throw industry on the mercy of the market. A subsidy financed by the *razverstka* (and later by the food-supply tax) was essential to stave off collapse.

The security motive behind the Bolshevik insistence on a burdensome grain collection has been even more neglected than the economic motive, partly because the Bolshevik leaders were loath to publicize their own vulnerability. Preservation of a fighting force was deemed essential even after the end of the war with Poland in summer 1920. Only after a determined forcing of the diplomatic pace by Lenin in early 1921 was it possible to contemplate the collapse of the Red Army that marked the early years of NEP.

Could the *razverstka* system be abandoned while collection targets remained relatively high? When the top leaders turned to their food-supply experts with this question in 1920, they got a resounding 'no'. The experts based their argument on their own weakness: the state did not have enough industrial goods for state-sponsored exchange, the bureaucracy was not good enough to make satisfactory individual assessments, and state collection efforts would be swept away by the black market (whether decriminalized or not) if grain producers had the right of free disposal over a significant part of the surplus. The reasoning of the food-supply officials is much more cogent than is usually realized: the experience of 1921 shows that it was indeed impossible to keep the free market within bounds and that state-conducted exchange could only obtain pitiful amounts.

Only after the top leaders made the decision to lower grain targets in early

1921 could they contemplate dismantling the *razverstka* system. Given lower collection targets, the food-supply establishment was able to go along somewhat grudgingly with the proposed changes. The most vocal protest came from *Narkomprod* official Moishe Frumkin, who accepted everything except the decriminalization of the market. Why abandon the monopoly ideal, he asked, just at the time when a reviving industry could begin to make state-conducted exchange a reality? But the consensus among Bolshevik economic experts was that it was pointless to adopt a tax system if free trade was still prohibited.

Frumkin need not have worried: the monopoly ideal was not abandoned. The Bolsheviks only revised their strategy for attaining it. Overgeneralizing from the wartime situation, they had earlier assumed it would only be possible to build up a genuine monopoly if it was protected from the competition of the private market by outright repression. When Lenin later referred to a crucial 'mistake' in the previous Bolshevik outlook, he seems to have been talking about this strategy (and not, as he is usually interpreted, the failures of the *razverstka* system as a wartime measure). After 1921, the Bolsheviks reverted to the logic of Preobrazhenskii's 'slow and steady' alternative by tolerating the private market until it could be 'squeezed out' and replaced. In 1927, Bukharin remarked that 'the grain monopoly was repealed with the introduction of NEP. But now, on the basis of the growth of our economic organizations, on the basis of their competition with the private middleman, we have squeezed private capital out of grain procurements, and we have arrived, so to speak, at a state monopoly from the opposite direction and on a new basis.'

Agricultural policy

The course of Bolshevik agricultural policy also reveals a growing clash between ideals of structural transformation and pressing political and economic necessities. In contrast to the grain monopoly, Bolshevik rethinking about peasant agriculture was conducted in the open and indeed with much fanfare.

It is hard to imagine that the Bolsheviks could have come to power in 1917, much less held on to it, if they had not given wholehearted support to peasant land hunger. From an orthodox socialist point of view, this was a dangerous concession, since it entailed breaking up large-scale estates and even the larger peasant farms. The Bolsheviks admitted that this policy pushed them back economically to a lower starting point, but they thought it was justifiable because it liquidated the landowners as a class and thus removed the main barrier to progress.

The Bolsheviks were confident in 1918 that the road was now open to rapid progress toward socialization in agriculture. The economic crisis would serve as a prod, while actual examples of socialist agriculture would serve as attractive models. A few landowner estates that were preserved intact from the flood of peasant revolution became state farms or *sovkhozy* that would demonstrate the advantages of large-scale production.

The Bolsheviks assumed that poor peasants would be in the forefront of the movement toward collective associations, and so great hopes were placed on the *kombedy* or Committees of the Poor formed in spring 1918. The main impetus for the creation of these committees was the food-supply crisis, but they also fit into a long-standing Bolshevik scenario about the political evolution of the peasantry. According to this scenario (worked out in greatest detail by Lenin himself), the peasantry as a whole worked together only in order to overthrow 'feudal' relations in the countryside. Once the common enemy was gone, economic evolution would lead to greater and greater conflict between peasants-in-the-process-of-becoming-proletarians and peasants-in-the-process-of-becoming-bourgeois. It was the task of the party to support the peasantry as a whole during the 'bourgeois' revolution against the landlords, but also to create special institutions for the poor peasants as soon as possible.

The Committees of the Poor of 1918 were based on this logic, but they proved to be an almost catastrophic disappointment: they came closer to uniting the village against the Bolsheviks than splitting it to their advantage. The Committees of the Poor were disbanded in late 1918; in later years the phrase *kombedovskii period* (the time of the Committees of the Poor) had a much more ominous ring than 'war communism' (usually dated 1918–21).

The disbandment of the Committees of the Poor was part of a larger shift that can be called 'the discovery of the middle peasant'. The term 'middle peasant' (*seredniak*) was notably absent from Bolshevik revolutionary rhetoric until early summer 1918, but after that it became more and more central until it was enshrined in the party programme adopted at the Eighth Party Congress in 1919. Lenin's speech at this congress became the main source of 'pro-peasant' rhetoric throughout the 1920s.

Western historiography has not been particularly interested in either the causes or the effects of the turn toward the middle peasant, perhaps because it conflicts with the overall image of proletarian militancy during the civil war. Yet it was arguably one of the most significant shifts in the outlook of the Bolsheviks after they took power. The shift was not in the characterization of the peasant, whom Marxists had long viewed as split between a labouring soul and a property-owning soul. But until the shift in 1918–19, the Bolsheviks had assumed that they would either work with the peasantry as a whole or with peasants who had already chosen to identify themselves with their labouring soul. The vacillating middle peasant was thus less interesting for what he was than for what he would become. Only after they took power and realized (as Preobrazhenskii put it in *Pravda* on 7 November 1920) that their fate depended on the choice made by the middle peasant did they start to accept the fact that they would have to work out some long-term *modus vivendi* with the middle peasant, vacillations and all.

The next party-wide discussion of relations with the peasants came in late 1920 with the establishment of sowing committees (*posevkomy*). The sowing committees were primarily a response to a pressing emergency (maintaining production despite lack of incentives and preserving seed stores in the face of the approaching drought). The discussion sparked off by the new committees reveals some of the conclusions the Bolsheviks had drawn from their earlier disillusionment. The party economist Iurii Larin coined the term '*krekhozy*' for the ordinary, individual-owner, peasant farm, and insisted that the *krekhozy* must be the centre of attention in the foreseeable future (*Pravda*, 12 December 1920). The emphasis on the *krekhozy* was accompanied by an apotheosis of the 'industrious owner' (*staratelnyi khoziain*) and a condemnation of lazy peasants (*lodyri*). To critics inside and outside the party, it seemed as if the Bolsheviks had reversed their earlier fierce stand on the relative merits of kulak and poor peasant.

The fall from grace of the *sovkhozy* and peasant collective experiments had now become orthodoxy. The attractive power of socialism was no longer expected to manifest itself by means of collective experiments within agriculture, but rather by the power and beneficence of state industry. In the short run, state aid was envisioned as a first repayment on the forced loan the Bolsheviks had extracted from the peasantry. (The loan metaphor dominated Bolshevik rhetoric about the peasantry in 1920.) In the long run, socialism would win over the peasantry via tractors and electrification.

At the time of the sowing committee legislation (late 1920), the Bolsheviks did not expect ever to decriminalize the grain market, and so they saw the winning-over of the industrious owner as a process occurring within a mandatory state-organized framework. The poverty of the state in 1920 also meant that for the most part it could only offer organization backed up by coercion, although the Bolsheviks assumed that the existing framework would slowly be filled with material content as industry revived. This scenario was revised in 1921 with the adoption of NEP and the emergence of a private grain market and the 'nepmen' who profited from it. The state now granted the private market a greater role in providing material incentives for increased production. Still, the revised scenario of NEP had the same basic plot as the scenario of 1920: the peasants would be won over to socialism via the might of socialist industry. But now the battle for influence over the peasantry was fought against a tolerated bourgeoisie rather than a bourgeoisie driven underground.

We can now identify three major changes in the Bolshevik conception of the path toward a transformed Russian countryside: the middle peasant replaced the poor peasant as the party's major companion on this journey; the task of demonstrating the advantages of socialism was taken away from *sovkhozy* and peasant collectives and given to industry; the bourgeois tempters of the vacillating middle peasant were allowed to emerge from the underground so that they could be 'squeezed out' more efficiently. None of these shifts challenged the Bolshevik axiom of moving to higher economic forms only by means of demonstrated material advantage – an axiom that was not violated on a large scale until Stalin's coercive collectivization, and even then shamefacedly and ·hypocritically. To overestimate the discontinuity that occurred in 1921 is to underestimate the more fundamental discontinuity that occurred in 1930.

Conclusion

We can now return to the two images of Bolshevik policy outlined earlier: the one that sees Bolshevik policy as an aggressive attack on the peasantry and the other that sees it as a series of concessions. We cannot choose between them merely on the basis of our estimation of the brutality and material suffering caused by the civil war, since different observers put this suffering into different overarching narratives.

According to Kautsky, the suffering was caused by the Bolshevik betrayal of Social-Democratic teaching about the conditions needed for socialist revolution. Although Bolshevik leaders accepted most of Kautsky's Marxist presuppositions about agriculture, they wove them into a story of class leadership: policies that were economically regressive were justified if they shored up peasant political support. For the Bolsheviks, even the suffering that arose directly from the exactions they made was ultimately due to the counterrevolution that imposed war and blockades on the country.

These contrasting stories by socialist participants converge on an image of Bolshevik concessions to the peasantry. Today we know what observers at the time did not know: the catastrophe waiting for the Soviet peasantry just around the corner, the permanent failure of Soviet agriculture to make good its claim to be a 'higher' economic form, and the final collapse of the whole Soviet experiment. Since we see the sufferings of the civil war as a rehearsal for the horrors to come, we can hardly help seeing Bolshevik peasant policy as a story of national tragedy.

Although we know more about the outcome than the participants themselves, we should not forget what they knew: the visions and unquestioned axioms of Marxist revolutionaries. The more we understand these axioms, the less we will see the policy changes of 1921 as a fundamental turning point: the Bolshevik outlook contained about the same mixture of generosity and cruelty, pragmatism and illusion, before as after. In our effort to tell the story of national tragedy in all its human complexity, we should not simply reject the old stories but rather incorporate them into our own.

Further Reading

Debo R., *Survival and Consolidation: The Foreign Policy of Soviet Russia 1918–1921* (Montreal, McGill-Queens University Press, 1992).

Figes O., *Peasant Russia, Civil War: The Volga Countryside in Revolution (1917–1921)* (Oxford, Oxford University Press, 1989).

Iurkov I. A., *Ekonomicheskaia politika partii v derevne 1917–1920* (Moscow, Mysl', 1980).

Kabanov V. V., *Krest'ianskoe khoziaistvo v usloviiakh 'voennogo kommunizma'* (Moscow, Nauka, 1988).

Kingston-Mann E., *Lenin and the Problem of Marxist Peasant Revolution* (Oxford, Oxford University Press, 1983).

Lih L. T., *Bread and Authority in Russia, 1914–1921* (Berkeley, University of California Press, 1990a).

Lih L. T., *The Bolshevik Sowing Committees of 1920: Apotheosis of War Communism?* (Carl Beck Paper No. 803, University of Pittsburgh Center for Russian and East European Studies, 1990b).

Patenaude B., 'Peasants into Russians: The Utopian Essence of War Communism', *Russian Review* 54 (October 1995), pp. 552–70.

Pershin P. N., *Agrarnaia revoliutsiia v Rossii*, 2 vols. (Moscow, Nauka, 1966).

Poliakov Iu. A., *Perekhod k NEPu i sovetskoe krest'ianstvo* (Moscow, 1967).

Wesson R., *Soviet Communes* (New Brunswick, NJ, Rutgers University Press, 1963).

Yaney G., *The Urge to Mobilize: Agrarian Reform in Russia 1861–1930* (Urbana, University of Illinois Press, 1982).

Problems Of Social Welfare and Everyday Life

WILLIAM G. ROSENBERG

Problems of social welfare and everyday life, a complex of phenomena encapsulated in Russian by the single term *byt*, constituted a vast range of hardships and agonies in the period between 1914 and the end of the civil war, a human ordeal which affected fundamentally the constitution and development of the early Soviet state. Although much less studied than the ideologies that interpreted them and the politics that created and then tried to contain them, radical changes in everyday social relations and life processes *were* the revolution for millions of future Soviet citizens in every category and position. For most, their impact was far more powerful than that of revolutionary politics and it is far better captured by the poetry of a Dr Zhivago than by economic and social statistics. To highlight demographic changes and mortality rates or to review shifting wage patterns, the rising cost of living, and the increasing problems of basic subsistence is to suggest only in barest outline the depth of emotional and psychological devastation endured in the period.

One must start by situating the problem of *byt* within the overall context of demographic change and population movement precipitated by seven years of near constant warfare. The most thorough study of aggregate population changes between 1914 and 1923 indicates a population loss from all causes of approximately 30 million, including the horrific famine that followed the end of the civil war in 1921 (Volkov, 1930, p. 262). As analysed by the respected American demographer Frank Lorimer, a loss of approximately 11 million persons can be attributed to the war years 1914–17; the larger remaining loss occurred during the civil war and its immediate aftermath, with the most traumatic moment coming not during the 1922 famine, as one might expect, but from the ravaging disease and hunger that accompanied the fierce fighting in 1920 (Lorimer, 1946, pp. 29–43). The sharpest population shifts occurred in Moscow and Petrograd. From somewhat over 2 million inhabitants at the time of the February revolution in 1917, the population of Petrograd fell to approximately 740,000 by 1920; in

Moscow, from 1,850,000 to 1,100,000. In both cities birth-rates halved, death-rates almost doubled (Prokopovich, 1930, pp. 18–27). These changes only exemplified, however, a universal demographic catastrophe, greater even than that brought by World War II. Severe declines occurred in every region and every population group, and especially among the industrial labour-force that Bolsheviks saw as their principal base of power (Rashin, 1923, pp. 64, 70).

Enormous social dislocations were, of course, in process well before the Bolsheviks came to power. In July 1914, 1,423,000 men were in the tsarist army, the largest in Europe. During the next three and a half years, an additional 14,375,000 men were mobilized, a staggering number by any absolute or comparative measure (TsSU, *Rossiia*, 1925, p. 4). By one estimate, this figure represented almost one half of all able-bodied men, and 22 per cent of the entire male peasant population (Lubny-Gertsyk, 1926, p. 26). In terms of the population as a whole without regard to age or sex, approximately 112 persons out of 1,000 found themselves in military service at some time before Russia's withdrawal from the war in 1918 (TsSU, *Rossiia*, 1925, p. 4). According to official figures, more than a third (775,400) were killed, 348,000 were 'maimed or mutilated', approximately 5 million were wounded and 3,343,900 were taken prisoner (TsSU, *Rossiia*, 1925, p. 4).

These figures hint at the traumatic social consequences of the World War independent of its relation to the revolution: any government responsible for political reconstruction in the war's aftermath would have faced grave problems of social and cultural reconstruction as well. In the event, civil war only continued the trauma. New mobilizations now affected many who were previously exempt, and new losses were inflicted by the various contending armies with a brutality far worse than the Germans'. Desertion, brigandage and the impressment of labour created chaos everywhere. Disease was rampant. There was a horrific shortage of food. According to one estimate, 1.2 million men and women died fighting for the Bolsheviks alone; 3.3 million more died from disease (Lubny-Gertsyk, 1926, p. 27).

A pervasive and devastating 'crisis of everyday life' thus accompanied the great political events of the 1914–21 period, shaping meaning and memory every bit as much as the revolution's many villains and would-be heroes. For those not directly caught up in the fighting, the crisis commonly centred on difficulties related to the production and distribution of essential goods, a condition that brought near chronic anxiety and social insecurity. Every industrial branch without exception suffered huge losses, especially between the end of 1916 and 1921. The output of coal, for example, fell from 29.1 million tons in 1913 to 8.6 million in 1920; pig-iron from 4.2 million to 100,000 tons; cement from 1.5 million to 36,000 tons; copper from 31,100 tons to 1,170, according to data for production on territory governed by the USSR before 1939 assembled by R. W. Davies' International Work-Group (Davies, 1990, p. 298). Declines were equally steep or steeper in the production of cotton and woollen fabrics, in agricultural output, and in the area of transport. From 2,582 million linear metres in 1913, cotton fabric production fell to just 120 million in 1920; and whereas some 132 million tons of commodities had been hauled in Russia's railroads in 1913, only half of this tonnage was transported over the same lines as late as 1923/24 (*Materialy*, 1927, p. lxix). Of the 15,000 locomotives in operation when the Bolsheviks took power in October 1917, fewer than 6,100 were in service by 1920. The decline in usable freight cars was even more precipitous (Klemenchich, 1920, p. 5; Golopolosov, 1920, p. 29). The consequences of chronic shortages of all kinds rippled through every aspect of daily existence, both before and after October: from the need to supplement incomes to absenteeism, the intensification of labour conflict, and the constant search for adaptive ways to survive. In one estimate, the average real monthly wage for industrial workers in constant roubles fell from between 30 and 49 roubles in 1913 to between 12 and 15 in 1921–22; in another, the purchasing power of the rouble in October 1920 was no more than 1 per cent of what it had been in October 1917 (Nove, 1982, p. 114; Dobb, 1948, p. 100). One can reasonably surmise that a great many anti-government protests throughout this period were conducted on nearly empty stomachs, whatever the strength of their political motivation.

As Barbara Clements has demonstrated, the burdens of this 'time of troubles' fell heavily on women (Clements, 1989, pp. 105–22). In the countryside, peasant women were often forced to farm their allotments alone; in urban areas, the wages of women workers were always lower than men's, and often insufficient alone to provide for their families. Everywhere, the anguish of home life compounded the uncertainties and hardships of work. Clements believes that, in the long term, the civil war contributed to Soviet Russia's evolution towards more nuclear family relations because of the destruction of so many extended families as places of collective labour and mutual support. By 1920, women constituted some 55 per cent of the country's urban population, precisely the reverse of the situation before 1913 (Kvitkin, 1923, p. 77); and in addition to the scourge of civil warfare, women in larger cities, particularly those who were formerly well to do, found themselves in the grip of a terrifying lawlessness in which their families' resources, whether meagre or substantial, could be destroyed in moments.

This did not mean, however, that recognizable urban life entirely collapsed during the revolutionary and civil war years, as Daniel Brower has recently admonished historians of this period. While emphasizing the severity of Russia's transportation crisis for urban areas and recognizing the devastating consequences of typhus and other epidemics, Brower argues that townspeople showed a remarkable facility for adaptation (Brower, 1989, pp. 58–80). Still, dramatic changes in available resources and the everyday patterns of life could not help but affect virtually every aspect of existence in Russia's cities and towns throughout the empire in these years. Nizhnii

Novgorod, Pskov, and several other large cities suffered population losses comparable to Petrograd and Moscow; Tiflis, Kiev, Baku, Tashkent and other non-Russian cities endured comparable upheavals in production and commerce; and virtually every town and city of more than 50,000 suffered the loss of at least one-quarter of its population (TsSU, *Trudy*, 1924, pp. 18–29).

A radical inversion in social status and privilege accompanied these demographic changes, making labourers out of members of the intelligentsia, petty traders out of those who had once presided over corporate institutions and large commercial enterprises. And as those identified as 'bourgeois' sought 'honest' work, the ranks of white-collar employees swelled along with the burgeoning soviet bureaucracy. Meantime, efforts to discriminate in the distribution of food rations on the basis of social status resulted in an artificial swelling of those representing themselves as 'workers'. To escape the vagaries and depredations of factory life in these conditions, many in the factory joined other townspeople in supporting themselves through petty trading, or set up their own small production shops as primitive entrepreneurs. In Brower's view, a petty capitalist economy may thus actually have been strengthened in this turmoil, rather than destroyed, and with it a relative homogenization of social circumstances and mentalities, forged around self-sufficiency and suffering. Brower suggests that an entrepreneurial approach to survival may even have contributed to the Bolsheviks' eventual decision to legalize private trade and small craft production with the introduction of NEP (Brower, 1989, p. 73).

Such momentous changes were scarcely forecast during what we might call the first phase of this prolonged crisis in everyday life, the months between July 1914 and the end of the old regime, although some signs of future trouble were quickly apparent. Here one can locate the initial difficulties brought on by tsarist mobilization policies, the decline in transport, grain requisitioning, and major shifts in the patterns of industrial production. Critical sectors of the economy were affected immediately. Imports of essential equipment and raw materials fell precipitously; consumer-goods industries like textiles and leather had to convert quickly to meet the needs of the army without having secured their own sources of supply (A. L. Sidorov, 1973, esp. pp. 363–8).

For the families of industrial workers, the most significant consequences of the war after mobilization itself related to the differential impact the needs of military production had on different industrial branches. As a result of these needs, a complex process of segregation began to occur, separating industries and enterprises the state decided to protect from those left to fend for themselves. Metalworking and chemical production increased significantly, for example, but virtually all other areas of production declined, in some sectors (glass-making, ceramics, cement production, wood products) from 40 to more than 50 per cent (TsSU, *Trudy*, 1926: 1, pp. 153–5). In the autumn of 1914, moreover, the government issued contracts for huge amounts of munitions to only a handful of large plants; small or medium-size producers were almost entirely neglected. Even in the metals sector almost 20 per cent of the enterprises working in 1914 had shut their doors by the end of 1915 (A. L. Sidorov, 1973, pp. 28–9).

While some workers found new jobs and were able to earn higher wages because their skills were in demand, most found themselves caught in an inflationary spiral and increasingly stringent work conditions, Many had difficulty finding work at all. More than 300,000, mostly unskilled, were processed by the Moscow labour exchange alone between October 1915 and June 1916, its first months of operation, while in Russia as a whole at least one-third of all industrial workers employed in January 1914 had left their jobs by February 1917 (K. F. Sidorov, 1927, pp. 217–18; Koenker and Rosenberg, 1989, chap. 1). Nominal as well as real wages began to decline, especially after large numbers of women and younger workers entered the workforce to replace those called into the army. The decrease was as much as 15 per cent overall by 1916, and as high as 20–25 per cent in some sectors (TsSU, *Trudy*, 1926: 1, pp. 153–5). According to one set of data, in Moscow metalworkers themselves were spending as much as 74 per cent of their family wages on food and clothing by 1916, and textile workers as much as 105 per cent, more that is, than their current income (Balabanov, 1928, pp. 15–16).

These conditions were not without opportunities for skilled workers able to avoid military conscription and for young and unmarried women. Yet they also served to sharpen social differentiations and reinforce the ways in which access to increasingly scarce goods was linked to one's role in production, private source of income, or the often arbitrary will of one's employer. Although the power of social identities in this period remains a subject of some contention, there is little question that social conflict in imperial Russia was increasingly framed in these terms. Bolshevik rhetoric became increasingly comprehensible precisely in terms of everyday life experience.

We can identify a second phase in this long social crisis beginning with the February revolution, whose proximate cause was the anxiety and anger that erupted among Petrograd working-class men and women over food shortages, wages, working conditions and welfare, however much these pressures were rooted in deeper and longer-term problems of social transformation. In considerable measure, addressing the problems of *byt* and their relation to Russia's continued participation in the war was the principal task of the new regime, one that was every bit as important to the future of political democracy as the construction of viable democratic institutions.

Almost immediately there was some relief. In the turbulence of the moment, many employers were not unwilling to improve working conditions and to negotiate over wages, especially after the Petrograd Society of Factory and Mill Owners agreed, in early March 1917, to the creation of factory committees. In a number of enterprises, work rules were modified and the most objectionable foremen removed. So were the harshest systems of fines and penalties that sometimes took as much as a third of a worker's wages and occasionally landed them in jail (Rosenberg, 1981, pp. 983–7). A brief spurt of optimism and energy also helped temporarily to ease the transport crisis.

Because these improvements proved short-lived, however, the hopes they generated only compounded popular distress when living costs continued to rise and economic circumstances deteriorated further. Without new revenues, employers struggling to keep their plants in operation were understandably resistant to increase wages, even though prices were rising rapidly. (For the market basket of goods consumed by an average worker, prices were 28 per cent higher in June 1917 than in May, an almost unprecedented rate of inflation) (Kokhn, 1926, pp. 10, 23–26). The wave of strikes that began soon after the formation of the first coalition government in May, and which occurred in part in the expectation that the new government would provide some relief, was overwhelmingly concerned with economic issues (Koenker and Rosenberg, 1989, p. 167).

Summer, however, only brought more hardships. As manufacturing groups insisted the regime take 'decisive measures' to restore industrial order, some firms resumed the pre-revolutionary practice of locking out dissident employees. Worker protests escalated, which in turn led to further economic deterioration. Between 1 March and 1 August 1917, as many as 568 factories closed permanently, leaving more than 100,000 unemployed (Kleinbort, 1925, p. 267). By summer's end, production even in favoured defence plants had fallen to as little as 60 per cent of February levels. Supplies of cotton and other textile resources virtually disappeared. More than 240,000 fewer freight cars moved on the rails compared to 1916. In Moscow, food prices increased on the average more than 20 per cent between August and September and were 62 per cent higher than in May. A reduction in the daily bread ration to half a pound (*funt*) per person in Moscow touched off new street demonstrations in August and September. Echoing the events of February, women demonstrators hurled insults and threats at local officials from the Commissariat of Food (Koenker and Rosenberg, 1989, chap. 8).

By September, as the Bolsheviks rapidly gained authority and organizational support, Russia faced the spectre of mass unemployment and the possibility of economic collapse. And with land seizures now common in the countryside, many underpaid or unemployed workers making their way back to family villages to 'get their share' found themselves unwelcome, just as many who returned from the front to their old places of work found those who had taken their jobs were quite unwilling to give them up. In September, the country estate of the former Kadet Minister of Agriculture, A.I. Shingarev, was looted and sacked. His wife died shortly afterwards. Well before the Bolsheviks came to power, everyday life at all levels of Russian society was beset with anxiety and tension. A 'civil war mentality' presaged additional horrors to come.

In this respect as in others, one of the most important aspects of the October revolution itself was that nothing changed for the better, even for those among the Russian proletariat who counted themselves as Lenin's strongest supporters. To be sure, for a few short weeks in November 1917, as managers disappeared from their enterprises and employees gained access and control over remaining inventories and resources, the illusion of betterment emerged in some places to reinforce the euphoric hopes of 'Land, Peace, and Bread!'. In so far as it occurred, however, this temporary relief came at the expense of further dismantling the infrastructure of production. Aside from the state itself, Russian enterprises in virtually every branch and sector were soon without adequate or effective credits, capital investment, a sufficient supply of materials, or an adequate market system for the distribution of their output. When goods and funds in the pipeline began to dry up in December and early January 1918, Petrograd and other major cities ceased functioning as commercial centres. Between January and April 1918, the supply of goods coming into Petrograd dropped catastrophically: meat and meat products by more than 85 per cent; eggs by 90 per cent; sugar and salt by more than 70 per cent; coal and other fuel to a level equal only to one-fourth of what the city had received the previous year (*Novyi put'*, 1 Sept. 1918). Unemployment spread rapidly, especially to the large privately owned plants that had earlier been among Russia's most stable and productive. The greatest declines by far were in chemicals (including rubber) and metals, 79 per cent and 74 per cent respectively by April 1918 in comparison to January 1917 (*Statistika Truda*, 15 Aug. 1918, pp. 8–14). In all, between December and June 1918, the Bolshevik government evacuated more than 100,000 unemployed workers and their families from places where production had completely stopped. Between January and September 1918, 833,616 persons sought work in the 153 labour exchanges of the Russian republic (Isaev, 1924, pp. 14–15; *Statistika Truda* 15 Oct.–15 Nov. 1918, p. 9).

It is hard to overestimate the magnitude of this crisis in either objective or subjective terms, and its effect on the quality of everyday life and the hopes of ordinary men and women about their future. In cities and towns all over the new Soviet Russia factories tried to hold on despite the lack of formal orders for goods, and turned urgently to the Bolsheviks for assistance. Supplies and materials were soon consumed. Funding stopped. Pilfering and theft became common. Decrees from the centre about factory administration, meanwhile, were largely ignored, especially those that attempted to reimpose a centralized management. Productivity continued to fall, and the more mechanized a plant, the greater the problems of maintaining production given the lack of fuel and spare parts. Workers were soon selling off plant equipment not because they were unaware of the longer-term consequences, but because their immediate need was to feed and support their families. When Red Guards opened fire in May 1918 on workers protesting shortages of food and jobs near Petrograd, a generalized anger and resentment spilled out in Moscow, Tula, Nizhnii Novgorod, Tver' and other industrial centers. In Petrograd, thousands gathered at meetings in the factory districts. Twenty-one plants sent delegations to the victims' funeral (*Novyi Den'*, 15, 16 May 1918; *Novaia Zhizn'*, 30 May 1918).

The spring of 1918 was also the period of massive exodus from Petrograd, and to a lesser extent from other cities as well. Research by Diane Koenker for Moscow gives some indication of the social consequences of this migration, and the ways it portended a more generalized 'de-urbanization' during the civil war. Between 1918 and 1920, 70 per cent of the 700,000 who left Moscow were children and non-working women between the ages of 20 and 59; of the workers who left, more than 90,000 were men, only 9,600 women (Koenker and Rosenberg, 1989, pp. 81–104; *Statisticheskii ezhegodnik*, 1927, pp. 46–51). Koenker argues that this placed a new emphasis on personal and local relations and identifications, and suggests that in these conditions of deprivation and stress, neighbourhoods may well have replaced the factory as the focus of working-class identity. In the process, it is possible that family ties, at least as they are reflected in marriage statistics, may have actually become stronger rather than weaker, as the literature often portrays, although the evidence here is mixed. In Moscow at least, the absolute number of registered marriages doubled in 1919 compared to 1918, and the relative number leapt from 54 per 10,000 in 1917 to 75 in 1918 and 174 in 1919. But by 1920, according to Barbara Clements, more than half of all marriages were also ending in divorce (Clements, 1989, p. 115; Koenker and Rosenberg, 1989, p. 97).

By the summer of 1918 even workers who were nominally employed were frequently absent from work, either because of illness or family problems, or because of the long hours now required to find adequate provisions. Workers were often forced to obtain food out of town on their own, 'requisition' fuel and raw materials, and perform independently and anarchically tasks ordinarily done by others. Illness accounted for approximately 25 per cent of the absentee rate, but more than half of all lost workdays were the result of workers having to procure goods for themselves and their families, as well as in many places for their factories. 'We must protest against the Centre's policies' even workers who carefully described themselves as 'conscious' and 'patiently starving revolutionaries' telegraphed Moscow from Ivanovo-Voznesensk late in 1918. 'Everything is taken from us. Nothing is provided ... We have not a pound of reserves ... We can accept no responsibility for what happens if our needs are not met' (*Ekonomicheskaia zhizn'*, 16 Nov. 1918). More than 5,000 similar complaints were received by party authorities in the course of 1919, according to official records, even from such Bolshevik supporters as the Central Committee of the Metalworkers' Union (*Izvestiia Gosudarstvennago Kontrolia*, 1 Nov. 1919). The drastic restrictions of the ration-card system had even 'left workers engaged in hard physical labour comparatively worse off than other social categories' (*Statistika Truda*, 1–4 (Jan.–Feb.) 1919, p. 34).

As we know, the winter of 1918–19 was devastating almost everywhere in Russia: in areas controlled by White forces in Siberia and South Russia, in the Ukraine, and in the centres of Bolshevik power. In Petrograd the months from December 1918 to March 1919 were the worst in the city's history in Mary McAuley's judgement. December was 'breadless', with only oats available for distribution for a time. Sickness and hunger were everywhere. Death-rates increased above 80 per 1,000. Calorie consumption was less than 1,500 per day, 800 less than the accepted minimum. By the end of the year, more than 50,000 apartments were vacant (McAuley, 1991, pp. 265–7, 280–1). Here and elsewhere most enterprises still functioning shifted to some form of piecework, with official wages determined by centralized norms and paid in kind. When goods themselves could not be obtained, wages went into arrears and workers and their families went hungry. Even the price of tea was four times higher than it was at the beginning of 1916; bread, six times more; meat, almost 20 times greater (Rabinovich, 1923, pp. 45 ff; *Statistika Truda*, 1 (15 July 1918), p. 10). Vegetables were in such short supply even in the summer that their prices in the aggregate in 1918 were 50 times the prevailing rates of the summer of 1916 (*Statistika Truda*, 1 (15 July 1918), p. 10).

Again, the flattening quality of these statistics masks a deep and pervasive suffering, as if the anxieties of everyday life could be objectively aggregated. When we learn that more than 1,250,000 workers registered as unemployed in 48 provinces of Soviet Russia during 1919, and that the figure grew to 1,703,000 for 46 provinces in 1920, we need to recognize the magnitude of this dislocation in the lives of individuals and families (Isaev, 1924, p. 31). Absenteeism even among employed workers may have run as high as 65 per cent throughout 1919, while in the first third of 1920, more than 40 per cent of work time may have been lost. For the year, the figure was more than 30 per cent (Rabinovich, 1923, p. 36; Frolov, 1920, p. 20). In the metals sector, once the bastion of Bolshevik activism, another fourth of the workforce was dismissed in 1920 both to reduce production costs and to lower the welfare obligations assumed by employment; in textiles, more than half of those employed in 1918 lost their jobs (Rashin, 1922, pp. 67–8). Those still working were now largely paid with army rations, a considerable privilege.

It is only by 1920 that one can begin to discern a degree of stabilization in everyday urban life in Soviet Russia, brought on finally in part by the Bolsheviks' increasing military success in the civil war, in part by the fact that the dramatic changes which had already occurred had left a residual population somewhat able to cope. Declines in food supply and production levelled off. In some areas there was even a demand for new workers. This small semblance of stability did little, however, to improve day-to-day conditions to any significant degree, and nothing to assuage increasingly bitter feelings, even among the workers of Petrograd who were nominally the Bolsheviks' strongest supporters. On the eve of the Kronstadt rebellion in early 1921, strikes and labour protests here were among the most threatening of the entire civil-war period.

As is well known, moreover, it was also during these latter months of the civil war that much of the Russian countryside lapsed into almost complete chaos. Food production in many places virtually stopped; towns and villages were overrun with deserters and marauding bands. As the civil war itself came to a close in 1921, consequently, the years of revolution and warfare reaped their final devastating toll. The famine which ravaged 33 provinces in 1921–22 directly affected more than 40 million, an extraordinary figure for a country that had only recently been one of the world's largest agricultural producers. Between 1 July 1921 and 30 June 1922, some 850,000 were forced by hunger to leave their villages, the largest numbers coming from Simbirsk, Samara and the region around Kazan (Bukhman, 1923, pp. 4–6). Eight hundred thousand people are estimated to have died from typhus, typhoid, dysentery and cholera, adding to the more than one million persons who succumbed to these diseases in 1920 (Lorimer, 1946, p. 41). Meanwhile, in urban areas, unemployment during 1921–22, especially among women, again became critical as military production largely came to an end and a new wave of dismissals occurred. In July 1922, it may have been as high as 43 per cent, with women constituting almost 70 per cent of all those unable to find jobs (Rashin, 1922, pp. 77–8). In Moscow, only about a fourth of those without work received benefits; in Petrograd, only around 5 per cent (Isaev, 1924, pp. 72–3).

One can augment these figures in many ways for this last phase of Russia's everyday life crisis: by detailing a new rise in mortality statistics; by describing further the new deprivations experienced by women and especially children, seven million of whom may now have been homeless and without families; by attempting to measure in some reasonable form the level of trauma that reduced peasants in some areas to cannibalism, and allowed roving bandits to visit tortures and mutilations on those they held 'responsible' with a cruelty difficult to imagine (see esp. Figes, 1989, chap. 7; Ball, 1994, *passim*). Far more important in terms of understanding everyday life in this momentous 'time of troubles', however, and in ultimately understanding its long-term consequences, is to grasp, however tenuously, the underlying subjectivities that made the upheavals of war and revolution in Russia a period of such profound human suffering and loss.

Further reading

Balabanov M., 'Rabochii klass nakanune revoliutsii', in A. Anskii, ed., *Professional'noe dvizhenie v Petrograde v 1917 godu* (Leningrad, Ist Prof: Izd. Len. Obl. Sov. Profsoiuzov, 1928).

Ball A. M., *And Now My Soul is Hardened: Abandoned Children in Soviet Russia, 1918–1930* (Berkeley and Los Angeles, University of California Press, 1994).

Brower D. R., '"The City in Danger": The Civil War and the Russian Urban Population,' in Koenker *et al.*, eds., *Party, State and Society in the Russian Civil War* (Bloomington, Indiana University Press, 1989).

Bukhman K. N., 'Golod 1921 goda i diatel'nost' inostrannykh organizatsii', *Vestnik Statistiki* 4–6 (1923).

Clements B. E., 'The Effects of Civil War on Women and Family Relations', in Koenker *et al.*, eds., *Party, State, and Society in the Russian Civil War* (Bloomington, Indiana University Press, 1989).

Davies R. W., ed., *From Tsarism to the New Economic Policy* (Ithaca, NY, Cornell University Press, 1990).

Dobb M., *Soviet Economic Development Since 1917* (New York, International Publishers, 1948).

Figes O., *Peasant Russia, Civil War: The Volga Countryside in Revolution (1917–1921)* (Oxford, Oxford University Press, 1989).

Frolov K. I., 'Proguly, rabota i zarabotnaia plata rabochikh za 1920 god', *Izvestiia Ivanovo-Voznesenskogo Gub. Ekon. Soveshchaniia* 1 (December 1920).

Golopolosov A. I., *Obzor zheleznodorozhnogo transporta (po dannym chrezvychainoi revizii 1919 g.)* (Moscow, Nar. Kom. Rab. Kres. Inspektsii, 1920).

Haimson L., Rosenberg W. G. and Rieber A., discussants, 'The Problem of Social Identities in Early Twentieth Century Russia', *Slavic Review* 47, 1 (1988).

Isaev A., *Bezrabotitsa v SSSR i bor'ba s neiu (za period 1917–1924 gg.)* (Moscow, Izd. 'Vosprosy Truda', 1924).

Kleinbort L. N., *Istoriia bezrabotitsy v Rossii, 1857–1919 gg.* (Moscow, Izd. VTsSPS, 1925).

Klemenchich V., *Itogi raboty zheleznykh dorog za 3 goda (1917–1920)* (Moscow, Lit-Izdat. Otdel Tsekhran i Politupravl. NKPS, 1920).

Koenker D. P., 'Urbanization and Deurbanization in the Russian Revolution and Civil War', in Koenker *et al.*, eds., *Party, State, and Society in the Russian Civil War* (Bloomington, Indiana University Press, 1989).

Koenker D. P. and Rosenberg W. G., *Strikes and Revolution in Russia, 1917* (Princeton, Princeton University Press, 1989).

Kokhn M. P., *Russkie indeksty tsen* (Moscow, 1926).

Kvitkin O., 'Naselenie gorodov Evropeiskoi chasti RSFSR po perepisam 1897, 1917, 1920, 1923 gg.', *Biulleten'* TsSU (Moscow, 1923).

Lorimer F., *The Population of the Soviet Union: History and Prospects* (Geneva, League of Nations, 1946).

Lubny-Gertsyk L. I., *Dvizhenie naseleniia na territorii SSSR za vremia mirovoi voiny i revoliutsii* (Moscow, Gosplan SSSR, Izd. 'Planovoe Khoziaistvo', 1926).

Materialy po statistike putei soobshcheniia (Moscow, NKPS, 1927).

McAuley M., *Bread and Justice: State and Society in Petrograd, 1917–1922* (Oxford, Oxford University Press, 1991).

Nove A., *An Economic History of the USSR* (London, Penguin Books, 1982).

Prokopovich S. N., 'Dinamika naseleniia SSSR', *Biulleten' Ekonomicheskogo Kabineta Prof. S. N. Prokopovicha* 7(80) (Moscow, 1930).

Rabinovich A. I., *Trud i byt rabochego* (Moscow, Izd. VSNKh, 1923).

Rashin A., 'Perspektivy bezrabotitsy v Rossii', *Vestnik Truda* 4, 22 (1922).

Rashin A., 'Dinamika rabochego sostava v promyshlennosti za 1913–1922 gg.', *Voprosy Zarabotnoi Platy* (Moscow, Izd. VSNKh, 1923).

Rosenberg W. G., 'The Democratization of Russia's Railroads', *American Historical Review* 86, 5 (December 1981).

Sidorov A. L., *Ekonomicheskoe polozhenie Rossii v gody pervoi mirovoi voiny* (Moscow, Izd. Nauka, 1973).

Sidorov K. F., 'Rabochee dvizhenie v Rossii v gody imperialisticheskoi voiny', in M. N. Pokrovskii, ed., *Ocherki po istorii oktiabr'skoi revoliutsii*, Vol. I (Moscow and Leningrad, Gosizdat, 1927).

Statisticheskii ezhegodnik goroda Moskvy i moskovskoi gubernii, issue 2 (Moscow, Biuro Stat. goroda Moskvy, 1927).

TsSU (Tsentral'noe Statisticheskoe Upravlenie), 'Sbornik statisticheskikh svedenii po Soiuzy S.S.R.', *Trudy* (Moscow, 1924).

TsSU, *Rossiia v mirovoi voine 1914–1918 goda (v tsifrakh)* (Moscow, 1925).

TsSU, 'Fabrichno-zavodskaia promyshlennost' v period 1913–1918 godov', *Trudy* 26, issue 2 (Moscow, 1926).

Volkov E. Z., *Dinamika naseleniia SSSR za vosem'desiat let* (Moscow, 1930).

War Communism

SILVANA MALLE*

The term 'war communism' is generally used to describe the period from summer 1918 to spring 1921, a period during which the Communist Party was to fight a civil war and emerge as the only political power in the country. This periodization, consecrated by the pioneering works of E. H. Carr, Maurice Dobb and E. G. Gimpel'son, still holds if one focuses on the main features of war communism: nationalization of industry and redistribution of land, centralization of power, obligatory quotas for delivery of foodstuffs to the state (*prodrazverstka*), and the naturalization of the economy. If, however, the focus falls on the origin of the new system, on values and projects, policy-making and deeds, this periodization is unsatisfactory and misleading. It is unsatisfactory because it does not identify the endogenous causes of the transformation, and misleading because the civil war inevitably becomes an exogenous and determining factor in institutional developments. Understanding the origins of war communism helps one to understand its legacy – the development and the collapse of the Soviet system. The origins of war communism must be looked for, first of all, in the projects and aims of its protagonists.

Ideology

The ideological framework is important: this was indeed 'communism', as theorized by many influential Bolsheviks before and immediately after the seizure of power and perceived as such by close observers. Military emergency may have been the necessary condition for war communism, but it was not sufficient. The distinguishing feature of communism, as an alternative to the market and individualism, was that production should be separated from distribution: 'from each according to his ability, to each according to his needs'. This goal was shared by socialists in general. The *Communist Manifesto* had seen the abolition of private property in banking and the means

---

* The views expressed in this article are those of the author and do not necessarily reflect those of the OECD.

of production as a prerequisite for socialism. Marx never gave more than a sketch of the system which would replace capitalism, suggesting a state framework for decisions on capital depreciation, investment and distribution out of the social consumption fund. Most Bolsheviks, like many European radical socialists, thought that by the turn of the century capitalism was ripe for collapse, that the World War was a sign of this collapse and that socialism should, indeed, get ready to replace capitalism. Under the influence of Karl Kautsky, Lenin further stressed the need for state power in *State and Revolution* and in *Can the Bolsheviks Retain State Power?*, and added his own contributions: the theory of the vanguard party and the use of violence against capitalist resistance. Workers' organizations under party leadership were expected to check the work of specialists, whose support for the revolution was not taken for granted, but whose necessity was by and large appreciated by the Bolsheviks. Lenin had in mind a kind of police state in which the party would mobilize workers, and would, with these workers, use coercion when the continued existence of capitalist ideas made this necessary. In the words of Lenin's post-Soviet biographer, Dmitrii Volkogonov, 'Lenin reinforced his "mainline" Marxism with everything that made that teaching uncompromising, harsh and radical.'

Marx and Engels had dismissed as 'barrack-room communism' models based on frugality and egalitarianism, sharing of canteens and dormitories, and rule by top committees, in which 'contempt for ordinary life acquires the highest meaning'. For many Bolsheviks, however, including Lenin and Trotsky, communism was indeed 'war communism', as their contemporary Aleksandr Bogdanov presciently put it, that is, a combination of rule from above and strict obedience from below, distribution of goods through rationing and decisive opposition to any form of individual appropriation. This simulacrum of communism emerged during World War I. (Lenin used the term *ex post* to distance himself from the experience.) What Bogdanov clearly perceived was that the institutionalization of coercion was implicit in the Bolshevik 'approach to any task as a question of shock work rather than organization'.

Anti-market approach

Coercion, indeed, was embodied in any socialist ideal to the extent that distribution by the market was not accepted. This explains the initial support that the Bolsheviks found among socialists in Russia and abroad. The desire to control the market was widely shared in the socialist camp for quite a long time, although not everyone realized that compulsion cannot be avoided if incentives anchored in individual property rights are not replaceable in society as a whole by high individual moral standards and self-sacrifice. This is why many blamed individuals rather than ideals and methods for the use of coercion.

The war-communist experience after October 1917 can be understood as an unsuccessful but continuous effort to control markets by decree, starting with the goods market and ending with labour, and to force society to accept increasing state control, from distribution to production, irrespective of performance. As government control over distribution increased, industrial supply shrank, the area under cultivation contracted, illegal markets mushroomed, and corruption became pervasive. This in turn prompted tighter control over the trade in and production of a wider range of goods and the expropriation of any possible surplus, particularly in foodstuffs.

Six major decisions mark the Bolshevik determination to fight the market: the order of 17 February 1918 issued by Trotsky to all local soviets, railway committees and patrols to fight *meshochnichestvo* (bagman trade) by means ranging from confiscation to execution on the spot, followed by the decree on railways of 23 March 1918 'to curb the anarchy of the market and create a wide basis for its regulation by the state'; the decree of 19 January 1918 on mandatory membership of citizens in consumers' communes, as the first step towards state-controlled distribution; the decree of 2 April 1918 'on commodity exchange to strengthen food supply' giving the food commissariat (*Narkomprod*) monopoly rights over trade in a number of consumer goods used in exchange for food and placing these goods under the control of the rural poor in the localities; the decree of 14 May on food dictatorship, authorizing the use of armed force in food collection; the decree of 21 November 1918 on the organization of supply to the population of all products and consumer goods, extending *Narkomprod*'s monopoly of supply to non-monopoly goods by giving it the right to nationalize, requisition and confiscate trade enterprises. By the autumn of 1918 in three-fifths of Russian provinces private wholesale trade had already been shut down, and in one-third of the provinces even retail trade had stopped working. The progressive shut-down of trade outlets went along with policies to control distribution in kind and a heavily bureaucratized network of consumer cooperatives.

The main steps towards the naturalization of commodity exchange taken in 1918 prepared the ground for policies of armed food and fodder requisition in 1919 and 1920. This is crucial for understanding both how a leading party with a small constituency survived the civil war and the nature and intensity of the revolts which in 1921 prevented any further anti-market leaps forward.

The social base of the Communist Party

The Bolshevik Party was responsible for the most important decisions taken after the revolution, although its limited social base meant that it had initially to compromise with other parties such as the Left Socialist Revolutionaries (Left SRs) and the Mensheviks on several policy issues. At the beginning of 1918 most of the 400,000 or so members of the Bolshevik Party were workers and employees (56.9 per cent and 22.4 per cent respectively) with peasants accounting for only 14.5 per cent. In the September 1917 elections for 455 of Russia's 643 urban dumas, the Bolsheviks got 7 per cent of the vote; at the uezd level they got 2.2 per cent. The socialist bloc, Mensheviks and Socialist Revolutionaries (SRs), and the Constitutional Democrats fared much better. The local non-party groups, with 50.3 per cent of the vote and wide representation, which Lenin thought could be won over to communism, were difficult to categorize in the early stages of democracy.

Thus, after taking power, the Bolsheviks could not have an immediate impact all over the country, nor would it be correct to regard any major economic and institutional development after the revolution as their responsibility alone. For quite a while collective decision-making at each soviet level was the practice. Factories and enterprises were confiscated and their products requisitioned by the local authorities, before central decisions on nationalization had been approved and even against the wishes of the centre. The Bolsheviks had the support of the Left SRs until March 1918. Even in the period between the repudiation of the the the Brest-Litovsk Treaty (3 March) by the other socialist parties and the expulsion of these parties from local soviets in June–July, the Left SRs numbered from 20 to 35 per cent in many soviets. They promoted the practice of egalitarian land partitioning, which productivity-oriented Bolshevik leaders looking forward to large-scale farming disliked. The Left SRs, by and large, were in favour of the naturalization of the economy and supported the programme of collective commodity exchange.

Communist takeover of the state

In spite of its electoral weakness, the Bolshevik government was able to create and run the central organs of power: the Council of People's Commissars (*Sovnarkom*) presided over 13 ex-ministries transformed into commissariats. On 2 December 1917 VSNKh (the Supreme Council of the National Economy) was founded with the task of planning and coordinating the economy. VSNKh was empowered to carry out confiscation, requisition and sequestration, to mandate trusts for branches of industry and to issue mandatory orders to any local government economic department. VSNKh prepared and carried out the nationalization of all joint-stock companies in June 1918. It acquired the status of a People's Commissariat in August 1918. After the approval of the July 1918 constitution, other commissariats, including that of State Control, were added to the government. From the autumn of 1918 a small council, later to become the Council of Labour and Defence, took over many of the functions of the *Sovnarkom* in policy-making. The centralization of government functions proceeded along with the strengthening of Communist control over all state bodies.

The Communists invaded the state organs. As early as March 1918 some 200,000 party members had been placed in the state administration and between spring and August 1918 they took over state institutions *en masse*. The highest concentration was in the commissariats of the interior, foreign affairs and in the Cheka. In the Commissariat of Justice 23.1 per cent, and in VSNKh 22.3 per cent of the staff were Communists. Although not a majority, the Communists held the highest positions. In 1920 the Communists were proportionally better represented in the provincial (gubernia) soviet congresses, than at the uezd level (76 per cent versus 42 per cent), and the 30 per cent proportion of Red Army representatives was an additional contribution to the military communistization of power.

Industrial management

In the aftermath of the revolution the Bolsheviks needed the factory committees, in which they were better represented than in the trade unions. Workers' control bodies and congresses were institutionalized on 14 November and were granted the right to issue binding decisions on management. This was a contested decision imposed by Lenin, who weighed the advantage of having the *longa manus* of Bolshevik power in private industry against the disruption which these bodies could bring in production. Supported neither by the trade unions, nor by the VSNKh technocrats, the factory committees had no major impact on economic developments, apart from scattered individual initiatives confiscating plants and requisitioning stocks in early 1918. When the nationalization of large-scale industry took place in June 1918, the former managers were obliged to remain at their posts, under political control, and one-man management became the rule. Three decrees on management were issued between 1918 and 1920. Workers' participation was reduced to *ex post* supervision, undertaken by the trade unions which by 1920 had become 'transmission belts' for political orders. The institution of political commissars in most factories helped the leadership to maintain its control over industry. This system proved to be more effective than collegial management. It outlasted war communism.

Legacies: structures and plans

Given the Communists' lack of skill and experience in economic matters, the organizational legacies of tsarism and of the short-lived but active Provisional Government became important. VSNKh replaced the Chief Economic Committee created under tsarism, and took over the branch chief committees (*glavki*) which the latter had coordinated and which controlled prices and distributed products for military orders. The *glavki* became the backbone of VSNKh's industrial organization, its production sections and later its branch central offices. It was they who in practice collected and coordinated enterprises' estimates and decided on financing, plant closures and the relocation of equipment. Thus the industrial conglomerates created under tsarism provided the structure (and the departmental approach) of the war-communist system.

The Communist leaders also inherited the theoretical premises of a general plan for the economy and labour developed by imaginative economists, one of the most radical of whom was V. G. Groman, who had chaired the Food Board of the Petrograd Soviet from March 1917. The plan assumed that by fixing state monopoly prices for industry and agriculture it would be possible to work out non-market state commodity price ratios and extract the agricultural surplus at below market prices. Consumption norms of peasant farms were worked out on the basis of local budget surveys, after which the agricultural surplus was calculated on the basis of the cultivated area. This plan worked out in 1917 provided the economic principles for the Communist policy of collective commodity exchange and food collection – an experiment which was tried in March 1918. The policy ended in failure, not only because the price ratio was totally out of touch with reality, but also because the Bolsheviks imposed collective exchange, meaning that the local community had joint responsibility for delivery of grain stocks, but industrial goods were to be delivered, under the control of the rural poor, in proportion to the population, rather than in proportion to each farm's contribution. The macroeconomic plan of exchange and distribution on which highly qualified economists continued to work during war communism was also the basis for the single economic plan in 1921.

By mid-1918 the Communists were already in control of existing consumer cooperatives, former Menshevik strongholds which served three-quarters of the population. By the end of 1919, a central Section of General Distribution presided over what was, in principle, a nationwide network of state-controlled cooperatives. The section's local bodies estimated local demand, taking into account population and industry, informed the centre and redistributed shipments of goods and products. The main organ in charge was *Narkomprod*. For the purpose of distribution the population was divided into six class-based categories with different ration entitlements. The distribution plan for 1920–21 embraced 37,520,300 people, of whom about 8.4 million were industrial workers and their families.

In parallel with plans of distribution, plans of utilization were devised. In spring 1919 a Commission for Utilization, created at VSNKh in November 1918, started working on material estimates of stocks of products and current output. In 1920 the plans of utilization apportioned the output of some 325 products among the population and industry in terms of physical units. These plans also included reserves and set factory, wholesale and retail prices. Industrial demand was computed taking into account effective utilization of capacity and technical coefficients of production. For consumer goods, tables of equivalents were used, in order to allow for some flexibility in payment in kind. These plans were far from realistic and the percentage of fulfilment did not suggest that industry was working in conformity with them. However, work done in this field was carried out with determination and in the belief that once the war was over, the economy, including agricultural output, could be planned from above.

In December 1920 a law was approved to form sowing committees, with the purpose of replacing farmers' decisions by central mandatory commands with targets down to the district level. This was to be achieved by redistributing means and materials of production among individual units. At the same time the Commissariat of Finance and the *Sovnarkom* approved a decision to work out a new accounting unit based on labour as a measure of value, on which work was done in the first part of 1921.

In the increasingly uncompromising political mood of 1920, the victorious Communist government was seriously considering implementing a single plan of production and distribution, but peasant revolts and workers' unrest, culminating in the sailors' mutiny in Kronstadt, halted the leap forward to full-scale communism. The revolts could no longer be blamed on opposition sabotage. Many Communists understood that a single plan could not be realized without further compulsion. For those most determined to go ahead, the further step that was needed was the collectivization of land, an idea which the Bolsheviks had never discarded.

Coercion

N. D. Kondrat'ev, who worked in the team of economic advisors to the Provisional Government, stressed that the Communists did not change the food procurement plans prepared under the Provisional Government. They only introduced a qualitatively new element justified by class struggle: coercion, which neither the Mensheviks nor the Left SRs were ready to approve. The use of force against the propertied class, marked by the decrees of December 1917 on the nationalization of banks and on the abolition of payment of dividends, could be interpreted as a component of the revolution – the dispossession of one class by another. Coercion in food procurement, on the other hand, which was proclaimed in May 1918 with the decree on the food procurement dictatorship, must be understood as an organizational means which characterizes both the approach to, and the methods of, tackling economic problems under war communism. This would be a lasting legacy for the Soviet system. The decision to centralize the supply of foodstuffs to the urban population in the hands of *Narkomprod*, and to keep monopoly purchase prices fixed at the August 1917 level, in spite of rampant inflation (the market price was about 8–10 times the fixed price), was adopted even though many Bolsheviks knew that a price increase would help procurement. This decision was, in fact, overruled by some local soviets which lifted the ceiling on purchase prices. As long as private channels remained open, people found ways to augment their meagre rations. The fight against *meshochnichestvo*, which Bolsheviks blamed as the cause rather than the effect of the shortage, did not help, particularly in late 1919 when the Cheka also began to be involved in fighting illegal trade (*otpustnichestvo*). More than once limited private trade was authorized after workers' unrest. It was only in the winter of 1920–21, in order to prepare a consumption fund large enough to implement the single economic plan, that the right to purchase in the private market was restricted to Soviet institutions and cooperatives working for *Narkomprod*. After *Sovnarkom*'s decision to prohibit the utilization of agents and intermediaries in state supply and the closure of the famous Sukharevka market in Moscow, famine spread across the country.

In food procurement, the Bolsheviks used the rural poor against the rest of the peasantry. In one sense, the creation of Committees of the Rural Poor (*kombedy*) in early June 1918 aided the Bolsheviks since they provided local organizations which could be made responsible for uncovering food and, with the help of Red Guards, armed food detachments and the military units of the Cheka, for extracting it from the villages. But the 'rural poor' were often not even local inhabitants; the attempt to use them actually reinforced the social cohesiveness of the peasantry as a whole; and after securing a parcel of land, the rural poor themselves shared the same interests as the other peasants. The authorities faced severe resistance both before and after the institutionalization of the *kombedy*. And even after the *kombedy* had been abolished, and an amnesty had been granted in 1919 to the middle peasants who had taken part in protests, the revolts did not stop. In the areas under counterrevolutionary government the peasants also revolted against the authorities. The question of where the peasants stood during the civil war has been long debated. The correct answer is probably that what the peasants actually wanted was to be let alone. This mood got bolder after the end of the civil war. In the second half of 1920, 64 anti-Soviet revolts occurred in which a large number of peasants took part. The best known of these was the one led by Antonov in Tambov province, which had been particularly savaged by food requisitions.

The Communist government succeeded in requisitioning considerable amounts of foodstuffs, a large part of which went to the Red Army, but, even with coercion, it did not do better than past governments, and did not succeed in providing sufficient and equitable distribution to the urban centres. Part of the food stocks spoiled in state warehouses, part was lost or stolen. By the end of 1920 large-scale pilfering was widespread in the state institutions. Under war communism the illegal market continued to supply between 65 and 70 per cent of the food necessary for survival. At the same time the peasants' losses were dramatic. As a whole in 1920–21, their direct and indirect payments, including requisitioning of cattle and similar taxes, were at least twice the pre-war level.

Economic organization

Even before the spring of 1918, besides nationalizing the banks and the land, the government also approved the cancellation of domestic and foreign state debt, the nationalization of the commercial fleet, the institution of local and provincial labour exchanges through which hiring was made mandatory, as well as the subordination of the consumers' cooperatives to state control. With the nationalization of the oil industry and of the joint-stock companies in June 1918, the Communist government was in control of the major part of industrial inventories and output and could dispose of large stocks of weapons. It also had the greater part of the population on its territory. These facts gave it superiority in the civil war.

By the end of 1920, the peak of war communism, there was state control over all sectors of the economy and most products. Few private retail traders remained, although some small-scale private trade and industrial undertakings survived, particularly in the areas which later came under Soviet control. The economy was largely, but not fully naturalized. The steps towards naturalization of the economy were by and large independent from monetary policy and skyrocketing inflation. Money continued to be printed to finance the state budget. Inter-enterprise transactions in the state-controlled sphere did not involve the use of money, but were recorded in accounts at prices fixed by VSNKh. Cash was still authorized and used for current operations outside the state sphere. The illegal wholesale and retail trade market survived together with pilfering, bribery and corruption.

The organization of the economy was geared to sustain the civil-war effort from the autumn of 1918. But the organization of military production operated as an enclave within the general economic organization. To assist military industry special organs were created to establish direct links between military and civilian industry. These bodies were directly subordinated to the Council of Labour and Defence. They advanced funds to enterprises working on military orders, and those enterprises' liabilities were written off when output was delivered. Political commissars used informal links to ensure the supply of fuel, foodstuffs and raw materials. With the creation of the Council of War Industry (*Promvoensovet*) in August 1919, which was given broad powers to open and close military factories and to assign extra-budgetary funds for the implementation of military orders, the organization of supply was completed. Besides the centralized military organization, a large number of private craftsmen worked for the army. They were important for the supply of personal equipment.

Labour conscription, which was enshrined in the 1918 constitution and in the Soviet Labour Code, was implemented according to needs rather than plans and was accompanied by a differentiation of wages and salaries in kind. However, by the end of the civil war the militarization of labour had become the foundation of the programme of reconstruction. Call-up lists of all able-bodied workers were compiled, and industrial workers had to register at a special military bureau. Failure to register was regarded as desertion. The army was supplied, but the population starved. In 1918 at least one-third of Soviet government outlays were spent on the military. In 1919 the Red Army claimed 40 per cent of the bread produced in Soviet territory and in 1920 the Red Army was a major consumer of the national product. From 1915 to 1923 wars, famine and epidemics caused a population deficit of 30 million. Approximately two-thirds of this deficit occurred between 1918 and 1923. Dreadful living conditions and widespread epidemics made 1920 the year that cost most lives.

War communism and command economy

It has often been argued that if the civil war had not interfered with the process of building communist institutions, the New Economic Policy, which was approved by the Tenth Congress of the party in March 1921 and marked the end of war communism, would have been applied from 1918. Lenin's writings in April of that year concerning the need for bourgeois specialists, for productivity increases and for Taylorism, and the party debate on those issues, it has been argued, could have been a turning point in the approach to the construction of socialism. But the same writings show that Lenin himself had nc clear ideas on how to provide incentives to produce, and compulsion was never ruled out. When he was at the head of VSNKh and the issue of increasing productivity was raised, Lenin argued that labour conscription, to which workers were already *de facto* subject, could only be extended to the bourgeoisie; to increase labour discipline among workers, he stressed, would require special inspectors selected from the ranks of the trade unions, and the enforcement of criminal punishment.

The stages in the development of the communist organization of the economy were marked by both ideological preconceptions and expediency. The means used to transform the market system were coercion against enemies and potential opponents, and mobilization within the party ranks. Commands replaced incentives and state bureaucracy replaced owners and specialists. Coercion and mobilization could not be effective without a high degree of political centralization. Effective administrative centralization of the economy was never attained, but political centralization provided a surrogate which worked during and after war communism. The foundations of the command economy were laid down in the first years of Soviet power, as were the means for its survival. The use of specialists in government and industry and of tsarist officers in the army was crucial for ensuring the level of performance required to survive and win the civil war. In both civilian and military institutions a passive acceptance of hardship and terror – the logic of collective action – was ensured by vigilant party members and political commissars. The large number of military deserters, 1,761,105 in 1919, does not suggest highly motivated support in all ranks.

The most comprehensive Western account of the civil war, that of Richard Pipes, concludes that the survival of Communist power was due to the unrestrained brutality of the Bolsheviks, who prevented their troops from retreating, and to disunity and an inability to conceive political alternatives on the part of the counterrevolutionaries. Casualties were very high, both among the Red Army, which suffered much greater losses than the Imperial Army in World War I, and among the civilian population, which accounted for 91 per cent of the victims. The population fell more in areas under Bolshevik control than in the areas under the control of the White armies.

War communism left the country impoverished and prostrated. There are no fully reliable data on the fall in output, but the data available show a dramatic fall, particularly in the central regions which were under Soviet rule. The output value of semi-finished products in 1920 was less than 20 per cent of the corresponding value in 1912. The total area under grain cultivation declined by some 25 per cent, in part because of the parcellization of the land among small farms and lack of implements, and in part in response to *prodrazverstka*. The cultivated area of the Lower Volga, which remained under Soviet control throughout the war, fell much more than the Middle Volga area which underwent changes of rule.

The New Economic Policy announced in March 1921 was marked by the replacement of *prodrazverstka* with a tax in kind (*prodnalog*). The same party congress also approved a ban on factionalism within the party. *Prodnalog*, the total amount of which was set in advance, was to be based on the contribution of individual farms, and sustained by a limited re-opening of local markets. The market helped the reconstruction of the economy in the 1920s. But the debate which preceded the launching of the first Five-Year Plan echoed many of the arguments raised during war communism in favour of a single economic plan. The protagonists were the same, most of them unrepentant, the belief in the vanguard party unshaken, and the Communist Party stronger than ever.

Further reading

Astrakhan Kh. M., 'Partinnost' naseleniia Rossii nakanune Oktiabriia (po materialam vyborov v gorodskie dumy v Mae-Oktiabre 1917)', *Istoriia SSSR* 6, (1987).

Bogdanov A. A., *Voprosy sotsializma* (Moscow, Izdatel'stvo politicheskoi literatury, 1990).

Bradley J., ed., 'War Communism', *Russian Studies in History* 33 (Summer 1994).

Carr E. H., *The Bolshevik Revolution, 1917–1923*, 3 vols. (London, Macmillan, 1950-3).

Dmitrenko V. P., *Sovetskaia ekonomicheskaia politika v pervye gody proletarskoi diktatury* (Moscow, Nauka, 1986).

Dobb M., *Soviet Economic Development after 1917* (London, Routledge and Kegan Paul, 1951).

Drobizhev V. Z. and Pivovar E. I., 'Kommunisty v tsentral'nykh organakh upravleniia RSFSR', *Voprosy istorii KPSS* 4, (1985).

Gimpel'son E. G., *Voennyi kommunizm: politika, praktika, ideologiia* (Moscow, 1973).

Gimpel'son E. G., 'Nachalnyi etap skladivaniia administrativno-komandnoi politicheskoi sistemy (1918–1920)', in V. P. Dmitrenko, ed., *Formirovanie administrativno-komandnoi sistemy* (Moscow, Nauka, 1992).

Kabanov V. V., *Krest'ianskoe khoziaistvo v usloviiakh 'voennogo kommunizma'* (Moscow, Nauka, 1988).

Malle S., *The Economic Organization of War Communism, 1918–1921* (Cambridge, Cambridge University Press, 1985).

Medvedev A. V., *Neonarodnichestvo i Bol'shevizm v Rossii v gody grazhdanskoi voiny* (Nizhnii Novgorod, 1993).

Morozov S. K., 'Nekotorye voprosy partiinogo rukovodstva sovetami v 1918–1920 gg.', *Voprosy istorii KPSS* 9, (1989).

Pipes R., *Russia under the Bolshevik Regime, 1919–1924* (Hammersmith, Fontana Press, 1994).

Remington T. F., *Building Socialism in Bolshevik Russia: Ideology and Industrial Organization, 1917–1921* (Pittsburgh, University of Pittsburgh Press, 1984).

Sakwa R., *Soviet Communists in Power: A Study of Moscow during the Civil War 1918–1921* (London, Macmillan, 1988).

Volkogonov D. A., *Lenin: Life and Legacy*, trans. and ed. Harold Shukman (London, HarperCollins, 1994).

NATIONALITY AND REGIONAL QUESTIONS

Nationality Policies

RONALD G. SUNY

From at least the moment of Ivan IV's conquest of Kazan (1552), there has been a peculiar connection between the forms of state power in Russia and the often dismissed 'national question'. When in the mid-sixteenth century Russia ceased to be a relatively homogeneous ethnic polity and became a multi-national one, the relations between the governing elite, made up largely of ethnic Russians and Russified non-Russians, over subordinate non-Russian peoples, variously referred to as *inorodtsy* or *inozemtsy*, were always unequal ones of subordination and superordination in which those with Russian cultural competence held privileged access to power and prestige. Though access to the elite was never closed off entirely to non-Russians, the degree of difficulty for upward social movement differed among the non-Russian peoples. While Baltic Germans had relatively easy *entrée* to the circles of power, other peoples, notably the Jews, Muslims of Central Asia, and Armenians after 1885, found their way blocked. The tsarist practices which both distinguished the core ethno-religious community, the Russians, from the 'others', and at the same time kept those peripheral 'others' in a subordinated relationship to the core nationality can be characterized as imperial.

Though a proto-autocracy existed in Muscovy before Ivan IV, the very longevity of autocracy and its accompanying ideological rationalizations were connected to the political imperative of maintaining state unity and the hierarchical social and ethnic structure in the face of the ethnic heterogeneity of the Russian empire. As long as peoples were understood to be ethnically or culturally superior and inferior, multi-nationality in a context of inequitable and exploitative inter-ethnic relations was a key structural impediment to the development of alternative political forms. The conservative support for basically inequitable, 'imperial' relations between peoples made devolution into more liberal constitutional forms difficult and rendered democratic reforms utopian. Though some Russian political leaders recognized, however reluctantly, that maintaining the empire precluded the likelihood of a representative political system, others, from liberals to Bolsheviks, attempted to force a marriage between the unitary state that tsarism had created and some form of democratic politics.

The variety of political entities within the Russian empire, from the Grand Duchy of Finland and the Viceroyalty of Caucasia to the khanates of Bukhara and Khiva, were indelible reminders of the stages of expansion that continued until the last days of Romanov rule. Held together both by military force and by the idea of loyalty to the tsar, the empire was not conceived in ethnic terms (*russkaia imperiia*) but as a cosmopolitan collection of peoples and polities (*rossiiskaia imperiia*) under a single sovereign. The ruling elite was equally cosmopolitan: Russian-speaking to be sure, but made up of members of many nationalities – Poles, Germans, assimilated Georgians and Tatars, among others – who once they had become loyal servitors of the emperor lost much of their identification with the people from which they had come. Ethnic elites were coopted into imperial service, and for much of the eighteenth and nineteenth centuries Russian policy was extraordinarily successful in deracinating those who might have been the leaders of resistance to central state rule.

Non-Russian peoples were governed in a contradictory system that involved indirect rule in some places, direct military government through local elites assimilated into the Russian administrative system in others, and various forms of constitutionalism (in the Grand Duchy of Finland and, until 1863, the Kingdom of Poland). Among the effects of tsarism was the imposition of a new state order on societies that had little contact with strong state structures, new regulations and laws, the spread of serfdom to certain regions, such as Georgia, and the enforcement of new taxation. This administrative 'Russification', the extension of bureaucratic absolutism over non-Russian subjects, was accompanied by a spontaneous self-Russification that many non-Russians found advantageous in the first two-thirds of the nineteenth century. But after 1881, when the government adopted more stridently anti-national and anti-semitic policies that threatened a forced cultural homogenization, even ethnicities which had been Russophilic, such as the Armenians, turned hostile to the tsarist regime.

The February revolution was marked by an extraordinary confidence in the power of juridical solutions to ameliorate deep social and ethnic conflicts. The evils that had led to class and nationality hostilities were laid at the doorstep of tsarism, and it was argued that proper legislation in the Western, liberal direction would remove obstacles to harmony. In one of its first acts (on 8 March) the Provisional Government restored the constitution of the Grand Duchy of Finland. The manifesto emphasized the illegality of tsarist regulations that contradicted the laws of Finland. Four days later the newspapers announced that the government intended to abolish all legal restrictions based on religion, nationality and 'class' (here referring primarily to official estates and ranks, *soslovie* and *chin*). When Prime Minister L'vov signed the law on 20 March, it was greeted by an editorial in the conservative *Novoe vremia* ('New Times') that expressed both the fear that 'the developing centrifugal forces and separatist aspirations of the nationalities that compose Russia' presented a 'real danger of the gradual decomposition of the state into its component parts' and the hope that '[n]ow all obstacles to mutual understanding among the peoples of Russia have withered away in the light of liberty dawning over the country'. Such optimism that 'liberty will unite' demonstrated faith in juridical solutions but also prepared the ground for bitter disappointment when problems associated with nationality proved to be far more intractable than imagined.

Towards the end of March, when the government worked out its provisions for local self-government, the principle of nationality was taken into consideration in two ways. In carving out a northern part of the province of Livland to be fused with Estland in the new province of Estonia, the demarcation line was to be an ethnic (Estonian/Latvian) one. In extending the zemstvos to Siberia and Arkhangel'sk province, the government exempted those areas occupied by the nomadic Samoeds, various other *inorodtsy*, and Cossacks, for whom special regulations and institutions would be implemented. Special laws were issued for Turkestan (where local authorities would decide if zemstvos were appropriate for various districts and peoples), the Kalmyk steppe and the lands of the 'Kyrgyz' (Kazakh) Inner Horde. Plans for extending zemstvos to Transcaucasia and the Cossack regions of southern Russia were still being formulated when the Provisional Government was overthrown.

Nationality was clearly a consideration in the formulation of policy, but the government and the principal parties with influence within and over it were much more concerned about the unity of the state in a time of acute danger. Rather than acceptance of the radical implications of the principle of national self-determination, liberal and conservative politicians maintained a paternalistic attitude towards most of the non-Russian peoples. And moderate socialists were willing to go along with the government's consistent delaying of hard choices until the convening of the Constituent Assembly.

The leading liberal party, the Kadets, opposed national territorial political autonomy, a federal structure for the new Russia, and any form of separatism. Representation would be geographic, rather than based on nationality. Proclaiming themselves for 'Russia, One and Indivisible', the Kadets saw manifestations of nationalism as signs of pro-German disloyalty. Pavel Miliukov told his fellow Kadets in May that:

the Party of the People's Freedom will endeavour to find a solution that, while giving an opportunity to the various regions of Russia to create their local autonomy on the principle of local legislation, will not at the same time destroy the unity of the Russian State. The preservation of the unity of the Russian State is the limiting factor conditioning the decisions of the Party. The division of the country into sovereign, independent units is considered by the Party as absolutely inadmissible.

The Kadets thus saw themselves as the champions of equal rights of individuals, rather than of peoples. Miliukov supported Russian hegemony in a multi-national state, though he wanted to end nationality restrictions such as those imposed under tsarism, for they inhibited the process of natural assimilation of minorities. Even more conservative than the Provisional Government, which promised independence for Poland, the Kadets were prepared to grant only autonomy to Poland and drew the line at the Ukraine. Miliukov and F. F. Kokoshkin told a delegation from the Ukrainian National Congress in late April that territorial autonomy was a danger to Russia's unity and that Ukrainians were not ready for independence.

To a greater degree than their leaders in the capital, provincial Kadets saw the February revolution 'as a means of "liberating" non-Russian nationalities; and despite the party programme's adherence to a non-federal, centralized system of government, some Kadets expressed themselves locally in favour of a new republican federation'. 'To some extent', William G. Rosenberg writes, 'the rights of Ukrainians, Georgians, and other national minorities were subordinated in Kadet practice to those of Great Russians, a posture of internal imperialism which had long characterized the tsarist regime itself, and which would cause Kadet leaders no end of difficulty in 1917, even within the ranks of their own party.' By the autumn of 1917, not surprisingly, leading Kadets had become political allies of the Cossacks, the traditional defenders of Russian statehood.

Just as on the issues of war and peace and questions of political and social legislation, so on the problem of the non-Russians, the leading organ of the *demokratiia*, the Petrograd Soviet, was seldom in agreement with the government. Even during the period of coalition the representatives of the moderate socialist parties developed a distinctive policy towards non-Russians that reflected both the pre-revolutionary positions of their parties and a greater sensitivity to the aspirations of the non-Russians. The Party of Socialist Revolutionaries had declared at its First Congress, in Imatra, Finland, in 1906 the 'unconditional right' of national self-determination, which included the right to political separation from Russia. Though some isolated voices called for subordination of the rights of nations to the mission of the socialist revolution, they were effectively silenced by an overwhelming majority. While the 'national question' was not a major concern for the neo-populists, the party was clear about its commitment to federalism – in contrast to the Social Democrats who supported a unitary state – and its opposition to coercion in order to preserve the empire. But, as Oliver Radkey writes, 'In 1906 the SRs were a party without responsibility; in 1917 they had achieved responsibility; and, as they surveyed the nationalities problem from the vantage-ground of offices of state, they came to conceive of it in a less generous spirit than during the years preceding the triumph of the revolution.'

In 1917 the party continued to favour federalism but now opposed separation. At the Third Party Congress, in May 1917, the rapporteur on state organization, the right SR M. V. Vishniak, envisioned Russia as Switzerland writ large, a federal state with a collegial executive, but, nevertheless, a single state – a *Bundesstaat* rather than a *Staatenbund*. Maximal national autonomy would be accommodated within the federation (even separate coinage and postal systems, but without tariff barriers), but secession was impermissible. Within these limits autonomy would be determined on the basis of mutual agreements. Only Poland was to be granted independence; Finland would remain tied to Russia for strategic reasons. When questioned about this anomalous treatment of Finland, Vishniak answered that Finnish independence would set a dangerous precedent and encourage separatist pretensions among other nationalities. On the national question the party as a whole followed the line of the right and rejected the left's support for secession. Even the centrist Viktor Chernov agreed that the All-Russian Constituent Assembly would first have to lay down the criteria within which national assemblies could elaborate their own claims to autonomy.

Social democracy was committed to national self-determination, and Lenin took that slogan farthest – to separation from the empire. In contrast to the Jewish Bund and the Armenian Dashnaktsutiun, which advocated the Austro-Marxist position of extraterritorial national-cultural autonomy for ethnicities (each nationality represented in parliament no matter where its members lived), the Bolsheviks rejected the idea of cultural autonomy in favour of non-ethnic regional autonomy. Lenin was also firm in his resistance to federalism. In the revolutionary year the Bolshevik position gave nationalities a stark choice: either full independence and separation from the rest of Russia or becoming part of a unitary socialist state with all cultural and civil rights guaranteed for working people. Lenin believed that national separatism would be reduced by Russian tolerance and support for full national self-determination to the point of independence. Only in 1918 did the Bolsheviks shift their position and come out in favour of a federal state in which nationalities would have their own national territorial homelands.

Both the Provisional Government and the Petrograd Soviet were committed to formal and complete independence for Poland. Since Germany was in control of most of Poland by early 1917, political support for Polish independence in no way threatened the war effort. But the concession to Poland only increased the appetites of the Finns and the Ukrainians, and the inherent conflict between the principle of national self-determination and the commitment of the leading political actors to the unity of the Russian state emerged into open political struggle within the first weeks of the revolution.

The manifesto of the government restoring Finland's constitution recognized the full 'internal independence' of the former Grand Duchy, but declared the Petrograd government 'the possessor of full sovereign power'. The Social-Democratic leadership of the Finnish parliament soon proposed that with the fall of the monarchy sovereignty should pass to the Finnish government, while conceding that the Provisional Government would continue to decide foreign and military policy for the time being. The future Bolshevik Otto Kuusinen concluded that this draft constitution gave Finland 'all that one could wish and is better than independence'. The reaction in Petrograd to the Finnish move, however, was quick, sharp, and negative. Russian policy, as initially formulated by Kerensky, rejected any firm pronouncement on the final status of Finland until the convening of the All-Russian Constituent Assembly.

The government's position was ultimately supported by moderate socialists in the soviets. When in early April the Finnish Social Democrats met with the Russian Menshevik leaders, the latter recognized Finland's right to self-determination but held that only the Constituent Assembly could ultimately determine the issue. The only major party to support Finland's full independence was the Bolsheviks. As early as 11 March, Lenin, still in Switzerland, had argued that 'the Russian proletariat will guarantee to a Finnish republic complete freedom, including the freedom to secede'. Lenin told the Seventh Conference of the Bolsheviks in April: 'Our attitude towards the separatist movement is indifferent, neutral.... We are for Finland receiving complete freedom because then there will be greater trust in Russian democracy, and the Finns will not separate.'

The attitude of the Petrograd authorities stimulated even more support for independence in Finland, and through May and June the Finnish Social Democrats pushed for a law (the *valtalaki*) that ascribed sovereignty to the Finnish Seim (parliament). The Russian socialists, however, hoped to delay the final disposition of Finland until the Constituent Assembly. In June, the First All-Russian Congress of Soviets adopted a broad resolution on the national question, proclaiming its support for decentralization of the state and broad political autonomy for regions that differ ethnically and socioeconomically from one another. It called on the government to issue a declaration recognizing the right of self-determination of all peoples, including separation, but left the final disposition of the various regions to be realized through a covenant with the national Constituent Assembly. Until the very last days of its existence the Provisional Government refused to concede full independence to Finland and proved willing to use armed force to enforce its policy in Finland.

The Provisional Government subordinated the principles of self-determination and democratic choice to preservation of the territory of the late empire. Moderate socialists in the soviets concurred with the government's strategy. Most of the peoples of the Russian empire were not determined in 1917 to secede from the new democratic state. Their faith lay in a constitutional solution within a renewed multi-national state, which overrode the risky choice of going it alone in time of war. In Kiev, however, a locally elected assembly, the Rada, issued its First Universal declaring autonomy for the Ukraine and itself the supreme political authority. Late in June delegates from the Provisional Government conferred in Kiev with representatives of the Rada, and after heated discussions the Petrograd delegation reluctantly decided to recognize the Rada's competence to work out reforms in the Ukraine and to run the region until the convocation of the Constituent Assembly. This attempt at compromise aggravated the July Crisis in Petrograd, when several members of the Kadet Party resigned from the government in protest over the concessions made in favour of Ukrainian autonomy.

Nationalism was relatively weak during the first revolutionary year, and was still largely centred among the ethnic intelligentsia, students and the lower middle classes of the towns, with at best a fleeting following among broader strata. Among Belorussians, Lithuanians and Azerbaijanis, rather than a sense of nationality, the paramount identification was with people nearby with whom one shared social and religious communality. Among these peoples neither nationalism nor socialism was able to mobilize large numbers into the political struggles that would decide their future. For several other nationalities, including the Latvians and Georgians, class-based socialist movements were far more potent than political nationalism. For still other nationalities, like the Ukrainians and the Estonians, nationality competed with a sense of class for the primary loyalty of workers and peasants with neither winning a dominant position. Among Armenians a socialist-nationalist party, the Dashnaktsutiun, dominated, and faced by the threat of annihilation at the hands of Ottoman Turks, Armenians rallied around an inclusive, all-class nationalism.

The choice for revolutionary Russia in 1917 was between keeping the empire or creating a new democratic state, which required allowing those nations that chose to secede to do so. Since the time of the French revolution, the discourse of the nation has included ideas of popular sovereignty and equality under the law. Nationalism rejects the unequal relations inherent in empire and pushes for full legal equality and representation of subordinated peoples. Both liberals and socialists believed in national self-determination as a political language, but when non-Russians opted for separation interests of state took precedence over principle.

Further reading

Carrère d'Encausse H., *The Great Challenge: Nationalities and the Bolshevik State, 1917–1930*, trans. Nancy Festinger (New York, Holmes and Meier, 1991).

Kazemzadeh F., *The Struggle for Transcaucasia (1917–1921)* (New York, Philosophical Library, 1951).

Pipes R., *The Formation of the Soviet Union: Communism and Nationalism, 1917–1923* (Cambridge, MA, Harvard University Press, 1954).

Radkey O., *The Agrarian Foes of Bolshevism: Promise and Default of the Russian Socialist Revolutionaries, February–October 1917* (New York, Columbia University Press, 1958).

Raeff M., 'Patterns of Russian Imperial Policy Toward the Nationalities', in E. Allworth, ed., *Soviet Nationality Problems* (New York, Columbia University Press, 1971).

Rosenburg W. G., *Liberals in the Russian Revolution: The Constitutional Democratic Party, 1917–1921* (Princeton, Princeton University Press, 1974).

Suny R. G., *The Revenge of the Past: Nationalism, Revolution, and the Collapse of the Soviet Union* (Stanford, Stanford University Press, 1993).

Upton A. F., *The Finnish Revolution 1917–1918* (Minneapolis, University of Minnesota Press, 1980).

Zaionchkovskii P. A., *Rossiiskoe samoderzhavie v kontse XIX stoletiia: Politicheskaia reaktsiia 80-kh – nachala 90-kh godov* (Moscow, Mysl', 1970).

The Revolution in the Baltics: Estonia and Latvia

OLAVI ARENS AND ANDREW EZERGAILIS

This chapter deals with the 1917 revolution in Estonia and Latvia. Lithuania, because it was occupied by German forces in 1915, was not directly involved.

The eastern Baltic area has historically been a borderland on the fringes of the Holy Roman Empire, of Poland–Lithuania, of Sweden, and of the Russian empire. Although after 1881 the Baltic provinces of Estland, Livland and Kurland had undergone severe Russification, which considerably reduced the political autonomy of the provinces based on the rights of the Baltic German nobility, in 1917 they still retained some cultural and administrative residues of the past in education, in religion (Lutheranism), and in the presence of a large German-language and German culture oriented public. The three provincial *Landtage* were technically still the highest self-governing institutions of the provinces. The literacy rate, even among the peasants, was more than 90 per cent.

Ironically it was precisely during the years of Russification that the existence of Estonian and Latvian culture and civic society became an irreversible reality. Estonian and Latvian political, intellectual and cultural life – the press, arts, literature and music – all burgeoned. An Estonian and Latvian middle class and intelligentsia emerged in the towns and cities to challenge the political position of the Baltic German bourgeoisie in urban self-government. As elsewhere, this intelligentsia divided into those who saw the future development of the provinces in terms of liberal values and advanced ideas of political and economic reform and those who adopted a Marxist or peasant socialist mode of thinking and sought solutions in revolutionary socialism. Marxism became especially strong in Latvia. Indeed, a Latvian Social-Democratic Party was established in 1904 from a merger of two existing Latvian social-democratic groups. From 1906 onward the party was affiliated to the Russian Social-Democratic Labour Party. In 1914, as a result of Lenin's efforts, the Bolshevik faction of the party emerged dominant. Except for a brief period in 1905–06, no separate

Map 4. The Baltic region 1917–1921

Estonian social-democratic party existed until one was established in 1917 on a combination of Kautskyite and Menshevik positions.

Peasant emancipation in the Baltic provinces had followed a pattern of its own and had produced a rural economic order and society different from that of Russia. Russia's two basic socio-political institutions, the village commune (*mir*) and the zemstvo, were absent in the Baltic provinces. A failed landless form of emancipation of 1816–19 was followed in 1856–60 by laws which provided for the purchase by some peasants of farms as private property. Although by the turn of the century an economically viable rural economy had evolved based on the large estates of the Baltic German nobility and an Estonian and Latvian landed peasant class, major rural social problems existed. About 50 per cent of all land in the provinces remained in the hands of the Baltic barons and a large landless and tenant-farmer peasant population had come into being. During the late nineteenth and early twentieth century industrialization led to urbanization and the growth of a factory worker population.

During the 1905 revolution, the intelligentsia in Estonia was split on whether to pursue revolutionary activity or not, while in Latvia intelligentsia leadership fell into the hands of Bolshevik social democrats and peasant socialists, which led to repeated confrontations with the authorities. In the Baltic urban centres the revolution began with the killing of 73 demonstrators and wounding of more than 200 in Riga. It ended in October with the killing of 90 demonstrators and the wounding of over 200 in Tallinn. The most conspicuous feature of the 1905 revolution in Latvia and Estonia, however, was the burning of the baronial manor houses. The latter led tsarist Russia to declare martial law in the region and to send in punitive expeditions. It is estimated that by 1908, when the punitive expeditions ended their work, approximately 300 Estonians and over 2,000 Latvians had been executed. Approximately 8,000 Latvians were deported to Siberia or fled abroad.

World War I made the eastern Baltic a battlefield and put Russia's control of the area at risk. The Russian army used Lithuania and Kurland (south Latvia) as a staging-post for an attack on East Prussia. The ensuing German counter-offensive led to German occupation of Lithuania and Kurland, and called into question the political future of those areas.

As the Russian army retreated, it pursued a scorched-earth policy. In Kurland, grainfields were burned and thousands of Latvian peasants and Jews were ordered to leave their domiciles. As the German army approached Riga, the city's factories and workers were evacuated. One result of the evacuation was that Latvian workers and revolutionaries were dispersed all over Russia's cities, from Pskov to Omsk. While the Latvians living in the territories under Russian domination participated in the 1917 Russian revolution, those under German control were unable to do so and were subject to German military authority headed by General Ludendorff.

Political changes in Latvia and Estonia followed quickly on the heels of the February revolution in Petrograd. During the early weeks the pattern of events in the two began to differ. Estonia's road to statehood and liberal democracy was more direct, in Latvia more circuitous. The presence of the front dividing Latvia in half served to radicalize Latvian politics.

The first success of the Estonian liberal and moderate socialist politicians in 1917 was to persuade the Russian Provisional Government to issue a decree establishing self-governmental institutions with wide-ranging authority for Estonia. The decree provided for the division of Livland along an ethnic (Estonian/Latvian) line and for the unification of an ethnically Estonian northern Livland with Estland to form a new province of Estonia. The 30 March statute also provided for an elected provincial Diet (*Maapäev*) which was to take over the property and functions of the Estland and Livland (the northern part) *Landtage*. Because of a failure to develop a common Estonian-Latvian approach on Livland, the *Maapäev* was only successful in securing a satisfactory agreement with the corporation of the Baltic German nobility in Estland, the *Ritterschaft*.

The *Maapäev* adopted Estonian as its working language and in July began to develop an administrative system to control education, local tax collection and lower-level self-governmental institutions. The *Maapäev's* goal was to secure control over all administrative activity in Estonia, and complete political autonomy. Friction soon developed between the *Maapäev* and the Provisional Government, supported by the remnants of Russia's bureaucracy in Estonia, whom the revolution had marginalized.

The late spring and summer of 1917 was a period of elections in Estonia. First, there were the two-stage elections to the *Maapäev*. The result was an almost even split between liberal-democratic and moderate socialist (non-Bolshevik) blocs (five Bolsheviks were also elected). Elections based on universal suffrage were also held at other levels of self-government: the *vald* (rural commune) councils and city and town assemblies. All this activity encouraged the formation of political parties, although none obtained a dominant role.

As elsewhere, soviets came to be organized in Tallinn and other towns in Estonia. Besides socialist activists, the soviets represented Russian garrison soldiers and Estonian and Russian factory workers. Since the Russian soldiers had substantial representation in the soviets, the language used in the soviets was Russian. The Tallinn Soviet, the most important one in Estonia, was dominated until August by a Russian SR–Menshevik bloc. Bolshevik politics in Estonia were directed by a small group of Estonian intellectuals drawn to Bolshevism after 1905. Their radical vision appealed first to some Estonian workers and later in the autumn of 1917 showed some success among the rural poor. In practice, the Bolsheviks opposed the policies of the *Maapäev* and all efforts at national self-assertion. Thus, the Bolsheviks opposed elections to the *Maapäev*, the naming of an Estonian liberal, Jaan Poska, as commissar (governor) in Estonia, and the formation of Estonian military units. Before the autumn of 1917, however, the Bolsheviks proved to be too weak to block any of these developments.

Unlike Estonia, Latvia began to tread a Bolshevik path from the early days of the revolution. Although the war had led to the evacuation to Russia of both the liberal and Bolshevik pre-war leaderships, it was the Bolsheviks who recovered first and showed superior organizational and rhetorical skills. The Bolshevik ascendancy in Latvian politics proceeded along two tracks: through the various soviets that arose in unoccupied Latvia in the first hours of the revolution, and in various provisional and elected councils. Initially the Bolshevik power-base was in the soviets which emerged during the early weeks of the revolution in the cities, among the landless peasants (farm-hands), and among the *strelki* (sharpshooters). From here, the Bolsheviks moved to control other institutions that in Leninist theory were regarded as bourgeois.

In Riga during the early weeks of the revolution three alternative governing institutions arose: the Riga Soviet, dominated from the beginning by Bolsheviks; the Council of Organizations which at first excluded Bolsheviks, but included a variety of socialists; and the traditional Riga City Council. Pending city elections, the Bolsheviks in the soviet suggested that a Provisional Riga City Council should be organized. Towards that end they drew up a list of deputies to be coopted, consisting mainly of non-Bolsheviks. Of 60 seats the Bolsheviks took only ten, and even these ten participated only as observers. This arrangement in effect placed the governance of Riga in abeyance until the elections on 13 August. Nominally the liberals ruled in Riga, but in fact the Bolsheviks did so through the Riga Soviet.

The fate of the administration of Vidzeme Province (southern Livland) was similar. A. Krastkalns, considered a conservative, was chosen by Petrograd as the commissar. The Bolsheviks, however, mounted a campaign against Krastkalns, and on 19 April 1917 he was replaced by A. Priedkalns, a Social Democrat who had served in the Third Duma. The Vidzeme Provisional Land Council, which was to exercise self-governmental functions equivalent to a provincial zemstvo, was organized by an assembly of deputies representing mostly non-Bolshevik organizations and political parties that met in Valmiera on 12–13 March. Of the 48 council seats, 12 each went to the landless peasants and small landowners, four each to the large landowners and the free professions, eight to both the cities and the cooperatives. An eight-person board served as a permanent Executive Committee.

In order to gain control over the Vidzeme Provisional Land Council the Bolsheviks convened, on 16 March, an assembly of landless peasants. In the end the Soviet of Landless Peasants obtained parity with the Vidzeme Provisional Land Council through the device of joining the two councils. In the elections to the Vidzeme Land Council on 20 August, the Bolsheviks actually won the majority of the seats. In October when the liberal faction walked out the Bolsheviks gained absolute domination of the Council.

The most important institution that the Bolsheviks brought under their control in 1917 was the soviet representing the Latvian *strelki* units. The executive committee of the *Strelki* Soviet was called *Izkolastrel*. Although the tsarist government traditionally was against separate national formations within the imperial forces, in 1915 it agreed to allow the organization of Latvian *strelki* battalions. Latvian conscripts fought well in the early battles of the war on the East Prussian front, and, once the war in 1915 moved into Latvia, the Russian military leadership was persuaded to allow the organization of two Latvian battalions. It was argued that Latvians fighting on their own soil against what they had come to regard as their historical enemy would perform better than Russian forces. The opposing argument of the Baltic Germans, remembering the 1905 revolution, that it would be dangerous to create Latvian military units, was overridden. By 1917 the *strelki*, now 30,000 strong, were organized into nine regiments. They were commanded by Latvian officers and displayed Latvian insignia.

The Bolshevik takeover of the *Strelki* Soviet proceeded more directly and expeditiously than that of the non-military institutions. The Bolsheviks did not enjoy the exclusive role in the establishment of the *Strelki* Soviet that they did in the case of the Riga Soviet, although radical Marxist opinions dominated in the assembly of *strelki* deputies on 13 March. The *Strelki* Soviet did not become an adjunct of the party, like the Riga Soviet and the Vidzeme Soviet of Landless Peasants, until 17 May. A full Bolshevik takeover took place during the Second Congress of *Strelki* Deputies, on 12–17 May. At this congress a Bolshevik resolution was accepted condemning the Provisional Government and the continuation of the war. This was one of the first such resolutions in any frontline military formation. Due to the importance of the *strelki* in Latvian consciousness at the time, the Bolshevization of the *Strelki* Soviet was of momentous importance.

Without exaggeration one can say that by June 1917, even before any elections, the Bolsheviks were in control of the governmental institutions in unoccupied Latvia. They reaffirmed their control by winning the four major elections held in Latvia: to the Riga City Council; the Vidzeme Provincial Land Council; the district land councils; and the Russian Constituent Assembly.

The most vigorously contested election was that to the Riga City Council. Altogether about 23 parties, organized into 13 rival lists, took part. The Bolshevik slate received 41 per cent of the votes securing 49 deputies out of 120. The Bolsheviks, however, did not have a chance to exploit their victory because the German assault on the Riga front commenced on 17 August and the city fell on 20 August.

The elections to the Vidzeme Provincial Council were slated for 20 August and for the Vidzeme district councils on 27 August. Unlike the one in Riga, the Vidzeme election campaign was basically a two-party struggle: the Bolsheviks versus the Farmers' Union Party. The Bolsheviks won the election comfortably by about 60 per cent to 40 per cent, assuring them of complete control of the Vidzeme Provincial Council, with 24 of the 40 seats. In the district elections the turnout was low in comparison to the provincial and Riga elections, but here the results were even better for the Bolsheviks.

The final election of 1917, the Russian Constituent Assembly election of November, actually had no real importance for the governance of Latvia, but was indicative of the trend towards Bolshevism. The Bolshevik victory margin was 71.85 per cent to 23 per cent for the Farmers' Union. Latvian Mensheviks received less than 2 per cent. The Bolsheviks sent three representatives to the Assembly (Pēteris Stučka, Fricis Roziņš, and Jānis Berziņš). The Farmers' Union was represented by Jānis Goldmanis.

By the end of the election process the Bolsheviks were in a commanding position in unoccupied Latvia, both in the soviets and in the other elected institutions. Liberal politicians, who were forced out of Latvia in the autumn of 1917, began to operate from Petrograd where they organized a Provisional National Council and, after the German occupation of Riga, they also operated underground in Riga, where the so-called Twelve Men Bloc was organized. If until October the Latvian liberals thought about Latvia's future in terms of federal arrangements within Russia, thereafter their alternative became independence, for which they began to prepare the ground, domestically and internationally. The international situation that evolved after the Treaty of Brest-Litovsk (3 March 1918) in fact began to favour their alternative.

Iskolat, the acronym for the Latvian Soviet of Soviets, came into existence in July 1917 at the Fifth Congress of the Latvian Social-Democratic Party and it gradually matured during the autumn. On 8 November the *Iskolat* proclaimed full sovereignty for itself within the unoccupied part of Latvia. The Bolsheviks had to choose between the elected councils or the network of soviets as their vehicle to power, and chose the latter. The *Iskolat* Republic was a unique organization within the former Russian empire. Its Executive Committee became the first *de facto* socialist government of Latvia, before vanishing in February 1918 when Germany occupied the remainder of Latvia. Thousands of Latvian Bolsheviks then sought refuge in Russia. It is significant that the *Iskolat* Republic was an independent Latvian Bolshevik entity, comprised of ethnic Latvians, which did not depend on Petrograd or the Council of People's Commissars (*Sovnarkom*) for its existence. The *Iskolat* received no aid from Russia. Indeed, if anybody sent aid, it was the Latvians themselves, dispatching a considerable military force to Petrograd to stabilize Lenin's shaky *Sovnarkom*.

Latvian Bolsheviks thus came to play an important role in the Russian revolution outside Latvia. The first contingent of *strelki*, the 6th Regiment, 2,500-men strong, arrived in Petrograd on 25 November. It was quartered in the Malaia Okhta barracks on Vasilievskii Island. Thirty days later, as the Bolsheviks were preparing for a stand-off with the Constituent Assembly, the regiment was moved to more aristocratic quarters on Galernaia Street, in the vicinity of the Winter Palace. The regiment performed general guard duties, including at the Tauride Palace.

On 26 November, the second 320-man *streļki* contingent arrived in Petrograd and was housed in the Smolny Institute. As a result, it came to be called the Smolny battalion. This group consisted of volunteers and hand-picked Bolsheviks. Their assignment was to guard the Bolshevik government in the Smolny and to perform special tasks in the city. Later the battalion's strength was raised to 500 men. After the establishment of the Cheka, the battalion performed tasks for Feliks Dzerzhinskii's organization in addition to guarding the government's headquarters. It was this Latvian battalion that guarded Lenin's entourage as the Soviet government moved to Moscow in March 1918. In Moscow the battalion was renamed the 1st Latvian *Streļki* Communist Battalion and until May 1918 continued to guard the Lenin–Trotsky government in the Kremlin. As the Bolsheviks' problems grew on a variety of civil-war fronts, the Kremlin Communist Battalion was reorganized into a full regiment, the 9th Latvian *Streļki* Regiment, and in May 1918 transferred out of Moscow. Throughout the civil war, the 9th Latvian Regiment was known as one of the fiercest military units in the Kremlin's service. Nor was it the only prominent Latvian regiment. The 1st Latvian *Streļki* Regiment played the major role in defeating the Polish Corps led by General Dowbor-Musnicki on 1 February in the Mogilev region, while the 3rd *Streļki* Regiment was sent from Petrograd to the Rostov front in early February 1918.

The Latvian *streļki* formed the first Bolshevik military force, before the Red Army was organized. All the other Bolshevik 'helpers' in October 1917, the sailors and the Red Guards, petered out in time. The *streļki* alone remained. Their significance is especially noteworthy from October 1917 to about August 1918, during the fledgling months of the Bolshevik order. As the German forces commenced their assault on the northern front after the breakdown of the Brest-Litovsk talks, all of the *streļki* regiments retreated into Russia. The question they faced was whether to obey the *Sovnarkom*'s order to demobilize. The Latvian political leadership in the *Izkolastrel*, consisting of staunch Bolsheviks, resisted demobilization.

Meanwhile, during the summer and autumn of 1917, Estonian politics continued to follow a different route from the Latvian. By August 1917 the changing international and Russian political landscapes led Estonian political leaders to more urgent discussion of Estonian national goals. For one, in August (following the fall of Riga) there was a renewed threat of German occupation of the entire Baltic region. Kornilov's failed coup was another portent of the possible disintegration of the Russian state. By September Estonian political leaders were becoming more and more estranged from their Russian counterparts, since the Provisional Government and Russian political leaders seemed to show a lack of interest in and support for the development of Estonian autonomy and federalizing the Russian empire. Consequently, Estonian politicians increasingly disassociated themselves from Russian political parties and established distinct Estonian ones representing ideologies of agrarianism, national liberalism, social democracy and varieties of labour and socialist populism. The only exception to this separatist tendency was the Estonian Bolsheviks.

Following the October revolution in Petrograd, Bolsheviks in Estonia attempted to assert power by using their control of the soviets (secured in August) and by organizing a Military-Revolutionary Committee. The move was rejected and resisted by other political forces, with only a small Estonian Left Socialist-Revolutionary group cooperating with the Bolsheviks. On 15 November 1917 the *Maapäev* declared itself 'the sole bearer of supreme authority in Estonia', assigning this authority to its Committee of Elders when it was not in session.

It must be noted that the Bolshevik programme in Estonia, and also in Latvia, was different in a number of ways from the one the party decreed for Russia. The Bolsheviks in 1917 judged the Baltic provinces to be at a higher stage of capitalist development than Russia and hence more ripe for the transition to a socialist system. This view especially prevailed in Bolshevik agrarian policy. They considered Estonian and Latvian agriculture to be in a capitalist phase of production with efficiently-run large estates of the nobility and with peasants already divided into owners and farm-hands (or landed and landless). From this analysis, essentially based on the views of Karl Kautsky on the state of agriculture in Germany, the application of the Soviet Land Decree of 26 October 1917 was considered regressive in the Baltics. The Bolshevik agrarian programme for Estonia and Latvia anticipated the elimination of Baltic German ownership of estates as a first step in establishing communism. There were also differences of substance between Lenin's views and the views of Baltic Bolsheviks on the nationality question. While the programme of the Russian party emphasized the right of nationalities to separate from Russia, the Bolshevik programme in Estonia and Latvia emphasized the need to join the Russian revolutionary community.

In Estonia, as in Latvia, the period between October 1917 and February 1918 was full of contradictory developments. The Bolsheviks in Estonia tried to copy the pattern of developments in Petrograd, using their control of the soviets and searching for support among factory workers, farm-hands, soldiers and sailors. They disbanded many elected institutions of self-government, their functions supposedly to be taken over by Bolshevik-dominated soviets. In a more original vein the Bolsheviks in December 1917 and January 1918 dispatched teams of activists to the countryside to seize control of Baltic German estates and set up soviets of landless peasants. They declared that these estates would be operated as large agrarian communal farms.

How much authority did the Bolsheviks exercise in Estonia during the period? Certainly more than other political groups or institutions. There was a steady growth of Bolshevik power from October 1917 to January 1918, and a constant struggle against persons and institutions that did not recognize Bolshevik control. On the other hand, the Bolsheviks never controlled the district of Haapsalu where the First Estonian Regiment was located, and non-Bolshevik political activity in Estonia continued throughout the period, some of it clandestinely.

In the November elections to the Russian Constituent Assembly the Bolsheviks secured 40 per cent of the vote in Estonia, showing that Estonian society was badly split. Despite their revolutionary activism and electoral success the Bolshevik position had major weaknesses. By opposing Estonian national issues and by advocating political terror, Bolshevism failed to attract Estonian intellectuals. Fatal to the movement was its failure to understand the realities of international relations by misreading the negotiations at Brest-Litovsk and ignoring the impending threat of German occupation.

Baltic German politics, and in particular the politics of the Estland and Livland *Ritterschaften*, was a separate, but ultimately connected factor in the Estonian-Latvian equation. The Baltic nobility had representatives in Berlin who lobbied for German occupation of the Baltic provinces and for their annexation to Germany. On 15 January 1918, a representative of the Estland and Livland *Ritterschaften* handed declarations of independence by the two provinces to the Soviet embassy in Stockholm, as a preliminary to an anticipated German occupation. The aims of the Baltic Germans were supported by General Ludendorff and Kaiser Wilhelm, but opposed by the Foreign Secretary, Richard von Kühlmann. Kühlmann wanted Germany to share the Baltic provinces with Russia by splitting them along the Daugava (Dvina) river. Because of the rift between the German military and the Foreign Office, German demands for Estonia and the rest of Latvia were not raised directly at the Brest-Litovsk conference. Bolshevik diplomatic ineptness at Brest-Litovsk, and Ludendorff's determined policy to exert maximal German control of the entire eastern Baltic area, crowned the Baltic German lobbying efforts with temporary success. In February 1918 German forces occupied Estonia and the remaining part of Latvia. In order to save the revolution and to consolidate Bolshevik power in Russia, Lenin was willing to give up the entire Baltic region.

Ultimately it was legitimacy that escaped the Bolsheviks in Estonia. Victory in the scheduled Estonian Constituent Assembly elections at the beginning of February 1918 would have given the Bolsheviks a claim to legitimacy which their control of the soviets did not. In January 1918 all political parties in Estonia – the Democratic Bloc, the Labour Party, the Estonian Social Democrats, the Estonian Socialist Revolutionaries and the Bolsheviks – engaged in an election campaign in which the major issue turned out to be Estonian independence. The reasons for the advocacy of Estonian independence were: a desire to remove Estonia from the impending chaos and civil war brought on by the disintegration of Russian state authority; a rejection of Bolshevism and the seizure of power in Petrograd; and the Bolshevik failure at the Brest-Litovsk conference to end the war and remove the threat of a German occupation. The non-Bolsheviks wished to declare Estonia an independent, neutral buffer state between Germany and Russia. The non-Bolshevik bloc, supporting Estonian independence, gained more than 60 per cent of the vote. The Bolshevik vote declined from the 40 per cent achieved at the All-Russian Constituent Assembly elections to 37 per cent.

A kind of 'end game' in Estonian politics was played out in February 1918. Since the Bolsheviks did not permit the convening of the Estonian Constituent Assembly, the Committee of Public Safety set up by the Committee of Elders of the *Maapäev*, basing its legitimacy on the elected *Maapäev*, issued a declaration of independence on 24 February 1918. The Committee of Elders, which was composed of representatives of the non-Bolshevik Estonian political parties, had taken the decision to seek independence for Estonia on 1 January 1918. Recognition for Estonian statehood was sought from Germany, Britain and France. The Bolshevik answer to the assertion of Estonian independence and the impending German occupation was terror. Specifically, the Bolsheviks carried out a mass arrest of Baltic German nobility and of political opponents. After the negotiations collapsed at Brest-Litovsk on 28 January 1918, the German government dispatched a military force to Estonia. What Soviet power existed collapsed as the Bolsheviks fled to Russia. The German occupation of Estonia helped Estonian diplomats in March 1918 to secure *de facto* recognition of independence from Britain and France. The Western powers did not want to see German domination of the eastern Baltic, a major sea route to Russia.

The events of 1917–18 in the Baltics represented a confluence of internal and external developments. As in other periods of history when the balance of power had shifted in northern Europe, the eastern Baltic became a battleground between contending armies. Even without the revolution, the World War itself – a German military thrust northward – raised a strong possibility that Russia would lose territory on the Baltic littoral. The revolution of 1917 in the Baltics exhibited similarities to Russian events but also brought to the fore distinctly Estonian and Latvian cultural, national and social factors. The Leninist programme ultimately had limited applicability in the Baltics. In a fundamental way Bolshevism in Estonia never fully recovered from the inept politics pursued in 1917–18. In Latvia, where in 1917 Bolshevik power foreshadowed that in Russia, Bolshevism proved to be of short duration – a passing phenomenon. Although in the early phase of the revolution there were differences between Estonia and Latvia, in the end the cultural similarities, similar social and political conditions and a similar international situation led to a similar solution in 1919–20: the establishment of independent, liberal, nation-states.

In the final analysis, the fate of Estonia, Latvia and Lithuania was perhaps decided on the western front in November 1918 and by the ensuing international politics. The Estonians, Latvians and Lithuanians managed to organize effective governments and sufficiently large military forces to counter Bolshevik efforts to incorporate them into the Soviet-Russian empire in 1919.

Further reading

Arens O., 'The Estonian Question at Brest-Litovsk', *Journal of Baltic Studies* 25, 4 (Winter 1974).

Arens O., 'The Estonian Maapäev during 1917', in V. S. Vardys and R. J. Misiunas, eds., *The Baltic States in Peace and War, 1917–1945* (University Park, Pennsylvania State University Press, 1978).

Bērziņš V., *Latviešu strēlnieki: drāma un traģēdija* (Riga, 1995).

Ezergailis A., *The 1917 Revolution in Latvia* (New York, Columbus University Press, 1973).

Ezergailis A., *The Latvian Impact on the Bolshevik Revolution* (New York, Columbus University Press, 1983).

Ģērmanis U., *Oberst Vācietis und die lettischen Schützen im Weltkrieg und in der Oktoberrevolution* (Stockholm, Almkvist and Wiksell, 1974).

von Hehn J., von Rimscha H. and Weiss H., eds., *Von den baltischen Provinzen zu den baltischen Staaten*, vol. 1 (Marburg/Lahn, J.-G. Herder Inst., 1971).

Kaimiņš J., *Latyshskie strelki v bor'be za pobedu Oktiabr'skoi revoliutsii 1917–1918*, trans. D. Dmitriev (Riga, Latviiskoe gosudarstvennoe izdatel'stvo, 1961).

Page S., *The Formation of the Baltic States* (Cambridge, MA, Harvard University Press, 1959).

von Rauch G., *The Baltic States: The Years of Independence*, trans. G. Onn (London, C. Hurst and Co., 1974).

Toman B. A., *Za svobodnuiu Rossiiu, za svobodnuiu Latviiu: latyshskie strelki i krasnogvardeitsy v pervyi god Sovetskoi vlasti* (Moscow, Politizdat, 1975).

The Revolution in Central Asia

MARTHA BRILL OLCOTT

Imperial Russia's vast Central Asian territories, stretching all the way from the Caspian Sea to the Chinese border in the east, comprised two governor-generalships – Turkestan, enveloping the protectorates of Khiva and Bukhara, and the Kazakh Steppe to the north. According to the census of 1897, about 11 per cent (13 million) of the empire's population were Muslim by faith and spoke Turkic languages, and over half of these lived in Central Asia. They were coming under increasing pressure from Russian settlers: by 1911 settlers constituted 40 per cent of the population of the Kazakh Steppe, and P. A. Stolypin's government opened the way for large-scale Russian settlement in Turkestan too. Resentment against the settlers fuelled a major uprising against the tsar in summer 1916, the immediate cause being the Russian government's decision to end their exemption from military conscription and mobilize half a million for labour service. The regime succeeded in crushing the revolt, and the tsar's fall a few months later came as a shock to the region. As a consequence, the relatively small number of politically active Central Asians were slow to take advantage of the opportunities which the revolution presented.

The Provisional Government brought to power by the February revolution was a creature of the Duma, a parliament chosen through electoral laws which had permitted the Central Asians – and Muslims in general – only minimal representation. There was a Muslim Caucus in the Duma, which did try to represent the interests of the empire's Muslim population, but without much effect. The caucus held an initial conference in March 1917, and a full congress two months later, but little consensus emerged because the group was split between pan-Islamists and pan-Turks, and between those who advocated the preservation of a unitary state and those who advanced the cause of territorial autonomy for their respective peoples. The small group of Central Asians who attended took the latter position, one of its most forceful advocates being the Kazakh Halel Dos Muhammedov, who later became a leader of the *Alash Orda* independent Kazakh government.

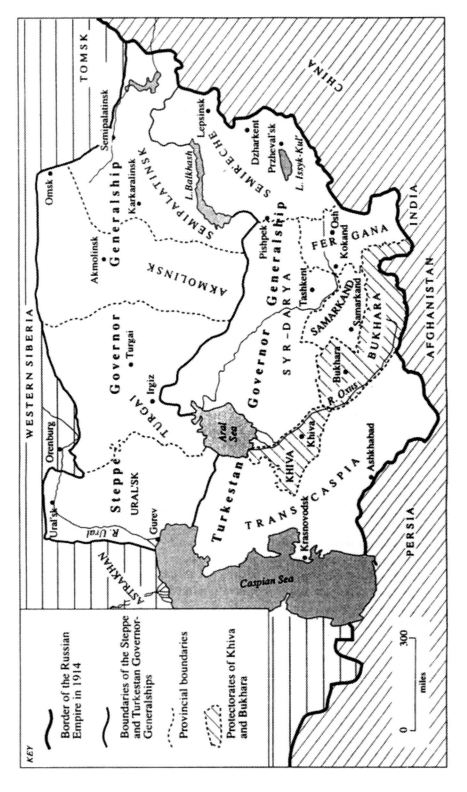

Map 5. Central Asia in 1917

Even if it had been more unified and decisive it is unlikely that the Muslim Caucus would have had much impact on the direction of the Russian revolution, since most Russian policy-makers were little inclined to give serious consideration to the opinions of their Muslim colleagues. A few prominent Muslim Kadets (Constitutional Democrats) did serve on regional staffs of the Provisional Government in Turkestan and in the Kazakh Steppe, but when the Muslim Caucus proposed Muhammad Tynyshpaev, a Kazakh from Turkestan, for the post of Minister of Agriculture of Russia, his candidacy was not deemed worthy of serious consideration.

The successive cabinets of the Provisional Government recognized that the post-imperial 'national question' had to be resolved, but self-rule for the Muslim areas was never regarded as such a pressing issue as it was for the European regions of the empire. As a result, while Socialist Revolutionaries (SRs) and pro-Bolshevik Social Democrats set about trying to create local soviets among the Russian workers of southern Siberia (including the Kazakh Steppe) and Central Asia, the Provisional Government remained content to rule these regions through local provisional committees, with some reorganization of personnel who had served in the local colonial administration.

The revolution in the Kazakh Steppe

Although the new authorities were little concerned with them, the Central Asians themselves, and particularly the Kazakhs, were beginning to develop definite views about how they should be ruled. Unlike nationalists in Finland, the Baltic states, Poland and Ukraine, Central Asian nationalists did not argue for full independence for their regions, but rather advocated the creation of autonomous territorial formations for the Turkestanis and Kazakhs. In general, the Kazakhs were more involved in the political debates of the Provisional Government period than were the Turkestanis. There was no single Kazakh position, and no single revolutionary or nationalist leader who might be said to define the Kazakh national ideal. Steppe Kazakhs like Dos Muhammedov and Ali Khan Bukeikhanov lobbied for Kazakh territorial autonomy in Moscow and Petrograd, as did Tynyshpaev. These three men, who were all loosely tied to the Kadets, joined Ahmed Baitursunov and Mir Jakup Dulatov in April 1917 to form the party of *Alash*, which held its first formal congress in July 1917, and which in November 1917 organized itself as the *Alash Orda* government.

Not all Kazakh intellectuals supported this effort at self-rule. A second group of Kazakhs, which included Saken Seifullin and Soviet Kazakhstan's first president, Seitgali Mendeshev, were pro-socialist. Initially sympathetic to the SRs, they later joined the Bolsheviks. Although less numerous in the beginning, it was this second group which eventually emerged victorious; when they did, they turned against the members of *Alash* with the full force of Soviet power (which a few years later Moscow would in turn use against them).

For all their mutual hostility, neither group was particularly successful in articulating a concept of Kazakh nationhood. Kazakh intellectuals agreed that their people were dying out, pushed from the best pasture lands by the Russians; they disagreed, however, on the question of how critical the survival of traditional authority structures was for the preservation of the Kazakhs. Most of the *Alash* leaders were from aristocratic families, and believed that the Kazakh people must not permit their traditional leadership structure to atrophy, whereas the leaders who gravitated toward the socialists did so primarily because they were attracted to the egalitarianism of socialist doctrine. Both groups, however, understood that the Kazakhs had to gain access to political power, ideally in the form of self-rule, if they were to address their people's growing pauperization.

The Kazakhs' leaders felt strongly that the Russians did not see preservation of a Kazakh nation as even desirable, let alone pressing; Russian interest in the Kazakhs was so minimal that they even continued, incorrectly, to call them 'Kirgiz'. However, the Kazakh intellectuals of both camps were less concerned about symbolic issues such as their nomenclature than they were about more substantive ones, which might lead to some degree of economic recovery in the Steppe. They were also pragmatic enough to realize that they would accomplish nothing if they pitted themselves directly against the Russians who were already living among them; accordingly, they ensured that one-third of the members of the *Alash Orda* government were Russians.

Despite this Russian participation, the *Alash Orda* government was designed to be a Kazakh government, mandating Kazakh-language education, a Kazakh militia, and a social-welfare structure that used the Kazakh *aul*, or village, as its basic unit. Its party and government programme called for an end to further settlement of Russians and the redistribution to poor Kazakhs of those lands seized but not yet allocated by the Russian authorities.

Subsequent Soviet-era vilification of the *Alash Orda* makes dispassionate assessment of the popular support for and the potential viability of this government extremely difficult, but existing source materials make it clear that during 1918 and early 1919 the *Alash Orda* did attract a considerable following among local Kazakhs. Even Soviet source materials admit that the authority of the *Alash Orda* government was recognized not only in all four oblast's of the Steppe territory, but also in the two Kazakh oblast's of northern Turkestan, and in the Kazakh settlements of Samarkand and Fergana oblast's, while the *Alash Orda* committees in Uralsk and Semipalatinsk enjoyed enough popular support, in the form of Kazakh tax payments, to enable them to mount an army when the civil war came to the region in 1918.

Even so, not all Kazakhs recognized the authority of the *Alash Orda*. Support was weakest in the western part of the Steppe territory, where the regional committees were dominated by members of the princely families of the tribal federations, the Small Horde and Inner Horde. This caused many, though by no means a majority, of the poor Kazakhs in the region to throw in their lot first with the SRs and then with the Bolsheviks, accepting the argument that Kazakh national interests would be best protected by a regime whose primary goal was to end the gap between rich and poor. Unlike in Turkestan, the first Soviet organizations in this region were not anti-native. The local working-class Russians who supported Soviet power agreed that this was the best way to protect both the national and the class interests of the local poor. During the civil war members of these groups fought with the Red Army under the leadership of Amengeldy Imanov and Alibai Dzhangel'din.

Russian farmers and the colonial administrative service class, by contrast, backed the White forces, led by commanders of the Cossack divisions that were posted to the Steppe. Orenburg was the headquarters of Cossack opposition in the region, with Uralsk a second centre. The White Cossack groups did not oppose *Alash Orda* rule, and after an accord signed in May 1918 by Ataman Dutov for the Cossacks and Ali Khan Bukeikhanov for the Kazakhs, the Cossacks and Kazakhs occasionally fought joint actions.

Relations between the leadership of the two communities were quite cordial, despite acute economic decline and periodic clashes between landless Kazakhs and local Russian farmers, giving little reason to suppose that had they been victorious the Whites would have turned against the *Alash Orda*. While the Cossacks would never have granted the *Alash Orda* authority over the European population, they might well have tolerated a degree of Kazakh self-government monitored by unobtrusive Russian overseers, allowing the Kazakhs to live much as the Cossacks themselves had lived during the time of the tsars.

The revolution in Turkestan

In the Kazakh Steppe, although there were considerable tensions between the two national groups, the civil war and the establishment of Soviet rule did not simply pit Russians and Kazakhs against one another. By contrast, the battle for Turkestan was a classic, if unsuccessful, struggle to wrest the region from colonial control. Whereas the Kazakhs eventually ceded their sovereignty, accepting what proved to be the false promises of the Bolsheviks, the people of Turkestan were forcibly reconquered in a process of subjugation which was not complete until 1924, indeed, which persisted in scattered fighting until well after the completion of collectivization in the mid-1930s.

After the fall of the tsar, many officials in Petrograd and Moscow recognized that modifications in the form of government over the Muslims would have to be made in order to take some account of growing nationalist sensibilities. However, it was unthinkable for even the most progressive among them to accept that local Russians should ever be subject to rule by 'the natives', while most officials serving in Turkestan were totally against permitting the local population even limited self-rule.

In part, such attitudes were a reflection of disdain by colonizers for a colonized population of whom they were largely ignorant; it was only rare officials like V. Nalivkin, a student of Turkestani culture and briefly the chair of the Provisional Government's Turkestan Committee, who supported the idea of limited local self-government. However, even those few who understood and sympathized with Turkestani national ambitions also recognized that the Central Asians did not agree among themselves about how they should be ruled. Turkestani nationhood was even less well defined than the fragile concept of Kazakh nationhood, to say nothing of the possibility of separate nationhood for the various peoples within Turkestan – Uzbek, Tajik, Turkmen and Kyrgyz.

In addition to having no shared vision of their identity or of how they should be governed, the people of Turkestan suffered further confusion of identity because of the continued existence in the region of two quasi-autonomous city-states, Khiva and Bukhara; memories of a third, Kokand, were also still relatively fresh. Some factions argued for a single Turkestan, governed perhaps from Samarkand, the ancient capital of Timur (Tamerlane), while others argued for a restoration of the more recent tripartite division. There were also disagreements about how to apportion power between the region's sedents and the nomads.

Nevertheless, all these questions were insignificant compared to the one issue on which there was general agreement – that the Turkestanis no longer wished to be ruled by the Russians for the advancement of Russian self-interest.

Turkestanis and Russians had begun to fight even before Russian political institutions collapsed, but conflict escalated with the fall of the tsar. Tens of thousands of Kyrgyz who had fled to refugee camps in Chinese Turkestan following the uprising in 1916 began to return, intent on recapturing their lands, only to be met by armed Russian homesteaders. The two groups clashed, thousands of Kyrgyz were killed, and the region was placed under martial law.

The conviction among local Russians that they must rule the natives was intensified, and one result was to reduce the authority of the Provisional Government in Turkestan, which had dismissed General Kuropatkin (in charge of the bloody suppression of the 1916 uprising) and, in line with Kadet ideology, had appointed a ruling committee of equal part native and European. That, in turn, strengthened the authority of the Tashkent Soviet, initially pro-SR, whose membership was entirely Russian/European.

Slower to organize than the Russians, the Turkestanis did not hold a regional conference until April 1917, with a larger one, to include some 200 delegates from throughout Turkestan, planned for November. However, empowered by the Bolshevik revolution, the new Soviet government in

Tashkent, composed entirely of Europeans, banned the second gathering, which convened instead in Kokand, on 28 November 1917.

That meeting, attended both by Muslim reformers like Mahmud Khoja Behbudi whose supporters were grouped around the *Shuro i Islamiia* (Islamic Council), and by traditional clerics, who had their own organization, the *Shuro Ulema* (Council of Clerics), proclaimed the establishment of a Turkestan Autonomous Government, or Kokand Autonomous Government. Like the Kazakhs, the Turkestanis did not seek or claim full independence; rather, they declared Turkestan to be an autonomous territory, ruled by an elected executive council, two-thirds of whose members would be Turkestani and the remaining third Russian, each group to be elected by its respective community. State law would be based on *shari'a* (Muslim law), but the European community would be subject to its own communal law. In practice, little of what was adopted at Kokand ever came into existence, because the Kokand Autonomous Government lasted a mere six weeks.

The Bolshevik revolution created a new political climate in Turkestan, one marked by greatly increased antagonism between Russians and Turkestanis. The *Turksovnarkom* (Turkestan Soviet of Peoples' Commissars), a pro-Bolshevik government, was organized on 15 November 1917, made up of local Bolsheviks and Left SRs, in which intellectuals outnumbered workers. Not only was this government, as we have seen, wholly European, but its members were both ignorant of and opposed to Moscow's goals for the Turkestani Muslims. On 3 December 1917 Lenin and Stalin issued a joint appeal to the 'Working Muslims of Russia and the East', in which they promised that the Bolsheviks would respect religion and redress grievances committed against Islam by their Russian predecessors. Yet ten days later the Tashkent Soviet declared that street processions marking Mavliud (the celebration of Muhammad's birth) were anti-government protests, and fired upon the crowds to break them up. While Lenin and Stalin's later treatment of Islamic leaders, schools and property give reason to doubt the sincerity of that first appeal, it is clear that both Bolshevik leaders were interested in attracting Muslim support. But Turkestan had been a distant outpost in peacetime, and had only become more remote during wartime. While preparing to seize power in Russia, Lenin had paid no attention to the selection of personnel who would lead his cause in Turkestan. As a result, after October, the few Bolsheviks already in the region immediately became the vanguard and the interpretors of revolutionary doctrine. They took literally Lenin's words, offering his guarantees specifically to the 'toiling Muslims' of Turkestan. And whereas 'toiling Muslims' were virtually non-existent in the region, 'bourgeois nationalist Muslims' seemed to be everywhere. The greatest proof of this, in the eyes of the new authorities, was the Turkestan Autonomous Government, created after the *Turksovnarkom* had staked its claim to be the region's sole legitimate government.

The assertion of Soviet control over the Kazakh Steppe and the reconquest of Turkestan

In February 1918, the *Turksovnarkom* in Tashkent, which had already successfully taken control of the local Russian garrisons, attacked the seat of its rival, the fortress city of Kokand. Though substantially outgunned by the Russians, the Turkestanis held out for more than a week. This attack marked the beginning of the civil war in Central Asia. Already disinclined to accept the reimposition of Russian rule, the Central Asians now saw the Bolsheviks as even more intent upon destroying the region's traditional practices than their tsarist predecessors had been. This made the battle for the region a long and bloody one.

Buoyed by victory at Kokand, the Bolsheviks in late February 1918 authorized the Young Bukharans, Muslim reformers, to overthrow the emir of their quasi-autonomous city-state; however, it was the reformers, not the emir, who wound up fleeing. With British troops in Krasnovodsk, just to Bukhara's north-west, the Bolsheviks decided to accept the emir's authority for the moment, rather than risk that he would offer Bukhara to the British as a staging point for an attack on Turkestan.

Although the Bolsheviks in Moscow had felt compelled to give formal recognition to the independence of Bukhara in April 1918, they had decided to consolidate their control over the rest of the old colonial province of Turkestan, declaring the formation of a Turkestan Autonomous Republic as part of the Russian Federative Republic. Exclusively Russian in composition, this new republic's government sought to govern through the strict application of the Communist Party's principles.

A drive to nationalize the land was started. The Turkestanis, who had begun to cultivate grain in place of cotton when the Russian textile industry collapsed during the war, now found themselves with no means to feed their families. By March 1919 the Turkestan government classified a full seventh of the population as 'starving', three-quarters of them either Kyrgyz or Kazakh. The new restrictions on private landownership were applied with particular vigour to local mosques and Islamic seminaries; religious schools and courts were closed. The Tashkent government lacked sufficient authority to implement its policies everywhere in Turkestan, but it did start seizing ecclesiastical properties in the region's largest cities, and shut the bazaars which had permitted unregulated trading in defiance of the policies of war communism. Though not yet strong enough to bend the population to their will, the Bolsheviks were able to cripple the major economic and social institutions in Turkestan.

The Turkestanis fought back using the militia hastily organized by the Kokand government as the nucleus of their resistance. The leader of the militia was named Irgash, and by summer 1918 he already had some 4,000 men under his command. This was a large enough force to allow Irgash and his allies to push the Bolsheviks from the cities of the Fergana Valley. As their successes increased, so too did the size of Irgash's forces, until by mid-1919 they numbered over 20,000 armed men.

The Soviets labelled these men *basmachi*, or 'plunderers', while the Turkestanis termed their fight the Freemen's Revolt, calling themselves 'fighters for the faith' or simply 'fighters' (*kurbashi*). Although the Bolsheviks had no wish to lose control of Turkestan, the Fergana revolt was a relative side-show compared to the many parts of the old Russian empire where, by early 1919, the Red Army faced a well-organized and armed opposition, often bolstered by Allied support of both arms and men. The *kurbashi* got almost no White assistance, while the British provided only minimal military assistance through Krasnovodsk, which was held by White forces loyal to the Orenburg Cossack leader Aleksandr Dutov until summer 1918, and gave virtually none across the Afghanistan border.

Moscow did not turn its attention to the reconquest of Turkestan until the middle of 1919, when the Fourth Red Army under Mikhail Frunze was sent to retake Western Siberia and parts of the Kazakh Steppe, some of which had been under White rule since spring and summer 1918, and then Turkestan itself. By this time the local economy had all but collapsed. These conditions and the population's general war-weariness worked to the Bolsheviks' advantage. After the Fourth Army took Orenburg in mid-February 1919, its successor force, the newly organized Turkestan Army, encountered decreasing resistance as it marched across the northern Kazakh Steppe. Here, Moscow tried to persuade as well as to conquer; in March 1919, for example, Lenin offered the members of the *Alash Orda* 'amnesty' if they voluntarily agreed to accept Bolshevik rule; some did, but most refused until December, when the offer was renewed by the *Kirrevkom* (Kirgiz Revolutionary Committee). The *Kirrevkom* had arrived to supervise the administration of the territory in June 1919; almost immediately it fell out with the existing pro-Soviet Kirgiz Autonomous Government, in part because the *Kirrevkom* now included *Alash Orda* leaders Baitursunov and Bukeikhanov among its membership. By January 1920 the Kazakh Steppe was fully under Bolshevik control, and in August 1920, Lenin authorized the creation of the Kirgiz Autonomous Soviet Socialist Republic within the RSFSR, to be headed by Seitgali Mendeshev. This decision was disputed by Russian Bolsheviks on both sides of the Siberian–Kirgiz (now Kazakh) border, who considered the northern regions of what today is Kazakhstan to be part of Siberia.

The situation in the Kazakh Steppe had improved enough by September 1919 to allow Frunze to shift troops south in order to begin the process of reclaiming Turkestan. A twofold strategy was attempted, with part of the forces sent to the Fergana Valley, the southern end of which was controlled by Irgash, while the northern end (Osh and Jalal-abadd) was now controlled by a Peasant Army led jointly by a Russian colonel named Monstrov and Madamin Bek (who had resigned as head of the Margelan militia when the Soviets ordered the razing of local mosques and holy sites). The remainder of Frunze's forces were dispatched to Khiva, to engage the forces of Turkmen Yomud tribal leader Junaid Khan, whose protection was sustaining the figurehead ruler Seid Abdullah Khan.

Frunze underestimated the strength of the poorly armed but numerically superior *basmachi* troops, and made little headway in recapturing Turkestan's most populous valley. He fared better in Khiva, although it took four months for the Red Army to take the city, which fell in February 1920. The Khorezm People's Soviet Republic was formed two months later, composed largely of members of the Young Khivan caucus, who with Bolshevik prodding had reorganized themselves as the Khivan section of the Communist Party of Turkestan in July 1919.

Refusing to recognize this new government, Junaid Khan fled into the desert, along with some 7,000 armed supporters. His army successfully kept the Soviet forces from consolidating their hold over the Khivan countryside until late 1924, even briefly retaking Khiva in January 1924. Eventually Junaid Khan fled over the border to Iran, but he continued to launch forays into Turkmenistan until 1927 and later returned to Turkmenistan to lead opposition to Stalin's collectivization policy.

The remainder of Turkestan was placed under the direct supervision of a Turkestan Commission, which Moscow charged with achieving both the political and the military defeat of the *basmachi*. Frunze quickly realized that the Bolshevik authorities would have to make major policy concessions to the Turkestanis if their resistance movement was to be defeated. To that end the Turkestan Autonomous Republic government was reorganized in July 1920, headed by Turar Ryskulov, a Kazakh who had joined the Bolsheviks in September 1917.

A major military campaign was launched against Irgash and the Peasant Army, while full amnesty was promised to those who surrendered. Madamin and Monstrov were both killed during the first months of 1920, and Irgash's troops suffered major defeats. As Bolshevik policies changed, popular toleration of the new rulers began to increase. NEP permitted freer trade and limited private ownership everywhere in the country, and at the same time the Turkestan government made a series of specific concessions to Islamic authorities, returning some *waqf* (clerically held) lands, permitting some religious schools to reopen, and giving limited jurisdiction to religious courts. Trade between Turkestan and the centre was slowly being restored, grain supplies increased and local elites regained partial control of irrigation canals, on which their traditional authority was largely based.

The relative peace such changes brought vanished again when the Bolsheviks took Bukhara later in the year. The Red Army invaded on the 'invitation' of the Young Bukharans, whom the Bolsheviks had been funding since 1918 and most of whom had just followed their leader, Faizullah Khojaev, into the newly formed Bukharan Communist Party. After five days of heavy fighting and great loss of life, Frunze entered Bukhara on 2 September 1920, and was met by a staged victory parade. The emir fled to

Afghanistan, after authorizing Ibragim Bek, a Lokai tribal leader, to try to retake the city. Although the new People's Republic of Bukhara remained in Soviet hands, the anti-Bolshevik resistance in Turkestan in 1921 and 1922 was larger, better led and more united than it had been elsewhere in the region. By mid-1921 a well-armed resistance movement controlled most of the countryside west and south of Samarkand and north of Kokand, leaving the Bolsheviks in control of the major cities, and of a hundred-mile radius around Tashkent.

Even the Turkestanis who had helped to drive out the emir soon had cause to regret their complicity, as it quickly became clear that Moscow intended to exert full control over the new states, despite the formal recognition which the Kremlin had given to the putative independence of Khorezm and Bukhara. The channels for this control were the local communist parties. The Bukharan party was subordinate to Moscow from the outset, while the party in Khorezm remained independent until 1922, but in both republics Young Bukharans and Young Khivans who were unwilling to renounce their *Jadid* (Muslim reformist) ideology were quickly pushed out of senior posts. By mid-1921 the social and economic policies of these supposedly independent states mirrored those of Turkestan, including far greater restrictions on private property and religion than the pre-revolutionary *Jadid* reformers and even many secular nationalists found acceptable.

Though many local communists stayed and continued to work with Faizullah Khojaev in Bukhara and A. Akchurin in Khorezm, several members of the respective ruling executive committees joined the opposition forces, especially after the November 1921 arrival in the region of Enver Pasha, a leader of the ousted Young Turk government. Enver Pasha had come to Turkestan at Lenin's invitation to help calm the situation, but once there he decided to direct the anti-Bolshevik opposition instead.

Enver's presence provided the anti-Bolshevik forces with new legitimacy. Renewed and more effective resistance groups sprang up throughout the region, including a new 'Army of Islam' of more than 20,000 men in the Fergana Valley. Here the resistance to the Bolsheviks now took on an explicitly religious character, as Sufi leaders began to organize and fund several large detachments of fighters. Although the opposition to the Bolsheviks was far from united, communications and supply lines linking Khiva, Bukhara and the Fergana Valley were established.

By January 1922 Lenin and Stalin recognized the situation in Turkestan was completely out of control and a Politburo resolution ordered local military and civilian authorities to take whatever steps were necessary to defeat the *basmachi*, now the collective term Moscow used for all these resistance movements. The Red Army forces in the region were upgraded, while at the same time Frunze and the Turkestan Commission were ordered to make new concessions to the Turkestanis. The food stores and arms depots of the 'Army of Islam' were destroyed, and its leaders hunted down, driving most of the fighters to slip back into the population from which they had come. By late 1923 Fergana's main *kurbashi* had all been defeated, although periodic skirmishes remained common through most of 1924.

Bukhara became the major theatre of operations, first in the flatlands of the west, and then in the mountainous terrain of the east, where Enver was tracked down and killed in August 1922. This proved to be the turning point in the fight for Turkestan, although even with the arrival of additional reinforcements in 1923, it still took the Red Army two more years to defeat and roust the last opposition from the hills of what is now southern Tajikistan.

National demarcation and Soviet rule

As the Bolsheviks began to conquer Central Asia, they had to decide how they were going to rule the territory. Although Stalin was Commissar for Nationalities from 1917 to 1924, the key decisions were made by Lenin himself as long as his health permitted. An internationalist, Lenin genuinely wanted to draw supporters from all the empire's nationalities, although he also assumed that, having made the revolution, Russians would continue to form its vanguard. Ideally each nationality would be led to socialism by its own leaders, but along a single path, with at most minor modifications, and under the direction of the Communist Party in Moscow – a view reflected in the 1922 Constitution of the Union of Soviet Socialist Republics.

This goal proved difficult to realize in practice. Nearly all the non-Russian Communists were convinced that they alone could understand how socialism should be achieved among their respective peoples, and because of the later vindictiveness of Lenin and, especially, Stalin, the dispute cost the lives of some of the most able political figures in Central Asia. Lenin's major opponent was Turar Ryskulov. Ryskulov became a member of the bureau of the Turkestan Communist Party in 1919, and then head of its Muslim Bureau and Chairman of the Executive Committee of the Turkestan Republic in January 1920, effectively making him head of state. In this position he soon clashed with Frunze, and then with Lenin himself, by calling for the creation of an independent Turkic Communist Party, to rule an independent Turkic Republic. Ryskulov's argument was that Central Asians and socialism would both best be served if these peoples were all gathered together in a single independent state. In his own mind at least, Ryskulov was not a Pan-Turk, because the ruling Turkic Communist Party would be internationalist, not pan-nationalist, and so would keep the various ethnic communities from developing into European-style nations.

Frunze rejected Ryskulov's proposition immediately, and in May 1920 so did Lenin, who saw this as evidence of how deeply rooted the 'bourgeois-nationalist' mentality was among Central Asians. Ryskulov was reassigned to Moscow, only to be reappointed chairman of Turkestan's Executive

Committee in autumn 1922, during the campaign against the *basmachi*. However, Ryskulov refused to break publicly with his friend and colleague, Tatar Communist Party leader Muhammad Sultan-Galiev, who was purged as a national-deviant in 1923 for his proposal to join parts of Afghanistan, Persia, Bashkortistan, Tatarstan and Central Asia into a Turan Republic, to serve as the vanguard for launching communism in the east.

Ryskulov's plan for an independent Turkic republic, Sultan-Galiev's demand that the Bolsheviks look eastward rather than westward, and the break with the Bolsheviks in 1920 by Bashkir Communist Party leader Zeki Validov (who fled to Istanbul after flirting briefly with the *basmachi*) all strengthened the arguments of local European Bolsheviks like F. I. Goloshchekin (*Kirrevkom* member and future party boss of Kazakhstan) that revolution would come to Turkestan and the Steppe only if it was imported.

As Lenin failed and Stalin took over, life became even harder for the Muslim revolutionaries. By 1922 Young Bukharans and Young Khivans were being forced either to conform or to leave their republic communist parties, and nationalist leaders like A. Fitrat or Baitursunov who refused to join the Communist Party were removed from senior government posts. All were men who had sided with the Bolsheviks in the hope that, as enemies of their tsarist enemies, the Bolsheviks would help their peoples gain the power and sovereignty which the tsar had denied them.

Even after Ryskulov's defeat in 1920, it appeared for a while that Moscow might grant the republics some sort of local autonomy. However, as the plans began to solidify for the new constitution (promulgated in December 1922 but not operative until January 1924), it became plain that Moscow would be the seat of power. Indeed, as part of the Russian Republic, Turkestan and Kazakhstan were not even signatories of the 1922 document.

In spring 1924, after the Twelfth Party Congress, the Central Asia Bureau of the Communist Party took up the question of how to organize Central Asia, asking the three affected communist parties to offer their ideas. The re-drawn map which emerged – formally in October 1924, though some scholars now claim that it was not agreed upon until February 1925 and that the documents were back-dated – divided the region into five republics, the Soviet forerunners of today's independent countries. The Kirgiz Republic, still an autonomous republic within Russia, was renamed the Kazakh Republic, and had appended to it the two historically Kazakh provinces of Syr Darya and Semirech'e, until then in Turkestan. Turkmenistan, made up of western Khiva and the Turkmen autonomous region of Turkestan, and Uzbekistan were both made into Union Republics. The latter also included the Autonomous Republic of Tajikistan, which was upgraded to full republic status in 1929, with Uzbekistan's capital moving from Samarkand to Tashkent. Finally, the Kara-Kirgiz autonomous oblast' was carved from an earlier autonomous oblast' of Turkestan; it was subsequently upgraded to the status of Autonomous Republic in 1926, and became the Union Republic of Kirgizia in 1936.

Further reading

Allworth E., *Central Asia: A Century of Russian Rule* (New York, Columbia University Press, 1967).

Bacon E., *Central Asia under Soviet Rule* (Ithaca, Cornell University Press, 1966).

Olcott M. B., *The Kazakhs*, 2nd edn (Stanford, Hoover Institution Press, 1987).

Park A. G., *Bolshevism in Turkestan, 1917–1927* (New York, Columbia University Press, 1957).

Sokol E. D., *The Revolt of 1916 in Russian Central Asia* (Baltimore, Johns Hopkins University Press, 1954).

Wheeler G., *The Modern History of Soviet Central Asia* (New York, Praeger, 1964).

Zenkovsky S. A., *Pan-Turkism and Islam in Russia* (Cambridge MA, Harvard University Press, 1960).

The Jews

JOHN D. KLIER

One of the first actions of the Provisional Government, on 9 March 1917, was to order the Minister of Justice, Aleksandr Kerensky, to devise a bill abolishing all national and religious restrictions. The resultant act was promulgated on 20 March 1917, accompanied by a list of 140 distinct laws and regulations, in most cases restrictive, which applied to the Jews at the end of the tsarist empire. This action ended the Jewish question *de jure*, but hardly *de facto*, as the revolution was left with the legacy of a century of economic and social change affecting the Jewish community.

The social setting

In the first imperial census of 1897, 97 per cent of the empire's Jews gave Yiddish as their native language. This oft-cited statistic is extremely misleading, because the census offered no option to indicate bi- or multilingualism. There is no doubt, however, that many Jews spoke a non-Jewish language. Invariably it was an 'imperial' language, such as Russian or Polish, rather than the language of an emergent nationality, such as Ukrainian or Belorussian. This was a simple reflection of the balance of political power in the empire, but it did not preclude a casual knowledge of a 'peasant' language for mercantile purposes.

Under the influence of the *Haskalah*, the Jewish Enlightenment movement, limited numbers of Jews sought acculturation, a desire expedited after 1847 through the agency of a state-sponsored, non-traditionalist Jewish school system. Service in the post-reform army after 1875 also served to spread Russian among the empire's Jews. Jews of the younger generation sought education in state institutions, and began to enter the professions on a limited scale. The religiously orthodox leadership responded to the threat of acculturation by seeking ways of revivifying traditional learning, most notably through the *Musar* movement, a reform of *yeshivot*, the schools of higher talmudic study.

Political tendencies

Despite the claims of Russian reactionaries, the vast majority of Russian Jews remained passive and politically loyal to the Russian imperial state. Student youth, exposed to the same influences as their non-Jewish class-mates, and subject in addition to restrictive legislation, moved into political activism in the late 1870s. By the end of the century Jews were to be found in every Russian political movement and tendency save the extreme right, whose anti-semitic ideology specifically excluded them. Jews also devised their own distinctive political movements. The programmes of all the Jewish political parties were essentially permutations of a specific set of ideological dichotomies: liberal/socialist; Zionist/anti-Zionist; autonomist/non-auto-nomist; internationalist/nationalist. Socialists sub-divided into Marxists and non-Marxists, while Zionism split into Palestinophilism and Territorialism. Jewish political activists fell into four general categories as follows.

Liberals

A number of Jewish professionals, such as M. M. Vinaver and G. B. Sliozberg, played prominent roles in the liberal Liberation Movement prior to the revolution of 1905. They pursued a parallel interest in the fate of the Jewish community by establishing, in 1905, the Union for the Attainment of Full Equality for the Jewish People in Russia. After the October Manifesto, the Union fragmented. The Jewish National Group, led by Vinaver, Sliozberg and others, was closely tied to the Constitutional Democratic Party. It was staunchly anti-Zionist, and pursued Jewish 'national interests' only through demands for full civil rights, legislative recognition of Jewish communal structures based on democratic principles, support for Jewish language and culture, and economic development of the impoverished Jewish population. A rival Jewish Democratic Group, led by L. M. Bramson, A. I. Braudo and others, was linked to the Trudovik faction in the State Duma. The group espoused extreme democratic principles which they wished to see introduced into Jewish communal life, heretofore dominated by the communal rich. The Jewish National Party (Volkspartei) was not an electoral organization as such, but a group dedicated to publicizing the the-ories of the historian and activist S. M. Dubnow, known as autonomism. Autonomism demanded guarantees for the national-cultural life of minor-ities within the Russian empire, exemplified by a system of autonomous self-government to be established at the national and local level. After the February revolution, Jewish liberals created a Jewish National Group whose moderate demands included a school system which would safeguard Jewish religion, language and culture, and limited use of Jewish languages in public life. The attitude of Jewish liberals was exemplified by Vinaver's plea that 'what is necessary is not just love of freedom, but also self-control'. As the revolution moved to the left, Jewish liberals quickly became politically irrelevant.

Socialists

The Bund (the General Jewish Labour Union in Lithuania, Poland and Russia) was one of the founding members of the Russian Social-Democratic Labour Party (RSDRP) in 1898. Together with its general commitment to class struggle, the Bund claimed an additional, specific mandate to carry out work among the Jewish proletariat wherever Jewish workers might be found in the Russian empire. This was mandated, Bundists argued, by the special needs of the Jewish proletariat (Yiddish-language propaganda) and circumstances (the situation of the Jews as an especially persecuted minority within the empire). The Bund was a tightly organized, conspiratorial and centralized movement, which boasted the largest mass following of any social-democratic grouping. These typical social-democratic features were accompanied by an untypically strong democratic tradition. Challenged by the rise of Zionism, and the spectre of foreign and domestic anti-semitism, the Bund developed a special programme to deal with the Jews, rather than leave the solution of the Jewish question to a socialist revolution. In 1901, the party accepted the principle of full national autonomy for national minorities, regardless of the territory which they occupied. The Bund specifically claimed nationality status for the Jews. In later years Bundist theoreticians spelled out demands for national-cultural autonomy, envisioning a Yiddish-based secular Jewish culture, to be supported and protected within a federated Russian state. The Bund organized Jewish self-defence groups to oppose pogroms, and insisted that social democracy must specifically fight the restrictive legislation imposed on Jews. The Bund proved resistant to internal schisms, and tried to play a mediating role between antagonistic party factions. The ideological intransigence of the 'Iskraist' faction with the RSDRP led to the withdrawal of the Bund from the party between 1903 and 1906. Upon re-admission, the Bund tended to be closer to Menshevik than Bolshevik positions. The Bundists' vaunted (or detested) ability to compromise was tested throughout 1917, and finally shattered after October.

Zionists/Socialists

The Bund faced a growing rivalry from other leftist Jewish parties, especially those which incorporated some form of Zionism or Territorialism in their programmes. The Jewish Socialist Labour Party (SERP, ES, *Seimovtsy*), founded in 1906, was originally a party which combined non-Marxist socialism and autonomism. The mechanism for autonomy was to be a Jewish National Council or Seim, elected by local units. The Seim would serve as the 'highest organ of Jewish self-government and as the representative of a united Russian Jewry'. The *Seimovtsy* were unwilling to cooperate with Jewish bourgeois autonomists.

The Zionist Socialist Labour Party (SSRP, SS), founded in 1905, pioneered the participation of Zionists in the Russian political struggle, as opposed to the 'neutralism' of the general Zionist movement. It initially advocated cultural autonomy, but was dismissive of national autonomy as a bourgeois utopia. The movement was represented in the World Zionist Congress in Basel in 1905, which split over the issue of the establishment of a temporary Jewish refuge in Uganda. The movement evolved into a Marxist, territorialist party which perceived its objective as safeguarding the interests of the Jewish proletariat within the bourgeois-dominated Zionist movement.

In May and June 1917 SERP and the SS merged to create a new entity, the United Jewish Socialist Labour Party, known as *Farainigte* (United). The party urged creation of a federated Russian republic, with a three-tiered system of a central parliament to serve as a national government, national seims overseeing education and social concerns, and regional assemblies charged with local economic concerns. The Jewish national Seim was to be elected by universal, equal, secret, proportional and direct suffrage. A local communal structure (a *kehillah*) would be created wherever there were 300 Jews. Class struggle would be carried on within the various national organs.

The Jewish Social-Democratic Party (Poale Tsion) (ESDRP – Workers of Zion), created in 1906, built on the ideas of Ber Borochov to create a party which was simultaneously strictly Zionist and Marxist. Jews must correct the economic and social abnormalities of the diaspora by going to Palestine, a backward, undeveloped country, and participate in the development and resultant class struggle which would lead to the 'normalization' of Jewish life. In the diaspora, Poale Tsion was committed to the attainment of broad national and cultural autonomy for the Jewish community.

Zionists

Political Zionism, the movement of Theodor Herzl and his World Zionist Organization, grew slowly in Russia as the government wavered between toleration and repression. Russia did become a centre for Orthodox support of Zionism with the founding by Rabbi Yitzhak Reines of a religious-nationalist party, Mizrachi, in Vilna in 1902. The party was allied to the World Zionist Organization, and sought to resist secularizing trends within Zionist-sponsored educational programmes. The traditional political neutralism of the Zionist movement was strained by the upheavals of 1904–06, which witnessed both anti-Jewish pogroms and Jewish political initiatives. The Third Conference of Russian Zionists, meeting in Helsingfors in November 1906, promulgated a programme which combined political involvement within the empire and work towards settlement in Palestine. The Helsingfors Programme demanded a democratic Russian state based on an elected parliament, with regional autonomy and the protection of the rights of national minorities. The programme demanded the recognition of the Jews in Russia as a united people, with the right of self-government in national matters, and full protection for the use of the Jewish language in schools, courts and social life. Jews demanded the right to maintain Saturday as their day of rest. The conference called for the convocation of a Jewish national assembly in Russia in order to develop the basis for national organizations. This remained the Zionist programme in Russia until the February revolution. Political reaction after 1906, however, forced much of the movement's activity underground.

Economic circumstances

Jews were an integral part of the quasi-feudal economic system which had reigned in the territories seized by Russia from the Polish-Lithuanian Commonwealth. They were an important mercantile element in both the villages and the private towns (the *shtetl*) of the Kingdom of Poland. In the Ukraine, Jews, possessing personal mobility and liquid capital, were an integral part of the noble latifundia economy, serving as estate managers, agents and go-betweens for the lords. Jews leased feudal prerogatives, especially *propinacja*, the production and sale of alcoholic beverages. The Jewish tavern-keeper was an archetypal figure in Eastern Europe. Jews settled in private towns also dominated artisan activities.

At the turn of the eighteenth century, the Russian state restricted Jewish access to the Russian interior, creating residence restrictions known as the Pale of Settlement. The dramatic growth of the Jewish population, from less than a million to over five million in the course of the nineteenth century, created residential and occupational overconcentrations, resulting in growing Jewish impoverishment. A steady foreign migration movement failed to halt this trend.

Post-Emancipation (1861) economic development was a mixed blessing for Jews. While a number of Jewish entrepreneurs, such as the banker Evzel Gintsburg and the railway magnate S. S. Poliakov, amassed substantial fortunes, Russian Jewry never approached the economic influence of Jews in the Austrian or German empires. While a few Jews entered the Russian middle class and the professions, most remained poor and underemployed. Railway construction destroyed the traditional transportation infrastructure which employed many Jews. In Russian Poland, on the other hand, and a few cities in the Pale, Jews did find employment as factory workers, and the rise of a Jewish working class made possible the growth of the Bund.

Official policy

The Russian government distrusted the Jews because of their alleged 'religious fanaticism' which kept them apart from the rest of the population, and made them bad subjects who did not scruple to live by 'economic exploitation' of the unsophisticated peasantry. The Jewish question was thought to be remediable, however, and was the target of reformist policies until the last decades of the nineteenth century. As a conservative ideology evolved in Russia, the Jews were increasingly demonized and seen as an alien element intent upon the destruction of Russian civilization. Jews became a convenient scapegoat for all the stresses and contradictions of modernization. Official prejudice and restrictive legislation grew in the face of both Jewish political activity and public order concerns posed by the outbreak of pogroms in 1881–2. In the period of the revolution of 1905, Jews became a convenient target for reactionary political activity, exemplified by the excesses of the so-called 'Black Hundreds' (extremist right-wing paramilitary groups). Despite the promise of the October Manifesto, after 1905 Jews were systematically excluded from the constitutional rights promised to all Russian subjects.

Impact of World War I

The outbreak of war exacerbated the Jewish question still further. The theatre of war included much of the Pale of Settlement, and Jews were made scapegoats for military reverses amidst charges of spying and disloyalty. In 1915, the military took the quixotic decision to evacuate the Jewish population near the front to the Russian interior, culminating in the resettlement of more than 600,000 persons. Faced with this *fait accompli*, the Council of Ministers formally expanded the Pale of Settlement, although the legal status of the refugees remained very ambiguous. The occupation of much of the Kingdom of Poland and the Baltic provinces by German forces meant that Polish Jewry was lost to Russian control. The chaotic removal of the Jewish population from the front created the opportunity for Jewish political leaders to act to organize relief operations, in a manner analogous to the role of zemstvos in supporting the war economy.

In the revolutionary year 1917, Jewish parties debated issues of war and peace, the nature of the revolution, and the nature of Jewish life in the new Russia. After October, the Jewish parties were forced to stand for or against the Bolshevik seizure of power. Further confusion attended the large Jewish population of the Ukraine, which had to resolve questions of the status of

Jewish life there as Ukrainian nationalists moved from demands for autonomy, to separatism, and then independence.

The Jewish response to the February revolution

The pent-up energies of the Russian Jewish community (reduced from 5.5 million to 3.5 million as a consequence of wartime territorial and population losses) exploded into a torrent of political, social and cultural activity in the post-February period. The already mobilized Jewish wartime aid societies, dominated by liberals, took the lead in calling for an empire-wide congress of Jews to formally create autonomous institutions for Jews and to prepare a set of demands in anticipation of the convocation of the Constituent Assembly. A pre-congress, the All-Russian Jewish Conference, was elected and met on 3 July 1917 to establish guidelines for the national meeting. The congress itself, elected after the Bolshevik revolution, never met.

There were numerous opportunities for Jewish political parties to judge their electoral appeal: there were national elections to the Jewish Congress and to the Russian Constituent Assembly, as well as elections to regional congresses in the Ukraine, and local elections to newly democratized *kehillot* boards.

Orthodox politics

The vast majority of the empire's Jewish population was nominally Orthodox, and politically inert. On the eve of the World War some efforts had been made to mobilize the Orthodox masses. In May 1912, representatives of German, Austrian and Russian Jewry met in Kattowitz to form an Orthodox political movement, Agudas Israel. In the wake of the February revolution, Orthodox representatives, including elements of the Orthodox Zionist party Mizrachi, met in Moscow on 3 April 1917 and founded the movement Mesoret ve-Herut (Tradition and Freedom). It called for Jewish national autonomy, based on democratic principles, a Saturday rest guarantee, and governmental financial support for the *kehillot*. In the summer of 1917, the Orthodox chose a seven-man committee of rabbis – including the heads of two Hasidic dynasties, the Lubavitch and Bobroisk – to prepare for the All-Russian Jewish Congress.

Despite its innate conservatism, even the Orthodox community found itself pushed to the left. A meeting of local religious political groups, meeting in Moscow in July 1917, not only asked for state funding of religious education, but demanded an eight-hour working day, the right to strike, freedom .of conscience, and a radical land distribution programme. The Orthodox were also active on the regional level: in the Ukraine, religious parties merged to form Akhdus (Unity) in 1918, while Agudas Israel achieved political successes in Belorussia.

The Orthodox never succeeded in creating a strong political movement. This may have been due to internal rivalries and disorganization, regional and religious differences (especially between the Hasidic movement and their non-Hasidic Orthodox opponents), and the absence of any truly national institutions throughout the period of Russian rule. Moreover, the Orthodox were challenged on their home ground, the local community, by secular parties which saw control of the *kehillot* as the surest route to political power 'on the Jewish street'. Thus, in no elections did Orthodox parties succeed in garnering more than 15 per cent of the Jewish vote. Jewish liberals, for whom the securing of equal rights had always been a *raison d'être*, fared even worse. As the revolution turned leftward they, like their gentile counterparts, declined into political insignificance.

Zionism

By all indicators – formal membership, local branches, percentage of votes in all elections – Zionism was the most potent ideology among the Jews of the empire after February 1917. The movement claimed 300,000 *shekel* holders (those who had made a small symbolic offering to the movement) at the end of 1917. Petrograd hosted the Seventh Congress of Russian Zionists (11–18 May 1917), which brought together 522 delegates representing 140,000 members in 340 towns and *shtetlakh*. Zionist parties received by far the largest percentage of the vote in communal elections in the Ukraine, in elections to the Ukrainian Provisional National Congress in August 1918, and to the Jewish National Congress elected in 1917–18. In elections to the Russian Constituent Assembly, Zionists received 417,215 votes out of the 498,198 cast for Jewish parties. Yet the practical consequences of these efforts were surprisingly slight, and suggest that the achievements of the Zionists were largely symbolic: the declaration of an emergent Jewish nationalism in the midst of a fundamentally conservative and religious population. Part of the Zionists' success came from their ability to assemble joint electoral lists with religious parties in the Ukraine. Zionism never found a completely coherent role in the Russian revolution, a reflection of the movement's need to pursue two objectives which were, in the long run, fundamentally contradictory. For example, at the Seventh Congress, the Zionist leader Yehiel Chlenov pledged the Jewish soldier 'to follow the call of the revolutionary democracy to defend Russia against her enemies'. At the same time, the congress agreed that it would not participate in the proposed All-Russian Jewish Congress unless the question of *Erets Israel* (Palestine) was placed on the agenda. The Bund, in opposition, branded such concerns as a counterrevolutionary fantasy. A compromise was reached by the two camps during the July pre-congress.

Arguably the political impact of Zionism was diminished because the energies of activists were channelled into 'organic' work, which sought to create the cultural and social pre-conditions for the Jewish colonization of Palestine. The most impressive accomplishments were those of the cultural movement, *Tarbut*, which created a network of over 250 Hebrew-language schools and educational organizations. A Hebrew-language theatre, Habima, enjoyed popular and critical success. The movement also sustained over 50 newspapers in Yiddish, Hebrew and Russian, and the activities of He-Haluz, designed to train would-be emigrants in agricultural techniques. The Balfour Declaration in November 1917 (NS) was welcomed with wild enthusiasm in Russia, with street demonstrations and celebrations. The crowd in Odessa greeting the declaration was reported to have numbered more than 100,000. What the Zionist movement did not produce was widespread emigration to Palestine: the total settlement during the so-called Third *Aliyah* (1917–21) numbered only 35,000 persons.

The Jewish response to the October revolution

No Jewish socialist party was close to the Bolsheviks, the Bundists being most comfortable on the Menshevik left wing. All Jewish parties initially opposed the October revolution. The Bolsheviks and their Jewish rivals alike were forced to modify their ideological stances. The assimilationist rhetoric of Bolshevik nationality policy, which envisioned the Jews as ethnic material to be speedily assimilated by the larger society, had to deal with the reality of millions of Jews, with a sharpened, not lessened, national-cultural identity. The Jewish political parties, for their part, had to develop a realistic response to October. This meant choosing, in the first instance, between Bolsheviks and their soviet-based opponents. As parties fragmented on this point, other forms of organization were debated. Jews on the left debated merger with the Communist Party and the question of autonomous forms of party membership and activity. The Jews of the Ukraine had to develop responses to specifically Ukrainian political events.

A number of totally assimilated Jews – Trotsky, Zinoviev, Kamenev, Sverdlov – played leading roles in the Bolshevik movement. Acculturated Jews also provided important assistance after October, when they helped to break the boycott of the new regime by the Russian intelligentsia. Denied public employment under tsarism, Jews flooded into the state apparatus. In Lenin's words, 'they sabotaged the saboteurs'. As a persecuted minority Jews, like the Letts, were especially welcomed into the Cheka, and many Jews made successful careers in 'the Organs' until the purges of the 1930s.

Ironically, the regime failed completely to find collaborators in the field of purely Jewish work, where socialists (excepting a small leftist faction of Poale Tsion), Zionists and the Orthodox alike spurned the Bolsheviks. Efforts to propagandize the Jewish population were initially left to foreign *émigré* employees of the propaganda section of the Commissariat for Foreign Affairs. This solution was clearly ineffective, and in early 1918 the regime created a Commissariat for Jewish Affairs (the *Evkom*) under the leadership of a veteran Bolshevik, Semen Dimanshtain. This was followed by the creation, in August 1918, of Jewish sections of the Bolshevik Party (the *Evsektsiia*), also headed by Dimanshtain. Initially the *Evsektsiia* had great difficulty in recruiting cadres or combating the existing Jewish parties. But during the 1920s, the *Evsektsiia* played a major role in mobilizing Soviet Jewry through a militant anti-religious campaign, efforts at industrialization and agricultural colonization, the Sovietization of existing Jewish communal institutions, and the creation of a Soviet Jewish culture, Yiddish in form and socialist in content.

The Jews in the Ukraine

The majority of Jews in the Russian empire lived in the Ukrainian provinces, where they constituted 9 per cent of the overall population (and 29 per cent of the urban population). Relations between Ukrainians and Jews were highly ambivalent: Jews were an integral part of the village economy with all the consequent elements of daily interaction. In times of national crisis the Ukraine was a focus for anti-Jewish rioting, the pogroms. The relations between Ukrainian intellectuals and Jews were extremely problematic, for the largely Russified Jewish intelligentsia had little sympathy for Ukrainian culture. The threat of Ukrainian 'separatism' had special risks for Jews: it threatened to split the empire-wide Jewish community, reducing both its political influence and cultural opportunities; to interfere with the free exchange of goods between Russia and the Ukraine (of particular concern to mercantile Jews); and to make possible the coming to power of anti-semitic political elements. There was no consensus within Ukrainian Jewry as to how best to confront these threats. The masses were politically apathetic and maintained a low level of political participation. Any common activity was complicated by the sharp disagreements between Zionists and diaspora nationalists. The relatively small Jewish socialist groups achieved a higher level of political organization and influence which prompted their claim to represent all Ukrainian Jewry. The Zionists challenged this assertion, predicting – correctly – that democratic elections would reveal majority support for them.

The Ukrainian national movement was slow to demand outright independence, professing a preference for substantial political and cultural autonomy within a democratic, federated Russian union. The Ukrainian revolutionary government, the Rada, sought the support of national minorities by granting them substantial territorial autonomy. Thus the Rada's General Secretariat created three vice-secretaries for nationality affairs (Jewish, Polish and Russian), each operating through a National Council.

The first Vice-Secretary for Jewish Affairs, Moshe Zil'berfarb, offered equal representation to all the major Jewish parties, which gave overrepresentation to socialists (and none at all to the ill-organized Orthodox). The Zionists, ambivalent in any case at being drawn into the ruling coalition, boycotted the National Council until the summer of 1918, when they participated in elections to a Provisional Jewish Assembly, conducted through the democratized *kehillot* of the Ukraine. The resultant assembly, which met from 3–11 November 1918, had a Zionist majority. The assembly's decision to send a delegation to the Paris peace talks to speak in the name of east European Jews as a national minority led to a boycott of Jewish institutions of government by the non-Zionist parties.

The Rada government responded to the October revolution on 7 November by declaring the Ukraine to be a People's Republic (although still within a putative all-Russian federation). In early January the Rada passed a bill on national-personal autonomy, which was considered a generous concession to the Ukraine's national minorities, and a corresponding response was anticipated. However, when the Rada voted to declare Ukraine an independent, free, sovereign state on 12 January 1918 in response to an attack by Bolshevik forces, nationalists considered the conduct of the Jewish parties to be most disappointing. The Bund voted against independence, and most of the other parties abstained. Ukrainian nationalists saw this response as a Jewish betrayal of the national cause.

For the next four years, the Ukraine was, at one time or another, the scene of warfare between Bolsheviks and various Ukrainian nationalists, between German occupation forces and anti-German partisan bands, of civil war between Bolsheviks and the White Army, of Entente military intervention, and of war between Ukrainians and Poles and Communists and Poles in 1920. The Jewish population became a special target for plunder and pogroms. Anti-semitism was a major mobilizing principle for the White armies, which invaded the Ukraine in June 1919. Many Polish forces viewed their enemy as 'Communist Jews'. Some Ukrainian nationalists considered Jews as traitors to the cause. Irregular forces of every ideological persuasion saw the Jews as a vulnerable target for forced requisition and brutalization.

A vigorous historiographical debate still rages over the scale of and responsibility for the approximately 1,000 pogroms which wracked the Ukraine between 1918 and 1921. Perhaps as many as 40,000 Jews were murdered outright, and the total casualties numbered over 100,000. The White forces were particularly prone to pogrom activity. The irregular and partisan forces of the Directory, led by local warlords, the so-called *otamany*, gained special notoriety for pogrom excesses. Although the overall commander of Directory forces, Symon Petliura, condemned the pogroms, he was held by many Jews to be morally responsible. Controversy still surrounds the person of Petliura, who was assassinated in Paris in 1926 by a Jewish assailant. The Red Army, although not blameless of anti-Jewish violence, had the best record, and was viewed by many Jews as their principal safeguard. Disillusionment with the failures of the various Jewish parties, together with the impact of the pogroms, drove many Ukrainian Jews onto the side of the Red Army and thus into the Communist camp.

Jewish cultural life

The revolutionary period encompassed more than pogroms and Jewish suffering. There was an explosion of Jewish cultural and artistic activity. Besides the initiatives of the Hebrew-language *Tarbut* educational movement mentioned above, the revolutionary era witnessed a revival of the Yiddish press and of Yiddish literature influenced by the latest literary trends, exemplified by the 'Kiev Group', which included David Bergelson, der Nister (Pinkhos Kaganovich), Peretz Markish and David Hofshteyn. There was a revival of the Yiddish stage, exemplified by the Moscow Yiddish State Art Theatre (GOSET), founded by Aleksandr Granovskii, starring the stage actor Solomon Mikhoels, with sets designed by Marc Chagall. Chagall also participated in a 'people's art academy' in Vitebsk from 1918 to 1920, where a circle also formed around the painter Yehuda Pen.

Summary

The responsiveness and adaptability of Jews to the multi-faceted impact of the revolution on their lives, which has been chronicled above, give the lie to the legend of Jewish political passivity in the diaspora. The availability of a cadre of Jewish activists – centre and left – to participate in the events of the revolution demonstrates the ongoing impact of modernization on traditional east European Jewish society at the dawn of the century. Even the religiously Orthodox were forced to develop the techniques of political mobilization in order to counter their secularist opponents.

This phenomenon of Jewish political participation promised a vigorous political battle for the collective heart and mind of the Jewish street in post-revolutionary Russia, similar to that which emerged in interwar Poland. However, the political realities of the new Soviet state soon put paid to the hopes and fears of Orthodox and radical Jews alike. Communism in power soon proved itself to be good for the Jew, but bad for the Jews.

Further reading

Abramson H., 'Jewish Representation in the Independent Ukrainian Governments of 1917–1920', *Slavic Review* 50, 3 (1991), pp. 542–50.
Aronson G., Frumkin J. *et al.*, *Russian Jewry, 1917–1967* (New York, Thomas Yoseloff, 1969).

Fishman D., 'Preserving Tradition in the Land of Revolution: The Religious Leadership of Soviet Jewry, 1917–1930', in J. Wertheimer, ed., *The Uses of Tradition: Jewish Continuity in the Modern Era* (New York and Jerusalem, Jewish Theological Seminary of America, 1992), pp. 85–118.

Frankel J., *Prophecy and Politics: Socialism, Nationalism, and the Russian Jews, 1862–1917* (Cambridge, Cambridge University Press, 1981).

Gassenschmidt C., *Jewish Liberal Politics in Tsarist Russia, 1900–14* (London, Macmillan, 1995).

Gitelman Z., *Jewish Nationality and Soviet Politics: The Jewish Sections of the CPSU, 1917–1930* (Princeton, Princeton University Press, 1972).

Hunczak T., 'A Reappraisal of Symon Petliura and Ukrainian-Jewish Relations, 1917–1921', and Z. Szajkowski, 'A Rebuttal', *Jewish Social Studies* 31, 3 (1969), pp. 163–213.

Kochan L., *The Jews in Soviet Russia since 1917* (Oxford, Oxford University Press, 1970).

Levin N., *The Jews in the Soviet Union*, 2 vols. (New York and London, New York University Press, 1988).

Maor I., *Sionistskoe dvizhenie v Rossii* (Tel Aviv, Biblioteka-Aliia, 1977).

Pinkus B., *The Jews of the Soviet Union: The History of a National Minority* (Cambridge, Cambridge University Press, 1988).

Potichnyi P. and Aster H., *Ukrainian-Jewish Relations in Historical Perspective* (Edmonton, Canadian Institute of Ukrainian Studies, 1988).

Silberfard M., *The Jewish Ministry and Jewish National Autonomy in Ukraine*, trans. David H. Lincoln (New York, Aleph Press, 1993).

The Revolution and Civil War in Siberia

ALAN WOOD

The February and October revolutions were essentially a metropolitan affair. However, what happened on the streets of Petrograd in 1917 quickly reverberated throughout the stricken empire, affecting the most far-flung regions of the country. Among the furthest-flung were Russia's vast North Asian territories of Siberia – the name traditionally given to the huge continental land mass which stretches from the Ural mountains to the Pacific littoral, and from the Arctic Ocean to the borderlands of northern China. Historically, it includes the island of Sakhalin and those regions known today as the Russian Far East. Its total area is roughly five million square miles, i.e. about one-twelfth of the planet's land surface. Given its size and the crucial role it has played in the historical development of the Russian state and society, not least as a major theatre of the civil war, it has until recently attracted relatively little attention among Western historians. And in the popular imagination, even in Russia, it conjures up images of a limitless frozen wasteland, remote, inhospitable, and made the more dreadful for its reputation as a huge penal colony inhabited by convicted criminals and exiles. The full picture is, however, rather different, and to understand the impact of the revolution and civil war in Siberia, it is necessary to sketch in something of its pre-revolutionary development, and outline its administrative, social and economic structure on the eve of 1917.

Siberia before 1917: from conquest to revolution

The traditional date for the beginning of Muscovy's subjugation and settlement of Siberia is 1581–82, when a Cossack chieftain – Ermak Timofeevich – led his warriors across the Urals to conquer the tiny Tatar khanate of Sibir on the river Irtysh. In little over a century, Russian servicemen (*sluzhilye liudi*), hunters, merchants, fugitive serfs, exiles, criminals and adventurers trailblazed their way across the continent, forging a chain of fortified

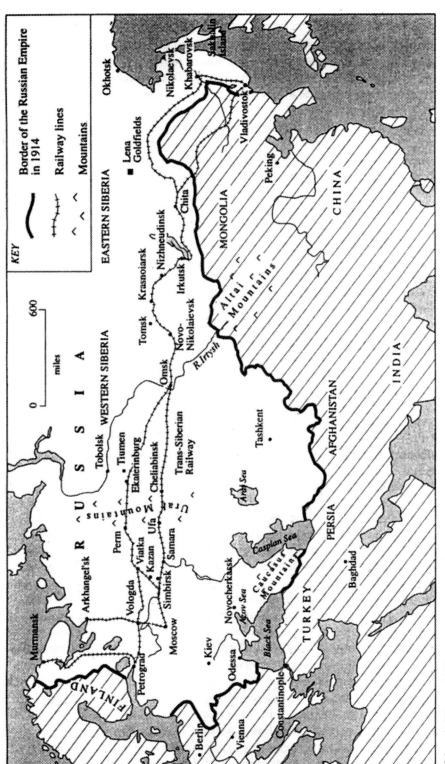

Map 6. Siberia, 1917

settlements (*ostrogi*) from Tiumen in the west to Okhotsk on the Far East coast. These were the sites of Siberia's future major towns and administrative centres. The economic impetus for this *Drang nach Osten* was the lucrative Siberian fur trade – furs being the most valuable commodity on Russia's internal and external market. Government officials, military commanders and their staff administered Muscovy's new territories as agents of the tsar, but in an arbitrary, corrupt, rough-and-ready manner typical of frontierland societies, reducing the conquered aboriginal peoples of Siberia to the status of tribute-paying vassals. The discovery in the eighteenth century of rich mineral deposits (silver, lead, copper, gold, etc.) led to further exploitation of the territory's great natural wealth for the benefit of the central exchequer. Put simply, Siberia was treated primarily as a 'resource frontier' of metropolitan Russia, subject to all the classic abuses of a colonial status.

In the eighteenth and nineteenth centuries, the rural population of Siberia was vastly expanded by the voluntary influx of waves of peasants fleeing the oppression and misery of serfdom in European Russia. For many, Siberia's notoriety as a land of penal servitude was offset by its promise of boundless opportunity, fertile land and personal liberty. The waves of fugitives swelled into a high tide of eastwards migration at the beginning of the twentieth century as the completion of the Trans-Siberian Railway (Trans-Sib) and a change in the government's agrarian policy after the turmoil of 1905 facilitated this massive demographic shift. The millions of new immigrants (*novosely*) were often resented by the old settlers (*starozhily*), but this was only one respect in which peasant society was different in Siberia from that in European Russia. The Siberian peasantry was more prosperous, farmed more land with more highly mechanized machinery and was more familiar with capitalist farming and marketing methods. Moreover, Siberia was relatively free of the historical legacy of serfdom and landlordism, and the system of communal land redistribution was rare. Among the most successful and well-off sections of the agrarian population were the Cossack communities, many of whom owned much larger farms than even the wealthy kulaks, and were to play a dramatic role in the civil war. Indeed, maverick Cossack atamans (chieftains) were among the most bloodthirsty of anti-Bolsheviks. In the early twentieth century, Siberia was transformed into one of the most productive agricultural regions of the empire. Its peasantry proved more resourceful, secure and independent-minded, and thus less susceptible to revolutionary activity and propaganda than those in European Russia. Neither the peasants' overwhelming support for the Socialist-Revolutionary Party in the Constituent Assembly elections of November–December 1917, nor the strength of the producers' and consumers' cooperative movement in the region should be taken as an indication of political radicalism, still less of a desire for socialism.

Siberian society was in general less rigidly class-ridden than that of European Russia; apart from the peasantry and the conservative urban middle classes, the very small industrial working class in Siberia and its underdeveloped manufacturing industries meant that there was only a very slender socio-economic base on which to build the structure of a Marxist 'proletarian-socialist revolution'. All the more remarkable therefore was the fairly rapid spread of 'Soviet power' across Siberia after the Bolshevik revolution.

More alive than any other grouping to the geographical, historical, economic and ethnic peculiarities of Siberia were the Siberian 'regionalists' (*oblastniki*). Starting among circles of 'expatriate' intellectuals at St Petersburg in the 1860s, there developed during the late nineteenth century a distinct school of regionalist thought (*oblastnichestvo*) which produced a rudimentary programme for the welfare, civic development, prosperity and local autonomy of the people of Siberia. Its major objectives were:

• the abolition of the exile system which was deemed to be harmful to the security of Siberia's free citizenry who were constantly terrorized by bandit gangs of escaped convicts;
• the lifting of discriminatory internal customs barrriers which acted against the economic interests of the Siberian merchantry;
• a more purposeful programme of land distribution and rural settlement;
• development of a proper educational and cultural infrastructure;
• adoption of humane policies to improve the material circumstances and civil rights of the Siberian indigenous peoples.

Calls for Siberia's complete political independence were rare, and the occasional manifestation of "separatism' was swiftly repressed. While Siberian society was hardly homogeneous – indeed, the revolution and civil war opened a Pandora's box of deep-seated divisions and antagonisms – and despite the recrudescence of industrial unrest after the 1912 massacre of striking workers in the Lena goldfields, in early 1917 there were few portents beyond the Urals of the revolutionary cataclysm into which the whole country was soon to be plunged.

Siberia: February 1917–May 1918

The abdication of Nicholas II on 2 March caught the whole country, including Siberia, unawares and created a power vacuum which in the capital was filled by the Provisional Government and the Petrograd Soviet, and throughout the rest of the country, especially in the borderlands, with a kaleidoscope of politically diverse groupings, institutions, committees, assemblies, local soviets and self-styled regional governments. At one point, there were at least nineteen different 'governments' operating between Cheliabinsk and Vladivostok. Over the next four years, the only quality which these bodies shared was their ephemerality. The collapse of Romanov rule and the crumbling of its agents' authority meant that for the first time since the sixteenth century Siberia was free from the direct rule of Moscow or St Petersburg.

The opportunity thus arose for the public assertion of a range of political and regional agendas. Apart from right-wingers and monarchists, the main political contenders were the Constitutional Democrats (Kadets), the regionalists (*oblastniki*), the Socialist-Revolutionary Party (PSR, SRs), and the Social Democrats (both Menshevik and Bolshevik).

Support for the extreme right was initially negligible, only gaining ground after the spring of 1918 during the so-called 'democratic counterrevolution'. Its only mainstay came from the superannuated officials of the tsarist establishment, rich businessmen and officers of the old Imperial Army. Even at the peak of its ascendancy (May 1918–November 1919) it had no clear political programme nor effective social or economic policies which appealed to the bulk of the population – a major cause of the Whites' ultimate defeat.

The Kadets' limited backing came from sections of the urban middle class, though many professional people and the intelligentsia also favoured the regionalists' programme, however amorphous. The Kadets suffered in this respect from their suspicion of the *oblastniki*'s populist preoccupation with local issues, whereas the more 'worldly' Kadets dismissed what they regarded as this petty parochialism in favour of championing a centralized Great Russian state. As Kadets, they were also tainted with the failure of the Provisional Government to deal effectively with the two most urgent problems of the day – land redistribution and Russia's participation in the war. During the civil war the Kadets moved further to the right of the political spectrum, even espousing the idea of one-man dictatorship.

The regionalists not surprisingly pressed their demands for greater autonomy for Siberia, with a regional government acting independently within a Russian federation to promote the discrete interests of Siberia itself as opposed to those of central government. There was little talk of all-out separatism, but a number of enthusiastic meetings, assemblies and congresses were convened which adopted regionalist slogans, called for greater regional independence, raised the green and white regionalist flag, and advocated elections to a Siberian Regional Duma. However, despite the progressive tenor of the regionalists' rhetoric, it found little resonance among the mass of the people, and knowledge of their activities was largely confined to an insubstantial circle of Tomsk-based intellectuals.

The party which won most support from the Siberian peasants (over 90 per cent of the population) was the PSR. In the elections to the Constituent Assembly, the SRs achieved 50 per cent of the Siberian vote (compared to the Bolsheviks' 10 per cent). However, the SRs, far from forming a solid, unified bloc, presented a patchwork of contending allegiances, factions and splinter groups, with no common leadership and no coherent programme of action. Eventually there occurred a *de facto* split in the party between the right SRs who gravitated more towards the Kadets or regionalists, and the Left SRs, some of whom even made common cause with the Bolsheviks. Marxist commentators insisted that the PSR essentially represented the interests of the 'petty bourgeoisie', with no roots in the working class or the non-kulak peasantry.

The schism in the Social-Democratic Party (RSDRP) was less clear-cut in Siberia than in other parts of the country, and Bolsheviks and Mensheviks regularly cooperated at both rank-and-file and local leadership levels. A number of senior Bolsheviks were in Siberia as political exiles at the time of the February revolution, but used this occasion to return to the centre of events in European Russia. Party discipline and organization in Siberia were therefore quite weak, though their strength fluctuated from town to town and from town to countryside. In the villages the major source of Bolshevik support came from soldiers returning from the battlefront (*frontoviki*). These were mainly young, battle-hardened, radicalized ex-conscripts who were attracted to the Bolsheviks by their slogans of peace and land. A combination of *frontoviki* and *novosely* was chiefly responsible for the wave of spontaneous peasant uprisings and illegal land transfers which swept the countryside in the summer and early autumn of 1917. Of the towns, the most militant and pro-Bolshevik was Krasnoiarsk ('Red Krasnoiarsk'), where 5,000 activists met in August and founded the Central Siberian Regional Bureau to direct party work in Siberia and gain control of local soviets.

After the October revolution, the Bolsheviks managed to establish 'Soviet power' in most of the major towns with astonishing speed, given the numerical weakness of the urban working class and the looseness of party organization. Two factors facilitated the Bolsheviks' early success – the involvement of the Bolshevized, armed *frontoviki*, and the opportunistic use of the Trans-Sib which acted as a conduit for the rapid spread of revolutionary activity through the towns and stations along its track. Soviet power was declared in Red Krasnoiarsk by the end of October, quickly followed by Tomsk, Irkutsk, Omsk, Chita, Khabarovsk and Vladivostok. There were, to be sure, sporadic instances of opposition in the shape of organized protests and mutinies, but overall lack of coordination and political cohesion among the opponents of Bolshevism contributed considerably to the advance of Soviet power. In the Far East, the most ferocious expression of anti-Bolshevism was the *atamanshchina* – a blood-curdling campaign of inhuman atrocities led by wild Cossack atamans such as G. M. Semonov, I. P. Kalmykov and R. F. Ungern-Sternberg. Some of the worst acts of gratuitous butchery during the entire civil war were perpetrated by these savage warlords in their attempts to exterminate 'Bolsheviks' – which meant almost anyone opposing their criminal depradations.

At the end of January, the Central Executive Committee of Siberian Soviets (*Tsentrosibir'*) ordered the dispersal of the Siberian Regional Duma, recently established in Tomsk. However, the consolidation of Soviet power throughout the region was a formidable task, bedevilled by remoteness from the political centre in Moscow, lack of outstanding local leadership, conflicts of interest among different party organizations, the

growing confidence of the anti-Bolshevik opposition, and the increasing
unpopularity of the government's policy of grain requisitioning (*prodrazverstka*) which was regarded as a re-activation of tsarist high-handedness and cupidity. By the late spring of 1918, the Bolshevik grip on Siberia
had already begun to weaken; however, two unforeseen events were to
cause it to break – the landing of Japanese military forces at Vladivostok
in April, and the revolt of the Czech Legion in May.

The 'democratic counterrevolution':
May–November 1918

Japan took advantage of the central government's weakness in the Far East
to press its own territorial ambitions in that region. On 5 April a Japanese
expeditionary force retaliated against the killing of three Japanese nationals
by disembarking at Vladivostok, closely followed by a much smaller British
contingent. This was the thin end of the interventionist wedge; over the next
few months thousands of troops from many nations – Japan, China,
America, Britain, France, Canada and more – poured into the Russian Far
East, ostensibly to support the Czechs and to protect their own national
interests and assets in the region, but without any shared practical political
agenda. American forces, for instance, were ordered not to take sides in
Russia's internal struggle, although in practice all their considerable
material assistance went to the Whites. This powerful foreign backing was
one of the triggers for the re-energizing of the various anti-Red forces
throughout Siberia.

The other was the mutiny of Czech ex-prisoners of war travelling via the
Trans-Sib to Vladivostok, from where they were to return to Europe in
order to join the Allies in the war against Germany. These men were no rab-
ble: they were well disciplined, well educated, and well armed. When
Trotsky sent a telegram to the local soviets in Siberia with orders to disarm
them and shoot any still bearing weapons, the Czechs, fearing betrayal, rose
in rebellion and began the systematic takeover of all the major towns along
the railroad. One after another, Novonikolaevsk, Cheliabinsk, Tomsk,
Omsk and all stations east to Vladivostok were seized.

In June they captured Samara on the river Volga. Czech control of the rail
link from the Urals to the Pacific was to be a crucial factor during the next
stage of the conflict in Siberia, the largest and arguably the most important
arena of the civil war.

The Czechs' easy victories persuaded the Allies to raise the level of their
support for anti-Bolshevik forces, which, with enhanced foreign backing,
now profited from the Siberian soviets' *débâcle* by creating a number of new
government authorities and institutions. In the west, the two most important of these were the SR-dominated Committee of Members of the

Constituent Assembly (*Komuch*) in Samara, and the Provisional Siberian Government (PSG) in Omsk, which was to become the virtual headquarters of the Whites' 'democratic counterrevolution'. 'Counterrevolutionary' (i.e. anti-Bolshevik) these bodies may have been, but there was little about their mandate or their policies to qualify them for the label 'democratic'. While *Komuch* adopted a moderate socialist stance (red flag and all) and raised a modest 'People's Army', the PSG was politically much further to the right, enjoying the support of the Kadets and the officer class, introducing anti-trade union measures and returning expropriated property to private landowners. Many of the increasingly restless and influential army officers who backed the PSG scarcely distinguished between SRs and Bolsheviks. Not even widespread peasant resistance to Moscow's hated *prodrazverstka*, nor outbreaks of working-class opposition to the Bolsheviks could unite *Komuch* and the PSG on a common platform.

Lack of unity in the White camp was not confined to the Samara/Omsk rivalry. In Transbaikalia and the Amur and Maritime provinces the *atamanshchina* continued its bloody course with Japanese underwriting of Semenov, Kalmykov and company's reign of terror, which served, if anything, to subvert the PSG's claim to represent the best hope for Russia's salvation from the godless Bolsheviks.

Meanwhile the Bolsheviks themselves suffered further reverses, being forced in July and August to abandon Simbirsk (Lenin's birthplace) and Kazan, the repository of the imperial gold reserves worth around 750 million roubles. This was now sequestrated by the Whites and trans-shipped to Omsk. A notable casualty of the Red retreat was the ex-tsar, Nicholas II, and his family, executed by Bolshevik guards on 16 July in Ekaterinburg as Czech and White troops threatened to take the town. Recognizing the gravity of the situation, Moscow inaugurated a vigorous campaign of military recruitment and reinforced its armies on the eastern front under the new command of I. I. Vācietis.

As the tide of war began to turn again in the Red Army's favour, the Allies, including the Czechs, applied fresh pressure on the feuding Whites to settle their differences and establish a concerted, united military and political front to halt the Red advance. Some urgency was given to their appeals with the Bolsheviks' recapture of Kazan in September, just as the various White factions were assembling at Ufa in an attempt to reach an agreed course of action. The result was the formation on 23 September of the All-Russian Provisional Government (ARPG), with a five-man Directory which included two Samara SRs and was headed by N. D. Avksent'ev, Minister of the Interior in Kerensky's last Provisional Government. In October the new government moved its seat to Omsk and established a Council of Ministers which included the recently arrived Admiral A. V. Kolchak as Minister of War and Navy. Within six weeks, Kolchak was catapulted from his new post to the position of military dictator, grandiloquently styled 'Supreme Ruler of all Russia'. A new phase in the conduct of the civil war had begun.

The regime of Kolchak:
November 1918–February 1920

Despite their democratic trappings, the ARPG and Directory were never popular and never wielded effective power. Moreover, as the Reds continued their advance, and as the ineffectualness of the Directory became more obvious, the notion of appointing a strong military leader – a dictator who would establish law and order, defeat the Reds and re-establish the unitary Great Russian state – became more and more attractive to Omsk's reactionary establishment, leading Kadets, Cossacks and chauvinistic military officers. Eventually, during the night of 17–18 November, Cossack officers arrested the SR members of the Directory, and on the following morning the Council of Ministers – with only one dissenting vote – elected Kolchak as Supreme Ruler (*Verkhovnyi Pravitel'*). Kolchak accepted and immediately declared his main objectives to be the organization of an effective army and the triumph over Bolshevism. It was no easy task, and one that was to end in his own defeat and death.

Kolchak's title as Supreme Ruler of all Russia was, of course, a conceit. Central Russia was always under Soviet control, and Transbaikalia remained the virtual fiefdom of the ruthless independent atamans, still bankrolled by the Japanese who had not abandoned their own expansionist aims on the mainland. Reactions to the coup were as to be expected: the right (including the Kadets) enthusiastic; the left, appalled; the Allies, cautious (there is no direct evidence of British involvement); the peasants, unconcerned; and to the often-forgotten native peoples, it was a matter of indifference. Despite some early military successes which placed Kolchak's forces in striking distance of Simbirsk, Samara and Kazan, his 'reign' was fraught with difficulties and obstacles to the military victory which was so essential to political triumph. For example, he was geographically separated by hundreds of miles from the armies of other White generals (e.g. Denikin in the south); after the 11 November armistice in Europe, military justification for Allied intervention disappeared and support was gradually withdrawn, further exacerbating Kolchak's vulnerability; what supplies of military *matériel* were delivered to the Far East were regularly plundered by the atamans for their own use; the Czechs, too, wished to disengage and return home to the newly independent Czech Republic; furthermore, Kolchak controlled only about 500 miles of the 4,000-mile Trans-Sib as far east as Omsk. He was, therefore, increasingly isolated.

He was also temperamentally unsuited to his new role. A distinguished admiral, he had no knowledge or expertise of land warfare, still less of politics, economic planning or international statesmanship. He was unswervingly patriotic, though not necessarily a monarchist; he was also irascible, easily offended, neurotic and seemingly addicted to alcohol and narcotics. His administration, too, was sabotaged by incompetent and venal subordinates; even his military commands were occasionally ignored. Most serious, he enjoyed no mass popular support or loyalty; the economy was in ruins – despite his stewardship of the imperial gold reserves – and with the loss of the Urals he had no industrial base; his conscript troops were unreliable at the front, and in the rear a constant thorn in his flesh was the unrelenting guerrilla warfare of hundreds of peasant partisan bands fighting for their own interests in the face of Kolchak's contradictory land policies. These peasant partisans ('Greens') were also distrustful of Bolshevik intentions, but overall their sympathies lay more with the Reds than with the Whites who were still identified with a return to the pre-revolutionary order. Their instincts were reinforced by the Kolchak regime's use of terroristic methods to enforce its policies, including floggings, pogroms and mass executions.

By November 1919 a combination of all these problems and failures, aggravated by the reinvigorated Red Army's inexorable thrust across the Urals, panicked Kolchak and his government ministers into abandoning their headquarters in Omsk and fleeing via the Trans-Sib to Irkutsk. Kolchak's train was impeded by unsympathetic railway workers, delayed by disgruntled Czechs, harried by bands of partisans and encumbered by the burden of the imperial gold reserve. Meanwhile the Red Army, under its competent new commander, M. V. Frunze, was forging eastwards and rapidly catching up on Kolchak. The latter was finally halted at Nizhneudinsk, short of Irkutsk, which was now in the hands of a new left-leaning government calling itself the Irkutsk Political Centre (IPC). Kolchak's end was near. On 15 January, he was handed over by Czech legionaries to the IPC, which shortly afterwards surrendered power, and Kolchak, to the Bolsheviks. An investigating commission interrogated the former Supreme Ruler for several days and finally on 7 February – as White forces mounted a last-ditch attempt to rescue him – Admiral Kolchak and his last prime minister, V. N. Pepeliaev, were executed by firing squad and their bodies shoved beneath the ice of the river Ushakovka, a tributary of the Angara.

The Bolsheviks and the Red Army now controlled Siberia from the Urals to Lake Baikal. It was to take another two and a half years to reach the Pacific.

Far Eastern finale:
February 1919–October 1922

With Kolchak disposed of, the Bolsheviks were faced with the task of pacifying and sovietizing one of the most highly volatile areas of conflict in the civil war. The whole territory from Baikal to Vladivostok was chaotically administered by a constantly shifting variety of political and military factions, the battleground of mutually hostile local Reds, Whites, SRs, Kolchakovites, peasant partisans, Czechs, Japanese, Americans and marauding Cossacks led by their brutal atamans. In the short term, Lenin chose to surrender Far Eastern space in order to gain time to settle more urgent problems closer to home by redeploying Red Army units to his European fronts. However, unwilling completely to sacrifice Russia's eastern provinces to the Whites and the Japanese, Moscow sanctioned the setting up of a nominally independent state in Transbaikalia called the Far Eastern Republic (FER), which would act as a kind of buffer regime interposed between Soviet Siberia and Japan. Founded exactly two months after Kolchak's death, its capital was originally located at Verkhneudinsk, from where it shifted to Chita after Semenov was forced to abandon the headquarters there of his Buriat-Mongol republic. After a brief sojourn in Dauria he was again forced to decamp, this time to Manchuria. The *ataman-shchina*, which had brought so much mayhem and bloodshed to the Far East, was soon to be at an end.

Not everyone was happy with the new moderate socialist FER, and it was not until the end of 1920 that most of the large urban centres grudgingly recognized its authority, though bitter hostilities were to rage throughout the region over the next eighteen months, often accompanied by terrifying atrocities. For instance, in January 1920 Red partisans slaughtered almost an entire Japanese garrison at Nikolaevsk-na-Amure, only to be visited by reprisals in other Far Eastern towns, during which nearly 3,000 suspected Bolshevik sympathizers were killed. Four thousand more Russians were later massacred by the partisans in Nikolaevsk itself as Japanese troops attacked the town. Similar horrors continued to be perpetrated on all sides. A murderous deadlock seemed to have set in. It was not to be broken until international pressure finally persuaded Tokyo to announce that it would evacuate all its troops from the mainland by the end of October 1922. Without sustained outside support, the rag-tag-and-bobtail remaining anti-Soviet forces began to disintegrate.

One last desperate throw by two Vladivostok businessmen, the brothers S. D. and N. D. Merkulov, to reverse the increasingly powerful pro-Bolshevik tide had taken place during the summer. Having successfully overthrown the Vladivostok agents of the FER, they and their supporters announced the formation of a new Provisional Priamur Government. However, faced with the Japanese retreat, it was compelled to give way to the imposition of a brief period of martial law under a former officer of the Czech Legion, M. K. Dieterichs. This in its turn collapsed, and on 25 October FER and Red Army troops entered Vladivostok under their new commander, I. P. Uborevich, parading in triumph through the city as the last Japanese ships left the Golden Horn. Thousands of Russians fled abroad as emigrants, while remaining oppositionists were mopped up by the security forces of the FER. The independence of the latter had been a sham from the start and on 15 November it yielded what little sovereignty it had had, and was formally incorporated into the Russian Soviet Federated Socialist Republic. Despite some sporadic resistance in the far north and the continuing Japanese occupation of northern Sakhalin (which did not end until 1925), to all intents and purposes the revolution, counterrevolution and civil war in Siberia, as elsewhere, were over.

Conclusion

After the formation of the USSR on 30 December 1922, Siberia and the Far East were destined to play a major role in the economic development of the Soviet Union. However, local resentment at this continuing role as a resource frontier, and a persistent sense of Siberian particularism have not, following the disintegration of the USSR, been extinguished. The core/periphery tension between Moscow and the Siberian regions, so tragically fought out between 1917 and 1922, is still a prominent issue in the politics of the post-Soviet world.

Notwithstanding recent increased scholarly interest in Siberia in the West, a large number of problems still demand further investigation, based on new methodologies and fresh information. Many of the traditional explanations given by Western and Soviet historians for the Communist victory in the east require re-examination. Among the objective factors needing to be considered are: Siberia's geographical remoteness from the centre and the awesomeness of its climate and terrain; the superior military experience of the White armies' officer class; the traditions of suspicion and hostility on the part of most Siberians towards metropolitan Russia; and the impact and extent of the foreign intervention in supporting those sworn to overthrow Lenin's government. Given all these apparently adverse circumstances and impediments to Red victory, it is ironic that the anti-Bolshevik 'Whites' and the peasant partisan 'Greens' – both colours traditionally symbolic of Siberia's snows and forests – should have been finally superseded by the incarnadine colour of Soviet communism.

Further reading

Lincoln W. B., *Red Victory: A History of the Russian Civil War* (New York and London, Simon and Schuster, 1989).

Maksakov V. V. and Turunov A. N., eds., *Khronika grazhdanskoi voiny v Sibiri (1917–1918)* (Moscow, Gosizdat, 1925).

Mawdsley E., *The Russian Civil War* (Boston, Allen & Unwin, 1987).

Okladnikov A. P. and Shunkov V. I., eds., *Istoriia Sibiri s drevneishikh vremen do nashikh dnei*, vol. 4 (Leningrad, Nauka, 1968).

Pereira N. G. O., 'Soviet Historiography of the Civil War in Siberia', *Revolutionary Russia* 4, 1 (1991).

Pereira N. G. O., *White Siberia: The Politics of Civil War* (Montreal, McGill-Queens University Press, 1996).

Smele J. D., *Civil War in Siberia: The Anti-Bolshevik Government of Admiral Kolchak, 1918–1920* (Cambridge, Cambridge University Press, 1996).

Snow R. E., *The Bolsheviks in Siberia, 1917–1918* (Rutherford, Fairleigh Dickinson University Press, 1977).

Stephan J. J., *The Russian Far East: A History* (Stanford, Stanford University Press, 1994).

White J. A., *The Siberian Intervention* (Princeton, Princeton University Press, 1950).

Wood A., ed., *The History of Siberia: From Russian Conquest to Revolution* (London and New York, Routledge, 1991).

The Revolution in Transcaucasia

RONALD G. SUNY

The Russian revolution was at one and the same time a political, social and a 'national' revolution, a conflict of political elites, social classes and nationalities. All three aspects of the revolution were present in the mountainous isthmus south of the Caucasus mountains. The revolutionary and civil war years were a period in which local nationalities and social groups forged clearer identities and ideas about their political futures. As new political leaderships emerged to express the aspirations of social and ethnic groups, the very constituencies that they represented became more clearly defined, developing their own identities, political profiles and goals. Lines of conflict and cleavage between workers and industrialists in Baku, Armenians and Georgians in Tiflis, and Muslims and non-Muslims in Erevan, Elizavetispol', and Baku provinces grew sharper. And social differences, which had been most intense in 1917, were for a time dissolved in the solvent of nationalism in the subsequent years of civil and inter-state war.

This region, a multi-ethnic isthmus lying between the Black Sea and the Caspian Sea, had often been depicted in the poems and stories of Russians as a land of temperament and passion, revenge and generosity, noble mountaineers and treacherous natives. The three major ethnicities – the Georgians in the north and west, the Azerbaijanis (usually referred to as 'Tatars' before the revolution) in the east, and the Armenians to the south – had managed to live together in relative peace during the 100 years of tsarist rule and occasionally, as in 1905, clashed with each other. In the century since the annexation of Transcaucasia, the Russian autocracy had integrated the noble elites of the Georgians and the Muslims into the seigniorial political and economic order of the empire, and had developed ties of economic interest with the local industrialists and merchants, but had failed to solve the land hunger of the peasantry or to deal adequately with the material and political demands of the newly emerging working class in the cities of Baku, Batumi and Tiflis (Tbilisi). By the indices of industrialization, urbanization and literacy, Transcaucasia was a region less developed than Russia proper,

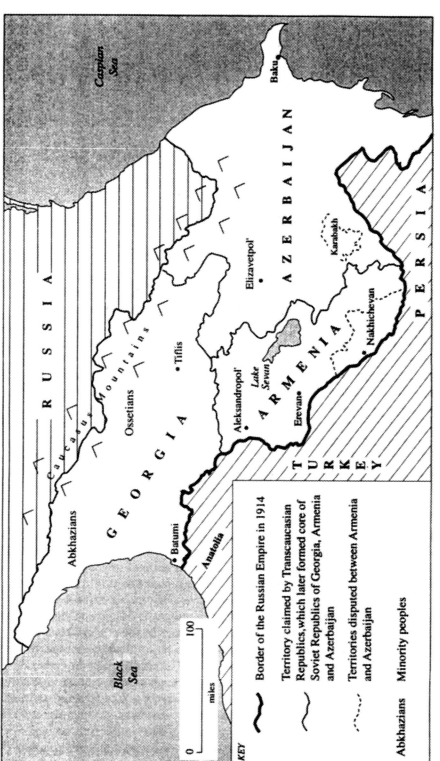

Map 7. Transcaucasia 1917–1921

KEY

— Border of the Russian Empire in 1914

〜 Territory claimed by Transcaucasian Republics, which later formed core of Soviet Republics of Georgia, Armenia and Azerbaijan

⸝⸝⸝ Territories disputed between Armenia and Azerbaijan

Abkhazians Minority peoples

and social grievances were compounded by ethnic distinctions, stereotypes and prejudices.

Divided by language, culture, and religion from one another, the peoples of Transcaucasia were also stratified socially and economically. Ethnicity and class reinforced one another, accentuating the differences between the major nationalities. The Muslims, the largest group (1,791,000 or 24 per cent of the population, according to the 1897 census), were primarily peasants little influenced by urban culture or secular nationalism. In so far as they possessed group consciousness and public expression, it was strongly influenced by the Shi'i Muslim clerisy. Russians and Armenians considered the Muslims to be a 'dark', unenlightened people, and legal restrictions were promulgated to keep the Muslim majority from political influence in the oil-producing city of Baku. By the turn of the century a small number of Azerbaijani entrepreneurs and intellectuals had emerged in Baku, creating a self-consciously Europeanized and 'modern' public sector that tried to promote the culture and political claims of the local Muslims.

The Georgians (1,741,000 or 23 per cent) were a people in rapid social transition. The Russians had abolished their 2,000-year-old monarchy at the beginning of the nineteenth century and, after half a century of bringing noble–peasant relations into line with the Russian practices of serfdom, abolished landlord serf-holding in their Georgian provinces. As a result the Georgian noble elite declined as both a political and economic force in the second half of the nineteenth century and were displaced as the political leaders of the nation by a new generation of Marxist intellectuals, the so-called *mesame dasi* (Third Generation). Led by Noe Zhordania, the Georgian Social Democrats joined the Menshevik wing of the Russian Social-Democratic Workers' Party and broadened their support by organizing rebellious peasants in western Georgia. Georgian Social Democracy was the first significant Marxist party in the world to lead a massive national, peasant and worker-based social movement.

The Armenians of Transcaucasia (1,685,000 or 22 per cent) were a dispersed and divided people. A majority were poor peasants barely making a subsistence living in Erevan province, while a small but powerful middle class had become by the early twentieth century the dominant economic force in several cities in Transcaucasia. Armenians were seen as the most entrepreneurial, the most 'bourgeois' nationality in the region, and in the ethnic mosaic of Baku and Tiflis social conflicts between workers and property-owners quickly took on ethnic aspects. Georgian and Muslim workers confronted Armenian and Russian employers, while Armenian peasants defied Muslim landlords. At the same time Armenians lived on both sides of the Russian–Turkish border, with the great majority in the Ottoman empire. Much of Armenian political energy, under the leadership of the Armenian Revolutionary Federation or Dashnaktsutiun, flowed from Transcaucasia into the historically Armenian provinces of eastern Anatolia in an effort to 'liberate' Turkish Armenians from Ottoman despotism.

On the eve of the First World War an acute observer would have noticed that Georgians were largely united around their Menshevik leadership; Armenians were divided between a majority following the nationalists and a minority aligned with the Russian socialist parties; and Muslims were still largely indifferent to national politics. With Menshevik intellectuals firmly established as the acknowledged leaders of the majority of the Georgian people, Bolshevik and Socialist-Revolutionary (SR) activists were confined to the oil-producing centre, Baku, where the largest concentration of industrial workers was to be found. Here socialists organized and led two general strikes of oil workers in the two years before the First World War, and their impact was felt as far away as St Petersburg. While ethnic identity had long been part of the loyalties of many in Transcaucasia, political nationalism grew slowly, and quite late, but by the second decade of the twentieth century it was growing as a potential rival to internationalist socialists. The small Georgian Federalist Party advocated national autonomy for Georgians, and Armenian nationalists spoke of a 'free Armenia' within each of the two major empires in which Armenians lived. Still confined to small coteries of nationalist intellectuals and politicians, nationalism presented an alternative vision to the class ideologies of the socialists that powerfully shaped the political discourses of the pre-revolutionary period. Only among the Armenians had one discourse – that of the socialist nationalist Dashnaktsutiun – managed to monopolize political expression among oppositional elements.

On 1 March 1917, a cryptic message was telegraphed by the Mensheviks in the State Duma to their comrades in Tiflis: 'Mtavrobadze is dead.' The Caucasian socialists understood that the government (*mtavroba* in Georgian) had fallen, and within hours the viceroy of the Caucasus, Grand Duke Nikolai Nikolaevich, called in the mayor of Tiflis, Aleksandr Khatisov, to inform him of the end of the Romanov regime. Two days later elections to soviets of workers' deputies were organized by the socialists in Tiflis and Baku. At the same time, in both cities, so-called 'executive committees' ostensibly representing all classes were appointed to operate in place of the now defunct tsarist officials. As in Petrograd, so in the major cities of Transcaucasia, two rival organs of power existed in the first few weeks of the revolution. The first, the soviets, were the elected voice of the workers and soldiers; the other, the executive committees, claimed authority from the Provisional Government and were nominally representative of all strata of the towns. But *dvoevlastie* (dual power) in Transcaucasia, as in Petrograd, masked only temporarily the fact that real decision-making power was located in the soviets. Only those bodies elected by workers and soldiers had the authority to call people into the streets or to issue effective orders to the garrison. What formal power the executive committees and the Special Transcaucasian Committee (*Ozakom*), appointed by the Provisional Government, enjoyed in the spring of 1917 derived from the sanction received from the soviets controlled by moderate Socialist

Revolutionaries and Mensheviks, who wanted to preserve social unity and maintain the war effort. Most Mensheviks conceived of the revolution as 'bourgeois-democratic', and this view was accepted by the SRs. Although suspicious of the Provisional Government, they were willing to support it as legitimate and to restrain workers from seizing power in the name of their soviets.

The one major local group opposed, first to dual power and from May to October to the coalition government, was the Bolshevik wing of social democracy. Led by Stepan Shahumian and centred in Baku, the Bolsheviks conceived of the revolution as developing into a socialist revolution under the impact of events in Europe. They opposed the 'revolutionary defencist' policies of the moderate socialists who favoured continuing the war effort until a 'democratic peace' could be achieved, and they called for a government of the whole 'democracy' (the lower classes). Urged on by the central Russian Bolshevik leadership, local Bolsheviks stimulated a formal break with the Mensheviks, which came relatively late in Transcaucasia (6 June in Tiflis, 24 June in Baku). Though they remained a powerful political force in Baku, as a result of the party schism the Bolsheviks were reduced to an impotent sect in Georgia, where the party organizations and soviets were firmly in the hands of the Mensheviks led by Zhordania.

During the government crises of April and May, when the coalition government was formed in Petrograd, the Mensheviks of Georgia came out against their comrades in Russia on the question of power. Under Menshevik urging the Tiflis Workers' Soviet voted overwhelmingly on 29 April to keep socialists from entering a coalition government. Zhordania preferred a purely 'bourgeois' government, though without Kadet leader Pavel Miliukov and others who favoured annexationist war aims. But the workers' soviet was not supported by the soldiers' soviet, led by the SRs, which on 16 May voted to support the coalition government. The conflict between the workers in Tiflis, largely Georgian and Menshevik, and the soldiers, primarily Russian and favouring the SRs and even Bolsheviks, came to a head on 25 June at a demonstration organized by the Bolsheviks. An estimated 10,000 soldiers shouted down Menshevik orators and adopted a Bolshevik resolution condemning the Kerensky military offensive and calling for a government based on the soviets. The Tiflis Mensheviks, fearful that the militants might try to seize power in the city, banned meetings of soldiers in the Alexander Garden, warned the public of the danger of counterrevolution, and made peace with Petrograd by approving the coalition government.

As in Russia proper, so in Transcaucasia, the pace of the revolution quickened towards the end of the summer as the mood of both workers and soldiers grew ever more hostile towards collaboration with the propertied classes (*tsenzovoe obshchestvo*). On 2 September, the Tiflis Soviet once again came out against coalition with the bourgeoisie and advocated a 'democratic socialist government' made up of all the socialist parties.

But it was primarily the Bolsheviks who benefited from the deteriorating economic situation, the inconclusive war, and the increasing suspicion of the upper and middle classes. After months of fruitless negotiations, industrialists in Baku provoked a general strike of oil workers in September, and in just six days well-organized, Bolshevik-led strikers forced the industry to capitulate. In the aftermath of General Kornilov's abortive attempt to establish a military dictatorship in Petrograd, Bolshevik resolutions found new support in Transcaucasian soviets. As militant opponents of the war, the Leninists gradually garnered support from soldiers, displacing the SRs in the Baku and Tiflis garrisons and at the Caucasian front in the autumn of 1917. And as the most vocal critics of the feeble coalition government and the local executive committees and dumas, the Bolsheviks gained credence as social antagonisms between the *verkhi* (top) and *nizi* (bottom) of society grew sharper. As Shahumian exclaimed in early October: 'Unrest is growing everywhere, and land is being seized, etc.; our task is to stand at the head of the revolution and to take power in our hands.'

When news of the October revolution reached Tiflis, reports circulated that the Bolsheviks would attempt to seize power in Baku. But in Transcaucasia the Mensheviks proved to be much more decisive than the local Bolsheviks. Shahumian hesitated to provoke an inter-ethnic bloodletting by instigating civil war in Baku, but Zhordania's forces seized the Tiflis arsenal at the end of November, thus disarming the pro-Bolshevik garrison. With their own Red Guard, the Mensheviks resisted the Bolsheviks' efforts to propagandize the soldiers. The balance of social forces in central Transcaucasia shifted in December, as the Caucasian front dissolved and Russia's soldiers 'voted with their feet' to end the war and return home. The Bolsheviks lost their most potent supporters outside Baku, the Russian soldiers, and one of the most important elements favouring preservation of the link to post-October Russia. Armenians, fearful of the Turkish threat, remained the most pro-Russian element in Transcaucasia. The Armenians in Baku, led by the Dashnaks, voted with the local soviet to remain loyal to Soviet Russia, but the Armenians in Tiflis, also under Dashnak influence, sided with the other local parties and worked within the autonomous and later independent political institutions.

Early in 1918 Soviet Russia withdrew from World War I, and the Ottoman Turkish armies launched a campaign into Transcaucasia towards Baku. In February a Transcaucasian parliament, the Seim, began to meet, but it soon became clear that relations between the three major nationalities were becoming increasingly strained. Pressured by the Turks, Transcaucasia gradually broke its ties to Russia. The Turks occupied Batumi, and a week later, on 22 April 1918, Transcaucasian leaders declared an independent 'federative republic', the *Zakavkazskaia Federativnaia Respublika*, and sent off a delegation to negotiate with the Turks. But the Turkish advance continued, taking Aleksandropol' on 15 May. Armenians organized their own defence in Karakalissa and Sardarabad, and the Turks moved around the Erevan enclave towards Baku.

With the Turks advancing through Transcaucasia, the federative republic based in Tiflis became untenable. Armenians were actively fighting the Turks, while Azerbaijanis were allied with them. Georgians were gravitating towards the Germans, while Armenians preferred the Western Allies. The Transcaucasian Republic disintegrated into three separate independent states at the end of May 1918. Rather than leading to a Transcaucasia united with a democratic Russia, the intense social and political conflicts of the first revolutionary year had led to conflict between socialists and nationalists, fragmentation along ethnic lines, and three small republics adrift between an expansionist Ottoman empire and a retreating Russia.

Baku remained an outpost of Soviet Russia under a Bolshevik government that styled itself 'the Baku Commune'. Led by Shahumian, 'Alesha' Japaridze, Ivan Fioletov and Meshadi Azizbekov, the Bolshevik-dominated Baku Soviet came to uncontested power by putting down a Muslim rebellion in March and allying itself with the Armenian troops commanded by the Dashnaks. A relatively benign government, the Baku Commune attempted to export the Soviet revolution westward, only to fall back before nationalist Muslims from Ganja (Elisavetpol') and their Turkish allies. Shahumian's government retired rather than invite in British troops from Iran, but the city was finally overwhelmed by the Turkish Army on 14–15 September 1918. Thousands of Armenians were massacred, and Shahumian and his closest comrades, the fabled 'twenty-six commissars', perished in the deserts of Turkmenistan, victims of anti-Bolshevik separatists.

The period of independence for Azerbaijan, Armenia and Georgia lasted only as long as civil war and foreign intervention prevented Bolshevik Russia from imposing its authority over Transcaucasia. Azerbaijan gravitated from being a Turkish satellite to a British ward before falling to the Bolsheviks in April 1920. The Azerbaijani nationalists who had declared this new state independent were treated as satraps by the pan-Turanist Ottoman government, as highly suspicious collaborators with the Central Powers by the British, and as agents of Turkish and British imperialism by the Soviets. However, the British, who returned to Baku in the autumn of 1918, backed the Azerbaijan government of Fath Ali Khan Khoiskii, even taking its side against the territorial claims of the Armenians to mountainous Karabakh, Zangezur and Nakhichevan. But once the British left most of Transcaucasia in August 1919, the weakness of the social base of the Azerbaijani government became apparent. The government had failed to restore the economy; conflicts with Armenians raged in the borderlands; and Baku, with its large Armenian and Russian working-class population, had never reconciled itself to separation from Russia and dominance by the Azerbaijanis. In April 1920, with little pretence about an internal domestic revolution, Red Army units crossed the frontier and proclaimed the Soviet Republic of Azerbaijan.

Armenia was the least viable of the three states. The government, formed in Tiflis, arrived in its capital Erevan several months after it had declared independence to discover a country inundated by refugees from Turkey, plagued by epidemic diseases and hunger, and threatened by the resurgent Kemalist movement in Anatolia. The frontiers of the new state were contested by its neighbours, Turkey, Georgia and Azerbaijan and Armenia found itself at war with each of them. Armenia's lifeline was the sympathy it enjoyed among the Allies, particularly President Wilson, and American aid accounted for Armenian survival in its first winters. The Dashnak government carried out democratic elections and the establishment of an embryonic state apparatus, while attempting to secure international recognition of Armenian statehood and territorial claims. In 1920 the Armenians entered into conflict with the Kemalists and quickly had to retreat. To save what was left of their republic, Dashnak leaders entered into negotiations with Soviet authorities and agreed to create a coalition government with the Communists. On 2 December 1920, the Red Army crossed into Armenia, and within days the Dashnaks were expelled from government. The militant policies of the Communists provoked a Dashnak-led rebellion in early 1921. Though quickly repressed, the revolt sobered the Soviet regime, which, under Lenin's instructions, soon adopted a more ameliorative policy towards its Armenian subjects.

Georgia, under Menshevik rule for two and a half years (May 1918 to February 1921), managed to evolve a democratic constitutional political system, though it never achieved full economic stability and physical security. The republic did not secure the loyalty of the Abkhaz and Osetin peoples of the west and north, however, and Georgian troops bloodily repressed separatist movements. At the same time the Georgians faced General Denikin's White forces in the north-west and fought a brief war with Armenia over border regions. Despite the economic decline and social unrest in the country, the Social Democrats retained their popularity with the ethnic Georgian majority and managed to combine democratic politics with mild social reforms. Elections were held to a Georgian Constituent Assembly, in which non-Georgians were also represented, and the government distributed land to the peasants. Bolshevism had little support within the country, and the Mensheviks secured a treaty with Soviet Russia recognizing Georgian independence. But early in 1921, the Georgian Communists Stalin and Sergo Orjonikidze pushed for the overthrow of the Mensheviks. Lenin opposed the move but eventually recognized the *fait accompli* carried out by an invading Red Army. By April 1921 all of Transcaucasia had come under the rule of local Communists.

The period of revolution, civil war and foreign interventions in Transcaucasia was a period of physical destruction and social devastation. The promises of multi-national democracy and socialist emancipation fell victim to the exigencies of war and the limits of underdevelopment. Social stress contributed to ethnic conflict, despite the best efforts of the

Mensheviks and Bolsheviks. The brief experience of independent statehood, however, had a far-reaching impact. The new Soviet republics were based on the independent republics, which in turn became, 70 years later, models for a second experiment in sovereign statehood.

Further reading

Hovannisian R. G., *Armenia on the Road to Independence, 1918* (Berkeley-Los Angeles, University of California Press, 1967).

Kazemzadeh F., *The Struggle for Transcaucasia (1917–1921)* (New York, Philosophical Library, 1951).

Suny R. G., *The Baku Commune, 1917–1918: Class and Nationality in the Russian Revolution* (Princeton, Princeton University Press, 1972).

Suny R. G., *Looking Toward Ararat: Armenia in Modern History* (Bloomington, IN, Indiana University Press, 1993).

Suny R. G., *The Making of the Georgian Nation* (Bloomington, IN, Indiana University Press, 1995).

Swietochowski T., *Russian Azerbaijan, 1905–1920: The Shaping of National Identity in a Muslim Community* (New York, Cambridge University Press, 1985).

Swietochowski T., *Russia and Azerbaijan: A Borderland in Transition* (New York, Columbia University Press, 1995).

Zhordania N. N., *Moia zhizn'* (Stanford, Hoover Institution Press, 1968).

Ukraine

MARK VON HAGEN

The revolutionary events in Ukraine illustrate very clearly the limitations of the traditional understanding of both the 'Russian revolution and civil war' and the 'Ukrainian revolution' *per se*. The contemporary understanding of Ukraine, as a geopolitical, cultural and national unit, was itself the product of contested and often violently conflicting perspectives against a backdrop of constant international and civil war. The very circumstances that permitted the various contenders for power to imagine that their political dreams were finally within their reach (whether those goals were nation-building or socialist revolution) were the same ones that made it nearly impossible to fulfil their ambitious projects. Even the familiar chronological boundaries of 1917–21 omit some of the most important processes that shaped politics in the volatile region.

The historian needs to balance at least the following perspectives (and in so doing risks imposing far more coherence and consensus than actual circumstances suggest) to begin to make sense of the dramatic shifts in political power that shaped the destinies of the communities concerned.

1. Generally speaking, the Russian imperial authorities, the leadership of most of the all-Russian political parties (with little significant variation from left to right) and their allies, the ascendant Bolshevik movement and the anti-Bolshevik White movements that operated on the territories of the former Russian empire all viewed the lands claimed by the Ukrainian movement as an integral component of the Russian empire, its south-west provinces, and the Ukrainian ethnic populations as a branch of the Slavic family, together with the Great Russians and Belorussians. These parties generally held the preservation of the Russian state or the social gains of the revolution to have priority over any nationalist claims.

2. The Ukrainian movement, on the contrary, viewed these lands and populations as distinctive within eastern Europe, although there were wide differences within the movement over the political future envisaged, ranging

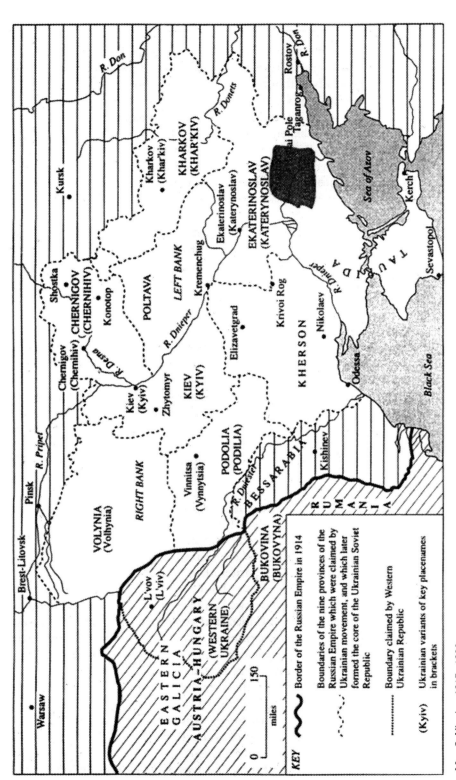

Map 8. Ukraine, 1917–1920

KEY

〜〜〜 Border of the Russian Empire in 1914

Boundaries of the nine provinces of the Russian Empire which were claimed by Ukrainian movement, and which later formed the core of the Ukrainian Soviet Republic

Boundary claimed by Western Ukrainian Republic

(Kyiv) Ukrainian variants of key placenames in brackets

from greater autonomy within a federated Russian democratic republic (the Ukrainian Socialist Revolutionaries favoured this platform) to independence, generally within the framework of a protectorate relationship, with Austria-Hungary, Germany (the Union for the Liberation of Ukraine advocated this solution), and Poland as the most popular candidates. The Ukrainian parties reached a high degree of consensus in claiming nine provinces: Kyiv, Podilia, Volhynia, Chernihiv, Poltava, Khark'iv, Katerynoslav, Kherson and Taurida. In addition, Kholm, Kursk, Voronezh and other provinces also had large Ukrainian populations. In the Austrian Empire, the Ukrainian movement claimed authority over eastern Galicia, Bukovyna, and Transcarpathia.

3. The Austro-Hungarian imperial authorities, their wartime German allies, the Polish national movement and eventually the Polish state held a third crucial perspective on Ukrainian affairs, generally hoping for a pliable Ukraine as a bulwark against a menacing Russia, whatever its political regime.

An important development during these years that shaped the context of the various revolutions in the lands between the Russian and Habsburg empires was the increasing acceptance of the principle of national self-determination, whether in its Wilsonian (14 Points) or Leninist version. Of course, this principle continued to meet opposition from traditional western and central European elites who resisted the transformation of great power politics. These various perspectives require that the revolution in Ukraine be considered at once as part of the history of the Russian (in the broader, imperial sense of the word (*rossiiskaia*) rather than the narrow, ethnic sense (*russkaia*)) revolution, of Ukrainian history, and of eastern European history more generally in the years 1914–23.

It is important to re-emphasize that 'Ukraine' in the first two decades of the twentieth century was a political, territorial, ethnic and cultural symbol that was contested and was therefore constantly changing. In other words, there was no Ukraine on which all the concerned parties could agree at any given time, and even individual parties often had at best inchoate platforms. The Ukrainian movement itself was bifurcated between organizations and institutions with a fairly sophisticated and long-term political experience in the Habsburg lands of eastern Galicia and more hesitant ones in the Russian provinces of the Kiev governor-general, where legal political parties dated only from after the 1905 revolution and the Duma was at best a quasi-parliamentary body with a highly restricted franchise.

The wartime occupation of Galicia by the Russian army in 1914 forced the first unification of these two parts, but that unification lasted only until the combined German-Austrian forces expelled the Russian armies eastward the next year. In the context of occupation policies which often pitted one ethnic community against others and of the wartime competition among the belligerent powers for the loyalties of the various subject peoples of the multi-national dynastic empires, nationality as an organizational principle for everyday survival acquired new meaning among social groups beyond the traditional intelligentsia elites of the pre-war period. Ukrainians in both belligerent camps, while preserving loyalty to their respective imperial overlords, were among the communities whose identities were affected and who began to dream of a post-war unified nation.

However, by 1917 the very different traditions which had developed within the Ukrainian movement in the two empires created a set of conflicts that would never be overcome. The fortunes of the Ukrainian movement(s) were further complicated by the presence of deeply rooted and substantial minorities of non-ethnic Ukrainians on the territories claimed by them, especially Russians, Poles, Jews and Germans. These groups, too, were affected by the rise of national politics. At the same time, nationalism offered only one of several poles along which communities articulated their revolutionary aspirations. Another very important pole was that of social class, and class-based parties and movements often cut across ethnic and national lines.

The February revolution and the Rada

The abdication of Tsar Nicholas II and the assumption of power by the Provisional Government began a radical restructuring of imperial politics that quickly escaped the control of the liberals and moderate socialists who headed the Dual Power arrangement, and subsequently the coalition cabinet in Petrograd. This initial coalition appealed to 'society' to enact their own revolutions and thereafter to safeguard the fragile revolutionary initiatives. In Kiev (in Ukrainian, Kyiv) several entities quickly competed for authority to act in the name of the revolution: liberals and some moderate socialists organized an Executive Committee of Public Organizations (IKSOOO); other socialists tried to divert the aspirations of workers, soldiers and peasants into soviets; the Ukrainian parties of various stripes, but primarily liberal and moderate socialist (Socialist Revolutionaries (SRs), Social Democrats and Socialist-Federalists), formed a Rada (Council, 'Soviet' in Russian) on 4 March from prominent pre-1917 professionals and intellectuals grouped around the Society of Ukrainian Progressives (TUP). The national movement, based at first in the intelligentsia, was soon joined by soldiers and peasants. All these organizations sought to expand their initial prerogatives, especially as the breakdown of authority across the empire proceeded apace. In April an All-Ukrainian National Congress empowered the Rada to begin organizing a union of all peoples in the empire who demanded national and territorial autonomy. The Rada remained at the centre of the movement to reform the empire along democratic and federalist lines; in September it convened a Congress of Autonomists in Kiev, whose achievements, however, were quickly overshadowed by the Bolshevik coup in Petrograd.

The Rada gradually emerged as the most important focus for an all-Ukrainian movement and claimed increased authority over processes in the nine provinces of the south-west governor-generalcy. The most prominent Rada politicians included Myhailo Hrushevs'kyi, a historian; Volodymyr Vynnychenko, a writer; and Symon Petliura, a publicist and specialist on military affairs. Its programme incorporated most of the demands of the pre-1917 Ukrainian movement in the Russian empire, focusing on expanded autonomy for local government; the use of the Ukrainian language in education, local government and the courts; a separate resolution of the land question for Ukrainian peasants. During the course of 1917, new demands were added, such as the recognition of Ukrainian representatives at the future peace talks to resolve the issue of Galicia, the formation of military units made up primarily of ethnic Ukrainians, the use of the Ukrainian language in military units, and their transfer to the two 'Ukrainian' fronts, the south-western and Romanian fronts.

The Petrograd Soviet and Provisional Government attempted to set bounds to these local initiatives and appointed their own commissars. Moreover, in preference to the Rada they encouraged a rival coalition body, the IKSOOO, to supervise the transformations that were occurring. Very quickly issues of peace, social justice and national autonomy pitted the Petrograd authorities and their local representatives against many of the Kievan counter-authorities. But because of the unstable coalitions and political identities that were especially characteristic in the peripheries of the Russian empire, the Petrograd politicians were always able to find some local support for their politics of temporizing. Several 'constitutional' crises during 1917 drove the wedge between Kiev and Petrograd ever deeper. As the Rada took further steps to institutionalize its authority by expanding its membership to include representatives of the Russian, Polish and Jewish communities, the Petrograd authorities countered with an instruction restricting the competence of the Kiev proto-government. Throughout the summer and early autumn the Rada and the increasingly impotent Provisional Government clashed over the terms of Ukrainian sovereignty.

The evolution of the Ukrainian movement can be traced in the series of proclamations, so-called 'Universals' (in honour of the Cossack legacy of the early modern Hetmanates) issued by the Rada during 1917 and 1918. The First Universal (10 June) established a skeletal governmental structure to the Rada headed by a General Secretariat with responsibility for military and nationalities affairs, but no power to tax and no local officials. The Second Universal followed negotiations in late June and early July between the Rada and a delegation from the Provisional Government, which promised concessions on Ukrainian autonomy. The agreement, however, provoked a crisis in the coalition government in Petrograd, after which the Kadet ministers resigned. The new coalition government took a harder line towards the Rada's demands. In Kiev the Rada moderates in turn faced charges of capitulation from militant Ukrainized army units. After the

Polubotok Regiment attempted a coup against the Rada, the latter was forced to call on another Ukrainized unit, the Khmel'nits'kyi regiment, to restore order. Soldiers came to play an increasingly important part in all the proto-governments that would claim authority over the Ukrainian lands.

The October revolution and the declaration of independence

Meanwhile the conservative opposition to Aleksandr Kerensky's failing coalition government in Petrograd pinned their hopes on General Lavr Kornilov to reverse the radicalization of politics and disintegration of the empire. The Kornilov incident reinforced the Rada's growing realization that Russian liberalism was an unreliable ally. So hostile were relations with Kerensky's government that, following the Bolshevik coup in Petrograd, the Rada and its military units briefly joined with the Kiev Bolsheviks in a Territorial Committee for the Defence of the Revolution in Ukraine and fought against the local troops loyal to the Provisional Government, despite heated opposition from Russian Mensheviks, Kadets and SRs, as well as the Jewish Bund. The Kiev Bolsheviks were soon ordered to withdraw from the committee, but the Rada and General Secretariat forced the 'counterrevolutionary' forces of the Provisional Government to withdraw from Kiev. The Rada issued its Third Universal (7 November), proclaiming the Ukrainian People's Republic (UNR) and demanding a Ukrainian Constituent Assembly, various social reforms, and the principle of national-personal autonomy, but it fell short of proclaiming independence, instead maintaining a tie to a democratic, federal Russia. The Rada acceded to the Bolshevik Decree on Land, itself derived from the SR programme, but failed to win much peasant support with this belated response to demands for land reform. Petliura also tried to consolidate the Rada's authority over the south-western and Romanian fronts and won the sanction of General Dukhonin for their unification into a Ukrainian front.

During the elections to the All-Russian Constituent Assembly in November, the Ukrainian SRs and the Ukrainian Peasant Union won a substantial majority in those provinces claimed by the Rada, (53 per cent of all votes cast in Ukraine and 71 per cent of the rural vote), which the Rada took as evidence of its legitimacy. Those who voted for the Ukrainian parties seemed to be attracted to the slogans of peace, a separate Ukrainian land fund for the promised agrarian reforms, and Ukrainian autonomy within a reformed Russian federation. The Rada, however, failed to translate that support into much genuine or widespread authority; it made virtually no effort to establish contact with the provinces outside Kiev and the agrarian Right Bank. It was also weakened by the divisions among the three major Ukrainian parties and the numerous Russian, Jewish and Polish parties, as well as by the personal antagonisms between the leading Social Democrats in the Rada, Vynnychenko and Petliura.

A more meaningful test of the Rada's authority came in its confrontations with the new government in the north. Lenin's government in Petrograd issued an ultimatum to the Rada on 4 December not to allow Ukraine to be used as a transit zone for hostile forces. Simultaneously in Kiev the Bolsheviks called an all-Ukrainian Congress of Worker, Soldier and Peasant Soviets, but an overwhelming majority at the congress protested against the ultimatum and appealed to their Russian comrades for a socialist federation. After the Bolsheviks failed to overthrow the Rada in Kiev, they withdrew to Khar'kiv, where they called another Ukrainian Congress of Soviets, which proclaimed the Rada dissolved and organized the first of several Soviet governments, the People's Secretariat of the Ukrainian National Republic. The Bolsheviks in Ukraine, like their counterparts in other parties, were split between a more Moscow-loyal (the Don Basin–Krivoi Rog organization based in Khar'kiv) and a more Ukrainophile wing (the south-western organization based in Kiev). These differences complicated the relationship between the local organizations and Lenin's government. To bolster the position of the Khar'kiv Soviet government, in mid-December Colonel M. A. Murav'ev led a Soviet Russian army of 30,000 men, joined by Red Guard detachments from Khar'kiv and the Donets Basin, in an invasion of Ukraine.

The invasion proceeded against the backdrop of the peace negotiations between the *Sovnarkom* in Petrograd and the Central Powers in Brest-Litovsk. The Rada pursued a separate peace which was signed while Red Guard units were seizing major Ukrainian cities. The Rada, in its Fourth Universal (9 January 1918), declared the independence of the Ukrainian People's Republic, but still held out hope for future federal ties with a democratic Russia. Ukrainian Bolsheviks and Left SRs protested against the onerous terms of the treaty and attempted a coup against the Ukrainian government, but the Ukrainian military commander arrested the leading conspirators and thwarted their efforts. The treaty's concessions to the Germans and Austrians provoked a government crisis, with a new SR cabinet headed by Volodymyr Holubovich replacing Vynnychenko's SD-dominated government. After shelling Kiev for 12 days, the Bolsheviks seized the capital and occupied it for three weeks. Following the Red victory, however, serious differences split the Soviet Ukrainian government which had moved from Khar'kiv to Kiev; several Ukrainian members resigned to form an opposition against the Russian Bolsheviks. The Rada, which had fled to Zhytomyr, returned with the German Army and the Sich Sharpshooters to expel the Bolshevik forces and preside over the Central Powers' occupation regime/protectorate. As part of their concessions at Brest, the Bolsheviks agreed to recognize Ukrainian independence, to withdraw all Red troops, and to halt their efforts to form a Soviet Ukrainian government. As they fled Ukraine at the end of April, the more

Ukrainophile wing of the Bolsheviks convened a founding meeting of the Communist Party of Ukraine.

The Hetmanate

The Rada's socialist agrarian legislation soon brought them into disfavour with both the German occupiers and the landlords who began organizing punitive expeditions against the peasants. In April the supreme commander of German forces in Ukraine, Field Marshal von Eichhorn, and the German commandant, General Wilhelm Groener, entered into a conspiracy against the Rada with the sanction of the League of Landowners and installed as Hetman of Ukraine Pavlo Skoropads'kyi, a former aide-de-camp to Nicholas II and commander of the first Ukrainized army corps in 1917. The Sich Sharpshooters offered little resistance to the assault on the Ukrainian People's Republic, which was quickly replaced with Skoropads'kyi's Ukrainian State (*Ukrains'ka Derzhava*). The formidable project of creating a Ukrainian nation-state was now assumed by the Provisional Government of Ukraine, which was formed from representatives of the liberal and conservative landowning and business elites, including Kadets and Octobrists. The Ukrainian socialist parties refused to cooperate with the Hetmanate and grouped around a Ukrainian National Union to defend their nationalist agenda and the independence of the Ukrainian state.

Although Skoropads'kyi's regime made considerably more progress in state-building and even Ukrainization than had the Rada during its short existence, it alienated the nationalist movement, enraged both the peasant majority with its policies to restore private property and many former landowners with its inability to protect their property, and lost the support of organized labour with its ban on strikes. As Russian elites fled the Bolshevik north, the Russian influence waxed in Kiev, where the *Russkii Soiuz* ('Russian Union') and officers' organizations aided the White movement, and fed the fires of national opposition. The Hetmanate's conception of Ukraine was a civic and territorial one, though not strictly confined to ethnic Ukrainians, whereas many members of the cabinet of the Provisional Government of Ukraine were of the firm conviction that Ukraine should serve as the base for an anti-Bolshevik movement to re-establish a united Russia. Not surprisingly, all Skoropads'kyi's overtures to the Ukrainian parties to collaborate with him were met with boycott.

During the summer *otoman* (in Russian, *ataman*) Yuriy Tiutiunnik led peasant uprisings against the Skoropads'kyi–Central Power regime. Relations within the occupation regime were also becoming strained. The Germans refused to allow the Ukrainians to form their own army, while the Austrians refused to support the Ukrainians in their irredentist claims on eastern Galicia. Just before the Central Powers acknowledged their defeat in the Great War, Skoropads'kyi was able to bring several National Union members briefly into a coalition government. Shortly thereafter, however, the Hetman's overtures to the Whites provoked the Ukrainian opposition forces in the National Union to launch an insurrection against him, and he was forced to flee with the retreating German armies. Petliura proclaimed the formation of a Directory and issued his own Universal as supreme commander; he led the Sharpshooters and peasant volunteers towards the capital, which in the end was defended by only a force of Russian officers. The Directory finally arrived in Kiev on 19 December and proclaimed a new Ukrainian National Republic in the name of the toilers and allied itself to the international revolution underway. Because the two leading Social Democrats in the Directory, Vynnychenko and Petliura, were at loggerheads over the radical politics of the new regime, considerable authority in Kiev rested with the Sich Sharpshooters' commander, Evhen Konovalets.

The Directory and the failure of united Ukraine

The retreat of the Central Powers' armies opened up the possibility of uniting the two Ukraines, but not without provoking the hostility of Polish national irredentism. Even before the Austrian and German capitulation, the new Habsburg emperor Karl had proclaimed his empire transformed into a federal union of free peoples. Ukrainian parliamentary leaders in the Austrian Imperial Council responded by convening in L'viv a Ukrainian Peoples' Council (*Ukrains'ka natsional'na rada*), which declared itself a constituent body and assumed command over all soldiers of Ukrainian nationality. When the Austrian authorities in L'viv refused to transfer authority to the Ukrainians, a Ukrainian Central Military Committee seized the principal government buildings and shortly thereafter the leadership of the Ukrainian political parties proclaimed the Western Ukrainian National Republic (ZUNR). In response, Polish military underground organizations in L'viv launched an uprising, which quickly chased the Ukrainians out of L'viv and marked the beginning of the Ukrainian-Polish War.

While an initial approach for help by the Galician Ukrainians to the Hetman had been rebuffed, the Directory in Kiev proved to be more responsive. On 22 January 1919, in the midst of the chaos of a new invasion from Bolshevik Russia, an Act of Union was agreed by which western Ukraine, while retaining considerable autonomy, joined the Ukrainian National Republic in a very short-lived 'united Ukraine'. The fate of the western Ukrainian experiment was settled by the Allied peace negotiators and the demands of newly independent Poland for sovereignty over what its leadership viewed – more than ever – as eastern Galicia rather than western Ukraine. The Poles launched a general offensive in early 1919; the western Ukrainian government responded to the emergency by investing Evhen Petrushevych with dictatorial powers and by appointing a new army commander to repel the Polish army. Despite Allied protests, the Polish army chased the Galicians into eastern Ukraine during the summer of 1919, where 40,000 of the retreating soldiers reinforced Petliura's now desperate armies.

Very shortly after its creation and throughout 1919, the new Ukrainian National Republic faced two formidable rivals for authority in a Bolshevik Provisional Workers' and Peasants' Government of Ukraine and the Volunteer Army to the south. The Ukrainian Bolsheviks had been exiled in Moscow during the months of the Hetmanate. After the Bolshevik invasion of Ukraine launched in December 1918, peace negotiations were pursued in vain and on 16 January 1919 the Directory declared war on Soviet Russia. Within two weeks the Bolsheviks had chased the Directory from Kiev and installed a Provisional Workers' and Peasants' Government of Ukraine. This second Soviet Ukrainian government was headed by Georgii Piatakov, whose rule was marked by efforts at centralization, re-Russification and the suppression of the 'bourgeois' Ukrainian nationalist movement. The ongoing divisions within the Bolshevik movement in Ukraine led to a reorganization of the government as the Ukrainian Soviet Socialist Republic, with Khristian Rakovskii as its chairman, but the pressure from Moscow for subordination of the Ukrainian government continued to grow. An experiment in coalition rule was made with the *Borot'bist* Party, a left-wing splinter group from the Ukrainian Socialist Revolutionaries which advocated peasant socialism, Soviet federalism, and the protection and dissemination of Ukrainian culture. The coalition survived only until the end of summer 1919, however, when the Soviet government was expelled by advancing White and Ukrainian forces.

The Directory, meanwhile, moved to its temporary capital in Vynnytsia, where Petliura's proto-government saw little option but to turn to the Entente powers for aid. But it came under increasing domestic criticism from the leaders of the Ukrainian SR and Social-Democratic parties, who insisted on pursuing peace with Soviet Russia and on establishing a Ukrainian Soviet Socialist Republic. Vynnychenko offered to ally Ukraine with a union of soviet republics from Hungary to Russia against the Entente powers, Poland and Romania. The chances of the Entente coming to the aid of the Directory were slim. The Allies were aiding the White movement centred around the Volunteer Army, whose leadership brooked no intention of abandoning their slogan of 'Russia, One and Indivisible'. After the collapse of Kerensky's regime, the conservative opposition in the former Russian empire had targeted the Ukrainian movement as a threat to their dream of restoring a united 'Great Russia' and rejected all efforts at forming a joint anti-Bolshevik coalition with successive Ukrainian governments until all these forces were defeated by the Red Army. French troops briefly occupied Odessa, but the Allies had little sense of local politics and even less of a coherent set of diplomatic and military objectives. No major power was prepared to recognize Ukraine at the Paris Peace Conference and Poland's insistence on a very generous understanding of 'historic Polish lands' contributed to the failure of the Ukrainian delegations' efforts to secure a state from the victors at Versailles.

General Anton Denikin, commander of the Volunteer Army, chose spring 1919 to launch his major campaign on Moscow and dispatched his troops through Ukrainian territory. The Galician commanders who had fled eastward following the Polish offensive formed an uneasy alliance with Petliura and together they marched on Kiev, just as Denikin's army was also entering the devastated capital. But this 'joint' occupation led to new conflict because the Whites, while willing to deal with the Galicians, were unwilling to negotiate with the representatives of the Directory, whom they considered to be traitors; the treaty that the Russians signed with the Galician commanders, who placed their troops under the South Russian forces for the common battle against the Bolsheviks, was denounced as a betrayal by their east Ukrainian would-be compatriots. Denikin, meanwhile, tried to roll back the Ukrainian revolution; he appointed a new government with Russians in all the key positions, suppressed the agrarian cooperative movement, banned the use of the Ukrainian language and refused to acknowledge the existence of a Ukrainian nation, preferring instead the theory that Ukrainians were really the Little Russian branch of the Russian family.

With Ukraine having become a primary object for the major contenders for power in post-war eastern Europe, and with a series of very weak proto-governments in Kiev, the year 1919 saw the triumph of *otomanshchyna*, a Ukrainian version of warlordism and guerrilla insurgency. During late spring the peasants rose up against the Ukrainian Soviet government's agrarian policies, which resembled those that had been abandoned months earlier in Soviet Russia itself. Armed peasant bands, often advised by SR intellectuals and led by men with professional military experience, roamed the countryside in the name of the peasants' revolution and against all outside forces. Their colourful leaders included Nestor Makhno, Danylo Zeleny and Mykola Hryhoriv; several of the *otomany* appointed extensive staffs to handle the issues of governance in the regions they provisionally occupied. None of the major claimants to power in the region could count for long on the *otomany*'s loyalties. Depending on their own sense of strategic advantage and the degree to which they had been betrayed by their most recent allies, they might switch their loyalties from the Bolsheviks to Petliura to the Whites to fighting against all of them. Although many of the peasant armies fought under the slogans of independent Ukraine or the socialist revolution, their primary politics was one of survival and self-defence. The absence of a firm central government also opened the door to the reign of lawlessness and violence, including a wave of anti-semitic pogroms in the villages and towns of the former Pale of Settlement.

Conclusion

The experience of 1919 suggests that the idea of a unified Ukraine had failed to take sufficient root or win any widespread consensus even among the political and military elites of the contested lands. The major split between the two communities (western and eastern Ukraine) was illustrated by the different orientations of their leadership during their brief proto-unification; Petliura, motivated by an intensely anti-Russian version of Ukrainian politics, was ready to deal with the Poles if it meant survival, while his counterpart in Galicia, Petrushevych, saw the greater evil in Poland and was willing to ally with the Russian Whites. In emigration, Galician activists formed a Ukrainian National Committee that strove in vain for 'the complete resurrection of Ukraine within its ethnographic frontiers united federally with a strong Russia', whereas Petliura was willing to join forces with the Poles to drive out the Bolsheviks in spring 1920, despite the Poles' clearly expansionist aims and their arrest of the remaining loyal Sich Sharpshooters. By this time, many of Petliura's forces had abandoned his cause for the Red Army or one of the *otomany*. Moreover, among eastern Ukrainians, too, seemingly irreconcilable political differences over fundamental issues of domestic and foreign policy prevented united action at several key junctures. During the Soviet-Polish War of 1920, a war waged primarily on lands claimed by the Ukrainian movements for their own, Petliura re-entered Kiev to form his last, short-lived cabinet before the Bolsheviks occupied the city again in June. That war only exacerbated the conflicts among the various surviving Ukrainian parties and rendered futile any efforts at state- and nation-building by any of them.

In preparation for the third invasion of Ukraine by Soviet armies, Grigorii Petrovskii was designated as head of a provisional government, the All-Ukrainian Revolutionary Committee in December 1919. By March 1920 Soviet forces were in control of most of the provinces of eastern Ukraine. The third Ukrainian Soviet government appeared to have learned some hard lessons from the first two disastrous experiments. At least part of the Bolshevik leadership deemed it politically expedient to make some accommodation with the nationalist movement in the name of combating historic Russian 'great-power chauvinism'. They accepted a form of coalition rule with the *Borot'bisty*, who were none the less forced to disband as a separate party, while simultaneously purging the Bolshevik Party of Ukrainian federalists. The prominent place of the former *Borot'bisty* in the Soviet Ukrainian government largely explains the success of the policy of Ukrainization (the local variant of *korenizatsiia* or nation-building) during the 1920s. That policy included promotion of the Ukrainian language and culture in official business, affirmative action for ethnic Ukrainians in public offices, and other measures to promote Ukrainian identity. Ironically, these were measures that had been advocated by the Ukrainian movement almost from its origins and had been pursued more or less successfully by each Ukrainian government during the years 1917–20. In this important sense, the legacy of the Ukrainian movement continued to shape Soviet rule in Ukraine well after the revolutions.

Further reading

Adams A., *Bolsheviks in the Ukraine: The Second Campaign, 1918–1919* (New Haven, Yale University Press, 1963).

Antonov-Ovseenko V., *Zapiski o grazhdanskoi voine*, 4 vols. (Moscow, Vysshii voennyi redaktsionnyi sovet, 1924–32).

Borys J., *The Sovietization of Ukraine 1917–1923: The Communist Doctrine and Practice of National Self-Determination*, 2nd edn (Edmonton, Canadian Institute of Ukrainian Studies, 1980).

Davies N., *White Eagle, Red Star: The Polish-Soviet War, 1919–1920* (New York, St Martin's Press, 1972).

Doroshenko D., *Istoriia Ukrainy 1917–1923 rr.* (Uzhhorod, Nakl. O. Tsiupki, 1930–2).

Doroshenko D., *History of the Ukraine*, ed. and introduction G. W. Simpson, translated and abridged Hanna Chikalenko-Keller (Edmonton, The Institute Press, 1939).

Eley G., 'Remapping the Nation: War, Revolutionary Upheaval and State Formation in Eastern Europe, 1914–1923', in P. J. Potichny and H. Aster, eds., *Ukrainian-Jewish Relations in Historical Perspective* (Edmonton, Canadian Institute of Ukrainian Studies, 1988).

Himka J. P., 'The National and the Social in the Ukrainian Revolution of 1917–20', *Archiv für Sozialgeschichte* 34 (1994), pp. 95–110.

Hunczak T., ed., *The Ukraine, 1917–1921: A Study in Revolution* (Cambridge, MA, Harvard University Press, 1977).

Khrystiuk P., *Zamitky i materialy do istorii ukrains'koi revoliutsii 1917–1920 rr.*, reprint (New York, Vid-vo Chartoriis'kikh, 1969).

Procyk A., *Russian Nationalism and Ukraine: The Nationality Policy of the Volunteer Army during the Civil War* (Edmonton and Toronto, Canadian Institute of Ukrainian Studies, 1995).

Reshetar J., *The Ukrainian Revolution, 1917–1920: A Study in Nationalism* (Princeton, Princeton University Press, 1952).

Vynnychenko V. K., *Vidrodzhennia natsii*, 3 vols. (Kyiv, Vyd-vo politychnoi literatury Ukrainy, 1920).

Glossary and abbreviations

apparatchik	member of party or state political machine
ataman	Cossack chieftain
burzhui	pejorative version of 'bourgeois'
CC	Central Committee
CCFC	Petrograd Central Council of Factory Committees
census society	propertied society
Cheka	Soviet secret police (later succeeded by GPU, OGPU, NKVD and finally the KGB)
chinovnik	bureaucrat, official
Comintern	The Third (Communist) International, founded 1919
desiatina (pl. *desiatiny*)	measurement of land equalling 1.09 hectares or 2.7 acres
EC	Executive Committee
Glavlit	main censorship organization
Gosplan	State Planning Commission
gubernia	province
GULAG	concentration camp administration
intelligenty	intelligentsia, intellectuals
Kadets	Constitutional Democrats
kombedy	Poor Peasant Committees
Komsomol	Communist Youth League
Komuch	Committee of Members of the Constituent Assembly; SR anti-Bolshevik government on the Volga in 1918
Krug	Cossack assembly
kulak	rich/exploitative/capitalist peasant
Mezhraionka	Interdistrict Organization of the RSDRP
mir	village commune
MRC	Military-Revolutionary Committee
Narkomprod	People's Commissariat of Food Supply
Narkompros	People's Commissariat of Education
Narodnaia volia	The People's Will, revolutionary organization of the 1870s/1880s
nomenklatura	Soviet elite; the list of responsible appointments requiring the party's approval

NSs	members of the Popular Socialist Party
oblast	region
Octobrists	members of the Union of 17 October Party founded in 1905
Okhrana	tsarist secret police
Pale of Settlement	area to which tsarist authorities sought to restrict Jewish residence, consisting of ten Polish provinces and fifteen in the west and south-west
proizvol	arbitrary rule
Proletkul't	Russian Proletarian Cultural-Educational Association
PSFMO	Petrograd Society of Factory and Mill-Owners
PSR	Socialist-Revolutionary Party
pud (pl. *pudy*)	weight equalling 16.38 kg
Rada	Ukrainian elected assembly
raznochinets	non-noble member of the intelligentsia
Revvoensovet	Revolutionary-Military Council
RSDRP	Russian Social-Democratic Labour Party
RKP(b)	Russian Communist Party (Bolshevik), later CPSU
ROVS	Russian All-Military Union, organization of White army soldiers founded by Baron Wrangel in 1924
RVSR	Revolutionary-Military Council of the Republic
SDs	Social Democrats
Sobor	Church Council
soslovie	legal estate
Sovnarkom	Council of People's Commissars
SRs	Socialist Revolutionaries
stanitsa	Cossack village
starosta	village elder
Stavka	army headquarters
TsIK	Central Executive Committee
uezd	district; sub-division of gubernia
uprava (pl. *upravy*)	executive(s)
voisko (pl. *voiska*)	Cossack self-governing community
volost	small rural district
vozhd'	leader
VSNKh	Supreme Council of the National Economy
VTsIK	All-Russian/All-Union Central Executive Committee
WIC	War Industry Committees
Zemgor	Joint Committee of the Unions of Zemstvos and of Towns for the Supply of the Army
zemstvo	elected local government assembly
Zhenotdel	Women's Department of the Communist Party
Zimmerwaldists	adherents of the anti-war resolution passed at the Internationalist Conference in Zimmerwald, Switzerland, in 1915

Index of names

Note: names in brackets signify birth names except when contained in inverted commas, where they indicate *noms-de-plume* used at some stage. Figures in bold refer to substantive entries.

Index of subjects

Note: figures in bold refer to substantive entries

Printed in the United Kingdom
by Lightning Source UK Ltd.
130587UK00001B/1-3/A